Short Stories
for Students

National Advisory Board

Short Stories
for Students

Presenting Analysis, Context, and Criticism on Commonly Studied Short Stories

Volume 19

Ira Mark Milne, Project Editor

GALE®

THOMSON
★
GALE

Detroit • New York • San Diego • San Francisco • Cleveland • New Haven, Conn. • Waterville, Maine • London • Munich

THOMSON

GALE

Short Stories for Students, Volume 19

Project Editor
Ira Mark Milne

Editorial
Anne Marie Hacht, Michelle Kazensky,
Timothy J. Sisler, Jennifer Smith

Rights Acquisition and Management
Margaret Abendroth, Jacqueline Key,
Ann Taylor

Manufacturing
Lori Kessler

Imaging and Multimedia
Lezlie Light, Daniel William Newell,
Kelly A. Quin

Product Design
Pamela A. E. Galbreath

ISBN 0-7876-4271-1
ISSN 1092-7735

Printed in the United States of America
10 9 8 7 6 5 4 3 2 1

Table of Contents

Why Study Literature At All?

Short Stories for Students is designed to provide readers with information and discussion about a wide range of important contemporary and historical works of short fiction, and it does that job very well. However, I want to use this guest foreword to address a question that it does *not* take up. It is a fundamental question that is often ignored in high school and college English classes as well as research texts, and one that causes frustration among students at all levels, namely—why study literature at all? Isn't it enough to read a story, enjoy it, and go about one's business? My answer (to be expected from a literary professional, I suppose) is no. It is not enough. It is a start; but it is not enough. Here's why.

First, literature is the only part of the educational curriculum that deals directly with the actual world of lived experience. The philosopher Edmund Husserl used the apt German term *die Lebenswelt*, "the living world," to denote this realm. All the other content areas of the modern American educational system avoid the subjective, present reality of everyday life. Science (both the natural and the social varieties) objectifies, the fine arts create and/or perform, history reconstructs. Only literary study persists in posing those questions we all asked before our schooling taught us to give up on them. Only literature gives credibility to personal perceptions, feelings, dreams, and the "stream of consciousness" that is our inner voice. Literature wonders about infinity, wonders why God permits evil, wonders what will happen to us after we die. Literature admits that we get our hearts broken, that people sometimes cheat and get away with it, that the world is a strange and probably incomprehensible place. Literature, in other words, takes on all the big and small issues of what it means to be human. So my first answer is that of the humanist—we should read literature and study it and take it seriously because it enriches us as human beings. We develop our moral imagination, our capacity to sympathize with other people, and our ability to understand our existence through the experience of fiction.

My second answer is more practical. By studying literature we can learn how to explore and analyze texts. Fiction may be about *die Lebenswelt*, but it is a construct of words put together in a certain order by an artist using the medium of language. By examining and studying those constructions, we can learn about language as a medium. We can become more sophisticated about word associations and connotations, about the manipulation of symbols, and about style and atmosphere. We can grasp how ambiguous language is and how important context and texture is to meaning. In our first encounter with a work of literature, of course, we are not supposed to catch all of these things. We are spellbound, just as the writer wanted us to be. It is as serious students of the writer's art that we begin to see how the tricks are done.

Seeing the tricks, which is another way of saying "developing analytical and close reading skills," is important above and beyond its intrinsic literary educational value. These skills transfer to other fields and enhance critical thinking of any kind. Understanding how language is used to construct texts is powerful knowledge. It makes engineers better problem solvers, lawyers better advocates and courtroom practitioners, politicians better rhetoricians, marketing and advertising agents better sellers, and citizens more aware consumers as well as better participants in democracy. This last point is especially important, because rhetorical skill works both ways—when we learn how language is manipulated in the making of texts the result is that we become less susceptible when language is used to manipulate us.

My third reason is related to the second. When we begin to see literature as created artifacts of language, we become more sensitive to good writing in general. We get a stronger sense of the importance of individual words, even the sounds of words and word combinations. We begin to understand Mark Twain's delicious proverb—"The difference between the right word and the almost right word is the difference between lightning and a lightning bug." Getting beyond the "enjoyment only" stage of literature gets us closer to becoming makers of word art ourselves. I am not saying that studying fiction will turn every student into a Faulkner or a Shakespeare. But it will make us more adaptable and effective writers, even if our art form ends up being the office memo or the corporate annual report.

Studying short stories, then, can help students become better readers, better writers, and even better human beings. But I want to close with a warning. If your study and exploration of the craft, history, context, symbolism, or anything else about a story starts to rob it of the magic you felt when you first read it, it is time to stop. Take a break, study another subject, shoot some hoops, or go for a run. Love of reading is too important to be ruined by school. The early twentieth century writer Willa Cather, in her novel *My Antonia*, has her narrator Jack Burden tell a story that he and Antonia heard from two old Russian immigrants when they were teenagers. These immigrants, Pavel and Peter, told about an incident from their youth back in Russia that the narrator could recall in vivid detail thirty years later. It was a harrowing story of a wedding party starting home in sleds and being chased by starving wolves. Hundreds of wolves attacked the group's sleds one by one as they sped across the snow trying to reach their village. In a horrible revelation, the old Russians revealed that the groom eventually threw his own bride to the wolves to save himself. There was even a hint that one of the old immigrants might have been the groom mentioned in the story. Cather has her narrator conclude with his feelings about the story. "We did not tell Pavel's secret to anyone, but guarded it jealously—as if the wolves of the Ukraine had gathered that night long ago, and the wedding party had been sacrificed, just to give us a painful and peculiar pleasure." That feeling, that painful and peculiar pleasure, is the most important thing about literature. Study and research should enhance that feeling and never be allowed to overwhelm it.

Thomas E. Barden
Professor of English and
Director of Graduate English Studies
The University of Toledo

Introduction

Purpose of the Book

The purpose of *Short Stories for Students* (*SSfS*) is to provide readers with a guide to understanding, enjoying, and studying short stories by giving them easy access to information about the work. Part of Gale's "For Students" Literature line, *SSfS* is specifically designed to meet the curricular needs of high school and undergraduate college students and their teachers, as well as the interests of general readers and researchers considering specific short fiction. While each volume contains entries on "classic" stories frequently studied in classrooms, there are also entries containing hard-to-find information on contemporary stories, including works by multicultural, international, and women writers.

The information covered in each entry includes an introduction to the story and the story's author; a plot summary, to help readers unravel and understand the events in the work; descriptions of important characters, including explanation of a given character's role in the narrative as well as discussion about that character's relationship to other characters in the story; analysis of important themes in the story; and an explanation of important literary techniques and movements as they are demonstrated in the work.

In addition to this material, which helps the readers analyze the story itself, students are also provided with important information on the literary and historical background informing each work. This includes a historical context essay, a box comparing the time or place the story was written to modern Western culture, a critical essay, and excerpts from critical essays on the story or author. A unique feature of *SSfS* is a specially commissioned critical essay on each story, targeted toward the student reader.

To further aid the student in studying and enjoying each story, information on media adaptations is provided (if available), as well as reading suggestions for works of fiction and nonfiction on similar themes and topics. Classroom aids include ideas for research papers and lists of critical sources that provide additional material on the work.

Selection Criteria

The titles for each volume of *SSfS* were selected by surveying numerous sources on teaching literature and analyzing course curricula for various school districts. Some of the sources surveyed include: literature anthologies, *Reading Lists for College-Bound Students: The Books Most Recommended by America's Top Colleges*; *Teaching the Short Story: A Guide to Using Stories from around the World*, by the National Council of Teachers of English (NCTE); and "A Study of High School Literature Anthologies," conducted by Arthur Applebee at the Center for the Learning and Teaching of Literature and sponsored by the National Endowment for the Arts and the Office of Educational Research and Improvement.

Input was also solicited from our advisory board, as well as from educators from various areas. From these discussions, it was determined that each volume should have a mix of "classic" stories (those works commonly taught in literature classes) and contemporary stories for which information is often hard to find. Because of the interest in expanding the canon of literature, an emphasis was also placed on including works by international, multicultural, and women authors. Our advisory board members—educational professionals—helped pare down the list for each volume. Works not selected for the present volume were noted as possibilities for future volumes. As always, the editor welcomes suggestions for titles to be included in future volumes.

How Each Entry Is Organized

Each entry, or chapter, in *SSfS* focuses on one story. Each entry heading lists the title of the story, the author's name, and the date of the story's publication. The following elements are contained in each entry:

- **Introduction:** a brief overview of the story which provides information about its first appearance, its literary standing, any controversies surrounding the work, and major conflicts or themes within the work.

- **Author Biography:** this section includes basic facts about the author's life, and focuses on events and times in the author's life that may have inspired the story in question.

- **Plot Summary:** a description of the events in the story. Lengthy summaries are broken down with subheads.

- **Characters:** an alphabetical listing of the characters who appear in the story. Each character name is followed by a brief to an extensive description of the character's role in the story, as well as discussion of the character's actions, relationships, and possible motivation.

  Characters are listed alphabetically by last name. If a character is unnamed—for instance, the narrator in "The Eatonville Anthology"—the character is listed as "The Narrator" and alphabetized as "Narrator." If a character's first name is the only one given, the name will appear alphabetically by that name.

- **Themes:** a thorough overview of how the topics, themes, and issues are addressed within the story. Each theme discussed appears in a sepa-

rate subhead, and is easily accessed through the boldface entries in the Subject/Theme Index.

- **Style:** this section addresses important style elements of the story, such as setting, point of view, and narration; important literary devices used, such as imagery, foreshadowing, symbolism; and, if applicable, genres to which the work might have belonged, such as Gothicism or Romanticism. Literary terms are explained within the entry, but can also be found in the Glossary.

- **Historical Context:** this section outlines the social, political, and cultural climate *in which the author lived and the work was created*. This section may include descriptions of related historical events, pertinent aspects of daily life in the culture, and the artistic and literary sensibilities of the time in which the work was written. If the story is historical in nature, information regarding the time in which the story is set is also included. Long sections are broken down with helpful subheads.

- **Critical Overview:** this section provides background on the critical reputation of the author and the story, including bannings or any other public controversies surrounding the work. For older works, this section may include a history of how the story was first received and how perceptions of it may have changed over the years; for more recent works, direct quotes from early reviews may also be included.

- **Criticism:** an essay commissioned by *SSfS* which specifically deals with the story and is written specifically for the student audience, as well as excerpts from previously published criticism on the work (if available).

- **Sources:** an alphabetical list of critical material used in compiling the entry, with bibliographical information.

- **Further Reading:** an alphabetical list of other critical sources which may prove useful for the student. It includes bibliographical information and a brief annotation.

In addition, each entry contains the following highlighted sections, set apart from the main text as sidebars:

- **Media Adaptations:** if available, a list of film and television adaptations of the story, including source information. The list also includes stage adaptations, audio recordings, musical adaptations, etc.

- **Topics for Further Study:** a list of potential study questions or research topics dealing with the story. This section includes questions related to other disciplines the student may be studying, such as American history, world history, science, math, government, business, geography, economics, psychology, etc.

- **Compare and Contrast:** an "at-a-glance" comparison of the cultural and historical differences between the author's time and culture and late twentieth century or early twenty-first century Western culture. This box includes pertinent parallels between the major scientific, political, and cultural movements of the time or place the story was written, the time or place the story was set (if a historical work), and modern Western culture. Works written after 1990 may not have this box.

- **What Do I Read Next?:** a list of works that might complement the featured story or serve as a contrast to it. This includes works by the same author and others, works of fiction and nonfiction, and works from various genres, cultures, and eras.

Other Features

SS*f*S includes "Why Study Literature At All?," a foreword by Thomas E. Barden, Professor of English and Director of Graduate English Studies at the University of Toledo. This essay provides a number of very fundamental reasons for studying literature and, therefore, reasons why a book such as SS*f*S, designed to facilitate the study of literture, is useful.

A Cumulative Author/Title Index lists the authors and titles covered in each volume of the SS*f*S series.

A Cumulative Nationality/Ethnicity Index breaks down the authors and titles covered in each volume of the SS*f*S series by nationality and ethnicity.

A Subject/Theme Index, specific to each volume, provides easy reference for users who may be studying a particular subject or theme rather than a single work. Significant subjects from events to broad themes are included, and the entries pointing to the specific theme discussions in each entry are indicated in **boldface**.

Each entry may include illustrations, including photo of the author, stills from film adaptations (if available), maps, and/or photos of key historical events.

Citing Short Stories for Students

When writing papers, students who quote directly from any volume of SS*f*S may use the following general forms to document their source. These examples are based on MLA style; teachers may request that students adhere to a different style, thus, the following examples may be adapted as needed.

When citing text from SS*f*S that is not attributed to a particular author (for example, the Themes, Style, Historical Context sections, etc.), the following format may be used:

"The Celebrated Jumping Frog of Calavaras County." *Short Stories for Students*. Ed. Kathleen Wilson. Vol. 1. Detroit: Gale, 1997. 19–20.

When quoting the specially commissioned essay from SS*f*S (usually the first essay under the Criticism subhead), the following format may be used:

Korb, Rena. Critical Essay on "Children of the Sea." *Short Stories for Students*. Ed. Kathleen Wilson. Vol. 1. Detroit: Gale, 1997. 42.

When quoting a journal or newspaper essay that is reprinted in a volume of *Short Stories for Students*, the following form may be used:

Schmidt, Paul. "The Deadpan on Simon Wheeler." *Southwest Review* Vol. XLI, No. 3 (Summer, 1956), 270–77; excerpted and reprinted in *Short Stories for Students*, Vol. 1, ed. Kathleen Wilson (Detroit: Gale, 1997), pp. 29–31.

When quoting material from a book that is reprinted in a volume of SS*f*S, the following form may be used:

Bell-Villada, Gene H. "The Master of Short Forms," in *Garcia Marquez: The Man and His Work*. University of North Carolina Press, 1990, pp. 119–36; excerpted and reprinted in *Short Stories for Students*, Vol. 1, ed. Kathleen Wilson (Detroit: Gale, 1997), pp. 89–90.

We Welcome Your Suggestions

The editor of *Short Stories for Students* welcomes your comments and ideas. Readers who wish to suggest short stories to appear in future volumes, or who have other suggestions, are cordially invited to contact the editor. You may contact the editor via E-mail at: **ForStudentsEditors@thomson.com**. Or write to the editor at:

Editor, *Short Stories for Students*
The Gale Group
27500 Drake Road
Farmington Hills, MI 48331–3535

Literary Chronology

1882: James Joyce is born on February 2 in Dublin, Ireland.

1894: James Thurber is born on December 8 in Columbus, Ohio.

1901: Zora Neale Hurston is born on January 7 in Eatonville, Florida.

1903: Morley Callaghan is born on February 22 in Toronto, Ontario, Canada.

1911: Bienvenido Santos is born on March 22 in Tondo, Manila, the Philippines.

1914: James Joyce's "Eveline" is published.

1923: Nadine Gordimer is born on November 20 in Springs, South Africa.

1925: Flannery O'Connor (born Mary Flannery O'Connor) is born on March 25 in Savannah, Georgia.

1926: Zora Neale Hurston's "Sweat" is published.

1931: Alice Munro is born on July 10 in Wingham, Ontario, Canada.

1932: John Updike is born on March 18 in Reading, Pennsylvania.

1933: James Thurber's "The Night the Ghost Got In" is published.

1936: Morley Callaghan's "All the Years of Her Life" is published.

1941: James Joyce dies on January 13 in Zurich.

1944: Alejandro Morales is born on October 14 in Montebello, California.

1948: T. Coraghessan Boyle is born on December 2 in Peekskill, New York.

1949: Jane Smiley is born on September 26 in Los Angeles, California.

1954: Flannery O'Connor's "A Circle in the Fire" is published.

1957: Lorrie Moore is born on February 13 in Glens Falls, New York.

1960: Zora Neale Hurston dies in a Florida welfare home.

1961: James Thurber dies on November 2.

1964: Flannery O'Connor dies on August 3 in Milledgeville, Georgia.

1967: Jhumpa Lahiri is born in London, England.

1968: John Updike's "The Slump" is published.

1977: Bienvenido Santos's "Immigration Blues" is published.

1982: John Updike receives the Pulitzer Prize for literature.

1986: Alejandro Morales's "The Curing Woman" is published.

1987: Jane Smiley's "Long Distance" is published.

1989: Lorrie Moore's "You're Ugly, Too" is published.

1989: Nadine Gordimer's "The Ultimate Safari" is published.

1990: Morley Callaghan dies on August 25.

1990: Alice Munro's "Meneseteung" is published.

1991: Nadine Gordimer receives the Nobel Prize for literature.

1991: John Updike receives the Pulitzer Prize for literature.

1992: Jane Smiley receives the Pulitzer Prize for literature.

1996: Bienvenido Santos dies on January 7 at his home in Albay, the Philippines.

1998: Jhumpa Lahiri's "A Temporary Matter" is published.

1998: T. Coraghessan Boyle's "The Underground Gardens" is published.

2000: Jhumpa Lahiri receives the Pulitzer Prize for literature.

Acknowledgments

The editors wish to thank the copyright holders of the excerpted criticism included in this volume and the permissions managers of many book and magazine publishing companies for assisting us in securing reproduction rights. We are also grateful to the staffs of the Detroit Public Library, the Library of Congress, the University of Detroit Mercy Library, Wayne State University Purdy/Kresge Library Complex, and the University of Michigan Libraries for making their resources available to us. Following is a list of the copyright holders who have granted us permission to reproduce material in this volume of *Short Stories for Students (SSfS)*. Every effort has been made to trace copyright, but if omissions have been made, please let us know.

COPYRIGHTED MATERIALS IN *SSfS*, VOLUME 19, WERE REPRODUCED FROM THE FOLLOWING PERIODICALS:

Boulevard, v. 17, fall, 2001. Copyright © 2001 by Opojaz, Inc. Reproduced by permission.—*Explicator*, v. 51, spring, 1993. Copyright 1993 by Helen Dwight Reid Educational Foundation. Reproduced with permission of the Helen Dwight Reid Educational Foundation, published by Heldref Publications, 1319 18th Street, NW, Washington, DC 20036–1802.—*Pacific Coast Philology*, v. 19, November, 1984. Copyright 1984 by Pacific Ancient and Modern Language Association. Reproduced by permission.—*Publishers Weekly*, v. 233, April 1, 1998. Copyright 1998 by Reed Publishing USA. Reproduced from *Publishers Weekly*, pub-

lished by the Bowker Magazine Group of Cahners Publishing Co., a division of Reed Publishing USA., by permission.—*Salmagundi*, winter, 1997. Copyright © 1997 by Skidmore College. Reproduced by permission.—*Silliman Journal*, v. 28, First and Second Quarters, 1981. Copyright 1981 by Silliman University. Reproduced by permission.—*Southern Literary Journal*, v. 26, spring, 1994. Copyright 1994 by The University of North Carolina Press Journals. Reproduced by permission.—*Southern Quarterly*, v. 40, fall, 2001. Copyright © 2001 by the University of Southern Mississippi. Reproduced by permission.—*Studies in Canadian Literature*, v.19, 1994. Copyright © 1994 by the author. Reproduced by permission of the editors.—*Studies in Short Fiction*, v. 30, fall, 1993. Copyright 1993 by Newberry College. Reproduced by permission.

COPYRIGHTED MATERIALS IN *SSfS*, VOLUME 19, WERE REPRODUCED FROM THE FOLLOWING BOOKS:

Beck, Warren. From *Joyce's Dubliners: Substance, Vision, and Art*. Duke University Press, 1969. Copyright 1969 by Duke University Press. Reproduced by permission.—Casper, Leonard. From an introduction to *Scent of Apples: A Collection of Stories by Bienvenido N. Santos*. University of Washington Press, 1979. Copyright 1979 by University of Washington Press. Reproduced by permission.—Conron, Brandon. From "The End of an

Era," in *Morley Callaghan*. Twayne Publishers, Inc., 1966. Copyright 1966 by Twayne Publishers, Inc. Reproduced by permission of Simon & Schuster.—Detweiler, Robert. From "More Fiction of the Seventies: The Exertions of Eros," in *John Updike*. G. K. Hall, 1984. Copyright © 1984 by G. K. Hall & Company. All rights reserved. Reproduced by permission of The Gale Group.—Howells, Coral Ann. From "On Lies, Secrets, and Silence: 'Friend of My Youth'," in *Alice Munro*. Manchester University Press, Manchester UK 1998. Copyright © 1998 by Coral Ann Howells. Reproduced by permission.—Kim, Elaine H. From "New Directions," in *Asian American Literature: An Introduction to the Writings and Their Social Context*. Temple University Press, 1982. Copyright 1982 by Temple University Press. Reproduced by permission.—Larsen, R. B. From "R. B. Larsen," in *John Updike: A Study of the Short Fiction*. Edited by Robert M. Luscher. Twayne Publishers, Inc., 1993. Copyright © 1993 by Twayne Publishers, Inc. All rights reserved. Reproduced by permission of The Gale Group.—Lowe, John. From "'Cast in Yo' Nets Right Here': Finding a Comic Voice," in *Jump at the Sun: Zora Neale Hurston's Cosmic Comedy*. University of Illinois Press, 1994. Copyright © 1994 by the Board of Trustees of the University of Illinois. Reproduced by permission.—Morsberger, Robert E. From "The Romantic Imagination," in *James Thurber*. Twayne Publishers, Inc., 1964. Copyright © 1964 by Twayne Publishers, Inc. All rights reserved. Reproduced by permission of The Gale Group.—Seidel, Kathryn Lee. From "The Artist in the Kitchen: The Economics of Creativity in Hurston's 'Sweat'," in *Zora in Florida*. Edited by Steve Glassman and Kathryn Lee Seidel. University of Central Florida Press, 1991. Copyright © 1991 by the Board of Regents of the State of Florida. Reproduced by permission of the University Press of Florida.—Smith, Rowland. From "Rewriting the Frontier: Wilderness and Social Code in the Fiction of Alice Munro," in *Telling Stories: Postcolonial Short Fiction in English*. Rodopi, 2001. Copyright © 2001 by Editions Rodopi B. V. Reproduced by permission.—Trotter, Robert, II, and Juan Antonio Clavira. From *Curanderismo: Mexican American Folk Healing*. University of Georgia Press, 1981. Copyright © 1981. Reproduced by permission.—Updike, John. From "Getting the Words Out," in *John Updike: A Study of the Short Fiction*. Edited by Robert M. Luscher.

Twayne Publishers, Inc., 1993. Copyright © 1993 by Twayne Publishers, Inc. All rights reserved. Reproduced by permission of The Gale Group.—Walsh, William. From "Morley Callaghan," in *Manifold Voice: Studies in Commonwealth Literature*. Chatto and Windus, 1970. Copyright © 1970 by Chatto and Windus. All rights reserved. Reproduced by permission of Random House Group, Ltd.

PHOTOGRAPHS AND ILLUSTRATIONS APPEARING IN *SSfS*, VOLUME 19, WERE RECEIVED FROM THE FOLLOWING SOURCES:

Boyle, T. Coraghessan, photograph by Jim Cooper. AP/Wide World Photos. Reproduced by permission.—Callaghan, Morley Edward, photograph by Jerry Bauer. Reproduced by permission.—Filipino immigrant boy working with labor gang near Santa Maria, California in March of 1937, photograph by Dorothea Lange/Corbis. Reproduced by permission.—Gordimer, Nadine, photograph. AP/Wide World Photos. Reproduced by permission.—Hurston, Zora Neale, on porch in Eatonville, Florida with musicians. © Corbis. Reproduced by permission.—Hurston, Zora Neale, wearing hat and feather, photograph by Carl Van Vechten. Reproduced by permission of Carl Van Vechten Trust.—J. Sherman Drug Store in Flemington, New Jersey, taken 1935. © Bettmann/Corbis. Reproduced by permission.—Joyce, James, photograph. The Library of Congress.—Lahiri, Jhumpa, photograph by Suzanne Plunkett. AP/Wide World Photos. Reproduced by permission.—Mexican Indian healer blowing on woman's head. © Viviane Moos/Corbis. Reproduced by permission.—Moore, Maria Lorena, photograph © Jerry Bauer. Reproduced by permission.—Mozambican refugees flee the war and resettle at a refugee camp Malawi, photograph. © Peter Turnley/Corbis. Reproduced by permission.—Munro, Alice, photograph by Jerry Bauer. © Jerry Bauer. Reproduced by permission.—O'Connor, Flannery, photograph. Corbis-Bettmann. Reproduced by permission.—Sailing ships stand by the Custom House in the dock of Dublin, Ireland, circa 1890, photograph. © Sean Sexton Collection/Corbis. Reproduced by permission.—Santos, Bienvenido, photograph by Wig Tysmans. Reproduced by permission.—Smiley, Jane, photograph. AP/Wide World Photos. Reproduced by permission.—State Street in Columbus, Ohio in 1901.

© Corbis. Reproduced by permission.—Thurber, James, 1954, photograph by Fred Palumbo. NYWTS/ The Library of Congress.—Updike, John, 1990, photograph by Wyatt Counts. AP/Wide World Photos. Reproduced by permission.—Women harvest grapes in a vineyard in San Joaquin Valley, California, on September, 15, 1942, photograph. © Bettmann/Corbis. Reproduced by permission.— Yankee Stadium, November 24, 1963, photograph. © Bettmann/Corbis. Reproduced by permission.

Contributors

Bryan Aubrey: Aubrey holds a Ph.D. in English and has published many articles on twentieth-century literature. Entries on *All the Years of Her Life*, *The Curing Woman*, and *Immigration Blues*. Original essays on *All the Years of Her Life*, *The Curing Woman*, and *Immigration Blues*.

Catherine Dybiec Holm: Dybiec Holm is a freelance writer and editor. Original essays on *Long Distance* and *You're Ugly, Too*.

Curt Guyette: Guyette is a longtime journalist who received a bachelor's degree in English writing from the University of Pittsburgh. Original essay on *The Underground Gardens*.

Jeff Hill: Hill is a freelance writer and editor who specializes in literature. Original essay on *The Underground Gardens*.

David Kelly: Kelly is an instructor of creative writing and literature at several Illinois colleges. Entries on *The Night the Ghost Got In* and *The Slump*. Original essays on *The Night the Ghost Got In* and *The Slump*.

Candyce Norvell: Norvell is an independent educational writer who specializes in English and literature. Entries on *A Circle of Fire* and *A Temporary Matter*. Original essays on *A Circle of Fire* and *A Temporary Matter*.

Ryan D. Poquette: Poquette has a bachelor's degree in English and specializes in writing about literature. Entries on *Long Distance*, *Meneseteung*, and *The Underground Gardens*. Original essays on *Long Distance*, *Meneseteung*, and *The Underground Gardens*.

David Remy: Remy is a freelance writer in Pensacola, Florida. Original essays on *Meneseteung* and *A Temporary Matter*.

Ericka Marie Sudo: Sudo is currently pursuing a master's degree. Original essay on *You're Ugly, Too*.

Scott Trudell: Trudell is a freelance writer with a bachelor's degree in English literature. Entries on *Eveline* and *Sweat*. Original essays on *Eveline* and *Sweat*.

Mark White: White is the publisher of the Seattle-based literary press, Scala House Press. Entries on *The Ultimate Safari* and *You're Ugly, Too*. Original essays on *The Ultimate Safari* and *You're Ugly, Too*.

All the Years of Her Life

Morley Callaghan

1936

"All the Years of Her Life" is a short story by Canadian writer Morley Callaghan. It was published in his second collection of short stories, *Now That April's Here and Other Stories* (New York, 1936). "All the Years of Her Life" is a straightforward story with only three characters, written in an economical, unpretentious style typical of Callaghan's work. A young man, Alfred Higgins, is caught by his employer, Sam Carr, pilfering items from the drugstore where he works. Instead of immediately calling the police, Mr. Carr sends for Alfred's mother. The story focuses on Mrs. Higgins's psychological state, which by the end of the story turns out to be quite different from how it first appears. When Alfred observes this change in his mother, he has a moment of insight in which he understands something about her he never before noticed. In just a few pages, Callaghan manages to tell a moving story of a mother's devotion to her wayward son and the son's sudden acquisition of a new maturity. The story ends on a note of quiet hope.

Author Biography

Edward Morley Callaghan was born February 22, 1903, in Toronto, Ontario, Canada. He was the second son of Thomas and Mary Callaghan and was raised in a middle-class home where literature was revered.

Morley Callaghan

From 1921 to 1925, Callaghan attended St. Michael's College, University of Toronto, graduating with a bachelor of arts degree in 1925. During these years, he wrote his first fiction. He also took summer jobs at the weekly *Toronto Star,* where he became friends with Ernest Hemingway.

In 1925, Callaghan enrolled at Osgoode Hall Law School, graduating in 1928. He never practiced law, however, because by then he had published several stories and his first novel, *Strange Fugitive* (1928). This work was followed by a collection of short stories, *A Native Argosy* (1929).

In 1929, Callaghan married Loretto Florence Dee. They honeymooned in Paris, remaining there for seven months. The couple had two children together.

The early and mid-1930s were a prolific period for Callaghan. He wrote a novella, *No Man's Meat* (1931), and five novels: *It's Never Over* (1930), *A Broken Journey* (1932), *Such Is My Beloved* (1934), *They Shall Inherit the Earth* (1935), and *More Joy in Heaven* (1937). He also published a collection of short stories, *Now That April's Here and Other Stories* (1936), which contains the story ''All the Years of Her Life.''

In 1938, with his reputation growing and critics and readers praising his distinctive style, Callaghan's creativity dried up, and he stopped writing novels and short stories. He tried his hand at playwriting, but the two plays he wrote in 1938 had to wait a decade before being produced. He wrote little more until 1947. Instead, Callaghan took up other occupations. He was a sports columnist for *New World Illustrated;* he joined the staff of the Canadian Broadcasting Corporation (CBC) radio program *Things To Come;* and in 1947, he joined the panel of the CBC radio quiz show *Beat the Champs.* Callaghan also wrote a screenplay for the National Film Board of Canada.

Callaghan resumed writing short stories and novels in 1947. His novel *The Loved and the Lost* (1951) won the Governor General's Award for fiction. Four years later, Callaghan won the *Maclean's* magazine fiction prize for the novella *The Man with the Coat,* which Callaghan adapted into the novel *The Many Colored Coat* (1960).

In 1958, Callaghan covered the death of Pope Pius XII in Rome for the *Toronto Star* weekly magazine. This article formed the basis for his novel *A Passion in Rome* (1961). His third collection of short stories, *Morley Callaghan's Stories,* was published in 1959. In 1963, Callaghan published *That Summer in Paris: Memories of Tangled Friendships with Hemingway, Fitzgerald and Some Others,* a memoir of his relationship with Hemingway and F. Scott Fitzgerald in the summer of 1929.

In his later years, Callaghan continued to write, publishing *A Fine and Private Place* (1975), *Close to the Sun Again* (1977), and *A Time for Judas* (1983). In 1982, Callaghan was appointed Companion of the Order of Canada. In 1983, he won the Author of the Year Award from the Canadian Booksellers Association. *A Wild Old Man on the Road* (1988) was his last novel. Callaghan died August 25, 1990, at the age of eighty-seven.

Plot Summary

''All the Years of Her Life'' is set in a drugstore in an unnamed city that may well be New York. The story begins one evening in late summer when Alfred Higgins, who works in the drugstore, is putting on his coat, ready to go home. The owner of the drugstore, Sam Carr, says he wants to have a word with Alfred before he leaves.

Alfred knows something is wrong because of the tone of voice in which his employer speaks. His heart begins to beat fast. Mr. Carr asks him to remove some items from his pocket, including lipstick and toothpaste.

Red-faced, Alfred tries to protest. Then he grows frightened and does not know what to say. He removes the items from his pocket. Mr. Carr asks him how long he has been stealing from the store, and Alfred says he has never done it before. But Mr. Carr knows Alfred is lying. Alfred is always getting into trouble at work, and he cannot hold a job.

Mr. Carr reproaches Alfred, saying he had been willing to trust him. He does not immediately want to call the police. He indicates he will call Alfred's father, but Alfred says his father is not at home. Over Alfred's protests, Mr. Carr decides to call Alfred's mother instead. He explains to her that Alfred is in trouble and asks her to come to the store.

They wait in silence until Mrs. Higgins, Alfred's mother, arrives. Mr. Carr explains that Alfred has been pilfering small items from the store. Mrs. Higgins asks her son whether the accusation is true, and he admits that it is. The only explanation he can give for what he has done is that he has been spending money with his friends.

Mrs. Higgins turns to Mr. Carr and speaks with a simple earnestness. After Mr. Carr explains that he intends to call the police, Mrs. Higgins gently says she thinks a little good advice is what her son most needs. Alfred is surprised by how calm and composed his mother sounds, and he senses she has made a favorable impression on his employer.

After Alfred's mother has spoken, Mr. Carr says he does not want to be harsh, and offers simply to fire Alfred and not take the matter any further. Mrs. Higgins says she will never forget his kindness. She and Mr. Carr part on warm terms.

As mother and son walk home together, Alfred is afraid to speak. He is relieved to have escaped so lightly, but he wonders what his mother is thinking. When he finally speaks, he promises not to get into such a situation again. His mother responds angrily, saying he has disgraced her again. She tells him to keep quiet.

When they arrive home, his mother reproaches him again. She tells him to go to bed and never mention the incident to his father.

While he is undressing in his bedroom, Alfred hears his mother moving around in the kitchen. She is making a cup of tea. He feels a kind of wonder and admiration for her strength. Then he goes to the kitchen, and at the door he sees her pouring a cup of tea. She is no longer the calm woman she was at the drugstore. Her face looks frightened, and her hand trembles as she pours the tea. She looks old.

Alfred realizes this is how it has been for his mother every time he has gotten into trouble. He now understands everything she may have been thinking when they walked home in silence. Just by looking at the way her hand trembles as she raises the cup to her lips, he thinks that he knows all she has experienced in her life. He feels that he is looking at her for the first time.

Characters

Sam Carr

Sam Carr is the small gray-haired owner of the drugstore where Alfred works. He is a shrewd man, not easily fooled, and he has been aware for some time that Alfred has been pilfering items from the store. Mr. Carr also possesses some patience. He does not explode in anger at Alfred but remains polite and courteous, even though his manner is stern. He gives the impression of being a tolerant, kindly man. He says he likes Alfred and is quite ready to trust him, and he is in no rush to call the police when he finally confronts the young man about his petty crimes. He just wants to do the right thing.

Alfred Higgins

Alfred Higgins is a young man possibly in his late teens. He has two older brothers and a younger sister who have married and left home, while he still lives with his parents. Alfred is an incompetent, immature young man who has difficulty holding a job. As the story begins, he has been working for six months in a drugstore, but he is about to be confronted by his employer about his habit of pilfering from the store. At first he tries to bluff and then lie his way out of the situation. When that does not work, his mother has to come and rescue him. However, the selfish Alfred grows psychologically during the course of the story. He realizes how hard his mother's life is, and he seems to be ready to make a new, more mature start to his own life.

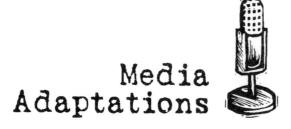

Media Adaptations

- "All the Years of Her Life" was adapted as a film by the same name in 1974. It was directed by Robert Fortier and stars Carl Marotte, Walter Wakefield, and Mary Gay Pinatel.

Mrs. Higgins

Mrs. Higgins is Alfred's mother. She is plump, with a friendly manner. When Sam Carr calls and tells her of the situation with her son, she goes immediately to the drugstore, without even changing her clothes. She is obviously devoted to her son, although she is also fully aware of how badly he behaves and what trouble he causes her. She says nothing of this in her dealings with Mr. Carr, with whom she is charming, humble, and dignified. She succeeds in softening Mr. Carr's heart. On the way home with Alfred, however, Mrs. Higgins reveals another side of her personality when she speaks angrily to him, saying he has disgraced her. All in all, Mrs. Higgins is a woman under great strain. Her son is always getting into trouble, and her daughter, who is even younger than Albert, married against Mrs. Higgins's wishes. Mrs. Higgins often manages to project an image of strength, but in reality she is weak and almost at a breaking point.

Themes

Motherly Love

Mrs. Higgins displays a mother's devotion to her son. Her devotion is so great she is able to overcome the immensity of her own worries, frustrations, and traumas in order to come to his rescue.

It is clear from Mrs. Higgins's distressed manner in the kitchen after she and Alfred have returned from the drugstore that she is living under a great strain. She seems to be at a breaking point. This

makes the reader appreciate the heroic effort she has just made to present a calm exterior to Mr. Carr. It must have taken a huge amount of focused will for her to do so. It was late at night when she received the call from the drugstore, and she left the house without getting properly dressed. The only thing on her mind was the welfare of her son. Whatever needed to be done, she would find the way to do it. She deals with Mr. Carr, who is justifiably angry, with a touching delicacy and a keen sense of what approach will work. She is not above using subtle feminine charm in order to persuade him to be lenient with her son. She makes no demands, and she does not challenge Mr. Carr. She merely offers an opinion (that at certain times good advice rather than punishment is what a boy needs). Her calm dignity becomes the dominant presence in the drugstore, and Mr. Carr softens.

Alfred notices what his mother is doing, but he does not understand why. He knows that if they were at home and someone suggested he be arrested, his mother would become very angry. But Mrs. Higgins has a mother's intuition about what qualities she needs to demonstrate at this moment. Her love for her son, the maternal love for which no sacrifice is too great, no task too hard, gives her the words she needs.

The striking nature of the change Mrs. Higgins undergoes when they arrive home only serves to highlight by contrast the supreme effort it must have taken to ease her son, who has disappointed her so many times, out of a difficult position. Her actions demonstrate the triumph of love, even in the most trying of circumstances.

Empathy, Knowledge, and Growing Up

At the beginning of the story, Alfred is an unimpressive young man with little to commend him. He has no empathy for others and does not feel it is wrong to steal from his employer. He steals just so he can keep up appearances with his friends. He seems shallow and incompetent. And yet by the end of the story, he has grown immensely. The growth begins when he goes to the kitchen, planning to thank his mother for the dignity and strength she showed in dealing with Mr. Carr. But Alfred finds out that his impression of his mother was not reality. The calm strength she projected was solely for his sake. Internally she was someone different. Alfred's sudden awareness of this fact completely arrests him. He has an insight into what his mother has had to go through in her life; he understands all her silent

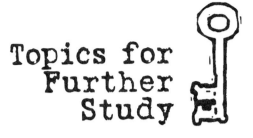

Topics for Further Study

- Describe an incident in your own life when you had a moment of revelation about someone. What truth did you see that was not apparent to you before, and how did it change the way you behaved afterwards?

- Do you think that Mr. Carr should have turned Alfred over to the police? Would Alfred have been better off in the long run by being prosecuted, or is his realization of how much his mother is suffering going to be sufficient for him to change his ways? Explain your answer based on events in the story.

- Write a short story approximately two pages in length that follows the structure of many of the stories in Callaghan's collection *Now That April's Here and Other Stories*. Your story should consist of a brief prelude, in which the situation is explained, followed by a confrontation. The confrontation should lead to some moment of realization (or revelation) on the part of the protagonist

in which he or she reaches a new understanding of life or a fresh understanding of his or her relationship with someone else. Limit the story to three characters or fewer.

- Research the Great Depression of the 1930s. What were the causes of the depression? What was life like for those who were unemployed or underemployed? How did people survive such hardships? What changes did the Great Depression bring about in social and economic policy in the United States and Canada?

- Rewrite "All the Years of Her Life" from the point of view of Mr. Carr. Show how he reacts to what happens. Show what he thinks and feels. For the final scene, after Mrs. Higgins and Alfred have left, show Mr. Carr reflecting on what has happened and wondering whether he made the right decision. Give him a moment of revelation, when he realizes something about life that had not struck him before.

---

tragedies. He also knows what she must have been thinking about as they walked home together. In this moment of empathy, knowledge, and insight, Alfred makes a leap beyond his own personal world, with its petty, selfish concerns, into the world of another person. He learns how to feel the pain of another person and, in so doing, glimpses a more mature way of living and being. In that moment, Alfred Higgins starts to grow up.

Style

Point of View

The story is told from the point of view of a selective omniscient narrator. This means that although the narrator, who is not a character in the

story, can enter the mind of any character and relate what the character is thinking, in practice he limits himself to focusing on one character.

For example, the narrator gives little information about what Mr. Carr is thinking, since the drugstore owner's thoughts are obvious from his words and actions; he is annoyed at having a thief as an employee. Any more attention given to the workings of Mr. Carr's mind would distract the reader's attention from where the author wants it, which is on the mind of Alfred. Alfred is the main character, and the narrator's knowledge of what is going on inside Alfred's mind enables the reader to observe him from the inside as well as the outside.

The narrator also chooses not to see into the mind of Alfred's mother. The effectiveness of the scene in the drugstore depends on the reader's ignorance of Mrs. Higgins's true state of mind. The insight into Mrs. Higgins's inner world has to come later through Alfred. It is this fact that gives the story its forceful, moving conclusion, because what is important is not Mrs. Higgins's state of mind *per se,* but the effect it has on her son when he perceives it for the first time.

Realism

The story belongs to the literary movement known as realism. The writer of realism seeks to give the impression that he is presenting life as it is. The opposite of realism is romantic fiction, in which life is presented in a more adventurous or heroic light. Realism deals with commonplace characters engaged in ordinary day-to-day activities (working in a drugstore, for example) and going through experiences that might happen to anyone. It would be hard to find three more ordinary, undistinguished characters than Alfred, his mother, and Mr. Carr. And yet, as sometimes happens in realist fiction, Alfred's mother, through a great effort of will, manages to rise to a level that if not quite heroic, certainly has some nobility.

Historical Context

Canadian Literature in the 1920s and 1930s

Canada did not officially become a country until 1867, so it has had a relatively short period to develop a distinctive literature of its own. Before Callaghan arrived on the scene in the late 1920s, few Canadian short-story writers had achieved any distinction. As Walter Allen points out in *The Short Story in English,* most pre-1920s Canadian literature also dealt either with pastoral life or with life in the wild, neither of which theme interested Callaghan, who grew up in an urban area.

The best respected Canadian literary predecessor to Callaghan is usually considered to be Duncan Campbell Scott (1862–1947). Scott was aware of the work of the best European writers of his time, such as Flaubert and Guy de Maupassant, which enabled him to produce work of above-average quality. Scott's best-known work of the three short-story collections he published is *The Village of Viger* (1896).

Another Canadian writer of short stories, as well as poetry and novels, is Callaghan's contemporary, Raymond Knister (1899–1932). His stories are notable for their clarity and sharp realism. Callaghan

himself acknowledged the high quality of Knister's work, but Knister's promising career was cut short by his premature death (he drowned in Lake St. Clair, Ontario, at the age of thirty-three). According to Allen, however, it is Callaghan whose work marked a new beginning for Canadian literature.

Callaghan made his living during the 1930s, publishing in the United States, not Canada. It was not easy for a Canadian writer of that period to get published in his own country. In ''The Plight of Canadian Fiction,'' an essay Callaghan published in 1938 in the *University of Toronto Quarterly,* Callaghan advises young Canadian writers that, even if they have talent and write honestly, they will not get published in their own country unless they first are published elsewhere. Callaghan points out that the only Canadian writers who publish in Canada are those who are willing to shape their work into a predictable formula that will fit in with the demands of the ''slick'' mass-market magazines. According to Callaghan, the Canadian literary writer who is not prepared to compromise his own integrity to suit the needs of the marketplace will have no outlet for his work. The only reason Callaghan was able to make a living from his writing was because he published in what he called the ''quality'' magazines in the United States, such as *Harper's, Scribner's,* the *Atlantic, Esquire* and the *New Yorker.* His book publisher in the 1930s, Random House, was also an American company.

In the 1940s, more distinctive Canadian fiction began to emerge, published by Canadian publishers, in the work of Sinclair Ross (1908–1996) and Hugh Maclennan (1907–1990). These writers did not base their work on American or British models but on Canadian themes and Canadian identity. This development took some time to filter into the Canadian education system. A distinguished Canadian novelist, Margaret Laurence (1926–1987), recalled that when she was in high school in the early 1940s, she was not assigned a single book by a Canadian author. She believed that Canadians of that period seriously undervalued the literature written by their fellow Canadians.

Critical Overview

During the 1930s, Callaghan's short stories were highly regarded by critics and reviewers. His work was compared to that of Russian writers Leo Tol-

Compare
&
Contrast

- **1930s:** Canadian literature is still in its infancy and is not known for having distinctive characteristics of its own. English-speaking Canadians tend to read mostly British or American fiction, but Callaghan brings a new voice to Canadian fiction.

  Today: Canadian literature is in the forefront of world literature. Writers such as Alice Munro, Margaret Atwood, Michael Ondaatje, Yann Martel, Alistair Macleod, and Carol Shields have won such international awards as Britain's prestigious Booker Prize and the American Pulitzer Prize for their work.

- **1930s:** The political situation in Europe is rapidly deteriorating. In 1936, the year Callaghan's *Now That April's Here and Other Stories* is published, German troops under Adolf Hitler's leadership march into the Rhineland. The three-year civil war in Spain also begins in 1936. In 1939 World War II begins.

  Today: Europe has overcome many of the consequences of the events of the 1930s and 1940s. Germany is no longer divided into East and West Germany. The Iron Curtain no longer divides eastern and western Europe. Spain is a democracy. The European Community is steadily expanding, and the North Atlantic Treaty Organization (NATO) is gradually increasing its membership to include nations that were formerly members of the communist Soviet bloc.

- **1930s:** The Great Depression creates hardship for millions of people in North America. At the height of the depression in Canada in 1933, unemployment is at 27 percent. Between 1929 and 1933, Canadian gross national product drops 43 percent. The depression ends in 1939.

  Today: Canada enjoys far greater economic stability and its citizens enjoy more security than was the case in the 1930s. Today's laws, which regulate a standard work week and a minimum wage as well as programs such as Medicare and unemployment insurance, arose from depression-era needs. The Bank of Canada, a central bank that manages the money supply and creates financial stability, also grew out of the Great Depression.

---

stoy and Anton Chekhov, both of whom were masters of the short-story form.

Wyndham Lewis favorably reviews the collection *Now That April's Here and Other Stories*, in which "All the Years of Her Life" appeared. The following comment from Lewis's review, which appears in Brandon Conron's *Morley Callaghan*, captures the essence of "All the Years of Her Life": "These are tales very full of human sympathy—a blending of all the events of life into a pattern of tolerance and mercy." Lewis admires the way almost all the stories in *Now That April's Here and Other Stories* end gently on a note of reconciliation.

Conron notes that the relationship between parents and children is the theme of many of the stories in *Now That April's Here and Other Stories*, and he highlights also the "double exposure" of Mrs. Higgins in "All the Years of Her Life." By this he means the contrast between the courageous display she puts on in the drugstore and the "frightened despair and trembling weakness" she exhibits in her home afterwards. Callaghan's stories, Conron observes, follow a certain pattern:

> They are all self-contained anecdotes. Their opening is usually a declarative statement that sets the stage for a drama that most frequently is psychological and involves little action. A problem is posed and, by description, dialogue and internal monologue, the story moves with easy economy through a climax to an ending which may not resolve the dilemma but invariably leaves it haunting the reader's mind.

"All the Years of Her Life" clearly follows this formula.

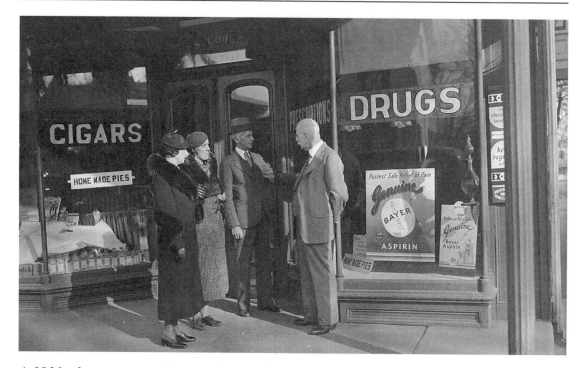

A 1930s drug store similar to Alfred's place of employment in "All the Years of Her Life"

Criticism

Bryan Aubrey

Aubrey holds a Ph.D. in English and has published many articles on twentieth-century literature. In this essay, Aubrey discusses the style and structure of Callaghan's short stories, and considers the importance of the psychological moment of revelation experienced by the protagonists, especially Alfred in "All the Years of Her Life."

Sometimes there are moments in a person's life that open a door to revelation; moments when life discloses a great truth that had previously been hidden, and huge personal growth and change suddenly become possible. Such moments are surprising, often unasked for, and may well shake up and transform rigidly held perceptions and beliefs. They may be more valuable for a person than months or years of dull, predictable day-to-day living. Such a moment is the essence of Callaghan's "All the Years of Her Life," which seems like a slight story until the last paragraph, when one single perception on the part of Alfred changes his life completely. There are so many implications in that one moment

of heightened perception and understanding that the story becomes almost a coming-of-age tale. It also puts in mind what literary critics call the "Romantic Moment," a moment of illuminated perception of a mundane event or object that is found preeminently in the poetry of William Wordsworth but also in modern prose writers, contemporaries of Callaghan such as James Joyce, Henry James, Joseph Conrad, and Virginia Woolf. Woolf called such moments "moments of vision," the "little daily miracles, illuminations, matches struck unexpectedly in the dark" (quoted in M. H. Abrams, *Natural Supernaturalism: Tradition and Revolution in Romantic Literature*).

A match struck in the dark is a perfect metaphor for the sudden illumination that comes to young Alfred. It is an inner rather than outer change that he undergoes (although outer change will no doubt follow). In "All the Years of Her Life," as is often the case in Callaghan's stories, not much happens on the surface. The external events can be related in a sentence: a young man is caught pilfering from his employer, but his mother persuades his employer not to call in the police. The reader's interest in the story does not focus primarily on the plot, nor does it center on Callaghan's style or his descriptive

What Do I Read Next?

- *Such Is My Beloved* (1934) is widely considered to be Callaghan's finest novel. It tells the story of a young priest who tries to rescue two prostitutes, depicting a world where cynicism and betrayal are common but also where a divine love redeems the fallen.

- *The Oxford Book of Canadian Short Stories in English* (1986), edited by Margaret Atwood and Robert Weaver, contains forty-one short stories written during the nineteenth and twentieth centuries. Authors include Mordecai Richler, Alice Munro, Sinclair Ross, Stephen Leacock, and Callaghan, as well as other, less well-known writers.

- Alice Munro's *Selected Stories* (1997) is a representative selection of the work of a Canadian writer considered one of the greatest contemporary short-story writers. Her subject matter is often the troubled lives of women in small-towns in Ontario, but her art transcends its rather narrow base and has universal appeal.

- *The Complete Short Stories of Ernest Hemingway: The Finca Vigia Edition* (1998) is the definitive collection of Hemingway's stories and can be used to compare his work with that of Callaghan, his friend and contemporary.

---

powers. The style is terse and unadorned, devoid of metaphor or figurative language of any kind. The diction is also plain, and the characters are described with a minimum of physical details. All the reader learns of the physical appearance of the characters is that Sam Carr is little and gray-haired; Alfred's mother is "large and plump, with a little smile on her friendly face"; and Alfred has a thin face with pimples, and his mother describes him as a "big fellow." Most creative-writing teachers would demand more of their students than this!

But Callaghan was fully aware of what he was doing. He had very clear ideas about the way he wanted to write. He stated his credo in his memoir, *That Summer in Paris*, in which he noted that as a young man he rejected many of the most popular writers of the day, including Edith Wharton and H. G. Wells, as "show-off writers; writers intent on proving to their readers that they could be clever and had some education." His goal as a writer was to concentrate on "revealing the object as it was." Elaborate language only took attention away from the object or event described and put the focus on the writer himself. Callaghan's language therefore resembles the economical, objective style of a reporter (as Callaghan was for a short time) rather

than a literary writer. "Tell the truth cleanly," was his watchword. He remembers listening one evening at twilight to the sound of birdsong and a woman's voice, and making it his task to describe what he heard in a way that did not sound like literature.

If Callaghan's style is direct and to the point, the structure of "All the Years of Her Life" follows a formula that characterizes many of the stories in the collection *Now That April's Here*, as Victor Hoar has pointed out in his book *Morley Callaghan*. Hoar identifies this structure as "prelude, confrontation, revelation." The prelude contains the exposition and also starts off the action, which quickly builds to a quarrel or disagreement or some kind of misunderstanding (confrontation). Then follows a resolution in which the protagonist reaches a usually positive new understanding of some important aspect of life (revelation).

What sticks in the reader's mind is usually the revelation. Often, as in "All the Years of Her Life," this comes right at the end of the story. In Callaghan's "Possession," for example, the only bright spot in the life of Dan, an unemployed young man, is his growing friendship with a young woman named Helen. He is devastated when Helen tells him she

> Between these two extremes--the healthy and unhealthy personality type-- there is a gap the size of the Grand Canyon, and Alfred shows in his breakthrough moment that he can make the leap."

must leave town to care for her sick mother. After he sees her off on the subway, Dan feels alone, with nothing in the world to call his own, and he reproaches himself for allowing Helen to leave. But then comes the mysterious moment with which the story ends. As he walks along the street, Dan feels the life of the city surging within him, with all its noise and traffic, and he suddenly realizes that his happiness did not depend on Helen at all: ''He felt he held it all in him, he felt all the joy of full possession, and he could never be alone again.''

Another example of a moment of revelation occurs in Callaghan's story ''Younger Brother.'' It is particularly interesting because to create the moment, Callaghan repeats a plot device that is central to ''All the Years of Her Life.'' It occurs when the protagonist observes another character, or in the case of ''Younger Brother,'' two characters, without the character or characters being aware of it. What the protagonist sees shocks him. In ''Younger Brother,'' young Jimmie comes home and finds his elder sister Millie sitting on the sofa with her boyfriend, an unpleasant man whom Jimmie dislikes. As Jimmie watches and listens unobserved, the couple appears to quarrel and the boyfriend slaps Millie lightly across the face. Jimmie expects his feisty sister to strike him back, but instead she begins to cry. Seeing this, Jimmie's world begins to crumble: ''Everything important and permanent in Jimmie's life now seemed beyond him.''

Although the plot device and the moment of revelation are similar, the content and effects of Jimmie's moment are quite different than those of Alfred in ''All the Years of Her Life.'' Whereas Alfred grows in knowledge, Jimmie lapses into

confusion (although by the end of the story Jimmie has managed to adjust to new realities).

This analysis shows that what counts in Callaghan's stories is a change in perspective on the part of the protagonist. Before the critical moment, the protagonist sees his life in a certain way, with certain structures and meanings. But after the moment of change comes, everything becomes different. The whole meaning of life undergoes a seismic shift. In no story is this shift more apparent than ''All the Years of Her Life.''

Perhaps one way of looking at Alfred's moment of transformation is to analyze it in terms of healthy or unhealthy personality types. At the beginning of the story, Alfred does not look like promising material. He gives every impression of being thoroughly selfish and unaware of the effect of his actions on others. He has little awareness of the strain his mother is under, or what her life is really like, until that extraordinary moment when he observes her trembling hand as she raises the tea cup to her lips. In that moment he makes a huge transition to healthy adulthood (''his youth seemed to be over'') because he has learned to empathize with another human being. Empathy is the beginning of compassion, for it is hardly possible for a fully developed individual to see into the suffering of another, as Alfred does here, and not feel compassion. The opposite of the empathetic individual is what psychologists call a narcissistic personality. The narcissist is easily recognizable as the person who always steers a conversation back to himself. In the eyes of the narcissist, everything revolves around him, and he is largely unaware of the needs and perspectives of other people. This is also true of the sociopath, who is incapable of empathy and merely uses others to gratify his own needs.

Between these two extremes—the healthy and unhealthy personality type—there is a gap the size of the Grand Canyon, and Alfred shows in his breakthrough moment that he can make the leap. He is helped by the situation upon which he stumbles, because it gives him the chance to observe a familiar person when that person is unaware of his presence. In social situations, humans often disguise themselves, whether consciously or unconsciously. The face they present to others may not reflect the thoughts and feelings they are really experiencing. In many situations this may be entirely necessary, and in the story Mrs. Higgins shows in the drugstore that she is a master of such disguises, or masks, when the need arises. Equally, however, the masks people wear may stifle real communication. And naturally when people think they are alone they tend to drop the masks they habitually wear in other situations. Therefore Alfred's mother, thinking she no longer has to keep up appearances, unwittingly helps to facilitate the crucial moment when Alfred sees her in a new light. Alfred, of course, must still have the perceptiveness and maturity to notice the difference and allow the implications of it to sink deeply into his mind.

The irony of human life is that two people can often spend many years in close proximity to each other and never have an ''Alfred moment''—that is, never have much insight into the essence and reality of the other person's life. This often leads to a lack of communication, and eventually a wall is built up between them that is impossible to penetrate. There can be great distance in proximity, as appears to have been the case for Alfred and his mother. It is particularly significant that the incident in the story involves a parent and child. Since adolescents are so fully occupied trying to find their own place in the world, they may find it hard to see their oh-so-familiar parents as individuals in their own right, with feelings and needs of their own. Often those whom a person most needs to see in a fresh light are the ones closest to them.

This is why the last line of the story, ''It seemed to him that this was the first time he had ever looked upon his mother'' is so moving. The challenge of life is always to see anew, not to let the film of habit or custom dull or distort perception. The image of the trembling hand holding the teacup, and the effect this has on Alfred, is surely a secular version of an epiphany—the illuminated, transforming moment in which a spiritual reality shines through a mundane object. In *Stephen Hero,* James Joyce defined such a moment (quoted in Abrams, *Natural Supernaturalism*):

> By an epiphany [Stephen] meant a sudden spiritual manifestation, whether in the vulgarity of speech or of gesture or in a memorable phase of the mind itself. He believed that it was for the man of letters to record these epiphanies with extreme care, seeing that they themselves are the most delicate and evanescent of moments.

Although Callaghan was a realist through and through, a secular not a spiritual mind, he obeyed Joyce's injunction. The nonliterary literary man preserved that delicate moment of epiphany in an exquisite work of art, the short story, ''All the Years of Her Life.''

Source: Bryan Aubrey, Critical Essay on ''All the Years of Her Life,'' in *Short Stories for Students,* Gale, 2004.

William Walsh

In the following essay excerpt, Walsh discusses ''All the Years of Her Life,'' focusing on the ''moment[s] of consciousness—of true recognition'' in the story.

It would be hard to find a writer who contrasts more vigorously with Katherine Mansfield than the Canadian Morley Callaghan, whom I wish to consider now. For one thing he works at a much greater psychic distance from, and with a considerably lower degree of sympathy for, the English literary tradition, in which Katherine Mansfield felt so intimately at home. For another, there is in his work, as in that of other Canadians writing in English, a further strain, an implicit sense of oppression by the powerful tradition of the United States. Moreover, Morley Callaghan is a writer whose intentions are simpler than those of Katherine Mansfield, and whose achievement is more restricted—a difference manifested in the contrast of their prose styles: where hers is poetic and suggestive, his is crabbed; where hers is light and gliding, his is stiff. And how extraordinarily discrepant are the materials they treat and the worlds they construct. The world evoked in Morley Callaghan's work is a bleak, industrial one, and its gritty presence rubs off even on the countryside. It is a shut-in, remorseless place in which the individual person even when he lives in a family is painfully isolated. Morley Callaghan's characters in the short stories, with which I shall begin, are mostly drawn from the middle and lower reaches of society: the bereaved poor, the workman, the forsaken wife, the widow, the hard-up young man, the nervous curate and the elderly parish priest, the part-time pugilist, the small girl with a dying mother, the amateur criminal, the drug-store keeper, the apprentice reporter, the cocky young man, the pianist in the tavern. His style is plain to the point of drabness and often painfully clumsy, and yet, in spite of the raw, northern world, the graceless manner and the dreary ordinariness of the characters, the reader is increasingly conscious of an awkward, stubborn and unfashionable conscience, and of a bluntly honest endeavour to dig out and to hold on to some evasive human truth.

'To dig out': as I use the phrase to convey something of Morley Callaghan's hard, blow-by-blow prose, it comes to me that the words say more about him than I had thought. They carry with them a sense of investigation and reporting, and

" A moment of consciousness--of true recognition, not the usual routine registration--is necessary to clinch the existence of an event ... and as it were, to sanction the disturbance it will produce."

Callaghan's stories strike one precisely as reports—as reporters' reports, in fact. They give the feeling of pre-1914–18 provincial newspaper chronicles, and sometimes of provincial newspaper prose, too. (In fact, Morley Callaghan began his career as a reporter on the *Toronto Star* when Ernest Hemingway was working on the same newspaper.) The storyteller's function as Morley Callaghan practises it is in keeping with this bias in his work. It is to impose an arrest upon time, and to outline for a moment an interruption in the flow of life, which, it is clear, continues as before once the observer's eye is withdrawn. His is a restrictive, framing technique. He is concerned with events, which are shown as instances and images of experience, while the people involved are planed down to an extreme simplicity. A Morley Callaghan story presents a special combination of realistically rendered happening and of people denuded of complication, who are seen as strangers are seen in the street in a single concentrated glance, as types and illustrations. Realism, and a somehow surprising strain of formality, blend in a drily personal way. Indeed, as the reader begins to find his way about the stories, he becomes gradually aware—the effect is slow and cumulative—of an authentic individuality strong enough to show through the plain prose and the straightforward narrative technique.

The reader's sense of that presence is arrived at by continuous application. The unremarkable medium, which has none of the literary sophistication of Hemingway, one of Callaghan's early heroes, takes time to make its mark. And yet it is exactly suited in its unpretentiously humdrum way to the intention on which all this work is sprung, the effort at scrupulous fidelity to the facts of the case. And

the 'case' in these stories is the mysteriousness of the ordinary, the inexplicable sequences of feeling, the bewildering discrepancies of human fact, *and* the logic, 'as severe as it is fleeting' as Coleridge has it, which the imagination can elicit from these frictions and inconsequences.

Short stories by Morley Callaghan appeared in 1929 (*A Native Argosy*), 1931 (*No Man's Meat*), and 1936 (*Now That April's Here*), and in the two-volume collection (*Morley Callaghan Stories,* 1959). Most of them are strikingly uniform in quality and even a random choice provides the characteristic Callaghan combination, an undistracted concentration on essentials, a rather grouchy but unquestionable honesty, a grave sobriety of mood and treatment and a naturally discriminating moral imagination. Let me look for a moment at the first story, *"All the Years of her Life,"* in the 1959 collection. The dim and oddly innocent Alfred Higgins is caught by his employer pilfering from the drugstore in which he works silly little objects which he sells for spending money. From this thin, commonplace situation there springs a movement towards complexity, not through analysis but by the natural growth of the action. Alfred's crime, at first denied, and then admitted, becomes an event, a phenomenon, which is gravely scrutinised by Mr Carr, the employer, Alfred himself, who from now on is the registering instrument rather than an active protagonist, and Mrs Higgins, Alfred's mother. She is large and plump with a little smile on a friendly face and seems an intensely positive person beneath her deference. The employer is dislodged from his position of moral superiority, which he had indeed begun to enjoy. Alfred realised that 'Sam Carr was puzzled by his mother, as if he had expected her to come in and plead with him tearfully, and instead he was being made to feel a bit ashamed by her vast tolerance. While there was only the sound of the mother's soft, assured voice in the store, Mr Carr began to nod his head encouragingly at her. Without being alarmed, while being just large and still and simple and hopeful, she was becoming dominant there in the dimly lit store.' The mother's contained strength deflects the angry proprietor. His expression of regret at what happened is almost an apology to her. When Alfred and his mother return to their home he begins to see that the force she showed in the shop was not what it seemed to be. It was not some intrinsic strength of character but a force which issued out of a passion for protection, and once home, with the crisis over, it collapses. As she drinks her tea her hand is trembling and she looks very old. 'He watched his mother, and he never spoke, but at that moment his youth seemed to be over; he knew all the years of her life by the way her hand trembled as she raised the cup to her lips. It seemed to him that this was the first time he had ever looked upon his mother.'

A moment of consciousness—of true recognition, not the usual routine registration—is necessary to clinch the existence of an event, like Alfred's petty crime, or a state of feeling like the mother's weary anxiety, and as it were, to sanction the disturbance it will produce.

Source: William Walsh, ''Morley Callaghan,'' in *A Manifold Voice: Studies in Commonwealth Literature,* Chatto and Windus, 1970, pp. 185–88.

Brandon Conron

In the following essay excerpt, Conron provides overviews of the stories in Now That April's Here, *including ''All the Years of Her Life.''*

Callaghan's second collection presents thirty-five selected stories written between 1929 and 1935. All of these had already been published in North American magazines except the title piece. It appeared in *This Quarter* (October–December, 1929) as the result of a bet which Edward Titus made with Callaghan and Robert McAlmon in Paris encouraging both to write a story expressing each's contrasting views about two young men familiar in the Montparnasse of 1929. McAlmon never did write his story.

''Now That April's Here'' comes fourth in the arrangement of the book. Its two chief characters, Charles Milford with his ''large round head that ought to have belonged to a Presbyterian minister,'' and his younger companion Johnny Hill with his ''rather chinless faun's head'' arrive in Paris in the late autumn. They have left their native Middle West city convinced that the American continent has ''nothing to offer them.'' They spend their afternoons wandering around the streets, admiring in art gallery windows such *objets d'art* as ''the prints of the delicate clever unsubstantial line work of Foujita.'' In the evenings they sit together at the cafés, snickering at the conversation of other customers. Aspiring writers, they look forward to the stimulating spring days of April.

The story traces in dramatic interludes this autumn introduction, a winter in Nice and their eager return to Paris at the beginning of April. Ironically that month frustrates their expectations.

> Her public display of courageous dignity and calm strength as she dissuades his employer from prosecuting are balanced in her own home by a private expression of frightened despair and trembling weakness."

For it brings cold and disagreeable weather, a temporary separation of the two friends as Johnny visits in England, and an irrevocable rift in their intimate relationships when Constance Foy, ''a simple-minded fat-faced girl with a boy's body and short hair dyed red'' becomes part of this unconventional love triangle. During the bright clear days while ''Paris was gay and lively'' as though in mockery of their romantic hopes, the boys are ''sad and hurt and sorry.'' On the evening of the rainy day when Johnny leaves to return home to the United States with Constance, Charles sits forlornly at a café with his overcoat wrapped around him and wearing his large black American hat for the first time in Paris.

Throughout his depiction of these youths Callaghan carefully builds up details which authenticate the atmosphere of intimacy that surrounds his main figures as they move about the left bank circle: ''People sitting at the café in the evening when the lights were on, saw them crossing the road together under the street lamp, their bodies leaning forward at the same angle and walking on tiptoe.'' Charles' nervous habit of ''scratching his cheek with the nail of his right forefinger till the flesh was torn and raw,'' his way of raising his eyebrows, Johnny's manner of snickering with his finger over his mouth, and even their bedroom conversations all develop a concrete picture of their strange world. Callaghan's handling of this detail is full of clever suggestion and insinuation. Even the title has an appropriately ironic twist in terms of Browning's original application in ''Home Thoughts from Abroad,'' as Johnny's April visit to England brings not spring joy but the autumnal decay of disintegrating family relationships, and the two boys never do ''recapture / The first fine careless rapture.'' Yet the story has an overall mocking brittleness of tone, which is not evident in the deft treatment of a somewhat similar theme in *No Man's Meat,* and which is different from Callaghan's customary compassionate or even detached interpretation of human aberrations.

Seven of the stories in *Now That April's Here* are included in J. Edward O'Brien's *The Best Short Stories* annual editions of 1930 through 1936. Set against selections of other writers, these tales provide a criterion of Callaghan's comparative skill in the genre as well as an indication of changes in his own technique. They also treat a variety of themes which are representative of his 1936 collection: young lovers' quarrels and problems; relations between parents and children; religious and miscellaneous subjects.

"The Faithful Wife," which appeared in the December 28, 1929 issue, was the first thirty-nine of Callaghan's stories to be published in *The New Yorker.* It is included not only in the 1930 edition of *The Best Short Stories* but also in O'Brien's *50 Best American Short Stories 1915–1939* (1939), as well as in Martha Foley's *Fifty Best American Short Stories 1915–1965* (1965). This piece catches a mood of poignant frustration. A young woman Lola, whose husband is a war invalid, invites a youthful lunch counter attendant George to her apartment on the last night before he leaves to enter college. The early winter setting is suggestively portrayed: the shoddy restaurant near the railway station, warming-up base for "brightly dressed and highly powdered" girls who are sharply contrasted with "gentle, and aloofly pleasant" Lola, and the older counter men with their knowing ways who urge on the naïve George, are realistically depicted. George's unexpected invitation to Lola's apartment and his nervous expectation are skilfully exploited as he finds Lola dressed in a tight fitting sweater and "almost savagely" responsive to his initial overtures. Yet for her these embraces are terminal. She has correctly assessed George's temperament—that he will "not spoil it for her." The story is typical of Callaghan in its moving insight into spiritual kinship, its sharpness of detail, and the final shift of frustration from the faithful wife Lola to the reluctantly noble young man.

"The Young Priest," originally published in *The New Yorker* of September 27, 1930 and included in the 1931 edition of *The Best Short Stories,* was later modified and expanded into a chapter in *A Broken Journey.* As noted already, this episode is a sensitive treatment of a young and inexperienced priest's introduction to the ugly actualities of life.

"The Red Hat," first published in the October 31, 1931 issue of *The New Yorker* and included in the 1932 edition of *The Best Short Stories,* expresses a frustrated yearning typical of the Depression era and appropriate to the autumn background against which it is set. A young wife Frances yields to the impulse to spend a great part of her weekly salary on a little red hat. Since her actor husband Eric, out of work for four months, "had been so moody and discontented recently she now thought with pleasure of pleasing him by wearing something that would give her a new elegance, of making him feel cheerful and proud of her and glad, after all, that they were married." Her eager modelling of the hat, however, precipitates a violent quarrel with Eric over the sensitive subject of money. Anxious to conciliate him, she sells the hat to the landlady for a third of its original price.

The structure moves neatly in a circle with Frances' emotions being described in both the opening and the conclusion in similar language. Just as she had let her fancies wander in front of the silver-faced and red-lipped mannequin in the shop window, so she lets her hopes rise that she can buy the hat back from Mrs. Foley and feels "an eagerness and a faint elation; it was a plain little red hat, the kind of hat she had wanted for months, elegant and expensive, a plain felt hat, but so very distinctive." Frances' desire, hesitation and finely shaded rationalization are concretely conveyed. The scene in the shop, where the "deep-bosomed saleswoman, splendidly corseted, and wearing black silk" ingratiatingly smiles approval, and Frances' vision of her own face in the mirror resembling the mannequin's face, is neatly balanced by the home scene with Eric slumped disconsolately in his chair and savagely deflating Frances' dream of his admiring approbation.

"A Sick Call," which appeared in the *Atlantic Monthly* of September, 1932 and was included in the 1933 edition of *The Best Short Stories,* probes a Roman Catholic priest's dilemma of conscience. Called to the bedside of a sick and frightened woman who has left the Church, old Father Macdowell meets the sullen opposition of her husband, John Williams. Behind the screen of his deafness, shortness of breath and tired legs, the priest succeeds in entering the bedroom which symbolically reminds him of a little girl's room with its light wall-paper with tiny birds in flight. John's protest against the priest's attempt to disrupt their spiritual kinship is futile in the face of Father Macdowell's patient persistence and even guile. Requesting a glass of water, he quickly hears Mrs. Williams' confession and gives absolution during the brief period in which her husband is out of the room getting the drink.

Throughout the story Father Macdowell is the focal figure. The significant details of his physical appearance and tolerant disposition are briefly sketched in the opening paragraph: his ''wheezy breath,'' large build, ''white-headed except for a shiny baby-pink bald spot on the top of his head,'' his florid face with its ''fine red interlacing vein lines'' and his tenderness with those who come to confess. All of these details are relevant to the bedroom scene and play a part in his battle of wits with John. Appropriately the conclusion returns to the priest as he goes home from the brief call pondering uneasily ''whether he had played fair with the young man,'' whether he has come between the two, alternating ironically between ''rejoicing amiably to think he had so successfully ministered to one who had strayed from the faith,'' and admiring sadly the staunch—if ''pagan''—beauty of John's love for his wife.

''Mr. and Mrs. Fairbanks,'' first published in *Harper's Bazaar* (September, 1933) and included in the 1934 edition of *The Best Short Stories,* is a miniature drama of misunderstanding between two young married people. Walking arm in arm together in the park, they share their mixed emotions over the discovery that Helen Fairbanks is expecting a baby. Bill's pride and pleasure in his wife's condition gradually overcome her uncertainty and fear until they are both glowing with contentment. At this crucial moment they pass a bench where a tired, shabby old man is sitting looking like a beggar. In an impulsive gesture of generosity Helen offers him a quarter which he declines with simple dignity. This silent rebuke arouses in her a mood of humiliation and injured pride that Bill's logically comforting remarks only accentuate. The happy contentment of a few moments before evaporates, the afternoon sunlight becomes ''hot and withering, drying up the little bit of freshness there was in the park,'' and fear of future poverty and old age pervades her thoughts. As the couple turn homeward, keeping ''a step away from each other, so their elbows would not touch,'' they hurry past the bench where the old man is seated. Glancing back Helen sees him ''looking after them, and suddenly he smiled at her, smiling gently as if he had noticed in the first place that they had been happy and now were like two

lovers who had quarrelled.'' This understanding rapport restores the mutual glow shared by husband and wife.

In his portrayal of the Fairbanks Callaghan catches and registers how fragile human relationships may be. Although the background of the Depression sharpens their fears and anxieties in contemplation of the responsibilities of parenthood, the emotions represented have a universal application. Even man's response to the weather is conditioned by his feeling of the moment.

''Father and Son,'' published in *Harper's Bazaar,* June, 1934 and included in the 1935 edition of *The Best Short Stories,* explores the feelings of a father who after a four year interval visits a young son and his mother. Greg Henderson, moderately successful New York lawyer, is drawn by an inexplicable compulsion to the old stone farmhouse in Pennsylvania where his former wife Mona lives with her husband Frank Molsen. From the moment of his arrival Greg feels uneasily aware of how unimportant he has become in the life of Mona and his own son Mike, who is ignorant of his real parent's identity. Despite the natural antagonism between himself and Frank, Greg is able to establish a companionable relationship with Mike. Although he contemplates taking his son away with him, Greg realizes how wrong such an action would be, and takes a kind of resigned pride in the fact that Mike is a ''fine boy.''

This is a story of strong contrasts both in natural setting and in human characteristics. The dark hill and the shadow cast by the huge old barn stand out sharply in the moonlight and the flood of light from the window; the silence of the mist-laden valley is a sudden change for Greg who is accustomed to city noises. Tall and dark in expensive clothes, Greg is in physical contrast with Frank, short and fair in his leather jacket. Temperamentally, the distinction between the two is even more marked. Urban Greg seems lonely, wretched and out of place in the simple farm home of Mona, with her peaceful assurance, and of Frank, with his social revolutionary enthusiasm. The latter looks on this ''no-account lawyer, a little bourgeois,'' as though ''he were an old enfeebled man who had been a slave all his life.'' This sense of himself creeps into Greg's own mind as he listens to the symbolical sound of ''the trickling of water in the nearly dried-up creek.'' Yet his pleasant day with his son and Mike's warm and spontaneous farewell bring a surge of joy to Greg which fills his emptiness and somehow unites him spiritually with Mona and Frank.

"The Blue Kimono," first published in the May, 1935 issue of *Harper's Bazaar* and included in the 1936 edition of *The Best Short Stories,* conveys with restraint the powerful feelings of a young couple when their son falls ill. Waking at dawn, George finds his wife Marthe nursing their feverish boy Walter, whom she suspects of having infantile paralysis. This new calamity triggers an outburst of bitterness from George over the bad luck which had dogged them ever since coming to the city. The corrosive effect of six months' unemployment on their bright dreams and aspirations, their fine resolutions and plans, seems to him to be symbolized by his wife's tattered blue kimono:

> The kimono had been of a Japanese pattern adorned with clusters of brilliant flowers sewn in silk. George had given it to her at the time of their marriage; now he stared at it, torn as it was at the arms, with pieces of old padding hanging out at the hem, with the light-coloured lining showing through in many places, and he remembered how, when the kimono was new, Marthe used to make the dark hair across her forehead into bangs, fold her arms across her breasts, with her wrists and hands concealed in the sleeve folds, and go around the room in the bright kimono, taking short, prancing steps, pretending she was a Japanese girl.

As the boy's temperature drops under the effect of an aspirin, however, both father and mother gain new hope. Mutual concern for their child deepens their own love for each other. The quiet implications of this changed mood are subtly indicated as Marthe, taking off the kimono, is suddenly sure that she can "draw the torn parts together and make it look bright and new."

In "Day by Day" the discouraging effect of unemployment is particularly evident. This compact story, originally published in *The New Yorker* of August 20, 1932, treats the theme of suspicion and jealousy nourished by economic distress. Pretty young Madge Winslow, after an innocent afternoon of window-shopping, relaxes peacefully in the park and dreams of recapturing with her husband John the eager spontaneity of their days of romance. Uncomplaining of the failure of their plans "or that her husband went from one job to another and the work was always less suited to him," she timidly asks "God to make her husband content, without any suspicion of her." Arriving home late, by her very animation and inner warmth she excites a jealous outburst from John. When he walks out of the house angry and embarrassed by his violence and lack of faith, Madge sits down to await his return:

> Tears were in her eyes as she looked around the mean little kitchen. She had such a strange feeling of guilt. White-faced and still, she tried to ask herself what it was that was slowly driving them apart day by day.

Accentuated by the conditions of the Depression era, the dilemma, frustration, paradox and disillusionment involved in the adjustment of a married couple are all subtly suggested or concretely portrayed; the very beauty which attracts a young man can also make him a suspicious husband; the cruel misunderstandings of married life are in stark contrast with the carefree gaiety and trust of courtship; youthful hopes often dissolve in the harsh actualities of experience; and hope itself may sometimes seem an affront to the miserable. More pervasively than many of the pieces in Callaghan's collection, "Day by Day" reflects the mood of pessimism of the thirties which intensified the age-old problems of young lovers.

When he was requested in 1942 to select his own favorite story for Whit Burnett's collection of "over 150 self-chosen and complete masterpieces" from "America's 93 living authors" published in *This Is My Best* (1943), Callaghan submitted "Two Fishermen." This story treats a typically Callaghan theme of human justice through an interesting series of ironic contrasts. Young Michael Foster, only reporter for the small town *Examiner,* discovers the identity of the man K. Smith who has arrived to hang Michael's old acquaintance Thomas Delaney, convicted of killing his wife's molester. In an evening of fishing together Michael and Smitty come to understand each other. The next morning after the hanging in the jail Smitty magnanimously gives to Michael two fish caught that morning. Shortly afterwards outside the jail yard these same fish are seized by one of the angry crowd and thrown at the hangman.

The peaceful setting of Collingwood on Georgian Bay, with "the blue hills beyond the town . . . shining brilliantly on square patches of farm land," seems incongruous with the hangman's grim purpose. In his explanation of why he chose this story for inclusion in *This Is My Best* Callaghan comments on the warm human relationship which developed between the young reporter and the executioner, as well as

> the hangman's rather wistful attachment to his despised job and his realization that it gave him an opportunity to get around the country and enjoy himself as a human being and a fisherman. And then after I had written it I saw that it had a certain social implication that I liked. The hangman, a necessary

figure in society, a man definitely serving the public and the ends of justice, was entitled to a little human dignity. In fact he saw himself as a dignified human being. But of course as an instrument of justice he became a despised person, and even his young friend, who understood his wistful humanity, betrayed that humanity when the chips were down. If I had started out to write the story with that in mind it might have become very involved but I wrote it very easily and naturally and without any trouble at all.

The contrast between Smitty in his human aspect and Mr. K. Smith as a public official is striking. As a fisherman dressed in casual clothes he is a small shy man "with little gray baby curls on the back of his neck," proud father of five children and an amusing raconteur. As an executioner "dressed in a long black cut-away coat with gray striped trousers, a gates-ajar collar and a narrow red tie" he walks with military precision and carries himself "with a strange cocky dignity." These two aspects of his personality are neatly brought together in the image of the two fish which he gives to Michael. They exemplify for both Michael and Smitty the fact that man is not only an individual but is also a creature of society. The fish, symbolical evidence of friendship, also become in the closing episode instruments of human betrayal and shameful rejection.

The stories of *Now That April's Here* have a remarkably uniform quality. The themes of the remaining twenty-five will be briefly noted. Several treat a variety of dreams, misunderstandings or entanglements of lovers: "The Rejected One," a family's disapproval of a young man's gaudy belle as a suitable marriage partner; "Guilty Woman," a young woman's stolen moment of love with her older sister's sweetheart; "Let Me Promise You," the attempt to recapture a former beau by an expensive birthday present; "Ellen," an unmarried pregnant woman's hope that her lover will return; "Timothy Harshaw's Flute," a young couple's impractical dream of moving to Paris; "The Snob," a lovers' quarrel resulting from a young man's sense of shame in snubbing his poor father; "The Two Brothers," the complex influence of a prodigal upon his older brother's love affair; "The Bride," the need for mutual attention in marriage; "One Spring Night," the natural warmth and the frustration of adolescent love; "It Must Be Different," the stifling effect of parental suspicion on young love; "Younger Brother," a boy's ignorant confusion about his sister's attitude to men; "Three Lovers," an older man's loss of his loved one to a younger rival through lack of trust; "The Duel," a former beau's failure to win back his girl; "Silk Stock-

ings," a frustrated attempt to win a girl's approval by a birthday present; "Rigmarole," the need to preserve in married love the sentimentalities of courtship; and "Possession," the recognition that a woman's genuine concern for her lover is superior to mere physical surrender.

Other stories in the collection reflect Callaghan's understanding of family life and the relationship between parents and children. The initial story, "All the Years of Her Life," which was included in *Short Stories from The New Yorker* (1940), presents a double exposure of a mother whose son is detected in petty larceny. Her public display of courageous dignity and calm strength as she dissuades his employer from prosecuting are balanced in her own home by a private expression of frightened despair and trembling weakness. The effect of family dissension on both parents and children is portrayed in "The Runaway," in which the quarrels of his father and stepmother so magnify a boy's own little failures that he runs away. "A Separation" reveals the unhappy result of a broken home and the tensions which arise between a deserted husband and his son.

The remaining pieces concern diverse aspects of human aspiration, disappointment and adjustment. In "Shining Red Apple" a fruit dealer gives vent to his resentment over not having a son by tormenting a hungry boy. "Lunch Counter" dramatizes the suspicions of a frustrated sensualist and his prudish wife who spoil an innocent friendship between a cook and a teen-age girl. In "Rocking Chair" the symbol of a young widower's love for his deceased wife is misinterpreted by an aggressive female friend as a token of favor toward her. "An Old Quarrel" contrasts the significance of petty animosities of bygone days with the richness of memories of happy times together. A priest's visit in "Absolution" arouses in an alcoholic woman "a faintly remembered dignity" of past respectability. In "Sister Bernadette" an illegitimate baby becomes the symbol of the sacrificed motherhood of a hospital nun.

Now That April's Here indicates both continuity and change in Callaghan's fictional technique. As in his earlier *A Native Argosy,* the stories, although distinctive and individual in flavor, do follow a recognizable formula. They are all self-contained anecdotes. Their opening is usually a declarative statement that sets the stage for a drama that most frequently is psychological and involves little action. A problem is posed, and, by description, dialogue and internal monologue, the story moves with easy economy through a climax to an ending which may not resolve the dilemma but invariably leaves it haunting the reader's mind. Sometimes the conclusion returns full cycle to the same emotional attitudes introduced initially, and these are then perceived in the light of a changed situation. Few violent passions are depicted, and little humor is displayed except in the quiet irony which pervades the style. A sure sense of significant detail and mood, and an unobtrusive use of symbolism contribute suggestive overtones of universality.

There are, however, obvious changes in the stories of this second collection. The chronological duration is briefer. The settings are authentically American, since many of the stories were actually written in New York about that city, and its streets are often mentioned by name. The tales reflect the conditions of the Depression era. The depiction of family life involving children is more frequent. The syntax is tighter and the overall structure more artful than in *A Native Argosy*. The characters, although still unpretentious and ordinary people, are generally more intelligent and more sophisticated than the bewildered persons of earlier stories with whom the average reader has difficulty identifying himself. Callaghan interprets this cross-section of humanity with sympathy yet detachment. His tales have a restraint, an unstressed reticence and a deceptive gentleness that subtly convey to the reader the quiet implications of the awkward emotional predicaments and fluctuations between happiness and despair which occur in intimate relationships. In his adroit handling of those commonplace actions that involve failure to adjust to circumstances or personalities, Callaghan in these later stories leaves the reader with a profound awareness of a universal truth: respect for individual dignity, patience and understanding love provide the best solution to the problems of life.

Source: Brandon Conron, ''The End of an Era,'' in *Morley Callaghan,* Twayne Publishers, 1966, pp. 97–108.

Sources

Abrams, M. H., *Natural Supernaturalism: Tradition and Revolution in Romantic Literature,* Norton, 1971, pp. 418–27.

Allen, Walter, *The Short Story in English,* Oxford University Press, 1981, pp. 201–09.

Callaghan, Morley, *Now That April's Here and Other Stories,* Random House, 1936, pp. 9–16.

———, ''The Plight of Canadian Fiction,'' in *University of Toronto Quarterly,* Vol. 7, 1938, pp. 152–61.

———, *That Summer in Paris: Memories of Tangled Friendships with Hemingway, Fitzgerald and Some Others,* Penguin, 1979, pp. 19–22.

Conron, Brandon, *Morley Callaghan,* Twayne, 1966, pp. 97–108, 168.

Hoar, Victor, *Morley Callaghan,* Copp Clark Publishing, 1969, p. 21.

Jones, Joseph, and Johanna Jones, *Canadian Fiction,* Twayne, 1981, pp. 57–61.

Further Reading

Boire, Gary, *Morley Callaghan and His Works,* Canadian Author Studies series, ECW Press, 1990.
   This short seventy-page study contains a concise biography of Callaghan, a description of the tradition and milieu that influenced him, a survey of criticism, an essay on his most important works, and a bibliography of primary and secondary sources.

———, *Morley Callaghan: Literary Anarchist,* ECW Press, 1994.
   This biography emphasizes Callaghan's early years through the 1940s. Boire addresses the claim made by Edmund Wilson that Callaghan has been unjustly neglected. Boire regards Callaghan as a literary anarchist, by which he refers to the writer's fierce individualism. The book includes a chronology of Callaghan's life, but there is no index.

Cameron, Donald, ''Morley Callaghan,'' in *Conversations with Canadian Novelists,* Part 2, Macmillan, 1973, pp. 17–33.
   This work contains an interview with Callaghan in which he talks about the importance of independence to a writer, the sources of his inspiration, his interest in Christian theology, the attitude of Canadians to their own literature, and other topics.

Lynch, Gerald, and Angela Arnold Robbeson, eds. *Dominant Impressions: Essays on the Canadian Short Story,* University of Ottawa Press, 1999.
   The introduction highlights issues in short-story theory and provides a concise history of Canadian short fiction in English. The essays deal with the period before the 1960s and examine the sociological, historical, and cultural aspects of Canadian short stories from the nineteenth century through the 1940s.

Wilson, Edmund, ''Morley Callaghan of Toronto,'' in *New Yorker,* Vol. XXXVI, No. 41, November 26, 1960, p. 224.
   At the time that noted literary critic Wilson wrote this article, Callaghan's reputation was in a slump, but Wilson argues that Callaghan was the most unjustly neglected novelist in the English-speaking world. Wilson regards Callaghan as superior to his more famous contemporaries Ernest Hemingway and F. Scott Fitzgerald.

A Circle in the Fire

Flannery O'Connor

1954

Flannery O'Connor's short story "A Circle in the Fire" was originally published in 1954 in *Kenyon Review*. At the time of its publication, O'Connor was on the verge of being recognized as one of America's greatest short-story writers, her first story having been published in 1946. In 1955 "A Circle in the Fire" appeared in three volumes, which together assured O'Connor's place in the literary canon: *A Good Man Is Hard to Find* (O'Connor's first published collection); *Prize Stories 1955: The O. Henry Awards;* and *The Best American Short Stories of 1955*. The story later appeared in the posthumous collection *The Complete Stories,* which was published in 1971.

Though "A Circle in the Fire" is not among O'Connor's best-known stories, it is characterized by the same grotesque characters, religious undercurrents, and dark humor found in her famed works "A Good Man Is Hard to Find," "The Life You Save May Be Your Own," and "Everything That Rises Must Converge." "A Circle in the Fire" is set on a farm—probably in Georgia, since the visitors live in Atlanta—and seems to be set at the time of its writing.

Author Biography

Flannery O'Connor was born Mary Flannery O'Connor on March 25, 1925, in Savannah, Georgia. O'Connor preferred to use her middle name

Flannery O'Connor

rather than her first name. Her father, Edward F. O'Connor, was in the real estate business. Her mother, Regina L. (Cline) O'Connor, came from a prominent Georgia family; Regina's father was a longtime mayor of the small town of Milledgeville, Georgia. The O'Connors were devout Catholics in a region that was at the time overwhelmingly Southern Baptist.

When O'Connor was twelve, her father became ill with lupus, a debilitating blood disease, and the family moved to Milledgeville. O'Connor's father died when she was only fifteen. She graduated from the local public high school and then earned a degree from the Women's College of Georgia (now Georgia College). O'Connor edited the college magazine and won admittance to the famed writers' workshop at the State University of Iowa (now Iowa State University). In 1947, O'Connor earned her master of fine arts degree, by which time she had already published her first short story, ''The Geranium.''

O'Connor moved to New York, where she wrote and published short fiction, including parts of what would become the first of her two novels, *Wise Blood* (1952). In 1950, O'Connor was, as her father before her, stricken with lupus. O'Connor returned to the family home in Milledgeville, where she

essentially lived the rest of her life with her mother and wrote as much as she was able to write.

''A Circle in the Fire'' was first published in 1954 in *Kenyon Review*. It was reprinted in *Prize Stories 1955: The O. Henry Awards* and in *The Best American Short Stories of 1955*. The story appears in the first collection of O'Connor's short fiction, *A Good Man Is Hard to Find* (1955), as well as in the posthumous collection of her work, *The Complete Stories* (1971).

A Good Man Is Hard to Find won O'Connor recognition as a master short-story writer. Her health, however, continued to deteriorate. Beginning in the mid-1950s, O'Connor was able to walk only with crutches. O'Connor's second novel, *The Violent Bear It Away*, was published in 1960. O'Connor died August 3, 1964, in Milledgeville, at the age of thirty-nine.

A second collection of short stories, *Everything That Rises Must Converge*, was published posthumously in 1965, and a collection of letters, *The Habit of Being*, was printed in 1979.

O'Connor continues to be honored as one of the best American short-story writers. Three of her stories—''Greenleaf'' (1957), ''Everything That Rises Must Converge'' (1963), and ''Revelation'' (1965)—won O. Henry awards. *The Complete Stories* won the National Book Award in 1972.

Plot Summary

As ''A Circle in the Fire'' opens, Mrs. Cope, the owner of a large, prosperous farm, is weeding a garden as Mrs. Pritchard, who works on the farm along with her husband, tells Mrs. Cope about the funeral of a distant relative. Mrs. Pritchard, a pessimist, dotes on calamity; Mrs. Cope, an optimist, tries vainly to raise the tone of the conversation. Mrs. Cope's twelve-year-old daughter Sally Virginia listens to the conversation from the window of her upstairs room. Through the girl's thoughts, readers learn that the one chink in Mrs. Cope's armor of optimism is her constant fretting about the possibility that a fire will start in the woods and destroy her farm.

When Mrs. Cope sees Culver, an African American hired hand, driving the tractor around a gate to avoid stopping to open it, she tells Mrs. Pritchard to stop him so that she can reprimand him. Culver listens to Mrs. Cope and obeys her command to open the gate and drive the tractor through it, but he refuses to look at her. In response to this exchange, Mrs. Cope says, "I thank the Lord all these things don't come at once. They'd destroy me." Mrs. Pritchard heartily agrees. Mrs. Cope responds by declaring that trials do not all come at once and that everyone has much to be thankful for and should say a prayer of thanksgiving at least once a day. She also speaks of her hard work and its role in keeping disaster at bay, saying, "I don't let anything get ahead of me, and I'm not always looking for trouble."

Mrs. Pritchard continues to insist that if trouble did all come at once, there would be nothing Mrs. Cope could do about it. As they are having this exchange, a truck stops nearby and lets off three teenage boys, who begin to walk up the dirt road toward the women. One of the boys is carrying a suitcase. From her window, Sally Virginia is the first to see the boys, and then the women see the boys coming toward them.

When the boys come face to face with the women, they stare sullenly. The boy carrying the suitcase says, "I don't reckon you remember me, Mrs. Cope." She does not, but he explains that he is Powell Boyd, whose father once worked on the farm. He says his father is dead, his mother has remarried, and the family now lives in a "development" of apartment houses in Atlanta. Powell introduces his friends, a big boy named Garfield Smith and a smaller one named W. T. Harper.

Mrs. Cope says it is "sweet" of Powell to stop and see her. W. T. volunteers that Powell has been telling the other boys about the pleasures of the farm, especially riding horses, and has told them they can ride the horses. Mrs. Cope tells them the horses are not shod and it is too dangerous for the boys to ride.

W. T. next tells Mrs. Cope that Powell has said he wants to come to the farm when he dies. Mrs. Cope's response is to offer the boys soft drinks and food. When she and Mrs. Pritchard go into the kitchen to get refreshments, Mrs. Pritchard warns Mrs. Cope that the suitcase means the boys intend to stay. Mrs. Cope replies, "I can't have three boys in here with only me and Sally Virginia. I'm sure they'll go when I feed them."

As she serves the food, Mrs. Cope sees Garfield spit a lighted cigarette onto her lawn. Calling him "Ashfield," she tells him to pick it up; he does, correcting her pronunciation of his name at the same time.

W. T. tells Mrs. Cope that Powell fantasizes about having one of her horses in Atlanta and that he says he would "bust this concrete to hell riding him!" Mrs. Cope says she is sure Powell does not use such language. Powell informs her that the boys intend to spend the night in Mrs. Cope's barn and that Powell's uncle, who dropped them off, will pick them up in the morning. Mrs. Cope says they cannot do that since she fears their cigarettes would start a fire. Powell suggests the woods, and she says, "I can't have people smoking in my woods." She finally tells them that they can sleep next to the house. Garfield mutters, "Her woods." The boys walk away as Powell says he is going to show them the place. They leave the food uneaten.

At sunset, the boys return to the house. When Mrs. Cope offers them guinea to eat, they say they do not eat such things. Still they wolf down the sandwiches she brings them. It is clear from their appearance that the boys spent the afternoon riding horses, which they deny. W. T. tells Mrs. Cope that Powell once locked one of his brothers in a box and set fire to the box. Mrs. Cope says she is sure Powell would not do that. Mrs. Cope asks the boys if they thank God every night "for all He's done for you," and the boys respond with silence. Sally Virginia makes a choking noise from her window so that the boys notice her for the first time. Garfield says, "Jesus, another woman." Later Mrs. Cope assures her daughter the boys will be gone in the morning.

In the morning, Powell tells Mrs. Cope that his uncle is not coming and that they have their own food. Mrs. Cope says, "You boys know that I'm glad to have you, but I expect you to behave. I expect you to behave like gentlemen." She reminds them, "this is my place."

The boys walk away. Mrs. Pritchard arrives and tells Mrs. Cope how her husband Hollis had tried unsuccessfully the day before to keep the boys from riding the horses. She also reports that the boys have been drinking milk from cans in the barn and that they argued with Hollis over whether Mrs. Cope owned the woods. When Mrs. Cope says she "cannot have this," Mrs. Pritchard tells her there is nothing she can do about it. Mrs. Cope says she is going to find the boys and tell them to hitch a ride on the milk truck when it comes. Sally Virginia says she will "handle" the boys, making a strangling gesture.

The boys tell Mrs. Cope they will leave on the milk truck, but they disappear when it comes and run away from Mrs. Cope when she tries to confront them after the truck leaves. Mrs. Pritchard reports that the boys let the bull out of its pen, drained the oil out of three tractors, and are now throwing rocks at the mailbox. Mrs. Pritchard all the while reminds Mrs. Cope there is nothing she can do about the boys' actions. Mrs. Cope gets into the car along with Mrs. Pritchard and Sally Virginia, and drives to the mailbox to confront the boys. She tells Powell his mother would be ashamed of him, that she (Mrs. Cope) has tried to be nice to them, and that if they are not gone when she returns from town she is going to call the sheriff. Mrs. Pritchard warns that Mrs. Cope has made the boys mad and ''it ain't any telling what they'll do,'' but Mrs. Cope is sure she has frightened the boys and they will leave immediately.

The women do not see the boys for the remainder of that day or the next morning. Sally Virginia puts on overalls, places two pistols in a holster, and sets off to find the boys, determined to get rid of them. When she finds them bathing in a cow trough, though, she hides and listens to them. W. T. says he wishes he lived on the farm; Garfield says he is glad he does not. Powell says that if the farm were not there, they would not have to think about it anymore. They get dressed, and Powell suggests they set fire to the woods. As the fire quickly spreads, Sally Virginia runs back to the house.

When Mrs. Cope sees the fire, she screams at the workers to hurry to put it out. Culver, knowing it is futile, responds, ''It'll be there when we git there.'' The story ends with the narrator describing the boys' joyous yells, which sound ''as if the prophets were dancing in the fiery furnace, in the circle the angel had cleared for them.''

Characters

Powell Boyd

Powell is a teenage boy about thirteen years old whose father used to work on Mrs. Cope's farm. Powell's family moved away from the farm sometime before the story occurs. His father has died, his mother has remarried and is working outside the home, and the family is living in an apartment complex in Atlanta. Powell arrives on the farm unannounced, along with two friends. It becomes clear that his only happy memories are of his childhood on the farm and the horses he rode there. Left alone all summer in what sounds from the

boys' descriptions like a tenement, Powell longed for the farm and regaled his friends with stories about it. According to Powell, his uncle has driven the boys to the farm for a visit.

From the moment of the boys' arrival on the farm, it is clear to readers, and the other characters, that Powell and his friends despise Mrs. Cope for what she has that they do not and for her false courtesy. Powell is well aware that with his friends in tow, Mrs. Cope is powerless to stop him from doing as he pleases on her farm. He has come to the farm realizing there is nothing to keep him from fulfilling his dream of enjoying all it has to offer, albeit temporarily.

Mrs. Cope

Mrs. Cope seems to be a widow. She owns a large farm and has several people working for her, including Mr. and Mrs. Pritchard and at least two African Americans. She is a small, thin woman whose large eyes give her the appearance of someone who is ''continually being astonished.''

Mrs. Cope has a neat conception of the world and her place in it, a conception rooted in religious ideas. She believes that hard work, optimism, and thanking God every day for all she has will keep calamity at bay. She views virtually every other human being and every event as either an irritation or a threat, but she is convinced that all these problems can be overcome as long as she is diligent and superficially pleasant. Authentic compassion and a true understanding of human nature are not among her resources.

It becomes clear that Mrs. Cope's neat vision of the world is mistaken. When the boys show up on the farm, all her responses to them are based on a complete misapprehension of their feelings and intentions. Therefore, every encounter she has with the boys makes her ruin more inevitable.

Sally Virginia Cope

Sally Virginia is Mrs. Cope's twelve-year-old daughter. She is fat and pale and wears braces. She is a sullen, sour girl who spends a lot of time in her room upstairs, listening and watching out the window as the story unfolds. This child is as aware of her mother's ignorance as are the adult characters in the story, and her response is to be rude and unresponsive toward her mother. However, she also hates the boys. Taking two pistols with her, she sets off threatening to track down the boys to force them to leave—that is, to do what her mother has failed to do—but instead she hides when she finds them and sees them set the fire. Her inability to exert her will over the boys makes her miserable, and for the first time she sees the similarity between herself and her mother.

Culver

Culver is an African American hired hand—identified in the story as a Negro—who works for Mrs. Cope. He listens to her but refuses to look at her, showing a bare minimum of respect. When the fire has been set and Mrs. Cope orders him to hurry to try to put it out, Culver only replies, "It'll be there when we git there."

W. T. Harper

W. T. is one of the boys who visit the farm with Powell. He is the smallest of the three boys. Shortly after arriving, W. T. tells Mrs. Cope that Powell has told the others he will let them ride the horses at the farm. This statement is an early indication that Powell has no intention of respecting Mrs. Cope's authority.

Just before the boys start the fire, W. T. says he wishes he lived on the farm. This remark, an acknowledgement of what all the boys feel, leads Powell to start the fire so that this paradise they long for no longer exists for anyone.

Hollis Pritchard

Hollis is Mrs. Pritchard's husband. During the course of the boys' visit, Mrs. Pritchard reports to Mrs. Cope her husband's futile efforts to keep the boys from causing trouble.

Mrs. Pritchard

Mrs. Pritchard, along with her husband, works for Mrs. Cope on the farm. She is described as being Mrs. Cope's physical opposite, a large woman with small, beady eyes. She is, in fact, Mrs. Cope's foil in every way. Mrs. Pritchard expects catastrophe and revels in it when it comes. Though Mrs. Cope clearly thinks that Mrs. Pritchard is her inferior in every way, Mrs. Pritchard judges the boys and their intentions correctly at every turn, and she repeatedly tries to warn Mrs. Cope that disaster is imminent.

Garfield Smith

Garfield is one of Powell's friends who visit the farm with him. He is the biggest of the three boys, smokes cigarettes, and has a tattoo. Just before the boys start the fire, when W. T. says he wishes he

Media Adaptations

- Victor Nunez produced and directed a film adaptation of "A Circle in the Fire" that was released by Perspective Films in 1976. The film, which shares the story's title, stars Betty Miller, Ingred Schweska, Katherine Miller, Mark Hey, Casey Donovan, and Tom Horkan. It is not widely available.

lived on the farm, Garfield says that he is glad he does not live there and that "it don't belong to nobody." These denials are an attempt to make himself and the other boys feel better about the reality that they cannot live on the farm.

Themes

Wisdom versus Ignorance

Mrs. Cope is convinced of her own wisdom, while everyone around her recognizes her ignorance. Mrs. Cope is far wealthier than all the other characters, and she believes that her material superiority is a result of her greater wisdom, diligence, and religious devotion. In reality she is completely lacking in wisdom, and her constant carping about the importance of being grateful to God sounds more like an attempt to appease an impetuous divinity than an expression of real gratitude toward a kind one.

Mrs. Cope misjudges the boys' intentions at every turn, while her less refined employee Mrs. Pritchard perfectly understands human nature. Mrs. Cope substitutes wishful thinking for good judgment; she is sure—against all evidence—that Powell does not curse and that the boys will leave the farm after she offers them soft drinks and crackers. After the confrontation at the mailbox, she is sure she has frightened the boys and they will leave. Mrs. Pritchard, however, understands that the boys are

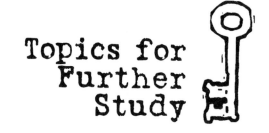

Topics for Further Study

- In the story, Powell and his friends consider the farm a paradise; they much prefer being there to being in the city, where they live. Do you think that this would be true for most thirteen-year-old boys in the twenty-first century? Why or why not?

- The boys live in a "development" in Atlanta. It is clear from their descriptions that they live in apartments and that they do not like living there. Research housing in the 1950s. Find out what these urban apartment developments were like and what life was like for the people who lived in them.

- Discuss the significance of Mrs. Cope's name. Why do you think O'Connor chose this name for her character? Do any of the other characters' names have particular significance?

- O'Connor makes clear that from the time the boys arrive at the farm Mrs. Cope makes one blunder after another. Her actions make the destruction of her farm virtually certain. What should Mrs. Cope have done differently? According to Mrs. Pritchard, there was nothing Mrs. Cope could have done. Do you agree or disagree? Explain what you would have done if you had been in Mrs. Cope's situation.

- At the end of the story, Sally Virginia identifies with her mother for the first time, although she recoils when she does so. What do you think is meant by this sentence describing Sally Virginia as she looked at her mother's face: "It was the face of the new misery she felt, but on her mother it looked old, and it looked as if it might have belonged to anybody, a Negro or a European or to Powell himself"?

---

angry, not scared, and that their hostilities will only escalate.

Mrs. Cope fails to understand the difference between authority, which she has as owner of the farm, and the power to enforce it, which she lacks. It is Mrs. Cope's own ignorance that sparks the boys' resentment and incites them to start the fire.

Style

Foreshadowing

O'Connor makes frequent use of foreshadowing, so that the reader may guess the story's ending almost from the story's start. On the story's second page readers learn that "Mrs. Cope was always worrying about fires in her woods," thus making it clear that the word "fire" in the story's title is not incidental. Each time Mrs. Pritchard warns that sometimes trouble comes in overwhelming waves, it enforces the idea that Mrs. Cope's trouble may come in the form of fire. Garfield spits a lighted cigarette into the grass, and a flustered Mrs. Cope mistakenly calls him "Ashfield." By this point in the story, the reader suspects the farm's fate is sealed.

The predictability that O'Connor creates heightens tension rather than quashing it. Readers may feel as if they are on a roller coaster, careening inexorably toward a final, heart-stopping drop. They know the drop is coming, they just do not know exactly when, or what the approach to the drop will be like. Tension is created by contrasting the inevitable conclusion with Mrs. Cope's immovable, incomprehensible confidence that all will be well. Her inability to grasp the reality of looming disaster becomes more incredible the nearer the disaster draws.

Biblical Allusion

The story's title and its last sentence are biblical allusions (indirect references to a biblical tale or event). The final image of Mrs. Cope watching her woods burn as Sally hears ''in the distance a few wild high shrieks of joy as if the prophets were dancing in the fiery furnace, in the circle the angel had cleared for them'' is an allusion to the third chapter of the Old Testament book of Daniel. This chapter tells the story of Shadrach, Meshach, and Abednego, three Jews who lived in Babylon during the reign of King Nebuchadnezzar. In the story, the king orders all his subjects must worship a golden idol he has had erected. Anyone who refuses to worship the idol is to be burned alive in a ''fiery furnace.'' Shadrach, Meshach, and Abednego refuse despite this threat, telling the king that their God will protect them from the fire. The three men are therefore tied up and thrown into the furnace. The heat is so intense that the soldiers who throw the three into the fire are killed by the fire. Yet the fire does not burn the three Jews. King Nebuchadnezzar looks into the furnace and is shocked to see Shadrach, Meshach, and Abednego walking around unharmed. The king orders the men to come out of the fire and then converts to their religion.

By placing allusions to this story at the beginning and end of ''A Circle in the Fire,'' O'Connor makes the biblical story the context for her own story and thus provides a clear direction for interpreting it.

Historical Context

Southern Gothic

O'Connor is among the writers associated with the southern gothic style of writing. This style features settings in the American South and characters who are bizarre, grotesque, and often outcast. Recurring themes include isolation, confusion, and the search for meaning. O'Connor's fiction focuses on the theme of confusion, especially confusion between wisdom and ignorance and between outward appearances (i.e., the facade of politeness, religious devotion, and conventionality) and inner reality (a meanness of spirit and egotism).

O'Connor is noted for populating her fiction with particularly grotesque characters and for crafting stories that cast them in a harsh light. Unlike some other southern gothic writers, such as Carson McCullers, O'Connor has no sympathy for her twisted characters and her casts include no heroes.

In addition to McCullers, other writers associated with southern gothic writing include Tennessee Williams, William Faulkner, Katherine Anne Porter, and Truman Capote.

Southern gothic is an offshoot of an earlier gothic style in European fiction that featured similarly peculiar themes and settings, such as eerie castles and dark, threatening woods. ''A Circle in the Fire'' shares with European gothic the use of woods as a place of danger and dark deeds, an untamed place from which destruction comes.

Civil Rights

The 1950s saw the beginnings of the Civil Rights movement that would gain momentum and make great strides in the 1960s. The movement began in the South and was largely centered there, since the abuses it sought to address—segregation of schools and other public facilities, intimidation at the voting booth, etc.—were severe and widespread in this region where less than a century had passed since the end of slavery.

When ''A Circle in the Fire'' was written, African Americans were still subject to discrimination in the South and often were forced to put up with mistreatment ranging from disrespect to physical abuse in order to be allowed a job and a place to live. While race is not a central issue in the story, O'Connor makes clear that Culver, the African American worker, has less status than anyone else on the farm. When Mrs. Cope sees Culver driving a tractor around a gate to avoid getting off to open the gate, she does not even call out to Culver herself. Instead she orders her white employee to get Culver's attention. After she reprimands Culver, Mrs. Cope says to Mrs. Pritchard, ''It's nothing to them. They don't have the responsibility.''

Women's Postwar Independence

The 1950s was a time of dramatic social and economic change. World War II had recently ended. During the war, large numbers of women had worked in factories for the first time and had functioned independently while husbands and fathers were away at war. Women were to some degree unwilling to give up the freedoms and responsibilities they had experienced during the war, which led to adjustments for both genders when men returned, expecting to pick up where they had left off. Some men were resentful of women's newfound independence.

Compare & Contrast

- **1950s:** Hitchhiking is a common way to travel, especially for poor people in rural areas where public transportation is not available.

  Today: Hitchhiking is illegal in many places and is rare even where legal. It is considered dangerous to be either a hitchhiker or a driver who might be willing to give a hitchhiker a ride.

- **1950s:** Fire is the greatest fear for farmers, ranchers, and others who live in rural wooded areas. Out of reach of urban fire departments and water supplies, people can lose their homes, livelihoods, and even their lives as a result of an act of nature such as a lightning strike or an act of human carelessness or meanness.

  Today: Residents in wooded rural areas still fear wildfires and arson. Although more resources are available to fight rural fires—such as water dropped from airplanes—fires may still burn out of control and lay waste to vast tracts of land.

- **1950s:** Three teenage boys traveling away from home without an adult is not considered unusual or suspicious.

  Today: Three teenage boys traveling away from home without an adult would most likely draw the attention of concerned citizens and law enforcement officials. In some areas, local laws restrict the activities of minors. Parents may even be held legally responsible for criminal acts committed by their children or be charged with negligence if their children are hurt.

In "A Circle in the Fire," Powell is clearly unhappy about being left alone in an apartment with younger siblings while his mother goes to her job, and Garfield repeatedly expresses contempt for women—especially for Mrs. Cope, who has wealth and authority as sole owner of the farm.

Economic Boom

The 1950s were also a time of a growing economy. Middle-class Americans enjoyed a fast-rising standard of living as new technologies led to the availability of laborsaving appliances. Buying on credit also became commonplace, allowing more people to buy the new products. More Americans than ever before were able to own their own homes, buy cars, take vacations, etc. While many Americans benefited from these changes, those who did not felt even poorer than they had before. There were more and more things they could not afford. In "A Circle in the Fire," Powell and his friends are resentful of all that Mrs. Cope has. Powell feels poorer in his Atlanta "development" than he did as the child of farm workers living on Mrs. Cope's farm. His standard of living has gotten worse, not better.

Critical Overview

"A Circle in the Fire" has drawn scarce critical comment as an individual story, but O'Connor's short fiction has been widely reviewed and analyzed as a whole. In the 1950s and 1960s when most of O'Connor's stories were first published, opinions of her work varied. Many critics and scholars immediately recognized that her work dealt with universal themes in a highly individual way and felt it would have lasting appeal. Others reviewers, however, criticized the stories for their grotesqueness and insisted that O'Connor was merely a regional writer of passing interest. As time has passed, respect for O'Connor's work has grown, and her early admirers have proved prescient.

In a 1965 review of O'Connor's collection *Everything That Rises Must Converge*, critic Irving Howe writes in the *New York Review of Books* that O'Connor's stories

> stand securely on their own, as renderings and criticisms of human experience. And as such, they merit a considerable respect. The writing is firm, economical, complex: we are engaged with an intelligence, not merely a talent.

Reviewing the same collection the same year, Webster Schott writes in the *Nation:*

> Artistically her fiction is the most extraordinary thing to happen to the American short story since Ernest Hemingway. . . . Flannery O'Connor was among those few writers who raise the questions worth thinking about after the lights are out and the children are safely in bed: What is reality? What are the possibilities for hope? How much can man endure?

Forty years after her death, O'Connor's place alongside Hemingway at the summit of the American literary pantheon is seldom questioned. Scholars continue to examine her work from new perspectives. In an essay in *Flannery O'Connor Bulletin,* Lisa S. Babinec analyzes the mother-daughter relationship in "A Circle in the Fire" and in two other O'Connor stories. Babinec concludes that the former story is "the most extreme example of maternal domination" in all of O'Connor's work. In an essay in *Southern Literary Journal,* Melita Schaum discusses "A Circle in the Fire" as a trickster narrative in which Powell Boyd is a caricature of Satan himself. Schaum admires the story as a "parable of property and loss, order and disruption" and declares that it "represents one of O'Connor's darker and more perplexing tales of grace."

Pulitzer Prize–winning author Alice Walker, who once lived just down the road from Flannery O'Connor's home in Milledgeville, has written that she considers O'Connor "the first great modern writer from the South." In an essay on O'Connor in her book *In Search of Our Mothers' Gardens: Womanist Prose,* Walker writes:

> her characters are new and wondrous creations in the world, and . . . not one of her stories . . . could have been written by anyone else. . . . After her great stories of sin, damnation, prophecy, and revelation, the stories one reads casually in the average magazine seem to be about love and roast beef.

Criticism

Candyce Norvell

Norvell is an independent educational writer who specializes in English and literature. In this essay, Norvell discusses the lack of a hero in "A Circle in the Fire."

Think of the body of Flannery O'Connor's fiction as a patchwork quilt. The quilt's backing—the large piece that underlies the patches and holds them together—is O'Connor's much-written-about Catholic theology. Each patch, cut from a cloth with a unique pattern, represents an individual story. Yet all the patches share something in common: the stitches that crawl across the squares are most irregular. Where they should march in a neat line, they jut unpredictably. They are tiny and puckered here, and long and loopy there. They are irreparably crooked and contorted. They are O'Connor's characters, and they are all villains and ne'er-do-wells. It has been said that in all of O'Connor's stories and her two novels, there is not a hero to be found.

"A Circle in the Fire" is not one of O'Connor's most written-about stories and is not considered one of her masterpieces. But as an illustration of her ability to craft a powerful, affecting tale without a hero—or even a single sympathetic character—it serves as well as any other story.

If "A Circle in the Fire" had a traditional structure, its main character, Mrs. Cope, would be its hero. She would be the good woman beleaguered by bad boys. She would contend with them wisely and bravely, and she would either be victorious (a comedy) or endure defeat with grace (a tragedy), comforted by the knowledge that she had fought with honor. Win or lose, a hero is somehow changed for the better by the struggle; he or she gains wisdom or compassion or some other virtue through the events of the story.

In this story, of course, it is none of the above. Mrs. Cope is its main character; she is not its hero. She demonstrates neither wisdom nor courage. She has neither understanding of human nature nor of human relationships. She fails to see that while she has authority on the farm; the boys have all the power. She assumes that her superior wealth makes her superior in wisdom, and she has no compassion for the many who have less than she does. Worse than all of this, Mrs. Cope refuses to learn from experience or to be changed by her struggle with the boys. She persists in her self-satisfied ignorance even as the other characters in the story recognize that she is creating the conditions for her own ruin. Mrs. Cope has none of the qualities of a hero.

Mrs. Pritchard, on the other hand, has one such quality: she is as savvy as Mrs. Cope is dense. Her assessment of the boys and their intentions is on target at every turn. She looks at the facts—the boys' ages, their poverty, their fearless sullenness—

What Do I Read Next?

- *The Complete Stories* (1971), by Flannery O'Connor, contains all thirty-one of O'Connor's short stories and has been reprinted more than forty times. The book includes two of her best-known stories: "A Good Man Is Hard to Find" and "Everything That Rises Must Converge."

- *Wise Blood* (1952) is one of only two novels O'Connor wrote. It is a piercing satire of humanism in general and American society in particular. The book was made into a film starring and directed by John Huston.

- *Collected Stories of Eudora Welty* (1982) includes all forty-one of Welty's published short stories. Like O'Connor, Welty was a twentieth-century southern writer and was recognized primarily for her short fiction. Elements of humor and southern gothic style appear in both writers' work, yet their sensibilities were quite different.

- *Collected Stories of William Faulkner* (1950) gathers forty-two stories—far from a complete collection—by the man many consider the best southern writer of the twentieth century and one of the greatest writers of his time. Known for his use of stream-of-consciousness style and symbolism, Faulkner won two Pulitzer Prizes and the Nobel Prize for Literature.

- *The Heart Is a Lonely Hunter* (1940), by Carson McCullers, is a critically acclaimed novel by a writer who was O'Connor's contemporary and, like O'Connor, a native of Georgia. It is the story of John Singer, a deaf-mute living in a southern mill town in the 1930s.

- *To Kill a Mockingbird* (1960), by Harper Lee, is the story of eight-year-old Scout and her older brother Jem growing up in the South during the Great Depression. The novel won a Pulitzer Prize.

---

and makes faultless predictions about what kinds of behavior these combined elements will produce.

Yet Mrs. Pritchard does not qualify as a hero. Although she possesses wisdom, she does not value it. A hero would be eager to use wisdom as a weapon to overcome challenges. Mrs. Pritchard is a prophet of doom who is convinced that challenges cannot be overcome. She enjoys her wisdom for the sense of superiority it gives her over Mrs. Cope and because it allows her to relish the certainty of Mrs. Cope's coming ruin—hardly heroic impulses.

Mrs. Cope's daughter, Sally Virginia, makes a halfhearted stab at heroic action. Having watched and listened to her mother's mishandling of the boys, Sally is finally overcome by frustration. Arming herself with two pistols, she sets off to find and deal with the invaders. But the pistols are only toys, and Sally is just a child. When she finds the boys, her bravado melts into fear, and she hides and watches them instead of confronting them. Even when she knows they are about to set fire to the

woods, she does nothing. For a time, she is not even able to run.

At twelve, Sally is already smarter than her mother. But her idea that she can "handle" the boys is as much a fantasy as her mother's idea that they will go away of their own accord. Sally is only a child, and it seems unfair to place the burden of conquering three teenage boys on her shoulders. But children can certainly be heroes, and often are in literature. If she had somehow followed through on her desire to confront the boys, she would have been heroic even if she had failed to save her home from them. It is her lack of courage and determination that deny her the hero's role. As she realizes at the end of the story, she is very much like the mother she despises.

That leaves the boys, Powell, Garfield, and W. T. They cannot be the story's heroes because they are its villains. They invade Mrs. Cope's farm, camp there against her will, and respond to every request and command by becoming increasingly destructive. They are juvenile delinquents who finally commit a serious crime that destroys Mrs. Cope's property, wealth, and livelihood. If they had acted in the service of some ideal or cause, the boys might be seen as antiheroes in the tradition of Robin Hood. But their actions are purely impulsive, selfish, and destructive.

The boys are neither heroes nor antiheroes, but in O'Connor's judgment they are, of all the story's characters, most deserving of mercy. In a biblical allusion that echoes the story's title, O'Connor ends the story with the narrator reporting that Sally ''stood taut, listening, and could just catch in the distance a few wild high shrieks of joy as if the prophets were dancing in the fiery furnace, in the circle the angel had cleared for them.''

In this image, the boys are not invaders or delinquents or criminals but ''prophets.'' In the Old Testament world that O'Connor has conjured up, prophets were righteous men who warned the worldly of divine punishments to come if they did not change their ways. While the fire consumes everything around them—everything that they longed for and could not have—the boys are described as dancing in ''the circle the angel had cleared for them.'' Only the boys, of all the story's characters, receive divine favor and protection. The irony of this is heightened by the fact that Mrs. Cope has repeatedly reminded those around her that she thanks God every day for all He does for her. Further, when she asked the boys if they too thanked God every day, they responded with silence. O'Connor's God, it seems, looks at something other than people's words when deciding their fates.

That the story's cast of characters is bereft of a hero is not surprising. That there are a few among them the author deems worth saving is a little more so. But the real shock, at first, is whom she chooses to save. In a story populated with ignorant, pathetic people, in the end what distinguishes the boys is not that they are the worst of a bad lot but that they alone may be redeemable. O'Connor draws readers in not by giving them a hero who represents all the best of humanity but by shaking up their notions about who represents the worst.

Source: Candyce Norvell, Critical Essay on ''A Circle in the Fire,'' in *Short Stories for Students,* Gale, 2004.

Peter A. Smith

In the following essay, Smith discusses dual gender roles present in O'Connor's women characters in ''A Circle in the Fire'' and other stories.

''O'Connor draws readers in not by giving them a hero who represents all the best of humanity but by shaking up their notions about who represents the worst.''

In a Jungian analysis of three key works of short fiction by Flannery O'Connor, ''A Circle in the Fire,'' ''The Displaced Person,'' and ''Greenleaf,'' Mary L. Morton claims that these stories ''dramatize the ludicrosity of women who have denied the spirit of femininity, the *anima*'' and that the sympathy that O'Connor generates for the protagonists of these stories is a ''trick on some readers.'' In fact, these characters, as well as other O'Connor characters in similar positions, do not really deny their femininity, they exploit it, sometimes to the point that they seem to be parodying it. And they *should* arouse in most readers not only sympathy but also a grudging respect. Unlikable as these women may appear, all deserve credit for employing a clever strategy in attempting to survive in a man's world while essentially manless, and all deserve sympathy because they are faced with an impossible task in having to synthesize aspects of both gender roles in order to maintain their livelihoods.

While these ''managerial types,'' as Morton terms them, or ''assertive widows,'' as Suzanne Morrow Paulson refers to them, are all overly demanding of their hired hands, all are justified in their aggressiveness by their common economic situation. As Louise Westling has observed, O'Connor's South of the fifties is nearly as hostile to the plight of widows managing farms as the South of the immediate post-Civil War period had been, when ''widows who attempted to manage their own affairs were regarded as arrogant.'' While these women may have ''consciously adopted a masculine ethic,'' thereby denying an essential part of their own femininity, there is really little choice involved; O'Connor's empowered women all sincerely believe that typically masculine, aggressive behavior is the only way to overcome the misogyny inherent in the lower class male workers they must control in order to keep their farms operating. Each

> Unfortunately for Mrs. Cope, she initially misjudges the boys and tries to control them in a purely maternal fashion, in contrast to the managerial tone she adopts with her workers."

woman is forced by necessity to channel whatever nurturing instinct she has into assuring the survival of her "place," a significant term used by each.

In fact, the women from the above stories display a rather admirable adeptness at manipulating the myth of the "Southern lady" to help them survive in a patriarchal society. These women firmly maintain that, as "ladies" in the traditional Southern sense of the term, they are entitled to the respect, protection and labor of those around them, particularly those of a lower caste. They lay claim to all of the privileges due a "Southern lady" while also having assumed all of the economic power of an absent male. This proves to be an effective combination for a time, allowing this character to feel that she can—and must—be as "iron-handed" as any male property owner while still feeling perfectly entitled to sympathy for having to debase herself by running things. Her stature as a "lady" entitles her to complain about being abused and disrespected by her subordinates because she is "only a woman," yet this complaint serves as a weapon to encourage others to be far more tolerant than they would otherwise be toward a male superior.

The basic situation in these stories is the same: all of these characters are, presumably, widows who have inherited farms—but little money—from their departed husbands and are left to manage on their own, quite in conflict with what their upbringings have told them is the proper place for a "lady." The economic support traditionally provided by the husband is gone, and all three of these women are left to fill the power vacuum; they are forced to take on the completely unladylike position of manager/employer. It is a role that each woman is actually quite adept at, and each is able to keep her "place" running well for a time, despite uncooperative employees. The

farms that these women inherit provide unique venues for them, since these farms constitute a confluence of the private, domestic sphere in which female empowerment is unquestioned, with the public, economic sphere in which Southern ladies traditionally have had no role. Thus each woman is able to view and run her "place" as an extension of her home.

In "A Circle in the Fire" this attempt to combine both feminine and masculine authority can be seen in Mrs. Cope's attempts to make her three uninvited visitors both "act like gentlemen" and display the same amount of obedience that she has come to expect from her employees. Unfortunately for Mrs. Cope, she initially misjudges the boys and tries to control them in a purely maternal fashion, in contrast to the managerial tone she adopts with her workers. Expecting the boys to be polite and deferential around a lady who is also a social superior, Mrs. Cope is shocked when the three refugees from an Atlanta housing development refuse to respond to her insincere maternal solicitude. As Margaret Whitt has noted, "the stern, businesslike woman farmer is nowhere to be found in Mrs. Cope's handling of the boy intruders. She speaks to them as a Southern lady would." Even after being informed of Powell's dismal home life, Mrs. Cope still attempts to control his behavior by reminding him of his defiance of accepted social standards: "I'm sure your mother would be ashamed of you." Mrs. Cope's language here makes clear that she is still viewing her empowerment as owner of the farm in domestic terms, with herself acting as a surrogate "mother" trying to discipline unruly children. If Sally Virginia's unruly behavior is any indicator, though, Mrs. Cope is ineffective as a controlling parent—as are most of O'Connor's single mothers.

What puzzles Mrs. Cope about the boys is that they are not only ungrateful to her for her attempt to be domestically gracious to them by offering food, but they also flatly reject her economic authority, refusing even to acknowledge her ownership of the land. The boys are clearly responding to the lack of a legitimate male authority figure, as they express disgust at the presence of a female "ruling class" on the farm. As one of the boys says to Mr. Pritchard, "I never seen a place with so many damn women on it, how do you stand it here?"

Mrs. Cope has every reason to believe that her tactics will work on the boys. After all, Powell's mother had once been an employee of Mrs. Cope's, and, presumably, she was able to control her as she controls her successor, Mrs. Pritchard. Although Mrs. Cope initially believes that she can control all of the "destructive and impersonal" forces on her farm, such as her black workers and the nut grass, this is only because none of these "forces" can question her authority. We can recognize in her paranoia about fire her awareness of how tenuous her control really is. Once she encounters a "force" that clearly challenges her feminine authority, she can only resort to the ineffective threat of summoning male authority, the sheriff, to regain control.

In donning male clothes and strapping on pistols to chase off the boys, Sally Virginia reveals that she, like Mrs. Pritchard, understands what her mother cannot: that the boys have no use for the Southern code of behavior by which a lady is owed deference, that their broken homes give them little experience in knuckling under to domestic authority, and that they will respond only to pure masculine power. Unfortunately, the only form of masculine power on the farm is in the destructiveness of the boys themselves. In fact, Powell's arson touches off a rebellion on the part of the male workers, as they refuse Mrs. Cope's final order to "hurry" to put out the fire. The male force triumphs and Mrs. Cope ultimately finds herself without any sort of authority at the most crucial time.

In a similar fashion, Mrs. McIntyre of "The Displaced Person" eventually loses control of her workers and ends up, like Mrs. Cope, losing her farm. Initially, though, Mrs. McIntyre's control grows to previously unknown levels thanks to the presence of another who, like herself prior to her marriage, had been without a "place." Irked by the same perception of disrespectful incompetence on the part of her workers that Mrs. Cope complains about, Mrs. McIntyre begins to gain a sense of strength and power once she finally hires a truly hard working, honest and knowledgeable hand. She holds the example of Mr. Guizac up to her other workers in order to create a kind of sibling rivalry among her employees to spur productivity: one can clearly hear a why-can't-you-be-like-your-brother admonition to Mr. Shortley when she compares him to Guizac. When she adds to this the substantial economic threat of firing the entire Shortley family, it is easy to see how the atmosphere of paranoia on the farm comes to exist. Mrs. McIntyre reaches the apex of her economic empowerment and comes to exploit her new-found authority with her workers. Finally, she has found a worker "who *has* to work," that is, one who has to knuckle under to her dubious authority, and she proclaims that the long line of

"white trash" families who have parasitized her and then left is now over. But she finds that her visions of freedom from worthless "poor white trash and niggers" who have "drained [her] dry" are short lived, as she must engage in a silent conspiracy with males of both of those groups to rid herself of Mr. Guizac.

Just as Mrs. Cope has her paranoia of losing all through fire, so does Mrs. McIntyre fear the loss of the social order which empowers her, hence the unlikely conspiracy to rid herself of her "favorite son." Because Mrs. McIntyre lacks any true maternal authority, since she is merely the childless young widow of a much older man, the social basis of her authority is of paramount importance to her. While Mr. Guizac continues to be a fine worker, his attempt to marry his cousin to Sulk, the younger black on the farm, is an affront to the social system that she just can't bear. While she herself had married in order to gain social and economic advancement, her union did not involve miscegenation, thus she cannot perceive a parallel. She had been willing to endure the laziness of the "white trash" and the stealing of the "niggers" because, in her view, these traits were to be expected of these classes; these acts merely reinforce the established order which puts the blacks on the bottom of the social scale, the poor whites in the middle and herself firmly on top. She admits her dependence on this order when she tells Guizac, "I will not have my niggers upset. I cannot run this place without my niggers." To her mind, her black workers are the equivalent of weak-willed children who can always be counted on to recognize her authority as a white woman.

Mrs. McIntyre is not alone in this belief, either, as all of O'Connor's empowered women rely absolutely on their black workers' recognizing whites as their superiors—even if these women complain that blacks don't grant this recognition as readily as they once did, as Mrs. Turpin claims in "Revelation," for instance. "The Enduring Chill" provides an interesting view of the consequences of the erosion of the social division that all of O'Connor's empowered women claim *should* exist between blacks and whites. The basic situation in this story is identical to that of the above stories, with a widowed land owner, Mrs. Fox, relying upon her black workers, Randall and Morgan, to keep her dairy farm running and wanting her son to keep the social barrier in place. But Asbury, as defiant as any child of any of O'Connor's single mothers, succeeds in breaking down the barrier by enjoying a forbidden smoke with the black workers in the milking barn; the act results in "one of those moments of communion when the difference between black and white is absorbed into nothing." But when he tries to push the "communion" further by drinking unpasteurized milk over Randall's objections that Mrs. Fox has strictly forbidden it, he is struck down with undulant fever and eventually pushed even further away from the black workers when his attempt to communicate with them while on his sickbed fails utterly and he must look to his mother to be "saved" from them. Asbury's attempt to defy the social hierarchy results in disaster; it leaves him ill for life and accomplishes nothing beyond what he intended all along—to annoy his mother.

We can see in Mrs. Fox's frustration with Asbury's strange desires the same emotion that is behind Mrs. McIntyre's exasperation with Guizac's failure to comprehend and bow to the accepted standards of her society and Mrs. Cope's frustration at the unwillingness of the boys to act like "gentlemen" after she has been "nice" to them. Mrs. McIntyre's words to Mr. Guizac even echo Mrs. Cope's reminder to the boys: "This is my place . . . I say who will come here and who won't." In the paranoia displayed by these women over seemingly harmless plans we can see that they realize the more profound implications of the disruption of the social order which supports their tenuous claims of authority. Without this order and the accompanying rules of conduct which restrain their workers, none of O'Connor's empowered women could function effectively as "bosses."

These characters are among a number of empowered female protagonists from O'Connor's short fiction who rigorously defend what they perceive to be the hierarchy of social classes in the South, primarily because of their own relatively lofty positions in this hierarchy. Perhaps the most obvious example is Mrs. Turpin of "Revelation," whose hobby of "naming the classes of people" who exist in her perception of the world is reinforced by the high status of the home-and-land owner class, to which she and many of O'Connor's other female protagonists belong. Although Mrs. Turpin has a husband, Claude is characterized throughout the story by his meekness and compliance with his wife's wishes, so Mrs. Turpin's life on her farm involves the same sort of pride in ownership and exasperation at having to deal with non-compliant help as the lives of the empowered widows. This she makes clear in her waiting room conversation, where she brags about her crops and livestock and be-

moans her inability to find good help: "You can't get the white folks to pick [cotton] and now you can't get the niggers—because they got to be right up there with the white folks." Although she readily admits to herself that her envisioning of a hierarchy based upon race, class and money is flawed, as it fails to account for richer people who are morally or racially inferior to herself, she still insists upon defending it and envisioning it—and her own position in it—even in the face of Mary Grace's "revelation" of Mrs. Turpin's true moral status.

Similarly, while having fallen from the land owner class, Julian's mother in "Everything That Rises Must Converge" also remains preoccupied with defending the social hierarchy against all of its enemies—including both Julian and the "misguided" blacks who don't agree with her pronouncement that they should be "rising" only "on their own side of the fence." Once again, the defense of this hierarchy is clearly a defense of the protagonist's own sense of "place" in it. While Julian is all too aware that his mother's life has been "a struggle to act like a Chestny without the Chestny goods," he doesn't seem to understand that her racist beliefs are an integral part of "knowing who she is." Without the inherited home and land, all Julian's mother has left of her former sense of empowerment is her breeding—particularly her ability to be gracious to those she believes to be social inferiors. To Julian's mother's mind, her ability to engage in conversation with those whites on the bus who are clearly "not our kind of people" and to be patronizingly kind to black children is her badge of social superiority; her sense of identity enables her to be "gracious to anybody."

In Julian's mother's firm belief in her own elevated position in the hierarchy, evidenced by her ability to graciously interact with her inferiors in the manner of a true Southern lady, we can hear the echoes of the voices of several of O'Connor's empowered women who point to their relationships with the families of their tenant farmers as proof of their magnanimity. For instance, we are told of Mrs. Hopewell, the farm owner in "Good Country People," that she "had no bad qualities of her own but she was able to use other people's in such a constructive way that she never felt the lack." This attitude of condescending charity can be seen in what Mrs. Hopewell regards as her masterful handling of Mrs. Freeman's intrusive personality by allowing her to be "into everything," and in her defending of the Freemans' worth despite her evident belief in their inferiority to herself: "they were not trash. They were good country people.'' This is a term that Mrs. Cope might apply to the Pritchards and Mrs. McIntyre might apply to the Guizacs, both of whom rate above the ''white trash'' employees of their past experience but below themselves.

It is in the defending of her vision of the hierarchy that both Mrs. Hopewell and her daughter experience their downfall. Just as both Mrs. Cope and Mrs. McIntyre contribute to their own defeats by their constant assertions about the social hierarchy, so does Mrs. Hopewell open the door to calamity by enthusiastically defending her opinion of the relative worth of ''good country people.'' Because of their belief in the hierarchy, both mother and daughter are equally duped by Manley Pointer, the travelling Bible salesman, who metaphorically keeps his foot in Mrs. Hopewell's door by claiming that Mrs. Hopewell is the type of person who doesn't ''like to foot with country people like me!,'' relying upon Mrs. Hopewell's condescending denial. Even Joy-Hulga, who seems opposed to all of her mother's ratings of the worth of fellow human beings, has bought into the idea of the hierarchy, as she sets out to seduce the salesman because she perceives him as ignorant (and thus inferior to herself), and becomes convinced that she ''was face to face with real innocence.''

For all of these women, it is the persistent belief in their own superiority that entitles them to denigrate their fellow human beings, that constitutes a spiritual defect as apparent as Joy-Hulga's physical defect. Manley Pointer is mocking the notion of his conforming to the Hopewells' stereotypical view of the ''good country person,'' as he tells Joy-Hulga that he belongs to that class. He maintains, however, that ''it ain't held me back none. I'm as good as you any day in the week,'' points out how the belief in any social hierarchy always carries with it a belief in one's own superiority to others. His retort also belies the built-in assumption of superiority on the part of both of the Hopewells. He's not as ''good'' in the moral sense, of course, but in the social sense; he makes his living from exploiting the patronizing, superior attitude of the ''upper'' class, who imagine themselves to be superior in every way. And belief in a social hierarchy characterizes nearly all of O'Connor's female characters, regardless of rank. Even ''white trash'' women such as the one in the waiting room in ''Revelation'' and the one on the bus in ''Everything That Rises'' agree with the protagonists that the blacks' struggle for equality is a sure sign that the world has gone terribly awry (after all, it is a threat to their own status as at least

one step up from the bottom of the scale). In stealing Joy-Hulga's artificial leg and strolling off under the unsuspecting eye of Mrs. Hopewell, who is convinced that he has been trying to sell Bibles to ''the Negroes back in there''—the implication being that such a ''simple'' boy could only be an effective salesperson among social inferiors—Pointer is pointing to how inane the belief in such stereotypes can be. Mrs. Freeman's sarcastic retort, ''some can't be that simple . . . I know I never could,'' also reflects the fact that it is the Hopewells who are simple and who see the world in black-and-white terms. The hoodwinking of both members of the Hopewell family (the upper class in the hierarchy) proves how silly the notion of a hierarchy is: if ''good country people'' can be defined by their ''simplicity,'' then it is surely the Hopewells who are ''country people.''

Another flaw in the proposition that these upper caste Southern ladies are superior, as they all seem to claim, concerns their common belief in their own graciousness and politeness toward others. Even if we can grant that graciousness is a sign of proper breeding, as many of O'Connor's protagonists claim, we have to question just how a ''gracious'' person can irritate virtually everyone she interacts with—including her own offspring. Mrs. Hopewell is typical in this respect, since she has divorced a husband, cannot get along with her own daughter, and has apparently been through a succession of tenant workers: ''Before the Freemans she had averaged one tenant family a year.'' The latter is apparently a trait of Mrs. Cope and Mrs. McIntyre as well, as both have had problems with retaining employees—we know that at least one family preceded the Pritchards on Mrs. Cope's farm, and Mrs. McIntyre and Astor mention three families that preceded the Shortleys on her farm. This common attribute indicates a basic inability on the part of these women to deal with the needs and concerns of workers, a lack of true maternal solicitude.

Mrs. May of ''Greenleaf'' not only shares with other O'Connor characters an inability to get along with her own offspring and workers but also assigns the same amount of importance to the established social order as O'Connor's other empowered women. Noting the unnatural rise of the ''white trash'' Greenleaf boys in the world, she bemoans the possibility of the Greenleafs becoming ''society,'' thus being beyond her control. But unlike most of the other female land owners, Mrs. May does have men on her farm who are capable of helping her run things; unfortunately, Scofield and Wesley have no interest whatsoever either in keeping the farm up or in helping to perpetuate their family. Although Mrs. May defensively refuses to admit them as such, her sons represent more of a threat to the established order than the Greenleafs do. Both are openly rude and contemptuous of their mother, and both refuse to marry and become "respectable," as O. T. and E. T. Greenleaf have done. Mrs. May complains as much as Mrs. Cope, Mrs. McIntyre and Mrs. Fox about her shiftless, lazy and parasitic tenant workers; however, Mrs. May is also burdened with two sons who are even worse than the workers. In Mrs. May's failure to get her sons to help with the farm by trying to wield domestic authority alone, we can see how these other women would be likely to fare if they lacked the additional weapon of economic authority. We can recognize that the admonishing tone used by Mrs. May when addressing her sons is identical to the tone used by the other ladies in addressing their workers, but Scofield and Wesley do not rely upon their mother for their livelihoods: each has a job which is entirely independent of the farm. The result is that they have the freedom to reject maternal authority without fear of economic consequences.

Because she is essentially left "manless" by her sons' apathy, Mrs. May, like Mrs. Cope and Mrs. McIntyre, views the survival of the farm as the product of her hard work alone. The three women virtually echo each other in this respect: Mrs. Cope asserts that she has "the best kept place in the county and do you know why? Because I work. I've had to work to save this place and work to keep it"; Mrs. McIntyre likens her efforts to run her farm to Mr. Guizac's "struggle" to survive his displacement, since "she had had a hard time herself. She knew what it was to struggle"; Mrs. May believes that "before any kind of judgement seat she would be able to say: I've worked, I have not wallowed." All three women classify their efforts to keep their farms afloat as "work," yet none do any real physical labor—as befits a "lady." While they may "constantly mouth shallow beliefs in the Puritan work ethic," they surely do not adhere to this ethic themselves. To them, "work" means wielding masculine authority by continually issuing orders and admonitions. Even Mrs. Cope's physical attack on the nut grass is not the act of a "worker," as O'Connor points out with the symbol of the sunhats, introduced in the first paragraph of the story: Mrs. Pritchard's is "faded and nut of shape while Mrs. Cope's [is] still stiff and bright and green," indicating that Mrs. Cope is the one who need not wear out her sunhat because she is the one in charge.

As with many of O'Connor's empowered women who speak as if their workers are more of a challenge and an affront than essential to economic survival, Mrs. May discounts the role played by her hired help, viewing the Greenleafs as a trial of her ability to assume the domineering role of the male required to keep her "white trash" workers in line. Mrs. May correctly senses that Mr. Greenleaf hesitates to recognize her authority, though she cannot see that this is partly because he has witnessed the complete breakdown of her maternal authority over her disrespectful sons, who are a stark contrast to his own respectful twins. Furthermore, the May farm lacks an underclass of black workers whose automatic deference to a white employer might serve to establish Mrs. May as an authority figure.

While Mrs. May bemoans the lack of a "man running this place" and claims that the Greenleaf brothers ignore her demands for the removal of the bull because of her gender, it is clear that the treatment she receives is only partly due to her status as a member of the "weaker sex." Mrs. May is ignored simply because she tries too hard to compensate for the lack of a strong male figure by being overly demanding and critical. As is the case with many of O'Connor's empowered women, Mrs. May's relationship with her workers consists of little more than constant demands and complaints of noncompliance. Having been raised on a steady diet of Mrs. May's whining and now being free from their economic dependence upon her, the Greenleaf twins are glad to be able to turn even more of a deaf ear to her than their father does. Although Mrs. May imagines that she is an effective authority figure because of her ability to rule the farm with "an iron hand," Scofield's mocking of this notion by holding up his mother's hand, which resembles a "broken lily," demonstrates how weak her authority actually is.

Like Mrs. Cope and Mrs. McIntyre, Mrs. May mistakes hurling verbal abuse for strength and giving commands for struggle. This is the respect in which O'Connor's empowered women are ultimately failures. While they are temporarily successful at using the power which comes as the result of land ownership and the ability to employ workers, all cross the line that separates managing workers from abusing them. If the Southern lady is to be characterized by her ability to charm and delight others, as the stereotype would seem to indicate, then these ladies fall short of the mark. In their efforts to be effective in a traditionally male role, they sacrifice an essential part of the traditional female role for people of their stature and social class. Similarly, these women are just as ineffective in translating maternal authority into managerial authority: their employees come to resent being scolded and regarded as children and come to ignore their orders. Even if this transfer of domestic power to the workplace were possible, the fact remains that Mrs. McIntyre had never established her domestic authority in the Judge's household, and Mrs. Cope, Mrs. Fox, Mrs. Hopewell and Mrs. May are all weak as maternal authority figures, as all fail to control the actions of their own children.

As is the case with Mrs. Cope and Mrs. McIntyre, Mrs. May also finds herself abandoned by her worker at a crucial time: Mr. Greenleaf is wandering off, ignoring her demand for the bull's death (just as all other males, both May and Greenleaf, ignore her incessant demands) when the bull charges her. As Paulson has noted, Greenleaf's inattention to the bull constitutes revenge upon the "castrating woman [who has] emasculated him." As is the case in the other stories, true male power ultimately wins out. As she warns her sons repeatedly, her demise means the demise of the farm as well.

In the end, Mrs. Cope, Mrs. McIntyre and Mrs. May wind up losing their hold on the "places" they had managed to grab from the partriarchy because they ultimately fail to fully synthesize the necessary aspects of both traditional gender roles. All three end up, in essence, "displaced persons." They are, in Westling's terms, "rendered passive by punishment." But while Westling asserts that "O'Connor seems to be demonstrating that independent female authority is unnatural and must be crushed by male force," the fact is that these women's authority was never fully independent due to their absolute reliance upon a thin veneer of social propriety. Despite our distaste for these women, there is something undeniably pathetic about their fate: there is no sense of a "natural" order being restored, only a sense of destruction and loss.

While these women may seem unsympathetic in their handling of power, it should be noted that O'Connor has her disempowered women fare no better than her empowered characters—as illustrated by the fate that befalls Julian's mother at the end of "Everything That Rises," after she has her belief in the social order that elevated her literally knocked our of her. Another helpful text to look at to illustrate the plight of the widow who owns land but is completely lacking in power is "The Life You Save May Be Your Own," in which Mrs.

Crater lacks the economic ability to hire workers or have repairs made. O'Connor symbolizes her disempowerment by having her show Shiftlet that she literally has no teeth (i.e. no authority) and that she and her daughter are going nowhere, as her automobile had "quit running" the day her husband died. Mrs. Crater is forced by poverty to barter her own daughter in order to get someone to work for her; she must give Shiftlet a share in the farm in order to get him to stay.

Her willingness to make any deal to secure a son-in-law who will agree to stay on the place is seen in her willingness to deal with Shiftlet, even though he openly admits he could be lying to her about his identity because "nowadays, people'll do anything anyways," and though she knows nothing about him other than his declaration, "I'm a man." But a man is exactly what Mrs. Crater feels she needs to keep her farm running. O'Connor signals this by having her "wonder if a one-armed man could put up a new roof on her garden house" from the outset and by having her offer Shiftlet as "bait" the means to flee (the automobile) as part of the "package" for her daughter—despite her demand that he remain on the farm. Her ordering of items in this package deal also reveals what she knows is truly important to Shiftlet: "you'd be getting a permanent house and a deep well and the most innocent girl in the world." But once Shiftlet assumes the power of her late husband by fixing the car, Mrs. Crater has no way to hold him to the bargain, and her innocent daughter ultimately pays the price for her lack of power. Unlike O'Connor's empowered women, who have the means to shelter and provide for their ungrateful children even well into their adult years, Mrs. Crater can't protect a daughter who is even more vulnerable than she. Disempowerment hardly seems an attractive alternative.

Perhaps O'Connor's stories should be taken as commentaries upon the impossibility of a woman of this society successfully negotiating her way through a patriarchal power structure, since no amount of "masculine" behavior can compensate for the fact that these empowered women are still inferior in the eyes of those they must control in order to survive. As women, their claims upon authority are dubious at best, and the males who destroy them recognize this. If O'Connor is satirizing these characters, it is only because they are too blind to realize that any attempt to mix masculine and feminine roles is destined to fail. Because they can obtain only toleration, but no true respect, from the males upon whom they must depend as a matter of economic necessity, these characters wind up being successful neither as "ladies" nor as bosses. In trying to act both gender roles, these women fail to completely fill the requirements of either. Flannery O'Connor's empowered women are eventually foiled by the representatives of a society unwilling to embrace the paradox they represent.

Source: Peter A. Smith, "Flannery O'Connor's Empowered Women," in *Southern Literary Journal,* Vol. 26, No. 2, Spring 1994, pp. 35–47.

Louise Westling

In the following essay, Westling explores the "radically different views toward femininity" found in a comparison of "A Circle in the Fire" and Eudora Welty's Delta Wedding *within the context of "the old mother/daughter story of Demeter and Persephone."*

Bookish southern girls a generation ago were likely to have saturated themselves with Greek and Roman mythology in childhood, because Southern culture has had a long love affair with the classics. Not surprisingly, that kind of early imaginative experience turns up in the fiction of two very different women writers, Eudora Welty of Mississippi and Flannery O'Connor of Georgia. Both writers echo the Demeter/Persephone story in dramatizing strong maternal figures who preside over pastoral settings. But while Welty celebrates the feminine power and fertility of what mythographer G. S. Kirk calls "the most pervasive of all Greek divine tales," O'Connor invokes the old patterns in order to deny their force. Welty is comfortable with her femininity and thus is able to imagine an attractive mother figure, while O'Connor seems to have only loathing for her gender and wish to deny the legitimacy of adult female authority.

"I've lived with mythology all my life," Welty told an interviewer. "It is just as close to me as the landscape. It *naturally* occurs to me when I am writing fiction." Flannery O'Connor relied chiefly on Biblical sources for imagery, but she also used myth consciously in at least one story and explored it seriously in her adult reading. Her personal library included a number of well-used books of mythology, including Bulfinch, and her friendship with Robert Fitzgerald stimulated her close reading of Homer and the Greek tragedians whom he translated. Like Welty, O'Connor was interested in mythic patterns associated with fertility, and both writers saw these as relevant to contemporary life.

Critics have called our attention to mythic elements in much of Welty's fiction, and Frederick Asals has established O'Connor's careful parallels of Christian and pagan symbols in "Greenleaf." With his previous work as a background, I want to look specifically at Welty's *Delta Wedding* and O'Connor's "A Circle in the Fire" to show how radically different attitudes toward femininity are expressed in their use of the old mother/daughter story of Demeter and Persephone.

Before looking specifically at the fiction, we should recall the major elements of this oldest recorded myth of feminine fertility and renewal in the "Homeric Hymn to Demeter." This was the source for Bulfinch's and most other modern versions in popular circulation. The story describes the abduction from a flowery meadow of Demeter's virgin daughter Kore or Persephone by Hades or Pluton, god of the underworld. Demeter's grief, the aid of her sister Hecate of the underworld, the punishment of all creation for the rape by the Great Mother's withholding of fertility, then finally its restoration on the return of Persephone—all these events define the ancient motif. The setting for the rape turns out to be highly symbolic. Deborah Dickmann Boedeker has shown that typical sites for rape in Greek myth and cult were meadow-like dancing grounds where circle dances promoted fertility and associated maidens with growing plants. These sites are protected by mother goddesses, as in the Homeric Hymn "To Earth the Mother of All." The hymn sings of the great nourisher of all life and of her gift of "fruitful land" (aroura), a word often used metaphorically to denote woman as bearing seed and fruit. Those blessed by Mother Earth have children who are like the fruits of the soil. In particular, "their daughters in flower-laden bands play and skip merrily over the soft flowers of the field." This scene is much like the blissful meadow where Persephone and her maiden companions gathered flowers where Hades suddenly appeared.

Such a fecund landscape is the setting for Welty's *Delta Wedding*—that famous bottomland in Mississippi whose name recalls ancient shapes denoting female fertility. Furthermore it is a world ruled by women: "In the Delta the land belonged to the women—they only let the men have it, and sometimes they tried to take it back and give it to someone else. . . . All the men lived here in a kind of sufferance!" Ellen Fairchild is the organizer and sustainer of domestic life in the plantation world of the novel, and matriarchal ancestor Mary Shannon Fairchild rules family tradition even from the grave.

The plot is constructed of a series of feminine rituals which prepare for the most important ritual of all—the wedding of Ellen's eighteen-year-old daughter Dabney to the mysterious and slightly sinister overseer who seems to walk right in from the fields to the ceremony.

Others before me have seen overseer Troy Flavin as a "field god" and have alluded to the ritualistic movement of the novel's plot, but the full significance of these associations has not been explained. We first see Troy through Dabney's eyes as she rides horseback with two girlish companions across Mound Field, site of the Indian mound for which the plantation is named. Dabney thinks of the field as "the pre-eminent place" where she first noticed Troy a year before, and her association of him with dark and explosive forces helps us realize that this place is symbolically the pre-eminent meadow with its *omphalos,* entrance to the underworld where the earth yawned and Hades emerged to snatch Persephone front her innocent, flowery play. Now, just a few days before her wedding, Dabney sees Troy as a distant figure riding across her path on his black horse, his arm raised in greeting like a gun against the sky. She shuts her eyes and sees "a blinding light, or else it was a dark cloud—that intensity under her flickering lids." "She thought of him proudly (he was right back of the mound now, she knew), a dark thundercloud, his slowness rumbling and his laugh flickering through in bright flashes. . . ." Welty knows that storm and earthquake, attributes of Zeus anti Poseidon, could be associated with their brother Hades. Indeed, Hades was often called Zeus. If Troy Flavin's positive qualities can be stimulated, he like Hades/ Pluton will become a source of new riches from the feminine earth. When Persephone returned from her underworld marriage, her mother welcomed her like a Maenad and the land burst forth in fruit. All this is possible for Dabney and Troy, as Welty suggests when she has Troy appear with a womb-like sack full of his mother's quilts which symbolize both the traditional feminine art of the mountain people from whom he descends, and also the fertility of the landscape which he and Dabney will imitate. As Troy displays the quilts, he declares his choice of one called Delectable Mountains to cover the marriage bed; "that's the one I aim for Dabney and me to sleep under most generally, warm *and* pretty." The sexual connotations of the bedroom landscape are not lost on Troy's audience, especially when he says Dabney should wait to thank his mother until she has tried the quilts. "That's what

> **The association between the contours and reproductive capacities of the earth and those of the female is as old as the human imagination. . . ."**

will count with Mammy. She might come if we have a baby, sure enough." By now, even the maiden aunts are beginning to quiver.

Before Troy's embarrassingly candid hopes can be realized, however, a serious threat to the wedding must be removed by ritual actions which parallel the Eleusinian Mysteries of Demeter. These rituals involve mythic figures not ordinarily seen as part of the Demeter/Persephone story—chiefly Dionysian ones—but their elaboration in the plot is too complex to describe here. An outline of the rituals themselves should indicate how richly Welty has endowed her novel with mythic meaning. We begin at the hearth, with the baking of a coconut cake by the white matriarch Ellen Fairchild. The recipe is a feminine family secret, and Ellen remembers a scene of marital eroticism as she works with the ingredients, hoping that such joy awaits her daughter. Later in the novel a complementary magic cake is baked by the black matriarch Partheny; hers is a black aphrodisiac patticake which Troy tastes before the wedding. The bride and two pubescent attendants make a ritual journey to the virgin grove where the spinster guardians of family history initiate them into matriarchal family traditions. A mystic encounter of mother and archetypal daughter in the bayou woods is followed by a trip by virgin daughters into a topographically complex underworld where the dead are visited and a lost Kore figure is found and restored to the world of light. Then the bride and groom's house is blessed in a strange rite where bees swarm in the central room, as if pollinating a flower. This fertile event is followed by a symbolic baptism for a nine-year-old girl which prepares her to serve as a flower girl in the wedding. Finally the wedding itself is celebrated in a pastoral motif with bridesmaids carrying shepherds' crooks and Troy coming in with flaming hair from the side door, "indeed like somebody walking in from the fields to marry Dabney." *Delta Wed-*

ding ends with a picnic three days after the wedding, in which the whole extended family is reunited with the newly married couple just back from their honeymoon down in the exotic nether world of New Orleans. Persephone has been restored to her mother, and a new vitality stirs in the family.

Whether or not Flannery O'Connor meant to reiterate the underlying pattern of the Demeter-Kore myth, it is the only literary precedent which can illuminate the obsessive theme of masculine invasion in her mother-daughter farm stories. "A Circle in the Fire" is the fullest exposition of the theme, revealing parallels to the myth which are surprising at the very least.

A triad of females is established as the essential population of the farm at the opening of the story. Mrs. Cope works vigorously in her flowerbed, as Mrs. Prichard [sic], her ally and the tenant farmer's wife, looks on and chats about a woman who died having a baby in an iron lung. Twelve-year-old Sally Virginia Cope spies on the two women from an upstairs window. In a very general way the group parallels the Eleusinian trinity of Mother Demeter, Kore, and Hecate the dark goddess of death, all guardians of earth's mysteries in the famous Greek cult. Mrs. Cope is custodian of the land and guardian of her daughter; Mrs. Prichard's fascination with disease and funerals allies her with the gloomy deity who led initiates to symbolic death in Demeter's awesome rites.

Weeding the invading nut grass from her flowerbed as if the plants "were an evil sent directly by the devil to destroy the place," Mrs. Cope is suddenly confronted by much more serious agents of destruction in the form of three thirteen-year-old boys who will claim the farm as their own and wreak havoc in defiance of the "damn women" whose province it has been. For Powell Boyd, the leader of the invading trio, the farm is a paradise, lost when his tenant farmer father moved the family to Florida. Powell has brought his friends from his new home in an Atlanta slum to see the place he wants to go to when he dies, a heaven of horses to ride and open pastures to roam. O'Connor equates these hungry children with suffering European refugees and clearly intends to dramatize and finally punish Mrs. Cope's lack of real Christian charity towards them. But from the outset the boys' claim on the farm is so relentless and coldly misogynist that no possible kindness offered by Mrs. Cope could disarm their determination to have the whole place to themselves. The first thing we learn about

Powell is that his gaze seems to come "from two directions at once as if it had [Mrs. Cope and Mrs. Prichard] surrounded." All three boys have "white penetrating stares," and Powell's seems to pinch Mrs. Cope like a pair of tongs. Their arrival is an assault which becomes more and more obvious as Mrs. Cope tries politely but vainly to keep them under control. When she refers to "her" woods, one boy echoes her in a sarcastic mutter. The next morning when she tells them she expects them behave like gentlemen, they stand looking away from her as if waiting for her to leave. "After all," she says in a voice strained with anxiety, "this is my place!" In her response to her authority they turn their backs on her and walk away.

The boy's resentment of women in general and Mrs. Cope's claim to the farm in particular is twice made very clear. Sally Virginia has been fascinated by her mother's increasingly exasperated dealings with Powell and his friends. Red in the face with excitement which gradually turns to rage, she peers down on the unfolding drama from the safety of an upstairs window and finally crosses her eyes, sticks out her tongue, and says "Ugggghhrhh." "The large boy looked up and stared at her. 'Jesus,' he growled, 'another woman.' She dropped back from the window and stood with her back against the wall, squinting fiercely as if she had been slapped in the face and couldn't see who had done it." Later Mrs. Prichard reports that the boys have been disputing Mrs. Cope's ownership to the farm in a, conversation with Mr. Prichard. "She don't own them woods," one boy said. The same boy who had insulted Sally Virginia complained, "I never seen a place with so many damn women on it, how do you stand it here?"

The farm is under a siege whose sexual danger Mrs. Cope senses. At Mrs. Prichard's suggestion that the boys might want to spend the night, she gives a little shriek and exclaims, "I can't have three boys in here with only me and Sally Virginia." Repeatedly she warns her daughter to stay away from the visitors, but she won't say why. O'Connor does, explaining to her friend "A" that Sally Virginia risks sexual attack if she goes near the boys. "They would do it because they would be sharp enough to know that it would be their best revenge on Mrs. Cope; they would do it to humiliate the child and the mother, not to enjoy themselves." Sexual violence is the most potent form of masculine assault, whose ominous potential Mrs. Prichard describes when she tells Mrs. Cope, "You take a boy thirteen years old is equal in meanness to a man twict his age. It's no telling what he'll think up to do. You never know where he'll strike next.''

Sally Virginia finally disobeys her mother's protective warnings and marches off to confront the boys in the woods where the climactic scene of destruction takes place. Flannery O'Connor told ''A'' that the boy's attack takes another form than the sexual one Mrs. Cope fears, but the woods they destroy are so closely identified with the child that the effect is almost the same. Sally Virginia adopts male dress to stalk her enemy, but the overalls she wears over her dress and the toy pistols she waves in the air are ridiculously inadequate defense. She comes upon the boys performing a curious rite in the back pasture behind the woods, and she hides behind a pine tree to watch. They are bathing in the cow trough which O'Connor likens to a coffin so that we will not miss the significance of their baptismal rebirth in the symbolically female meadow. Their conversation is a litany of claims for possession of the place. The biggest boy says the farm ''don't belong to nobody,'' and the smallest boy chimes in, ''It's ours.'' At that signal Powell jumps out of the water and begins a celebratory race around the pasture, tracing its boundaries in a circular path. As he passes the trough again, the other boys leap from the water to follow him. Their long naked bodies glint in the sun and their masculinity must be obvious in its simplest form to the frightened girl behind the tree. The side of her face is so closely pressed against the trunk that ''the imprint of the bark [is] embossed red and white'' upon it. When the boys dress and move into the woods to set them on fire, we should remember that earlier in the story Sally Virginia had registered the big boy's contemptuous ''Jesus, another woman'' as if she had been slapped in the *face.* Her face carries the mark of her humiliated feminity just as it carries the imprint of the tree that identifies her with the ravaged woods.

Although Sally Virginia symbolically shares Kore's fate as object of male assault, the attackers' motivations differ profoundly in the Greek myth and in O'Connor's story Like Kore, Sally Virginia is wandering outside her mother's protection when the violation of the garden occurs; the attack in both cases circumvents the mother's power. But while Pluto or Hades is motivated by positive desire for Demeter's daughter as his mate, Flannery O'Connor's boys hate women and seek revenge rather than sexual union. Demeter herself makes the land barren in retaliation against her daughter's rape; her authority is never challenged. In contrast, as we

have seen, that kind of authority is exactly the object of male retribution in ''A Circle in the Fire.'' By burning Mrs. Cope's woods, O'Connor's boys humiliate the daughter and her mother, bringing the fiery devastation Mrs. Cope has feared throughout the story and destroying the female integrity of the land. For O'Connor, the boys are agents of divine retribution, prophets dancing in the fiery furnace, ''in the circle the angel had cleared for them.'' Thus the story ends, with Mrs. Cope's pride humbled by a God who forces her to share the homeless misery of European refugess, Negroes, and hungry children.

So much emphasis is placed in this story upon the terrified impotence of mother and daughter to prevent disaster that the failure of charity which O'Connor wants us to accept as justification for the boys' vengeance is simply not sufficient cause. Unlike Eudora Welty, who not only accepted but *celebrated* maternal control of the pastoral landscape, Flannery O'Connor has dramatized its gleeful destruction in eerie male rituals which seem an inversion of the flowery circle dances of maidens protected by the mother deity which Boedeker described as traditional in ancient Greek religion. The circles the boys trace around the pasture in their naked race are statements of possession, and the final circle in the fire is a charmed spot at the center of a holocaust.

The association between the contours and reproductive capacities of the earth and those of the female is as old as the human imagination, lying at the root of almost every religious tradition that derives from prehistoric times and continuing to find expression in contemporary life. It should not be at all surprising to find women writers especially sensitive to landscapes, and indeed Ellen Moers has revealed in *Literary Women* how from George Eliot to Willa Cather and Gertrude Stein they have associated their sexuality and autonomy with symbolic landscapes. Moers opened a whole rich mine of literary discovery when she wrote her provocative final chapter suggesting distinctively feminine metaphors which could be explored by future scholars. So far not very much has been done to develop and expand her discussion of feminine landscapes, but I hope that here I have demonstrated how differently the identification of the mother with the fruitful land can be treated in fiction. Because both Eudora Welty and Flannery O'Connor echoed the myth of Demeter and Kore/Persephone, its original focus upon the mother's fertile power invests both *Delta Wedding* and ''A Circle in the Fire'' with imaginative reverberations that are both ancient and profound. Why Welty uses them to affirm feminine identity and O'Connor to humiliate it—that is another question.

Source: Louise Westling, ''Demeter and Kore, Southern Style,'' in *Pacific Coast Philology,* Vol. 19, Nos. 1–2, November 1984, pp. 101–07.

Sources

Babinec, Lisa S., ''Cyclical Patterns of Domination and Manipulation in Flannery O'Connor's Mother-Daughter Relationships,'' in *Flannery O'Connor Bulletin,* Vol. 19, 1990, pp. 9–29.

Howe, Irving, ''Flannery O'Connor's Stories,'' in *New York Review of Books,* September 30, 1965, pp. 16–17.

O'Connor, Flannery, *The Complete Stories,* Noonday Press, 1972, pp. 175–93.

Schaum, Melita, '''Erasing Angel': The Lucifer-Trickster Figure in Flannery O'Connor's Short Fiction,'' in *Southern Literary Journal,* Vol. 33, No. 1, Fall 2000, pp. 1–26.

Schott, Webster, ''Flannery O'Connor: Faith's Stepchild,'' in *Nation,* Vol. 201, No. 7, September 13, 1965, pp. 142–44, 146.

Walker, Alice, *In Search of Our Mothers' Gardens: Womanist Prose,* Harcourt Brace Jovanovich, 1982, pp. 42–59.

Further Reading

Bloom, Harold, ed., *Flannery O'Connor: Comprehensive Research and Study Guide,* Bloom's Major Short Story Writers series, Chelsea House, 1999.

    This introduction to O'Connor's short fiction features some of her best-known stories, including ''A Good Man Is Hard to Find'' and ''Everything That Rises Must Converge.'' Bloom includes a biography of the author along with analyses of the stories.

Cash, Jean W., *Flannery O'Connor: A Life,* University of Tennessee Press, 2002.

    This recent biography focuses on presenting the facts of O'Connor's life rather than attempting to interpret it. Cash catalogs even minute details of her subject's life, such as what college courses she took.

O'Connor, Flannery, *The Habit of Being,* edited by Sally Fitzgerald, Noonday Press, 1988.

    This is a reprint edition of a collection of O'Connor's correspondence that was first published in 1979. Arranged chronologically, the letters take up nearly 600 pages and comprise the closest thing readers have to an autobiography of O'Connor.

Ragen, Brian Abel, *A Wreck on the Road to Damascus: Innocence, Guilt, and Conversion in Flannery O'Connor,* Loyola Press, 1989.

    This volume is one scholar's attempt to explain O'Connor's Catholic beliefs and their effects on her work—especially to readers who do not share those beliefs.

Rath, Sura P., and Mary Neff Shaw, eds., *Flannery O'Connor: New Perspectives,* University of Georgia Press, 1996.

    This collection of essays by eleven scholars, including the editors, examines O'Connor's short stories and novels from both traditional and contemporary perspectives, including issues such as gender politics and trends in academia and criticism.

The Curing Woman

Alejandro Morales

1986

Alejandro Morales's short story ''The Curing Woman'' was first published in 1986 in *The Americas Review*. It was reprinted in the anthology *Short Fiction by Hispanic Writers of the United States* (Houston, 1993). ''The Curing Woman'' draws on the traditional Mexican folktale, but it also possesses elements of social realism and magical realism. Set in the late nineteenth and early twentieth centuries in Spain, Mexico, and California, it describes the life of Doña Marcelina Trujillo Benidorm. Marcelina is a young woman who leaves her home at the age of thirteen to be reunited with her mother. Her mother, who is a traditional healer or *curandera,* trains Marcelina in the healing arts. Marcelina then travels to Mexico, where she apprentices herself to two more master healers. She then makes her way to Simons, California, where she becomes widely known for her practice of the art of *curanderismo.* The story centers on one cure in particular, that of a boy named Delfino, who suffers from a malady that cannot be explained or cured by other doctors.

Author Biography

Alejandro Dennis Morales was born October 14, 1944, in Montebello, California. His parents, Delfino Morales Martínez and Juana Contreras Ramíriz, had immigrated to California from Guanajuato, Mexico. Morales grew up in East Los Angeles, where he attended elementary and secondary schools.

Morales married H. Rohde Teaze on December 16, 1967.

Morales earned a bachelor of arts from California State University in Los Angeles and a master of arts and Ph.D. in Spanish in 1971 and 1975, respectively, from Rutgers University in New Jersey.

Morales is known primarily as a novelist who records and interprets the Mexican American experience. His first novel, *Caras viejas y vino nuevo*, was written in Spanish and published in 1975 in Mexico City. It examines the conflict between generations in a Mexican American community. It was revised and edited before being translated as *Old Faces and New Wine* (1981). *La verdad sin voz* (Mexico City, 1979) was translated as *Death of an Anglo* (1988). It continues the theme of the earlier novel, drawing on actual accounts of conflict between Chicanos and Anglos in the town of Mathis, Texas.

Reto en el paraíso (*Challenge in Paradise*) was published in a bilingual edition in 1982. It was based on a hundred years of Mexican American history and myth.

In 1986, Morales published two short stories, "Cara de caballo" and "The Curing Woman," followed within a few years by two novels in English. *The Brick People* (1988) examines the lives of two families—one family owns a brick factory and the other family includes an immigrant laborer who works at the factory. The story begins in the nineteenth century and is based on real events. *The Rag Doll Plagues* (1992) consists of three self-contained but thematically related stories about outbreaks of disease in different time periods in Mexican and Mexican American history. The first story takes place in colonial Mexico, the second in present-day Mexico and southern California, and the third is set in the mid-twenty-first century in the high-tech society of Lames.

Morales is a professor in the Spanish and Portuguese Department at the University of California, Irvine, where he has taught since 1975.

Plot Summary

"The Curing Woman" tells the story of Doña Marcelina Trujillo Benidorm. Marcelina is born into a rich, aristocratic family in Spain. Her mother is one of the family's servants. When her mother is forced to leave the service of the family at the end of her ten-year term, Mrs. Trujillo Benidorm, the wife of Marcelina's father, refuses to let her take nine-year-old Marcelina with her.

Marcelina is heartbroken. When she looks at her mother's face as her mother is leaving, she realizes it is like looking into a mirror; it is as if her mother had given birth to her own twin.

For four years Marcelina is well cared for and receives a good education. Then one morning a servant brings her a piece of paper, and the information contained on it leads Marcelina to travel to a place called Alhambra. In one of the caves in the hills that overlook the town, she meets her mother again, whom she has not seen or heard from for four years.

Marcelina spends seven years with her mother, learning the art of healing. When her mother realizes Marcelina has learned everything she has to offer, she sends her away. Marcelina, now age twenty, travels on a ship to Veracruz on the Gulf Coast of Mexico. In Veracruz she is met by a man called "El Gran Echbo," who is a teacher and a healer. Marcelina is apprenticed to him for several years. Near the end of that period, she meets María Sabina, a saintly woman renowned for her healing abilities. María Sabina teaches Marcelina everything she knows, and then the two of them travel to Mexico City by an ancient route known only to a few.

The journey is hard on Marcelina, and she falls into a trance-like state. She awakens in María Sabina's shack in the poorest section of Mexico City. María Sabina tells her that the city is dangerous and that in four days' time Marcelina must leave and journey north. Then María Sabina disappears.

Marcelina travels north through a country ravaged by the violence of political revolution. She treats the sick and wounded. She finally crosses the border into the United States, and travels by train for three months until she reached Simons, California.

Some time elapses. Concepción Martínez and her eldest son Delfino walk toward Marcelina's home. She is now known as Doña Marcelina, the *curandera*. The two women have been friends for years, and Concepción is taking her son to Marcelina for treatment. Delfino has a strange illness. He is losing weight and is weak and delirious, but the doctors can find nothing physically wrong with him. The illness may be the result of a fire that consumed the family home. Delfino thought his family had perished, and the shock may be causing the malady. But no one really knows.

When Marcelina greets them at her house, Delfino for a moment sees her as both an old woman and a beautiful young girl. Marcelina guides Delfino into a small room, and his mother waits behind. Delfino notices a painting on the wall of a man sitting on a wheelbarrow with a woman sitting on a block in front of him. Under the painting is a wheelbarrow with a black block in front of it. Marcelina asks Delfino to sit in the wheelbarrow. Then she sits on the black block in front of him. She prepares potions and sings a litany of prayers and incantations.

Concepción watches from the doorway as Marcelina struggles to defeat the spirit that is eating away at Delfino's body. Delfino's physical appearance changes until he looks like Marcelina.

After a while a grotesque form appears on Marcelina's lower back. It becomes like an octopus and wraps its tentacles around her waist. Marcelina eventually makes it disappear. Delfino reappears in his own body, and feels refreshed and free again. He recalls nothing of what has happened. He is surprised to find that he is wearing Marcelina's jacket. He takes it off and places it in the wheelbarrow.

Later Marcelina gives Concepción some potions which Delfino is to take for the next nine days. Delfino waits while the two women talk. He looks back into the room where he was treated. He notices that the painting on the wall has changed. The man has disappeared. He turns around to tell his mother, but finds himself in front of his own home waiting for his mother to open the door.

Characters

Doña Marcelina Trujillo Benidorm

Doña Marcelina Trujillo Benidorm is the protagonist of the story. She is born into an aristocratic, Catholic, Spanish home, the daughter of Trujillo Benidorm and a female servant of the family. Her servant mother is sent away from the family home when Marcelina is nine years old, but Marcelina has to stay behind. Four years later Marcelina goes in search of her mother and finds her near the town of Alhambra. Marcelina then begins a long apprenticeship to become a *curandera,* or traditional healer. She has three teachers: her mother; a man named El Gran Echbo, whom she meets in Veracruz, Mexico; and María Sabina, a woman who is known for her healing abilities. When her apprenticeship is over,

Marcelina travels with María Sabina to Mexico City, and then quickly travels north. As she goes north she treats the wounded from the civil war ravaging the country. Continuing to travel north, she crosses the border into the United States and reaches Simons, California, where she sets up a practice as a *curandera.* She earns a reputation amongst the townspeople as a mysterious woman, and the local children avoid her. One of the patients she successfully treats is Delfino. Marcelina remains in Simons for the rest of her life.

Mrs. Trujillo Benidorm

Mrs. Trujillo Benidorm is the wife of Marcelina's father. She has three sons of her own, but she is not Marcelina's mother. She and her husband are well respected in their society, and they are known for their charitable works. But they are also snobbish and keep company with only a few select aristocratic families.

El Gran Echbo

El Gran Echbo is a wise man and healer who takes in Marcelina as an apprentice upon her arrival in Veracruz, Mexico. He teaches her everything about the spirit of the New World, adding to the knowledge she learned from her mother.

Concepción Martínez

Concepción Martínez is a friend of Marcelina's in Simons, California. Concepción is in awe of her friend's knowledge and abilities, and she takes her son Delfino to her for treatment.

Delfino Martínez

Delfino Martínez is the eldest son of Concepción Martínez. He suffers from a malady that doctors cannot cure. The illness may have been caused by the shock of the fire that consumed his home, in which he believed at first that all his family had been killed. Delfino's mother takes him to see Marcelina. It is their last hope, and it is rewarded. Marcelina cures him.

María Sabina

María Sabina is a woman with saintly qualities. She is also a renowned healer with a deep knowledge of plants and animals. Marcelina meets her in Veracruz, and María Sabina becomes Marcelina's final teacher, instructing her in all the ancient wisdom she knows. María Sabina takes Marcelina with her to Mexico City, where she leaves her, giving her instructions to travel north.

Yerma

Yerma is Marcelina's mother. She is a servant in an aristocratic house but is asked to leave when her ten-year term expires. She then marries and trains to become a healer, a *curandera*. She bears no other children. When Marcelina finds her in Alhambra, Marcelina stays with her for seven years, learning everything her mother knows about the healing arts. After Marcelina leaves Yerma for Veracruz, the two never meet again.

Themes

Spiritual Healing, Magic, and Cosmology

"The Curing Woman" is about the power of a great traditional healer to cure physical illness by working on the spiritual level. The work of Doña Marcelina rests on a dualistic theory of the universe in which there are good and evil powers. There is also a fluid interchange between spiritual and physical worlds. What this means in practice is that a person's illness may have causes other than merely physical ones. Since natural and supernatural worlds interact, evil spirits can take over a person's body and cause illness. But a skilled healer who understands how the cosmic forces operate can overcome these evil spirits.

The traditional (as opposed to modern medical) knowledge Marcelina learns from her mother in Spain is very eclectic, drawn from Moslem, Jewish, and Christian sources. All these religions have strong roots in Spain. Within the Christian tradition, there was a system of healing known as "white magic," which used the occult (hidden) properties of natural things, such as herbs, plants, and minerals, to effect cures through "sympathies" and "antipathies" that were believed to exist between those natural things and elements within the human body. White magicians would also use other esoteric methods, including chants and incantations (as Yerma does in the story), and formulas that would take into account astrological influences. The tradition of white magic in Europe was undermined by the rise of science, but it lived on in practitioners such as Yerma.

When Marcelina arrives in Mexico she learns something new: the wisdom and cosmology of the Aztecs, the civilization that flourished in Mexico until the arrival of the Spanish colonizers in the early sixteenth century. The clue to the fact that Marcelina learns Aztec wisdom is in the language that María Sabina speaks and which she teaches Marcelina. It is Natuatl, which was the language of the Aztecs (still spoken in parts of Mexico today). Aztec cosmology, like the religious traditions Marcelina absorbed from her mother, is dualistic. One of the forms that dualism takes is between male and female forces. Marcelina mentions Ometechuhtli-Omecihuatl, which are the primordial deities in Aztec cosmology. They are known respectively as "Lord of duality" and "Lady of duality." Additionally, the "four suns of the mandala" that Marcelina contemplates may be a reference to the sequence of four world ages in Aztec cosmology, known as Jaguar Sun, Wind Sun, Rain Sun, and Water Sun, each age ruled by a different god.

It is only by immersing herself in this knowledge that Marcelina is able to effect the cures she does. Because she understands how all the cosmic forces work within her own person and is able to magically transform the patient's body so that it resembles her own, she is able to locate the nature and form of the invasive spirit. The healing process incorporates strong elements of Christianity. These include the prayers Marcelina says before she begins her work and the signs of the cross she makes as she prepares another potion. The pulling out of the evil spirit seems to resemble a Christian exorcism. Thus her work as a *curandera* seems to fuse elements of Christianity with indigenous Mexican folk healing.

The story also suggests that although this kind of traditional healing may be a gift, it also requires long training. Doña Marcelina has to go through many years of training to acquire her knowledge of how to heal others, which involves learning from people who are themselves masters of their art. It is a wisdom that cannot be learned from books.

The Mystery of Identity and the Self

The story has several mysterious elements that cannot be rationally explained. For example, when she is nine years old, Marcelina has a realization that she is not only her mother's daughter but also her twin. She looks in a mirror and sees that she looks exactly like her mother. Perhaps the explanation for this is that for a moment, the spiritual dimension of life shines through. Just as in the future, her mother will study and become a *curandera,* so will Marcelina; their roles in life become identical. As a

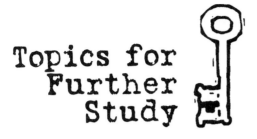

Topics for Further Study

- Are traditional methods of healing, such as *curanderismo*, a valuable complement to modern medicine, or are they made up mostly of outdated superstitions? Explain your answer based on your research.

- Research the Mexican Revolution of the 1910s that is mentioned in "The Curing Woman." Why did the revolution take place, and what was the outcome?

- What role, if any, do faith and belief have in healing? Should a cure work regardless of whether the patient believes it will?

- Provide a definition for "magical realism" along with some examples of other writers who have used this element in their stories. Does magical realism take the reader closer to the truth about all aspects of life in a way that simple realism cannot? If so, in what sense?

- Research and discuss some aspects of traditional Mexican culture and belief. Is it important for Mexican Americans to preserve their cultural heritage? What are the advantages and/or disadvantages for any immigrant group in preserving their cultural heritage?

---

young girl, Marcelina has a foretaste of this spiritual level of their relationship.

Another mysterious moment which also involves the breakdown of the apparently solid walls of the individual self is when Delfino, in the course of his treatment, takes on the actual physical appearance of Marcelina. This is startling for Concepción, who gazes at her son in the form of her friend. This mysterious transference suggests there is more to life than the accepted, common sense belief that individuals are completely separate and different from one another. There is no rational explanation why Delfino finds himself wearing Marcelina's jacket, other than the fact that it serves as a symbol for what happens in the process of healing. Within the tradition of *curanderismo* it appears that it is possible for two individuals to temporarily merge into one.

This mystery of psychic and even physical transference extends further, into the realm of art. Just as the separation between natural and spiritual worlds, and the boundaries between individual selves, are not fixed and absolute, nor is the division between life and art. The details of the painting that Delfino sees at the end of his treatment are different from the way they were before. The man, who surely represented the sick Delfino, has been re-

moved from the painting. Perhaps this suggests that the way art is viewed is entirely dependent on the perceiver, who will see it differently according to his own state of mind. Another possible meaning is that art can imitate or reflect life in ways that cannot be rationally explained.

Metaphor of the Journey

After she leaves her home when she is thirteen years old, Marcelina undertakes many journeys. She travels to find her mother in another part of Spain, and then after seven years goes south to the port city of Cadiz, where she sails for Veracruz, Mexico. After some time, she travels again, this time to Mexico City. Then she undertakes the longest journey of all, to Simons in California. The many journeys she takes, although they are literal journeys, are also metaphors for her inner journeys, her mental and spiritual preparation for the calling she is to pursue, that of a healer.

The symbolic nature of the journey is strongly suggested by the description of the route that Marcelina and María Sabina take on their way to Mexico City. It is a "an ancient secret path known only to a chosen few," which is also a perfect description of the extensive training Marcelina has undergone in order to become a *curandera*. The spiritual nature of this inner journey is emphasized when, on the way along this "secret path" to Mexico City, Marcelina gains insight into the divine principles that operate in the cosmos. The final stage of both the outer and the inner journey (which she must make alone) is to Simons, California, which is the fulfillment of the journey. Marcelina spends the rest of her life putting into practice the wisdom she has attained.

Style

Folktale, Social Realism, Magical Realism

The story combines elements of the folktale with social realism and the style known as magical realism. The opening sentence, "This is the story that Doña Marcelina Trujillo Benidorm told her friend Concepción Martínez when they met in Simons, California," makes the story sound as if it is part of a tradition of oral storytelling. The folktale elements include the brevity of the story, its wide time span, the dignified, noble emotions ("infinite sadness," "immense sorrow") and the simplicity of many of the descriptions: the rich aristocratic family, the "beautiful" servant, the "beautiful" daughter, the "lovely" mother, the "saintly" healer. In literary fiction, as opposed to folktales, adjectives such as "beautiful" are used very sparingly and are usually amplified with more specific details.

Countering the timeless folktale elements is the social realism of the setting, which is especially noticeable when Marcelina travels through Mexico. The realistic setting allows the time period of the story to be pinpointed. Marcelina's journey through Mexico takes place during the Mexican Revolution, which began in 1910 and continued for much of the following decade. In the second part of the story, the realism increases, which can be seen in the detailed descriptions of Doña Marcelina's house, for example.

Finally, the magical realism can be seen in the unexpectedness and sheer impossibility, from a rational viewpoint, of Doña Marcelina's cure, which is nonetheless embedded within the realistic framework of the story. The final line also, in which Delfino finds himself suddenly in front of his own home, as if he has been magically whisked there, gives another nonrational twist to the story. It is almost as if Delfino has dreamed the whole incident, or imagined it.

Historical Context

Curanderismo

Curanderismo is the Mexican American system of folk healing. The word comes from the Spanish word *curar,* which means "to heal." *Curanderismo* has a long history, and it is still practiced in the twenty-first century in Mexican American communities, as an alternative system of healthcare to mainstream Western medicine.

Historically *curanderismo* has evolved through many influences. It incorporates practices that go back to Arabic medicine introduced in medieval Spain. (The Spanish connection is emphasized in "The Curing Woman," since it is in Spain that Marcelina's mother accumulates her knowledge of healing.) The Arabic practices were brought to Central America by the Spanish conquerors in the sixteenth century. The Spanish also brought Christianity with them, which is another major influence on *curanderismo.* The *curandera* (female healer) or *curandero* (male healer) may utilize symbols and rituals drawn from Christianity (for example, Doña Marcelina prays and makes the sign of the cross as she prepares to heal). The Bible has plenty of information about the healing properties of plants, and Christianity rests on a dualistic universe of good and evil that also underlies the beliefs central to *curanderismo.*

The Spanish conquerors also assimilated from Native Americans and the Aztecs in Mexico further knowledge of the medicinal properties of herbs and plants. Another influence on *curanderismo* was European witchcraft. According to Robert T. Trotter II and Juan Antonio Chavira, witchcraft involved the belief that "supernatural forces can be controlled by man himself, rather than their having undisputed control over him." Supernatural power can be tapped into by those "who possess the correct incantations, prayers, and rituals."

Curanderismo makes a distinction between "natural" and "supernatural" illnesses. As one researcher of *curanderismo* writes (quoted in Trotter and Chavira), "A harmonious relationship between the natural and the supernatural is considered essential to human health and welfare, while disharmony precipitates illness and misfortune." For those who believe in *curanderismo,* supernatural illnesses cannot be treated by Western medicine. Thus in "The Curing Woman," Delfino cannot be cured by the psychiatrist that his mother takes him to see.

Such supernatural illnesses may be caused by a *brujo* (witch or sorcerer) or *espiritus malos* (evil spirits).

Curanderos therefore conduct healing on the spiritual as well as the physical level. They usually believe that they are doing the work of God, and that their healing powers are a gift from God; healing is only done through God's mercy. However, in spite of this religiosity on the part of the healers, they are sometimes regarded as being agents of Satan, which makes some people wary of seeking their help. In the modern world, the hostility to *curanderos* often comes from evangelical Christian churches. Other, nonreligious people may oppose *curanderismo* because they believe it is only a collection of old superstitions that should be disregarded.

Although many of the illnesses treated by *curanderos* are recognized by Western medicine, there are also some that are known as ''folk diseases'' and appear to be exclusive to *curanderismo.* Four diseases in particular are frequently diagnosed: *mal de ojo* (evil eye), *envidia* (extreme jealousy), *mal puesto* (hexing), and *susto* (extreme fright or fear). In *mal de ojo,* a look, glance, or stare from an enemy or stranger can be interpreted as an attempt to give this illness to someone. *Mal de ojo* results in headaches, irritability, and other symptoms. *Envidia* may produce symptoms similar to those found in a variety of anxiety disorders. *Mal puesto* may be inflicted by someone who knows witchcraft; symptoms include paranoia and gastrointestinal problems, among others. Finally, *susto* produces symptoms that are like post-traumatic stress disorder: fatigue, restlessness, withdrawal, depression, and change in appetite. It is *susto* that Delfino suffers from in ''The Curing Woman,'' although in the story *susto* is used also to describe the evil spirit that is causing the condition.

Another aspect of *curanderismo* apparent in ''The Curing Woman'' is that the healer always works from his or her home and shares the same cultural background as the people he or she treats. As Martin Harris points out in his paper ''*Curanderismo* and the DSM-IV'': ''In addition to sharing their clients' geographic location, the curers share patients' social/economic, [sic] class, background, language, and religion, as well as a system of disease classification.'' So in the story, Doña Marcelina and Concepción Martínez are friends. They share the same beliefs, as does the patient, who is Concepción's son. The fact that the patient shares the worldview of the *curanderismo,* especially regarding the supernatural element in disease, is an important factor that allows healing to take place.

There have been a number of famous *curanderos.* Don Pedrito Jaramillo (?–1907), who lived in Falfurrias, Texas, was famous for his cures that often made use of water. A shrine to Don Pedrito was built around his tomb, and pilgrims continue to visit this shrine, seeking cures. ''El Nino'' Fidencio Constantino (1898–1938) of Espinazo, Nuevo Leon, Mexico, was a self-taught *curandero* whose healing powers, which he believed came from God, were apparent very early in his life. El Nino would perform surgeries using only shards of glass and sewing needles, while the patient remained fully conscious. Thousands flocked to see him, and chapels to him have been set up in Mexico and in the United States, as far north as the state of Washington.

Critical Overview

Morales has chosen to concentrate principally on the novel rather than the short story. His novels such as *The Brick People* (1988) and *The Rag Doll Plagues* (1992) examine and interpret the experience of Mexican Americans in a variety of contexts. His critical reputation as one of the most important of contemporary Mexican American writers rests with his novels. Morales's short-story output, which consists only of ''Cara de caballo'' and ''The Curing Woman,'' is too small to attract critical attention. However, it is clear from ''Cara de caballo'' and *The Rag Doll Plagues* that Morales has more than a passing interest in *curanderismo.* Like ''The Curing Woman,'' the plot of ''Cara de caballo'' includes magic potions and mysterious transformations. There is an emphasis on events that cannot be rationally explained. *The Rag Doll Plagues* is notable for the magical realism also found in ''The Curing Woman,'' and it presents an aspect of *curanderismo* that has not received much attention from historians: the persecution of the *curanderos* by the Spanish after their conquest of Mexico.

Criticism

Bryan Aubrey

Aubrey holds a Ph.D. in English and has published many articles on twentieth-century literature.

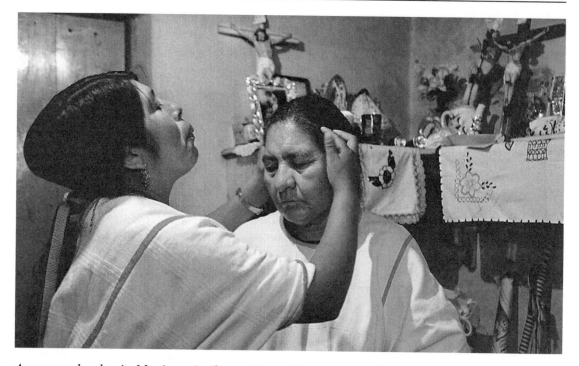

A woman healer in Mexico, similar to Marcelina, a curandera in "The Curing Woman"

In this essay, Aubrey discusses magical realism and shows how other fiction by Morales reveals his interest in curanderismo *and sheds further light on "The Curing Woman."*

Morales is known as a writer who explores the Mexican American cultural heritage and often uses the techniques of magical realism to do so. Magical realism deals with the "transformation of the common and the everyday into the awesome and the unreal," writes Angel Flores in the essay "Magical Realism in Spanish American Fiction." This describes exactly what happens in "The Curing Woman," and it is not surprising that a magical realist writer should be fascinated by the topic of *curanderismo.* Morales's interest in the topic is apparent not only in "The Curing Woman" but also in the only other short story he has published, "Cara de caballo." *Curanderismo* also plays a part in his novel *The Rag Doll Plagues* (1992).

All *curanderos* are magical realists who can transform reality and blur the boundaries between the natural and the supernatural. This is their job, their calling. In "The Curing Woman," not only is Doña Marcelina able to heal through a strange process whereby the body of her patient, Delfino,

takes on her own physical characteristics, she is the means whereby Delfino's universe (and therefore the reader's too) suddenly becomes magical. It no longer obeys the rules Delfino has come to expect. A painting magically changes its composition, and he is inexplicably transported to a different location in time and space. This event takes place within an utterly realistic framework, as can be seen by the matter-of-fact, detailed way in which Doña Marcelina's house is described. Doña Marcelina can therefore be seen as the catalyst that makes life full of magical possibilities. Her art of *curanderismo,* like magical realism, breaks the mold of rational expectation.

As Zamora and Faris write in their introduction to *Magical Realism:*

> Mind and body, spirit and matter, life and death, real and imaginary, self and other, male and female: these are boundaries to be erased, transgressed, blurred, brought together, or otherwise fundamentally refashioned in magical realist texts.

In addition to strange magical transformations, "The Curing Woman" hints at an abundance of ancient, esoteric lore that over the years was incorporated into the practice of *curanderismo.* It is no accident, for example, that Marcelina spends "seven

What Do I Read Next?

- Morales's first English novel *The Brick People* (1989) makes use of magical realism as well as historical facts to tell the story of Mexican Americans in California from 1892 to the 1940s. The focus of the novel is on the brick factory owned by wealthy white Americans and the Mexican immigrants who work there.

- *Cuentos Chicanos* (1984), a revised edition edited by Rudolfo A. Anaya and Antonio Márquez, contains twenty-one stories that cover the full range of Chicano literature including stories derived from oral tradition and complex narratives. The anthology includes established writers, such as Anaya and Sergio Elizondo, as well as emerging new writers.

- *Mexican Americans, American Mexicans: From Conquistadors to Chicanos* (1993) by Matt S. Meier and Feliciano Ribera covers Mexican American history from the time of the Spanish conquest to the Civil Rights movement of the 1960s and recent immigration laws. The book includes maps and a glossary.

- Rudolfo A. Anaya's *Bless Me, Ultima* (1972) is not only one of the most popular Chicano novels ever written, it also provides a wealth of insight and information about *curanderismo.* The novel centers on Antonio Marez, who is six years old when Ultima, a *curandera,* comes to stay with his family in New Mexico. Through Ultima's knowledge and wisdom, Antonio discovers the richness of his cultural heritage.

---

happy years'' learning the healing arts from her mother. Seven is a sacred number in many religious traditions, including Judeo-Christian tradition. It often symbolizes completion, or the whole of something. Examples include the seven years of plenty and the seven years of famine in Egypt (Genesis 41: 53–54), and the seven churches, seven golden candlesticks, seven angels, seven thunders, and seven heads, to name just a few examples from the Revelations of St. John the Divine, in the New Testament. The number seven often occurs in folktales and myth, and it also has a symbolic value in magic and witchcraft.

Similarly, the number nine was sacred to the ancient Greeks, Romans, and Egyptians, as well as later European magicians, because nine is a multiple of the number three, which was considered to be the perfect number. As Trotter and Chavira point out in their book *Curanderismo,* the number nine figures prominently in *curanderismo.* It may designate the length of a cure or the number of times a ritual must be performed. So it is not surprising that the potion Doña Marcelina gives Delfino to complete his cure must be taken for nine successive days.

The exact purpose of this potion in ''The Curing Woman'' is not stated, but potions given not by a *curandera* but a *brujo* (witch) figure prominently in Morales's short story, ''Cara de caballo'' (''Horse face''). Like ''The Curing Woman,'' this story taps into traditional folk beliefs, and features a surprise magical transformation that shatters the everyday realism that normally governs life.

''Cara de caballo'' is a brief story, covering only four pages. It tells of the marriage between the beautiful Doña Arcadia Bandini and a wealthy, much older man named Abel Stearns. Both were from prominent families in southern California in the nineteenth century. Stearns had a reputation as one of the ugliest men in California; his face was disfigured, and he was called *cara de caballo.* The couple had no children; this was deliberate on Arcadia's part because she did not want to risk passing on her husband's ugliness. To ensure her infertility, she consulted local *curanderos,* who prescribed a regimen of special baths, herbs, and potions. She outlived her husband by many years and remarried. At the turn of the century, at the age of about seventy, she remained as beautiful as she

> In the modern Mexican American community, hostility to <u>curanderos</u> has not entirely disappeared. Those who embrace Western medicine believe <u>curanderos</u> are purveyors of ignorant superstitions. Others continue to link the <u>curanderos</u> with witchcraft."

had been when she was twenty. Legend had it that she was consulting a *brujo,* who gave her a potion made up of ground-up brown insects. She had to take the potion every day to conserve her beauty and her youth. One day she failed to drink the potion and her face was transformed into a *cara de caballo.* The few servants who witnessed the transformation lived only long enough to tell the tale.

"Cara de caballo" refers to both the *curandera* and the *brujo.* Their function in the story is different, but in Mexican American culture, *curanderos* were sometimes regarded as *brujos.* Although *brujos* would often use magic in service of harmful ends, they also had the capacity to heal the sick. In such cases, when both *brujos* and *curanderos* were able to heal, there remained, in theory, a vital difference: *brujos* were thought to use dark, Satanic forces to achieve effects that would not otherwise be possible, whereas *curanderos* worked only with holy powers. However, in practice this distinction was not always easy to perceive.

In "The Curing Woman" there is a small clue that *curanderos* and *brujos* were sometimes linked together in the minds of the people—when Delfino confesses he is somewhat frightened by the prospect of visiting Doña Marcelina's house: "Doña Marcelina had always been a mystery to the townspeople, someone the children stayed away from." It appears that the parents in Simons, California, were unsure of exactly what powers the *curandera* called upon to effect her cures. (In fact, the presence in Doña Marcelina's house of pictures of the Passion of Christ, and her making the sign of the cross as she prepares her potions, demonstrates that she is, so to

speak, on the side of the angels, but not all the locals appear to be aware of this.)

Historically, attitudes of hostility and suspicion towards *curanderos* go back to the Spanish conquest of Mexico in the sixteenth century. The Spanish persecuted the *curanderos.* A glimpse of what this must have been like is described in another work by Morales, his novel *The Rag Doll Plagues.* In the first of the three books that comprise the novel, Don Gregorio Revueltas, a physician and surgeon to the king of Spain, has been sent to Mexico City, where a plague is ravaging the people. The year is 1788. Don Gregorio is extremely prejudiced against the local Indian population. In particular, he dislikes the *curanderos:*

> These [Spanish-speaking] *curanderos* were dangerous and had caused the deaths of thousands. Worst of all were the Indian *curanderos* who practiced witchcraft in their native tongue. They had to be prevented from practicing their evil craft.

The native tongue Don Gregorio complains of is possibly Nahuatl, the language Marcelina learns from María Sabina in "The Curing Woman."

But *The Rag Doll Plagues* also shows that some of the Spanish rulers had a more enlightened attitude to *curanderismo.* Don Gregorio meets a Catholic priest, Father Jude, who after being badly wounded by pirates was taken in by a *curandero* who cared for him. Father Jude lived with the man and his family for five years. The *curandero* taught him everything he knew, and for the last year of his stay Father Jude became the principal practitioner of *curanderismo* in the village.

Later, Father Jude takes Don Gregorio to see Father Antonio, a distinguished and highly respected Spanish Catholic doctor. When Don Gregorio asks him what he would do to improve medical conditions in the country they call "New Spain," Father Antonio replies:

> The Holy Office must stop persecuting the *curanderos,* for they are an asset to us. Many are truly learned *texoxotla ticitl,* doctors and surgeons. It is not important that they speak Latin. They save more lives with their vulgar language than we do with our sanctified words.

Thanks to the wisdom of those such as the fictional Father Antonio, the Spanish colonizers' persecution of the *curanderos* gradually disappeared. Over the centuries there was a twofold cultural interchange. More of the Spanish learned the art of *curanderismo,* and, as Christianity spread, more and more *curanderos* incorporated aspects of Christian theology and devotional practice into their work, as "The Curing Woman" shows.

In the modern Mexican American community, hostility to *curanderos* has not entirely disappeared. Those who embrace Western medicine believe *curanderos* are purveyors of ignorant superstitions. Others continue to link the *curanderos* with witchcraft. On the other hand, among those who respect *curanderos,* there is a feeling that these healers are set apart from others, that they are different from ordinary people because of their special gifts. Either way, the practitioners of *curanderismo* are special figures in their communities. And from the way Morales presents his *curandera,* the fictional character Doña Marcelina, it is clear that the *curanderos* are the ones who can challenge and confound our own beliefs about what is possible and what is not.

Source: Bryan Aubrey, Critical Essay on "The Curing Woman," in *Short Stories for Students,* Gale, 2004.

Robert Trotter II and Juan Antonio Clavira

In the following essay, Trotter and Clavira provide background on curanderismo, *or Mexican American folk healing.*

At least six major historical influences have shaped the beliefs and practices of *curanderismo* by Mexican Americans in the Lower Rio Grande Valley: Judeo-Christian religious beliefs, symbols, and rituals; early Arabic medicine and health practices (combined with Greek humoral medicine, revived during the Spanish Renaissance); medieval and later European witchcraft; Native American herbal lore and health practices; modern beliefs about spiritualism and psychic phenomena; and scientific medicine. None of these influences dominates *curanderismo,* but each has had some impact on its historical development.

Judeo-Christian beliefs and practices provide the basic framework for *curanderismo,* just as for most Western cultural systems. The Bible and the teachings of the Church have been combined with folk wisdom to produce a foundation for the theories of both illness and healing that make up much of the structure of *curanderismo.*

The Bible has greatly influenced *curanderismo* through references made to the specific healing properties of animal parts, plants, oil, and wine (for example, see Luke 10:34). Humans are clearly instructed to use the resources, beginning with the general principle set forth in Genesis 1:29–31 that

> These healers explain that their healing abilities are a gift (<u>don</u>) from God, and that they heal through his power and through the patient's belief in God."

all the plants and animals were created for man's use and reinforced with the specific, statement, "The Lord has created medicines from the earth, and a sensible man will not disparage them."

The pharmacological information in the Bible is fairly extensive for that time, but it is less important in its influence on *curanderismo* than are the basic concepts of healing embodied in the Bible. The principal concept found there can be termed "God's power over man." There are two aspects to this concept: first, the belief that God can and does heal directly; and second, the idea that people with a special gift from God can heal in his name.

The first method, healing through divine intervention, is common in the Bible. It is often used as a sign of God's presence among the masses. Such signs include the examples of Jesus' healing found in the New Testament:

> Wherever he went, to farmsteads, villages, or towns, they laid out the sick in the market places and begged him to let them simply touch the edge of his cloak; and all who touched him were cured.

The second biblical foundation for folk healing, the healing power of faith, originates in the Apostles' instructions to the Church after Jesus' death. In these instructions, healing was directly linked to faith in God and in prayer:

> Is one of you ill? He should send for the elders of the congregation to pray over him and anoint him with oil in the name of the Lord. The prayer offered in faith will save the sick man, the Lord will raise him from his bed, and any sins he may have committed will be forgiven.

Similar passages provide the rationalization for the existence of Mexican American folk healers as individuals, not as a part of the organization of the Church itself. Several *curanderos* referred to the following passage in the Bible to justify and explain their activities:

> In each of us the Spirit is manifested in one particular way, for some useful purpose. One man, through the Spirit, has the gift of wise speech, while another, by the power of the same Spirit, can put the deepest knowledge into words. Another, by the same Spirit, is granted faith; another, by the one Spirit, gifts of healing, and another miraculous powers; another has the gift of prophecy, and another ability to distinguish true spirits from false; yet another has the gift of ecstatic utterance of different kinds, and another the ability to interpret it. But all these gifts are the work of one and the same Spirit, distributing them separately to each individual at will.

Today these biblical principles are found in the healing beliefs and practices of many (but not all) modern *curanderos*. These healers explain that their healing abilities are a gift (*don*) from God, and that they heal through his power and through the patient's belief in God.

The concept of the soul, which is central to the teachings of Christianity, also contributes to the *curandero*'s theories of healing, in particular those cures performed by *curanderos* working as spiritualists (*espiritistas* and *espiritualistas*). Belief in the soul affirms the existence of saints and devils, as well as the immortal soul of ordinary human beings. The belief that souls or spirits (*espiritos*) can either aid or hinder the healer promotes the desire or need for *curanderos* to contact them and petition them to use their powers for good or evil ends. While the idea of the soul has a strong biblical base, it was greatly expanded during medieval and modern times and has become a part of the shamanism and sorcery found in modern *curanderismo*.

Finally, the constant biblical theme of the dual worlds of light and darkness, good and evil, health and illness, life and death runs throughout the practice of *curanderismo*. This symbolic system links all of the areas of *curanderismo* together. To heal may be a sign from God, since health is linked to light and goodness. To harm someone is to work in the absence of light (*un trabajo obscuro o negro*). Such an act promotes evil and illness. This dichotomy between good and evil is expressed on each of the levels of power recognized by both the Bible and by *curanderismo:* on the human level the *curandero* heals and the *brujo* (witch or sorcerer) harms; on the spiritual level benevolent souls and saints can bring luck, health, and contentment, while malevolent souls and demons bring misfortune, illness, and misery; on the highest level of existence God (the light and giver of health) opposes Satan and his evil

works. Within *curanderismo* this duality presents a constant theme of oppositions integral to understanding it.

Preconquest Spain had the best-regarded system of medicine available in the Western world. The Spanish healing system combined earlier Greek and Roman practices of Hippocratic medicine with the highly successful Arabic medical practices introduced in Spain by the Moors. The Spanish medical theories and practices were brought to the New World at the time of the conquest and were eventually influenced by Native American healing practices.

Anthropologist George Foster (1953) notes the major theoretical components of the Hippocratic base of Spanish medical beliefs.

> The Hippocratian doctrine of the four ''humors''— blood, phlegm, black bile (''melancholy''), and yellow bile (''choler'')—formed the basis of medical theory. Each humor had its ''complexion'': blood, hot and wet; phlegm, cold and wet; black bile, cold and dry; yellow bile, hot and dry.... Natural history classification was rooted in the concept that people and even illness, medications, foods, and most natural objects had complexions. Thus, medical practice consisted largely of understanding the natural complexion of the patient, in determining the complexion of the illness or its cause, and in restoring the fundamental harmony which had been disturbed.

During the introduction of these medical beliefs into the New World, the duality of wet and dry was for all practical purposes lost. The continuing importance of the hot-cold syndrome has been emphasized repeatedly in the literature about Latin American folk medical beliefs. However, the importance of the hot-cold dichotomies varies from area to area and is especially weak in south Texas. Even though one can find in Mexican American communities in south Texas residual folk sayings and household beliefs that reflect this hot-cold dichotomy, it does not play a central part in the theoretical structure of *curanderismo*. This absence is noted by Madsen:

> Hippocratic medicine was introduced into Mexico in the 16th century and is still a basic part of Mexican folk medicine but is of little significance in Mexican American folk medicine of South Texas. Minor stomach upsets are believed to be caused by eating too many hot or cold foods in most communities, but the hot-cold complex is completely lacking in some localities.

Similar results were obtained from our own research, although a continuing emphasis was placed on both the hot-cold (and even with one *curandera,* the wet-dry dichotomies) by people knowledgeable about herbal remedies (*yerberos*).

The Hispano-Arabic medical system contributed two important theories to Mexican American folk medicine. First, it contributed the idea that health consists of a balanced condition. The lack of harmony with the environment (social and spiritual as welt as physical) produces illness, and the readjustment or removal of this imbalance becomes the primary function of the healer. Thus the basic tenets of *curanderismo* are to produce and protect a holistic relationship between the individual and his total environment. Second, Spanish medical theory contributed the idea that medicinal remedies can be discovered in plants and animals, an idea that is reinforced by the teachings of the Bible. This emphasis on herbal medicines caused many individuals to search out and experiment with new sources of medicine in both the Old World and the New. These two themes, the restoration of health through the restoration of balance to the patient and the experimentation with and use of herbal remedies, have had an enduring influence on the practice of *curanderismo*.

The major symbols used in the rituals of *curanderos* (numbers, words, and objects), the structure of those rituals, and the theoretical explanations given for success in healing substantiate the importance of Old World historical influences on Mexican American folk medicine. The symbols used in healing rituals are overwhelmingly part of the Western cultural tradition. The numbers most frequently used to designate the length of cures, number of times rituals are performed, and other magical sequences of activities are all within the Judeo-Christian system of symbolic numbers (primarily 3, 7, 9, and 11; occasionally 13 for certain negative magical rites). Many of the objects used to promote healing are of Old World origin: olive oil, lemons, garlic, chickens, camomile, votive candles, and the crucifix, to name a few. Finally, the structure and theory of the *curandero*'s healing arts come primarily from more recent European and New World sources of the theory and practice of witchcraft, spiritualism, psychic phenomena, and modern medicine, such as the *Grimoire* and the writings of Allen Cardec.

The ideas embodied in medieval and later European witchcraft have contributed heavily to the theoretical base of *curanderismo*. These ideas were constantly reinforced in the popular mind throughout the period of intensive witchhunting that lasted from the early fifteenth century, through its peak around 1600, and into its decline and final disappearance in the early nineteenth century. This coincides with the discovery, conquest, and colonization of the New World, and it can be assumed that these popular concepts accompanied the conquerors. Fortunately, the more ferocious and disgusting practices of the witch burners seem to have been left at home, with the brief exception of the Salem witch trials.

The basic theoretical premise of witchcraft and sorcery is the belief that supernatural forces can be controlled by man himself, rather than their having undisputed control over him. This belief, combined with the teachings of Christianity, creates a dual philosophical system within *curanderismo*. This duality is symbolized by the differences between a religious orientation and a magical orientation. That duality is aptly described by E. A. Hoebel:

> That which distinguishes religion from magic is neither the goodness of one nor the evil of the other, but the state of mind of the believer and his consequent modes of behavior.... In the religious state of mind, man acknowledges the superiority of the supernatural powers upon whose action his wellbeing depends. His attitudes are preponderantly those of submission and reverence.... The magician, on the other hand, believes that he *controls* supernatural power under certain conditions. He feels confirmed in his belief that if he possesses a tested formula and if he executes it perfectly, barring outside interference, he will get the results which that formula is specified to give. The supernatural power has no volition or choice of its own. It must respond. The magician works with a confidence similar to that of a student in the laboratory who knows that if he follows the manual instructions correctly, he will obtain a predictable result. The religious attitude and behavior are devout; the magician works with a kind of arrogance—or, at least, self-assurance.

These philosophies are not necessarily mutually exclusive. They can be and have been combined into a single belief system, where that theoretical system has many flexible facets and is not yet totally integrated into a single theoretical framework. This condition exists in modern scientific medicine, with its official acknowledgement of the physical, psychological, and spiritual components of human health and illness, and its unofficial acknowledgement of the "miracle" of faith. And *curanderismo* shares this theoretical flexibility, although the emphasis placed on the importance of each of these components of the system is somewhat different.

Two closely related concepts from European witchcraft continue to influence modern *curanderismo*. The first is a belief in the existence of a source of supernatural power that can be tapped by human beings who possess the correct incantations, prayers, and rituals. The ingredients used in the spells and the words or even the languages used for the spells may have changed somewhat through time, but many of the rituals used by both *curanderos* (to heal) and *brujos* (to harm) follow the structure of formulas from the Middle Ages and later.

The second is a belief in the ability of some *curanderos* to control or influence spirit beings. Control of spirit beings is exercised through the knowledge of various incantations, prayers, and rituals that can bring about direct human control over spirits. The structure of the spirit-controlling rites is similar to the structure of those designed to tap supernatural power.

One final influence on *curanderismo,* traced to medieval European beliefs about witchcraft and sorcery, has resulted in confusion within the Mexican American community over the ultimate source of the healing power demonstrated by folk healers. One group maintains that the power to heal comes from God; the other group, primarily members of fundamentalist religions, insists that the healing *curandero*'s performance is inspired through the power of Satan. This is a traditional dichotomy in Western tradition, as is pointed out by Givry:

> We find the theologians in opposition to the demonists. If cures have taken place at Lourdes or any other sanctuary consecrated by the Church, they are the undeniable work of the Deity. But, similar cures have so taken place in circumstances where the disapproval of the Church has been clearly shown; these cures according to the Church, are the work of the Devil. Hence, the Devil holds in his hands curative powers equal to those of God.

The possibility that the *curandero* may be working through the Devil causes some of the confusion over the moral rightness of seeking help from a proven healer in Mexican American communities. Powerful *curanderos* are restrained from practicing sorcery (antisocial magic) only by their own moral conscience. Each *curandero* has the option of working through good or evil sources, and many people fear them even when seeking their help. There is always the possibility that some spiritual harm may come to the patient even while he is being cured of his malady.

The belief that *curanderos* may be the devil's agents on earth is most pronounced among fundamentalist groups and pentecostal churches. These churches are growing rapidly in Mexican American communities, and their members seem to feel that all works of the folk healers are inspired by the Devil (with or without the knowledge of the healer). They quote appropriate passages from the Bible that demonstrate that the Devil is loose in the world and that these works (the healings) are the kind the Devil uses to subvert mankind by performing miracles. This attitude, combined with a fear of the unknown, and perhaps unknowable, source of the *curandero*'s power produces confusion about the morality of using the *curandero*'s services. The more powerful *curanderos* publicly admit that both good and evil sources of power are available to them, a fact that increases their reputations but does nothing to allay doubts about the morality of their calling.

Some of the most recent influences on *curanderismo* arise from the writings of the eighteenth-, nineteenth-, and twentieth-century European spiritualists and psychic researchers. The growing importance of the scientific method during the last few centuries, and the end of persecution for witchcraft, touched off intensive and wide-ranging investigations of the validity of ghosts, spirits, mediums, fortune tellers, telekinesis, and a hundred other psychic phenomena. Most of this research was anecdotal, with occasional exceptions such as the work done at the Rhine Institute at Duke University. Most researchers have been content to pile one report, one case, one anecdote on top of another in the hope that others will be convinced of the validity of psychic phenomena. Other writers have ignored the necessity for proof altogether by assuming these phenomena exist and have devoted their energies to sharing their knowledge with the other adepts through the reporting of ancient sources of knowledge or through writing of their own experiences and knowledge gained from direct experimentation. The publication of such works has created an enormous volume of information, misinformation, and speculation that is currently available to the general public and to believers. One result has been the spread of both spiritualist and psychic healers from Europe to the United States and Mexico.

The most influential spiritualist writer is Allen Kardec, who is directly responsible for the recent rapid growth of ''spiritual temples'' in Mexican American communities. Kardec has produced a series of works that explain the structure, maintenance, and function of spiritual healing centers and provide careful descriptions of the rituals, prayers, and incantations necessary to the temple ceremonies.

Another important spiritualist movement is based on the life, teachings, and spirit of a famous young folk healer (now dead) from northern Mexico, el Niño Fidencio. The *Fidencitas* have built large temples in several Mexican cities, with smaller ones scattered around Mexico and the United States (including Chicago). These *centros* are staffed by trance mediums who, often in flower-decked rooms, don purple robes, go into trance, and (in their words) let the spirit of el Niño descend on them, their bodies forming a link between the material and spiritual realms of existence. Through this linkage, the immortal spirit of el Niño performs cures, does consultations, even predicts the outcome of future events for the members of his cult.

Spiritualist healing is now taught in *centros espiritistas* in Mexico and by traveling adepts from these *centros,* as well as by local adepts. Many professional *curanderos* state that today many imporant parts of their healing knowledge come through spiritual training (*desarrollo*) and subsequent contact with the spiritual realm. They claim some of their cures are done through the use of spiritual knowledge that simply comes into their minds or comes from spiritual voices (*las voces*), while other cures are carried out directly through the agency of spirits themselves. These spirits are those who have agreed to aid the *curandero* in his or her work.

The phenomenon of psychic healing is also becoming more common among *curanderos.* It is said to be performed by the *curandero* directing psychic energies (*corrientes mentales*) directly at the afflicted organ—a form of mind over matter. The importance of psychic healing to the theories held by *curanderos* is rapidly growing, especially in urban areas.

The effects of the medical knowledge, beliefs, and practices of American Indian groups on *curanderismo* have varied significantly from area to area. The most important influence in all areas was the impact that the incredibly rich and extensive knowledge of medicinal herbs existing in Native American groups has had on European pharmacology. One of the first tasks undertaken by individuals in expeditions to the New World was to discover and classify new plants and animals, making careful note of their medicinal properties. The lack of sufficient doctors and medical facilities in the New World caused books about these newly discovered medicinal herbs, along with their Old World counterparts, to be disseminated throughout Mexico, especially in the frontier regions. The direct descen-

dants of these books are still widely used by both Mexican and Mexican American housewives.

The most important of the early botanical books and medical compendiums, according to anthropologist Margaritta Kay, was the *Florilegio Medicinal,* a three-volume set encompassing medicine, surgery, and pharmacology. Written by a Jesuit lay brother, Juan de Esteyneffer, this work had a lasting effect on the practices of folk medicine along the northern frontier areas of New Spain.

> The work of the 16th century natural historians of Mexico had already been incorporated into the knowledge of the European apothecary. These included Hernandez (via Ximinez 1615) who had been sent by Philip II of Spain to report on the *materia medico* available in New Spain, and Nicolas Monardes, the Spanish physician, who wrote knowledgeably about these herbs without ever leaving Spain. Sahagun's data were not available until 1829, but his influence was felt through Martin de la Cruz and Juan Badianus, who produced the beautiful Badianus manuscript of 1595 in which indigenous herbs are given humoral classification. For Esteyneffer, the most important writer of this kind was Farfan.

Farfan, mentioned in the above quote, had written a book in 1592, *Tractado Breve de Medicina* to aid the poor and people in rural areas by providing them with remedies and cures from both New and Old World medicinal herbs. This book may have inspired Esteyneffer to produce his own larger treatise on the same subject.

The *Florilegio Medicinal,* through Esteyneffer's teaching efforts among the Jesuits in the missions of northwestern Mexico, is at least partly responsible for the blending of Old and New World cures for many of the folk diseases and other illnesses recognized by Mexican Americans throughout the southwestern United States. It is also responsible for similar beliefs and practices among such different American Indian groups as the Papago, Pima, Yaqui, PaiPai, Tarahumara, and Tepehuan, among whom the Jesuits also had missions.

> Nentuig spoke of the "old Spanish women who have either set themselves up or have become in the natural course of the events the College of Physicians of Sonora." I think they used the *Florilegio Medicinal,* which compiled the herbal lore of various Indians of the Southwest, combined it with the *materia medica* of Europe, attached them to disease conditions that were scientifically recognized in the eighteenth century and diffused this knowledge throughout the Northwest of Mexico and the Southwest United States. For *pasmo, alferecia, empacho, mollera caida, tirisia* and *pujos,* which have first been explained by Esteyneffer

and are still diagnosed today, are cured by the same herbs.

Other bits of information were added to the immense herbal knowledge of *curanderismo* through direct contact with various American Indian groups, and through individual experimentation on the part of the Spanish settlers in the northern frontier areas. The fact that access to modern medical services is still limited by poverty, isolation, and discrimination in south Texas has encouraged the use of this herbal knowledge up to the present.

The other influences that Native American folk medicine has had on *curanderismo* are more difficult to isolate. In many of the border areas, such as the Lower Rio Grande Valley of Texas, the environment supported only scattered groups of hunters and gatherers before the influx of the Spanish. Thus, the amount of contact between settlers and Indian groups was far less than between the conquerors and the larger agriculturally based Indian populations in Mexico and parts of South America. In the Southwestern Pueblo Indian complex, where greater contact might have been possible, these exchanges were limited by suppression of Native American beliefs and activities and secrecy on the part of the Indians. Further Native American influences may be revealed to be a part of *curanderismo* as more research is done in this area, but as of now Mexican American folk medicine seems to have primarily a European historical and theoretical base.

Until the development of extensive irrigation works in the early 1900s, most of the southwestern United States was best suited for ranching and very small scale farming. People lived on scattered homesteads, isolated from the medical resources of the cities. Very few health-care professionals were attracted to the area because of the lack of facilities, small population, and the immense distances. Herbs, prayers, and faith in the *curandero*'s healing ability were often the only medical resources these people had to combat either illness or accident.

Urban centers grew as irrigation works were developed. These towns and cities were progressively linked by roads, telegraph, railroads, and other communication systems tying the Southwest more directly into the political and economic centers of the United States. Previously the region had been isolated or had been more directly linked to northern Mexican towns than to centers in the United States. New concentrations of people in the Southwest, and the wealth associated with the agricultural and mineral industries being developed,

have attracted growing numbers of doctors, nurses, and medical services to the area. Thus modern medical practices began to influence the practice of *curanderos* in areas like the Lower Rio Grande Valley. Yet even after modern medicine became established in the area, poverty, discrimination, prejudice, and cultural barriers to communication and understanding combined to deny many Mexican Americans access to the new medical system. For these excluded people the *curanderos* continued to provide the best available care.

Today *curanderos* in urbanized areas like south Texas recognize and accept the diagnosis of many, if not most, diseases defined by Western medicine. Some even use modern drugs, anatomical charts, and clinical facilities that closely resemble a doctor's office in their own practices. More commonly they simply recognize conventional categories of disease and refer patients to doctors for those diseases which modern medicine has proven highly successful in healing. In addition, they recognize certain diseases that mimic, for instance, tuberculosis, asthma, and cancer, but are thought to be caused by magical works placed on the patient by *brujos*.

Since the return of World War II veterans, more and more Mexican Americans have gained entrance into the mainstream of American society, including its medical system. However, too many people are still very poor, even though there is a growing middle and upper class made up mainly of businessmen and professionals. The result of this change is that some Mexican American patients now make use of both *curanderismo* and modern medicine. We shall now consider why people prefer one system to the other or, more commonly, use both simultaneously.

Source: Robert Trotter II and Juan Antonio Clavira, "The History of *Curanderismo*," in "*Curanderismo*": *Mexican American Folk Healing,* University of Georgia Press, 1981, pp. 25–40.

Sources

Flores, Angel, "Magical Realism in Spanish American Fiction," in *Magical Realism: Theory, History, Community,* edited by L. P. Zamora and W. B. Faris, Duke University Press, 1995, p. 114.

Garza, Mary Jane, "Healing Spirits: The Growing Acceptance of Alternative Medicine Enhances the Popularity of *Curanderismo*," in *Hispanic,* June 1998, pp. 36–38.

Harris, Martin, "*Curanderismo* and the DSM-IV: Diagnostic and Treatment Implications for the Mexican American Client," JSRI Occasional Paper #45, The Julian Samora Research Institute, Michigan State University, East Lansing, Michigan, 1998. http://www.jsri.msu.edu/RandS/research/ops/oc45.html.

Morales, Alejandro, "Cara de caballo," in *Short Fiction by Hispanic Writers of the United States,* edited by Nicolas Kanellos, 1993, pp. 151–54.

———, *The Rag Doll Plagues,* Arte Publico Press, 1992, pp. 11–66.

Trotter, Robert T., II, and Juan Antonio Chavira, *"Curanderismo": Mexican American Folk Healing,* University of Georgia Press, 1981, pp. 14, 31–32.

Zamora, Lois Parkinson, and Wendy B. Faris, eds., *Magical Realism: Theory, History, Community,* Duke University Press, 1995, p. 6.

Further Reading

Griego, José, Maestas Anaya, and Rudolfo A. Anaya, *Cuentos: Tales from the Hispanic Southwest,* Museum of New Mexico Press, 1981.

The twenty-three tales collected in this volume feature elements of magic and witchcraft that are also prominent in the work of Morales. The tales draw on the traditions of the early Spanish settlers and their descendants in New Mexico and southern Colorado.

Toor, Frances, *A Treasury of Mexican Folkways,* Crown, 1947.

Toor provides a wealth of information about the customs, myths, and folklore of Mexico, as well as its dances, fiestas, and songs. She also recounts her experiences of being treated on several occasions by *curanderos,* although her account is affected by her cultural bias, since she plainly does not believe that *curanderos* have much value to offer.

Torrey, E. F., *Witchdoctors and Psychiatrists,* Harper and Row, 1986.

Originally published in 1972 as *The Mind Game,* this book offers an overview of the psychiatric profession, which also compares the effectiveness of modern psychiatry and psychotherapy with the work of traditional healers such as the Zar priests in Ethiopia, the Menang healers of Sarawak in Indonesia, and the *curanderos* of Mexico. Torrey concludes that traditional healers get results just as effectively as psychiatrists and psychotherapists.

West, John O., *Mexican-American Folklore,* August House, 1988.

This is a reference book of Mexican American culture, its customs and traditions. It contains some useful information on *curanderismo.*

Eveline

James Joyce

1914

Groundbreaking in form and of great psychological depth, James Joyce's ''Eveline'' is a short but important story in Joyce's first major work of fiction, the short-story collection *Dubliners* (London, 1914). ''Eveline'' is a portrait of a young woman torn between her obligations to stay and look after her family or escape with her lover to a new life across the sea, and this struggle is developed intricately and realistically. But the story is also thematically ambitious and highly symbolic, containing allusions to Christianity, mythology, Irish politics, and Dublin's social conditions, and exhibiting many characteristics common to the newly developing literary movement of modernism.

Set in the closing years of nineteenth-century Dublin, Ireland, ''Eveline'' is very much about the political and social climate of this era. With its majority Catholic population suffering the disgrace and depression of economic and social decline and with no end to English rule in sight, Dublin Catholics were experiencing a spiritual and moral crisis. Part of a series of stories that portray the soul of this city, the publication of ''Eveline'' was delayed for nine years, until 1914, because publishers were worried about Joyce's controversial methods and themes.

Author Biography

Born February 2, 1882, in Dublin, Ireland, Joyce was the eldest of ten children in a family that went from prosperity to poverty in a short time. He attended two private Jesuit schools, and the religion he learned there influenced much of his writing. Joyce graduated in 1902 with a degree in modern languages from University College, Dublin, and then left for Paris to study medicine but instead spent his time writing. He returned to Dublin in 1903 because his mother was fatally ill. It was also during this time that Joyce began a lifelong relationship with Nora Barnacle, whom he married in 1931.

By the time Joyce brought Nora with him to continental Europe, he had already begun work on some of the short stories for *Dubliners*. In 1905, Joyce submitted the first version of this collection, including "Eveline," to the English publisher Grant Richards. Richards was afraid the stories were too controversial, however, and did not actually publish them until nine years later. In the meantime, while living mostly in Trieste (then part of the Austro-Hungarian Empire), Joyce published a book of poetry titled *Chamber Music*, fathered two children, and worked on a semi-autobiographical novel called *Stephen Hero*, which he ultimately discarded, turning its subject into an entirely new work that became *A Portrait of the Artist as a Young Man*. This novel, which helped define the form of European modernism, was published serially between 1914 and 1915 in Ezra Pound's *Egoist* magazine and was published in book form in 1916.

With the onset of World War I, Joyce and his family moved to Zurich, in politically neutral Switzerland, where they stayed until briefly moving back to Trieste after the war. They then moved to Paris to better negotiate the publication of what would become one of the most important novels of the century, *Ulysses*. This novel is a heavily allusive text following the lives of Stephen Dedalus and Leopold Bloom through Dublin in the course of a single day. Joyce had begun work on the novel while in Switzerland, and its first edition was published in 1922 in Paris.

By 1922, Joyce had already earned international fame, but he began to suffer from severe eye troubles and was distraught at his daughter's mental illness, which ultimately led to her institutionalization. For the next seventeen years, Joyce worked on his final book, *Finnegan's Wake* (1939), which examines a huge canvas of issues in Western civili-

James Joyce

zation and employs a completely new approach to language. He moved to unoccupied France during World War II. Joyce died January 13, 1941, shortly after he and his family had returned to Zurich.

Plot Summary

"Eveline" begins with a young woman gazing out the window to a Dublin street. Her name, Eveline, could be a reference to the title character of a nineteenth-century pornographic novel, or it could be a reference to a song by the Irish poet Thomas Moore; either way, the name is likely to connote a woman sexually active before marriage. Smelling the dust from "cretonne" curtains, a heavy cotton material that is usually brightly colored, Eveline reflects on her life, beginning with her childhood.

The Hill family, Catholic and working class, live in a "little brown" house distinct from the bright brick dwellings that stand on the old spot of Eveline's childhood playing field. A man from Belfast, a city that connotes the richer Northern Ireland that is largely populated by Protestants loyal to the English government, built the brick houses, and Eveline remembers the children that used to play on the field. She was happy then, when her father was less abusive and her mother was alive, and now, Eveline thinks, she is going to leave her home.

Looking at the objects around her that she might never see again, Eveline notices a colored print of promises made to Margaret Mary Alacoque, a French nun canonized in 1920, whose image was connected with domestic security and was common in Irish Catholic homes. Eveline remembers that the priest whose photograph is next to the print is in Melbourne now, which sends her thinking about whether or not she should leave home. She would not be sorry to leave her job; she works in the "Stores," a dry goods store in south Dublin, where her boss Miss Gavan is rude and embarrasses her.

Eveline considers what it would be like in a faraway country, where she would be married and treated with respect, unlike her mother who had been abused by her father. Still afraid of her father's violence towards her to the point that it gives her spasms of fear (which, it is implied, may lead to a nervous breakdown), Eveline considers that with her brothers gone she is no longer safe. Her father has been threatening her, particularly when she asks him for money on Saturday nights, even though she gives him all of her wages, does the shopping, and looks after her younger siblings.

So she plans for her departure with her lover Frank, a sailor fond of music who has taken her to an opera (about the fortunes of a "Bohemian girl" who is abducted by gypsies) and told her of the "terrible Patagonians," or Argentines, who represent decadent morality. A veteran of the "Allan Line," a sea route associated with exile, Frank is planning to take Eveline by night boat to Liverpool, England, and then across the sea to Buenos Aires, a city at the time associated with prostitution. Mr. Hill dislikes sailors, has quarreled with Frank, and, having guessed about the affair, has forbidden Eveline from seeing him.

Eveline continues smelling the dust from the curtains and considers two letters on her lap, one to her brother Harry (who is living in "the country," or southern Ireland) and one to her father. She reflects that her aging father—who sometimes can be nice, like the time he took their family to the pretty Hill of Howth in northeast Dublin—will miss her, and then she hears music from a street organ that reminds her of her mother's dying wish that Eveline stay home as long as she could. Then she remembers her father's racist remark to an Italian organ-player playing the same song and

her mother's final, "foolish" repeated phrase, "Derevaun Seraun," which is possibly nonsense and possibly corrupted Gaelic for a number of phrases including "the end of song is raving madness." Terrified, Eveline feels the necessity to escape to happiness with her lover.

The final scene of the story is on a crowded dock on the river Liffey, where boats leave for Liverpool. Without understanding what Frank is saying to her, Eveline is pale, distressed, nauseous, and praying to God to reveal her "duty." The boat blows a long whistle. A bell clangs, and Frank tries to pull her on board, but Eveline clutches an iron railing on shore, feeling that he will drown her in "the seas of the world." She cries out and grasps the railing tighter while Frank calls to her, and she turns her helpless face to him without a glimpse of "love or farewell or recognition," staying on shore as the boat pulls away.

Characters

Frank

Frank is a sailor planning to move to Buenos Aires and take his lover Eveline with him. He has told Eveline he intends to marry her, which may well be the case, but Frank is a mysterious character and there is some implication that his intentions are devious. He started his sailing career on a trade route associated with exile and full of stories about infamously savage tribes from Argentina. Also, "going to Buenos Aires" was a slang term for prostitution, and the night boat to Liverpool may have been a reference to the mythological journey over the Styx river to the pagan underworld—both of which are implications that Frank might have no intention of marrying his lover, but instead is planning bring her into a situation she will find immoral.

However, Frank is also described as "kind, manly, open-hearted" and is set up as Eveline's only way to happiness, so he may indeed have only the best intentions in helping his lover to escape from her abusive household and difficult job. In fact, the new lands and adventure into the outside world that Frank represents are perhaps the only hopeful elements of the story, especially considering Eveline's very bleak future at home. But Frank's character is left obscure so that, like Eveline, the reader is left nervous and guessing at what life would be like with him.

Miss Gavan

Eveline's supervisor at the "Stores," which sells a variety of dry goods in south-central Dublin, Miss Gavan nags and embarrasses Eveline, especially when other people are around. She is probably a Quaker because the "Stores" was owned by Quakers, a religious group known for being pacifist and often associated with trades people in Ireland.

Ernest Hill

Eveline's favorite older brother, Ernest, is dead at the time of the story. Eveline remembers him being too grown up to play with the other children in the field next to their house.

Eveline Hill

Eveline is the protagonist of the story; her psychology is profoundly developed and the majority of the story takes place in her mind. A complex and conflicted person, she leads a hardworking life taking care of her family and tending a shop in Dublin. Her main problem is her abusive father, who has been threatening, berating, and beating her, and she must decide whether to abandon him and her family for her own happiness. Her father has forbidden her from seeing her lover, a sailor named Frank, but Eveline has managed to sneak away and keep up the affair, to the point that he has promised to marry her and sail with her to a new life.

Tortured by the promise she made her mother to keep the home together as long as she could, and unsure of whether to leave her father, who will miss her, Eveline is trying to decide whether to attempt to "live" and be happy with her lover. She expresses some subtle doubts about Frank when she reflects that she had merely "begun to like him" and that he will only "perhaps" give her love, but this does not seem to be the major issue in her debate with herself. Eveline is principally concerned about her "duty" and her role within her family.

Although her name connotes the idea of a "fallen" woman, as does the concept of going to Buenos Aires, Eveline seems to be a rather modest and prudent person. She does the housework and the shopping, works faithfully at her job, and could be said to live in the image of her mother, in a life of "commonplace sacrifices." On the surface this term implies the difficult job of the person holding the family together. Eveline also thinks in a manner common to victims, justifying her father's abuse with three random acts of benevolence she remembers.

The last scene of the story renders Eveline's character rather enigmatic at the same time as it penetrates the deepest parts of her psychology. Unable to leave and petrified to return, Eveline is revealed to be a torn, devastated person by her difficult life and rigid value system. Like her mother before her, she is resigned to an abusive household that will, as we learn from her "palpitations" due to her father's violence, lead to her own nervous breakdown.

Harry Hill

Harry is the older brother to whom Eveline has written one of the letters she is holding during her scene of reflection. He works as a church decorator, lives somewhere in the countryside south of Dublin (which comprises most of Ireland), and regularly sends money to his sister. Harry and Ernest used to shield Eveline from their abusive father because he would "go for" them first, but now that Harry is living elsewhere and Ernest is dead, there is no one to protect her.

Mr. Hill

Mr. Hill is Eveline's abusive father. He has regularly beaten his wife and children in the past, and as he gets older he is becoming increasingly prone to violence towards Eveline. With her mother and older siblings gone, she is likely to take all of the abuse herself.

Eveline has a confusion of memories about her father; first she remembers him "hunting in" the children from their playing field with a walking stick, which is a rather worrisome image itself, and then she remembers in depth all of his increasing abuse. She finds it very difficult to get money from him (for the family shopping) because he says she wastes all of his "hard-earned" money, and he threatens to abuse her just "for her dead mother's sake." By this he could be referring to any number of real or imagined faults, including what seems to be a certain amount of time living out of wedlock, which was a major taboo in the Catholic community. Eveline also remembers two isolated examples of how her father is sometimes "very nice": when he read her a ghost story and toasts her, and when he made his children laugh at a picnic.

These positive memories are very tenuous evidence of Mr. Hill's good character. From the comment that he is usually "fairly bad of a Saturday night," it can be inferred that he has a drinking problem, and the fact that he would miss Eveline in his old age suggests he might be insecure and bitter about getting older.

Mrs. Hill

Eveline's mother was abused by Mr. Hill and treated with disrespect by the community, as becomes clear when Eveline muses that, unlike her mother, she will be married and therefore treated with respect. It is likely that Eveline's mother had an affair with Mr. Hill out of wedlock and later married him, but this is not explicitly mentioned in the story. Her life was one of sacrifices, according to Eveline's musings, probably for her children's sake, but it seems that these sacrifices and her husband's abuse eventually drove her crazy and to her death.

Mrs. Hill is particularly important for her somewhat conflicting dying advice to her daughter. Eveline has promised to "keep the home together as long as she could," but her repeated last words in "foolish insistence" seem to contradict the life of martyrdom that she has recommended to her daughter. "Derevaun Seraun," whether it means "worms are the only end," "the end of song is raving madness," something else in corrupt Gaelic, or nothing at all, inspires Eveline's terrified epiphany that she must escape. In fact, it is possible that Mrs. Hill's "final craziness" actually results in her most coherent advice, since keeping the family together seems very likely to drive Eveline to the same bitter end as her mother.

The Priest

Mr. Hill's school friend, the priest is only present in "Eveline" as a yellowing photograph on the wall. He has gone to Melbourne, which was known for its association with exiled Irish criminals as well as with the Irish Catholic priesthood.

Themes

Paralysis

Critics have long noted that one of the most important themes in *Dubliners* is the tendency for its characters to be frozen in a state of psychological and spiritual arrest, or "paralysis." As it is portrayed in the collection, Dublin suffers from harsh social conditions, the lack of moral hope, and spiritual emptiness, which combine to erode the impetus to positive change in many of its characters. And there is perhaps no example of this paralysis so

bleak as that of the seemingly doomed and completely immobile Eveline at the end of her story.

Eveline is unable to escape the paralyzed existence of the "duties" and inhibitions of home, living under her father's abusive control. Her mother's death, emblematized by the mysterious (but most likely morbid and fatalistic) Irish phrase "Derevaun Seraun," inspires Eveline's desperate and terrified desire to escape. But it also reminds her of her promises to stay at home, and Eveline's chance to flee to the freedom and motion of a new life across the sea fails, leaving her locked into the paralyzed role of housewife to an abusive father, poised for a nervous breakdown of her own. As Brewster Ghiselin notes in *Accent,* in *Dubliners* "the soul's true satisfaction cannot be exhibited in the experience of those who remain in Ireland"; distant countries and the sea to the east represent "the aspect of a new life" and the possibility of spiritual regeneration. Eveline is denied this possibility precisely because she is paralyzed, clinging to the iron railing at the harbor passively, "like a helpless animal" unable to move or even think of her own volition.

Joyce is careful to develop the complexity of Eveline's situation; the association of Buenos Aires with prostitution is an example of the implication that her fears of being drowned in the sea of her new life are justified. Also, Eveline might not even be in love with Frank; she says he would "perhaps" give her love, and her description of his character, which concentrates on the stories and adventures he tells her, may imply that she is more interested in the exotic new places Frank can bring her than in his true personality. This point is also important because it marks Eveline's conscious desire to leave her paralyzed state.

Ultimately, however, Eveline cannot enter the perilous sea. Ghiselin writes that she is paralyzed because she fails "in the cardinal virtue of fortitude," fourth in what he considers Joyce's systematic approach to the degeneration of the soul that is developed throughout *Dubliners*. Whatever the reason, Eveline is paralyzed into an enclosed island of suffering from which, Joyce implies, she is unable to escape.

Freudian Psychology

Eveline's central conflict is directly connected with the theories of Sigmund Freud, the father of psychoanalysis. Exhibiting the major symptoms of Freud's theory of the "Oedipal complex" (or Electra complex, the Oedipal complex occurring in women),

Topics for Further Study

- Many critics and readers wonder what would have happened had Eveline left Dublin with her lover. What is the significance of the destination of Buenos Aires in the story? Research the history of Argentina to discover what life might have been like in Buenos Aires for an Irish immigrant sailor and his wife. Were the economic and social conditions for Catholics better than they were in Dublin?

- Read Virginia Woolf's *The Voyage Out* (1920). How do you think Woolf's vision of a young woman's awakening differs from that of Joyce? Do you think Eveline would have undergone a similar fate to Rachel had she left with Frank for South America? Woolf and Joyce are both considered major modernist writers; what do their debut works have in common?

- Most critics now consider *Dubliners* a unified work of fiction. Read the other stories in the volume. How does ''Eveline'' fit into Joyce's greater scheme? Does it express or develop a certain theme common to the surrounding stories? Is it an extreme story, or does it fit subtly into the whole? Read a variety of critical essays proposing theories about *Dubliners* in order to formulate your answer.

- Research Irish history by examining books such as R. F. Foster's *Modern Ireland: 1600–1972*. What position does Joyce's text seem to take on the turbulent politics of the time? What kind of Dubliners would have read and enjoyed ''Eveline?''

- What do you think is the key to Joyce's status as perhaps the chief writer in changing literary style during the modernist era? Start by examining some basic techniques, like symbolism. Joyce was extremely well versed in both Christianity and mythology, and there are symbols from both of these in ''Eveline.'' Explore the symbolism in the story and discuss how it relates to the meaning.

Eveline is a classic example of a patient trying to escape from an attachment to her tyrannical father. Freud believed that children inevitably form an attraction to the parent of the opposite sex and a rivalry with the parent of the same sex, that can lead to a profoundly troubled adult sexuality. In her desire to stay with her father in her mother's role, Eveline is displaying what Freud would likely consider an ''Oedipal complex,'' or an inability to break from the attraction to the father and pursue other lovers. The fact that she considers Frank a protector and father figure who, she repeats, would ''save her,'' underscores the Oedipal drama in the story, since Freud thought girls only emerged from the crisis by finding lovers similar to their fathers.

The breakthroughs in psychology that Freudian theory allowed for modernist artists were particularly important to groundbreaking writers like Joyce. Joyce's portrayal of Eveline's psychology, developed with a minimum of elaboration, acquires a new dimension by employing Freud's insights into the workings of consciousness. Applying Freudian theory to ''Eveline'' reveals some of Joyce's ambitions with the story, such as underscoring the psychological paralysis (discussed above) of its main character. It also implies the sexual tyranny of her father, who is subconsciously involved in the violent struggle to maintain control over his daughter's body and mind, and allows the reader a clue as to the true nature of Eveline's choice to remain behind. Although Frank's intentions are possibly dubious and although Eveline does not even seem to love him, he is her one chance, in Freudian terms, to escape the Oedipal complex. The fact that she is unable to leave with him implies that she is in a state of a nearly inescapable psychological trauma.

Irish Politics

Although its treatment is often beneath the surface, ''Eveline'' attacks some of the most pressing issues in the Irish political climate of the time. By depicting the oppressed condition of Dublin Catholics and connecting the idea of staying in Ireland with devastating abuse and hardship, Joyce is editorializing on the condition of his country that would continue until well after the volume was published. It took Joyce nine years to publish *Dubliners* in no small part because of his frank treatment in stories such as "Eveline" of the dynamics of both political and domestic oppression.

Style

Epiphany

One of Joyce's stylistic trademarks is the use of a character's brief realization of truth and clarity, usually signaling a new direction and understanding of the world. Eveline experiences an "epiphany" after she remembers her mother's dying words "Derevaun Seraun" and makes the ecstatic resolution to escape to a new life, although she is unable to follow a new course when the time comes.

The word "epiphany" comes from the Greek for "manifestation," usually of divine power, and Joyce was very cognizant both of this root and the connotation of the January-sixth Christian festival of the Epiphany, which commemorates Jesus' baptism, the visit of the Wise Men, and the miracle at Cana. Each of these events is, for Christians, an instance of a manifestation of God's power, and the festival is second only to Easter in theological importance. In *A Portrait of the Artist as a Young Man*, Stephen's epiphanies are often overtly religious, and although Joyce expands the idea into other contexts, it carries Christian undertones throughout his works.

Because of this religious context, and because Eveline is seeking spiritual regeneration in her journey, the epiphany in the story can be read as a moment of divine clarity. Phrases like "sudden impulse" and "he would save her" clue the reader into the religious connotations of the moment. Since she fails to carry out a divine manifestation, Eveline could be said to be falling into spiritual decay when she is unable to follow the course revealed by a holy epiphany.

Joyce is unlikely to be providing a straightforward spiritual allegory, however, and he may even be bitterly ironic about the form of Eveline's divine epiphany and escape. Religion is a potentially dubious influence in the story, from the sickly yellow portrait of her father's priest friend to the fact that a perverse sort of religious duty confines Eveline to the home to the epiphany that guides her to the arms of a sailor she might not even love. Instead, the epiphany reveals Joyce's very subtle thinking about the actual resonance of this kind of religious imagery. He is likely to be using the religious reference to underscore and universalize the complications of Eveline's bleak choice, her confinement on all sides.

Symbolism

Although *Dubliners* was originally considered a strictly realist work, critics now largely place it alongside Joyce's later masterpieces and acknowledge its profound symbolism. "Eveline" is an extremely realistic and focused portrayal of two events in one important day, with a thoroughly developed psychological narrative. But the story also contains a variety of symbolic references that broaden its implications and possibly allegorize its content (turning it into a lesson for the reader to absorb).

The first symbol is overt, that of the print of Margaret Mary Alacoque. This prominent Irish Catholic symbol represents domestic security and piety, and Eveline notices it just as she is having her first doubts about leaving home. The print is beside a yellowing photograph of a priest who is Mr. Hill's friend and above a broken harmonium (a keyboard instrument with reeds), which may be meant to emphasize the disorder of the home or Eveline's discordant spirituality. The fact that the priest has emigrated is a particularly interesting detail, possibly implying that problems in domestic piety will follow Eveline elsewhere.

As discussed above, Brewster Ghiselin argues that the sea itself is a symbol for Christian rebirth and salvation, perhaps even representing the water of a baptismal font. He also writes that Eveline's failure to leave is a symbol of failure of the fourth cardinal virtue of Christianity—fortitude—and that "music symbolizes the motion of the soul toward life or the call of life to the soul." This might be why the music in the story—such as the Italian air from the street organ that reminds Eveline of her promise to her mother, Frank's sailor songs, and the boat whistle and bells that "clanged upon her heart"—is closely connected with the idea of leaving for faraway shores.

Compare
&
Contrast

- **1900:** Dublin is second to Belfast and is firmly under English rule with Catholics in an oppressed majority.

  Today: Dublin is the capital of independent Ireland, non-inclusive of Belfast and the northern counties that remain part of the United Kingdom.

- **1900:** Having endured a century of economic decline, Dublin's unemployment is massive and prospects are bleak. Although many Protestants enjoy relative prosperity, the Catholic majority in the city are poor and live in overcrowded districts, and the city has an extremely high infant mortality rate.

  Today: Ireland has the fastest growing economy in Western Europe and is held as a worldwide model for dramatically improved social conditions. Dublin is at the center of it all, with a high level of education and job prospects that have attracted a large immigrant population.

- **1900:** Ireland has a very religious culture. Chris-

tian values are pervasive in legal and social norms, although the population is divided between Catholic and Protestant interpretations of correct belief and practice.

  Today: Christian influence has somewhat declined. Abortion is still illegal in Ireland, but the government finally legalized divorce in 1996. Church attendance and membership has dropped dramatically in the last decade, and Ireland's large foreign community has brought an influx of new religions.

- **1900:** English publishers were liable to legal penalty if they allowed works considered offensive or immoral to be published. Joyce's *Ulysses* is banned in the United States until 1933 when the court declared it not obscene.

  Today: Although the Irish and British governments infrequently ban books outright, each government has provisions similar to the telecommunications bill passed by the United States Congress in 1996 that renders it illegal to make ''indecent'' material generally available.

Historical Context

Turn-of-the-Century Dublin

The world of *Dubliners* is based on the political and social climate of Dublin around the closing years of the nineteenth century, when Joyce was growing up. The author used Dublin as the artistic canvas for all his major writings, and each street name, political reference, or mention of different regions of Ireland holds a particular significance to what he is communicating.

Dublin was the capital of Ireland, although Belfast was to temporarily outgrow it in size by 1900, and the entire island was under strict English rule (a regime that would lead to nearly a century of violent conflict). At the heart of the economic and political hardships of the era, Dublin had a majority Catholic population, most of whom desired home rule for Ireland. These ''Nationalists'' were deeply disillusioned after the disgrace and death of the formerly championed Irish political leader Charles Stewart Parnell, who skillfully fought for home rule in the British Parliament until he was voted down as leader because of an affair with a married woman. Parnellite loyalists like Joyce's parents, living on the unfashionable north side of the river Liffey, were shamed and humbled after Parnell's death in 1891. Coupled with the longstanding economic decline of the city in general, Catholic families like the Joyces were often left in miserable social conditions.

At the top of this strict social order was Dublin's 17 percent Protestant population, closely tied to the English ruling class. Holding most positions of political power and business influence, this minority kept the class system rigid. One of the most overt signs of the religious discrimination that stemmed from their power was the worsening north side of the city, which was vastly overcrowded, poor, and almost entirely Catholic. The docks on the Liffey were another example, overflowing with the displaced and unemployed masses of the Catholic lower class and a symbol of the exploitative British colonial system; this is why it is not insignificant that the boat at the end of "Eveline" is leaving from the docks of the "North wall," and why it would be very resonant with Irish readers that she makes a meager seven shillings per week.

Modernism

The beginnings of the literary movement of modernism are generally considered to have coincided with World War I, an upheaval that caused a variety of assumptions and ways of thinking to drastically change. Many modernist writers, feeling they could no longer express themselves in old forms, responded with experimental techniques based most notably on post-impressionism (which dealt with a simplification of form in the visual arts) and naturalism (which dealt with a deterministic universe that often involved a brutal struggle for individual survival). Ezra Pound and T. S. Eliot were among the chief writers of the modernist movement, Pound's criticism often becoming more influential than his other writings and Eliot's poetry examining the spiritual decadence of the modern world by reconciling the idea of "tradition" with new artistic forms in works like *The Waste Land.* Later, American novelists such as F. Scott Fitzgerald and Ernest Hemingway moved to Paris and produced their own innovations in style, while in London, Virginia Woolf, who was associated with the "Bloomsbury Group," wrote novels dealing with feminism and new expressions of consciousness.

Joyce himself was probably the most influential author on the whole of the modernist movement. One of the first writers considered a modernist, he actually invented many of its new aesthetic methods, including the tendency to develop a multiplicity of viewpoints that lead to an "epiphany," or sudden moment of truth and understanding. *Dubliners* was written ten years before the main onset of modernism, and for a long time it was thought to be straightforward realism out of the naturalist movement. The Norwegian dramatist Henrik Ibsen, whose naturalist and proto-modernist tendencies depicted a somewhat dismal provincial world and its complex relationship to truth and light, was particularly

influential over *Dubliners.* As with many of Ibsen's plays, most critics now acknowledge the vast amount of symbolism in *Dubliners* and consider it one of the key modernist texts.

Critical Overview

Craig Hansen Werner writes in his book *"Dubliners": A Pluralistic World* that "the earliest critics of *Dubliners* were the editors and printers who seem to have shared a feeling that the book was in some sense obscene or dangerous." The collection did not, however, receive the antagonistic reception its publisher Grant Richards had feared. Although it tended to be eclipsed by what were considered Joyce's more radical works, *A Portrait of the Artist as a Young Man* and *Ulysses, Dubliners* had a warm reception in the literary climate of the time. Werner notes that its most influential critic, Ezra Pound, praised the collection's "clear hard prose" and, like other critics, concentrated on its effective realism. In his book *Axel's Castle,* Edmund Wilson calles the work "a straight work of Naturalistic fiction," which was the general view of *Dubliners* for twenty years.

One of the first critics to begin to explore the symbolic themes of *Dubliners* was Brewster Ghiselin. In his 1956 essay "The Unity of Joyce's *Dubliners,*" published in *Accent,* Ghiselin argues that the collection of stories should be understood as a unified whole and that its symbolism reveals "a sequence of events in a moral drama, an action of the human spirit struggling for survival under peculiar conditions of deprivation." Since Ghiselin's reading, critics have tended to deny that *Dubliners* is exclusively a work of realism. As with Joyce's major novels, critics have thoroughly examined it under almost every conceivable critical lens and raised it to the level of a modern classic.

Because of the trend to review the collection as a whole, "Eveline" has largely been considered within essays or books alongside theories about all the stories in *Dubliners.* While early critics focused on the psychological forces in Eveline's decision, Ghiselin, for example, discusses the story as an instance of the symbolism recurring through the collection, such as the sea as a symbol for freedom. Similarly, Garry Leonard's 1993 book *Reading "Dubliners" Again* analyzes the story as an example of how the text as a whole relates to the theories of the French psychologist Jacques Lacan.

Dock on the river Liffey in Dublin, Ireland, where Eveline and Frank parted in "Eveline"

Criticism

Scott Trudell

Trudell is a freelance writer with a bachelor's degree in English literature. In the following essay, Trudell examines the elements of Freudian theory beneath Joyce's psychological portrait of Eveline.

On either side of Eveline's major life decision about whether to leave her home is a suspect and potentially abusive man. Because of the manner in which Joyce has set up the story, however, she must choose one of them; and due in large part to what is probably the result of years of psychological and physical abuse, Eveline pictures both of these men as her potential protector. She seems to be searching for a tender father figure; somewhat illogically, she tries to balance her father's increasing capacity for violence by remembering three random acts of gentleness. And she pictures Frank in a similar way, as a savior and protector to "take her in his arms, fold her in his arms," repeating as if to convince herself that "he would save her."

In his 1993 book *Reading Dubliners Again,* in which he studies the collection from a Lacanian perspective (based on the theories of the psychologist Jacques Lacan, who is associated with the literary movement of postmodernism), Garry Leonard discusses Eveline's desire to subject her self to a "nice" father in terms of what Lacan would call a participant in the male-dominated symbolic world:

> The hope that Frank will be an unconditionally loving father is the result of a feminine fantasy on her part about belonging to a benevolent phallic economy that would regard her as a particularly valuable object of exchange.

In other words, in Eveline's subconscious mind, which is deeply infused with the sexism she has learned from her culture and from her abuser, she can only conceive of her "value" as the property of a father figure. Her choice, Leonard believes, is simply to find which masculine master would deem her of greater value as a sexual object (not even which one would treat her better). Elements of the story, such as Eveline concentrating on her duty to her father and concern that "he would miss her," as well as language like "He would give her life," in reference to Frank, use such passive language as to support the idea that she has a completely servile understanding of her self worth. Leonard then goes on to discuss the presence of Eveline's own sexual

What Do I Read Next?

- *A Portrait of the Artist as a Young Man,* Joyce's autobiographical first novel, was serialized between 1914 and 1915 in Ezra Pound's magazine *Egoist.* One of the most influential early modernist works, the novel took much critical attention away from *Dubliners* because of its radical innovations in form, and it is perhaps more accessible than Joyce's famous *Ulysses.*

- Henrik Ibsen's *Ghosts,* a domestic drama in which an ill young man returns to his mother's home and begins to uncover some of their dark family history, was very influential over Joyce's efforts to forge a new literary style. Written in 1881, *Ghosts* is a landmark in modern literature.

- Virginia Woolf's first novel *The Voyage Out,* published in 1915 but revised and republished in 1920, is the story of a young woman's emigration from England to South America and her confrontation with a patriarchal society. It shares many stylistic similarities with *Dubliners,* and its plot resonates strongly with that of "Eveline."

- Edited by T. W. Moody and F. X. Martin, *The Course of Irish History* (2002) offers a variety of essays by prominent historians on each major period of Irish history, evoking a broad understanding of Ireland's turbulent politics and social conditions.

- *In Our Time,* Ernest Hemingway's debut collection of short stories, published in 1925, employs a style very distinct from that of Joyce and reveals some of the further innovations in fiction prevalent when literary modernism was at its height.

---

desire and how it finds a form in the story, arguing that the final scene can be interpreted as Eveline's sexual orgasm that the male perspective of the story fails to understand.

This is where Leonard's analysis fails to ring true; despite his insistence that Eveline's "jouissance" (a word from postmodern theory that means orgasmic pleasure at the expense of others) cannot be understood from the male-dominated perspective of the story, the final scene is undoubtedly a devastating failure for Eveline. It is certainly true that she is, seemingly willingly, objectified into the property either of her father or her lover, but it is doubtful that the end of the story could in any way represent her orgasm. The bleakness of the situation and Eveline's dismal paralysis that will probably lead to her own nervous breakdown (signaled by the "palpitations" her father's abuse has already started to give her) imply, to the contrary, that she is stifling the orgasm Frank offers by repeating, "Come!"

Perhaps, then, despite Leonard's progressive insight into the ways that Joyce's story can be applied to more recent psychological theory, it will be more helpful to return to the discussion of earlier critics and examine the story in relation to the theories of the famous psychoanalyst that was Joyce's contemporary, Sigmund Freud. Already incredibly influential over the literary world at the time Joyce was writing "Eveline," Freud had in 1900 published *The Interpretation of Dreams,* which began to develop his ideas about the "Oedipal Complex" that would become central to his later work on sexuality. Joyce was very much aware of Freud's work, and psychoanalysis would come to be associated with some of the most fundamental explorations of the modernist forms that *Dubliners* helped to develop. Applying the Freudian Oedipal drama to "Eveline," therefore, will provide a fruitful understanding of the story's portrayal of psychological development.

According to Freud, attraction to a parent of the opposite sex and rivalry with the parent of the same sex represents an extremely important developmental stage for children. Psychoanalysis attributes much abnormal psychology in later life to a failure to successfully emerge from this role, highlights its prevalence in dreams and in primitive societies, and ultimately concludes that it is a central conflict for all of human psychology. Freud began with some ambiguity about the distinction between boys and girls in their enactment of the Oedipal drama, but as his 1916 "Development of the Libido and Sexual Organizations" lecture clarifies, he considered that

> things proceed in just the same way, with the necessary reversal, in little girls. The loving devotion to the father, the need to do away with the superfluous mother and to take her place, the early display of coquetry and the arts of later womanhood, make up a particularly charming picture in a little girl, and may cause us to forget its seriousness and the grave consequences which may later result from this situation.

Grave consequences indeed follow for Eveline, in whom the reader notices the key symptoms of an Oedipal complex: major problems in adult sexuality that relate to her parents. Joyce seems to be implying that Eveline has failed to emerge from a childhood attraction to her father, which is a vital element in Freud's analysis of the complex, in a number of ways. First, Joyce makes it clear that Eveline has a rather ungrounded attraction to her father when she says, "Sometimes he could be very nice," and remembers three instances of his tenderness. In fact, it is particularly interesting that Mr. Hill puts on his wife's bonnet because it was an important belief of Freud's that pre-pubescent girls are first attracted to their mothers before they begin their more prolonged attraction to their fathers.

Secondly, there is Eveline's fondness for her brothers, although they have disappeared as possible incestuous partners (consider Freud's remarks later in "Development of the Libido and Sexual Organizations" that incestuous partners are a detriment to emergence from the Oedipal complex: "A little girl takes an older brother as a substitute for the father who no longer treats her with the same tenderness as in her earliest years.") The fact that Harry and Ernest have departed from Eveline's life would imply, in Freudian terms, that she is now freer to find a non-incestuous, although father-like, sexual partner. For Freud, the only possibility of successful escape from the Oedipal drama is with a father-like lover that will eventually lead the female child to what Freud would consider "normality," or what Eveline might mean by "life." Of course, this lover is Frank; as has already been established, Eveline treats her lover as another version of her father, a new father that will protect her and "perhaps love" her but, more importantly, "give her life."

> " Confrontational with her mother's ghost but unable to disregard the promise to fulfill her duty, 'keep the home together,' and inhabit Mrs. Hill's own doomed role (including her nervous breakdown), Eveline is condemning herself to a life of Oedipal inhibition."

Perhaps the most convincing evidence that "Eveline" can be read as a Freudian Oedipal drama, however, is the influence of Mrs. Hill on the story. Eveline has taken her mother's place in exact parallel to Freud's theory. She acts as her father's housewife to the point where even Mr. Hill associates her with his late wife when he becomes abusive toward her: "latterly he had begun to threaten her and say what he would do to her only for her dead mother's sake." There is a perverse sense in this phrase, and throughout the story, that sex is always related to a violent exchange of property, that intercourse itself is implied in what he would "do to her." Confrontational with her mother's ghost but unable to disregard the promise to fulfill her duty, "keep the home together," and inhabit Mrs. Hill's own doomed role (including her nervous breakdown), Eveline is condemning herself to a life of Oedipal inhibition.

Joyce supports this idea, which many critics have termed Eveline's "paralysis," with sophisticated symbolism. The author is by no means straightforward in his implication that Eveline has failed to successfully emerge from her Freudian conflict via its only solution, her lover. Many suspicions about Frank's character are implied in the text, including his symbolic association with exile and questionable morality, since Buenos Aires was associated with prostitution and the "Patagonians" he describes were notorious for their barbarity. Also, the night boat journey from the "North wall" may be a reference to the mythological voyage through the river Styx to the Underworld and therefore Eveline's death (as opposed to the "life" of psychological normality she seems to desire).

But the main force of the symbolism in the story, including the sea as spiritual regeneration and baptismal font, is Ireland as Eveline's mother finally sees it: "Derevaun Seraun" (which probably means something like "worms are the only end" and certainly connotes terrifying oppression). Take the climax of Eveline's psychosexual development:

—Come!

All the seas of the world tumbled about her heart. He was drawing her into them: he would drown her. She gripped with both hands at the iron railing.

—Come!

No! No! No! It was impossible. Her hands clutched the iron in frenzy.

It is understandable why Leonard sees an orgasm here, but examined from the Freudian lens it is clear that this orgasm is Frank's, and that Eveline's is denied; instead of "Yes! Yes! Yes!" she experiences "No! No! No!" The orgasmic seas of the world, she feels, will drown her, so she grips the phallic alternative to Frank, the iron railing that echoes the first image of her father's "blackthorn stick." It is no surprise that, like her mother, gripping this iron railing representing Mr. Hill sends Eveline into a "frenzy" that reminds us of her palpitations and her mother's nervous breakdown.

Eveline has, in Freudian terms, become entirely frigid and failed to escape from the prison of her own psychology. The only method of emergence from the Oedipal complex, despite his suspect intentions and his own orgasm seeming to drown Eveline, is Frank, so it is no surprise that the final imagery of the story is one of suppression and regression to extreme infancy: "She set her white face to him, passive, like a helpless animal." Joyce is at one of his bleakest moments here, envisioning almost hopeless psychological oppression as Eveline is unable to break free of her abusive father.

Source: Scott Trudell, Critical Essay on "Eveline," in *Short Stories for Students*, Gale, 2004.

Joseph Florio

In the following essay, Florio explores how music informs "Eveline" and how Joyce turns the image of mythic Irish poetry upside down in the story.

The work of scholars such as Zack Bowen, Ruth Bauerle, and M. J. C. Hodgart has done much to illuminate the role that music plays in the works of James Joyce. I have found, however, that in their endeavors the researchers have paid too little attention to *Dubliners*. It is in these tales of grey existence that Joyce truly begins to display the talent for musical allusion that comes to full fruition in his later masterpieces, *Ulysses* and *Finnegans Wake*. It is my particular belief that their research has overlooked the importance of music in the theme of "Eveline." Although both Bauerle and Bowen cite Joyce's use of "Silent, O Moyle," neither recognized the significant implications of the music and lyric.

Thomas Moore borrowed the music for this song from the traditional tune "My Dear Eveleen" and altered the lyrics so as to convey a story based on Celtic myth. Subtitled "Song of Fionnulla" the song tells the tale of Fionnulla, the daughter of the Celtic god of the sea, Lir. She is transformed into a swan and condemned to wander over Irish lakes and rivers until the first sound of the Christian Mass bell gives the signal for her release.

Moore obviously believed that the song bespoke a "tale of woes," as the marking on the sheet music is "mornfully." Joyce was no stranger to Moore's works; he actually liked "Silent, O Moyle" so much that he recommended it to his son Giorgio, praising it as one of the "lovely arias for deep voices among Thomas Moore's *Irish Melodies*," and he was familiar enough with the mythological background of the song to have once remarked to his brother George that Fionnulla was one of three girls turned into swans, "condemned to fly over the leaden Moyle till the first Christian bell sounded in Ireland." Since this brother died in 1902, Joyce must have been aware of the myth prior to finishing "Eveline" in the summer of 1904.

Considering this evidence, it is possible to conclude that Joyce has named his protagonist for the "Dear Eveleen" of the original, traditional song. He contrasts Eveline's situation with that of Fionnulla and has very deftly constructed his "tale of woes" in close relation to the story that is told in the lyrics of "Silent, O Moyle":

Silent, O Moyle! Be the roar of thy water
Break not, ye breezes! Your chain of repose
While murmuring mournfully, Lir's lonely daughter
Tells to the night star her tale of woes. (Moore, lyric sheet)

The picture that Joyce paints of Eveline from the outset can undoubtedly be construed as one of a "murmuring lonely daughter." She is the only girl in the family. The reader is introduced to her "watching evening invade the avenue," leaning her head against the window, telling "the night star her tale of woes." Eveline is awash in the turbulent tides of choice, which the "roar" of the Moyle represents. It is important to keep Joyce's aversion to Catholic doctrine in mind, as well as his awareness of the role of the poet in Irish history, political and literary. M. J. C. Hodgart astutely points out Joyce's recognition of their contributions. He states that Joyce was very familiar with the ballads and folk verses of his country: "He valued this material not as a minor contribution to serious literature but as the natural expression of the Irish people."

Inasmuch as Joyce realized their importance he also realized the strong irony that could be conveyed by twisting the role of the Irish poet to one of intense self-scrutiny, and he does this by reversing the imagery and intention that Moore had when he altered "My Dear Eveleen." In "Eveline" the Moyle represents freedom, not imprisonment; heaven's "sweet bell" will not liberate, but serve as a call to stultifying obedience; and Joyce does not lament the predicament of his country and blame outside forces for its situation, but sees the paralytic paradigm of Ireland as being self-created. As Moore updated "My Dear Eveleen" to help him express his views on Irish life, so in turn has Joyce used Moore's version as a vehicle for a statement of his own.

> When shall the swan, her death note singing
> Sleep with wings in darkness furl'd?
> When shall heav'n, its sweet bell ringing
> Call my spirits from this stormy world? (Moore, lyric sheet)

In the last paragraph of the story, Joyce presents the animal side of Eveline to the reader, Eveline as swan: "She set her white face to him, passive, like a helpless animal." This revelation allows us to strengthen the ties between "Silent, O Moyle," "My Dear Eveleen," and Celtic mythology. Eveline is Joyce's version of Fionnulla. In the end she will still sing "her death note" and will continue to sleep with her "wings in darkness furl'd," primarily because she waits upon the "sweet bell," which actually calls her *to* that "stormy world." Again Joyce turns Moore's imagery around, as well as the traditional image of the Irish poet.

> Sadly' O Moyle, to thy winter-wave weeping,
> Fate bids me languish long ages away;
> Yet still in her darkness doth Erin lie sleeping
> Still doth the pure light its dawning delay. (Moore, lyric sheet)

Here we find Moore making the shift from myth to political reality, associating the plight of Fionnulla with the dark, uphill struggle of sleeping Erin. Joyce wants us to view Eveline as a symbol of Ireland, as well as an example of the powerless, grey souls that dot the Dublin landscape of his short story collection. But instead of portraying them as seekers of emancipation through Christianity he ironically conveys an image of a country and its citizenry hemmed in by Catholic dogmatism to the point that their fates and lives are paralyzed. The second and third lines of this stanza comprehensively imbue the reader with the endless hopelessness that engulfs the existence of both Eveline and Eire. Joyce believes, however, that the decision to "languish long ages away" does not rest in the hands of fate, as Moore would have us believe, but rather lies in the inability of individuals and nations to have the strength of heart and conviction to set out on the course that leads to self-determination. It is this lack of resoluteness of spirit that Joyce scrutinizes and, in the end, scorns. Ireland is a land that has now heard the "sweet bell" of Christianity. Eveline, a symbol of that green isle, still lies sleeping, and the dawn that should have granted her fulfillment and her country freedom still delays its "pure light" solely because Catholic doctrine stands between the luminescence and the receiver of its transforming rays.

> When will the day-star, mildly springing
> Warm our isle with peace and love?
> When shall heav'n, its sweet bell ringing,
> Call my spirits to the fields above? (Moore, lyric sheet)

In light of Joyce's own description of his tone in *Dubliners* as one of "scrupulous meanness," and the theme of paralysis that threads through all of the stories, it is easy to conclude that Joyce's answer to the two questions contained in this stanza would be

''Never.'' This could not be more evident than when we look at the closing moments of ''Eveline.'' The ''mournful whistle'' that blows into the mist (and here Joyce at least retains the tone of Moore's song) sets the stage for the ensuing drama. ''All the seas of the world'' tumble about Eveline's heart as Frank draws her toward the boat that will cross the forbidden waters of the Moyle. But it is a journey not meant to be, for the ''bell'' clangs ''upon her heart'': ''No! No! No! It was impossible . . . Amid the seas she sent out a cry of anguish!— Eveline! Evvy!''

By contrasting the stories of Eveline and Fionnulla, Joyce seeks to inform us that we must accept life ''as we see it before our eyes, men and women as we meet them in the real world, not as we apprehend them in the world of faery.'' He insinuates that real life in Ireland could not be further from the glory of myth and goes on to insist that the role of the Irish poet must now change; it is time to pick apart the myths and deal with reality. Joyce mocks the myth by altering the meaning of its imagery. The ''bell'' that clanged upon Eveline's heart signifies the presence of Catholic doctrine in her life. It does not induce joy and exultation but, on the contrary, dolor and burden, a reminder of the duties that Eveline subconsciously feels are hers. For Eveline, Christianity is an enchaining force. The calm and motionless lakes of Irish life recede from her when Frank takes her hand. The ''roar'' of the Moyle's ''waters'' becomes too much to bear; she realizes that escape is beyond her. In recognition of her predicament, she sends a most curious, animal ''cry of anguish'' out to the sea, curious because it is her own name! Paralysis has completely overtaken this tragic figure who yearns for fulfillment only to find herself unprepared for it. She cries out to her sister self, Fionnulla, to her mother country, where she leads a ''life of commonplace sacrifices'' that is destined to end ''in final craziness.'' The ultimate irony is that the ''sweet bell'' calls Eveline to Christianity, but not to ''heav'n,'' and in listening to it she denies her life the possibility of happiness.

The final lines of the story portray a girl totally shaken by the decision that she has made. White-faced, like a swan, she is rendered a ''helpless animal,'' not destined for flight, keeping a good distance from the place where the calm lakes and rivers meet the ''seas of the world.''

Source: Joseph Florio, ''Joyce's 'Eveline,''' in *Explicator,* Vol. 51, No. 3, Spring 1993, pp. 181–84.

Earl G. Ingersoll

In the following essay excerpt, Ingersoll discusses the idea of Eveline embodying the ''stigma of femininity.''

James Joyce made the intent of his organization of *Dubliners* clear in his famous letter to Grant Richards:

> My intention was to write a chapter of the moral history of my country and I chose Dublin for the scene because that city seemed to me the centre of paralysis. I tried to present it to the indifferent public under four of its aspects: childhood, adolescence, maturity and public life. The stories are arranged in this order. (5 May 1906)

Joyce's classification of the quartet beginning with ''Eveline'' and ending with ''The Boarding House'' as stories of ''adolescence'' seems patently problematic. At 19, Eveline is technically ''adolescent''; however, the central characters of the other three stories in this quartet—''After the Race,'' ''Two Gallants,'' and ''The Boarding House''— are hardly adolescents, unless we associate ''adolescent'' with ''unsettled,'' or ''unmarried.'' In the last of the quartet there is an adolescent, Polly Mooney, who is the same age as Eveline—19. In a group of stories whose characters' ages are tantalizingly withheld—how old *are* the boys of the first three stories, for example?—the link of Eveline's and Polly's ages cannot be mere coincidence. Instead, it offers an example of Joyce's subtle counterpointing of two women who bear the stigma of ''femininity'' in seemingly opposing yet perhaps similar fashions.

Before exploring that connection, it might be useful to construct a framework of recent observations about the fascinating relationship between the use of literary tropes and indications of gender. In *Reading Lacan* Jane Gallop explores the gender associations of the two key tropes in contemporary critical theory—metaphor and metonymy. She traces concern with these tropes back to the seminal work of Roman Jakobson, who saw connections between metaphor and poetry, especially the poetry of nineteenth-century Romantics and Symbolists, and connections between metonymy and the realist novel. Jacques Lacan followed Jakobson in connecting metonymy with realism and metaphor with poetry; he asserts: ''In a general manner, metonymy animates this style of creation which we call, in opposition to symbolic style and poetic language, the so-called realist style.'' Gallop hypothesizes that metaphor and metonymy have gender implications as well; she writes:

Metaphor is patent; metonymy is latent. The latency, the hiddenness of metonymy, like that of the female genitalia, lends it an appearance of naturalness or passivity so that realism . . . appears either as the lack of tropes, or as somehow mysterious, the ''dark continent'' [Freud's term for female sexuality] of rhetoric.

Drawing on the work of the feminist psycho-analyst, Luce Irigaray, who correlates the privileging of metaphor over metonymy in contemporary psychoanalytic theory with a ''phallocentric neglect of femininity,'' Gallop concludes:

> The most extreme and explicit form of metaphor's privilege in Lacan's text inhabits its association with liberation, which contrasts with metonymy's link to servitude . . . metonymy's ellipsis can be considered ''oppressive.'' . . . Metaphor, on the other hand, is ''the crossing of the bar.'' The word for ''crossing''—''franchissement''—has an older meaning of liberation from slavery, enfranchissement. The ''bar'' is an obstacle; metaphor unblocks us.

In this way Gallop extends Irigaray's suggestions of a connection between metaphor and the ''phallocentric'' on the one hand, and between metonymy and the ''feminine'' on the other, to imply that liberation, movement, and activity are associated with the ''masculine,'' while oppression, servitude, and passivity are associated with the ''feminine.''

For such readers of Lacan as Barbara Johnson, Shoshana Felman, and Jerry Aline Flieger, the ''feminine'' represents something other than conventional sexual identity. In her defense of Lacan's reading of Poe's ''Purloined Letter'' against Jacques Derrida's accusations of misreading, Barbara Johnson, for example, posits femininity as an indication of *position*. Discussing the repeated expropriations of the letter, Johnson comments on how the letter ''feminizes its purloiners by being successively purloined from them.'' In this context ''femininity'' cannot be attributed to just one sex, since it indicates a position of vulnerability for men as well as women.

One fascinating refinement of this effort at finding gender implications in Lacan's key tropes of metaphor and metonymy is offered by Naomi Schor in her article ''Female Paranoia: The Case for Psychoanalytic Feminist Criticism.'' Following in the male footsteps of psychoanalytic theorists like Lacan and Derrida in reading Poe's ''The Purloined Letter'' as an allegory of the signifier, Schor argues that Derrida ''inadvertently'' points out what Lacan missed in his purloined reading of Marie Bonaparte's reading of the Poe story—the little brass knob ''between the legs of the fireplace.'' That

> **❝ If the Joycean epiphany allows the subject an encounter with the metaphoric, or the power of movement across the bar, Eveline is a subject as incapable of the epiphanic experience as is conceivable.❞**

knob is the clitoris that male theorists tend to omit in their discourse. If, as Schor argues, ''the clitoris is coextensive with the detail,'' may we not legitimately propose a ''clitoral school of feminist theory'' ''identified by its practice of a hermeneutics focused on the detail, which is to say on those details of the female anatomy which have been generally ignored by male critics. . . .''

Taking off from Irigaray's identification of metonymy with ''the rhetorical figure of vaginal theory,'' Schor would associate her ''clitoral theory'' with ''synecdoche, the detail-figure.'' She suggests that it is no coincidence that in his reading of Jakobson's seminal study, ''Two Types of Language and Two Types of Aphasic Disturbance,'' Lacan erased synecdoche, which Jakobson had subordinated to metonymy. Schor concludes:

> Clearly in Lacan's binary structural linguistics, with its emphasis on the perfect symmetry of metaphor and metonymy, there is no room for this third trope, just as in his rewriting of Bonaparte's analysis of Poe, there is no room for the knob-clitoris. Let us now praise synecdoche!

This framework offers a useful context for a discussion of the *Dubliners* stories as they situate themselves within the dynamic of the metaphoric and the metonymic. It is possible to read *Dubliners* as an expression of the binary oppositions of ''symbolist poetry'' and ''realist prose,'' since the stories focus on both a ''scrupulous meanness'' in representing the details of everyday Dublin life and the transformative power of metaphor with which Joyce associated epiphany. It is more advantageous, however, to focus on the clear gender associations of these binary oppositions in the *Dubliners,* where the ''feminine'' is consistently associated with the constrained, restrained, and repressed position of those in the bourgeois "room," while the "masculine" is associated with the impulse to travel, to organize desire as a quest for a variously defined possession or goal.

In "Eveline" domesticity is clearly associated with details, with metonymy and synecdoche. The detail that will become Eveline's signature is the "odour of dusty cretonne," expressive of the eternal Hausfrau's world: Eveline cleans and cleans, but still there is the inevitable dust that settles in those curtains of cretonne, representing her marginal effort at gentility. This is the "home" she has decided to leave, a home that she associates with its objects: "She looked round the room, reviewing all its familiar objects which she had dusted once a week for so many years, wondering where on earth all the dust came from." Of the many "familiar objects" on which her gaze is fixed, two are foregrounded: the "yellowing photograph" of an absent priest whose name she was never able to identify and a "broken harmonium." In a home now merely a museum of memories for Eveline, it is details that have made her "tired." She has not only all those "familiar objects" to be dusted each week but also the Saturday night quarrels with her father over money, which "weary her unspeakably." She has been "feminized" by a concern for details, since she has become the keeper of the pitifully meager household funds.

Eveline, with her "black leather purse" that she held "tightly in her hands as she elbowed her way through the crowds," recalls the boy of "Araby," who carried the image of Mangan's sister "like a chalice safely through a throng of foes," perhaps on the very same Saturday nights. As a metonymy of her role as housekeeper for her family, the "purse" with its naturalistic function in the narrative is juxtaposed with the boy's metaphorical "chalice," neatly marking the tropological/gender differences in these two contiguously linked narratives. Accompanying his aunt, another woman responsible for the details of household maintenance, the boy of "Araby" may feel burdened by the "parcels" she asks him to carry; however, the loving burden he more genuinely bears is that iconic chalice of Mangan's sister's image. Eveline, on the other hand, has no avenue for such metaphoric transcendence of the marketplace. Instead of the boy's metaphoric "chalice," she clutches that metonymic detail of the "black leather purse," the incriminating stigma of her role as imprisoned housekeeper.

Frank, on the other hand, offers her the prospect of "travel." The narrative makes clear that the possible trip with him to Buenos Aires, where he claims to have a house, is a metaphor for a new realm of experience that his love promises to open for Eveline. In a statement suggesting how she herself might phrase it if this story were first-person narrative, we learn: "She was about to explore another life with Frank." In contrast to the stasis of her life at home, or at "the Stores" where she is also confined, Frank offers Eveline the possibilities of travel in a variety of modes. He "took her to see *The Bohemian Girl,*" just as he has taken her into the realms of desire, for she is "pleasantly confused"—a Joycean euphemism for "sexually aroused"—by the knowledge that others know they are courting, especially when he sings the song of the "lass that loves a sailor."

Most importantly, Frank takes Eveline with him imaginatively by telling her stories of his voyages. As though he fears that he will be the prisoner of the stereotyped sailor yarning a girl into his bed in every port, he offers her a profusion of details that neither her memory nor the narrator now particularizes—"the names of the ships he had been on and the names of the different services." However, she recalls his telling her of his first voyage on "a ship of the Allan line going out to Canada" and his earning a "pound a month" as a "deck boy." Furthermore, he tells her of having sailed through the "Straits of Magellan" and relates "stories of the terrible Patagonians." These details, which he may offer as a legitimation of his authenticity as a wooer—like some latter-day Othello courting Desdemona with his tales—are metonymies of her desire for his Frank-ness, for his being something more than the sailor of countless jokes with what Lily in "The Dead" will call "palaver."

Juxtaposed to Frank, whose company she has been forbidden after their courtship was discovered, is Eveline's father. Mr. Hill, in contrast to Frank's associations of menace, offers the comfort and security of the familiar. Indeed, now that he is growing old and perhaps less likely to have the strength to abuse her, as he did her mother, he seems to be moving in her consciousness toward another of those "familiar objects" on which the dust will soon be settling in her domestic prison. As the time approaches when she must leave to keep her appointment with Frank, she continues to sit with two letters in her lap—one to her brother Harry, who tends the houses of his Lord, and the other to her father. Eveline recalls details from her life with her father, just as she has recalled similar ones from her new relationship with Frank: the time her father made her toast when she was ill and read her a ''ghost story,'' and the family picnic to Howth when he put on ''her mother's bonnet to make the children laugh.'' Through the letters she has written and the ''ghost story'' that her father appropriately has read to her, Eveline is also implicated in textuality. However, she is a prisoner of ''prose,'' the servant of metonymy, and thus unable finally to travel, to move from the house of her father.

Even the detail of the returning Italian organ-grinder, whom Eveline associates with her mother's martyrdom and who seems to prophesy similar prospects for her own future, is insufficient to save her. The last paragraph of the major section of the story begins: ''She stood up in a sudden impulse of terror,'' and the first paragraph of the last section following a narrative strategy that seems like an extended ellipsis begins: ''She stood among the swaying crowd in the station. . . .'' However, the reader has no way of ascertaining that Eveline has actually moved to the ''North Wall,'' except in projecting herself forward to that scene of departure. Whether she stands on the quay being ''shouted at'' to come aboard or stands instead in her room fantasizing her inability to move forward in answer to his cry of desire is not important finally. What is important is the closing image of Eveline as one immobilized, one whose hands are frozen to the railing, one who loses humanness itself: ''She set her white face to him, passive, like a helpless animal. Her eyes gave him no sign of love or farewell or recognition.''

Central to this last scene is the iron railing ''gripped'' and ''clutched'' by Eveline's terrified hands. If the Joycean epiphany allows the subject an encounter with the metaphoric, or the power of movement across the bar, Eveline is a subject as incapable of the epiphanic experience as is conceivable. Offered the possibility of crossing that bar into the metaphoric, she cannot move or indeed even speak. All she can know in the end is the ''nothing'' to which ''all the seas of the world'' seem to be opening her up. More graphically than any of the Dubliners to follow, Eveline is the ultimate ''feminized'' subject. Perhaps because she has been lent for a time a prospect of enfranchisement—whether or not Frank was ''frank'' is a moot point—Eveline comes to embody the essence of the ''feminine'' in patriarchy. She has seen the possibility of ''travel,'' but she evades the opportunity of ''travel'' because she can associate it with only the very vulnerability

and loss to which, in the end, she ironically commits herself. Even if she never leaves her room at the end of the story—indeed *especially* if she does not—she has passed a life sentence on herself as a ''house-keeper,'' a servant of details. . . .

Source: Earl G. Ingersoll, ''The Stigma of Femininity in James Joyce's 'Eveline' and 'The Boarding House,''' in *Studies in Short Fiction,* Vol. 30, No. 4, Fall 1993, pp. 501–10.

Warren Beck

In the following essay, Beck focuses on Eveline's ''death of the heart'' as being symbolic of the greater theme of Ireland's paralysis and ''deadening influence'' in Dubliners.

In the story ''Eveline'' a far journey is projected, but the timid protagonist, paralyzed by ambivalence at the moment of embarking from Dublin's North Wall, never sets out. In the three preceding stories lesser journeys have been proposed, from their adjacent locales in one region of North Dublin, and all with a crossing of the river Liffey to the south. (''The Sisters'' locates the priest's house in Great Britain Street, now Parnell Street; ''Araby'' has its base in North Richmond Street; presumably the boys of ''An Encounter'' live in the same area, since they meet at the Canal Bridge, proceed to the North Wall, and then cross the river.) Father Flynn had ''had his mind set on'' a drive down to Irishtown—the poor region just south of Ringsend, adjacent to the harbor—''to see the old house again'' where he and his sisters had been Born, and the unfulfilled wish takes on natural pathos in Eliza's mention of it after his death. The boys of ''An Encounter'' did ferry across the Liffey but did not make it to their goal, the Pigeon House. He of ''Araby'' not only crossed ''the twinkling river'' by train, but got to the bazaar, yet to be the more frustrated by coming so close but failing to secure a gift for the girl. Eveline's crisis, more simply narrated, is most severe. On her proposed journey to Buenos Aires she gets only as far as the dock, and while the boy of ''Araby'' feels an ''anguish'' that makes his eyes burn, Eveline's mental ''Anguish'' causes her to cry out, and then reduces her to a state of shock.

This third-person story is continuously sustained in the brooding consciousness of its main character. Of its seven pages, almost six are given over to her eddying recollections as she sits by the window at dusk, and her only overt act there is finally to stand up, with impulse to escape. The last

> No longer seeing, she is seen in a helpless isolate animal passivity, with eyes that give her lover no sign, not even of 'recognition.'"

page shows her at the North Wall but unable to go up the gangplank to the ship that would carry her away with her lover. This scene too is realized in her consciousness as she subsides through painfully conflicting emotions into a rigidity that marks the numbing of feeling. At the last it is as if not only self-possession but self-awareness have been drained from her; here the point of view changes from her anguish to the climactically worded image of what Frank saw as he called in vain for her to follow—''She set her white face to him, passive, like a helpless animal. Her eyes gave him no sign of love or farewell or recognition.''

Who and what is Eveline that her life, in this most vital sense, should be ending before she is twenty? She is in one way a widely representative figure, in her presumable fate as one of that under-privileged and put-upon minority, the spinsters for whom love's proper tide is reversed and chilled into filial dutifulness, and whose care is required for the offspring of others' passion. More particularly, though, this is an Irish story; most pointedly it is Joyce's Dublin with its special injunctions and encirclements that holds Eveline and will not let her go. Religion is part of it, inculcating the pious obligations of family life, no matter how harsh its demands. On the wall is ''a coloured print of the promises made to Blessed Margaret Mary Alacoque''—she who will bless a home where her picture is exhibited—and at the dock Eveline's last act before she lapses into a fixed inaction is to murmur prayers ''to God to direct her, to show her what was her duty.'' The neediness that stalks so many of Joyce's Dubliners is in this story too. ''She always gave her entire wages—seven shillings'' to the family's support. Family demands in addition almost the whole of her life. Eveline's promise to her dying mother has left the nineteen-year-old girl responsible for two younger children, and subject to a domineering father.

This parental figure, from Joyce's view, is authentic Dubliner. Given to drink, he ''was usually fairly bad on Saturday night.'' Then he would be capriciously tyrannical, first refusing money for the household and finally giving it but blaming Eveline for the delay in buying Sunday's dinner. When as children she and her older brothers had played in the adjoining field, their father ''used often to hunt them in . . . with his blackthorn stick,'' and ''he used to go for Harry and Ernest.'' Now Ernest is dead and Harry, ''in the church decorating business,'' is away from home, and there is no one to protect her from this man who had treated her mother badly and whose threats have ''given her the palpitations.'' Like most autocrats, he is insular, damning the Italian organ grinders for ''coming over here,'' and he plays the proper heavy father, forbidding his daughter ''to have anything to say'' to that sailor chap, Frank.

Thinking of herself as ''over nineteen,'' Eveline looks back to what in her wearisome life seems ''a long time ago,'' before houses were built on the field where she and other children had played, and before those playmates had died or moved away. Then ''they seemed to have been rather happy,'' she recalls. This moderate memory, centers on two things—''Her father was not so bad then; and besides, her mother was alive.'' Since then Eveline has gone to work in the Stores, to bring back all her wage for the family's support, while it also de-volved upon her to see that ''the two young children . . . went to school regularly and got their meals regularly.'' She knows it to be ''hard work—a hard life,'' yet habit has so captured her that ''now that she was about to leave it she did not find it a wholly undesirable life.'' At an enervated pause there by the window in the little brown house, looking about the room, she is reminded chiefly of dutiful toil, regarding familiar objects as things she ''had dusted once a week for so many years.'' It is with such and like details that Joyce has gone on to substantiate the story's remarkable opening paragraph of three sentences:

> She sat at the window watching the evening invade the avenue. Her head was leaned against the window curtains and in her nostrils was the odour of dusty cretonne. She was tired.

The word ''invade,'' especially connoting the dusk, suggests a suspended mood without stressing it; ''was leaned'' conveys her passivity, and that effect is sustained by the parallel verb structure of ''in her nostrils was the odour of dusty cretonne.'' The rhythms of the first two sentences make way for the epitomizing of her lassitude in the simple brevity of the third.

Eveline's fatigue was more than physical; it was a dreadful weariness of spirit as she approached the verge of impasse. With the odor of dust in her nostrils and with bits of the distant and nearer past alternating in her mind, she was trying "to weigh each side of the question" of leaving her home and family. Against all her hardships she could find almost nothing to persuade her to stay. She made herself recall that sometimes her father "could be very nice." Not long before, when she was ill, he had read her a ghost story and made toast for her; but for more on that positive side she must go back to once when her mother was alive and they went to picnic on the Hill of Howth (her widest excursion, probably, no further than those few miles to the northern tip of Dublin harbor) and the father had donned the mother's bonnet to make the children laugh. There is little enough of past felicity to summon up in the room with the broken harmonium and the yellowing photograph of a priest notable for having gone to Melbourne. Of only one thing is she certain—"She would not cry many tears at leaving the Stores," where her superior is inclined to be severe. Eveline can explicitly reject the impersonal claims of a job, but obligation to family is not to be put aside without painful questioning.

Circumscribed by harsh authority and onerous necessity, in meekly complying she has developed timidity as a fixed characteristic, much like others among Joyce's Dubliners, such as Little Chandler, Maria, Jimmy Doyle, and Gabriel Conroy in their variously diffident ways. But Eveline is not simply timid; she is racked by inner conflict, finally to the point of distraction. Her father's inconsiderateness and the hardness of her laborious life are not, however, primary factors in this ambivalence. Its poles are a young girl's desire for the assurances of love with the security of marriage and, on the other hand, her submission under the weight of a promise made on "the last night of her mother's illness" that she would "keep the home together as long as she could." Furthermore, in her very remembrance of that pledge she is of two minds.

While she continued to sit by the window, though "her time was running out," still leaning her head against the dust-impregnated curtain, a street organ was playing outside, sounding from the world beyond Dublin "a melancholy air of Italy," just as on the night of her mother's death. Under music's spur to association she recalls not only her promise but her mother's "life of commonplace sacrifices closing in final craziness," and with this "pitiful vision" she hears again her mother's insistent cry, "Derevaun Seraun!" The words constitute a puzzle. To an inquiry one Irish scholar said that whatever this is, it isn't Gaelic. Another informally put it that it sounds something like what might mean "one end . . . bitterness" or, more closely, "end of riches . . . bitterness." Tindall, in *A Reader's Guide to James Joyce,* reports that Patrick Henchy of the National Library in Dublin "thinks this mad and puzzling ejaculation corrupt Gaelic for 'the end of pleasure is pain.'" Marvin Magalaner writes that the words "seem to be crazed ravings, the meaning of which I have been unable to determine." The phrase doubtless is to be read as unintelligible to Eveline, but that would have made it the more disturbing to her, and whatever the senselessness, the tone of despair would have been clear. Thus the memory triggered by the street organ's air involves both the solemn promise her mother had extracted from Eveline and the inference that if the promise is kept, she like her mother will be misused and deprived, and perhaps even driven to distraction. And the latter fear, for the moment, tips the scale in this ambivalence. In "a sudden impulse of terror" Eveline stands up, knowing she "must escape!"

She believes too that a way to life and rightful happiness is open—"Frank would save her." He is Irish, but is in Dublin "just for a holiday" in "the old country," from which he had shipped out as a deck boy, to Canada; since then he has seen the world and reports himself "fallen on his feet" in Buenos Aires, where a "home" awaits Eveline if she will go with him. This bronze-faced sailor had been attentive, he would meet her outside the Stores every evening to see her home, and he took her to *The Bohemian Girl.* At first for her there was the excitement of having "a fellow," and "then she had begun to like him." Primarily, though, he is a refuge and her salvation. She believes he "would give her life, perhaps love, too" but certainly "would . . . fold her in his arms . . . would save her."

Such details allow a supposition that Eveline's father might not have been all wrong in forbidding her to see Frank, though the reasons were mean—a stereotyped distrust of "sailor chaps" and an unrelenting claim upon his domestic drudge. As Eveline sees Frank, he is not only spirited but "very kind, manly, open-hearted." Yet it is not quite as one reader puts it: "Marriage and flight across the sea promise life and 'perhaps love too.'" For her to be a bride before the flight would require, if not a secret marriage in Dublin, an immediate ceremony in the captain's cabin—a most unlikely thing in the Catholic context of this story, and one which, had it been pending, surely would have entered into Eveline's reverie. Instead this inexperienced nineteen-year-old about to "run away with a fellow" thinks simply that she "was to go away with him by the night-boat to be his wife" and believes that "tomorrow she would be on the sea with Frank, steaming towards Buenos Ayres." However, "the night-boat" from the North Wall is probably the regular one to Liverpool, and while passengers might sail to Buenos Aires from there, Liverpool could be the sordid end of this journey for Eveline; or she could reach South America still unmarried and find Frank's promises false.

Joyce has given no further or more substantial grounds for suspecting Frank besides these slight implications in the details and phrasing. If the inference is made, it merely stresses the pathos of Eveline's situation; and to leave it at that would accord with the narrative's tone and intent. For Frank to have given Eveline more precise assurance or for the hint of possible betrayal to have been stronger would have made it another story, or an infringement upon the integrity of this one. It is one of its many delicate balancings, both in Eveline's mind and in the total effect itself, that Joyce makes it a matter of "perhaps love, too" but allows some uncertainty as to just what kind of escape is open to Eveline. There is a great deal of such selective economy and particular focusing in all the *Dubliners* stories, and in this technique they are still quite modern, sixty years after their composition. Indeed, in comparison it is Joyce's later and more experimental works that may seem "dated" by uniqueness and by a fixity less within the literary period than in the artist's own history.

More to the main point in "Eveline" is the nature of her indecision and her eventual paralysis. This intimidated girl perceives in sailor Frank's vitality and amiability something more pleasing and reassuring than anything in the Dublin life she has known, and it is not implied that she doubts him. What she doubts is herself. Too many burdens and restrictions have conditioned her to abandon hope and merely endure, with those bare consolations she weighs as "shelter and food" and "those whom she had known all her life about her." Ellmann reports, on the word of Joyce's sister, Mrs. Mary Monaghan, that an Eveline of North Richmond Street "did fall in love with a sailor" but "settled down with him in Dublin and bore him a great many children." Joyce

did not locate the story on that street or any other but only in a neighborhood where an adjacent field had made a place for the children to play until "a man from Belfast"—a foreign invader of a sort—"built houses in it." Apparently for this story all Joyce borrowed from North Richmond Street was a first name for a Dublin instance of early inescapable stunting, this downtrodden young woman who in her twentieth year already is girded about narrowly by what she "had known all her life." To that dead center she returns from her fluttering endeavor to escape, and there she is left, fixed in a confinement as strict as any in Joyce's several illustrations of Dublin's rigorous effect.

As Tindall has put it of this story, "The end is not a coming of awareness but an animal experience of inability." Thereby "Eveline" sounds a somewhat different note from the three tales preceding it. Derived from Joyce's boyhood and told retrospectively in first person, those all show a "coming of awareness," though with some differences. In the first two the boy knows a liberation—in "The Sisters" from clerical and social domination into intellectual detachment, and in "An Encounter" from the contagious staining of a sense for adventure into a real knowledge of honest comradeship. Something positive is thus achieved in both stories, and they imply that where limitations are incidental and particular they may be evaded or transcended. "Araby," based more deeply on universals in addition to the presence of obstructive environmental factors, suggests that ultimately limitation inheres in the tearful nature of things, discovered between the spirit's inordinate projections and reality's unaccommodating welter. "Eveline" merges such elements, in a most economical and pointed story, toward a most acute crisis. The barely more than one page which is the simple concluding scene sketches with urgent directness her descent through conflicting emotions into an almost cataleptic state, with her hands clutching the iron railing in something like a death grip.

What precipitated this ultimate seizure as Frank tried to draw her with him was the indefinable but terrifying sense that "all the seas of the world" in its strange far regions and ways are only an extension of what she already knows—the multiplicity of the disparate and unamenable which has brought her to a neurotic fatigue beyond any remedy but one, apathy. When she sends her "cry of anguish" from "amid the seas," these are real depths; nor is she out of them. Compared to the anguished boy in "Araby" she is more pathetic, and a much grimmer example of frustration, since her whole life has already fallen into so harshly restrictive a mold. The boy's grief is sharp but not paralyzing; he has a lively anger to arm him for the rebellion latent in his nature; the environmental pressures upon him are less direct and insistent; and he has somewhat more time, since his crisis has come earlier; and as a man-child he has more scope. His frustration is of a kind many have suffered in early adolescence and recovered from; Eveline's moment at the North Wall is crucial, with implication of lasting defeat. Passing beyond stories based in his own childhood, Joyce defined in Eveline not only a characteristically limited Dublin life but traced psychologically the onset of impasse, through conflict to submission, and from the unrest of a divided mind to the barren refuge of inaction.

Eveline's is a simple story, simply told, but it is not slight, nor in any sense skimped. The vividly dramatic closing scene can be brief because it is well based. The preceding pages, concerning Eveline as she muses by the window with the farewell letters to father and brother in her lap, are a masterful narrative deployment to bring a whole life into plain view, and by its own light. The movement is that of casual association, suggesting by its shifts the recurrent alternations in Eveline's ambivalent mood. There are brief passages of chronologically ordered detail, but the total order is that of discursive mental process, for realistic characterization and for thematic penetration. Eveline remembers childhood, then looks at this room now, then weighs the question of leaving home, but from that prospect she returns to her past, caught in an eddy of inconclusive reconsideration. In thinking of what they would say at the Stores, where she works, that more immediate situation led her to suppose "it would not be like that" when she was married—"People would treat her with respect then." The next sentence—"She would not be treated as her mother had been"—carries her back to her father's bullying, but as she thinks of hardships she is about to escape, the habitual makes its claim, for "now that she was about to leave it she did not find it a wholly undesirable life," and the imminence of a decisive break wakens timidity and indecision, sounding again the fatal note of ambivalence. Still she projects "another life" which she "was about to explore" and that returns her to her first meeting with Frank, his continuing attentions, and intimations of the great world his tales brought her; then her mind swings to her father's opposition to the sailor chap, and to her farewell letters in her lap for father and

brother, and so to her father's increasing age and dependence, and thus to remembrance that sometimes "he could be very nice," as when "not long before" he had been considerate of her in her illness or when, much longer before, he had been playful at their picnic on the Hill of Howth.

This is the point at which her repetitious medley of recollections is broken into by the street-organ music with its reminder of her mother's death; hence Eveline's wrench, from her remembered promise "to keep the home together as long as she could" to an impulse to escape that brings her to her feet. Yet while her musings have been freely associative and inconclusive, the narrative itself has not lapsed into rambling. The details of Eveline's history accumulate into shape and implication as unobtrusively yet solidly as the silting that shallows a river and underlies its meanderings. Unobtrusive yet crescive as thematic effect is the recurrent sway of Eveline's wavering regard. This prepares so well for the climax that Joyce can move into it directly, to show the pendulum finally stilled at dead center. It is not told what steps Eveline took after her standing up, "in a sudden impulse of terror" with intent to escape her present life, and until she stood in "the swaying crowd" at the North Wall at sailing time. The ellipsis is allowable, for evidently the impulse had sufficed to carry her straight on thus far, and her real story is not of direct progress but of haltings and stalemate.

Earlier in the evening, though she was aware that "her time was running out," Eveline had "continued to sit by the window"; now time has run out, she is at the point of embarkation, physically and psychologically. It is now that "a bell clanged upon her heart" as she feels herself about to be engulfed in "all the seas of the world." Now Frank, who she had thought "would save her," appears as one about to draw her into those seas and "drown her." This cannot be taken to mean she suspects him of bad faith. The story has given no hint that she had ever doubted him, and if she had, the probable reaction would have differed from that which follows, her freezing into a complete negation and unresponsiveness, to avoid taking the finally decisive step. This is marked by the fact that here her consciousness fails as the medium of the narrative. The rest beyond her silence can be said, however, in one paragraph of four short sentences. No longer seeing, she is seen in a helpless isolate animal passivity, with eyes that give her lover no sign, not even of "recognition."

Of all the traumatic experiences suffered by Joyce's Dubliners, this is the worst. Herself, too severely beset, has lost the sense of self with loss of volition. The boy of "Araby" at least can say "I saw myself," though only as "a creature driven and derided by vanity." Old Father Flynn in the double darkness of his confession-box was at least "wide-awake and laughing-like to himself." And even Mr. James Duffy's painful case of isolation is of another order, since as he "gnawed the rectitude of his life" he knows his own coldly wilful withdrawals are to blame for his finally feeling "outcast from life's feast." For Eveline the possibility of "life, perhaps love, too" has been eroded by an exacting sense of obligation. Self-sacrifice, inculcated as filial regard, has undone her even more severely than selfishness did for Mr. Duffy. At the quayside, glimpsing "the black mass of the boat" and hearing its "long mournful whistle into the mist," she prayerfully centers her mind on "what was her duty." This for her is the primary dilemma, of which her timidity is the effect not cause; she shows how frustration can produce indecisiveness. She proves too how the subservient finally have no point of reference except the authority which has dominated them; evil becomes what little good is left them, and their only pleasure, if any, would be a martyr's masochism. Frank held her hand and "she knew that he was speaking to her, saying something about the passage over and over again," but she scarcely heard these promises of liberation, and she "answered nothing," meanwhile silently imploring "God" to "show her" the clear path of "her duty." Hitherto basically guided by her promise to her dying mother, and conscious that her father, aging of late, "would miss her," now while her urgent lover is holding her hand what she thinks of is not love, even for him, but of something owed here too—"Could she still draw back after all he had done for her?"

Thus her life has come at last to nothing but a stark dilemma of duties, and either way will be a self-reductive subordination. Yet not to choose is to remain divided, which in the end is self-annihilating. So her final cry of "anguish" is not to Frank or to mother or father or God; if anything more than the scream of a trapped animal, it is to her dying identity amid those "seas of the world" that tumble in all their smothering contrariety "about her heart." She is paying an ultimate price, in unresolved paralyzing ambivalence, as that may be induced by too severe limitations and exactions. Concerning Eveline it has been observed by Hugh Kenner that "she is not a protagonist . . . but a mirror," placed in a

"masculine world (Dublin)" which has "given" what her mind must "feed on." It is a nice point, and the more so if it be allowed that Dublin as a masculine world includes the Church's authoritarian impact, especially on family life. It is also true that in some degree all of Joyce's Dubliners are pseudo-protagonists, in subjection to an environment insular, strict, and dominant. There is neither hero nor heroine among them, but whether or not they may be called "protagonists" they are actors; and all spirits, playing out illustratively Joyce's critical, melancholy view of life in Dublin, where degrees of paralysis are traceable to ambivalence more or less induced by various repressions upon the vulnerable.

The story does not tell whether Eveline's frenzied grip on the iron railing was held until the boat put off, or whether even then she had to be torn away from her clutch on an inanimate stability. If at the very best she could have found her way back to dutiful routines as housekeeper and store clerk, would other Dubliners (themselves relatively passive in a fatalistic acceptance) have seen anything about her "that made them think that there was something gone wrong," as was so mildly observed of Father Flynn? Joyce the artist, who has brought his account to a full stop with terrifying impact, states no prognosis of Eveline's case, but there is dark implication in the descending order of those closing words fixing her at that moment as one in whose eyes is "no sign of love or farewell or recognition." Had love's promise been strong enough and she not too enervated to answer to it, she would have followed Frank up the gangplank to at least something more than paralysis. Had she been capable of an unenforced, self-expressive decision not to go, at least she could have called farewell to the person who had persuaded her this far. The absence of recognition is the death of the heart.

And it is read as such through the eyes of one about to depart from Dublin. "Eveline," the second of Joyce's stories to be published, appeared in the *Irish Homestead* on September 10, 1904, and on October 8 Joyce sailed from the North Wall with Nora Barnacle, on a questing that was also in flight from deadening influence. Degrees of approach to the heart's death by various Dubliners are to be seen and shown by Joyce in the subsequent stories. In placing "Eveline" at their head, as example of the endemic Dublin disease in a classic, extreme, and in one sense fatal form, Joyce prepares for recognition of its less violent but at least partially disabling instances. Besides that, "Eveline" is a high particular artistic achievement of controlled intensity, a clearly implicative document in the onset of apathy, and a tragedy in the modern mode, brimming with the pathos of a little person's defeat under the pressures of an inimical order.

Source: Warren Beck, "'Eveline,'" in *Joyce's "Dubliners": Substance, Vision, and Art,* Duke University Press, 1969, pp. 110–22.

Sources

Freud, Sigmund, "Development of the Libido and Sexual Organizations," in *Introductory Lectures on Psycho-Analysis,* George Allen & Unwin, 1922, pp. 259–84.

Ghiselin, Brewster, "The Unity of Joyce's *Dubliners,*" in *Accent,* Spring 1956, pp. 75–87.

Joyce, James, *Dubliners,* Penguin Classics, 2000, pp. 29–34, 253–56.

Leonard, Garry M., *Reading "Dubliners" Again,* Syracuse University Press, 1993, pp. 95–112.

Werner, Craig Hansen, *"Dubliners": A Pluralistic World,* Twayne Publishers, 1988, p. 11.

Wilson, Edmund, *Axel's Castle,* Macmillan, 1991, p. 192.

Further Reading

Ellman, Richard, *James Joyce,* Oxford University Press, 1983.

> Originally published in 1959, Ellman's biography of Joyce remains the definitive insight into the life of the writer. It includes anecdotes about Joyce's notorious drinking bouts and selections from his letters.

Foster, R. F., *Modern Ireland: 1600–1972,* Penguin Books, 1990.

> Foster's book provides an excellent survey of Irish history since the seventeenth century, detailing the background and key figures of Irish independence.

Garrett, Peter K., ed., *Twentieth Century Interpretations of "Dubliners": A Collection of Critical Essays,* Prentice Hall, 1968.

> This thorough collection of analytical essays is helpful for further study on *Dubliners.*

Joyce, James, *James Joyce's "Dubliners": An Illustrated Edition with Annotations,* edited by Bernard McGinley and John W. Jackson, St. Martin's Press, 1993.

> With vivid illustrations and helpful notes, this edition of *Dubliners* contains a useful version of "Eveline."

Mosher, Harold F., ed., *ReJoycing: New Readings of "Dubliners,"* University Press of Kentucky, 1998.

> The collection of critical essays in this book, by a variety of key Joyce scholars and from a number of different schools of thought, are accessible for readers of any background.

Immigration Blues

Bienvenido Santos

1977

''Immigration Blues,'' by Filipino American writer Bienvenido Santos, won the award for fiction from *New Letters* in 1977 (an award that includes publication of the work as part of the prize) and is available in his short-story collection *Scent of Apples* (Seattle and London, 1979). Santos writes frequently of the Filipino experience in America, which is the subject of ''Immigration Blues.''

The story is a poignant study in the loneliness and sense of exile that have often been a part of the Filipino experience in the United States from the end of World War II through the 1970s, when the story was written. ''Immigration Blues'' also reveals the fact that many Filipinos desperately wanted to come to the United States and remain there, in spite of the difficulties. As the story relates, many Filipino women were prepared to do almost anything to achieve their goal of living in America.

''Immigration Blues'' is written in a simple style that belies the emotional subtlety it conveys. It was awarded the fiction award from *New Letters* and shows Santos's art at its finest.

Author Biography

Bienvenido N. Santos was born March 22, 1911, in Tondo, Manila, the Philippines, the son of Tomas and Vicenta (Nuqui) Santos. At the time, the Philippines was a colony of the United States, and the language of instruction at the school Santos attended was English.

Santos graduated from the University of the Philippines in 1932 and became an elementary and high school teacher. He began publishing his short stories in English at this time. When he left for America in September 1941 as a scholar of the Philippine Commonwealth government, Santos was an established writer in the Philippines. He enrolled at the University of Illinois in the master's program in English, graduating in 1942. Meanwhile, the United States had entered World War II, and Santos was unable to return to the Philippines, where his wife Beatriz, whom he had married in 1933, and their three daughters lived (they later had a son).

In the summer of 1942, Santos studied at Columbia University. From 1942 to 1945, Santos was a public relations officer at the Embassy of the Philippines in Washington, D.C. In 1945, Santos had his first fiction published in America, the short story "Early Harvest," which appeared in the magazine *Story*. After studying at Harvard in 1945 and 1946, Santos returned home to the Philippines, where he became professor and vice-president at Legazpi College (now Aquinas University) in Legazpi City. It was during this period that he published two collections, *You Lovely People* (short stories, 1955) and *The Wounded Stag: Fifty-Four Poems* (1956).

Santos returned to America in 1958 as a Rockefeller Foundation fellow at the University of Iowa Writer's Workshop. He remained at the University of Iowa for three years. During the 1960s, Santos divided his time between the United States and the Philippines. In 1965, his first two novels, *Villa Magdalena* and *The Volcano*, written with the help of a Rockefeller grant and a Guggenheim fellowship, were published in Manila. Also in 1965, Santos won the Philippine Republic Cultural Heritage Award for Literature.

In 1972, the Philippine government banned Santos's serialized novel *The Praying Man*, which is about government corruption. It was ultimately published in book form in 1982. Santos had intended to return permanently to the Philippines, but he now found himself again in exile. From 1973 to 1982, Santos was Distinguished Writer-In-Residence at Wichita State University. In 1976, Santos became a U.S. citizen. In 1979, *Scent of Apples*, which includes the short story "Immigration Blues," was published. It is the only book of Santos's short stories published in the United States.

Bienvenido Santos

Many more of Santos's writings appeared during the 1980s, including the novels *The Man Who (Thought He) Looked Like Robert Taylor* (1983) and *What the Hell for You Left Your Heart in San Francisco* (1987), as well as a collection of poetry, *Distances in Time* (1983), and a collection of stories, *Dwell in the Wilderness* (1985). Santos died January 7, 1996, at his home in Albay, the Philippines.

Plot Summary

One summer day in San Francisco, two Filipino women, one fat and the other thin, call on Alipio Palma, an old Filipino widower who lives alone. He has been an American citizen since 1945, after the Japanese surrender that ended World War II. Alipio has had a recent run of misfortune. His wife died, and then he was involved in a car accident that left him bedridden for a year. He now can walk, although he limps and must take great care as he moves around. He seldom sees or talks to anyone, so it is a surprise for him when two women he does not know arrive on his doorstep. He invites them in. The fat woman does most of the talking, while the thin one is silent. The former introduces herself as Mrs. Antonieta Zafra, the wife of Carlito, and says that

Carlito and Alipio had been friends in the Philippines. Alipio inquires about Carlito, and Mrs. Zafra says he is now retired and lives in Fresno. She introduces her elder sister as Monica. Monica has never been married. She looks uncomfortable. Alipio says he thought Carlito must be dead, since he never hears from him anymore. Alipio then reminisces about his dead wife, Seniang, who died of a heart attack. He addresses a remark to Monica, but she is still unable to speak.

Alipio invites the two women to stay for lunch. Mrs. Zafra offers to help him prepare it, but he says there is nothing to prepare. He likes to eat uncooked sardines with rice and onions. Mrs. Zafra tries to bring Monica into the conversation, but she is very shy. When Alipio shows them all the canned food he has in his cabinet, Mrs. Zafra says that all she needs is a cup of coffee. He shows them more food, and Monica, plucking up courage to speak, wonders why he keeps so much of it in the house. He replies that he watches for sales and then stockpiles items.

They eat a simple lunch. It is revealed through conversation that Mrs. Zafra was once a nun in a convent in California. She left the convent more than six years ago and then married Carlito. She tells Alipio her story. After leaving the convent, she could not find any work. More importantly she was then no longer entitled to stay in the United States, and the immigration office began to hound her. Many other Filipinos were in a similar position. She did not want to return to the Philippines, where she would have difficulty explaining why she left the convent. She then remembered it was possible to marry an American citizen and automatically be entitled to the status of permanent resident. At first she disliked this idea, but after an immigration officer told her she had to be out of the country within a week or face deportation, she decided she would indeed try to marry an American. She asked God how she should go about it. God told her to look for an elderly Filipino who was an American citizen and tell him the truth. She then met Carlito, and he was willing to do what she asked. They were married a day before the deadline expired. They lived simply and well, she says. Then she sent for Monica to come from the Philippines.

Alipio then explains that the woman who was to become his wife, Seniang, was in a similar situation to Mrs. Zafra. She had to find an American husband or face deportation. Alipio liked her anyway and thought it would be a good idea to get married. In those days, Seniang was slim—like

Monica—he adds. This prompts Monica to start talking, blushing as she does so. She seems more at ease now and goes unbidden to the kitchen to wash the dishes. But Alipio tells her not to; he will do them later.

Mrs. Zafra thanks Alipio for being such a good host to two strangers; he says they are not strangers because he and Carlito are friends. He recalls his youthful days with Carlito and admits he was a romantic in those days. In a moment of wistfulness, he wonders what has happened to all those friends of his youth. They are all old now, and are scattered throughout the United States and the world.

As he speaks, Monica watches him closely. Then she begins to speak, saying that she admires him because he has strength of character. She wonders whether it is hard for him, living alone all the time. Alipio loses track of the conversation and does not respond. Monica, discouraged, lets the conversation drop, which displeases her sister.

Alipio asks Monica how long she has been in the United States. Mrs. Zafra answers the question for her. Monica has been in the country for a year on a tourist visa, but now she has only two days left on her visa, and she does not want to return to the Philippines.

Alipio now realizes why the women have come to him. Mrs. Zafra admits it. They had found out all about him from other Filipinos who know him. She says Monica will accept any arrangement that suits him. Monica starts to weep and says they should leave. But Alipio invites them to stay longer. It seems he is not averse to the idea of marrying Monica. Mrs. Zafra goes out to get some groceries, leaving Alipio and Monica alone. When she returns, Monica takes some of the grocery bags and heads for the kitchen. It is clear that she and Alipio have agreed to marry.

Characters

Monica

Monica is Mrs. Zafra's sister. Mrs. Zafra says she is her elder sister, but Alipio thinks she looks younger. Monica is thin and very shy. She has never been married. In the Philippines, she works as a teacher. She is in the United States on a tourist visa and is desperate to find a way of permanently staying in the country. She and her sister therefore approach Alipio with the intention of convincing Alipio to marry Monica. Since he is an American citizen, marriage to him will entitle her to permanent resident status in the United States. At first when she meets Alipio she is too shy to speak, but she later finds her tongue and makes sure he knows how admiring and how helpful she will be to him.

Alipio Palma

Alipio Palma is an old Filipino man who has lived most of his life in California. He has been an American citizen since the end of World War II. Since the death of his wife Seniang, he has been lonely. He is also still suffering from the ill-effects of a car accident that happened shortly after his wife died. He was bedridden for a long time as a result, and now can walk only with some difficulty. Few of his friends are left to visit him, and sometimes he does not have enough to do to keep him busy. He watches television and sits out on the porch and observes the passersby. He reminisces about the friends of his youth and wonders where they all are now. The marriage he had to Seniang was a happy one, even though it was undertaken only so that Seniang could stay in the country. He has no real desire to marry again, but when he realizes what Monica and her sister have in mind, he seems ready to accede to it.

Seniang Palma

Seniang is the deceased wife of Alipio. They had a happy marriage, and he recalls her with fondness. He calls her his good luck. When they first met, it was she who approached him, because she already had marriage in mind. She needed to marry an American citizen to avoid deportation.

Mrs. Antonieta Zafra

Mrs. Antonieta Zafra is the Filipino wife of Carlito and sister of Monica. She and Monica visit Alipio, whom they have never met, in order to arrange for Monica to marry him. The idea is Mrs. Zafra's, and it is she who eggs on Monica. Mrs. Zafra is a big woman who does most of the talking. Before she met Carlito, she was a nun at a convent in California. But about six years before the story takes place, she left the convent. The religious lifestyle no longer suited her. But this meant that she was no longer entitled to remain in the United States. Threatened with deportation, she persuaded Carlito to marry her in the nick of time.

Carlito Zafra

Carlito is the husband of Mrs. Zafra. He does not appear directly in the story, but he is described by his wife and is also recalled by Alipio, who is his old friend. Alipio and Carlito came to America at the same time as young men. Carlito never had much interest in women, being more interested in cultivating his fighting cocks. But when Mrs. Zafra approached him, wanting marriage to secure her own status in the United States, Carlito agreed to the marriage, which turned out to be a reasonably happy one. They are now retired and live in Fresno, California, raising chickens and hogs.

Themes

Exile

Even though he has lived in the United States since he was a young man and is now a U.S. citizen, Alipio still thinks of his homeland in the Philippines. He gives the impression that he is not fully at home in America, in a culture so different from the one in which he grew up. His memories of the Philippines remain powerful. In the second sentence of the story, when he first sees his two female visitors, they remind him of the country girls in the Philippines ''who went around peddling rice cakes.'' The sound of the waves outside also reminds him of his home in the Philippines, where he lived in a coastal town. He used to tell his wife, ''across that ocean is the Philippines, we're not far from home.'' Even though he lives in the United States, he still thinks of himself as Filipino, not American. When he invites the women to take *merienda* (''picnic, afternoon tea''), he says, ''And I don't mean snacks like the Americans.'' Alipio is one of many such ''pinoys,'' as Filipino immigrants in America are known, who feel they are living in exile, even though they may have lived in America for many decades. There is a tone of wistful regret in Alipio's voice as he says, ''We all gonna be buried here.''

Loneliness and Aging

As an old man who lives alone following the recent death of his wife, Alipio is lonely. He is childless. He often thinks of his wife, and few friends come to visit him. On the day the two women visit, he has not talked to anyone all week, nor has his telephone rung. He spends a lot of his time listening to the radio or watching television.

Topics for Further Study

- Review the characters of Alipio and Monica, and then write a brief sketch set one year after they have married that portrays their partnership. Are they both satisfied with the arrangement they made, or is one partner more satisfied than the other? Are there any tensions between them? This is a creative exercise, but try to base your sketch realistically on the characters as they appear in the story, taking into account their personalities and motivations.

- Investigate the system that allows foreign nationals to become U.S. citizens by marrying a U.S. citizen. Do the arrangements made by the characters in "Immigration Blues" constitute an abuse of the system? Why or why not?

- Should recent immigrants to the United States from Asia or anywhere else in the world make an effort to fit in with American culture, or should they focus on preserving their own cultural heritage? Explain your answer.

- Research the war of 1898 to 1902 that established American rule in the Philippines. Why did the United States embark on this war? What were its goals, and how were they achieved? What have been the long-term consequences of the American colonization of the Philippines?

He admits his house is a mess, since he has no reason to keep it tidy. Often he has nothing to do. Sometimes he just sits on the porch for hours, nodding to passersby. He looks back fondly on the days of his youth and wonders where all his friends from the past are. In his reflections there is a poignant sense of the passing of time. Alipio also has his share of the infirmities of age. He is hard of hearing; he cannot walk well. This portrayal of Alipio's loneliness makes him a sympathetic figure to the reader.

Immigration

The story highlights the precariousness of the temporary immigrant (especially the female immigrant) to America, who must keep on the "right" side of immigration authorities. Although the story often hints at the difficulty of life in America as a Filipino immigrant, it also emphasizes the unwillingness of the immigrants to return home. Mrs. Zafra explains the plight of many Filipinos in a situation similar to the one that she faced and Monica now faces. They are forced to hide like criminals from the immigration agents. Those who are caught and forced to return to the Philippines have to cope with the "stigma of failure in a foreign land." Many become depressed and antisocial; some

even go mad or become criminals. So whatever the difficulty of living in a land and culture not their own, the Filipino immigrants still feel this feat is preferable to returning home.

Hope

Although the story is a study in loneliness and a kind of cultural alienation, it ends on a note of hope. Alipio will marry Monica. She will look after him and see to his needs. He did nothing to bring this situation about; it just happened to him. Alipio appears to be a religious man, and several times he suggests that life is in the hands of God ("God dictates"). God has been merciful to him in sending him a young wife. This suggests that even in unpromising circumstances, life may always take a turn for the better.

Style

Structure and Style

"Immigration Blues" is notable for the simplicity of its style and structure. The diction is simple, and there is little use of figurative language. The story unfolds in one scene only, in the same place, over the course of only a few hours.

Memory

Embedded within a simple frame are many stories, including that of Mrs. Zafra and her marriage of convenience to escape deportation, as well as the reminiscences of Alipio about his youthful adventures with his friend Carlito and his obviously happy marriage to his wife. It is largely through this technique of using memories related by the characters, rather than through anything Alipio does or says in the present, that the story creates empathy in the reader for its main character. Alipio's conversation is ordinary, but his memories have power to charm—memories of how he and Carlito were young gallants who wowed the girls with their cooking or how Seniang used to wear his jacket and his slippers when he was at work because "you keep me warm all day." These memories add richness and depth to the story and the characterization.

Historical Context

Filipino Literature in English

The first Filipino literature published in English in the United States was in the early 1930s, a decade before Santos's arrival in the country. The writer who made this breakthrough was José Garcia Villa (1914–1997), whose poems and stories were published by Scribner's in 1933 as *Footnote to Youth: Tales of the Philippines and Others.* Villa lived in the United States, and his short stories, which were highly praised by critics, were included in *Best American Short Stories of 1932* and *Best American Short Stories of 1933.* Despite the success of his fiction, however, during the 1930s Villa decided to write only lyric poetry. His *Selected Poems and New* was published in 1958. Although scholars acknowledge the merits of his pioneering work, Villa is little read today.

In the 1940s, poet and short-story writer Carlos Bulosan (1913–1956) came to the forefront of Filipino writers. Like Santos, Bulosan chronicled the lives of Filipino immigrants in the United States. His stories appeared mainly in magazines such as the *New Yorker.* His book of satirical, humorous poems, *The Laughter of My Father,* was published in 1944 by Harcourt, Brace and was warmly received by readers. It was followed by the autobiographical *America Is in the Heart* (1946), which remains an influential work today.

Also in the 1940s, Filipino immigrant N. V. M. Gonzalez (1915–1999) began publishing short stories, some of which appear in book form in *Children of the Ash-Covered Loam* (1954) and *Selected Stories* (1964). Gonzalez also wrote novels, including *The Winds of April* (1940), *Seven Hills Away* (1947), and *A Season of Grace* (1956). Like Santos, Gonzalez portrays the lives of Filipinos in the United States, although Gonzalez writes mainly of graduate students and other young or middle-aged people who visit but do not remain in the United States.

In the late 1950s, Linda Ty-Casper (1931–) began publishing. Her novel *The Peninsulars* (1964) is about the influence of Spanish colonization on the Philippines in the mid-eighteenth century. Ty-Casper has since published a total of ten novels and three short-story collections.

During the 1950s and 1960s, Santos wrote some of his best work, but it was published mainly in the Philippines. It was not until 1979 that Santos's collection *Scent of Apples* was published in the United States.

Much Filipino work published in the United States deals with the problem of Filipino identity. Filipinos are a people with a colonial past, having been ruled by Spain for 300 years, followed by half a century of American rule. Filipinos who immigrated to the United States had to face issues of exile, isolation, and racism. They had to forge an identity for themselves that could bridge the gap between their cultural and racial heritage as Filipinos and their new status as Filipino Americans, living in a culture very different from their own.

The Filipino Experience in America

The first wave of Filipino immigration to the United States occurred between 1906 and 1934, when Filipinos were recruited to California as agricultural workers. Alipio and his friend Carlito in "Immigration Blues" probably arrived in California during this period, although no details are given of their occupations. Filipinos also immigrated to Hawaii, where they worked on sugarcane plantations, and in the 1920s many immigrated to the

Compare & Contrast

- **1970s:** According to the 1980 census, there are 774,652 Filipinos living in the United States. This constitutes 0.3 percent of the total population.

  Today: According to the 2000 census, Filipino Americans number 1.9 million. This is up from 1.4 million in 1990. The largest Filipino population is in California, at 918,678. Hawaii, Illinois, New Jersey, New York, and Washington also have substantial Filipino populations. In Washington, the number of Filipinos has increased by 50 percent since 1990.

- **1970s:** Filipino immigration to the United States increases due to the Immigration Act of 1965, which loosened restrictions on immigration from Asia. Once in the country, Filipinos are allowed, like immigrants from other countries, to bring their immediate family to join them, subject to visa approvals.

  Today: Since the 1970s, the time necessary for approval of a visa application for a brother or sister has grown much longer. The process can literally take decades. Some Filipinos who immigrated during the 1980s are, therefore, still waiting for the immigration of their families from the Philippines to the United States to be completed.

- **1970s:** With Filipino American writers such as Santos and Linda Ty-Casper publishing their work in the United States, Filipino American writing begins to make its way into the mainstream of American literature.

  Today: A new generation of Filipino Americans is making its mark on literature, in a variety of literary forms and genres. Authors include Jessica Hagedorn (whose novel *Dogeaters* [1990] was nominated for the National Book Award), Ninotchka Rosca, Epifanio San Juan, and Michelle Skinner.

Pacific Northwest. Beginning in 1934, however, the Tydings-McDuffie Act severely limited Filipino immigration to the United States.

Many Filipino Americans served in the American armed forces during World War II. Although ''Immigration Blues'' does not mention it, the fact that Alipio received his U.S. citizenship after the end of World War II suggests that he may have fought in the U.S. Army, although it is possible he would have been too old to serve.

A new wave of Filipino immigration to the United States began after the passage of the Immigration Act of 1965, which loosened restrictions on immigration from Asia. Between 1965 and 1984, 664,938 Filipinos entered the country (in ''Immigration Blues,'' this is the period during which both Mrs. Zafra and Monica secure their immigration status by marrying American citizens). The rate of immigration increased in part because of political and economic uncertainty in the Philippines. This wave of immigration is sometimes called the ''brain

drain,'' because it consisted mainly of professionals, including doctors and lawyers.

Filipino Americans have at all periods faced discrimination because of their national origins. Many have been confined to low-status, low-income jobs. In Santos's story ''The Day the Dancers Came,'' which is published in *Scent of Apples*, a Filipino immigrant becomes an American citizen in 1945 and joins the workforce. This is his experience:

> To a new citizen, work meant many places and many ways: factories and hotels, waiter and cook. A timeless drifting; once he tended a rose garden and took care of a hundred-year-old veteran of a border war. As a menial in a hospital in Cook County, all day he handled filth and gore.

In the early days of Filipino immigration to California, Filipinos were sometimes banned from hotels, restaurants, and swimming pools. In 1926 antimiscegenation laws were passed in California that banned Filipinos from marrying white women. This kind of prejudice is apparent in some of Santos's stories. In "Ash Wednesday," for example (published in *You Lovely People*), a Boston family turns their daughter Muriel out of the house when she decides to marry a Filipino.

Santos refers to the early Filipino experience in America in his essay, "Pilipino Old Timers: Fact and Fiction":

> Prior to World War II and as late as the 1950s, the Pilipino immigrant was unwanted wherever he went, in the big and the small cities of the United States. As Pilipinos came in increasing numbers, they caused mounting resentment, particularly on the Pacific Coast where riots against them flared, which gave rise to violence and accusations.

Critical Overview

"Immigration Blues" won the *New Letters* award for fiction from the University of Missouri at Kansas City in 1977. In 1978 it was listed as an honorable mention in *Best American Short Stories*. In 1981 the second edition of *Scent of Apples*, the book in which the story appears, received an American Book Award from New York's Pre-Columbus Federation.

Anthony Tan, writing in *Silliman Journal*, calls the stories in *Scent of Apples* "emotionally poignant" and says "Immigration Blues" is "a story of understated pathos and the very human and selfish motive of marriage for convenience." He also notes that all the stories in *Scent of Apples* share the common themes of "exile, loneliness, and isolation."

Tan argues that the stories fall short of greatness because the characters are left groping in states of isolation, denied a moment of illumination that would enable them to make sense of their lives. However, Maxine Hong Kingston, writing in the *New York Times Book Review*, takes the view that Santos "places . . . rare incidents of joy at the center of his stories." She also praises Santos's "very delicate, very fine" writing that "gently" portrays the difficult experience of being a Filipino man in America.

"Immigration Blues" exhibits the simplicity of style that some critics in the Philippines have seen as a fault in Santos's work. But Miguel A. Bernad, writing in *Bamboo and the Greenwood Tree: Essays on Filipino Literature in English*,

A Filipino worker in California in the late 1930s, similar to Alipio in "Immigration Blues"

views this simplicity as a virtue. He writes of Santos's short stories:

> The language is simple but weighted with emotion. It is pitched in low key, but the emotion is implicit in the tone, atmosphere, narrative tempo, length or brevity of sentence, the rhythm that sometimes approaches musicality, and the sparing but carefully chosen imagery.

Criticism

Bryan Aubrey

Aubrey holds a Ph.D. in English and has published many articles on twentieth-century literature. In this essay, Aubrey discusses "Immigration Blues" as a study in old age and assesses the degree to which the story embodies or rejects the negative stereotypes of the old that are common in American culture.

Santos is known in the United States as a writer who chronicled the difficult lives of Filipino immigrants,

What Do I Read Next?

- Santos's *Dwell in the Wilderness: Selected Short Stories* (1985) contains eighteen stories from the early part of Santos's career. Written between 1930 and 1941, these stories are set in the rural towns and villages in the Philippines familiar to Santos in his youth and early manhood.

- *Growing Up Filipino: Stories for Young Adults* (2003), edited by Cecilia Manguerra Brainard, contains twenty-nine short stories, most of which have been written since the turn of the twenty-first century. The authors include those who live in the Philippines as well as American-born Filipinos. The stories reflect a wide range of issues that Filipino youth encounter.

- *Contemporary Fiction by Filipinos in America* (1998), edited by Cecilia Manguerra Brainard, includes work by prominent Filipino writers such as Linda Ty-Casper, N. V. M. Gonzalez, Cecilia Manguerra Brainard, Greg Sarris, Marianne Villanueva, Vince Gotera, Eileen Tabios, and John Silva.

- *From Exile to Diaspora: Versions of the Filipino Experience in the United States* (1998), by E. San Juan Jr, is the most comprehensive examination of the history and current status of Filipino Americans.

- *On Becoming Filipino: Selected Writings of Carlos Bulosan* (1995), edited by E. San Juan Jr, is the first collection of Bulosan's short stories, essays, poetry, and correspondence to focus on the Filipino American experience. Bulosan was one of the pioneer Filipino American writers, and his work covers the period from the 1930s through the 1950s.

---

especially those "old timers" (as they became known) who came to the country from the 1920s through the 1940s. The old timers remained in the United States for the rest of their lives, but they never lost their sense of exile from the Philippines, and they were often lonely and isolated.

"Immigration Blues" is one such story. The protagonist Alipio is an old timer who lives alone in California and still thinks often of his homeland. But more than being a study of a Filipino immigrant from a certain era, "Immigration Blues," as well as other stories by Santos, are studies in old age.

In American culture, the elderly do not generally occupy positions of honor and respect. In a society that values youth, success, and material productivity, the old are relegated to a position on the sidelines of life. What they contribute to society is not so easily measured as it is for those in the prime of life. In addition, popular culture, in everything from television to jokes (the cognitive lapses of the elderly often being the subject of humor), creates negative stereotypes of old people. Numer-

ous studies of attitudes to the elderly on the part of the young as well as the middle-aged suggest that old age is viewed as a time of helplessness, loneliness, dependence, senility, and passivity. Old people spend most of their time sitting around and doing nothing—or so many people appear to believe. Not all the studies suggest such a negative view, and over the last twenty years, as people live longer, more healthy, and more productive lives, this view of the old could well be slowly changing. But it remains deeply ingrained. The term "ageism" was coined to describe such biased attitudes to the old.

With that background in mind, how does Santos depict his old characters? Does he reflect the negative stereotype or does he undermine it?

The first thing to note is that Alipio is a character drawn realistically from life. When at the age of eighty-two Santos wrote his memoir *Memory's Fictions: A Personal History*, he confessed that in his old age he had come in some respects to resemble Alipio. Like his character he spent much of his time alone, and also like Alipio he was given to reminiscing, wondering whether his friends all over the world were well and knew he was still alive. "I have become my character, a character I created before I knew what direction my life would take," Santos writes. In his article "Pilipino Old Timers: Fact and Fiction," he again quotes a passage given to Alipio in "Immigration Blues" and uses it to point out that there is no difference between the "old timer" in real life and his fictional representation.

So what is the nature of that real life fictional representation? An examination of Alipio seems in some ways to suggest a negative picture of old age, one that confirms the kind of stereotypes that researchers in aging and advocates for the elderly deplore.

This is Alipio: he lives in the past a lot (exactly the way the old are routinely perceived); he is in poor health since his car accident; he is hard of hearing; he does not have enough to keep him busy. He even prepares lunch early because he has nothing else to do. He spends a lot of his time sitting on his porch watching construction work and nodding to strangers as they pass. He has few visitors, and he hardly speaks to anyone as there is no one to whom he wants to speak. Gerontologists (those who study the aging process) sometimes call this kind of withdrawal "retreatism" or "disengagement." In many cases it is considered a defense mechanism: the aged may convince themselves that they do not wish to participate in social life, or do not mind being alone, rather than face the painful fact that they, like most others, are dependent on other people, and not having enough people in their life is a cause of loneliness and distress.

There is a deep sadness about Alipio. He still broods over his wife's death, and since he has no children, he is truly alone in the world. When it transpires that often he whiles away the time by watching television or listening to the radio until he falls asleep, the impression given is of a man who has given up on life. This is a sign of what gerontologists call "alienation." As Zena Smith Blau describes it in *Aging in a Changing Society*:

> Alienation is an extreme form of maladaptation, characterized by the feeling that "there is just no point in living," by feelings of regret over the past, by the idea that "things just keep getting worse and worse," and by abandonment of all future plans.

Those at risk for developing an attitude of alienation include those who, like Alipio, have

"This story's ending shows that Alipio defies the stereotypical notion that the old are rigid and stuck in their ways."

recently lost a spouse. Being a husband or a wife is a major role in life, like that of having a productive occupation, which keeps people engaged in the world and sustains their morale, their sense of usefulness.

What it is like to be old and have neither of these things is also apparent from another of Santos's stories, "The Day the Dancers Came," which appears in *Scent of Apples*. The main character is a Filipino called Fil. He is fifty years old, which may not seem very old, but it is his age that is emphasized. He looks old, and he feels old. Old age has prematurely come upon him. This is how he experiences it:

> A weariness, a mist covering all things. You don't have to look at your face in the mirror to know that you are old, suddenly old, grown useless for a lot of things and too late for all the dreams you had wrapped up well against a day of need.

Fil lives in a Chicago apartment with another old timer named Tony, who is dying of a wasting disease. Fil is excited because a troupe of dancers from the Philippines is coming to Chicago. He plans to introduce himself to them, give them a tour of Chicago, and then invite them back to his apartment for a Filipino meal. But what happens when he tries to put his plan into action is nothing like what he imagined. When he arrives at the hotel where the dancers are to perform, they and their entourage are already milling around in the lobby. Fil feels unwelcome in the midst of all these beautiful young people. He is conscious of how old his face looks, and his "horny hands." Everyone is talking but he is able to talk to no one. The little speech he had rehearsed in his apartment now strikes him as foolish; they would only laugh at him. He eventually plucks up the courage to invite two of the young male dancers to his apartment, but they just walk away with hardly a word. Fil tries again, and is ignored again. He might as well be invisible.

Fil's story is a sad one, made even sadder by the fact that his friend Tony is dying. Soon Fil will be entirely alone. Can the old timers be redeemed? Is there anything about them that offers hope, or is old age everything the cultural negative stereotypes present it to be? The answer is yes, there is redemption, of a kind. Let us return to Alipio.

Alipio is a religious man. His explanation for the loss of his wife is that God took her. And in his eyes it was a matter of God's will regarding whether he would walk again after his car accident. Monica notices and comments on his strong belief in God. Toward the end of the story, Alipio twice uses the phrase, "God dictates." This does not seem merely to be a routine statement of faith but one that has real practical consequences for him. He is aware that life flows on, controlled by some force (which he chooses to call God) that is beyond the petty strivings of the individual. Individuals may have their plans and their designs, but there is a larger pattern at work too, the working of the divine in the world. Alipio is aware of this. One might call it wisdom. When many other things have departed forever, wisdom is there for the old. In this respect, despite his many failings, Alipio offers a glimpse of the archetype of the wise old man, the man who has lived long and knows the way things are. And in this lies his salvation. Look at how he reacts when Monica suddenly comes into his life. His response could not have been predicted from what has been shown of him up to this point. He had no thought of taking another wife, but when Monica arrives and her intentions become known, he goes along with what God sends. He has won a new lease on life.

This story's ending shows that Alipio defies the stereotypical notion that the old are rigid and stuck in their ways. The message is clear: there is still hope for new things, transformations can still happen and in the most unexpected of ways, even when one does not ask for them or seek them. Life is eternally unpredictable, and as Alipio shows, the old can be as swift as the young to adapt to new circumstances and accept what comes to them. Alipio deserves his new young wife. She may not be another Sensiang, his first wife, but one senses that he will no longer be falling asleep watching television, or aimlessly sitting around the house doing nothing.

In "Immigration Blues," then, Santos presents both sides of the coin, negative and positive images of old age. He shows that life is many-sided and cannot be put in a box with only one label.

Source: Bryan Aubrey, Critical Essay on "Immigration Blues," in *Short Stories for Students,* Gale, 2004.

Elaine H. Kim

In the following essay excerpt, Kim discusses Santos's focus on Filipino laborer exiles who came to the United States after World War II.

The theme of the immigrant as permanent exile has held a special fascination for Filipino immigrant writer Bienvenido N. Santos, whose short stories set in the Filipino immigrant community in America are attempts to give voice to the exile in Asian American literature. Santos is writing as one of them. He had come to this country as a cultural envoy immediately prior to World War II. Forced to extend his sojourn because of the war, Santos traveled widely in America. During this time, he says, he was profoundly moved by the lives of his Filipino compatriots here. Although he was supposed to work towards cultural understanding between the Philippines and the United States and to study English and American literature, he "studied instead the Filipino heart." When he returned to the Philippines after the war, Santos was "sad and disheartened . . . but full of stories about his lonely and lost fellow exiles in America."

"In memory of the Pinoys whose lives I shared," Santos published a collection of short stories, *You Lovely People,* in the Philippines in 1965. Santos' portrait of Filipino American life in the 1940s is a tale of men wandering, sometimes lost, in a hostile and sterile climate. It is a journey from bouyant innocence to degraded experience, which can only be endured because the exile still cherishes his memories of home.

An oldtimer helps the narrator of the stories, Ben, understand how the degradation of Filipinos in America has taken place: "I have seen many a child . . . lost in a thousand fogs of the big and small cities of the country. Those are stories for you, Ben, but they are all sad stories. All our stories are sad." Ben learns the story of Nanoy, who dies alone in a vermin-infested basement room; of Delfin, whose blonde wife keeps him waiting on the front steps of their apartment building while she seduces other men inside; of Pete, whose white wife drowns their sons in the bathtub when driven to distraction by their neighbors' racial taunts; and of Tan, whose white wife becomes an alcoholic after she is rejected by her friends and family for marrying a Filipino: "Lord, the things Filipinos do in this country. The things we say. What keeps us living on like this from day to day, from loveless kiss to loveless kiss, from venomed touch to venomed touch. . . . [T]hey are blessed ones like Nanoy, though it took him too long to die.''

The transformation of innocent, hopeful young Filipino immigrants eager for a life of freedom and happiness into a community of lonely exiles is gradual and irreversible. As the years pass, their glowing letters filled with ''bright hopes for the future and tales of the glitter of life in the new country'' cease, even while their aging parents continue to wait for the few dollars they hope to receive, ''weaving bright dreams of the future.'' Meanwhile, the son drifts from one menial job to another and is eventually engulfed by the depravity that surrounds him:

> Soon he was gambling himself, laughing with the men when they laughed about vulgar things he himself now knew. . . . Now the drifting from one city to another. Here would be new faces. would be a new lease on life. But it was the same brown face everywhere, the same shortcomings, the same pitfalls. And, the things he saw, the things he knew, the things he heard from the drunken lips of whores. Who was good, was there any good face, any good heart that remained so in this crowd?

The promise of America ultimately becomes a song repeated by cynical bellhops in their rooming houses for laughs. The monument to Lincoln, the poor boy who became president, becomes the background for souvenir photographs of Filipino men with their white girlfriends. The Gettysburg Address, which they had diligently memorized as school children in the Philippines, becomes, like the ''landmarks of American history . . . meaningless . . . meaningless.''

The illusion of America is replaced by a fleeting dream of the homeland, pastoral, lyrical, and no longer accessible to them. For Ben, it is the memory of bamboo groves and the fragrance of lime in his mother's hair. For some men it is the dream of carrying huge bags filled with silver dollars home to their families. For others it is the memory of their now dead wives' dark and trusting eyes. For one man, it is a faded, much-fingered photograph of an unknown Filipino girl, who has come to represent home to him. When Fabia asks Ben if the Filipina has changed during his twenty years of exile in America, Ben is careful with his answer because he knows that ''all these years, he must have held on to certain ideals, certain beliefs, even illusions peculiar to exile.'' Since there were so few Filipino women in America, years might pass during which

> ''Among the new immigrants, Santos says he feels like an 'oldtimer' and wonders if his presence makes them think of their old parents back home. Consistently, he returns to his interest in the older, laboring exile.''

a Filipino never saw a Filipino woman. Once, when Ambo is hospitalized, a Filipino nurse attends him. Just seeing her makes him want to live: ''[T]hrough his fevered mind, she was his sister, she was his mother, she was his sweetheart, she was his wife, ministering to him, talking to him with love and he was home again.''

The burden of the exile is the fear of dying alone in a hostile land. Kang had felt it keenly, and the terrible fear of dying among strangers far from home loomed ominously before him. What had kept Ambo from suicide in moments of profound despair and loneliness was the hope that he was remembered at home, more than ''a named mentioned now and then, casually, always without love,'' more than ''a blurred face in a picture fast yellowing with the years'':

> I've gone hungry for days and days in the Loop, looking vacantly at stores; in vermin-infested little rooms among the shiftless and unwashed; and I didn't care at all if I went to bed and woke up no more. . . . I thought of hurling myself into the river, but now I wanted to live; I mean, if I died, I wanted to die not here, please not here, in the faraway land, but somewhere in the islands where it is possible someone yet lives who loves me.

Even those who have lost real contact with their homes are gripped with a common anxiety when the fighting in the Philippines threatens even their distant illusions:

> Little brown men with sad, oily faces, lines deep under the eyes and around the mouth; frightened eyes, like those of a hunted deer; yellow figures and rough, hardened with labor, chafed from steaming water and the touch of hot plates and glasses. We have known of

hunger away from home, ten years, twenty, thirty, a lifetime. What place will be bombed next, we ask, what do you think? My hometown?

In the end, the Filipino in America survives the loss of his innocence and illusions because of his ability to accept reality. Ambo gives up pretending someone is waiting for him in the islands: perhaps the answer lies in "wanting to remain here forever, not wanting to go home no more. Six feet of sod's six feet of sod—anywhere—and worms look pretty much the same in any climate, under any flag."

The central contradiction of Filipino immigrant life during this period has been described as alienation or feelings of displacement among those who have left a traditional society where community, kinship, and mutual support are the basis of individual mental health:

> Filipinos . . . traditionally have enjoyed a highly developed sense of community (*bayanihan*) dependent on face-to-face (*damay*) relations. They have drawn their identity from extended family lines. . . . [In America, they faced] both physical distances between themselves and their motherland [which was evolving in their absence into a place to which they could no longer easily return], and the psychological distances between the Pinoys and earlier migrants from Europe and East Asia. . . . The Pinoy's expectation of *belonging* to others and not just to himself somehow had to be satisfied.

Finally, Ambo recognizes that his folk loyalty and community is the community of exiles to which he does in fact belong. This fraternity of shared suffering and common understanding is the most meaningful aspect of their lives; together they are the "homeless waifs . . . the forgotten children of long lost mothers and fathers, as grown up men without childhood, bastards in an indifferent country." But they are as kin to one another:

> The Filipino members of the orchestra were looking at Leo and Val; the boys acknowledged their glances and smiles passed through music. The glances said, Filipino? Yes. And the smiles said, countryman, do I know you, or have we met before, or shall we meet perhaps, it's a familiar face, Countryman; this music is for you; my steps are easy, happy moving steps because the music is for you, Countryman.

The themes in *You Lovely People* are brought together in one story that Santos wrote in 1966. "The Day the Dancers Came," which won the *Philippines Free Press* annual short story contest that year, is a concise and unified expression of the conditions of Filipino exiles in America and their fleeting confrontation with the ideal that has sus-

tained them through their years of exile. Filipino Acayan, retired special post office policeman, former hospital, hotel, and factory worker, waiter, cook, gardener, and bearer of "several jobs that born no names," had "never looked young." His life, emblematic of the lives of thousands of other Filipino men who came to the land of golden opportunity to eke out a living on its fringes, unable to make enough money to return to their native lands but prevented by anti-miscegenation laws from marrying and starting families, has passed him by unaware like an aborted foetus. Fil has not been permitted to develop a full life, and he suddenly finds himself an old man: "In the beginning, the words he often heard were: too young, too young; but all of a sudden, too young became too old, too late. What had happened in between? A weariness, a mist covering all things." Fil had worked as a menial in a Cook County hospital, tending a row of bottles on a shelf:

> [E]ach bottle containing a stage of the human embryo in preservatives, from the lizard-like foetus of a few days, through the newly-born infant, with the position unchanged, cold and cowering and afraid. Sometimes in his sleep, Fil dreamed of preserving the stages after infancy, but somewhere he drew a blank like the many years between too young and too old.

Fil Acayan's marginal existence has made his life a shadow, a recording to be played back on a portable tape recorder, which he calls his "magic sound mirror." In his isolation he has learned to make the lonely world around him meaningful through fantasy: staring at the ceiling over many years, he begins to see landscapes, and rivers in the stains and cobwebs. He imagines civilizations waxing and waning as the ceiling is changed by soot and age. Staring at the ceiling becomes a game he can play by himself while forgetting the passage of time.

When the dancers from Manila come to Chicago, he hopes to taste his lost youth and his homeland through them. He wants to invite them, his *paisanos,* to his apartment for *adobo,* to take them sightseeing in "his" Chicago. From the point of view of the dancers, it would be senseless to eat *adobo* with some old Filipino exile in Chicago. The decades Fil has lost between youth and old age divide them permanently. Fil, like many Meiji Japanese, Ch'ing Chinese, and Yi Dynasty Koreans, has been cut off from his homeland by the years between their arrival in America and today. Even his dialect, which he speaks in "florid, sentimental, poetic" style into the tape recorder, is the language of a past not known to the dancers and strange to their modern ears. Fil demands the impossible of them: he wants to relive through them the lost period between his infancy and old age, the period that spans his life in America. So the "beautiful people" reject his awkward, diffident advances, brushing past him, laughing and chatting at the hotel, their hair pomaded and exuding the fragrance of "long forgotten essence of *camia, ilang-ilang, dama de noche*." Rebuffed, Fil fantasizes that, if they had accepted his invitation, they would have returned to the islands to tell their countrymen of the kind, amusing old Filipino who took them into his apartment:

> They would tell their folks: We met a kind, old man, who took us to his apartment. It was not much of a place. It was old—like him. When we sat on the sofa in the living room, the bottom sank heavily, the broken springs touching the floor. But what a cook that man was! And how kind! We never thought that rice and *adobo* could be that delicious. And the chicken *relleno*! When someone asked him what the stuffing was—we had never tasted anything like it— he smiled, saying, 'From heaven's supermarket,' touching his head and pressing his heart like a clown.

Since the moment that would have served him as a memory of his relived lost youth remains only a fantasy, Fil records the dancers' performance on his tape recorder. He can then play back the performance, experiencing the clapping bamboo poles, the dancers' bare brown legs, "the sounds of life and death in the old country," the Igorots, the lovers, the gongs, and the feasts of his mislaid youth and distant homeland over and over again in the narrow confines of his apartment. Fil knows that he will never go back to the Philippines.

The only meaningful reality in Fil's life is his friendship with his roommate, a retired porter. Tony is Fil's only family; like *manong* Fil, he was brought to America for menial labor and then relegated to a life of poverty and isolation. The two men share their exile huddling together in their loneliness, suspended between a dimly recalled homeland and the inaccessible fringes of American society. Fil is the dreamer; Tony is the realist. Tony knows that they will die in America, alone and discarded, while Fil dreams of the islands. Tony does not even attend the dancers' performance.

Fil's fantasies are abruptly interrupted by his realization that Tony is really dying, that he may lose the only family and friend in his life, the only one who has shared his floating life, "stranded without help" in the middle of a shoreless and indifferent sea.

The intended audience for the stories is less the American reader than the intellectual in the Philippines, whose idealization of American life and culture and aristocratic dissociation from the low-born Pinoy Santos challenges in stories of the shared suffering and alienation of Filipinos of all social classes. There is an undertone of reproach in the portrayal of the contrast between the Filipino exile in America, who has sustained himself on dreams of the homeland, and the "beautiful people" of contemporary Manila, who little resemble the ideal cherished by the exile. In "The Long Way Home," rich Filipinos in posh coffee shops and bayside rivieras discuss in fluent Castilian or in "psuedo-Yankee twang" their plans to leave their war-torn mother country for Europe or America, "where everything can be bought for money." Santos is particularly concerned with the contrast between the Filipinos who are desperate to come to America and become completely assimilated into American life and the "oldtimers" who "did not want to become American citizens because they planned to return home to the Philippines, living the remainder of their days in the old villages, where their roots are." The irony is that most of the oldtimers never made it home again.

Although Santos has not devoted his literary attention exclusively to the Filipino American experience, the life of the exile has continued to haunt him. He made three more trips to America, at first as a Rockefeller and Guggenheim fellow and later as an Exchange Fulbright Professor. In 1972, he and his family were preparing to leave for the Philippines when martial law was declared. The novel that he had scheduled for publication was disapproved and canceled; and although he had been slated to teach in the fall semester, the schools had been closed. And so Santos himself has become an unwilling exile, living in America indefinitely, suspended between the same two worlds of the oldtimers about which he had so poignantly written.

For a time, he tried to write about the recent city-bred and middle-class Filipino immigrants, who have been settling in the United States according to the new Immigration and Naturalization preferences established in 1965. Santos tried a "funny novel," *What the Hell for You Left Your Heart in San Francisco,* about "the new breed of Filipino immigrants, professionals and businessmen who lived in mansions on hills above the babel of the narrow streets, or in the exclusive residential sections away from the smell of the harbor and the fish markets." But there is something prosaic and distasteful about this "new breed," who according to Santos are "independent, luckier, . . . smart," and callous:

> They know all the answers or seem to, anyhow; they glow with confidence, a beautiful people. . . . No loneliness for them. Loneliness is a disease, a terminal disease, they say in so many words, and they talk a lot. They hold glittering parties around their swimming pools, the diamonds on the fingers outshining the light in their eyes. No nostalgia for the new breed. The talk closest to home revolved around the current peso-dollar exchange, tax exemptions, loopholes in the tax laws and proven ways of circumventing [*sic*] them. Investments. New car models. At the last party I attended, they were comparing the relative power and clarity of their C.B. radios and how to keep them from being stolen.

Among the new immigrants, Santos says he feels like an "oldtimer" and wonders if his presence makes them think of their old parents back home. Consistently, he returns to his interest in the older, laboring exile:

> I could not forget the smell of decay and death in the apartments of the old-timers among my countrymen who sat out the evening of their lives before television sets in condemned buildings in downtown San Francisco. Then the grin in both story and writer kept getting twisted in a grimace of pain close to tears.

Santos cannot resist focusing on the old exiles, because "now I realize that perhaps I have also been writing about myself.

Source: Elaine H. Kim, "New Directions," in *Asian American Literature: An Introduction to the Writings and Their Social Context,* Temple University Press, 1982, pp. 265–72.

Anthony Tan

In the following essay, Tan discusses the stories in Santos's Scent of Apples *and their common theme of expatriation and its effects.*

Scent of Apples: A Collection of Stories (Seattle and London: University of Washington Press, 1979, 178 pages) is Bienvenido N. Santos's first book to be published in the United States, but fifteen of the sixteen stories in this collection have appeared before in two books published in the Philippines: eleven in *You Lovely People* (Bookmark, 1955) and four in *The Day the Dancers Came* (Bookmark, 1967). Thus, all the stories in this new collection are familiar to Filipino readers except the first one, "Immigration Blues," whose significance in the book, apart from its own separate virtue as a story of understated pathos and the very human and selfish motive of marriage for convenience, is that it brings

to the present decade the continuing story of Filipinos in America.

The common themes of these stories about Filipinos in America are universal themes of exile, loneliness, and isolation. Into these themes Santos has folded the special flavor of Filipino nostalgia for home, which, for the exiles, meant also the past. When Santos achieves a perfect blending of the universal themes and the indigenous sensibility, the results are such emotionally poignant works as the title story and the prize-winning "The Day the Dancers Came," two stories in which nostalgia accentuates the sense of exile and isolation.

For one reason or another Santos's Filipino expatriates stay on in America even when their dream of success in the land of plenty has finally vanished. Ambo, the narrator in many stories, has attempted to return, only to be disappointed at home, not so much by the yearly typhoon that plagues his home in the Bicol region as by the betrayal of a friend whom he used to help in Washington, D.C. So he seeks another passage, perhaps a final one, back to America. Celestino Fabia can never return to his native shore in the Visayas because, having stayed twenty years on a remote farm in Michigan, no one will remember him. His only link with the Philippines is a faded picture of a Filipina he does not even know. Filemon Acayan can only make a symbolic return by welcoming and attempting to entertain the Bayanihan Dancers in Chicago. When they turn down his offer to drive them around the city and to eat at his apartment, he makes what seems a desperate effort at preserving the last moorings with his country: he attends their show and records their songs and the sounds of their agile, dancing feet doing the *tinikling*. However, when he plays the tape recorder at his apartment for the benefit of his dying friend, another Filipino exile, Filemon presses the wrong button, and in one clumsy moment erases what he has tried so hard to preserve—his last link with his people and country—thus making his isolation more devastating and complete.

Many more like him never return, even symbolically, and many do not even dream of returning. Lost and confused in strange cities among strange people, they drift aimlessly, and to forget a weariness which is more than physical they play poker or billiards, and drink and seek momentary solace in the faithless arms of women. They have become spiritual drifters, suffering as much ruin as the war-ravaged Philippines. In a sense, they are the people to whom the words of Father Ocampo in "For These Ruins" accurately apply: "We have seen pictures of our blasted cities. But there are ruins other than the eyes can see."

It is the mark of Santos's genius as a fictionist to have portrayed these ruins in story after story, to have given a spiritual and cultural counterpart to the physical ruins suffered by the Philippines during the last war. To be sure, the stories of Santos in this collection are not about the Filipinos in the Philippines who, having suffered the physical effects of war, have also suffered its spiritual effects. The scarred psyche caused by the war remains for other Filipino writers to record, and many have attempted to do so. Having spent the war years in America, Santos could only write about those who have been, literally, far from battlefronts. Yet, it is a further measure of his genius that his stories are no less memorable and true, his characters no less lonely, for that fact.

If the outbreak of the war gave Santos the personal opportunity to travel and lecture extensively in America and enabled him to meet many Filipino expatriates, the consequent occupation of the Philippines by the enemy gave him the artistic fulcrum to elevate reality into art. It fired his imagination so that he began to see the war as one more dimension in the isolation of the expatriates. It became for him as a writer, if not as a man, the ultimate symbol of the *lostness* of his countrymen in America. I say this notwithstanding the fact that in the present book only three stories have something to do with the war, and even here the war is a mere backdrop: because in many stories he has transmuted the physical ruins of his country into the spiritual ruins of his countrymen abroad.

In exploring the many dimensions of the isolation of the expatriates, Santos, however, has not stopped with the war. War, after all, is a historically contained event, and although a people may suffer its consequences long after it is over, the isolation it imposes on its victims comes from the outside and from foreign enemies. Besides, the Filipinos about whom Santos has written were not direct victims of the war. If they suffered from isolation from their country as a result of the war, their isolation is somehow lessened by their own helplessness and by a great deal of historical inevitability. What is more painful is that isolation for which they were responsible and which to a certain degree they could prevent. In almost all the stories this is the kind of isolation that Santos has tried to explore.

> ... 'Immigration Blues,' whose significance in the book, apart from its own separate virtue as a story of understated pathos ... is that it brings to the present decade the continuing story of Filipinos in America."

There are at least four sources of this isolation. One is excessive nostalgia for the homeland. Another is betrayal by fellow men, by fellow-Pinoy. The third is the death of a dream of success, ironic in that the dream dies in the land which has caught the imagination of the world, and of Filipinos especially, as the land of promise, the land of opportunity. The characters of Santos, after a brief fling with the ideal, wake up one morning to find that America has turned out to be the land of unfulfilled promises, of lost opportunities. The last source of isolation is the confusion brought about by trying to live in two culturally different worlds.

Two of the best stories in this collection explore the pathos of nostalgia. In "Scent of Apples," Celestino Fabia travels thirty miles from his farm to the city just to listen to a Filipino talk about the Philippines. This certainly is not bad, but his keeping a picture of a Filipina when in fact he is married to an American is something else. It is not fair to his wife, to say the least. His wife happens to be a faithful woman, who saved him from freezing in the snow when he had appendicitis, and who worked as a scrub woman in the hospital to pay the bills. She is worthy of her namesake, the biblical Ruth. He has a good-looking son and an apple orchard which gives him more apples than he can sell. The surplus apples rot in the storeroom, and he gives them to the pigs. His wife, his son, and the apple orchard are abundance enough, but his excessive nostalgia for home, where nobody remembers him, makes him blind to all these blessings. He wastes his abundance, like the apples he gives to the pigs, throwing, so to speak, the proverbial pearls to the swine. Hence, we note in passing, the aptness of the apple-symbol and the title. This story should make the exile rethink his idea of home: not a place where you were born and grew up, but where you are at present, where your love is. But man, especially the exile, is an incorrigible dreamer. How often in the solitude of an exile do the images of home crowd into his lonely mind! And in this lies the pathos of the story.

Another such dreamer is Filemon Acayan in "The Day the Dancers Came." Growing old in a foreign country is sad enough, but if one could accept it as inevitable, if one tried to make the best of the situation, one would suffer less. This seems to be what Acayan is trying to do in Chicago until he hears of the coming of the Filipino dancers. Then he begins to dream: welcome the dancers, entertain them, show them around the city, invite them to eat Filipino dishes at his apartment, so that when they return to the Philippines they will remember him. But all his efforts at trying to establish a link with his countrymen are frustrated. When he accidentally erases what he has recorded in his "sound mirror" he loses the last link with what he knows as home. In a symbolic way, this underscores the irony and pathos of longing.

"The Door" and "Letter: The Faraway Summer" explore the other source of isolation. Betrayal, especially by a friend, is so crushing that it could burst even the mighty heart of a Caesar. This allusion to Caesar is not uncalled for. Santos himself deliberately, albeit implicitly, alludes to Caesar's "Et tu, Brute." In the story "The Door," Delfin knows that his American wife is unfaithful, but he cannot do anything, does not do anything, because he loves her. She entertains men in their apartment, and when he comes and finds the door locked, he waits on the stairs until her lover comes out. One Christmas evening, Ambo, a friend of Delfin and the narrator of the story, visits him and his two little daughters. Delfin is not at home, and Ambo, while waiting for him, takes time to fix the blinkers of the Christmas tree. The girls lock the door. When Ambo finally leaves the apartment he finds Delfin waiting outside. To Ambo's Christmas greetings Delfin can only ask the stabbing question in the dialect, "Why you also, Ambo?" (*"Bakit ikaw rin ba, Ambo?"* in Tagalog.) It is significant that Delfin expresses his most profound hurt in his mother tongue. The pathos is that Delfin does not know the truth, and it is cold comfort to say that at least Ambo has not actually betrayed his friend, because for Ambo it is as if he has.

In "Letter: The Faraway Summer" betrayal comes in the form of one man's, one Pinoy's, lack of *utang na loob* and the other man's sensitivity to such cold and general reference as "just one of those Pinoys" when friendship demands a warmer reference. In "For These Ruins" betrayal comes from one who does not understand the special value we Filipinos attach to *utang na loob*. Julia Flores, an uneducated Filipina, has a son by an American soldier whose life she has saved in Bataan. She is left by her husband and is driven away with her son from America by her in-laws.

Beginning with "And Beyond, More Walls" and ending with "Lonely in the Autumn Evening," seven stories must be taken as one long story (the stories being merely episodes); Santos here chronicles the aimless lives of Filipinos whose dream of success has come to naught. The focal story is that of Nanoy, a taxi driver, whose death brings the Filipinos together in communal suffering, and in whose misfortune they see their own. In these stories we see the resiliency, humor, and *bayanihan* spirit of the the Filipinos abroad, three qualities which sustain them and earn for them from their American friends the sobriquet "you lovely people." It is also in these stories that the real name of Ambo, Pablo Icarangal, takes on a larger significance, for it is he who goes around soliciting contributions in order to help defray the funeral expenses of Nanoy. Ambo's act may be seen simply as an expression of basic human sympathy and charity. As Filipinos we see it as a concrete example of the values of *damay* and *bayanihan*, of *awa*, or pity, for someone who has suffered at the hands of fate. In Ambo we see a praise-worthy Filipino who has not lost his soul even in a foreign land.

The other story that deals with frustrated dreams is "The Contender," the story of a former boxer who, doomed to sell pencils because he is going blind, loses in the larger arena of life.

The story that deals with the confusion of trying to live in two culturally different worlds is "Quicker with Arrows." In love with Fay Price (an unfortunate choice of name), Valentin Rustia cannot make up his mind whether he should marry this American cashier in a government cafeteria or a pampered Filipina heiress. As long as there is war and he is in America, he need not make a decision, but the war ends, he has to return to the Philippines and he has to decide. Unfortunately, the decision to marry Fay comes too late and he loses her; and the price for such procrastination, which in Rustia is a result of "cultural stress" (Leonard Casper's phrase in the Introduction to the book), is loneliness and isolation.

Memorable and sad as most of these stories are, they, nevertheless, leave the reader unsatisfied. Even "Scent of Apples" falls short of being great. The reason, I think, is that Santos, consciously or not, leaves his protagonists groping in the darkness of their isolation. He denies them that sudden moment of illumination of their condition, that "epiphany," as James Joyce calls it, that moment when the protagonist, provoked by an image, a sound, or a smell, realizes something about himself, or about the nature of life in general. It need not be a full awakening, an apocalyptic vision, such as we have in the novel or novella. An intimation, a glimpse, a flash, would suffice in a short story, provided that it allows the protagonist to experience a change in perception or attitude; to become, if slightly, a different person, though not necessarily a better one, at the end of the story from what he was at the beginning. A more useful term for this change than Mark Schorer's imprecise "moral evolution" would be Robert Frost's "momentary stay against confusion." This term suggests more accurately that the moment of illumination need not be, in a short story, as clear, final, and irrevocable as the shout of "Eureka!" or Mr. Kurtz's "the horror! the horror!"

The protagonists of Santos's stories draw us into their world by the force of their isolation and loneliness. Indeed, pathos is the most arresting emotional quality of these stories. Depending on one's aesthetics, it may or may not be enough. However, the stories of Tolstoy, Mann, Conrad, Kipling, Joyce, and Marquez show us that pathos can, artistically, be more poignant and satisfying if the protagonist is made aware of his condition, of some meaning in his experience or other people's. It does not matter if that meaning is not positive or wholesome so long as the protagonist becomes aware of it, and to a certain degree it clarifies an aspect of his experience. Reading the stories of Ivan Ilych, Aschenbach, Arsat, Dravot, Conroy, and Colonel Buendia elevates our sympathetic identification with them from mere pathos to tragic pity. The mature aesthetic experience does not remain in a nether world of feeling because the pain of knowing experienced by the protagonist illuminates both his understanding and ours. In his conscious suffering the protagonist elicits, if not actually demands, respect from the reader, and this respect expunges the temptation of the reader to feel, his pity, superior to the protagonist. An unconsciously suffering protagonist is looked down upon as somebody to be pitied without necessarily being respected. Shakespeare and the Greek tragedians understood this important psychological point in the aesthetic experience of literary art. If we examine our feeling of pity toward Fabia, Acayan, and Rustia, we will discover that we harbor a certain degree of superiority to them. Not so with Ambo, especially in "Letter: The Faraway Summer," because, even in his inarticulateness, he seems to know.

Santos, a professor of English and Distinguished Writer-in-Residence at Wichita State University, Kansas, is now an American citizen. But like many of his characters, he dreams of returning to the Philippines. He writes in the Preface that he has in fact made several attempts; the last one did not materialize because of the declaration of martial law. Whether he will ever return or not is not too important for Philippine literature. What is important is that he continue to write about the Filipinos whereever they are, in America, in the Bicol region, or in the slums of Sulucan. And whatever in the vast heartland of America stirs him to creative efforts, be it the scent of apples or that of "calamondin fruit and fresh papaya blossoms," be it a wintry landscape or the memory of a tropical skyline dominated by Mayon, the important thing, we need hardly remind him, is to carve in high relief the peculiar character of the Filipino soul.

Source: Anthony Tan, "You Lonely People: Exiles in the Stories of Bienvenido N. Santos," in *Silliman Journal*, First and Second Quarters, 1981, pp. 43–48.

Leonard Casper

In the following essay, Casper discusses the displaced person theme in Santos's work.

In the fall of 1942, Ben Santos was summoned from his studies at Columbia University and assigned a basement desk in the Information Division of the Commonwealth Building (now the Philippine Embassy) in Washington. Some of the upstairs officials preferred speaking Spanish and, on the avenues, passing as Latin Americans. Near Santos worked Jose Garcia Villa, mindlessly clipping news items about Bataan and Corregidor while lost in reveries about his first volume of poems, just released: *Have Come, Am Here*. Santos' own sentiments were fixed on his homeland and the immeasurable distances placed by war between it and not only the Philippine government-in-exile which he served, but also anxious *pensionados* like himself with endangered families still in the occupied islands.

> "This new loneliness, this latest fear of no longer belonging to a culture which itself seems at times to be wasting away, finds expression in the rhythm of arrangement provided by the selections in <u>Scent of Apples</u>."

His enforced separation from his wife and three young daughters brought him closer to fellow "exiles" whom he later met when the U.S. Office of Education asked him to tour America, lecturing on the worth and stamina of Filipinos as allies. "I loved my countrymen," he wrote, "the so-called Pinoys who were simple and good and trusting once they found you were not a snob." His stories about their anguish and strengths were eventually collected in *You Lovely People* (1955). But he has never really ceased to write about these "hurt men," whose isolation he was to share again in the postwar decades, as resident author on Midwest campuses.

The hard circumstances of prewar Filipino immigrants have been recounted too capably in Carey McWilliams' preface to Carlos Bulosan's *America Is in the Heart* to require repetition. For years, one of the most unnatural conditions imposed on the *sakadas* who cut Hawaiian sugar cane, or the truck-farm *cargadores* of the Imperial Valley, or the transient menials in the rundown neighborhoods of Chicago and New York, was the near absence of Filipino women among them. When women did occasionally appear, they had to defend themselves against attention turned desperate; and their caution, reinforcing Filipino decorum, was often misunderstood. In "Brown Coterie," one of the original collection's nineteen episodes, a number of educated "Filipina girls" are scolded for avoiding the "good-for-nothing boys who circulate around here." In their enforced loneliness, some Filipinos earned a reputation as "blonde chasers"; others sought in American women the virtues of fidelity and tenderness which they associated with the half-remembered, half-romanticized motherland. Novelist-critic

N. V. M. Gonzalez is surely correct in seeing this ideal as providing *You Lovely People* with "a heroine, the Filipino woman. Obviously, she is what no woman in the flesh can ever be; still, the hurt men are as if possessed. I suspect that it is their private vision of her which made them different, handsome in their awkward way, and which guaranteed survival of some kind."

Filipinos, like their agrarian counterparts elsewhere, traditionally have enjoyed a highly developed sense of community (*bayanihan*), dependent on face-to-face (*damay*) relations. They have drawn their identity from extended family lines, fortified by very real and multiple ritual godparenthood (*compadrinazco*), even when nearly four hundred years of Spanish overrule and half a century of American sovereignty prevented development of any clear image of national identity. Some of the psychological security derived from supportive family closeness had to be sacrificed by persons migrating to metropolitan Manila or to American fields and canneries, despite the fact that their earnings were shared with those left behind. The Pinoy's isolation became an extension of the pain of separation that other Filipinos felt when transported from one island (and vernacular) to another, or from rural barrios to makeshift *barong-barongs* dangerously propped on the edge of city railroad tracks or slowly collapsing into storm-sewer *esteros*. Furthermore, the feeling of uneasy identity, natural to the Commonwealth years of experiments in political independence, was multiplied among overseas Filipinos because of both physical distances between themselves and their motherland, and the psychological distances between the Pinoys and earlier migrants from Europe and East Asia. In addition to the usual difficulty that all humans have, of negotiating a single selfhood out of *being* and *becoming,* the Pinoy's expectation of *belonging* to others and not just to himself somehow had to be satisfied.

The wonder is that, under all this cultural stress epitomized by the war years' abrupt rupture of family communications, so many Pinoys managed to remain "lovely people." Like Bulosan, Santos can chronicle the varieties of pathetic frustration; the sense of abandonment associated with liberation from a colonial past; the wearing away of protective naivete. But, again like Bulosan, he captures the infallible faith, the resilience, the resurgent dream of self-recognition and esteem, the folk endurance of a people partially immunized against despair by so long a history of dispossession.

The difficulty of reconciling the Filipino dream of solidarity with the American dream of individualism, of unity risking and enriched by diversity, is implied in the mestizo form of *You Lovely People.* Many of its episodes are self-contained; others, with Ben at the circumference or Ambo (Pablo) at their center, provide a kind of continuity compatible with change. Ambo's trembling hands and poker face mirror the Pinoy's profound disquiet under a mask of serenity. Similarly, Ben's near-anonymity barely conceals the fact that whatever is missing in him has to be found in these others, their gentleness, their thoughtless betrayals, their confusions and confessions. Santos deliberately keeps center and circumference subservient to the circle of Pinoy compatriots—such is the book's socioesthetic. Both Ambo and Ben exist in that purest of compassions: shared suffering, as concelebrated offering.

In all of Santos' fiction, this compulsion to belong consistently raised images of departure and provisional return, of loss and attempted recovery. The structure of his second collection of stories, *Brother, My Brother* (1960), is generally recollective of an original flight from the Sulucan slums of Manila to the greater opportunities in the less crowded prewar barrios of Albay under the shadow of Mt. Mayon. Guilt that the relative ease has not been deserved or adequately shared creates an alternating current of tensions not unlike the expatriation/ repatriation/reexpatriation pattern in *You Lovely People.* The same longing for home and homogeneity serves as a central motif for his first novel, *Villa Magdalena* (1965), in which, driven by the smell of death in their tanneries, various members flee the decaying Conde-Medallada ancestral home, for Japan and America. Only years later do they recognize that mortality cannot be outrun, though mutual solicitude may offset it; and a family feeling is restored. A second novel, *The Volcano,* also published in 1965, dramatizes the Filipino crisis of identity by chronicling the lives of an American missionary family in the islands, between 1928 and 1958. Cross-cultural relationships at first rise smoothly; then, as a Philippine-American marriage is planned, abruptly drop. The sharp contours of the action resemble the perfect cone of Mt. Mayon, beneath whose picturesque slopes seethes a molten mass in perpetual threat of eruption. When ultranationalists violently demand that the Americans return to a country they have hardly known, for the first time they too experience (without quite appreciating) the Filipino's long-term sense of deprivation and homelessness.

In the May 1971–February 1972 issues of *Solidarity,* a Manila monthly, Santos serialized *The Praying Man,* a novel about a slum-dweller from Sulucan who becomes a multimillionaire by selling diluted drugs with the aid of government functionaries. (His wife remarks, "He has to meet, you know, the high cost of bribing.") But even though Santos implies that group-loyalty precious to Filipinos can so corrupt their feeling of community that it deteriorates into special-interest complicities, still he affirms its more positive side. What comforts the fugitive from justice is not the prospect of spending funds salted away in Swiss banks, but the trustworthiness he discovers in two persons from Sulucan, especially his best friend who is now a sculptor in Chicago. Penitent and unafraid, he returns from the States to face charges. The sculptor too is restored by that bond of friendship. He has been laboring on a cryptic memorial to a Sulucan eyesore, a man who daily lay naked and withered, "like the praying mantis," on a pallet near an open window: fatally diseased, yet refusing to die. Out of spite? Out of fear? By the end of the novel, the sculptor has recast his bronze in an attitude of courageous hope. Neither the millionaire's countless *queridas* nor the sculptor's affair of confused passion with Mabel, a student at Northwestern, has offered adequate "pain-killers for loneliness." However, the two men's friendship succeeds because it springs from Sulucan—symbol, in Santos, for folk loyalty and support; help from the helpless, in the absence of patrons.

The feeling of being a displaced person—of having lost or betrayed the traditional attitudes that ordered society—is inevitable in any society undergoing relatively rapid change. The reaction can be as violent as the revolutionary fervor which characterized the Sakdalista movement during the Commonwealth years, the postwar Huk uprising, and the civil unrest organized by the New Peoples' Army during the 1970s. All these had their origins partially in landlessness but just as significantly in absentee landlordism. According to both John Larkin's *The Pampangans* (1972) and Benedict Kerkvliet's *The Huk Rebellion* (1977), the paternalism of plantation owners diminished rapidly when they fled to the cities during the Japanese occupation. Class consciousness could be successfully appealed to, and then armed, only as the former familial relationship eroded. Indeed, class division has continued to increase as a result of postwar restrictions on land holdings, the sale of arable land for suburban development, reinvestment of subsequent profits in corporations clustered in high-rise Makati, and the increasing importance of industrial over agricultural portions of the gross national product. In addition, ex-tenants following ex-landlords to the metropolis have found fewer opportunities for personal services and therefore for patronage.

Changes such as these have caused a decline in the simple agrarian ideals that guaranteed cultural uniformity and stability. With diversification came a rise in expectations inadequately met by opportunities, so that large numbers of professionals who could not be absorbed by the Philippine economy or who preferred a meritocracy emigrated to the United States and Canada. After martial law was imposed late in 1972, political refugees swelled these numbers (Santos' novel- in-progress, *What the Hell For You Left Your Heart in San Francisco?*, uses material drawn from this group). Still more followed later, who considered regressive the autocratic rule of President/Premier Ferdinand Marcos and the rationalization of continuing "crisis government" under the guise of a New Society. By training, many of these later immigrants have been confident, self-possessed technicians, having little experience to share with earlier—and now older—Filipinos. Consequently, the "o.t.'s" (old-timers) may suffer from three kinds of distances at once: between themselves and their homeland; between themselves and their children who have known only America; and between themselves and recent arrivals whose Philippines, in some ways, is drastically different from their own.

Solomon King, in Santos' unpublished novel, The *Man Who (Thought He) Looked Like Robert Taylor,* feels bitterly this deterioration in the spirit of ethnic unity, which he himself will take to the grave. He has lived alone for thirty years in Chicago, surrounded by Poles and carefully preserved souvenirs of Sulucan where he was born and early orphaned. His father was a champion *arnis* fencer, using wooden weapons in "a silent duel of no touch." Solomon's life too has been spent in a kind of pantomime, so that he might pass unnoticed, untouched. But realizing that, like his idol Robert Taylor, he has not escaped the many little deaths that aging brings, he goes to Washington in search of whatever old friends may still be left. The lament of Solomon (a King Solomon less wise, and divided within himself) is played against a counterpoint of dialogues between anonymous Pinoys of his generation, at ease with one another but embarrassed by the better educated Filipinos now among them.

This new loneliness, this latest fear of no longer belonging to a culture which itself seems at times to be wasting away, finds expression in the rhythm of arrangement provided by the selections in *Scent of Apples*. "Immigration Blues" describes the still precarious situation of aliens and permanent residents, today. The segments of *You Lovely People* which follow are doubly retrospective, recovering incidents from Pinoy life during World War II, and folkways from a past even more remote. So receding a perspective could easily be considered nostalgic; or even elegiac; and the Pinoy characters, sentimentalists unable to adapt to the natural evolution of their dearest traditions. But the spiral motion of the final section makes it clear that Santos is offering an essentially timeless view of culture, which transcends history limited to the linear, the consecutive, and the one-dimensional.

Both "The Day the Dancers Came" and "The Contender" are contemporary accounts of how two old-timers, awkward before the beauty and surpassing sophistication of young travelers from home, recoil into one another's care for final comfort. They are poignant couples, but couples nonetheless. "Quicker with Arrows" is a tale of distraught Philippine-American lovers, in a roomful of opportunists who are planning how they will exploit the chaos in their country, just after the holocaust at Hiroshima. And in "Footnote to a Laundry List" a professor, recently returned from a ill-fated affair in the States, makes a sympathetic defense of a young female student, out of respect for what he remembers of love and innocence.

That this final sequence (present:present:remote past:recent past) is chronic, rather than chronological, suggests that Santos—throughout the entire collection—is less concerned with history perceived as ocean current or successive waves, than with culture as an entire archipelago of diverse islands in that stream. What he discerns is that any ethnic group consists of individual particles, no two of which are exactly identical (there are Filipinos, and Filipinos), but all of which have declared their commitment to participate, as if in some consummate entity. The declaration of a common bond, of course, tends to be more perfect than uneasy coexistence may actually turn out to be. Nevertheless, it provides a measure of meaning even for those who pay it lip service only.

This is the recurring theme in Santos' work: how hard it always is, yet how important, to be "Filipino" at heart, with all that that implies about human decency, good humor, and honor, considera-tion beyond courtesy, and putting both hands to a common burden; while at the same time trying to make a life out of being overseas Filipinos, Philip-pine-Americans, temporary "permanent residents" obligated to be buried "at home," or those assimi-lated beyond recovery of any heritage whatsoever.

As permeating as the scent of autumn apples is this single, persistent dream: the return of the Philip-pines to the man, whether or not a return to the Philippines is ever managed. Through dreams one presumes to distinguish the momentary from the momentous. For Santos, that ideal has too often been realized to be mocked as imaginary.

Source: Leonard Casper, "Introduction," in *Scent of Apples: A Collection of Stories by Bienvenido N. Santos,* University of Washington Press, 1979, pp. ix–xvi.

Sources

Bernad, Miguel A., *Bamboo and the Greenwood Tree: Essays on Filipino Literature in English,* Bookmark, 1961, pp. 33–41.

Blau, Zena Smith, *Aging in a Changing Society,* 2d ed., Franklin Watts, 1981, p. 139.

Kim, Elaine H., ed., *Asian American Literature: An Intro-duction to the Writings and Their Social Context,* Temple University Press, 1982, pp. 265–72.

Kingston, Maxine Hong, "Precarious Lives," in *New York Times Book Review,* May 4, 1980, pp. 15, 28–29.

Santos, Bienvenido, *Memory's Fictions: A Personal History,* New Day Publishers, 1993, p. 252.

———, "Pilipino Old Timers: Fact and Fiction," in *Amerasia,* Vol. 9, No. 2, 1982, pp. 89–98.

Tan, Anthony, "You Lonely People: Exiles in the Stories of Bienvenido N. Santos," in *Silliman Journal,* Vol. 28, Nos. 1–2, 1981, pp. 43–48.

Further Reading

Alegre, Edilberto N., and Doreen G. Fernandez, *Writers and Their Milieu: An Oral History of First Generation Writers in English,* De La Salle University Press, 1984.
This book contains a wide-ranging interview with Santos in which he discusses his career and his creative methods.

Campomanes, Oscar V., "Filipinos in the United States and Their Literature of Exile," in *Reading the Literatures of Asian America,* edited by Shirley Geok-Lin Lim and Amy Ling, Temple University Press, 1992, pp. 49–78.
This scholarly article examines themes of exile, iden-tity, and language in the literature of Filipino Ameri-cans. It includes a discussion of Santos's work, in-cluding his short stories.

Casper, Leonard, *New Writing from the Philippines: A Cri-tique and Anthology,* Syracuse University Press, 1966, pp. 127–33.
Casper provides an appreciative discussion of Santos's short stories, mainly those that record the disillusion-ing post–World War II return to Manila of many Filipino Americans.

Santos, Tomas N., "The Pinoy in Fact and Fiction," in *Solidarity,* Vol. 10, Nos. 5–6, 1976, pp. 132–36.
Tomas Santos (Bienvenido Santos's son) discusses Bienvenido Santos's short stories as a continuation of the work of Carlos Bulosan in chronicling the lives of Filipino Americans.

Long Distance

Jane Smiley

1987

Jane Smiley's "Long Distance" was first published in the *Atlantic Monthly* in January 1987 and then published later the same year in Smiley's short-story collection, *The Age of Grief*. Smiley wrote this book after she divorced her second husband, historian William Silag, an event that influenced the content of the stories—all of which deal with marriage and family in some regard. In the case of "Long Distance," which won Smiley her third O. Henry Award, the story examines one man's reaction to a failed relationship. During the course of a family holiday gathering, he is forced to confront his views of love, marriage, and responsibility, and in the process he realizes that his selfish actions have cheated others—and himself. Smiley wrote the story during a time when the concept of the American family was changing. Evolving roles of men and women—due in part to the influence of the modern women's movement and freer sexual attitudes for both men and women—were changing the structure of many families. Although *The Age of Grief* is not as well known as Smiley's novels, particularly her Pulitzer Prize–winning novel, *A Thousand Acres*, it has received overwhelmingly positive criticism. A copy of "Long Distance" can be found in the paperback edition of *The Age of Grief*, published in 2002 by Anchor.

Author Biography

Smiley was born on September 26, 1949, in Los Angeles, California. Her parents divorced when she was very young, and the author was raised by her journalist mother, Frances, in St. Louis, Missouri. Smiley benefited from the close contact of her mother's large extended family, whose stories have appeared in many of Smiley's own works.

After graduating from high school in 1967, Smiley attended Vassar College in New York, where she graduated in 1971 with a bachelor's degree in English literature. During this time, she also met John Whiston, a student at Yale University. The two were married in 1970. After graduation, they moved to Iowa City, where Smiley eventually began graduate work in English literature at the University of Iowa, earning her master of arts degree in 1975. At the same time, Smiley applied for admission to the university's prestigious Iowa Writers' Workshop but was initially turned down. After honing her technique, Smiley reapplied and was accepted in 1974, graduating in 1976 with a master of fine arts degree. In 1975, Smiley and Whiston divorced. During the 1976–1977 academic year, Smiley earned a Fulbright-Hays study grant and spent the year in Iceland, where she began her first two novels, *Barn Blind* (1980) and *At Paradise Gate* (1981).

In 1978, Smiley earned her doctoral degree from the University of Iowa and married her second husband, historian William Silag. In 1981, Smiley began teaching courses in literature and fiction writing at Iowa State University. From 1984 to 1985, Smiley began researching and writing her epic historical novel, *The Greenlanders* (1988). Smiley and Silag, who have two daughters (Phoebe and Lucy), were divorced in 1986. The emotional impact of this divorce manifested itself in Smiley's novella, *The Age of Grief*. This novella was collected in a book by the same name in 1987, which also included some of Smiley's short stories, including "Long Distance." Also in 1987, Smiley married her third husband, Stephen Mortensen, whom she had met when she was an undergraduate student.

Though critics have raved over her short fiction, Smiley is best known for her Pulitzer Prize–winning novel, *A Thousand Acres* (1991), which recasts William Shakespeare's *King Lear* tragedy in a modern, rural American setting. The book, which also earned a National Book Critics' Circle Award, tells the story from a feminist perspective and

Jane Smiley

includes some shocking twists. In 1996, Smiley stopped teaching at Iowa State and moved to Carmel Valley, California, to pursue full-time writing. During this time, she and Mortensen, who have one son (Axel James), divorced.

Unlike many writers who choose one genre and stick with it, Smiley set herself the challenge of completing a work in each of the four traditional literary forms: epic, tragedy, comedy, and romance. Smiley completed this long-term goal with the publication of *The All-True Travels and Adventures of Lidie Newton: A Novel* (1998), an unconventional romance. Smiley published the novel *Horse Heaven* in 2000.

Plot Summary

"Long Distance" begins with the main character, Kirby Christianson, in the shower, anxious about a visit from Mieko, a Japanese woman with whom he is having an affair. He finishes his shower and answers the ringing phone, annoyed; it is Mieko, calling from Japan. She tells him that she cannot make it to the United States to visit with him over Christmas because she has to stay with her father, who has lung cancer. This was the only chance that Mieko had to come to the United States because she had lied to her family and said that she was coming for a literature conference, a supposedly onetime event. The realization that Mieko will never be able to come to see him and that their relationship is effectively over has a strange effect on Kirby. He feels relieved because he was not sure that he could live up to Mieko's expectations, and now he does not have to. Now that their relationship is over, Kirby is no longer annoyed and can be a sympathetic listener.

After the phone call, Kirby gets on the road to drive to his brother's house in Minneapolis. During the trip he begins to think about the plans that he and Mieko had made to drive out West. Kirby drives into a blinding snowstorm, an event that makes him think about his own mortality. He thinks of several examples of people who have either frozen to death in similar winter conditions or who have overcome great odds to survive the elements. Kirby decides that the weather is not so bad that he should stop off at a rest stop, and, after he passes this exit, he starts to think of Mieko again. The thoughts of Mieko and their failed relationship distract him, and he misses the tourist center that he planned to stop at to ask about road conditions. He decides to drive past another potential stopping point, and, in an effort to keep his mind off morbid thoughts of dying in the cold, he daydreams about the time he spent in Japan as a teacher, where he met Mieko.

Kirby arrives at his brother Harold's house, and during dinner he thinks about the family members there, focusing especially on his brother Eric, an academic who specializes in writing about the family. Kirby thinks about how he and Harold often make fun of Eric, who they feel is overly pretentious. As he thinks of all of the people sitting at the table, Kirby wonders how Mieko would have fit in and decides that her meek Japanese demeanor would have made her an outsider. The next morning Kirby lies awake in bed, miserable. He fixes on images of furniture—in his brothers' homes, in his own home, and in the home of one of his teacher friends in Japan—but no image offers comfort. At breakfast, Kirby watches the way that Leanne, Harold's wife, bustles around the kitchen doing various domestic activities, and he begins to feel attracted to her. Since all of the others are involved in their own

activities, Kirby sits in the living room and begins drinking. The only person who visits him is Anna, Eric's daughter, who asks him if he is a socialist, an idea that Kirby realizes she got from Eric and his wife, Mary Beth.

As Kirby continues to drink, he first starts making fun of Eric in his mind and then starts to feel depressed because he does not have a family of his own as his two brothers do. At dinner, Kirby is still intoxicated from his all-day drinking session. When Anna stands up to her father, Kirby comes to her aid and starts an argument with Eric, venting his pent-up emotions by goading Eric into a discussion about the family. The dinner becomes uncomfortable for everybody else. After dinner, they open the family Christmas gifts, and everybody is impressed by Kirby's unique, Japanese gifts. Later on, Harold invites Kirby outside for some air, realizing that his intoxicated brother needs it. The two men do not talk about the dinner incident but discuss the weather instead.

Back at the house, Kirby realizes that Leanne and Mary Beth are arguing because Leanne wrapped the presents for her baby, Isaac, in the same wrapping paper as the gifts from Santa Claus. Worried that her own children will figure out there is no Santa, Mary Beth pushes the issue, and Leanne says she will rewrap the gifts. Kirby tries to go to bed but is too intoxicated to sleep. He gets up, and Leanne makes him a cup of cocoa to help him sleep. They talk, and Leanne takes Kirby's side in the argument that he had with Eric. Kirby opens up to Leanne about Mieko and says that he promised himself that he would not date Japanese women when he was abroad because it is a different culture. He worries that, by being affectionate and caring to Mieko—something that he says a Japanese man would never do—he has shown her a different way to live, which will make her even more miserable in Japan. Kirby also admits that he broke his promise to himself because he was lonely, without really taking the consequences into consideration. Leanne notes that, even though Eric is heavily criticized in the family, he does not try to get something for nothing—as Kirby has from Mieko, who will most likely never get married. Kirby waits for Leanne to say something to make him feel better, to absolve him of his guilt, but she does not. As the two walk upstairs in the dark to go to their respective rooms, Leanne kisses him on the cheek, a sign that, although she does not agree with the way that Kirby has treated Mieko, neither does she condemn him.

Characters

Anna Christianson

Anna is Kirby's niece and the oldest daughter of Eric and Mary Beth. Anna is only in the fifth grade, but when Kirby notices her spying on him, she seems much older. Anna tries to stick up for her sister Kristin to Eric but is unsuccessful until Kirby steps in to back her up.

Eric Christianson

Eric is Kirby's brother, Mary Beth's husband, and the father of Harold the younger, Anna, and Kristin. Eric is well educated but chooses to use his education not to teach, as Kirby does, but to write for a conservative think tank. Eric specializes in the family and becomes especially passionate when somebody challenges these views, as when first Anna and then Kirby criticize him for not letting Kristin eat whatever she wants. When Kirby draws Eric into this argument, he cites the necessity for authority when socializing children and talks about the effectiveness of a patriarchal, or male-dominated, society.

Harold Christianson

Harold is Kirby's brother, Leanne's husband, and the father of Isaac. Harold is an adventurous, self-made man who owns a store and who has spent his life skiing and ski-jumping. Harold is always open to making fun of his brother Eric, something that he and Kirby do often behind Eric's back. He is also more than willing to openly support Kirby when Kirby starts an argument with Eric. Harold is so critical of Eric that he never spends more than three days with him.

Harold "The Younger" Christianson

Harold the younger, so called to distinguish him from Kirby's brother Harold, is Kirby's nephew and Eric's son. The twelve-year-old Harold shares a bedroom with Kirby at Harold the elder's house during the holiday gathering.

Isaac Christianson

Isaac is Kirby's nephew and the son of Harold and Leanne. When Leanne wraps all of Isaac's presents—those from his parents and those from Santa Claus—in the same paper, Mary Beth is worried that her own children, especially Kristin, will notice this and realize there is no Santa Claus.

Media Adaptations

- Smiley's title novella from *The Age of Grief* was adapted in 2002 as a feature film titled *The Secret Lives of Dentists*. The film was produced by Holedigger Films and Ready Made Film and was directed by Alan Rudolph. It stars Campbell Scott, Denis Leary, Robin Tunney, and Peter Samuel.

- Smiley's novel *Good Faith* was produced as both an audiobook and audio CD in 2003 by Recorded Books Unabridged.

- Smiley's Pulitzer Prize–winning novel, *A Thousand Acres,* was adapted as a feature film by Touchstone Pictures in 1997. The film, directed by Jocelyn Moorhouse, featured an all-star cast including Jessica Lange, Michelle Pfeiffer, Jennifer Jason Leigh, Jason Robards, Colin Firth, and Keith Carradine. It is available on VHS and DVD from Buena Vista Home Video.

Kirby Christianson

Kirby is the protagonist in the story and the only single adult at a family Christmas gathering, where he is forced to confront his own views of love, marriage, and responsibility. In the beginning of the story, Kirby is relieved when Mieko, a Japanese woman with whom he has had an affair, cannot come to the United States to visit him, because he is worried that he cannot meet her expectations. During a road trip in a blizzard for a family holiday gathering at his brother Harold's house, Kirby worries he may die. When he arrives at Harold's house, Kirby is already on edge from his road stress and the breakup between him and Mieko, which has occupied his thoughts during much of the drive. Though Kirby adores Harold, neither of them gets along well with their other brother, Eric.

As the gathering progresses, Kirby begins to feel sorry for himself because everybody else has a family and he does not. He also begins to drink heavily. These factors come to a head during dinner one night when an intoxicated Kirby gets involved in a family dispute among Eric, Anna, and Kristin. Kirby tries to escalate the argument but backs off when it is clear that he has offended Leanne. Later on, in a conversation with Leanne, Kirby talks about his affair with Mieko and finally admits to himself, and to Leanne, that he feels he has destroyed Mieko's life and prospects for marriage. Since Kirby has treated her differently than a Japanese man would, she now has expectations that go against her culture. In a comment about Eric, Leanne essentially tells Kirby that he has been selfish for the way he has treated Mieko. Whereas he was relieved in the beginning of the story to be rid of Mieko, Kirby now feels guilty. He looks to Leanne to absolve him of his guilt, but the most she offers is a kiss on the cheek—a symbol that, although she does not agree with the way he handled the Mieko situation, she does not condemn him.

Kristin Christianson

Kristin is Kirby's niece and the youngest daughter of Eric and Mary Beth. Kristin is an energetic three-year-old, who gets into trouble when she refuses to eat her dinner. This defiance leads to her punishment, Anna's ill-timed attempt to stick up for her younger sister, and Kirby's drunken attempt to spin the incident into an argument with Eric.

Leanne Christianson

Leanne is Kirby's sister-in-law and Harold's wife. Throughout the story, Kirby notes that even though it is her house, Leanne defers to Mary Beth. When Mary Beth does not like the fact that Leanne has wrapped both the family and the Santa presents for Isaac, her son, in the same wrapping paper, Leanne rewraps them. But Leanne shows her quiet strength during the dinner argument between Eric and Kirby when she gets Kirby to back off and feel bad about instigating the fight. She also shows this strength during her conversation with Kirby. Though she tells Kirby that she takes his side in the argument with Eric, she says that she respects Eric for not being selfish—implying that Kirby has been selfish in the way he has treated Mieko. Still, Leanne does not condemn Kirby, as she shows by kissing him briefly on the cheek when she is leading him up the stairs in the dark.

Mary Beth Christianson

Mary Beth is Kirby's sister-in-law and Eric's wife. Although the Christmas gathering is at Harold and Leanne's house, Mary Beth puts herself in charge of everything, including pressuring Leanne to rewrap Isaac's gifts so that the ones from Santa Claus and the ones from the family are in separate wrappings.

Mieko

Mieko is a Japanese woman with whom Kirby had an affair while he was working in Japan. In the beginning of the story, Mieko calls to say that she cannot come to the United States to see Kirby because she must stay with her father, who has cancer. Mieko is distraught because Kirby is the only man who has ever listened to her and shown her affection—something that she has not experienced with Japanese men. Mieko has changed so much at the end of their affair that Kirby realizes she will probably remain an old maid for the rest of her life.

Themes

Distance

As the story's title implies, the main theme in this story is distance. Smiley explores this theme in two ways: physical distance and emotional distance. When the story begins, Kirby is anxious about seeing Mieko, a Japanese woman with whom he has had an affair in Japan. The two are attempting to continue seeing each other in a long-distance relationship. Kirby uses this distance to his advantage when she calls, and he acts as if there is a bad international phone connection—to mask the annoyance in his voice, which Mieko has picked up on: "So he says, 'Hello, Mieko? Hello, Mieko? Hello, Mieko?' more and more loudly, as if her voice were fading." Kirby is also thankful for the distance because it makes their breakup much easier, since Mieko's family situation will prevent her from making the global journey again: "She isn't coming. She is never coming. He is off the hook." After their breakup, when Kirby begins to reflect on their relationship as he is driving in the blizzard, he realizes that if he were to die, Mieko would never even know it: "And if she were to ever call him back, she would get only a disconnect message and would assume that he had moved." Even though Kirby is initially relieved that the relationship is

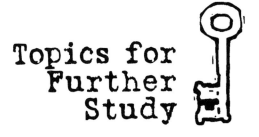

Topics for Further Study

- During his road trip, Kirby thinks about several instances in which people have been caught unaware in snowstorms. Research some real-life examples of people who have survived horrible winter conditions, and discuss the methods that they used for survival.

- Research the dating rituals in modern-day Japan, and compare them to the dating rituals in modern-day America. Imagine that you are a Japanese teenager, and write a journal entry that describes a day in your courtship, using your research to support your ideas.

- Research modern interracial relationships in at least five different countries other than the United States and Japan. For each country, write a short description of the prevalence of these interracial relationships, as well as the cultural challenges that these couples face.

- Research the history of the family in America, from the beginning of the twentieth century until today. On a chart, plot the major trends that have occurred in family structure, and identify the factors—social, technological, or otherwise—that have helped to bring about these changes. Discuss the family structure that you think is the most effective.

- In the story, Leanne references a study that says one-year-olds will choose a balanced diet when left to pick their own foods and that they will also choose to be toilet trained. Read a number of studies that address these ''nature versus nurture'' issues. Discuss which of one's skills and character traits you think are learned naturally and which are learned from one's environment, using examples from your research—and your own background, if you wish—to support your claims.

- Research any proposed legislation that could affect American families. Discuss how this law (or laws) could affect the family, as well as whether or not you think this legislation is a good idea. Write one of your representatives in Congress and express your views on this topic.

---

over, this morbid thought fills Kirby with great despair.

The story also explores the effects of emotional distance. Though Kirby and Mieko were in a long-distance relationship, it could have worked if they had connected emotionally. But they are on two different emotional levels. Kirby's strongest emotion concerning Mieko is his ''feeling of anxiety'' that he gets in the shower. It is only after he realizes that Mieko is not coming that he lets go of his anxiety and becomes a caring listener, so much so, in fact, that when Mieko is saying goodbye, Kirby begs her not to hang up and to call him again. Mieko, on the other hand, is focusing only on the happiness that she and Kirby could have had. ''I know that I am only giving up pleasure,'' she says. These two reactions indicate the emotional divide between Kirby and Mieko, which makes their union improbable. Kirby thinks about this after the breakup: ''The connection in her mind between the two of them, the connection that she allowed to stretch into the future despite all his admonitions and all her resolutions, is broken now.''

Family

Kirby is also emotionally distant from most of his family, which is one of the other major themes in the story. From the moment that Kirby sits down to dinner with his relatives the first night, he feels out of place: ''The other people at the table seem unfamiliar.'' For Kirby, this feeling manifests itself in the way he views his relatives, how they seem to ''waver in the smoky candlelight,'' a feeling that only goes away when Harold gives him a beer, which ''seems to adjust all the figures around the table so that they stop wavering.'' Kirby's single status makes him feel like an outsider. As the story progresses, Kirby finds himself increasingly yearning for the comforts of family, such as having a wife like Leanne to take care of him: "'sweetie'—he would like for Leanne to call him that."

When Kirby begins drinking, he sits, thinking, and first directs his frustrations at his brother Eric, an academic who focuses on "the family." But then Kirby gets depressed as he starts to reflect on the importance of family in a man's identity, and he realizes that, whereas he and his brother Harold were more alike as children because of their personalities, "It is Harold and Eric who are alike now." Harold and Eric both have families, houses, and other things that Kirby associates with adulthood. "Only Kirby's being does not extend past his fingertips and toes to family, real estate, reputation." Kirby wallows in self-pity, drinking past the point of reason, until he tries to lash out at Eric by confronting him on his ideas about the family. This move backfires when Kirby offends Leanne, and he "blushes and falls silent." Kirby feels even more depressed and out of place at the end of the meal, "and by the time they get up from the table, Kirby feels as if he has been sitting in a dim, candlelit corner most of his life."

Responsibility

Part of the reason for Kirby's status as an outsider is his lack of personal responsibility. All of the other characters in the story are responsible to a parent, a spouse, or a child. In fact, the story begins with a conflict in responsibility. Mieko cannot come to the United States to see Kirby and thus must end their relationship because she feels a responsibility to her family: "Kirby, I cannot come. I cannot go through with my plan. My father has lung cancer, we learned this morning." Due to her sense of responsibility to her father, Mieko feels she has to stay in Japan.

But Kirby is self-involved and allows his selfishness to direct many of his actions. First, he drinks too much, realizing he should stop but drinking more anyway. Then, during the fight with Eric, as Kirby goads him on, Mary Beth and Leanne look at Kirby, "no doubt wishing that he had a wife or a girl friend here to restrain him." Because Kirby is unattached and is responsible to nobody else, he says and does whatever he wants. Even the fight itself is about responsibility—in this case, the responsibility of a parent to teach children how to act, instead of letting them do what they want, poten-

tially hurting themselves, as in letting Kristin eat whatever she wants. "For a certain period of their lives others control them," Eric says, defending himself. "In early childhood others control their bodies. They are taught to control themselves," he continues. Not everybody agrees with this theory. Referring to some studies that back up her claims, Leanne says she thinks children inherently know how to take care of themselves: "You know, I don't agree with Eric about that body stuff. I think they naturally do what is healthy for them." Yet, even though she disagrees with Eric's views, she notes that he "never tries to get something for nothing. I admire that." Leanne's comment is intended to dig at Kirby, who only thinks of himself—first in getting involved with a Japanese woman, even though he knew it could make future relationships difficult for her, and then in lashing out at Eric in a drunken rage. "Leanne's cool remark has revealed his permanent smallness." Kirby realizes at the end that he has been selfish and irresponsible by not taking into account others' feelings or the potential consequences of his own actions.

Style

Point of View

Smiley chooses to use a form of narration known as third-person-limited point of view in "Long Distance." The story is told from the point of view of Kirby alone, by an outside narrator who refers to Kirby in the third person, either by his name, "Kirby," or by third-person pronouns such as "he" or "his." Another way to think about the point of view is that the story is told *about* Kirby, not *by* Kirby, as it would be in the first person. The third-person point of view is evident from the first line of Smiley's story: "Kirby Christianson is standing under the shower, fiddling with the hot-water spigot and thinking four apparently simultaneous thoughts."

Throughout the narrative, the reader continues to hear only Kirby's thoughts, as well as to experience the sights and sounds of the story only as Kirby experiences them. By filtering the action through one character, authors like Smiley force themselves to develop one character more than the others. That's not to say that the other characters aren't developed, but the reader's understanding of the other characters is limited by the main character's experiences with them, and so the reader can only use these clues to guess at what is going on in the supporting characters' minds. This is the opposite of a third-person-omniscient viewpoint, in which an author employs a narrator that can jump in and out of any character's thoughts and tell the story from any character's point of view at any time. In "Long Distance," the use of a third-person-limited viewpoint is very effective. By focusing on Kirby, and Kirby alone, Smiley helps to underscore his isolation from the rest of the characters.

Flashback

Throughout the story, Kirby has many flashbacks, or recollections, in which he remembers events from his past and thus illustrates these events for readers. These flashbacks serve two narrative functions in the story. The first is that they help Smiley with her exposition, or the revealing of the back story (the events that took place before the story's first scene). For example, when the story begins, the reader immediately learns of a character named Mieko but is given very few details about the relationship between her and Kirby. When Kirby gets on the road, he starts to daydream, recalling his past with Mieko, beginning with the plans that they made, which are now canceled since she cannot make it to the United States. Kirby has several other recollection daydreams on the trip, which are comforting and which help to take his mind off the bad weather. When he gets to his brother's house, he has more recollections. For example, when he is avoiding getting out of bed one morning, he occupies himself by thinking about the furniture at various places he has visited, including his friend's house in Japan. But whereas earlier in the story he thought about images of Japan as "the one tangible gift of his travels," now as he is beginning to explore the depth of his despair over the loss of Mieko, "even the Japanese images he calls up are painful."

This shift in Kirby's attitude highlights the second narrative function of the flashbacks. As the story progresses, Kirby begins to realize that memories from his past, even fond ones, can no longer help him cope with or avoid the pain of the present. In fact, the reverse is true: examining his past has revealed the consequences of his actions, which in turn leads to more pain. As he looks over the events of his life, especially his relationship with Mieko, he sees that he has made some choices that he wishes

he had not. "I was so careful for a year and a half. I didn't date Japanese women, and I was very distant," Kirby tells Leanne, as he talks about his past with Mieko. Unfortunately, Kirby was lonely in Japan, and so, against his better judgment, he started the affair with Mieko, which he now realizes has led to Mieko's inability to fit into her own culture. As he is talking to Leanne, he tells her that looking back "I see that, one by one, I broke down every single one of her strengths, everything she had equipped herself with to live in a Japanese way." Kirby is depressed, "and it seems to him that all at once, now that he realizes it, his life and Mieko's have taken their final form."

Historical Context

Japanese Culture in the 1980s

In the story Mieko starts weeping when she's on the phone with Kirby, after they both realize that their relationship is over. She tells him that he "should not have listened" to her cry, but Kirby, raised in an American culture, asks her, "How could I hang up?" To this, Mieko replies, "A Japanese man would have." Later, at the end of the story, when Kirby is telling Leanne about Mieko, he notes that Japanese women must make certain emotional concessions if they are to live "in a Japanese way." As Edwin O. Reischauer says in his book *The Japanese Today: Change and Continuity,* "Japanese men are blatantly male chauvinists and women seem shamefully exploited and suppressed," especially when viewed by Americans and other Westerners. Reischauer's book was published in 1988, one year after Smiley published "Long Distance," so his observations of Japanese culture help to better understand the world of the story. Whereas Japanese men largely followed their impulses, Reischauer notes that women, like Mieko, were expected to be composed at all times, "to have a strong character, to be always 'ladylike,' and to hold the family together." Women like Mieko were not supposed to weep uncontrollably, and it would not be out of place for a Japanese man to hang up on her if she did.

Though Japanese women were largely subservient to men, they did make certain advances in the 1980s. The most notable of these accomplishments was the Equal Employment Opportunity Law that

Compare
&
Contrast

- **1980s:** Thirty percent of Japanese women in their twenties are not married.

  Today: Fifty percent of Japanese women in their twenties are not married.

- **1980s:** Although Japanese women are still encouraged to marry in their twenties, it becomes socially acceptable for married women in certain classes to work part-time, as long as it does not interfere with their marriage duties.

  Today: Almost half of all Japanese women work outside the home, in full-time and part-time jobs. Yet, for the working women with children, it is more common to pursue part-time employment, unless their children are old enough that they do not require full-time care anymore.

- **1980s:** Following the modern women's movement of the 1960s and 1970s, many American women embrace their independence and choose to put child-rearing on hold while pursuing careers.

  Today: Many American women are torn between being independent and raising children, and some try to do both by working first and then having children later in life or by using services such as daycare to take care of their children during the day while they work. New fertility studies, which suggest that it is difficult for some women to have children after their late twenties, increase the pressure on many women to choose between work and family. At the same time, advancements in technology make working from a home office more feasible, and many employers offer flexible working arrangements, creating new opportunities for women who want to do both.

- **1980s:** About 50 percent of all American marriages end in divorce.

  Today: About 40 percent of all American marriages are predicted to end in divorce.

- **1980s:** In 1980, 18 percent of all births in America are to unmarried women.

  Today: In 1998, 30 percent of all births in America are to unmarried women.

---

was passed in Japan in 1986. This law created two work paths for Japanese women. Those who wished to have a less stressful work life could choose a general-track job, a menial job that tended to have less responsibility and more job security. Those who wished to have a more challenging career joined the integrated track, which placed them in the same job pool as men, with whom they competed for promotions and job security. Yet, even though the two-track work system led to more opportunities for women, Japan was still a male-focused society. Men were not given the option of the general track and were instead expected to join the integrated track. Furthermore, although young women often did work for several years after school in Mieko's time, many of them were not taken seriously and were looked upon as potential brides for the young workingmen. These attitudes have changed in recent years, and an increasing number of Japanese women are pursuing careers as more than just a diversion before marriage.

The American Family in the 1980s

While Japanese society was going through changes in the 1980s in regard to its treatment of women, Americans were experiencing radical changes in family structure—also due, in part, to changing attitudes toward women. To understand this change, one must look farther back into the past, to the post–World War II era in America's history. Following the devastation of this world war, which ended in 1945, many American families chose to seal themselves off from the world, focusing on family and marriage. During the 1950s, this intense focus on family and family values reinforced the idea of the nuclear family, two parents and children. Because women were expected mainly to reproduce and raise families, the American birth rate shot up until it was higher even than some undeveloped nations, creating the event known as the baby boom.

But many women were not happy with this social arrangement, which often limited their educational and social options. In 1963, Betty Friedan tried to debunk the myth that American housewives were happy in these limited, male-focused roles when she published her landmark book *The Feminine Mystique*. This book is widely credited with sparking the modern women's movement in the 1960s. This movement, coupled with other societal factors, such as the difficulty in the later decades of the twentieth century for families to survive on one income, encouraged more women to become educated and join the workforce. Attitudes toward sex also changed, and, especially after the sexual revolution of the 1960s and 1970s, premarital sex was not the social taboo that it once had been. People were also not as willing to stay in bad marriages, as some had during the 1950s, for the sake of the children.

As women gained independence and equal rights and both men and women explored their sexuality and freedom to choose the right relationship, the nuclear, patriarchal family became less and less common. In the story both Eric and Harold head up nuclear families. Eric and Harold work; their wives cook, clean, and take care of the children. Yet, just as Kirby ends the story alone, so did many in the 1980s. Due to the greater emphasis on finding the perfect relationship and on the social acceptance of premarital sex, an increasing number of people waited until later life to get married or never married at all. And even for those who did marry, the unions did not always last. An increasing number of marriages ended in divorce, which helped lead to the trend of single-parent families. The trend of the single parent was also helped by the prevalence of premarital sex among teenagers and young adults, which led to an increasing number of births to young, unwed mothers.

the major strengths of this quiet and unflashy collection by Jane Smiley is that in her stories things actually do happen.'' Kaveney also says that any moral commentary in the book ''comes from the fact that her characters are shown as lovable and their actions as things we just have to accept.''

Although other critics have noted the power of Smiley's understated style, some do not agree that all of Smiley's characters in the collection are lovable. In fact, as Thom Conroy says about ''Long Distance'' in his 2001 entry on Smiley for *Dictionary of Literary Biography*, ''Kirby emerges as one of Smiley's least sympathetic characters.'' Conroy notes that, unlike other Smiley protagonists, Kirby's ''emotional trauma is not brought on by naiveté, but by indifference.'' Conroy says that Leanne's biting comment to Kirby ''reveals the pernicious nature of Kirby's shortcoming,'' that he only cares about his own comfort and not about the feelings of others.

Though Kirby may not be the nicest character, other critics agree with Raymond Sokolov, who notes in his 1987 *Wall Street Journal* review of *The Age of Grief* that ''Ms. Smiley's best characters are men.'' Smiley herself has said that she does not find it hard to write from a male viewpoint and has offered an explanation why. ''I think partly because I'm 6' 2.'' I think being tall makes my femininity less of a disadvantage. . . . I live in a slightly different world than most women,'' Smiley says in a 1998 *Publishers Weekly* interview with Marcelle Thiébaux.

Critics such as Anne Bernays also tend to highlight the family theme—especially the theme of marriage—that pervades much of Smiley's fiction. In her 1987 review of *The Age of Grief* for the *New York Times Book Review*, Bernays says that ''Ms. Smiley is much occupied with marriage.'' Despite the unsympathetic protagonist, Bernays feels that ''Long Distance'' is ''the most compelling of the five'' short stories in the collection.

Criticism

Critical Overview

Both *The Age of Grief* story collection and ''Long Distance'' have captured the attention of critics. In Roz Kaveney's 1988 *Times Literary Supplement* review of the collection, the critic notes, ''One of

Ryan D. Poquette

Poquette has a bachelor's degree in English and specializes in writing about literature. In the following essay, Poquette discusses Smiley's use of narrative technique, imagery, and symbolism in

What Do I Read Next?

- In *Family: American Writers Remember Their Own* (1997), editors Sharon Sloan Fiffer and Steve Fiffer collect essays from several American writers recalling family members who have changed their lives. Contributors include Edward Hoagland, Alice Hoffman, Jayne Ann Phillips, and Deborah Tannen, and there is also an afterword by Smiley.

- In Joyce Carol Oates's 1996 novel *We Were the Mulvaneys,* an affluent, seemingly close-knit family gets torn apart after one of its members experiences a tragic event.

- Like Smiley, E. Annie Proulx is an American writer regarded as a critical success for both her short stories and novels. Proulx's short-story collection *Close Range: Wyoming Stories* (1999) includes a story titled "The Half-Skinned Steer." This story, like "Long Distance," depicts a man trying to make it through a brutal winter storm in the northern United States as well as the man's efforts to deal with his family issues.

- In *The Epidemic: The Rot of American Culture, Absentee and Permissive Parenting, and the Resultant Plague of Joyless, Selfish Children* (2003), child and family psychiatrist Robert Shaw examines the faddish child-rearing practices from the past three decades. Shaw believes that these practices, along with the effect of the media, are largely to blame for the increase in incidents such as the Columbine High School shooting, and he offers alternative solutions to help stem destructive trends among American children.

- In "Long Distance," Eric has a Ph.D. but does not teach, instead using his knowledge of the family to write for a conservative think tank. In Smiley's 1995 novel *Moo,* she satirizes life at a Midwestern university during the 1989–1990 academic year, incorporating then-current events into the plot, which features a pig as a main character.

- Smiley's Pulitzer Prize–winning novel, *A Thousand Acres,* first published in 1991, recast Shakespeare's play *King Lear* in a modern-day rural setting. The feminist revision of the story depicts an Iowa farmer who decides to divide his farm among his three daughters. The novel includes elements of sexual abuse and, like "Long Distance," examines sometimes painful family relationships.

"*Long Distance*" to enhance the story's dismal mood.

Smiley has become a successful author in part because many of her works contain characters that, while not very flashy, usually elicit sympathy from readers. As Thom Conroy notes in his entry on Smiley for *Dictionary of Literary Biography,* "Often passive and usually sympathetic, Smiley's characters salvage self-knowledge out of the intricate histories and traumas of their inner lives." Yet in "Long Distance," a story that *New York Times Book Review*'s Anne Bernays calls "the most compelling" of the short stories in *The Age of Grief,* readers are given a main character with whom it is difficult to sympathize. It would be very easy for Smiley to condemn Kirby, commenting on his selfish actions and pointing him out to her readers as an example of bad behavior. Instead, Smiley tells Kirby's story without making value judgments. As Roz Kaveney notes in the *Times Literary Supplement,* "Smiley's refusal to get angry with her protagonists, and the way this tolerance never becomes saccharine, are her most attractive virtues." That does not mean that Smiley has no opinion, however. In fact, by using a specific narrative style, as well as imagery and symbolism, Smiley amplifies the dark mood of the story.

The mood of a literary work refers to its defining emotional qualities, which reflect the author's attitude toward the work and its subject matter. Though Smiley does not condemn Kirby's behavior, she does work hard to show how this type of behavior can lead to unhappiness and despair. Even in the beginning of the story, before he has had the revelation that makes him regret the selfish choices he's made in his life, Kirby is not a happy man. He is emotionally distant, a quality that Smiley highlights through the narrative style she uses to describe Kirby's thoughts. In the first paragraph, readers go inside Kirby's head, while he is in the shower, and "hear" four short, simultaneous thoughts about the lack of hot water in his apartment, the abundance of hot water in Japan, the impending arrival of Mieko, and his inability "to control Mieko's expectations of him in any way." When he gets out of the shower, the phone is ringing, and when he answers it, it is Mieko, as he expected. Smiley describes Kirby's reaction as follows: "Perhaps he is psychic; perhaps this is only a coincidence; or perhaps no one else has called him in the past week or so."

This use of short, disparate thoughts in Kirby's mind, none of which register much emotional value or importance, continues throughout the story. When Mieko tells him, with regret, that she knows her sacrifice—not coming to America—could be pointless because her father might die, Kirby apologizes, but his thought patterns betray his indifference to Mieko's pain. "He understands that in his whole life he has never given up a pleasure that he cherished as much as Mieko cherished this one." He does not feel bad for Mieko, who is obviously in pain, and, as Conroy notes, "he offers her no consolation on the subject." Instead, Kirby feels "a lifting of the anxiety he felt in the shower" at not being able to live up to Mieko's expectations. Now that he is "off the hook" and Mieko's pain is clearly "her father's doing, not his," he feels he "can give her a little company after all." As this short, dispassionate style of narration illustrates, Kirby is only able to help others through their pain after he has determined that he is not the cause of it, and after his own needs have been met.

In fact, barring his drunken episode, it is only when the events of the story threaten to cause Kirby physical or emotional harm that he exhibits anything other than casual concern or annoyance. And even then, the emotions are not that powerful. When he is faced with the prospect of his own death as he is driving through a terrible snowstorm, he feels only "self-pity." He is depressed at the idea that if he died on the road, Mieko would never know about it. "He can think of no way that she could hear of his

> "... Harold's spacious house also symbolizes the emotional and familial wealth that Kirby does not possess. Kirby might be able to buy a house someday, but what he lacks--a warm, caring wife and children to fill it--he will never have, unless he learns how to put his selfish feelings aside and care for others."

death, even though no one would care more than she would." Mieko cares about Kirby, but it is obvious from these self-serving thoughts that he could not give her the same emotional support, and, if the situation were reversed and he learned of her death, his reaction would be different. As Conroy notes, later in the trip, "Kirby calls up pleasant images of his stay in Japan in order to divert his mind from a treacherous snowstorm, but he does not give a second thought to Mieko's emotional state."

This emotional indifference shelters Kirby from experiencing the type of pain and loss that Mieko feels, but it also limits his ability to experience some aspects of humanity to their fullest, a fact that becomes clear during the conversation with Leanne at the end of the story when Kirby realizes he has wasted his life and falls into a bitter despair: "it seems to him that all at once, now that he realizes it, his life and Mieko's have taken their final form." As Conroy notes, unlike other Smiley protagonists, Kirby's "emotional trauma is not brought on by naiveté, but by indifference."

Smiley adds power to this final, revelatory scene by employing imagery and symbolism that work together throughout the story to increase the tale's dark mood of despair. The most powerful of these images and symbols are related to the cold weather in which the story takes place. Winter is a season that is often used to symbolize, or represent, the idea of death. The story is saturated with winter imagery, beginning with the phone call between

Mieko and Kirby. As Mieko is telling Kirby that she cannot come to America, ''Kirby is looking out his front window at the snowy roof of the house across the street.'' Although this may seem like merely a casual observation, the timing is intentional on Smiley's part. The relationship between Kirby and Mieko is dying, just as the world outside is going through a season that traditionally symbolizes death. Snow and cold are also often used to describe somebody's lack of passion, as when the term ''frigid'' is used to describe a passionless person. Given Kirby's emotional indifference, the cold weather is an effective symbol for his own dispassionate state.

Later, as Kirby is driving through the blinding snowstorm, the winter elements take on even stronger associations with death: ''The utter blankness of the snowy whirl gives him a way of imagining what it would be like to be dead. He doesn't like the feeling.'' This thought leads to several vivid images that he calls up from his memory of people either dying in the cold or overcoming great odds to survive the elements. Then he imagines himself in such a scene. ''Were he reduced to his own body, his own power, it might be too far to walk just to find a telephone.'' Kirby not only lacks emotional drive; he also lacks the lively spirit and lust for life that others, such as his brother Harold, possess. When Kirby finally arrives safely at Harold's house, he does not mention the bad driving conditions because, ''Compared with some of Harold's near misses, this is nothing.'' Harold has lived an adventurous life, and even though some of his adventures ''show a pure stupidity that even Harold has the sense to be ashamed of,'' there is no doubt that his emotional strength and vitality would help him survive a storm. The most that Kirby can manage is self-pity, which, in a survival situation, would not be enough to save him.

Besides the weather imagery and symbolism, Smiley also uses domestic images to symbolize Kirby's isolation and lack of emotional fortitude. At his brother's house, he can't bear to get up one morning to face all of his relatives, so he lies in bed, thinking. ''As always, despair presents itself aesthetically.'' In this case, he thinks about images of furniture. On the surface, he is just comparing the various interiors of the homes of his family and friends to his own place. Symbolically, however, Kirby is weighing each lifestyle—as represented by the furniture—and trying to find one that fits him. Unfortunately, none does. He thinks of Harold's living room, with ''matching plaid wing chairs and

couch, a triple row of wooden pegs by the maple front door.'' The image is one of frontier, manly coziness and warmth. Indeed, when Kirby thinks later about the meaning of being a man, he says that Harold would define it as somebody who ''can chop wood all day and f—— all night, who can lift his twenty-five pound son above his head on the palm of his hand.'' This robust lifestyle is one that is alien to the emotionally unavailable Kirby.

Yet, Kirby also cannot relate to the pretentious lifestyle of Eric and Mary Beth, which manifests itself in their furniture: ''antique wooden trunks and high-backed benches painted blue with stenciled flowers in red and white.'' The image is one of comfortable, responsible stability. When Kirby imagines how Eric would define manhood, he notes that Eric would say it is someone ''who votes, owns property, has a wife, worries.'' Kirby does not relate to this other extreme either. These thoughts leave him in an unhinged state because he realizes that even the image of his own apartment, with an ''armchair facing the television, which sits on a spindly coffee table,'' does not bring him happiness.

The fact that Kirby lives in an apartment is an important symbol in itself. Whereas Harold's house has sturdy furniture, a symbol of permanence and stability, Kirby's apartment lacks this stability as the ''spindly'' coffee table indicates. When he thinks about Harold's house, he realizes that ''it is the house of a wealthy man.'' Though Kirby means material wealth, Harold's spacious house also symbolizes the emotional and familial wealth that Kirby does not possess. Kirby might be able to buy a house someday, but what he lacks—a warm, caring wife and children to fill it—he will never have, unless he learns how to put his selfish feelings aside and care for others. As Conroy notes of the conversation with Leanne at the end of the story, her comment about Eric not taking advantage of others reveals Kirby's shortcoming, which is much worse than any flaws the rest of his family, even Eric, may have. ''Though Kirby's brother Eric may be overbearing and narrow-minded, he does not value his own pleasure over the feelings of others,'' Conroy says.

In the end, Smiley chooses not to condemn Kirby for his selfish behavior, instead employing techniques in the story that illustrate the loneliness one risks when acting the way Kirby does. The story also ends on a positive note when Kirby ''feels a disembodied kiss on his cheek,'' a message from Leanne in the dark that, although she does not approve of Kirby's callous behavior or absolve him of his guilt, there is hope for him yet. Even the events immediately leading up to this kiss are presented in a symbolic way. Kirby is stumbling in the dark, "unable to see anything." Kirby is in the dark because he wants to change but does not know how. When Kirby stumbles, Leanne takes his arm "in a grasp that is dry and cool, and guides it to the banister." Leanne serves as a symbolic guide to help show Kirby to the stairs—which symbolize the emotional challenge that lies ahead of him if he truly wishes to change his ways—but he must make his way up these stairs himself.

Source: Ryan D. Poquette, Critical Essay on "Long Distance," in *Short Stories for Students,* Gale, 2004.

Catherine Dybiec Holm

Dybiec Holm is a freelance writer and editor. In this essay, Dybiec Holm traces the protagonist's journey toward discovering his personal identity.

At first glance, Jane Smiley's "Long Distance" appears to be a story about a long distance relationship and its implications. Kirby learns immediately in the story that his girlfriend in Japan will not be flying to meet him in the United States for Christmas. A deeper read, however, shows that "Long Distance" is actually about personal identity. Distance is both metaphorical and actual, as in the distance that Kirby needs to travel to define his own identity. Identity is a theme that runs through this story. Kirby searches for his identity, and other characters either lose part of their identity (Mieko) or clearly assert their own identities (Kristin, Anna, and Eric).

Kirby is a protagonist who often acts uncertainly or passively; who practices avoidance; a person with low-level fear; a person unsure of his identity. He cannot deal with the expectations that Mieko has of him, and he wishes the shower would wash his anxiety away. When Mieko calls on the phone, Smiley portrays Kirby's natural uncertainty in his thoughts: "Perhaps he is psychic; perhaps this is only a coincidence; or perhaps no one else has called him in the past week or so."

Kirby is uncertain of how to act on the phone when Mieko breaks down. "This attentive listening is what he owes to her grief, isn't it?" he wonders. Kirby is sure he would have disappointed her, no matter what he did, and would have failed to live up to her expectations. His own personal uncertainty outweighs the slight relief that he feels at her cancellation. As it turns out, the cultural divide

> " Kirby realizes, perhaps for the first time, the immensity of what he has done, even over a long distance. He has, without meaning to, lessened or injured Mieko's sense of identity."

between them shows Kirby another personal shortcoming that he didn't anticipate—his listening to her grief on the phone violated the unwritten rule of privacy that Japan values so highly. In one of Kirby's most revealing moments—at the end of the story—he realizes that in this unwitting, inept move on his part, he somehow lessened Mieko's identity.

During Kirby's road trip to Minnesota in the midst of a blizzard, he works himself into a state of fear, imagining all the things that could go wrong, all the ways he could die. Again, his uncertainty reveals itself: he cannot decide whether to pull off at the rest stop or to keep going; he wants to do both. Yet he still doesn't believe in himself or the essence of his own power. He is still not sure of his identity. "Were he reduced to his own body, his own power, it might be too far to walk just to find a telephone." When he gets through the storm and arrives at his brother's house, Kirby's thoughts sound extremely passive, as if he had nothing to do with getting himself safely to Minnesota. "His car might be a marble that has rolled, only by luck, into a safe corner." We get the sense that Kirby floats through life without identity—waiting for things to happen to him rather than directing his life.

Kirby's identity, or lack of it, is further tested once he settles in at his brother's home. Kirby doesn't dare talk about his dangerous experience driving through a blizzard on the interstate, simply because it could never stand up to some of the dangerous escapades his brother Harold has been through. "The last thing he wants to do is start a discussion about near misses. Compared with some of Harold's near misses, this is nothing."

Kirby may not be quite sure of his own identity yet, but he is sure of what he doesn't want to be. His alienation from the mannerisms and the lives of his extended family become obvious as the holiday gets underway. Kirby doesn't like the "sweet and savory Nordic fare" that is served at dinner. His brother Eric and his wife have molded their self-identities with a Nordic theme. As Kirby observes, Eric has developed "each nuance of his Norwegian heritage into a fully realized ostentation." All the furniture in Eric's house is "pretentious; they have antique wooden trunks and high-backed benches painted blue with stenciled flowers in red and white." But Kirby doesn't even care for the house of the brother he is closer to, and he finds that the image of Harold's and Leanne's living room is like the "interior of a coffin. The idea of spending five years, ten years, a lifetime, with such furniture makes him gasp."

The children of Kirby's extended family show a better sense of identity than does Kirby. Anna's "No!" is "glassy and definite" when she refuses to go outside and play with her brother. Kirby's self-assurance continues to waver. Instead of confronting Eric and Marybeth about their gossip regarding his politics and his life, "he knows that if he were to get up and do something he would stop being offended, but he gets up only to pour himself another drink." Drinking is one way to avoid his feelings of discomfort with himself and his family, and Kirby continues to drink through the rest of the story.

Kirby studies his brother Eric, whom he's never liked, and begins to make an internal judgment, noting that Eric is a "jerk," acts like an old man, and has put on weight. But ultimately, Kirby is uncertain of this opinion, and "his bad mood twists into him." Kirby wonders whether the definition of a man resembles the more traditional Eric or the more adventurous Harold, "someone . . . who can chop wood all day and f——k all night." Notably absent from Kirby's musings are what Kirby thinks. How does he define a man? Kirby cannot know, because he has not defined himself. Kirby realizes that his brothers are similar to each other and he is the odd person out: "Kirby's being does not extend past his fingertips and toes to family, real estate, reputation."

But finally, the beginnings of possible identity make an appearance in Kirby's actions. Interestingly, this is spurred by younger family members who assert themselves and are sure of their identities. The argument that arises at the dinner table concerns a question of identity. Three-year-old Kristin

refuses to eat her ham and, with cognizance that seems beyond her age, tells her father "I mean it." Older Anna defends Kristin and defies her rigid, traditional father by saying that Kristin can put whatever she wants into her own body, an issue related to one's concept of self and identity. "She should have control over her own body. Food. Other stuff. I don't know." Anna asserts her opinion, exposing her own identity by taking a risk. Anna is also defending a question of identity: Kristin should be allowed to make choices for herself, regardless of her age. Anna falters under her father's rage, and this is where Kirby begins to assert some identity by verbally defending Anna and Kristin.

During this interchange, something else happens that eventually leads Kirby to his biggest realization. While Eric is angrily airing his opinions about the function and purpose of the family unit, Kirby looks at Anna and sees a look that he has seen "on Mieko's face, a combination of self-doubt and resentment molded into composure." This is a huge wake-up call for Kirby, who seems to gain an understanding of the issues women face in patriarchal social systems.

During and after the argument, however, there are still subtle hints of Kirby's uncertainty. Smiley puts careful sentence construction and selection of words to good use to illustrate Kirby's hesitance. Kirby realizes "from the tone of his own voice that rage has replaced sympathy and, moreover, is about to get the better of him." Again, we have the sense that Kirby really is not yet in control of his own identity, that he's a passive observer watching himself spring into action, that rage could overtake him and he'd have no control in the matter. After the argument, "he cannot bear to stay here . . . he cannot bear to leave either." This resembles earlier instances of indecision in the story, such as his wanting both to pull off the highway and to keep on driving. In a way, the highway, or the long distance that Kirby travels to see his family, can be seen as a metaphor for Kirby's journey toward defining his own self-identity. All roads lead to his final, illuminating conversation with Leanne.

During this last scene, Kirby reveals more about himself and utters more dialog than he has at any previous point in the story. It seems that Kirby is beginning to crystallize his understanding of himself. Appropriately, perhaps symbolically, the conversation starts with Kristin, the little girl with a well-established sense of identity. Leanne also displays her own strong identity and her strong feelings for Kristin; Leanne has gone to some trouble to rewrap gifts so that Kristin will have a good Christmas.

But Kirby reveals that he's realized something that will lead to the key to his own identity: he's taken from Mieko everything she needed to protect herself. Kirby says, "I see that, one by one, I broke down every single one of her strengths, everything she had equipped herself with to live in a Japanese way." Kirby realizes, perhaps for the first time, the immensity of what he has done, even over a long distance. He has, without meaning to, lessened or injured Mieko's sense of identity. Again focusing on the topic of identity, Leanne points out that, as irritating as Eric can be, the identity that he projects and possesses is firmly established: "He never tries to get something for nothing. I admire that."

With Leanne's comment, Kirby comes closer than he ever has to understanding himself. He realizes that both his life and Mieko's have "taken their final form." Kirby admits the consequences of his actions, and Leanne reaffirms this when she says, "what people do is important." Smiley reinforces for the reader what the story is really about with the cadence of "And himself. Himself." Kirby has, throughout the story, struggled and journeyed toward identifying "himself," what he is about, his self-identity. Though Kirby feels that his "permanent smallness" has now been revealed, he is many steps closer to understanding himself and being more sure of himself, even if that understanding starts with a sense of sorrow for what he has done. At this point, the reader may not be sure about what will become of Kirby or whether he will ever get over his treatment of Mieko. Reviewer Joanne Kaufman, in *People Weekly*, calls the ending to this story "a letdown, as if the author had run out of steam." While the ending may raise more questions than answers, it is the termination of a particular road that Kirby had to travel.

In the end, Leanne does grant Kirby a sort of pardon by guiding him to the stairs and giving him "soft and fleeting . . . a disembodied kiss on his cheek." The use of the word "disembodied" is interesting: it recalls the disembodied tone at earlier points in the story when Kirby seemed to be passively watching himself be led through life. Perhaps the usage is intended as a symbolic falling away of Kirby's passivity. Or perhaps the kiss represents forgiveness across a long distance; the forgiveness of Mieko.

In an interview in *Belles Lettres: A Review of Books by Women*, Smiley said that for her, the writing process is "akin to having three or four interesting objects on your desk and you move them around until you can see some relationship among them." All in all, this story does a wonderful job of looking at a protagonist's journey toward self-identity, with undercurrents of family, gender issues, and distance (metaphorical and literal) pulled into the mix.

Source: Catherine Dybiec Holm, Critical Essay on "Long Distance," in *Short Stories for Students,* Gale, 2004.

Jane Smiley with Marcelle Thiébaux

In the following review-interview excerpt, Smiley comments on critical reception to her collection The Age of Grief *and discusses writing from the male viewpoint.*

We talk too about *The Age Grief,* whose title story, a novella, deals with a pair of dentists and their three small daughters. The marriage is foundering, the wife has a lover. Told from the husband's viewpoint, the novella gets inside modern family life with exquisite sensitivity. The husband senses that he has arrived at a grief which is "the same cup of pain that every mortal drinks from."

Smiley says she was incredulous when *The Age of Grief* was nominated as a finalist for the NBCC Award. "I think if they had actually chosen me I would have been appalled, but it was great, it was totally unlooked for, so it was like this completely positive and totally abstract experience." Even the splendid reviews took Smiley by surprise. "I was unprepared for the personal way that a lot of people took it. I received letters that in some ways were more astonishing than the reviews. Tons of men wrote me saying that [the title story] was very convincing. It seemed like a phenomenon, as if I had tapped into some deep nerve without expecting to."

She finds she has no difficulty writing from a male viewpoint. "I think partly because I'm 6′2′. I think being tall makes my femininity less of a disadvantage. In a big city I notice that I never get accosted or even spoken to. And I think I live in a slightly different world from most women because of my intimidating height."

Whether she is writing from a man's or a woman's perspective, in a medieval or a modern setting, the topic of family life preoccupies Smiley. Living with her third husband, screenwriter Stephen Mortensen, and young daughters Phoebe and Lucy,

> Whether she is writing from a man's or a woman's perspective, in a medieval or a modern setting, the topic of family life preoccupies Smiley."

Smiley finds that parenthood has had a powerful effect on her creativity. "The day my first child was born was a day in which my imagination became fully engaged. Now I'm interested in questions like: How do mothers grow to love their children, and what does that mean? I love books on theories of child-raising."

Source: Jane Smiley with Marcelle Thiébaux, "An Interview with Jane Smiley," in *Publishers Weekly,* Vol. 233, No. 13, April 1, 1998, pp. 65–66.

Sources

Bernays, Anne, "Toward More Perfect Unions," in *New York Times Book Review,* Vol. 92, September 6, 1987, p. 12.

Berne, Suzanne, "In an Interview," in *Belles Lettres: A Review of Books by Women,* Vol. 7, No. 4, Summer 1992, pp. 36–38.

Conroy, Thom, "Jane Smiley," in *Dictionary of Literary Biography,* Vol. 234, *American Short-Story Writers Since World War II, Third Series,* edited by Patrick Meanor, Gale, 2001, pp. 272–78.

Kaufman, Joanne, Review of *The Age of Grief,* in *People Weekly,* Vol. 29, No. 2, January 18, 1988, p. 14.

Kaveney, Roz, "Acceptable Behaviour," in *Times Literary Supplement,* March 18, 1988, p. 302.

Reischauer, Edwin O., *The Japanese Today: Change and Continuity,* Harvard University Press, 1988, pp. 175, 181.

Smiley, Jane, "Long Distance," in *The Age of Grief,* Fawcett Columbine, 1987, pp. 69–92.

Smiley, Jane, with Marcelle Thiébaux, "An Interview with Jane Smiley," in *Publishers Weekly,* Vol. 233, No. 13, April 1, 1998, pp. 65–66.

Sokolov, Raymond, "Them Too: A Family Affair," in *Wall Street Journal,* Vol. 210, No. 49, September 8, 1987, p. 30.

Further Reading

Caplan, Mariana, *When Holidays Are Hell. . .!: A Guide to Surviving Family Gatherings,* Hohm Press, 1997.
    In this comprehensive guide, Caplan examines the advantages and disadvantages of visiting relatives during the holidays and explores—from the viewpoints of both adults and children—the many negative situations that can occur during these times of heightened stress.

Crohn, Joel, *Mixed Matches: How to Create Successful Interracial, Interethnic, and Interfaith Relationships,* Fawcett Books, 1995.
    Crohn, a psychotherapist, uses several case studies to demonstrate the trends and unique challenges faced in interracial, interethnic, and interfaith relationships. Although this book is primarily intended as a guidebook for couples in these situations, it does draw on research to discuss these relationships, so it also serves as a good general resource for anybody interested in learning more about this timely topic.

Guldner, Gregory, *Long Distance Relationships: The Complete Guide,* Fawcett Books, 1995.
    This book examines the factors necessary to sustain a long-distance relationship, such as the one that Kirby and Mieko have in the beginning of "Long Distance." This book is primarily for couples, but it includes quality research into the trends and effects of long-distance relationships.

Kamachi, Noriko, *Culture and Customs of Japan,* Greenwood Press, 1999.
    Kamachi's book examines what life is like for people in Japan. The book includes sections on every major aspect of Japanese life, including thought and religion; literature and art; cuisine and clothing; women, marriage, and family; and social customs and lifestyle.

Nakadate, Neil, *Understanding Jane Smiley,* University of South Carolina Press, 1999.
    Nakadate's book offers a comprehensive critical and biographical study of Jane Smiley's works. Nakadate employs published criticism, interviews with Smiley, and the author's own commentary to examine Smiley's major interests and themes.

Meneseteung

Alice Munro

1990

Alice Munro's short story "Meneseteung" was published in the author's collection *Friend of My Youth* (1990). The meaning of the title "Meneseteung" is not certain: it is the name of the river that Champlain is credited with exploring, and it is also associated with the onset of the menses (menstrual flow) mentioned in section V. The story, like many of Munro's works, was based on her love of the history of rural Ontario, Canada, where she grew up. When one first reads the story, it might appear confusing. Munro employs an outside narrator, who jumps back and forth in time from the 1800s to the 1980s. This narrator includes external sources of information—such as newspaper clippings and excerpts from books—that interrupt the flow of the story and disorient the reader, and, at the end of the story, the authenticity of the narrator is called into question, which can make some readers question the point of the story. Yet, when one digs deeper, the reasons for these seemingly jarring narrative devices, which are another trademark of Munro's writing, become clear. Through its complicated structure and the use of a questionable narrator, "Meneseteung" ultimately explores many themes. As a result, Munro's story can be enjoyed on many levels. One can read the story as a historical piece, examining the life of a Canadian frontierswoman who lives in a male-dominated society and who encounters the baser aspects of the human experience. One can also concentrate on the narrator, who is reconstructing this tale by using historical bits of information and extrapolat-

ing to cover the gaps. Finally, one can focus on Munro herself and the author's attempts to describe the narrative process. A current copy of the work can be found in the paperback version of *Friend of My Youth*, which was published by Vintage Books in 1991.

Author Biography

Munro was born on July 10, 1931, in the small town of Wingham, Ontario, in Canada. Her father owned a silver-fox farm on the outskirts of the town. The author began writing stories as a teenager during her lunch hours at school because it was too far to walk home, as other students did. Since writing was not looked upon favorably in the small town, Munro never showed her writing to anybody, but she has described these early works as passionate stories, full of horror, romance, and adventure. Munro did well in school, and in 1949 she earned a scholarship to the University of Western Ontario in London, Ontario.

In 1951, Munro married James Munro, and the couple moved to the city of Vancouver, British Columbia, on Canada's west coast, where the author concentrated on raising a family, including Sheila (born in 1953) and Jenny (born in 1957). Munro also secretly began to write stories again, drawing on her experience in rural Ontario for many of them. In 1963, the couple moved to Victoria, British Columbia, where they opened a bookstore together and, in 1966, had another daughter, Andrea. Two years later, in 1968, Munro published her first story collection, *Dance of the Happy Shades*, which won her immediate critical and popular attention— as well as the Governor General's Award for fiction in 1969. In 1971, Munro published *Lives of Girls and Women*, an interconnected collection of stories.

Munro's relationship with her husband deteriorated, and, when they separated in 1972, she moved back to London, Ontario, with her two younger daughters. During the 1974–1975 academic year, Munro served as writer-in-residence at the University of Western Ontario. In 1974, Munro also published *Something I've Been Meaning to Tell You*, her third collection of short stories. In 1976, Munro's divorce from James Munro became official. The same year, she married Gerald Fremlin, a geographer, and the couple moved to Clinton, Ontario, about twenty miles from the author's childhood home of Wingham.

Munro has been consistent in her writing career, publishing a story collection every three or four years. In 1978, she published *Who Do You Think You Are?*, which was also published as *The Beggar Maid: Stories of Flo and Rose* (1979). From 1979 to 1982, Munro traveled throughout Australia, China, and Scandinavia, but this did not interrupt her publishing pattern. In 1982, she published the collection *The Moons of Jupiter*, which was followed by *The Progress of Love* (1986). The same year, Munro was awarded the first Marian Engel Award, which is given to a woman writer for an outstanding body of work. In 1990, Munro published her seventh book, *Friend of My Youth*, which included the story ''Meneseteung.''

Unlike many authors who write both novels and short stories, Munro continues to focus solely on short fiction. Munro has also published the following collections: *Open Secrets: Stories* (1994), *The Love of a Good Woman: Stories* (1998), and *Hateship, Friendship, Courtship, Loveship, Marriage: Stories* (2001).

Plot Summary

I

The first section, like all of the other sections of ''Meneseteung,'' starts out with a short piece of poetry by Almeda Joynt Roth, a nineteenth-century woman. The narrator, whose gender is never noted, gives some background about the publishing details of Roth's one and only book, *Offerings*, and then gives a description of Roth herself, based upon a photograph that the narrator is looking at in the front of the book. The narrator quotes from the preface of the book, which gives a short history of the poet's life, including her family's move to the frontier of Canada West (modern-day Ontario) and the death of her entire family. Roth talks about her love of poetry, which she turned to because she lacked the skill for other crafts common to women of her time, such as crochet work. At this point, the narrator takes over the story, giving a list of the various poems that are in the book, most of which are about nature or family.

II

The second section begins with the narrator talking about Roth's life in 1879, following her parents' death, when she lived alone in their house on Pearl and Dufferin streets. The narrator compares the home to the modern-day home, indicating that she is in the same area of Ontario as she relates the story. The narrator gives details about the daily life in Roth's small town, which the narrator read in the *Vidette,* the local newspaper. Some details include the fact that school is only in session four months out of the year, which leaves adventurous boys with time to harass others or otherwise get into trouble. One person whom the boys continually harass is a woman nicknamed Queen Aggie, a drunk whom they dump into a wheelbarrow and roll all over town. The narrator paints a picture of danger, noting the confidence men, thieves, and other disreputable types that inhabit the town. They are particularly prone to hanging out at the end of Pearl Street, which is farthest from Roth's home.

III

This section introduces the character of Jarvis Poulter, who arrived a few years ago and who lives two lots down from Roth. Poulter is a widower who is known for his tendency to take water and coal supplies, in an attempt to save money. This fact is alluded to in the *Vidette,* which, according to the narrator, spreads rumors and innuendos that would be libelous in today's newspapers. Poulter came to the town seeking oil but discovered salt instead and has become a wealthy businessman. Poulter and Roth are seen speaking together about his business, prompting a thinly veiled note in the *Vidette* that indicates they may be a couple. The narrator talks about the fact that Roth is not quite an old maid and that she is thinking she would like to marry Poulter but, as is proper for the times, is waiting for him to make the first move to indicate his interest. The narrator says that Roth does not want a man whom she has to mold as other women mold their husbands. Roth waits anxiously for a sign of Poulter's interest, but, at the same time, she would be disappointed if they were to go out on a countryside date, because she could not reflect on nature in silence as she usually does.

IV

The narrator says that Roth takes sedatives that her doctor has prescribed for sleeplessness but avoids nerve medicine drops because they give her vivid dreams. The doctor believes that Roth needs to be more active and that her problem would be solved if she got married. She decides one day to make some grape jelly, and when she goes to bed, the grape pulp is still straining. She wakes up to noises outside and realizes they are coming from the rowdy denizens of

Alice Munro

Pearl Street. She tries to ignore them but thinks she hears somebody being murdered. She plans to go check it out but falls asleep before she can get up the nerve to go. She wakes at dawn and in her half-awake state dreams she sees an imaginary bird that tells her to move the wheelbarrow. This word, which seems odd at first, recalls the wheelbarrow used by the youths to transport Queen Aggie.

Indeed, when Roth looks outside, she sees that there is a woman pressed against her fence, who Roth assumes is dead. In a panic she runs out of her house in her nightclothes and fetches Jarvis Poulter to come and help her with the dead woman. Poulter is at first annoyed and gets even more callous when he sees that the woman on Roth's fence is not dead but merely passed out from drinking too much. The woman's animal-like behavior shocks Roth and makes her feel sick, as does Poulter's callous behavior. Poulter, on the other hand, likes the vulnerability that he has seen in the desperate Roth and finally asks her to accompany him to church.

V

When Roth gets back to her house, she realizes that part of her sickness is from the bloating of premenstruation. She decides that she is not well enough to go to church and leaves a message for

Poulter on the front window stating this. She makes herself some tea and adds several drops of nerve medicine. The medicine affects her, making the room around her seem to come alive. In her delirious state, Roth starts to think about poetry and has the wish to create one poem that will contain all of her experiences. She is so caught up in her delirium that she does not notice the grape juice bin overflowing, and she is so far gone that she does not think anything is real anymore.

VI

Unlike previous sections, the final section is told entirely through two *Vidette* clippings and some present-day commentary by the narrator. The first news clipping describes the mental decline of Roth and her death, which the newspaper suggests was due to harassment by youths like those who used to harass Queen Aggie. The second news clipping describes the death of Poulter, less than a year later. In the final commentary, the narrator describes going to Almeda Roth's grave in the present day and talks about how people make connections from historical clues. Then in the last paragraph, the narrator shares a revelation, indicating that everything that has come before has also been extrapolated from historical clues and that the narrator does not know if the story really happened that way or not.

Characters

The Doctor

The doctor gives Almeda ''bromides and nerve medicine'' for insomnia. He advises her to do housework and to exercise but not to read. It is his opinion that ''her troubles would clear up if she got married,'' despite the fact that he prescribes nerve medicine most often for married women.

The Narrator

The narrator is a person of unspecified gender who relates the tale of Almeda Roth, the story inside Munro's short story, but who admits at the end that he or she is not sure the story happened that way, since he or she has guessed on many of the historical details. The narrator's presence is most noticeable at the beginning and ending of Munro's story. In between, the narrator gradually fades into the background, and the story focuses more and more on specifics in Roth's life that the narrator could not

possibly know, such as Roth's thoughts during individual events. At the end of the story, the narrator visits Roth's grave, where the authenticity of the story is called into question.

Jarvis Poulter

Jarvis Poulter is the initial love interest of Almeda Roth in the narrator's story. Poulter, a widower, arrived a few years before the main action of the story takes place. He lives two lots down from Roth and has only shown casual interest in her, talking with her on occasion but never making a formal show of interest, such as asking her to walk to church with him or accompany him on a trip to the countryside. Poulter has become rich through a number of businesses, most notably salt mining, but he still has the tendency to collect coal from alongside the railroad tracks and take water from the public pump. When Roth comes to him early one morning in a panic, telling him about the dead body against her fence, Poulter realizes that the woman slumped against Roth's fence is merely drunk and roughly makes the woman leave. Attracted to Roth's desperate vulnerability, Poulter asks her to church, but Roth ultimately refuses, and the two never pursue a relationship. Poulter dies less than a year after Roth.

Queen Aggie

Queen Aggie is the nickname for a drunk woman who gets harassed by youths who roll her around in a wheelbarrow before dumping her into a ditch.

Almeda Joynt Roth

Almeda Roth is the main character in the narrator's story. Roth is a historical figure whose life the narrator is reconstructing through old news stories and clues, such as the nickname on Roth's gravestone. In the beginning of the narrator's story, Roth is a respectable woman who has become famous in her small Canadian town for her book of poetry. Roth yearns to marry Jarvis Poulter, an idea that the rest of the town supports. Even Roth's doctor, who prescribes nerve medicine to help Roth with her sleeplessness, says she would be much happier if she were married. When Roth sees a drunk woman— who she presumes is dead—slumped against her fence, she appeals to Poulter for help. The woman is not dead, and Poulter treats her roughly. Poulter, who has been, up until this point, uninterested in Roth, now is drawn to her vulnerability, but Roth is turned off by the callous way that Poulter has treated the drunk woman, and she rebuffs his interest and retreats into the vivid delirium induced by her nerve medicine. Her mental health declines, and she meets her death after being harassed by youths in much the same way that Queen Aggie was. Because the narrator is guessing at much of Roth's life, the reader is left to guess how much of the story is true.

Themes

Roles of Women

Through the use of a sleuthing narrator who tries to re-create certain aspects of the life of a historical figure, Munro's story examines the expected place of women in Roth's society. While the *Vidette* claims Roth's poet status as a town asset, the narrator notes that "There seems to be a mixture of respect and contempt, both for her calling and her sex." In the nineteenth century, when Roth's story takes place, the expectation is that a woman will marry, have a family, and live to support her husband, none of which Roth has done. When the *Vidette* speculates about the prospect of Roth and Jarvis Poulter getting married, the newspaper says, "She is not too old to have a couple of children" and "She is a good enough housekeeper." In the minds of the townspeople, this is enough incentive for a man to marry her. The narrator further speculates about why Roth may have been passed over, using the *Vidette* article as a starting point: "She was a rather gloomy girl—that may have been the trouble." Beyond this depression, which Roth fell into after the death of her entire family, the narrator also surmises that it might be her vocation that has kept her an old maid: "And all that reading and poetry—it seemed more of a drawback, a barrier, an obsession."

Marriage is also viewed as the cure-all to many of women's problems, even when this logic does not make sense. For example, when Roth's doctor prescribes medicine for her sleeplessness, the narrator says that the doctor thinks she will not have this problem if she gets married. "He believes this in spite of the fact that most of his nerve medicine is prescribed for married women." Women are por-

Media Adaptations

- Munro's *Friend of My Youth* (1990) was produced as an abridged audiobook in 1990 by Random House Audio. It is currently out of print but is available through some libraries and used book stores.

- Munro's *Hateship, Friendship, Courtship, Loveship, Marriage: Stories* (2001) was produced as an unabridged audiobook in 2002 by Audio Partners. It was also produced as an unabridged audio CD in 2002 by Chivers Sound Library.

- Munro's *The Love of a Good Woman* (1998) was produced as an unabridged audiobook in 1999 by Chivers Audio Books.

trayed as weak and in need of men, as when Roth panics and rushes over to Poulter's house for assistance with the drunk woman. When she does this, it is the first time Roth has acted like a typical woman of her society—as opposed to the poised, confident woman that Poulter has known in the past, qualities that have not attracted him to her. "He has not been able to imagine her as a wife. Now that is possible." The narrator says that Poulter is "sufficiently stirred" and posits that it is most likely due to Roth's "indiscretion, her agitation, her foolishness, her need." Yet, as the narrator indicates, women are not powerless in marriage, and one of their primary roles in this era is "creating their husbands" by "ascribing preferences" to them. "This way, bewildered, sidelong-looking men are made over, made into husbands, heads of households." Roth cannot see herself doing this, which further separates her from the society in which she lives.

The Human Experience

The narrator's story also explores the darker aspects of the human experience. Although the tale starts out with Roth ignoring the most realistic parts

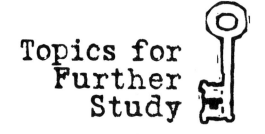

Topics for Further Study

- In "Meneseteung" the narrator creates a story by citing fictional news clippings and reconstructing the historical events this fictional paper discusses, filling in the blanks with guesswork. Pick a little-known historical event, and use the bits of information available to create your own historical short story, using your knowledge of the topic to fill in the blanks where necessary.

- In the story, Almeda Roth is a female poet. While the townspeople claim her literary gifts as a town treasure, they also believe that she should give them up to get married and take care of her husband. Choose another female writer from the late nineteenth century and write a short biography about her, focusing on how her talents were received by her society.

- Research the history of female painters in the nineteenth century, and compare the challenges

that they faced to the challenges that Almeda faces in the story.

- Draw a map of Canada, circa the late nineteenth century when the main events of the story take place. Identify the general region in which Almeda Roth lives, and, using the geographical clues in the story—as well as any relevant information from the author's own geographical background—try to pinpoint the specific area where Munro intends the story to take place.

- One of the final news clippings in the story describes Almeda as having become an unusual eccentric, but, given the details, it seems likely that Almeda has gone insane. Research the history of insanity in the late nineteenth century, and discuss several methods that were used to deal with the mentally ill. For each method, try to find an actual historical example to illustrate your idea.

---

of humanity, preferring to look at life through rose-tinted glasses, the incident with the drunk woman forces her to come face to face with the dark side of human nature, and she sees humans as little more than animals. When Roth first sees the woman, she thinks of her in animal terms: "Almeda can't see her face. But there is a bare breast loose, brown nipple pulled long like a cow's teat, and a bare haunch and leg." This bestial style of language continues when Poulter examines the woman and "nudges the leg with the toe of his boot, just as you'd nudge a dog or a sow." Roth's association of the woman with her base, animal nature becomes complete when the woman lifts her head, which is covered with blood and vomit, and begins to bang it against the fence. "As she bangs her head, she finds her voice and lets out an openmouthed yowl, full of strength and what sounds like anguished pleasure."

Though the description of the woman blatantly indicates the raw, animal nature of humanity, other

aspects of the story underscore dark elements of the human experience in more subtle ways. For example, throughout the story readers hear about incidents of violence, such as when the youths harass Queen Aggie or strangers, or when the fight takes place on the street outside Roth's fence. "And the people around are calling out, 'Stop it! Stop that!' or 'Kill her! Kill her!' in a frenzy, as if at the theatre or a sporting match or a prizefight." Besides murder, the story gives a litany of examples of ways that people die or become ill, so that, by the end of the story, Roth is so disillusioned with the human experience that she associates it with death. Following the incident with the woman, when Roth is locked away in her house, she hears everybody walking to church and thinks of them in morbid terms: "Tombstones are marching down the street on their little booted feet, their long bodies inclined forward, their expressions preoccupied and severe." At this point, long before the nerve medicine has started to affect her sense of reason, Roth has given

---

up on humanity. She locks herself away, and, as the last news clipping indicates, she never fully rejoins human society, instead choosing the comfort of living in an imagined reality.

Style

Point of View

The narration in "Meneseteung" is complex. At first it seems to be a typical third-person-omniscient point of view, one in which an outside narrator is given the ability to tell the story from the point of view of any character. In this viewpoint, the narrator can also move between time periods, as necessary, to tell the story. This differs from the third-person-limited point of view, which limits the telling to the perspective of a limited number of characters, usually just one. Beyond this basic structure, however, the narration in "Meneseteung" features another aspect that gives it greater complexity than the average third-person-omniscient story. The story uses an unreliable narrator, a narrator whose story cannot be trusted for some reason. This fact becomes most evident at the end of the story when the narrator says, "I may have got it wrong. I don't know if she ever took laudanum. Many ladies did. I don't know if she ever made grape jelly." By referring to two specific facts from the story that play a large part in the story's plot and then posing the idea that these events might never have happened, the authenticity of the narrator's entire story is called into question.

The Narrative Process

Point of view is one specific narrative aspect that Munro uses to shape her story, but, through her narrator's questionable storytelling methods, Munro also explores the narrative process itself—the actual process of creating a story. At the beginning of the narrator's tale, the story seems quite straightforward, and readers might suspect that they are going to hear a historical account of Roth's life. Though this happens to some extent, readers also learn more about the narrative process, an idea first introduced when readers are told about Roth's love of poetry.

"From my earliest years I have delighted in verse and I have occupied myself . . . with many floundering efforts at its composition," Roth notes in the preface of her book. Then the narrator discusses some of Roth's poems, listing their titles and basic themes in a straightforward manner, as if the narrator is cataloguing the poems. The style of the narrator's storytelling at this point is very factual and to the point, with little embellishment.

As the narrator digs deeper into Roth's life, however, the narrator sheds objectivity and begins to dig into the narrative process, creating a life for Roth that may have never existed. In the process, readers are taken along for the ride, thinking that they are hearing a historical account but in the end realizing that they have been duped and that the narrator has actually been creating the story while telling it to the readers. Munro also explores the narrative process through the specific ways she has her narrator describe Roth's delirium: "Soon this glowing and swelling begins to suggest words—not specific words but a flow of words somewhere, just about ready to make themselves known to her. Poems, even." This passage, and the ones that follow it, on the surface serves as a description of what goes through Roth's head during her delirium. Yet this language also attempts to describe the mystery of a writer's inspiration, the mental rush that suddenly makes connections in the writer's mind, leading to the formation of an original thought and ultimately to a literary work, such as the poem that Roth tries to create in her delirium.

Setting

The setting of the story is also extremely important to the narrative. The story is set in two different time periods, the late 1980s, when Munro is writing the story, and the mid-to-late 1800s, mainly 1879 when the main action of the story begins. This time change is important. More than a century has passed since the time of the story events, so the story cannot be simply told; it must be reconstructed from historical accounts. For this to happen, somebody has to be motivated enough—as the narrator is—to do the historical legwork. The narrator notes this quality of historical stories at the end of "Meneseteung" in a general comment about researchers: "You see them going around with notebooks, scraping the dirt off gravestones, reading microfilm, just in the hope of seeing this trickle in time, making a connection, rescuing one thing from the rubbish.''

Yet, while the story bounces back and forth between two time periods, the place does not change. In the narrator's time, the story takes place in modern-day Ontario, which, when Almeda Roth and her family moved there, was known as Canada West. The use of the same physical setting helps to add authenticity to the narrator's story since the narrator can cite specific details about the town in Roth's time and compare them to details that can be seen in the narrator's own time. For example, the narrator talks about Roth's house: ''The house is still there today; the manager of the liquor store lives in it.'' Since the house physically exists and is not just a figment of the narrator's imagination, it becomes one of the solid, factual details that anchors the story. Comparisons such as this also add to the effectiveness of the story. In 1879, the house is owned by Almeda Roth, who, in the beginning, is the picture of virtue. In the narrator's time, it is owned by somebody who sells alcohol, which in Roth's time was viewed as a vice. The contrast is intentional on Munro's part, as it helps to underscore the mental deterioration that Roth undergoes in the story.

Historical Context

In ''Meneseteung,'' Almeda Roth's family moves to ''the wilds of Canada West (as it then was)'' in 1854, as Roth notes in the preface to her poetry book. This simple statement is anything but simple when looked at in a historical context. In fact, the Roth family move is representative of a greater population shift that was taking place in Canada. As in the United States, this immigration was due in part to the establishment of railways and roads, which provided mass transportation into desolate areas. Yet, while Americans' version of moving west generally meant California and other states in the far West, moving westward for Canadians often meant moving to Canada West. The designation of this area, which is today known as Ontario, as ''west'' may appear to the modern reader to be somewhat of a misnomer, since it is located north of the American Midwest, not even half of the distance

across the vast country of modern-day Canada. But in this time period, much of western Canada was still undeveloped, and one did not have to travel too far to reach the frontier.

In the 1850s, the whole of modern-day Canada was still referred to as British North America—a collection of colonial provinces that was under British sovereignty. This governing arrangement changed in the 1860s, thanks to a large political movement that culminated in an event known as the Confederation. The push for confederation, which essentially united the disparate colonies into one political region, began for many reasons. Many leaders sought union as a way to overcome political differences and make it easier to pass legislation and accomplish other governmental duties. With each province separate and watching out for its own interests, it was hard for British North America to evolve and compete with other countries, most notably its southern neighbor, the United States, which was quickly becoming a world power. Economics also played a large part in the Confederation. Some visionaries realized that by unifying they could open up even more railways, which would lead to more immigration to desolate areas, which ultimately would lead to a stronger, more populous British North America—one that could compete with the United States.

British North America's troubled relationship with the United States provided another impetus for confederation. Although the two regions had enjoyed a thriving trade relationship, the American Civil War (1861–1865) threatened to change that. During the war, Britain had supported the American South in various ways, and so British North America was guilty by association—even though many of its citizens were against slavery to the point that some volunteered to fight on the side of the American North. So, distancing itself from Britain seemed like a good idea to British North America, which did not want to lose valuable trade dollars or get on the bad side of the powerful United States. From Britain's perspective, separating itself from its colonies in British North America also seemed like a good plan, since the vast territory was expensive to maintain and protect and the money that Britain made off the territory did not justify keeping it within its control. So, on July 1, 1867, the British Parliament passed the British North American Act, which officially severed the country's control of British North

Compare & Contrast

- **Mid-to-Late 1800s:** The various provinces of Canada are united into the British-affiliated Dominion of Canada in an event known as the Confederation. The move is completely supported by Britain through the British North America Act of 1867, although not all Canadian provinces agree with this move.

  1980s: In 1982, Britain passes the Canada Act, which formally removes the British North America Act of 1867 and grants Canada complete autonomy from Great Britain. The Canadian government drafts its first constitution in 1982, which leads to many political battles in Canada, most notably with residents in the province of Quebec, which refuses to sign the document, worrying that the specific needs of its distinct French-Canadian culture will not be preserved by the constitution.

  Today: Although Quebec has still not signed the constitution, it operates under this document, and the province is considered a part of Canada. That said, Quebec retains several distinct aspects that are influenced by its French-speaking heritage, including a different civil code and separate schools for French-speaking and English-speaking students.

- **Mid-to-Late 1800s:** The Confederation sets the stage for immigration into the western portions of Canada. Due to bad economic times, Canadians move westward, seeking better opportunities, and also southward to the United States.

  1980s: Due to a large influx of immigrants from Europe and Asia, as well as from the United States, Canada's population becomes increasingly multicultural. The overwhelming majority of these people settle in urban areas.

  Today: In terms of land area, Canada is the second-largest country in the world after Russia, but it is one of the most sparsely populated countries. Despite the massive migration west in the late nineteenth and early twentieth centuries, the greatest concentrations of people are still in Ontario and Quebec, formerly Canada West and East, respectively, and more than three-fourths of the population lives in urban areas.

- **Mid-to-Late 1800s:** Legislation is passed that restricts voting to property-owning males only, which, during the year of Confederation, equates to only about one-fifth of Canada's males. Women in Canada join the international women's movement, known as first-wave feminism, that is taking place in other areas of the world, most notably Britain and the United States. Women's suffrage becomes one of the main goals of this movement.

  1980s: Despite gaining the right to vote and making other advances through the modern women's movement in the 1960s and 1970s, women still struggle to achieve equal rights in certain areas, such as the workplace and education.

  Today: Some inequalities remain, particularly in the political sphere. Canadian women outnumber the men but do not have equal representation.

America—from that point on known as the Dominion of Canada. Although Britain was no longer in control of the Canadian territories, the new dominion was loosely affiliated with Britain and did not achieve full autonomy until 1982.

As expected, the Confederation led to even greater immigration into the frontier lands in Canada West, which was renamed the province of Ontario. As Munro's story demonstrates, life in these wild Ontario lands was dictated by extremes. The attitudes expressed by the townspeople in the story are indicative of the rigid morality that held sway in Canada during much of nineteenth century—a social attitude that was embraced by certain segments of the population in Britain. Because Canada was first ruled by Britain and then remained affiliated with it after the Confederation, the region tended to adopt many of the social customs of its parent country. This rigid morality often expressed itself in a focus on marriage and family—including the proper, dependent role of respectable women—and conservative sexual attitudes, like those expressed by the townspeople in the story.

But in Roth's town, as in areas of Britain, this code of morality was not followed by all. On the other extreme, there were violence, crime, and other forms of disreputable behavior. In fact, Roth's geographic location, on the border between the good and bad sections of the town, gives her a vantage point from which to view both the moral, good acts and the violent, terrible acts that often took place simultaneously in frontier towns.

Critical Overview

When *Friend of My Youth* was published in 1990, it was a critical success. As Judith Timson notes in her 1990 essay on the work, it "was an instant literary event not only in Canada but also in the United States, where the writer and her work have garnered rave reviews." Many of these rave reviews, including those that Munro earned for *Friend of My Youth*, are due to Munro's unconventional style. Anne Boston, in her 1990 review of the collection for *New Statesmen and Society,* remarks on Munro's "fine disregard for convention," saying that the author "spins her narratives decades back and forwards, gathering lifetimes and whole groups of characters into the space of 20 pages." Specifically, Boston notes that the use of a present-day narrator to tell a historical story gives "Meneseteung" "added depth and distance."

Besides the temporal span of her works, critics also cite Munro's ability to combine fictional and realistic elements in unique patterns. In a 1986 essay about Munro's fiction for *Queen's Quarterly,* George Woodcock calls this "a tension between autobiography and invention which she manipulates so superbly that both elements are used to the full and in the process enrich each other." Some critics note that the realistic elements of Munro's fiction take on near photographic qualities. "Details of place are strikingly, almost photographically evoked," Carol Shields says in her 1991 review of *Friend of My Youth* for *London Review of Books.* Likewise, Woodcock says, "The photographic ele-

ment in her presentation of scenes and characters as visualizable images is an essential factor in her writing."

Besides favoring Munro's use of photographic descriptions, critics also praise her unconventional use of realistic elements such as the news clippings she employs in "Meneseteung." "Munro has gone a long way toward reshaping the short story for her purposes, or rather unshaping it," Shields says. She references Munro's use of "newspaper articles, old letters, and, very often, seemingly random anecdotes beaded on a thin string of narrative." Timson speaks about the effect of these added elements, especially in a work like "Meneseteung." "It is a tricky work because parts of it, including excerpts from Roth's book of poetry and her obituary, suggest that she was a real person, brought to life from some dusty newspaper clippings." But as Timson notes, the entire story—clippings, poetry, and all—was fabricated by Munro.

Because Munro tends to take her reader back and forth through time and uses realistic elements in much of her fiction, disorienting the reader and sabotaging the flow of her stories, some critics refer to her works as plotless, though not in a bad way. In her 1986 entry on Munro for *Dictionary of Literary Biography,* Catherine Sheldrick Ross says, "Instead of plots, Munro's work offers arrangements of materials that shift our perceptions of ordinary events and make us see the ordinary in an extraordinary way." Ross, like many critics, believes that Munro's intentionally plotless works force readers to examine the specific, realistic details of the stories, in an attempt to make them "recognize and acknowledge discoveries" about their own selves. In addition, critics note that there is a silent elegance in Munro's seemingly haphazard stories. "As much is omitted or hidden as left in; and things are rarely what they seem," Boston says.

While critics note that all of the stories in *Friend of My Youth* share these universal qualities of Munro's writing, some have singled out "Meneseteung," for various reasons. For example, though Munro has always been fascinated by the narrative process, a fascination that permeates many of her stories, Shields says that "Meneseteung" is about fiction itself, "the materials that go into a narrative, the how of a story rather than the what." Critics also note the complexity of the story. In her

1990 review of *Friend of My Youth* for the *New Republic,* Mary Jo Salter calls "Meneseteung" "the most ambitious story in this volume." Citing Almeda's vision, Salter says it is "one of the most inspired moments in any of these extraordinary stories."

Criticism

Ryan D. Poquette

Poquette has a bachelor's degree in English and specializes in writing about literature. In the following essay, Poquette discusses Munro's use of external elements to enhance the narrative impact of "Meneseteung."

When one first reads "Meneseteung," it may seem as if Munro is as delirious as Almeda Roth, the nineteenth-century woman and main character in the narrator's story who succumbs to the blissful escapism of drugs by the end of the tale. Munro seems to indulge her every whim in the story, merging back and forth between two radically different time periods, including a narrator that calls into question the very authenticity of her own tale, and, most noticeably, inserting bits and pieces of historical information into the narrative, such as newspaper accounts and photographs. As Carol Shields says in the *London Review of Books,* "Munro has gone a long way toward reshaping the short story for her purposes, or rather unshaping it. Strange bits of the world go into her work: digressions of every sort." Shields also notes the "seemingly random anecdotes beaded on a thin string of narrative." Yet, nothing in Munro's work is random, including these external, historical elements. Rather, these devices serve several purposes.

The first and most noticeable effect of these external elements is that they jar the reader and disrupt the flow of the story, slicing the narrative into distinct and separate episodes. This episodic narration works against a reader's natural tendency to look for the organizing pattern, or plot, in a story. Most humans instinctively crave this order, which is

one of the reasons why traditional, well-constructed stories, stories that are bundled up into neat packages with clear themes and a coherent structure, bring so much enjoyment. But, as in much of Munro's fiction, there is no organizing, cohesive structure to "Meneseteung." In her entry on Munro for *Dictionary of Literary Biography,* Catherine Sheldrick Ross notes the effect of the plotless style that Munro uses, saying that it forces readers to look at the events in a different way: "Instead of plots, Munro's work offers arrangements of materials that shift our perceptions of ordinary events and make us see the ordinary in an extraordinary way."

Munro discusses the ordinary in many of her stories, including "Meneseteung," which includes long descriptions about the nineteenth-century frontier town in which Almeda Roth lived. "Only the main street is gravelled; the other streets are dirt roads, muddy or dusty according to season. Yards must be fenced to keep animals out." This is just one detail in a lengthy passage that also discusses what kinds of animals are in the town and the different types of droppings that these animals leave, which make "ladies have to hitch up their skirts." The story gains authenticity from these near photorealistic descriptions that the narrator uses. But these details, as the narrator says, are based upon accounts from the newspapers of the time. "I read about that life in the *Vidette,*" the narrator says. This sets up the idea that the narrator is using the newspaper accounts to re-create Roth's story.

From the very beginning, the narrator uses the newspaper in this way, as one of the main sources for her historical facts. In the first two sections of the story, the narrator tells the story almost entirely through factual sources such as the *Vidette* and the *Offerings* book that Roth published, which includes a publication date and a photograph of the author—lending the narrator's story even more authenticity. But at the end of the second section, the narrator merges into a more subjective role while shaping the story, re-creating Roth's thoughts—something that the narrator could not possibly know from newspaper accounts or even from the preface to Roth's book. "Almeda sleeps at the back of the house. She keeps to the same bedroom she once shared with her sister Catherine—she would not think of moving to the large front bedroom." In the third section, the narrator's re-creations get even more into the mind of Roth, and they also quote

What Do I Read Next?

- Sherwood Anderson's *Winesburg, Ohio* (1919) depicts everyday life in small-town Ohio. This collection of short stories was noted for its subtle, understated qualities and its use of unconventional structure.

- In "Meneseteung," the narrator imagines Almeda Roth in a nerve-medicine-induced delirium in which Roth locks herself inside her house and examines the wallpaper, which she thinks might move at any moment. In Charlotte Perkins Gilman's famous novella *The Yellow Wallpaper* (1899), the story consists of ten diary entries by Jane, a wife who gets locked into a room. Her physician husband thinks that the seclusion will help her get over what he assumes is depression. As the story progresses, Jane increasingly relates with a trapped woman whom she envisions living inside the room's yellow wallpaper.

- In Munro's first book, *Dance of the Happy Shades* (1968), several of the female narrators possess characteristics that keep them isolated from their communities, like Almeda in "Meneseteung."

- Munro's *Lives of Girls and Women* (1972), a collection of interconnected short stories that some critics refer to as a novel, examines the life of Del Jordan. Del is exposed to the underworld of crime and outcasts on The Flats Road, a seamy area like the Pearl Street region described in "Meneseteung." The book explores Del's coming of age as a woman and a writer, including her experiences with sex and religion.

- Several critics have noted the photorealistic qualities of Munro's fiction, including the stories in *Friend of My Youth.* In Susan Sontag's landmark essay collection *On Photography* (1977), the writer thoroughly explores the meaning of photography. Like Munro's examination of the roles of fiction and reality in the narrative process, Sontag explores the relation between a photograph and the real object that it is meant to represent, including how much truth there is in a photograph.

- Tom Stoppard's play *Arcadia* (1993) involves major characters from two different time periods in the same house who are involved in a mystery that takes place in both eras. Like "Meneseteung," the modern-day characters help to re-create the historical events. Unlike Munro's story, audiences see the events literally reenacted by the historical characters, as opposed to having them reconstructed through a narrator who is making educated guesses.

- Munro has often been called a regional writer, and she has noted that she was most influenced by another regional writer, Eudora Welty, a woman who set most of her stories in the American South and who also focused on the mundane aspects of everyday life. *The Golden Apples* (1949), an interconnected collection of stories, features a strong female protagonist who defies the conventions of her southern society by remaining a single and independent woman. Unlike Munro's works, which are subtle in their discussion of mythological elements and symbolism, this book, like much of Welty's work, incorporates a heavy dose of Greek mythology and symbolism.

---

specific, private conversations between Roth and Jarvis Poulter.

Now, in a normal story, readers understand that narrators, as a rule, can go inside the heads of fictional characters and present their thoughts as necessary, which is an essential technique for telling the story. But Munro does not set up "Meneseteung" like a traditional, fictional story. The historical accounts make it seem as if it really happened. Judith Timson notes this effect in

Maclean's, saying that the story "is a tricky work because parts of it, including excerpts from Roth's book of poetry and her obituary, suggest that she was a real person, brought to life from some dusty newspaper clippings." But, as Timson notes, "the whole thing, including the poetry, is out of Alice Munro."

Since Munro's narrator largely fades into the background as the story progresses, readers may not make these connections and realize that the entire story is fabricated. Yet Munro does provide clues that foreshadow, or predict, the story's ending. These clues include specific sections of the story that discuss the manipulation of truth. For example, in the third section, a clipping from the *Vidette* talks about Jarvis Poulter's tendency for stealing coal and water. This leads into a discussion of Poulter's background, which is the subject of many rumors in the town. Many of the townspeople believe that Poulter's wife has died in some horrible fashion. But, as the narrator says, "There is no ground for this, but it adds interest. All he has told them is that his wife is dead." Just as the townspeople are starting with a simple fact and adding on extra details to spice up this anecdote, so is the narrator—with the entire story. The narrator, when talking about how Roth views the countryside as she composes a poem about it, examines this idea of reality versus fiction and further foreshadows the ending. "The countryside that she has written about in her poems actually takes some diligence and determination to see. Some things must be disregarded." In other words, in the name of art, Roth observes the world but changes specific details that do not fit into the theme or feeling that she is trying to achieve in her poetry. Again, the narrator does this, as well, while re-creating the story of Roth.

At the end, the narrator realizes that the story, as it has been told, may be inaccurate: "I may have got it wrong. I don't know if she ever took laudanum. Many ladies did. I don't know if she ever made grape jelly." This narrator, like many of Munro's narrators, discovers the limitations in telling a story. As Katherine Mayberry notes in *Studies in Short Fiction,* "Eventually, most of Munro's narrators, both primary and secondary, come to recognize, if only dimly, the imperfection and inadequacy of their medium." Yet, in seeking out the gravestone of Almeda Roth, the narrator sees that it says "Meda," which confirms the narrator's supposition that this name, from Roth's poetry, was Roth's nickname. Getting this fact right gives the narrator a sense of accomplishment: "I thought that there

> Since Munro's narrator largely fades into the background as the story progresses, readers may not make these connections and realize that the entire story is fabricated. Yet Munro does provide clues that foreshadow, or predict, the story's ending."

wasn't anybody alive in the world but me who would know this, who would make the connection."

That, ultimately, is Munro's goal with the story—getting readers to make their own connections. By deliberately making the story lack a cohesive plot and feeding story content to readers in detached, episodic blocks, as well as by questioning the authenticity of her own narrator, Munro forces readers to focus on the details. As Ross notes:

> We say, yes, that is how life is; we recognize and acknowledge discoveries about our deepest selves. And this recognition is the purpose of the author's journeys into the past, undertaken with compassion and determination to 'get it right,' to get down the tones, textures, and appearances of things.

In the case of "Meneseteung," these appearances can be misleading or downright false. But whether these appearances are truth, fiction, or somewhere in between does not matter, since even in a story that never really happened, readers can find elements that resonate with their own lives.

Source: Ryan D. Poquette, Critical Essay on "Meneseteung," in *Short Stories for Students,* Gale, 2004.

David Remy

Remy is a freelance writer in Pensacola, Florida. In the following essay, Remy examines the narrative use of stereotype in "Meneseteung."

Like many other Alice Munro stories, "Meneseteung" explores the biases and obstacles an independent woman must face while living within a provincial culture. Almeda Joynt Roth, the story's protagonist, is a poet, the author of "ballads, couplets, [and] reflections" that are often sentimental, if not morose, in tone. In piecing together the many facets of Roth's biography, the narrator takes a view of the poet that is no different from that of her contemporaries during the latter half of the nineteenth century, a perspective that eventually leads to questions regarding the story's content. At first glance, Roth appears to fit the stereotype of the mad, tormented artist, the bohemian who lives her life with blatant disregard for convention. Relying upon a single volume of published poems and a few tidbits of information garnered from the archives of the local press, the narrator seems to confuse Roth's actual life with one imagined, thus proving to be an unreliable source of information as she perpetuates this stereotype for the reader.

From the beginning of the story, the narrator, for reasons unknown, adopts the identical mores and attitudes Roth struggled against during her lifetime. In examining a copy of *Offerings,* Roth's only published collection of poems, the narrator exhibits the same "mixture of respect and contempt" that the townspeople display toward Roth "both for her calling and for her sex—or for their predictable conjuncture." The artist, a solitary figure, is simultaneously revered and despised for being independent, for living outside the traditional roles established for a woman. The narrator outlines this difference by describing a photograph of Roth and by citing passages from a brief family history which the poet includes in the preface to her book. There are traces of a grudging respect in the narrator's tone as he or she—the narrator remains nameless throughout the story, though at times the narrator's opinions appear to be feminine—describes Roth's physical characteristics and mode of dress and uses them to speculate about the poet's life. The narrator begins by describing Roth's physical attributes, especially a "streak of gray hair plain to see," which emphasizes an unusual combination of youth and maturity in a woman of "only twenty-five." The narrator goes on to describe the poet as "[n]ot a pretty girl but the sort of woman who may age well, who probably won't get fat." After delivering this rather backhanded compliment, the narrator attempts to fathom the poet's personality with the aid of a few sartorial clues. "It's the untrimmed, shapeless hat, something like a soft beret, that makes me see artistic intentions," the narrator declares, "or at least a shy and stubborn eccentricity, in this young woman, whose long neck and forward-inclining head indicate as well that she is tall and slender and somewhat awkward." As intuitive as these observations are, they nevertheless amount to conjecture. Neither Roth's book nor her photograph offer any confirmation of what the poet's life was actually like. A stereotype has taken root that will flower by the story's end.

The narrator's imagination takes flight as she begins to piece together Roth's biography. Simultaneously, the narrator, who, based upon the above comments, may well be Roth's biographer or a graduate student researching a thesis, makes observations that distinguish Roth from her contemporaries yet relegate her to the ordinary and commonplace: "From the waist up, she looks like a young nobleman of another century. But perhaps it was the fashion," the narrator says dismissively. The narrator, like the townspeople of more than one hundred years earlier, regards Roth with admiration and, perhaps, a dose of envy. The combination of the two emotions at times makes it difficult for the narrator to distinguish between fantasy and reality, thus placing her account of events in doubt.

This ambivalent attitude, fueled by gossip and hearsay, also extends toward Roth's social life, which is a source of much speculation for both the townspeople and the narrator. Citing entries in the *Vidette,* the local paper that includes "sly jokes, innuendo, [and] plain accusation" as it maintains an insular stance against outsiders, even those like Roth whose family helped settle the town, the narrator mistakenly assumes that there must be a romantic link between Almeda Roth and Jarvis Poulter, her neighbor, based upon the simple fact that she is single and he is a widower. Why, asks the narrator, has Almeda remained unmarried for so long? Apparently unaware that she has adopted a preconceived idea of what the poet's life *should* be like, the narrator suspects that Almeda remains unmarried because she possesses a gloomy disposition and is weighted down by too many burdens, especially after the loss of her family. Rather than have Roth conform to the stereotype of the reckless hedonist, the narrator molds her into that of the "tormented artist," one who suffers dutifully for her art.

Furthermore, in a passage that reveals the narrator's adoption of Victorian attitudes about what a woman's literary ambition should be, Roth's poetry is regarded as more of a hobby than a vocation, an aimless activity to keep her mind occupied until her grief subsides.

And all that reading and poetry—it seemed more of a drawback, a barrier, an obsession, in the young girl than in the middle-aged woman, who needed something, after all, to fill her time. Anyway, it's five years since her book was published, so perhaps she has got over that. Perhaps it was the proud, bookish father encouraging her?

When Almeda's insomnia requires treatment by the local doctor, she is advised not to read or study; exercise and hard work are the proper antidotes for a nervous disposition. According to the narrator's account, one told through the kaleidoscope of history in which truth and myth play upon the imagination in equal measure, the doctor believes that a majority of Roth's preoccupations would disappear if she married. It is ironic, therefore, that the doctor believes this "in spite of the fact that most of his nerve medicine is prescribed for married women."

The narrator, grasping firmly onto the stereotype of the promiscuous, single woman, lets her imagination soar as she confuses the personal qualities of one character with another. After describing an incident whereby a drunken woman, whom Almeda naively mistakes for dead, is found near Almeda's home and revived by Jarvis Poulter, the narrator ignores the plight of the fallen woman and instead seizes the opportunity to elaborate further upon Roth's life, transferring the drunken woman's lewd character to that of her protagonist, a projection that only compounds the narrator's unreliability. Like one of the village women gossiping at the well, the narrator imagines that circumstance has freed Almeda and Jarvis from all social constraint and that they will act upon their desire.

> As soon as a man and a woman of almost any age are alone together within four walls, it is assumed that anything may happen. Spontaneous combustion, instant fornication, an attack of passion.

The scene remains vivid for the narrator, yet there is no record that the event actually took place as described in the story. Echoing the spirit of the times, the narrator's imagination quickly moves from erotic confinement to the less provocative scene of the couple walking to church together on a bright Sunday morning. The next logical stage in the development of the couple's relationship, the narrator suggests, is courtship and marriage.

Having brought Roth fully to life in her imagination, the narrator describes her protagonist as remaining at home, claiming infirmity, when the offer of an escort finally does come. Unlike the townspeople of Roth's day, the narrator under-

> "The artist, a solitary figure, is simultaneously revered and despised for being independent, for living outside the traditional roles established for a woman."

stands that Almeda is much too independent a person to take the trouble to mold a man, especially one as ambitious as Jarvis, into a husband. The poet fails to conform to one stereotype, yet this does not prevent the narrator from having Roth embody another. "Almeda Roth cannot imagine herself doing that. She wants a man who doesn't have to be made, who is firm already and determined and mysterious to her. She does not look for companionship. Men—except for her father—seem to her deprived in some way, incurious." Though her image of Roth changes constantly, the narrator seems intent on having her conform to a prescribed idea of what an artist's life should be—in this case, that of the loner who, like a celibate taking religious orders, has sacrificed her life for art.

Even though the narrator seems to understand that Almeda Roth was a complex individual, an author who assiduously practiced her craft as a vocation and not as a hobby, the narrator nevertheless subscribes to the fallacy that the poet found inspiration for her greatest poem, "Meneseteung," not through careful observation and the calculated juxtaposition of ideas but through the use of sleep medication. Just as Coleridge is said to have used opium to inspire one of his greatest compositions, "Kubla Khan," so too does the narrator imagine Roth using sleep medication to recreate the "deep holes and rapids and blissful pools," the "grinding blocks of ice thrown up at the end of winter," the "desolating spring floods" that arise from the eponymous river. The narrator imagines that all of Almeda's anguish, sorrow, and ambivalence is "channelled" into the poem, creating a river of emotion that rushes from her psyche down through the tip of her pen.

Indeed, by subscribing to the romantic notion of the poet being an afflicted soul who must seek inspiration through intoxicants or else risk being forsaken by the muse, the narrator, relying upon a biased conception of the writer's life, discredits Roth's artistic achievement. While the poet may well have been under the influence of medication to relieve her insomnia and the nervous condition that, as the narrator supposes, made interaction with Jarvis Poulter so difficult, this in no way undermines the task Roth must undertake of harnessing her thoughts and feelings to meet the linguistic and structural demands of composing verse. "The name of the poem is the name of the river. No, in fact it is the river, the Meneseteung, that is the poem . . . ," observes the narrator, aware that the poem, with its full title "Champlain at the Mouth of the Meneseteung," exploits the popular but untrue belief that the French explorer Champlain landed at the mouth of the river while sailing down the eastern shore of Lake Huron. Thus, by undermining her narrator's reliability, Munro underscores the way that myth, as exacerbated through ignorance and gossip like that spread by the *Vidette,* can be mistaken for truth. Munro dispels the stereotype of the mad poet who, through revelatory hallucinations, makes the world anew. The narrator acknowledges Roth's actual state of mind toward the end of section V:

> For she hasn't thought that crocheted roses could float away or that tombstones could hurry down the street. She doesn't mistake that for reality, and neither does she mistake anything else for reality, and that is how she knows that she is sane.

The poem endures, though any biographical aspects related to it remain pure speculation.

Confronted by the reality of Roth's poem, the narrator's perspective changes toward the end of the story as she searches for one last physical clue that will confirm her idea of what the poet's life was like. No longer does she rely upon conjecture and innuendo to imagine Almeda Roth's life but instead seeks a tangible reminder of Roth's relationship to her family, whose members frequently appear in her poems. With Roth's sole volume of poetry in hand, the narrator, who has stood in a cemetery the entire time she has related her account of Roth's life for the reader, removes grass and dirt from the flat stone that marks the poet's final resting place. "Meda" reads the placard that completes the family plot, and the narrator immediately establishes a relationship between Roth's nickname and the child being called out to play in "Children at Their Games." The narrator realizes that this gravestone is the one connection between Roth and her poetry that actu-

ally captures a "trickle in time." Everything else that the narrator has previously thought and felt about Roth's life amounts to nothing more than guesswork. The narrator's account thus far has proved unreliable. "I may have got it wrong," the narrator admits at the end of the story. "I don't know if she ever took laudanum. Many ladies did. I don't know if she ever made grape jelly."

Through the use of an unreliable narrator, "Meneseteung" quietly argues that literature be taken on its own terms, that its ability to achieve success as an enduring work of art does not rely upon aspects of the author's biography or circumstances that are mere interpolations of the reader's desire. As the narrator's experience aptly demonstrates, the relationship between the poet's life and work is much too subtle to accommodate romantic notions of creativity.

Source: David Remy, Critical Essay on "Meneseteung," in *Short Stories for Students,* Gale, 2004.

Rowland Smith

In the following essay excerpt, Smith suggests that for Munro's female protagonist Almeda the wilderness is less dangerous than the human male-dominated garrison.

In a well-known passage in *The Empire Writes Back,* the authors define one of the central problems in the literature of 'settler colonies' as that of the "relationship between the imported language and the new place." This need to find an appropriate language to deal with the reality of new landscapes in settler colonies (such as those in North America, Australia and New Zealand, where Europeans formed independent societies out of colonies originally subservient to the metropolitan, colonial power) is of a different order from the cultural assertions of colonized societies in Africa and Asia. In those colonies, the differences between the indigenous culture and the imposed colonial culture were always obvious:

> Whatever the particular nature of colonial oppression in Africa or India, and whatever the legacy of cultural syncretism, the differences confronted as a result of colonialism were palpable []. In the settler colonies, however, difference from the inherited tradition and the need to assert that difference were felt equally strongly.

An interesting development of the need to assert the differences in settler realities is the possibility of later writers from those cultures re-investigating the earlier, established models of settler myth. Do the long-established literary or cultural mythologies of settler difference adequately reflect the differing realities of current writers in settler countries, even as they look back on the settler past that has been inscribed as their authentic, non-metropolitan cultural identity?

The assumptions of settlers who first asserted a distinctly autochthonous reality can be seen by later writers to be devices that obscure uncomfortable aspects of settler culture while highlighting what makes it different. Edward Said has consistently argued that the way European explorers and colonizers depict otherness is only partly an attempt to understand or describe that different reality; it is also, invariably, an attempt to manage, contain, control it. Said discusses Western, colonizing habits of representation and the counterassertions of colonized peoples about creating a mythic, indigenous reality in opposition to that imposed on them. While not directly related to the practices of settler cultures, his comments are relevant to the non-belligerent attempts of early settler mythologizers (who did not have to fight wars of liberation) to assert cultural independence. Discussing the "constructions" of "insurgent 'natives' about their pre-colonial past," he writes:

> This strategy is at work in what many national poets or men of letters say and write during independence or liberation struggles elsewhere in the colonial world. I want to underline the mobilizing power of the images and traditions brought forth, and their fictional, or at least romantically colored, fantastic quality.

In discussions of the literary ethos of the settler culture of Canada, representations of the wilderness or the bush, and refuge from them in concepts of survival or the garrison, are commonplace constructs. In *Strange Things* (originally given as lectures at Oxford), Margaret Atwood links these motifs to the practice of an equally celebrated Canadian cultural icon, Alice Munro. Atwood discusses the mystique of the wilderness, particularly the North, in Canadian imaginative writing. She discusses patterns of Canadian reflection on the wilderness/North, and the different ways writers depict either the malevolence or the neutrality of that vast expanse. In passing, she comments on the difference between the perspective of male writers (with their male protagonists) and that of female writers (with female protagonists): "If the North is a cold femme fatale, enticing you to destruction, is it similarly female and similarly fatal when a woman character encounters it?" The continuing obsession with the

> " In 'Meneseteung,' the perspective moves between an almost celebratory, historical re-imagining of the growing prosperity of a frontier town and a straight-faced depiction of its human nastiness; the latter quality created implicitly in a narrative whose tone remains bland."

North in the Canadian psyche is one of her constant themes; it is this obsession that leads her to relate her own interest in the wilderness motif to contemporary urban life. And it is to Alice Munro that she turns for oblique explanation of her own focus. Atwood writes:

> The fourth lecture is called "Linoleum Caves," a title suggested by a sentence in Alice Munro's *The Lives of Girls and Women* "People's lives, in Jubilee as elsewhere, were dull, simple, amazing and unfathomable—deep caves paved with kitchen linoleum." I was intrigued by the contrast between the domestic linoleum and the natural and potentially dangerous cave, and in women-in-the-north stories there is often such a contrast—sometimes with the linoleum being the more treacherous feature.

The surface ease of Atwood's writing is, as always, deceptively straightforward. The well-known passage quoted from Alice Munro introduces elements of the "amazing and unfathomable" alongside those of the "dull" and "the domestic"—all concepts that intrude with increasing urgency in Munro's later work. But it is Atwood herself who raises the question of which is the more "treacherous" or "dangerous"; domesticity (with "linoleum" suggesting a certain kind of economically strained, or at least not lavish, domesticity) or the wilderness—hostile or otherwise. And it is Atwood who typifies, as Canadian, Munro's trait of idiosyncratic juxtaposing or combining of the wild and the domestic; the tamed and the untameable; the decorous and the depraved. Atwood recalls a complaint made in Oxford by a young Canadian about her subject-matter for the Clarendon lectures:

I should not be talking about the North, or the wilderness, or snow, or bears, or cannibalism or any of that [. . .]. these things were of the past, and [. . .] I would give the English a wrong idea about how most Canadians were spending their time these days.

It was "the literature of urban life" that this particular young man thought Atwood should be discussing in Oxford in the 1990s. Atwood's reply—as a by-product—recognizes the unique quality of Alice Munro's imaginative perspective on modern urban life:

I said I thought the English had quite a lot of urban life themselves, and that they didn't need to hear about it from me [. . .]. Given a choice between a morning spent in the doughnut shop and a little cannibalism, which would you take—to read about, that is? Alice Munro of course could handily work in both—but as a rule?

To posit as specifically Canadian an overriding awareness of the wilderness, or at least of natural hostility, is not far removed from familiar statements about survival or the garrison. The new element in Atwood's comments in *Strange Things* is the different uses to which male and female Canadian writers may put their common subconscious access to a mythology of the wild-at-the-door. Alice Munro seldom writes about the far North, but the settler origins of the culture she knows and explores form a substratum in her fiction. And the restrictions on her female protagonists of that early world are almost invariably more intense when created by humans than are those afforded by the roughing-it-in-the-bush motif of frontier literature.

The way the ethos of the past, whether distant or recent, permeates her protagonists' attitudes is a distinctive feature of her created world. And it is in this regard that her questioning is most consistent: how subjective are those memories and to what extent have they been sanctified as part of an imaginative need to create a special kind of mythologized experience of wilderness life in order to manage it and tame it emotionally?

Because her technique is often ironic, the bleakness in Munro's references to the distant frontier past can be muted in deadpan narration of events or customs. In "Meneseteung," the perspective moves between an almost celebratory, historical reimagining of the growing prosperity of a frontier town and a straight-faced depiction of its human nastiness; the latter quality created implicitly in a narrative whose tone remains bland.

The spinster-protagonist, Almeda Joynt Roth, is an amateur poet whose derivative verses treat conventional subjects. The European context of a poem dealing with a gypsy encampment outside town typifies the conventional struggle of a colonial writer to find an indigenous topic, let alone an indigenous language. But mingled with such literary sources are elements derived from Roth's own experience—a poem by her depicts the children's game of making angel wings in the snow, an explicitly Ontarian experience, even if the Victorian manner of reflection is borrowed:

White roses cold as snow
Bloom where those "angels" lie.
Do they but rest below
Or, in God's wonder, fly?

The sentiments may be borrowed, but the children's angels are indigenous.

A reflection on what is indigenous forms the topic of some of the protagonist's poems. "The Passing of the Old Forest" lists and describes the trees cut down in the original forest as well as providing "a general description of the bears, wolves, eagles, deer, waterfowl." This is wilderness-writing in content, although the tone of all her poems is drawing-room poetic. An instinct to define the local is more pronounced in a companion piece, "A Garden Medley," which is a "catalogue of plants brought from European countries, with bits of history and legend attached, and final Canadianness resulting from this mixture." Final Canadianness would be the goal of the most dedicated postcolonial settler-poet.

Almeda's interest in defining her connection to European roots exists side-by-side with an inability to create an indigenous style that is neither derivative nor romanticized. The title of the story itself, "Meneseteung," is taken from one of her poems, which epitomizes her penchant for mythologizing her environment. The narrator of the story gives this description of the poem: "'Champlain at the Mouth of the Meneseteung' [. . .] celebrates the popular, untrue belief that the explorer sailed down the eastern shore of Lake Huron and landed at the mouth of the major river." This is an example of Southwestern Ontario frontier myth. In it, the district's pioneering past is derived from the romantic voyage of a great European explorer, opening up its wilderness. The land of the noble adventurer is shared—through the use of the 'Indian' name of the river—with untroubled aboriginal people. From this idealized beginning, the later cosmetic historicizing of Almeda's nineteenth-century frontier town can develop.

The narrator of "Meneseteung" both speculates on life in Almeda's town and recounts the events recorded in contemporary issues of the *Vidette*. This mixture of the imagined ("perhaps petunias growing on top of a stump") and the recorded ("I read about that life in the *Vidette*") offers a shifting focus under the surface ease of the swiftly moving account of the ethos of the settler town, which explicitly resembles Northrop Frye's garrison:

> it's not going to vanish, yet it still has some of the look of an encampment. And, like an encampment, it's busy all the time—full of people [. . .]. full of the noise of building and of drivers shouting at their horses and of the trains that come in several times a day.

Here is the positive element of frontier myth: the wilderness driven back by human enterprise and determination. Mr Jarvis Poulter, the widowed businessman who interests Almeda, epitomizes the virtues of wilderness-into-profit; his salt-extraction enterprise is not only successful, but also uses technology to bring natural riches to the surface. In an area which is really "a raw countryside just wrenched from the forest, but swarming with people," he embodies the official values of the settlement, and they have all the elements of Victorian puritanism and taboo that (as cultural baggage carried well into the twentieth century) provide the restricted ethos from which Munro's twentieth-century protagonists attempt to break free.

But the reality of the frontier town is two-sided. Human endeavour can be seen in heroic terms; the wilderness is receding, prosperity is evident, decorous social norms are being established. At the same time, there is a norm of atrocious behaviour. The list of accepted acts of viciousness is endless: "Strangers who don't look so prosperous are taunted and tormented [. . .]. Be on your guard, the *Vidette* tells people. These are times of opportunity and danger. Tramps, hicksters, shysters, plain thieves are travelling the roads." Those who taunt and torment strangers are children, the boys of the town who "rove through the streets in gangs" and always pick on the weak or the socially unacknowledged ("strangers who don't look so prosperous"). The frontier idyll is at its least convincing in their treatment of the frailest in the encampment, its defenceless women: "one day they follow an old woman, a drunk named Queen Aggie. They get her into a wheelbarrow and, trundle her all over town, then dump her into a ditch to sober her up." These elements of the settlement culture are presented in

such a matter-of-fact manner that they appear on the surface to be part of the romance of imperial development.

Just as Almeda's penchant for romance disqualifies her from coming to terms with the raw side of life at the end of Pearl Street, so a romantic reading of these opening historical re-creations (by the narrator) of life in Almeda's town mask the rawness of the place; a rawness in which the town boys' treatment of Queen Aggie foreshadows their treatment of Almeda in old age when she has become a social oddity, conspicuously incapable of conforming to the decorum expected of her. In recording her death, the *Vidette* reports:

> She caught cold, after having become thoroughly wet from a ramble in the Pearl Street bog. (It has been said that some urchins chased her into the water, and such is the boldness and cruelty of some of our youth, and their observed persecution of this lady, that the tale cannot be entirely discounted).

According to the narrator, who controls access to both imagined and recorded events, the latter account in the *Vidette* dates from the twentieth century (1903) rather than the nineteenth (1879 is adduced as the date of the near-miss with Mr Poulter). The change in mood is reflected in the disapproval of the behaviour of "our youth" in 1903, whereas the same behaviour has been neutrally recounted by the narrator in an imaginative re-creation of the frontier town in 1879. When Mr Jarvis Poulter's death is recorded in the *Vidette* of 1904, however, the celebration of the pioneer spirit of enterprise which he is seen to have epitomized is on a par with the implicit enthusiasm for the energy of the frontier town of 1879 in the narrator's account. He is described as

> one of the founders of our community, and early maker and shaker of this town [. . .] [who] possessed a keen and lively commercial spirit, which was instrumental in the creation of not one but several local enterprises, bringing the benefits of industry, productivity, and employment to our town.

By this time, the frontier virtues have been codified.

Almeda cannot cope with either the decorum of the town or the raw side revealed in a Saturday night squabble-and-fornication on Pearl Street. While her own house faces on Dufferin Street, which is a street "of considerable respectability," her back gate opens onto Pearl Street, which degenerates block by block to the last "dismal" one: "nobody but the poorest people, the unrespectable and undeserving poor, would live there at the edge of a boghole (drained since then) called the Pearl Street Swamp."

I will not belabour the obvious imagery of what the society "faces" and what it "backs onto," but it is worth pointing to the unrelenting nastiness in the presentation of the human values of the frontier town. The poorest people are unrespectable and undeserving, and that's that.

Human constructs defeat Almeda on both levels. She cannot digest the rawness of the Pearl Street scene (which Mr Poulter can move aside with his shoe) and she is entrapped in the straitjacket of official social decorum: for Mr Poulter to walk with her to church (as opposed to walking her home from church) would be a sign of "a declaration." Her retreat into the romantic fantasy world of her poems, seen as a "drawback, a barrier, an obsession in the young girl," becomes for the middle-aged woman a way to "fill her time." And what fills her verses is the myth-building fantasy of an early 'Canadianness' composed of plants and bears and a great explorer's visit to her part of the world, to the total exclusion of Pearl Street, the cause of her turning away from normal social life and her final dowsing in the bog.

As Atwood suggests, it is not the wilderness that is fatal in this experience of a woman on the frontier. A similar inversion of the relative safety offered by the wild or the pioneers in it occurs later in "A Wilderness Station." A reworking, from many viewpoints, of the tale of a colonial bride sent to a remote Ontario site in the mid-1800s, the epistolary narrative constantly captures—without authorial comment—the unthinking objectification of the young woman as commodity in the wilderness settlement. The wilderness *per se* is in fact relatively friendly to its bride. After her husband's murder (by his brother) she is safer—in her eyes—roughing it alone than remaining in contact with her brother-in-law, whose own guilt could be revealed by her.

It is not only the guilty brother who frightens the widow/bride, however. Even the friendly neighbours are a threat because of possible social censure. The shame of her position is an equally important element in her choosing the solitude of the wilderness over social contact with its settlers. Annie has been beaten, and does not want her past or present vulnerability exposed:

> Mrs. Treece came and tried to get me to go and live with them the way George was living. She said I could eat and sleep there, they had enough beds. I would not go. They thought I would not go because of my grief but I wouldn't go because somebody might see my black and blue, also they would be watching for me to cry. I said I was not frightened to stay alone.

This is not the conventional plight of a woman widowed in the bush. The threat has in fact been turned inside out, and social life is the most menacing element in Annie's shocked condition. The point is made relentlessly. Annie stops sleeping in the house "where he could find me." She writes: "the flies and mosquitoes came but they hardly bothered me. I would see their bites but not feel them, which was another sign that in the outside I was protected." Those outside the immediate circumstances of Annie's plight can only explain her apparent abnormality in social terms. The conventional stresses of frontier life are judged to have affected her disposition. Letters from "good" males like the ailing Presbyterian minister in the region from which Annie flees, and the dutiful Clerk of the Peace in the village to which she flees, embody conventional attitudes toward women-on-the-frontier. The letter-writers cannot understand the nature of her plight and inscribe an inaccurate myth of frontier-woman problems as they fumble their way around the truth of her predicament. The bewildered Reverend McBain (who, as a mate, is consumed by a frontier fever whereas Annie lives on to old age) ponders on her apparent insanity:

> It may well be that so early in the marriage her submission to her husband was not complete and there would be carelessness about his comfort, and naughty words, and quarrelsome behaviour, as well as the hurtful sulks and silences her sex is prone to. His death occurring before any of this was put right, she would feel a natural and harrowing remorse, and this must have taken hold of her mind [. . .].

Mr James Mullen writes back with the views of a country doctor:

> His belief is that she is subject to a sort of delusion peculiar to females, for which the motive is a desire for self-importance, also a wish to escape the monotony of life or the drudgery they may have been born to.

This rewriting of the wilderness myth is not an end in itself. Munro is not merely re-interpreting the reality of settler culture. The plight of both Annie and Almeda embodies the value-system underlying the reactions of subsequent generations of Munro female characters to their parochial world. That world may cease to be part of the wilderness, but as a settled Victorian colony or a shabby-genteel mid-twentieth-century Dominion, or the liberated, Trudeau-era 'world-class' province, its puritan roots, patriarchal and materialistic, inform the existential predicaments of Munro's women. When the irrational and the unpredictable erupt—with increasing frequency—into the lives of the protagonists in Munro's later volumes, those flashes of quasi-insanity are almost without exception revealed in the context of the suffocating conventions of either nineteenth- or twentieth-century Ontario.

Annie's temporary retreat into an outdoor life to escape the threats of her society is seen as a kind of madness in the wilderness station. Almeda is accepted as ''odd'' once she retreats from the twin nightmares of Pearl Street and Mr Jarvis Poulter's respectable physicality. When Munro's contemporary protagonists attempt to escape the confines of their society, they themselves frequently see it as madness. The origins of this quite explicable turning to the non-rational are what Munro reveals in her re-imagining of the settler roots of their Ontario culture. . . .

Source: Rowland Smith, ''Rewriting the Frontier: Wilderness and Social Code in the Fiction of Alice Munro,'' in *Telling Stories: Postcolonial Fiction in English,* edited by Jacqueline Bardolph, Rodopi, 2001, pp. 77–90.

Coral Ann Howells

In the following essay excerpt, Howells argues that Munro reconstructs a member of the Canadian female literary tradition with Almeda, a poet who escapes from the confines of what society expects of her into the ''the wilderness space of her imagination.''

'Meneseteung' presents Munro's contribution to the feminist re-visionary project of reconstructing a female literary tradition by recovering the work of forgotten women writers. As Canadian critic Carole Gerson remarks in her essay on the disappearance of so many nineteenth-century Canadian women poets' names from twentieth-century anthologies,

> Tired of being cheated of recognition by the literary establishment, the early Canadian woman poet has deviously begun to re-enter our literature in fictional form, in Carol Shields' *Mary Swann: A Mystery* and Alice Munro's 'Meneseteung'.

Munro's story about a fictive nineteenth-century woman poet who lived in the small town of Goderich in southwestern Ontario pays attention to issues highlighted by feminist critics, such as social assumptions about femininity, women's domestic roles as daughters, wives and mothers, and also to the dualities experienced by women artists whose creative powers conflicted with conventional feminine expectations. The American critic Mary Poovey's study of eighteenth-century literary women *The Proper Lady and the Woman Writer* provides the focus for my discussion of Munro's exploration of that double role and its disruptive effects on a

" Evidently the contemporary narrator shares the historian's impulse to rescue obscure details from the past and to make connections, though in the last paragraph she seems to wish to withdraw from responsibility for the story she has just told, admitting she has made up the details of Almeda's life by inference only. . . ."

woman's life that her story becomes a critique of nineteenth-century Canadian colonial society and its attitudes to women and to 'poetesses' in particular. Yet precisely because it is a fiction and not a piece of literary criticism Munro is free to invent her character's life story, combining psychobiography with local history of place as well as a recognition of her own role as narrator. She is also free to highlight those topics which interest her most: the traditional Canadian trope of women and wilderness, issues of gender, sexuality and female bodies, and crucially women's pleasure in writing—be it history, fiction or poetry.

This story has an apparently decorous old-fashioned structure, beginning with a scrupulous account of the (fictive) historical evidence available, as the narrator describes the book of poems which she finds:

> *Offerings* the book is called. Gold lettering on a dull-blue cover. The author's full name underneath: Almeda Joynt Roth. The local paper, the *Vidette,* referred to her as 'our poetess.' (*FMY*)

The book, published 1873, has the author's photo as frontispiece as well as a preface giving details of her life. The photo is described in detail, as are a selection of her poems, stanzas of which are used to introduce each of the six sections into which the story is divided. Almeda's life and her poetry would seem to conform to colonial constructions of middle-class femininity with her family's pioneer history, her role as unmarried housekeeper for her widowed father, and her poems on conventional Victorian subjects like childhood, death and landscape; as Munro says, they are 'poems about birds and wild flowers and snowstorms' (*FMY*).

Yet there are striking oddities here: first the mysterious title of the story, and then Almeda's ambiguous challenge to gender construction in her portrait where she looks like 'a young nobleman of another century' as well as her fascination with heroic exploration narratives in a poem called 'Champlain at the Mouth of the Meneseteung'. (This is where we realise that the story's title is the ancient Indian name for the Maitland River, at the mouth of which Goderich is situated.)

Munro foregrounds the documentary evidence for her historical reconstruction, where in addition to the book of poems she refers to old photographs of the town and to reports in the local newspaper. (Curiously, the *Vidette* was the name of the local paper in Munro's home town of Wingham in 1883, though the name of the Goderich paper in this period was the *Signal Star*.) She pays attention to the town's economic and material development in the late nineteenth-century with the coming of the railway, local industries, sawmills and brickyards—all typical features of raw new towns built on the edge of the Canadian wilderness. The *Vidette* also supplies a skeleton outline of Almeda's life story after the publication of her single volume: her prospects of marriage to the respectable citizen and Civil Magistrate, Jarvis Poulter, followed by a brief news item on her discovery of a drunken woman's body near the back of her house, and then a gap of over twenty years till the notices of Almeda's death in 1903 and of Jarvis Poulter's in 1904. Apparently they never married. Munro's narrative effort is dedicated to filling in these gaps and to constructing a logic behind scraps of newspaper gossip. Only the first and last sections are set in the present, so forming a frame for the imaginative reconstruction of a woman's relation to place and to poetry, for this is the story of Almeda's transformations from sentimental poetess into romantic wilderness visionary and town eccentric.

Munro's story is a playful mixture of fact and fiction, an imaginative re-visioning of history. Just as Goderich is not named though easily identifiable from its situation on Lake Huron and its salt wells discovered in 1866, so I believe that Almeda is 'partly real' rather than 'wholly invented', as Claire Tomalin speculated in her review of *Friend of My Youth*. I would suggest that Almeda's shadowy parallel be found in the forgotten nineteenth-century poet Eloise A. Skimings (1836–1921), a native of Goderich and known locally as 'the poetess of Lake Huron'. Her photo appears in the Huron County Museum in Goderich as it does on the frontispiece to her one book of poems, *Golden Leaves,* published by Signal Press, Goderich, in 1904. Like Almeda's *Offerings,* the book also has a pale-blue cover with gold lettering on it. Her poems, many of them addressed to persons who had presented her with flowers (like 'a double golden petaled tulip' or 'gold and crimson water lilies') are full of Victorian sentimentality, though one of them is about 'the proud Maitland River' and another 'Reminiscence of Early Days' begins remarkably enough with the phrase 'friend of my youth' in its first line:

> Friend of my infancy, friend of my youth,
> Thou are just the same to me
> As when we roamed adown the glassy slopes
> Of old Huron's rippling sea.
> (*Golden Leaves*)

Skimings (known in her family as the diminutive 'Eliza') was unmarried too, though looking through her letters I could find no trace of a Jarvis Poulter figure. Indeed, their 'life stories' would appear to have been different, though both are buffed in Goderich cemetery. However, these sketchy similarities grounded in local history provide fascinating glimpses into Munro's fictional transformations of real material.

Almeda's story conforms to nineteenth-century convention with its descriptions of traditional feminine occupations and domestic spaces. However, her house has a double view for though its frontage is on the respectable main street, its back windows overlook a very poor quarter and a patch of undrained bogland, the Pearl Street Swamp. The wilderness is still there on the edge, and Pearl Street with its drunken disorder and violence marks the borderline of settlement beyond which glimmers the pristine wilderness. Almeda can see it like a mirage from her bedroom window:

> She can see the sun rising, the swamp mist filling with light, the bulky, nearest trees floating against that mist and the trees behind turning transparent. Swamp oaks, soft maples, tamarack, bitternut. (*FMY*)

Almeda Roth in her late thirties is still encased in her Victorian image of the 'proper lady', and her romantic aspirations are restricted to thoughts of marriage with Jarvis Poulter. Wanting a hero, she believes that he with his uncompromising masculinity would fulfil her desires:

> She wants a man who doesn't have to be made, who is firm already and determined and mysterious to her. She does not look for companionship. (*FMY.*)

Yet even as she decorously fantasises marriage and dreams of the public trappings of courtship like a drive with him into the country, a note of ambivalence creeps in for she knows that this relationship would interfere with her imaginative life and her labours of poetic composition: 'Glad to be beside him. . . . And sorry to have the countryside removed for her—filmed over, in a way, by his talk and preoccupations' (*FMY*). Almeda's landscape poetry (as we can tell from the quoted passages) is sentimental fabrication and highly selective of its raw materials; the countryside that she has written about actually takes 'diligence and determination to see'. In the way she measures loss as well as gain in her romantic fantasy we have a hint of Almeda's 'shy and stubborn eccentricity' which cannot easily be accommodated within conventional femininity.

This delicately nurtured feminine world is split apart by the incident of the drunken brawl and the woman's body against her back fence reported in the *Vidette*. For once, violence and carnality intrude into Almeda's consciousness on a hot summer night:

> It's as if there were a ball of fire rolling up Pearl Street, shooting off sparks . . . yells and laughter and shrieks and curses, and the sparks are voices that shoot off alone (*FMY*).

Almeda hears confused sounds of a man and a woman fighting, followed by 'a long, vibrating, choking sound of pain and self-abasement, self-abandonment' which in her innocence she interprets as murder but which are really the sounds of sex. When next morning Almeda goes out and finds the woman's body still there, she is so upset by the sight that she runs barefoot in her nightgown to ask for Jarvis Poulter's help. In his worldly wisdom he takes one look at the body, prods the bare bruised leg 'as you'd nudge a dog or a sow' (*FMY*) and shoos the woman home like an animal, rather coarsely remarking, 'There goes your dead body' (*FMY*). Though Almeda feels sick enough to retch, seeing this female body and how it is treated by men (including Jarvis Poulter) she suddenly becomes aware of her own sexuality through an odd sympathetic connection below the level of consciousness, just as paradoxically Poulter becomes aware of Almeda's sexuality as well. Now he makes the declaration which is tantamount to a marriage proposal: 'I will walk with you to church'—and she refuses him.

Her body becomes the site of resistance, and returning home she finds that she has begun to menstruate, so she locks herself inside her house and ignores Jarvis Poulter's knock at the door. Instead, she takes a dose of her nerve medicine (probably based on laudanum) with a cup of tea and spends the day in 'perfect immobility' sitting enclosed in her overdecorated colonial dining room. The only sound she can hear is the *'plop, plop'* of the grape juice falling from its swollen purple cheesecloth bag into a basin beneath, for she had started to make some grape jelly the evening before. This is Almeda's crisis, possibly diagnosable as a minor nervous breakdown though also possibly as a sign of her strange liberation—or through that state of drug-induced hypersensitivity Almeda finds access to her poetic imagination once more where 'Everything seems charged with life, ready to move and flow and alter. Or possibly to explode' (*FMY*). She begins to conceive a new poem which will 'contain everything', with all her former sentimental subjects supplemented by 'the obscene racket on Pearl Street' and the woman's body, as she makes the leap beyond sentimentality into a new world of imaginative excess where everything overflows and merges—history and prehistory, domestic details, her own unspeakable body fluids, the grape juice now overflowing and staining her kitchen floor. Together they form a river in her mind to which she gives the ancient name 'Meneseteung':

> The name of the poem is the name of the river. No, in fact it is the river, the Meneseteung, that is the poem—with its deep holes and rapids and blissful pools under the summer trees and its grinding blocks of ice thrown up at the end of winter and its desolating spring floods. (*FMY*)

Almeda slips out of the safe spaces of home into the wilderness space of her imagination, escaping from the orthodox feminine role through writing—or rather, imagining writing—a new kind of visionary poetry about the Canadian wilderness which is beyond words: 'a flow of words somewhere, just about ready to make themselves known to her. Poems, even' (*FMY*). Munro is situating Almeda within the tradition of English-Canadian women's wilderness writing. However this vision seems to spell the silencing of Almeda for we hear no more of her till the *Vidette* record of her death from pneumonia caught, ironically enough, after being chased by some louts into the Pearl Street bog. (Again, as Margaret Atwood claimed in *Survival* or

'Death by Landscape' the wilderness has claimed another of its victims.) The newspaper refers to her as a *'familiar eccentric, or even, sadly, a figure of fun' (FMY)*. Almeda has become an outsider in her own town, though the obituary goes on to restore to her the femininity and poetic reputation (*'with a volume of sensitive eloquent verse'*) which she has plainly abandoned. Whether Almeda ever 'found' herself, having succumbed to the ambiguous spell of the wilderness we do not know; all we witness in this reconstruction is her moment of cutting loose from Victorian conventions. Rather like Aritha van Herk's heroine in *No Fixed Address,* crossing over the frontier into wilderness territory makes it impossible to send back any messages at all.

The story ends with a return to the present as the narrator records her researches in the graveyard where she manages to find Almeda Roth's stone, marked with the one word 'Meda', in its place beside her parents and brother and sister in the family plot, unearthing it by 'pulling grass and scrabbling in the dirt with my bare hands' *(FMY)*. Evidently the contemporary narrator shares the historian's impulse to rescue obscure details from the past and to make connections, though in the last paragraph she seems to wish to withdraw from responsibility for the story she has just told, admitting she has made up the details of Almeda's life by inference only:

> And they may get it wrong, after all. I may have got it wrong. I don't know if she ever took laudanum. Many ladies did. I don't know if she ever made grape jelly. *(FMY)*

It is that final disclaimer (absent when the story was first published in *The New Yorker* in 1988 but added to this version) which foregrounds Munro's own hidden agenda as a woman writer, for the image of the swollen cloth bag full of grape pulp, the plop of the juice into the bowl, and the immovable purple stain on the kitchen floor when the basin overflows, provide the real connection between the story fragments. This connection highlights not femininity and 'the proper lady' but femaleness, linking a woman writer's domestic tasks with her menstrual flow and the purple bruise on the drunken woman's naked haunch, so making visible the unspoken hidden connections which unite all women regardless of social class or historical time. We may even see such imagery as Munro's version of *écriture féminine,* a way of writing the biological rhythms of the female body and so moving through metaphor beyond the body into the spaces of imagination, for grapes (even when made into jelly) carry connota-

tions of the Bacchantes and their orgiastic worship of Dionysus, an ancient European female wildness as untamed as anything to be found in the Canadian wilderness. This emphatically fictive element of the grape jelly is the attribution of the contemporary narrator, so that her revisionist project recovers a great deal more than the name and voice of a forgotten nineteenth-century poetess. It uncovers connections (or should we say 'makes the connection'?) between women's bodies and writing within the subjective spaces of wilderness, reappropriating Canada's most popular cultural myth as the elusive site of the female imagination. . . .

Source: Coral Ann Howells, ''On Lies, Secrets, and Silence: *Friend of My Youth,*'' in *Alice Munro,* Manchester University Press, 1998, pp. 101–19.

Dermot McCarthy

In the following essay, McCarthy contends that Almeda chooses ''marginality, rather than having it imposed upon her by the Victorian patriarchy.''

Alice Munro's short story ''Meneseteung,'' which Clare Tomalin has described as ''the finest and most intense'' (quoted by Redekop, *Mother*) of the stories collected in *Friend of My Youth* (1990), recounts a narrator's attempt to ''see'' someone in the past, and like a number of other contemporary fictions by Canadian women—for example, Carol Shields' *Small Ceremonies* (1976), Susan Swan's *The Biggest Modern Woman in the World* (1983), Jane Urquhart's *The Whirlpool* (1986) and *Changing Heaven* (1990), Katherine Govier's *Between Men* (1987) and Daphne Marlatt's *Ana Historic* (1988)—seems to present such vision as an enabling precondition for living through the present; for in all these works, it is the historian, more than the history, who comes to matter, and the narrator, for whom the historical narrative is the way into and out of history, who most commands our attention.

E. D. Blodgett has observed that the narrator in Munro's fiction ''so often represents the problem of knowing.'' In ''Meneseteung'' this ''problem'' is embodied in the figure of Almeda Joynt Roth, a genteel lady-poet of the mid-Victorian era living in Munro's fictionalized southwestern Ontario. Interpolating between a few ''facts'' gleaned from the town newspaper, and extrapolating from a reading of Roth's book of poems, Munro's narrator constructs a version of the other's life which becomes an envisioning, as she imagines Almeda's thoughts and feelings one August weekend when an incident in her back yard leads her to become what the paper describes as "a familiar eccentric."

"Meneseteung" is interesting as well because the author herself has told us what we should see in it. Munro has written that she consciously set out to create in Almeda a poet-figure in a small Ontario town "out at the edge of Victorian civilization," in whose poetry "you get a sense of claustrophobia and waste" ("Contributors' Notes"). She gave the character "just enough [talent] to give her glimpses, stir her up" and "wanted her to have choice." Munro describes Almeda at the end of the story as "half mad but not, I thought, entirely unhappy." Recent critical discussion of the story has taken its cues from Munro's statement of her intentions. What I want to suggest, however, is that "Meneseteung" is a story in which what we see may be something quite other than, perhaps even contrary to, what the author commands us, and that recent critical views of Almeda have ignored the significance of the "glimpses" the character experiences during that August weekend, as well as the "choices" that she may be seen to make. In particular, I want to suggest that Almeda, as a result of her back yard experience, *chooses* eccentricity: she elects marginality, rather than having it imposed upon her by the Victorian patriarchy represented by the town paper, because she intuits in the peripheral world of the Pearl Street Swamp the centre for her life that she (or, as we shall see, the narrator, *for* her) had been unconsciously seeking. For to consider Almeda-as-eccentric as a figure of marginal-peripheral womanhood is to see her exclusively from the point of view of the patriarchal centre, a viewpoint that by the end of the story is as "dis-arranged," to use Lawrence Mathews's term for Munro's structural technique, as it is discredited.

I

Almeda's house, as a symbol of the past, presents a conventional twentieth-century view of the nineteenth century. The Freudian intersection ("Joynt"?) where Father Roth (Wrath?) has built his house is the conjunction between the respectable and the rejected, the conscious and the unconscious, the superego and the id. The front "faces" on the respectable and patriarchally-named Dufferin Street, but the back windows "overlook" the ironically and female-named Pearl Street, the world of "the unrespectable and undeserving poor." Almeda lives at this intersection carefully locking and unlocking her doors and gates only to be, like Joyce's Mary, "surprised . . . in the rere of the premises" (Joyce).

> The symbolism of place in 'Meneseteung' radiates outward from Almeda Roth's house, but the house is just one of the symbols of the past in the story that the narrator is trying to recover."

The symbolic significance of the house's location is in its both/neither relation to the opposed worlds. Its position marks the inevitability of its inmate's need to choose, and when, at the end of section II, the narrator imagines that Almeda has refused to sleep in her father's "large front bedroom," preferring instead to sleep "at the back," where "she can see the sun rising, the swamp mist filling with light, the bulky, nearest trees floating against that mist and the trees behind turning transparent," we are given a proleptic glimpse of Almeda's ultimate choice of redemptive female eccentricity over confining patriarchal respectability.

It also needs to be emphasized that it is the narrator who imagines this refusal on Almeda's part. Munro's now well-known description of her understanding of a story to be "like a house" because "it encloses space and makes connections between one enclosed space and another and presents what is outside in a new way" ("What Is Real?") suggests that, as a metafiction, the relations between the narrator, the character, and the author in this story are a complex series of mirrorings in which identities slide into each other, are interchangeable. The narrator in "Meneseteung" gradually merges with the character, Almeda, an other whose temporal displacement in another century is crossed out as the narrator "crosses over" to her by means of her empathetic re-visioning. In this sense, the "story" of "Meneseteung" is the narrator's "dreaming-back" to the nineteenth-century woman in order to dream her forward into her own contemporary consciousness, a consciousness which identifies the other's eccentricity as her mystery and her saving difference.

The symbolism of place in "Meneseteung" radiates outward from Almeda Roth's house, but the house is just one of the symbols of the past in the story that the narrator is trying to recover. This recovery is achieved, with the irony and skepticism that attend all Munro's moments of recognition, as the narrator moves from the external view of Almeda Roth provided by the historical record to an internal view which comes with her imaginative merging with the character. In this process, the narrator seeks to connect the Almeda Joynt Roth whom she encounters in the local newspaper, the *Vidette,* with "Meda," who is her "dream" of another Almeda, based on the name she discovers in the book of poems. The Almeda of the *Vidette* is the eccentric spinster whose shelf-life expires 22 April, 1903, a life as closed and unknown to the townspeople as her book of poems. No less external is the initial view of the narrator, looking from the twentieth cenutury to the nineteenth, as if through the wrong end of a telescope, and seeing a life small and alien, inviting the *Gestalt* of stereotype—yet another madwoman in the century's attic, a victim of patriarchal oppression.

The inside view of Almeda is the narrator's dream of Meda, and the "plot" of the story is the project of freeing this imaginative ancestor from the patriarchal stereotype. Meda is not the spinster-eccentric, the failed phobic poet and madwoman suggested by Munro, but the "other" hidden within Almeda yet, paradoxically, there for all to see. The character's middle name encloses the "joy" the narrator's fantasy searches for in her dream of that other's life, and encodes the narrator's imaginative project of connecting objective, "historical" details and subjective dream. As much as Munro's story may suggest the authorially-imposed version of Almeda as half mad, it also suggests that she chooses her eccentricity, ironically, as a way of escaping the cyclopic social eye of the patriarchy and the identity it would assign her. The narrator's dream of Almeda's transformation one hot August weekend releases the character into a "floating independence" that moves her beyond the world of her ominous neighbour, Jarvis Poulter, beyond the gravity of the *Vidette's* conventions, which would fill her pockets with stones to pull her to the bottom of the social stream.

At the end of section II, the narrator has moved inside the house, beyond the realm of public knowledge of Almeda represented by the *Vidette,* to begin to see with the character's eyes. This merging continues in section III as the narrator imagines Almeda's feelings about Poulter, a widower who has prospered from developing a technique for extracting salt from underground. Poulter clearly belongs on Dufferin Street, and though he is considered "An eccentric, to a degree," his eccentricity is his miserliness. Almeda's is her imagination, and the contrast between them is evident when he tells her how his wells bring up the salt from beneath the earth. She alludes to "The salt of the earth," and then imagines "a great sea" covering the land long ago. Poulter is not interested in this kind of speculation, but Almeda's intuition of "the ancient sea" is what eventually leads her to the Pearl Street Swamp, just as it is her imagination which warns her against a future with Poulter.

Pearl Street, the narrator remarks, is "another story." But that other story *is* the story that is told, the story of the other that Almeda represents for the narrator, the "Meda" submerged in Almeda, and that the swamp-woman represents in the story for Almeda herself. This mysterious woman from Pearl Street, the swamp angel who turns up at Almeda Roth's back door, leads Almeda to a breakthrough rather than a breakdown because the marginal world of Pearl Street, with its apogee of exclusion, the swamp that "No decent woman" would dare approach, is not periphery but alternate centre. Because of the symbolism of place in the story, this significantly unnamed woman may be seen, to use Catherine Ross's metaphor, as an emissary from the lower world, a world Almeda has been conditioned by the world of her father to abhor (see Ross, "'At least part legend'"). The significance of her anonymity is, perhaps, that the patriarchy excludes her from its privilege of recognition because of the threat she poses to it, but also that her escape from the "public record" is itself evidence of her eccentric freedom, her slipping back to the "swamp" beyond patriarchal control. For the Pearl Street Swamp is an image of a wilderness or "wild zone" which demarcates woman's potential freedom, as well as her actual exclusion, from patriarchal order. Father Roth functions in the story as a compact symbol of Victorian patriarchy: "a harness-maker by trade, but a cultivated man who could quote by heart from the Bible, Shakespeare, and the writings of Edmund Burke." As "housekeeper to [her] father," Almeda is harnessed by her sense of love and filial duty. As the voice of the Bible, Shakespeare, and Burke, he embodies the culture that, as "poetess," she seeks to enter, but which already entombs her. Almeda appears to be a thoroughly submissive woman, self-deprecating, apologetic, obedient. But this is not the Meda whom the narrator goes on to imagine, and what she discovers this weekend may be understood as a knowledge against the Father, the beginning of a life of defiance which the patriarchy labels as ''eccentric.''

Almeda's attraction to Jarvis Poulter is partly her need to replace the dead father. She misses the harness of female service, ''misses . . . her father's appreciation, his dark, kind authority.'' When she imagines Poulter coming to her bed, ''a fit of welcome and submission overtakes her, a buried gasp.'' The narrator imagines Almeda wanting Poulter to walk her to church on Sunday morning, but when he does offer, following the scene in the back yard, she rejects him, locks the door and posts a sign she does not want to be disturbed. For the experience has left her ''trembling, as if from a great shock or danger.'' And it has been both: the woman-beast on all fours is a sign of her own ''buried gasp'' of womanhood, and Poulter's banishment of this messenger back to the swamp from which she came is a sign of the danger he represents to Meda.

II

The narrator's account of Almeda's dream-like experience in which she witnesses a violent sexual encounter involving a Pearl Street couple outside her bedroom window is the climax of ''Meneseteung.'' Awakened by the ''fracas,'' she goes to the window and immediately sees ''Pegasus . . . straight ahead, over the swamp.'' Below, ''It's as if there were a ball of fire rolling up Pearl Street, shooting off sparks—only the fire is noise.'' What she hears pouring from the man's and woman's mouths are the voices of the swamp: ''a rising and falling howling cry and a steady throbbing, low-pitched stream of abuse that contains all those words which Almeda associates with danger and depravity and foul smells and disgusting sights.'' She hears all the words she has never used in her verse, the anti-poetry buried within her polished and civilized confections, a ''gagging, vomiting, grunt-ing, pounding. Then a long, vibrating, choking sound of pain and self-abasement, self-abandon-ment, which could come from either or both of them.'' As she senses a quality of performance about the scene—''it is always partly a charade with these people''—Almeda becomes a spectator at the mystery play of her own unconscious.

She falls back to sleep but awakens into a profounder dream the next morning when another symbolic emissary appears to her: ''She thinks there is a big crow sitting on her windowsill, talking in a disapproving but unsurprised way about the events of the night before. 'Wake up and move the wheel-

barrow!' it says to her, scolding, and she under-stands that it means something else by 'wheelbar-row'—something foul and sorrowful.'' When she goes out to inspect what appears to be a dead body against her back fence, she finds that ''Spiders have draped their webs over the doorway in the night, and the hollyhocks are drooping, heavy with dew.'' Framed by the drooping sticky flowers she sees ''a bare breast let loose, brown nipple pulled long like a cow's teat, and a bare haunch and leg, the haunch showing a bruise as big as a sunflower. The unbruised skin is grayish, like a plucked, raw drumstick.'' The latter image makes it clear that the man called Poulter will know how to deal with this invasion of the elemental, and when Almeda fetches him he ''nudges the leg with the toe of his boot''; then ''a startling thing happens. The body heaves itself onto all fours, the head is lifted—the hair all matted with blood and vomit—and the woman begins to bang this head, hard and rhythmically, against Almeda Roth's picket fence. As she bangs her head, she finds her voice and lets out an openmouthed yowl, full of strength and what sounds like an anguished pleasure.'' '''Far from dead,' says Jarvis Poulter'': unimaginative patriarch that he is, he could not understand the full meaning of his words; on an unconscious level the more imaginative Meda does. This woman is Life in all its obscene splendour. She is an other Almeda must acknowledge. '''There's blood,' says Almeda as the woman turns her smeared face.'' Poulter discounts it. '''You stop that, now,' he says. 'Stop it.''' He means the yowling but it is as if he is ordering her to stop the blood. When Almeda goes back into her house, she discovers that she has started to menstruate. Poulter sends the woman on her way and says to Almeda, '''There goes your dead body,''' again unconscious of the meaning of his words; for, far from being a ''farcical resurrec-tion'' (Redekop, *Mothers*), this swamp angel points the way out of her death-in-life for Almeda, an-nouncing the end of a cycle which is also a beginning.

In her kitchen, ''The grape pulp and juice has stained the swollen cloth a dark purple''; Almeda's ''abdomen is bloated; she is hot and dizzy.'' ''*Plop, plup,* into the basin beneath. She can't sit and look at such a thing.'' It seems a parody of her own body. Earlier, the rhythmic dripping ''remind[ed] her of the conversation of the crow,'' in which she was ordered to '''Wake up and move the wheelbar-row!''' Again, if we remember that all of this is the narrator's imagining, then the crow-messenger may be as much a figure of narrative desire as of the disapproving patriarchal conscience. It is the narrator who wills Almeda to leave the *camera oscura* of her repressed self, to overcome her fear and enter the body of life outside the prison of the father's house. The "wheelbarrow" is her "dead body" (as long as she remains an inmate of the father's house) waiting to be taken up and possessed by her. In what follows, Almeda becomes hypersensitive to all the patterns she sees around her, "For every one of these patterns, decorations seems charged with life, ready to move and flow and alter." She spends the day trying to "catch" this flow and altering—"to understand it, to be part of it." Because she is a poet, "Soon this glowing and swelling begins to suggest words—not specific words but a flow of words somewhere, just about ready to make themselves known to her." And then she imagines the "one very great poem that will contain everything and, oh, that will make all the other poems, the poems she has written, inconsequential, mere trial and error, mere rags."

At this point, as Almeda "wakes up," in a sense, to the vocation of her body, the narrator in effect imagines the Victorian Almeda Joynt Roth into the twentieth century, for the poem she imagines her wanting to write is a modern, if not even modernist, poem of encyclopedic scope, of contraries and contradictions held in equilibrium, in the meaningful but fictive order of a constellation. Grape juice, menstrual blood, words—all flow into the image of the river, the Meneseteung, which Meda sees as the symbol and subject of the poem she needs to write. Carrington considers "this equation of menstruation and artistic creation [to be] deeply ironic . . . because menstruation signals the absence of conception—the lack of new creation" (*Controlling the Uncontrollable*). But I think this imposes the same patriarchal construction of woman upon Munro's character that the story shows her to escape. To interpret menstruation as "the absence of conception," and thus "creation," is to subscribe to definitions of creation/presence that we are now so sensitive to as ideological instruments of patriarchal oppression, and to fail to see how Munro, in this instance, "write[s] from within a woman's body without trapping that body inside old symbols" (Redekop, *Mothers*). Almeda's menstrual flow can be considered a "hopeful sign" because it signals a release from the false pregnancy of her hopes of marrying Poulter. Even from the patriarchal point of view, Almeda's menstruation can be taken as a sign of her continuing fertility, her potential to create future presence, rather than as a sign of past failure. Munro's story shows Almeda to

triumph by escaping such definitions: her life after this weekend is a life of eccentric creativity, a self-fashioning secret to herself and beyond the prying phallic eye of the patriarchal *Vidette*. And finally, can we not see the menstrual flow imagined by the narrator as her attempted "connection" with the ancestor/character, the woman's "period," "this trickle in time making a connection, rescuing one thing from the rubbish" that she describes in the closing lines of the story?

Almeda's "unresisting surrender to her surroundings" would seem madness from Jarvis Poulter's point of view, who represents the forces that would control the uncontrollable, in Carrington's terms. But is madness what *we* see? It is the narrator who is imagining this experience and who, as Almeda becomes Meda in that imagining, feels that the surrender "is alright. It seems necessary." This moment can be seen as the transformation of Almeda's loneliness into the pleasure of Meda's independence. To echo Yeats, when Almeda becomes Meda she recovers a radical innocence and learns at last that her happiness is self-delighting, self-appeasing, and self-affrighting. It may also be seen as the ultimate moment of identity between the narrator and the character. When she says that Almeda "cannot escape words. She may think she can, but she can't," it is the *narrator*'s words she cannot escape because, of course, Almeda is nothing but the narrator's words. Almeda discovers her identity as Meda, as river daughter, as the narrator completes her invention. Nor is she Munro's version of the modernist Eliots's Thames Daughter, who "can connect / Nothing with nothing." Meda's is a vision of liberating connection, of hope rather than despair.

To read this moment as the beginning of madness is to opt for "another story" altogether. The narrator emphasizes that Meda "hasn't thought that crocheted roses could float away or that tombstones could hurry down the street. She doesn't mistake that for reality, and neither does she mistake anything else for reality, and that is how she knows that she is sane." "No need for alarm," the narrator cautions, but who is she reassuring? Is she "speaking" as narrator or "thinking" as the character? The swamp ultimately kills Meda, but that is only how the *Vidette* would understand her death. She dies from pneumonia, which developed from a cold caught "from a ramble in the Pearl Street bog." But why not see joy and freedom in that "ramble"—the freedom that eccentricity marks in opposition to the centre?

In the narrator's dream of Meda, the night-world night-town of Pearl Street and its obscene but fecund life-forms flood the erstwhile ark, the safely fenced and locked house of her father. When Poulter, after shooing the Pearl Street drunk from Almeda's garden, says to her, "'There goes your dead body,'" he unknowingly points her in the direction of her freedom, just as the faint, ironic echo of the communion words suggests how that freedom will be achieved. The rough beast Poulter rouses in her yard slouches off to the Pearl Street world Almeda has always looked at from her back windows. In the next few hours, Almeda comes to recognize her repressed connection to that world. It is a breakthrough rather than a breakdown. Poulter's name suggests his fairy tale-like identity as keeper and killer, and, as Almeda becomes Meda, she seems to recognize this, realizing that the poem she must try to imagine, the "one very great poem that will contain everything," must contain "the obscene racket on Pearl Street and the polished toe of Jarvis Poulter's boot and the plucked-chicken haunch with its blue-black flower." The latter image recalls the drunken woman in her yard whom Jarvis drove away. Were Almeda to marry this man she would end strung up by the feet, plucked and bloodless, in a marriage of convention, and this is what she turns away from, choosing instead the dreaded "swamp" of her imagination and independence and the mask of eccentricity.

III

In "Meneseteung" Munro's representation of the past as a variety of texts—poetic, journalistic, photographic—waiting to be read and rewritten by the present facilitates the dissolution of the narrator into the character, which is the most important feature of the story's form; it also sanctions the convergence of the external reader with the narrator in a way that evokes the interpretation of Meda's breakdown as a liberation and triumph, contrary to the authorially imposed interpretation of the episode as signifying madness and failure.

The photo of Almeda described in section I represents a distant, silent past that looks out at the present, like Eurydice, waiting to be recovered. This Orphic disinterring of the dead woman continues as the narrator reads/quotes/writes Almeda's Preface to her book of poems. The story exemplifies the pun in the subtitle of Neuman and Kamboureli's *A Mazing Space: Writing Canadian Women Writing*. The narrator's dream of Meda Roth *corrects* the *Vidette* version of Almeda Roth's life. When Almeda

writes in her Preface that "I have occupied myself" with the effort of writing poetry, the phrase connotes more than the Victorian obsession with the immorality of idleness and the necessity of keeping busy. There is the sense that her writing has been an attempt to fill in an "unoccupied" space, a blankness in her sense of self. This returns as well upon the frame story, the narrator's "writing" as a filling in of an emptiness, a gap she wants to connect. Her remarks at the end of the first section about the forgotten knowledge of poetry, the mystery of masculine and feminine rhymes, link the character and the activity, a forgotten woman and a forgotten art, as a composite "mystery"—in the sense of an enigma (*mysterium*) and of a craft (*misterium*)—the character's identity and the narrator's activity.

But while Almeda's poetry in the story would seem to be crucial to the narrator's act of recovery of the symbolic foremother, I am not sure that it functions in a "positive" way. In my understanding of her fictive career/chronology, Almeda's only book is published in 1873, the year after her father's death. While this might suggest we interpret the poetry as an expression of her newfound independence, the "facts" would suggest that the poems were all written while Almeda was daughter/housekeeper to the patriarch. The narrator wonders (facetiously, for she is adopting the tone and viewpoint of the *Vidette*), "Perhaps it was the proud, bookish father encouraging her"; and in her Preface to the book, Almeda herself describes her writing as if it were a supplement/compensation for her inadequacies as a housekeeper; the book's title, *Offerings*, further implies a dispossessing humility. Also, I do not get the sense from the narrative that the poetry continues after the weekend in 1879 when the experiences that alter Almeda occur, and perhaps this silence is another ironic mark of her triumphant escape: she refuses to be the patriarchally approved "poetess," approved so long as she sings from within the gilded cage of the Victorian construction of the feminine. Moreover, it seems that "Meneseteung," the "one very great poem that will contain everything," remains unwritten as a Victorian poem—until, of course, the narrator presents its prose substitute, a late twentieth-century short story, an act which in itself confirms the paradoxical recovery/over-writing of the Victorian foremother by "the writing daughter."

What the narrator presents as Almeda's frame of mind during her breakthrough experience is very much her own in the closing lines of the story. "Meneseteung" ends as it begins with the narrator trying to see her subject in a text. She discovers the gravestone with ''Meda'' inscribed on it. The whole story has been the reciprocal staring of subjective narrator at narrative subject, and the uncovering of the inscription corroborates the truth of the narrator's belief in Almeda Roth's secret identity:

> I thought that there wasn't anybody alive in the world but me who would know this, who would make the connection. And I would be the last person to do so. But perhaps this isn't so. People are curious. . . . You see them going around with notebook, scraping the dirt off gravestones, reading microfilm, just in the hope of seeing this trickle in time, making a connection, rescuing one thing from the rubbish.

These lines are the original ending of the story, as it appeared in *The New Yorker,* and in them the narrator describes herself and her project. She has wanted to make a connection with this figure in the past. When she quotes from Almeda's poem, ''*Come over, come over, let Meda come over,*'' we can hear what Karen Smythe describes as the '''double voice' of fictive-elegy'' (*Figuring Grief*) the character imagines her dead family calling to her to join them, but the line also speaks the twentieth-century narrator's wish to bring the dead past into the living present. Like Marlatt's narrator in *Ana Historic,* Munro's has set out to rescue a woman from the rubbish of history because that is where woman has been put. Like Laurence's Morag Gunn in *The Diviners,* she knows that the rejected is the motherlode of women's stories.

Friend of My Youth is full of stories about connecting. The title story establishes the pattern as its narrator obliquely approaches a posthumous rapprochement with her mother by imagining the life of someone in her mother's past, eventually moulding this character into a kind of oracular dream-figure who silently speaks words of ironic revelation to her:

> I would have wanted to tell her that I knew, I knew her story, though we had never met. I imagine myself trying to tell her. (This is a dream now, I understand it as a dream.) I imagine her listening. . . . But she shakes her head. She smiles at me, and in her smile there is a degree of mockery, a faint, self-assured malice. Weariness, as well. She is not surprised that I am telling her this, but she is weary of it, of me and my idea of her, my information, my notion that I can know anything about her.

In Munro's fiction, the irony of revelation is not so much that nothing is revealed but that revelation does not bring salvation. In ''Friend of My Youth'' the vision that does not salve is the narrator's recognition that ''Of course it's my mother I'm

thinking of'' when she dreams the other, and thus her mother comes forward to affirm her own impenetrable otherness against her daughter's self-serving designs.

The version of ''Meneseteung'' in the collection ends with a similar unravelment. But instead of the ironic deflation's taking the wind out of the narrator's sail, it is the reader who is left drifting in indeterminacy. The narrator thinks of others who might seek, like her, to connect past and present:

> And they may get it wrong, after all. I may have got it wrong. I don't know if she ever took laudanum. Many ladies did. I don't know if she ever made grape jelly.

This ''un-writes'' all that has come before it. The episode with the laudanum and grape jelly is the central episode in the story in which Almeda finally connects with the world that has attracted and repulsed her all her life. But the admission is important not so much as metafictive signal as an expression that the patriarchal right/wrong, true/false views of history are not operative here. Woman's story in ''Meneseteung'' dares to be read by the patriarchal reader as ''hysterical,'' but in that daring it successfully achieves its own hearing, re-writing the dismissive ''our poetess'' of the opening paragraph into a reclamation of a necessary ancestor. Munro herself may read the episode as the beginning of Almeda's disconnection with reality, but I feel that this goes against the spirit of the story and what is presented. Why should we not imagine Almeda, like the dream-Flora of ''Friend of My Youth,'' listening but smiling in mockery and weariness at her author's idea of her and ''her notion that [she] can know anything about her''? This not to suggest that my critical reading of the story is ''truer'' or ''more insightful'' than the writer's own understanding of her work, only that Munro's house of fiction is so complex a fabrication that there is no one view of it—critic's or author's—that sees, or seizes, it all.

We cannot discuss Almeda Roth the way we discuss other fictional characters. She does not have the fictive existence of characters whose stories are told in the third person. The form of this story—the movement in the relation of narrator to character, from differentiation to identity to what might be called internalized differentiation—forces us to be aware of the activity of fictive construction, in particular, as a process of ''consolation.'' In her discussion of fictive-elegy, Smythe shows how ''self-consciousness functions as a trope of consolation'' (*Figuring Grief*). The narrator's confession to invention at the end of ''Meneseteung'' is part of a pattern in *Friend of My Youth* in which narrators or characters fantasize about another character's life or behaviour but admit that they will never know for sure if they understand the other character. The autobiographical (re)turn of the narrator at the end of ''Meneseteung'' reminds us that the story has been ''about'' her, as ''the writing daughter'' (Redekop, *Mothers*), as much as about Almeda, the absent foremother. The shifts from first- to third- and back to first-person narration, as well as the quotations from Almeda's poetry, configure the ''double voice'' of elegy, ''the voice of the absent as well as the voice of the survivor . . . figured in the performed and performative text'' (Smythe, *Figuring Grief*). The past is used in ''Meneseteung'' in ways that serve a feminist recovery of a lost history as well as a metafictional exploration of how narrative, like Penelope's tapestry, is as much what is unwoven as what is woven. Like the other women's works that use the nineteenth century mentioned at the beginning of this essay, Munro's ''Meneseteung'' also shows that these are one and the same project. Imagining/unravelling the other's past is an invention/weaving of the present, a present that is now, and then, connected and continuous with the mystery of woman coming to possess her own presence. In this sense, Munro's inventive recollection of the past exemplifies the moral imagination which Benjamin urges in his ''Theses on the Philosophy of History'': ''The past can be seized only as an image which flashes up at the instant when it can be recognized and is never seen again''; and ''every image of the past that is not recognized by the present as one of its own concerns threatens to disappear irretrievably.'' The centre of Munro's story is the apocalyptic flash of that ''ball of fire rolling up Pearl Street, shooting off sparks,'' apocalyptic for Almeda as well as for Munro's narrator; for from the image cast by that moment a complex recognition begins to arrange itself, and it is in that patterned reflection that Munro articulates some of her deepest ''concerns.''

Source: Dermot McCarthy, ''The Woman Out Back: Alice Munro's 'Meneseteung,''' in *Studies in Canadian Literature,* Vol. 19, No. 1, 1994, pp. 1–19.

Sources

Boston, Anne, ''Hidden Reasons,'' in *New Statesmen and Society,* Vol. 3, No. 1233, October 19, 1990, pp. 32–33.

Mayberry, Katherine J., '''Every Last Thing . . . Everlasting': Alice Munro and the Limits of Narrative,'' in *Studies in Short Fiction,* Vol. 29, No. 4, Fall 1992, pp. 531–41.

Munro, Alice, ''Meneseteung,'' in *Friend of My Youth,* Knopf, 1990, pp. 50–73.

Ross, Catherine Sheldrick, ''Alice Munro,'' in *Dictionary of Literary Biography,* Vol. 53, *Canadian Writers Since 1960, First Series,* edited by W. H. New, Gale Research, 1986, pp. 295–307.

Salter, Mary Jo, ''In Praise of Accidents,'' in *New Republic,* Vol. 202, No. 3930, May 14, 1990, pp. 50–53.

Shields, Carol, ''In Ontario,'' in *London Review of Books,* February 7, 1991, pp. 22–23.

Timson, Judith, ''Merciful Light,'' in *Maclean's,* Vol. 103, No. 19, May 7, 1990, pp. 66–67.

Woodcock, George, ''The Plots of Life: The Realism of Alice Munro,'' in *Queen's Quarterly,* Vol. 93, No. 2, Summer 1986, pp. 235–50.

Further Reading

Bothwell, Robert, *A Traveller's History of Canada,* Interlink Books, 2001.
> This brief history of Canada includes two chapters that cover the era in which ''Meneseteung'' takes place, including the major social and political changes. The book also includes historical maps, a chronology of major events, and lists of major political figures in the nineteenth and twentieth centuries.

Gilbert, Sandra M., and Susan Gubar, *The Madwoman in the Attic: The Woman Writer and the Nineteenth-Century Imagination,* Yale University Press, 2000.
> Sandra M. Gilbert and Susan Gubar originally published this groundbreaking volume of feminist literary criticism in 1979. The book offers revolutionary concepts in literary criticism about women and gives critical studies of the works of major nineteenth-century women authors, such as Jane Austen, Mary Shelley, and Charlotte Brontë. This latest edition includes a new introduction from the two authors.

Heble, Ajay, *The Tumble of Reason: Alice Munro's Discourse of Absence,* University of Toronto Press, 1994.
> Munro is known for the plotless, episodic quality of her fiction, which often does not examine ideas to completion, and, in fact, seems to purposely leave elements out. In Heble's book, he fills in the gaps in Munro's fiction, exploring the subtext behind these omissions.

Howells, Coral Ann, *Alice Munro,* Manchester University Press, 1998.
> This first book-length study of Munro's work gives a comprehensive overview of the author, including a discussion of her fictional small-town Canadian settings and photorealistic descriptions.

Ross, Catherine Sheldrick, *Alice Munro: A Double Life,* ECW Press, 1993.

This first book-length biography of Munro gives a chronological overview of the author's dual development as a wife/mother and professional writer and the challenges that she faced in balancing these two roles. Ross also examines how these autobiographical elements have figured into Munro's fiction.

Thacker, Robert, ed., *The Rest of the Story: Critical Essays on Alice Munro,* ECW Press, 1999.

Thacker, the editor of the *American Review of Canadian Studies,* includes essays from leading critics that collectively give a comprehensive critical and biographical discussion of Munro and her art.

York, Lorraine, *The Other Side of Dailiness: Photography in the Works of Alice Munro, Timothy Findley, Michael Ondaatje, and Margaret Laurence,* ECW Press, 1987.

Although published before *Friend of My Youth,* York's book is still a good source for anybody wishing to examine the use of photography in Munro's fiction. The book includes a discussion of Munro's *Lives of Girls and Women* as well as an exploration of works by the three other Canadian authors.

The Night the Ghost Got In

"The Night the Ghost Got In" is a prime example of the storytelling technique of James Thurber, who is widely considered one of the greatest humor writers that America ever produced. It was published in Thurber's 1933 book *My Life and Hard Times*, a fictionalized account of his childhood in Columbus, Ohio. Like most of Thurber's best works from that collection, the story combines events that are plausible with comic exaggeration and then adds responses that range from exaggeration to deadpan. The characters' inappropriate understanding of their world serves the dual purposes of amusing readers while revealing to them the uneven balances of the human mind.

The story centers on a common situation: the narrator (a first-person speaker, standing in for Thurber as a young man) hears a strange sound downstairs in the middle of the night. He assumes that it is a ghost, but his mother calls the police, who are thoroughly befuddled by the odd characters of the Thurber household and their way of life. By the time it is over, one of the policemen has been shot in the shoulder by the household's senile grandfather, and a local news reporter, told that a ghost is the cause of all the commotion, is left speechless. Since it is a light comedy, there are no serious repercussions in this story, and in the end life goes on in the household just as it had before.

My Life and Hard Times is still in print in paperback, more than seventy years after its first publication. This story is also included in the Library

James Thurber

1933

of America volume *James Thurber: Writings and Drawings*, edited by Garrison Keillor.

Author Biography

James Thurber was born on December 8, 1894, in Columbus, Ohio, the town that, throughout his travels and writing, he always referred back to and spoke fondly of as his home. Thurber's father was a clerk and minor politician and was often unemployed, a situation that caused the family to have many relatives living in the house at one time to help share the expenses. It was from his mother that Thurber received his subtle sense of humor. She regularly made up fantastic exaggerations of life in the Thurber household, which she would tell to unwitting guests with a straight face.

One of the most important events in Thurber's life occurred in 1901, when he was seven: While playing in the yard (varying accounts identify the game as William Tell or Cowboys and Indians), an arrow shot by his brother went into Thurber's eye. As a child, the weakness of his left eye drove him from play toward reading and academics; as an adult, his eyesight weakened until he was eventually blind.

Thurber went on to graduate from high school and enrolled in Ohio State University in 1913, where he wrote for the campus paper and became editor of the monthly campus magazine. Thurber did not finish his degree but instead became a code clerk for the State Department, which sent him to France from 1918 to 1920. Returning to America, Thurber worked as a reporter for the *Columbus Dispatch* for a while and then quit in 1924, returning to Paris to write, along with others of the post–World War I generation who are remembered today as the Lost Generation. The novel he wrote was never published, and Thurber took a job reporting for the Paris edition of the *Chicago Tribune*.

In 1927, Thurber was in New York when E. B. White, himself a famous writer, recommended Thurber to the editor of the *New Yorker*. Thurber was hired as a staff writer and soon distinguished himself for his short comic pieces. White was also responsible for taking a few of Thurber's doodles down to the magazine's famed cartoon department, giving rise to Thurber's secondary career as a cartoonist, which in itself would have ensured his

lasting fame had he not been such a respected writer. Thurber and White coauthored a book called *Is Sex Necessary?*, a parody of Freudian analysis, which was popular at the time; it was published in 1929. Thurber worked for the *New Yorker* from 1927 to 1933 and continued contributing stories and drawings to it for the rest of his life.

Thurber continued to write from the 1930s to the 1950s, becoming one of America's most treasured humorists. Collections of his stories and his cartoons consistently rode at the top of the bestseller lists. As the sight in Thurber's good eye failed, his literary production dwindled. Thurber fell into alcoholism in his later years and died of pneumonia following a stroke on November 2, 1961.

Plot Summary

"The Night the Ghost Got In" is a fictionalized account of life in the Thurber household while its author, James Thurber, was growing up. Early on, Thurber gives the exact date when the events related in the story take place: November 17, 1915. The story begins with a short introductory paragraph that prepares readers for the more colorful events that will unfold in the pages to come—his mother throwing a shoe through a window, his grandfather shooting a policeman—and then goes right into the events of that night.

It starts with the narrator, James Thurber, coming out of a bath at 1:15 in the morning and hearing a noise downstairs in the dining room. It sounds to him like footsteps, like someone walking quickly around the dining room table. He assumes that it is his father or older brother, just home from a trip, but after a few minutes have passed and the walking has not stopped, he goes to wake his brother Herman. Wakened suddenly, Herman is frightened when he is told that there is someone downstairs, although the story never does indicate whether he hears the same sound the narrator does. He goes back to bed, slamming the door. The noise downstairs is gone, and, Thurber explains, "None of us ever heard the ghost again." However, the slamming door brings their mother out into the hall.

The mother asks about all of the footsteps she has heard and then comes to the conclusion that there are burglars downstairs. Because the telephone is downstairs where she thinks the burglars are, she devises a scheme to contact the police: She throws a shoe through the window of the house next door, which is close to the Thurber house, waking Mr. and Mrs. Bodwell, who live there. At first, Mr. Bodwell thinks that she is telling him that there are burglars in his own house, but after a momentary confusion he calls the police and tells them to go to the Thurber house.

The arrival of the police blows the whole event out of proportion. Their group includes "a Ford sedan full of them, two on motorcycles, and a patrol wagon with about eight of them in it and a few reporters." They call out for the front door to be opened, and when no one in the house goes downstairs, they break it in. They go upstairs to find the narrator, still not dressed after his bath, and the mother insisting that there were burglars in the house, even though all of the doors and windows are bolted from the inside. To justify their trip, the police set about searching the house, moving furniture and emptying closets. At one point, a policeman's curiosity gets the best of him, and he points out an unusual old musical instrument, a zither, to another officer. The narrator adds to the confusion by adding the useless information that the family's old guinea pig used to sleep on the zither. The police are suspicious of this strange family. One points out that the son, Thurber, was "nekked" when they arrived and the mother was hysterical, or, as the policeman puts it, "historical."

When the narrator's grandfather, who sleeps in the attic, makes a slight noise, the policemen spring into action. They race upstairs to investigate. The narrator knows that this will lead to trouble because his grandfather is "going through a phase" in which he thinks that the Civil War is still going on. Grandfather is obsessed with the retreat of the Union army under General George Meade from the forces of Stonewall Jackson's Confederate army. When the policemen arrive at his door, he is convinced that they are Meade's army. He calls them cowards and tells them to go back to the battle. He slaps one of the policemen across the back of the head, sending him to the floor, and as the others leave their fallen comrade and run away, he takes the man's gun from his holster and shoots at him, hitting him in the shoulder. He fires twice more and then goes back to bed.

Back downstairs, the police are upset that there is nobody to arrest, but they are not willing to go back to the attic and risk being shot at again. The wounded officer's shoulder is bandaged, and they

James Thurber

start looking around the house again. A reporter approaches the narrator, who has not been able to find one of his own shirts and is instead wearing one of his mother's blouses. When the reporter asks what all of the commotion is about, the narrator answers, in all sincerity, that the problem is that they have had ghosts in the house. The reporter thinks about that for a while and then just walks away quietly.

The policeman who has been shot declares his intention to go up to the attic and get his pistol back, but the other officers just mock him. The narrator promises to get the gun from his grandfather in the morning and bring it down to the police station. When the narrator's mother is told that Grandfather shot a policeman, the only reason she is disturbed is that the officer is "such a nice-looking young man."

The next morning, the grandfather comes down to breakfast looking cheerful. Nothing is said about the commotion of the night before, and the family assumes that he has forgotten it, until he asks, "What was the idee of all them cops tarryhootin' round the house last night?" Thurber does not say when the grandfather realized that it was policemen, not soldiers, in his room, but the fact that he understands reality is accepted as a sign that all is fine in the house, and the story ends on that lighthearted note.

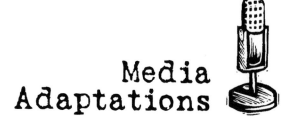

Media Adaptations

- Thurber's collection *My World, and Welcome to It* was adapted to a television series starring William Windom, Joan Hotchkiss, and Henry Morgan. It ran from 1969 to 1970.

- Thurber's play *The Male Animal* ran on Broadway for 244 performances in 1940 and is frequently revived today.

- Students can find references to books and articles by and about James Thurber at http://www.budgetweb.com/heather/thurber/Thurber.html.

Characters

Mr. Bodwell

Bodwell is the Thurber family's neighbor, a retired engineer. He is "subject to mild 'attacks,'" like most people whom the family knows. When the narrator's mother throws a shoe through the Bodwells' window and shouts to them that there are burglars in the house, Bodwell is momentarily confused, thinking that the burglars are in his house, before calming himself and calling the police.

Mrs. Bodwell

Mrs. Bodwell lives, with her husband, next door to the Thurbers. When a shoe comes through their window, before the Bodwells have a chance to realize that the narrator's mother threw it to get their attention, Mrs. Bodwell is heard shouting, "We'll sell the house and go back to Peoria."

Joe

The only policeman referred to by name, Joe does nothing that distinguishes him from the others. He examines an old zither with another policeman, and he is the one to say something when they hear the grandfather making noise in the attic. When the policeman who has been shot talks bravely about going to retrieve his gun from the grandfather, Joe mocks him and reminds him of the danger of approaching an armed and unstable suspect, which makes him change his mind.

Reporter

Near the end of the story, a newspaper reporter shows up and asks the narrator, "Just what the hell is the real lowdown here, Bud?" Told that the problem with the house is that it has ghosts, he just stares for a long time and then walks away.

Grandfather Thurber

The narrator's grandfather is a veteran of the Union army of the Civil War, which ended fifty-two years earlier. His bedroom is in the attic. When the police come to the house to search for an intruder, the grandfather thinks that they are soldiers who are deserting because they are losing to the South. He calls them "cowardly dogs" and "lily-livered cattle" and then reaches for a policeman's holster and shoots a man with his own gun. The police retreat, afraid of the crazy old man, but at the breakfast table the next morning, Grandfather seems perfectly aware of the previous night's situation, asking why so many police had been "tarryhootin'" around the house.

Herman Thurber

Herman is the brother of the narrator. He generally sleeps uneasily, always fearful that something might come and "get him" in the night. When the narrator comes to wake him, Herman hears the sounds in the dining room, which drives him to run back into his room and slam the door.

James Thurber

The narrator presents himself as acting reasonably, although his actions are unusual enough to raise the suspicions of the policemen. He is the first person in the household to hear the unidentified sound, as he is stepping out of the bathtub at 1:15 in the morning. After waking his brother Herman, he is the one who decides that the cause of the sound downstairs must be a ghost. When his excitable mother decides that the sounds must be caused by burglars, the narrator stays with her, thinking that she is beyond reason. He is still wrapped in a towel from his bath when the police arrive and only puts on pants when they point out his nakedness; later, when the reporter comes around asking questions, the narrator puts on one of his mother's blouses, explaining that it is the only thing that he can find. He decides to be honest with the reporter and tell him that the problem was caused by ghosts, but the reporter does not take him seriously. Later, when the policeman who has been shot by Grandfather wants to confront him and take his gun back, the narrator intervenes with calm sensibility and volunteers to take the gun over to the police station in the morning.

Mother Thurber

The narrator's mother is a highly excitable woman, scatterbrained in some regards yet practical when she needs to be. Hearing a sound in her house and suspecting that it is a burglar, she thinks of the clever plan of alerting a neighbor by throwing a shoe through his closed window. After he has gone to phone the police, however, she considers throwing the matching shoe, "because the thrill of heaving a shoe through a window glass had enormously taken her fancy." She is surprised to hear that Grandfather has shot a policeman, not because of the daring violence of the act, but because "He was such a nice-looking young man."

"Zither"

One of the policemen who search through the house finds an old zither and strums it in curiosity. The story later refers to this officer as "Zither," as well as "the zither-cop." When this officer goes to the attic to see what the noise up there is, Grandfather pushes him back and then shoots him with his own gun. Wounded in the shoulder, the zither-cop is upset, but he is logical enough to leave his gun with the angered grandfather so that the narrator can retrieve it for him the next day.

```
Topics for
Further
Study
```

- Interview a member of your local police department about what the proper procedure would be when responding to a call about a strange noise in a house, and report on it to your class.

- Take a tape recorder around with you for a few days and record any sounds that you have no explanation for. Create an audio essay about contemporary ghosts.

- If there is a ghost in the house that Thurber describes, it does not talk. Write a short story to function as a sequel to this one, explaining who the ghost is and why it is haunting this house.

- Research a contemporary culture that would not find the idea of a ghost in the house unusual, and write a report on the history of this belief among that culture's people.

- Discuss this short story with a lawyer, and find out what might be the modern legal ramifications of the mother throwing a shoe through the neighbors' window, the police breaking down the front door, the family turning in a false alarm, and so forth.

Themes

Supernatural

This story asks readers to accept the existence of the ghost mentioned in the title as a plausible, if uncommon, explanation for what occurs in this article. Many times, ghost stories offer readers evidence for natural explanations for the events that the characters themselves believe are caused by the supernatural. Although it seems very unlikely that a real ghost would have created a disturbance in the house, Thurber gives readers overwhelming evidence that the sounds that he heard were indeed supernatural. For instance, the police check the house and say that all of the doors and windows are locked from the inside; nothing in the house is said to have been taken by burglars; and the father and

brother, who are at first assumed do have come home from Indianapolis early, do not in fact appear in the story.

Like more traditional ghost stories, this one touches upon several possible explanations that would not force readers to accept supernatural causes. Herman's nervousness suggests that he may have been in a state of mind that would make up sounds and would accept things that go outside the bounds of normal reality. A nervous disposition is often used in ghost stories to explain why someone would make up the idea of a ghost, but, in this case, it is not only Herman who hears the ghost; it is heard by three people, including Thurber's mother, who shows no sign of believing in the supernatural. Also, Thurber makes a point of mentioning that it "did not enter my mind until later that it was a ghost," indicating that the supernatural interpretation is an act of his wandering imagination. Still, though he casts doubts on the idea of there being a real ghost, the evidence that he presents leads to the conclusion that there was.

Absurdity

The humor in "The Night the Ghost Got In" derives from the story's ability to show a world where absurdity rules. There are forces working to bring about order in this story, but they are easily outweighed and outwitted by the forces that struggle to create nonsense out of sense.

The sense of order is represented here in the authority held by the police force. When strange sounds occur in the dining room, both Thurber, who thinks the cause is a ghost, and his mother, who thinks it is burglars, rely on the police to take control. Their ability to impose order is far outweighed by the absurd elements in the house, though. These elements include the narrator's inability to find any clothes; the mother's urge to give in to the "thrill" of throwing a second shoe through the neighbors' window, even though the first had done its job; the grandfather's demented certainty that the policemen are deserters from Meade's army; and the grandfather's reversal of that dementia the next morning, when he implies that he knew they were policemen all along. The police themselves add an absurd element by their eagerness to find something amiss: They arrive at the house with too many men and are overenthusiastic about tearing through the family's front door and their personal effects, proving themselves to be a threat to the people they are there to protect.

The element that readers might expect to make sense of these events is the narrator. Because he is writing as an adult, Thurber might have, in a more serious work, explained that the absurd events that went on in his house may have seemed normal at the time but that he sees them differently now. He does not distance himself from them in this way, though; instead, he calmly asserts that it was indeed a ghost in the house. The narrative voice is just as involved in the absurdity as the members of the household.

Defiance

Though the characters in this story seem to be members of an ordinary family, they are defiant to forces from outside of the house that come to change them. The most obvious example of this occurs when Grandfather actually shoots a police-man. His remarks at the breakfast table give readers good reason to believe that the senility that excused his violence of the night before was just a ruse, that he may well have known what he was doing all along. He knows how to put up enough resistance to the police who have disturbed his sleep to make them go away, mixing the frightening prospect that he might shoot again with just the right balance of rationality so that they believe he will cause no more trouble if they leave the matter for his grandson to handle. In this way, he is successful in subverting the authority that the policemen show themselves so anxious to assert.

The narrator of the story shows his defiance in a more subtle, less confrontational way. His lack of clothing is explained insufficiently by the fact that he could find nothing to wear, in his own house, over the length of time that the story covers. It can also be read as an act of defiance against the representatives of society's authority. The fact that it bothers the police officers is clear when one of them mentions, after the narrator is dressed, that he had been "nekked" when they arrived. Later, he wears one of his mother's blouses, which shows a mocking attitude toward social gender norms that perplexes the outsiders. Lacking the respect that society would show to an aged war veteran like his grandfather, he is even less obvious about his defiance, explaining it to readers as if it were quite natural, but his casualness about it hides the fact that, in his own house, Thurber was free to flaunt society's customs.

Comedy of Life

Despite the eccentricities of the Thurber household, this story is drawn from the tradition of comedy that laughs at common, everyday occurrences. Most readers will not have had a ghost in their house, but they will know the experience of hearing a strange noise that has no rational explanation. And, while it is uncommon for carloads of policemen and reporters to arrive in answer to a call, almost everyone can identify with the idea of things spinning out of control, with officials, stuffed by their own self-importance, working hard to find more trouble than is actually there. And the grouchy old grandfather living in the past is a character familiar throughout the world's cultures, even though such a character is usually "ornery" or "cantankerous," not violent. American humor has a gentle strain, poking fun at the middle-class household that fits poorly into society's norms, and this story is a classic example of that type of humor.

Style

Folktale

Most ghost stories fall into one of two categories: horror or folktale. The main purpose of horror stories is to thrill readers. Folktales, on the other hand, serve to amuse readers while telling them something about the culture that is being described. In the case of "The Night the Ghost Got In," readers are introduced to the tiny subculture of a Columbus, Ohio, family where strange noises in the night are explained by acceptance of the supernatural. Most ghost stories from the folktale strain inform readers about the culture's relation to its dead members: The ghosts are manifestations of mourning, or guilt, or some other unfinished business. Thurber does not offer any explanation about why this ghost might choose to appear in this particular house at this particular time, but once he does introduce the ghost, it does, like ghosts in traditional folktales, illuminate the prevailing social situation. Of the younger members of the household, Herman fears it and Thurber is fascinated by it; the mother interprets its disturbance as a burglar, representing a threat from outside the house; the grandfather, to whom the ghostly armies of the Civil War are part of everyday reality, does not hear it; and the police and reporters think that it is just a sign of the Thurbers' mental instability.

Persona

The book that this story comes from, *My Life and Hard Times*, is based on Thurber's childhood, although liberties have obviously been taken with the facts. Many details in this story, from the number of policemen and reporters who show up to the existence of the ghost at all, are clearly exaggerations. The first-person speaker of the story should similarly not be mistaken for an actual representation of James Thurber himself, but should be looked at as a comic persona that resembles him.

The word "persona" comes from the Latin word for "mask." In most first-person short stories, the writer's persona is clearly recognizable as a different person. Usually, a character in a short story will not even have the same name as the writer. In this case, however, readers can become confused by the fact that "The Night the Ghost Got In" claims to be from Thurber's memoir and that the setting and events are similar to those he experienced in his life. The "I" who tells the story has much in common with the author of the story, but he is still a mask that the author created.

Stereotype

A stereotyped character is one that is written to represent some particular type of person, oversimplified, so that the character shows no internal depth. In literature, writers try to create their characters with the same range of emotion that ordinary humans have. It is also necessary, though, for literary works to be filled in with stereotyped, or "stock," characters who have little to do with the main story but interact with the main characters. Humorous writing, in particular, relies on stereotypical characters because it is easier for readers to laugh at the misfortunes of hollow representations of people than it is to laugh at characters who are well-rounded.

In "The Night the Ghost Got In," several of Thurber's characters represent familiar stereotypes. The policemen, for instance, are boorish and self-important, determined to justify their own authority by finding evidence of criminal wrongdoing even if it does not exist. None of them is able to understand or appreciate the quirky behavior of the people in the Thurber household because, as written, they lack the psychological depth to see beyond their own limited characterizations. The grandfather, as well, is humorous precisely because he plays the "senile old man" role. Shouting about a war that ended fifty years earlier, confusing the policemen for an army, and living out his faded glory by firing at an imagined enemy are all traits that would be considered pathetic, not funny, in a realistic portrayal. The ditzy mother who fails to recognize the seriousness of a man being shot is the same type of well-meaning, scatterbrained matron that shows up in situation comedies today. As long as the central character, the narrator, is psychologically complex, it is not necessary that any of these secondary characters should be, and in fact adding more depth to them would slow the story's humor down.

Epilogue

In the last paragraph of the story, Thurber adds a brief epilogue that tells readers what happened the next morning, when the daylight had come to shed light on things and the confusion had died down. An epilogue is usually not a part of the story but is included to let readers know what happened to characters as a result of the events that have taken place. Since this story is a comedy, there are no serious consequences to be faced in the morning. There is no sign of a ghost or whatever caused the initial disturbance; Mr. Bodwell from next door does not demand that his window be fixed; and the law does not show up to arrest the grandfather for shooting an officer. In fact, Thurber has the grandfather speak coherently (if angrily) about the policemen who were there, showing that he is not permanently out of touch with reality. The last line—''He had us there''—shows that the narrator is willing to consider the night's events baffling and inexplicable, but not serious.

Historical Context

The Great Depression

Thurber first published this story at the height of the Great Depression, when America was in the midst of one of the worst economic crises that it has ever known. By that time, about one-third of the labor force—16 million people—were unemployed. The country's gross domestic product, which is one of the main indicators that economists use to measure economic health, had shrunk nearly in half between 1929 and 1933, from $104 billion to $56 billion. Hundreds of people died of starvation every year, and thousands avoided starvation only by relying on government handouts.

The Great Depression had many causes, but the main factor that started it was the stock market crash on Thursday, October 4, 1929, a date that has come to be known as Black Thursday. During the 1920s, economic prosperity had given people a false sense of security, leading many to invest foolishly in stocks, often with borrowed money. When the value of the stocks fell sharply, debt holders were forced to default on their loans, which caused a rippling effect throughout the economy. Businesses folded, laying off workers who then had trouble paying for goods and services, forcing other businesses into bankruptcy, and so on. The economic crunch was worldwide, blocking any hope for relief: In Ger-

many, for instance, despair over the runaway economy gave Adolf Hitler and his Nazi party a platform for their rise to power.

The economy worsened for the first years of the 1930s. In 1933, Franklin Delano Roosevelt became president and initiated a long list of policies, collectively known as the New Deal, that were meant to stimulate the economy and help Americans deal with the problems of chronic unemployment. The economy rose slowly, and the depression never fully lifted until 1939, when World War II began in Europe.

Americans coped with the economic situation by finding ways to spend less. One way they did this was by moving into more cramped quarters. It was not uncommon for several generations of family members to live in one house, as older members, who once may have been able to afford to live on their own, found that their savings would not stretch, their pension plans were bankrupt, and the few employers who did have jobs gave them to younger workers. People also relied on their neighbors more to help out when they came up short, whether it was in borrowing cooking ingredients or calling for a hand in putting together food or furniture that they could not afford to buy from the store. Thurber's audience, therefore, would have been well familiar with the kind of household and community that he describes in ''The Night the Ghost Got In,'' many of them having been pushed together into similar close circumstances themselves.

Domestic Comedy

''The Night the Ghost Got In'' gains its humor from several trends in American humor. For one thing, it is the sort of family-oriented story that was popular during the depression. The major strains of humor throughout the country's history had always been political humor—as might be expected of a democracy that was built on the principle that those who govern are no better than those whom they rule—and racial or ethnic humor, owing to the country's immigrant nature. The late 1880s and early 1890s, however, saw the establishment of the middle class, a new category that was neither high nor low but was prime material for satire. Though satires of the upper and lower classes usually had an outsider's perspective, middle-class humor was gentler, if only for the reason that most writers and their readers were members of that category themselves.

Compare & Contrast

- **1915:** Mack Sennett's *Keystone Cops* comedies are popular at the movies, featuring a large group of bungling policemen running around and creating mayhem.

  1933: A string of movies about hard-boiled gangsters, including *Little Caesar* (1930), *Public Enemy* (1931), and *Scarface* (1932), has given policemen a sense of self-importance.

  Today: The trend in police dramas is toward the collection of minute pieces of evidence, in direct contradiction to the brutish destruction wrought by the officers in "The Night the Ghost Got In."

- **1915:** In the middle of World War I, many of the young men of Thurber's age are off in the trenches of Europe.

  1933: In the middle of the Great Depression, many family members who would otherwise have gone their own way are still living at home, unable to afford separate housing.

  Today: The past decade has brought a dramatic rise in the number of people moving back home after college, unable to find jobs and burdened with student loans.

- **1915:** Fifty years after the end of the Civil War, a veteran like the grandfather in the story can still use it as a point of reference.

  1933: Having been through World War I, the Civil War seems like a quaint antiquity to Thurber's readers.

  Today: Nearly thirty years after its end, Vietnam still remains America's point of reference for large-scale conflicts.

- **1915:** Spiritualists and mediums are popular and have achieved some credibility in upper-class social circles.

  1933: Many tricks that spiritualists have used to create the illusion of unworldly occurrences have been debunked. Magician Harry Houdini, in particular, has spent years revealing how such mysteries as phantom knocking and music from nowhere are created.

  Today: Spiritualists seldom use elaborate special effects but instead just make unverifiable claims about speaking to people who have died.

Thus, there was no audience for humor pieces that would portray homeowners and housewives as corrupt or inherently ignorant. The humor tended to laugh with them, not at them.

The *New Yorker,* for which Thurber wrote for most of his life, was a main influence for the growth of this type of writing. The magazine began in 1925 as a sophisticated journal for an urban audience. In writing for that audience, however, Thurber's mentor and friend, editor Harold Ross, assembled a stable of writers who wrote droll, understated pieces about the quirks of family life. Writers like Robert Benchley and S. J. Perlman spun witty stories about their difficulties as decent, ordinary fellows in coping with modern expectations. Clarence Day, whose version of the same material was collected into the book *Life with Father,* took a somewhat more sentimental view of the same material, whereas James Thurber was more likely to venture into the absurd. But at the core of the *New Yorker* style of humor in the 1930s was the bumbling middle-class man.

Domestic comedy grew over the years. The latter part of the decade saw the extravagant musicals, with which Hollywood had kept people amused during the beginning of the depression, give way to screwball comedies based on the idea that ordinary life was anything but ordinary. In order to develop continuing characters that people would want to revisit week after week, situation comedies were developed, placing their stars in ordinary households that home audiences could relate to. Movie studios started churning out series with low production budgets, such as the *Blondie* movies, based on the popular comic strip, and the *Andy Hardy* series. These, in turn, have given rise to the domestic comedies that proliferate on television today about ordinary, working-class people with eccentric family members.

Critical Overview

Throughout his long career, and ever since, James Thurber has been considered one of America's great humor writers, and *My Life and Hard Times*, the book that "The Night the Ghost Got In" comes from, is widely considered to be his best work. In 1933, the year that the book was published, Robert M. Coates wrote in the *New Republic* that it constituted "the pleasantest mixture of fantasy and understanding, one of the funniest books of recent times." More than half a century later, Robert Emmet Long writing in his book *James Thurber* still referred to that particular volume of Thurber's work as "one of the most striking and original books published in America in the 1930s."

The public never seemed to lose its appreciation for Thurber's comic pieces and his drawings, which came less and less frequently as his eyesight failed. What was unusual, however, was the sustained approval of literary critics. As he aged, critical appreciation for Thurber grew to almost mythic proportions. Three years before his death, Robert H. Elias wrote in the *American Scholar,* "For more than a generation James Thurber has been writing stories, an impressive number of them as well shaped as the most finely wrought pieces of Henry James, James Joyce and Ernest Hemingway." Elias went further, comparing his prose to that of H. L. Mencken and J. D. Salinger, his insights to those of poets E. A. Robinson and Robert Frost, pointing out the unfairness that Thurber had never been nominated for a Nobel Prize. The excess of such enthusiasm was recognized by Melvin Maddocks, who wrote in the *Sewanee Review* that "The superlatives applied by Thurber's colleagues and contemporaries seem excessive to the point of embarrassment today." Looking back on Thurber's career, Maddocks was able to identify a formulaic pattern to his stories, one that applied to other humor writers who wrote for the *New Yorker* as well. Like most critics today, Maddocks appreciated Thurber's comic innovation while accepting his limits.

Criticism

David Kelly

Kelly is an instructor of creative writing and literature at several Illinois colleges. In this essay, Kelly questions the description of this story as "autobiography," considering what it should properly be called.

In his "Afterward" to the current paperback edition of James Thurber's *My Life and Hard Times*, noted essayist and *Masterpiece Theatre* host Russell Baker calls the book "possibly the shortest and most elegant autobiography ever written." Now, generally, the words "biography" and "autobiography" are used to describe factual accounts of an individual's life. There are, in fact, cases in which a work of fiction is written in the first-person voice and the narrator refers to herself or himself as "I"; there are even such narratives that use the author's name for one of the characters in the book. But no matter how close they come to the facts of the author's life, these are still considered works of fiction, though their narrators quite naturally insist that the events they relate are "real."

It would seem that Baker did not take into account the whole scope of Thurber's book. One powerful clue to whether the book is actually an autobiography might be the chapter titled "The Night the Ghost Got In." The factual presentation of a ghost, in the title as well as in the story, is not the kind of thing that fits well into a memoir. Here, it should be enough to show that, regardless of how much the details of the book resemble the details of Thurber's own life, this is a work of fiction.

But there is one more element that has to be added to the assessment, as Baker most certainly knew. This book belongs in the category of "fiction," but it is also clearly meant to be humorous. Humor changes the responsibilities of the author, as well as the expectations that are held by his readers. In an autobiography that is presented without any irony, giving a twisted version of the events that occurred amounts to a criminal act, breaking a sacred trust between author and audience. In a work of fiction, readers actually expect events to be filtered through the author's imagination: The whole point of fiction is for readers to identify what has been spun from the author's imagination and to think about why particulars were added or left out. With humor, the audience is invited to join the author in a cooperative adventure. It is quite un-

Columbus, Ohio, in the early 1900s, provides the setting for Thurber's ''The Night the Ghost Got In''

likely that Russell Baker actually believed that a ghost haunted the Thurber household in 1915, but acting as if he does believe it, because Thurber's narrator presents it as a fact, is all part of being a good sport.

So, if Baker's use of the word ''autobiography'' is not exactly correct, it just shows that he is going along with the spirit of the book. The confusion is not his fault; he is just going in the direction pointed out by the author. Still, critics and readers ought to take the responsibility straight to Thurber, and when reading his book, demand to know, Why *isn't* this book an autobiography, or at least a fictionalized facsimile of one? If the presence of the ghost creates such a drastic change in the type of book this is, then maybe Thurber should have gone against his humorous inclination and not let it stand in the book.

Right away, care should be taken to point out how little this would change the overall story. Thurber could easily have added a line, or half a line, anywhere in ''The Night the Ghost Got In'' that would have given readers enough reason to believe that the ghost was just the projection of a youthful imagination. A simple mention if a stirring dog downstairs, or a family member that might have

been in the dining room at the time of the incident, or a draft down the chimney would have more clearly made this an imaginative autobiography, instead of a work of pure fiction.

It is very likely that Thurber might feel that he gave exactly such evidence, that his comic narrator is unreliable enough that readers certainly would not trust him when he talks about a ghost. Perhaps careful readers are not supposed to think that the author is telling them that there was a ghost in his house, only that the narrator, who witnessed the events as an impressionable young man, thought that there was. There are several good reasons not to believe the narrator's claim.

For one thing, *My Life and Hard Times* is chock-full of exaggerations, which Thurber uses to show the sort of humorous exaggeration that was common where he grew up, or at least the sort of comic exaggerations that mark his style of writing. In other chapters, the young Thurber tells such tall tales as electricity leaking out of sockets into the open air, a rumor of a crumbling dam stampeding a whole town, a man catching chestnut blight from a tree, and a car dropping its engine on the road and then driving back to get it. These are the sort of things that various characters believe, as if the

What Do I Read Next?

- Charles S. Holmes is considered one of the preeminent scholars of Thurber's literary career. Holmes's 1972 biography of James Thurber, *The Clocks of Columbus,* is a detailed examination of both the writer and his works. It is accepted by many as the definitive biography.

- Among contemporary humor essayists, Sarah Vowell and David Sedaris are among the most respected. Vowell's most recent collection is *The Partly Cloudy Patriot,* published by Simon & Schuster in 2002. Sedaris's masterpiece is "The Santaland Diaries," a Thurberesque account of his stint as an elf at Macy's one Christmastime, included in the 1994 collection *Barrel Fever.*

- Essays that Thurber wrote about the writing profession have been collected in *Collecting Himself: James Thurber on Writing and Writers,*

Humor and Himself, edited by Michael J. Rosen. It was published in 1989 by Harper & Rowe.

- Most of Thurber's best humor pieces, including "The Night the Ghost Got In," were collected later in his career in *The Thurber Carnival,* which is still in print in paperback, from Perennial.

- Robert Benchley was another *New Yorker* humorist, so keen of wit that Thurber once remarked, "One of the greatest fears of the humorous writer is that he has spent three weeks writing something done faster and better by Benchley in 1919." *The Best of Robert Benchley* was published in 1996 by Random House.

- In 1989, the University of Missouri Press brought together a collection of previously published interviews with Thurber in the book *Conversations with James Thurber.* It was edited by Thomas Fensch.

Columbus, Ohio, of Thurber's youth was in the grips of a mass hysteria. Readers are not expected to believe that any of them are true.

The ghost claim is different, though. For one thing, there is the conspicuous absence of a rational explanation. As mentioned before, it would have been a simple thing for Thurber to include something that might really have made the noise that the characters in the story attribute to the ghost. Most ghost stories do in fact include something to show readers where the idea of the ghost came from. It almost seems as if Thurber, as author, went out of his way to insist that his narrator is right in claiming a there is a ghost. The cleverness, the sense of fun, diminishes if the author has to force it like this.

The main problem with this, though, is that it breaks faith with the reader. The voice in which Thurber tells this story is not the voice of a teenage boy from a Midwestern town at the turn of the century—that is just the person that this grown-up narrator remembers once being. The voice that tells

"The Night the Ghost Got In" is polished and sophisticated. It is the kind of complex voice that can weave together a phrase like "the thrill of heaving a shoe through a glass window had enormously taken her fancy," combining the low vocabulary ("heaving") and high ("enormously") with the whimsical ("taken her fancy"). It is the kind of voice that knows to whet its readers' appetites with an introductory paragraph that lays out all of the high points of what is to come, as he does in several of the book's chapters. It is a voice that knows when to refer to the lawmen as "police" and when to call them "cops." In short, it is not the kind of naïve observer that actually would believe in a ghost.

For this narrator to claim a belief in ghosts is dishonest, which might not necessarily be something that, if asked, he would deny. He probably would not admit to it either. A wink would have to suffice. The dishonesty is part of the humor of this piece. An intelligent writer like Thurber swearing that a ghost invaded his house has the same basic design as a bald-faced lie, but a lie ceases to be a lie if no one is expected to believe it. That is when it becomes a comic exaggeration. The aforementioned effect that humor has to bring the reader in on the trick forces Thurber's readers to supply the information that he refuses to give them, making them draw a conclusion (that he, of course, does not think there was a ghost in his house) that his comic persona will not let him say out loud.

Calling *My Life and Hard Times* an "autobiography" still seems to be taking the joke a little too far. After all, critics and reviewers have a greater responsibility to the truth than writers and readers. It is easy to see, however, how anyone reading Thurber's wild exaggerations would want to join in on the fun. "The Night the Ghost Got In," in particular, represents a case in which Thurber's narrator, normally the cool observer who keeps readers informed about the bizarre behaviors and beliefs of the people who surrounded him in childhood, throws caution to the wind and joins in on the fun, stating beliefs that are just as daffy as, for example, his grandfather's. That old man, in fact, may be the best example of the spirit with which readers should take Thurber's narrator. He seems completely out of touch with reality, shouting that the policemen in the house are Civil War deserters and even shooting one, but the next morning, when they are gone, he is not confused about who they were and shows no sign that he ever was. If his family can accept his switch between delusion and clarity so quickly, then readers of "The Night the Ghost Got In" should probably follow their lead and accept the idea of a ghost as a "phase" that Thurber was going through when writing this particular exaggerated comic piece.

Source: David Kelly, Critical Essay on "The Night the Ghost Got In," in *Short Stories for Students,* Gale, 2004.

Robert E. Morsberger

In the following essay excerpt, Morsberger discusses Thurber's philosophy of fantasy.

V Facts and Fantasy

"Dis morning bime by," said his hired man Barney Haller, "I go hunt grotches in de voods." Such a statement set Thurber's mind on fire. "If you are susceptible to such things, it is not difficult to visualize grotches. They fluttered into my mind: ugly little creatures, about the size of whippoor-wills, only covered with blood and honey and the scrapings of church bells." The grotches turn out to be nothing more than crotched branches of trees, but

> " For this narrator to claim a belief in ghosts is dishonest, which might not necessarily be something that, if asked, he would deny. He probably would not admit to it either. A wink would have to suffice."

a world without grotches is a duller place. "There is no person," wrote Thurber, "whose spirit hasn't at one time or another been enriched by some cherished transfiguring of meanings"; and he gave as an example the youngster who thought that the first line of the Lord's Prayer was, "Our Father, who art in Heaven, Halloween be thy Name." "There must have been for him in that reading a thrill, a delight, and an exaltation that the exact sense of the line could not possibly have created."

A militant realist might scoff at such a mind as Thurber's; but, in so doing, he would miss much of the charm of life—like the patient bloodhound who went through the world with his eyes and nose to the ground and so missed all its beauty and excitement. The realist worries about heredity and environment, depression and taxes; Thurber too knew that life is perilous, but he worried about being "softly followed by little men padding along in single file, about a foot and a half high, large-eyed and whiskered." (For a picture of these little men, see *The Seal in the Bedroom.*) "Fantasy is the food for the mind, not facts," wrote Thurber; and one of his cartoons shows a social gathering in the midst of which sits an austere, scholarly looking man, chin in hand, scowling; while behind his back, one woman explains to another, "He doesn't know anything except facts."

Robert Louis Stevenson expressed what is essentially Thurber's position:

> There are moments when the mind refuses to be satisfied with evolution, and demands a ruddier presentation of the sum of man's experience. Sometimes the mood is brought about by laughter at the humorous side of life. . . . Sometimes it comes by the spirit

> " A militant realist might
> scoff at such a mind as
> Thurber's; but, in so doing, he
> would miss much of the charm
> of life. . . ."

of delight, and sometimes by the spirit of terror. At least, there will always be hours when we refuse to be put off by the feint of explanation, nicknamed science; and demand instead some palpitating image of our estate, that shall represent the troubled and uncertain element in which we dwell, and satisfy reason by the means of art. Science writes of the world as if with the cold finger of a starfish. . . .

Thurber recognized the dangers of carrying the imagination to extremes. While commenting that "Realists are always getting into trouble," he went on to say that "I do not pretend that the daydream cannot be carried too far." "You can't live in a fantastic dream world, night in and night out, and remain sane," he explained. Charlie Deshler in "The Curb in the Sky" tried to do just this and ended up in an asylum. In "A Friend to Alexander," Mr. Andrews, who took to dreaming constantly about Aaron Burr, withdrew farther and farther into his imagination, dreaming of finally wreaking vengeance on Burr, for whom he felt an intense hatred because the face of Alexander Hamilton resembled that of Andrews' dead brother. When he finally faced Burr's phantom in an imaginary duel, Andrews, identifying himself with Hamilton, dropped dead.

For all of his fantasy, Thurber satirized those who mistook illusion for reality. In his study of soap opera, he told of listeners who thought that radio characters were real and sent in wedding gifts and layettes to the studio when "Big Sister" got married or the daughter on "Just Plain Bill" had a baby. When another actor took over the role of the husband in "Pepper Young's Family," "Indignant ladies wrote in, protesting against these immoral goings on." Another woman listener, recognizing that Kerry Donovan, the husband in "Just Plain Bill," and Larry Noble, the husband in "Backstage Wife," were played by the same actor, wrote to the studio that she was aware of this double life and

threatened to expose the bigamy. Such a confusion of fact and fiction Thurber found pathetically absurd.

Thurber himself was certainly well grounded in reality. His work even more than Wordsworth's is full of concrete details and observations, sometimes interesting and informative, sometimes dead wood. Thurber had total recall, and once commented about himself: "He can tell you to this day the names of all the children who were in the fourth grade when he was. He remembers the phone numbers of several of his high school chums. He knows the Birthdays of all his friends and can tell you the date on which any child of theirs was christened. He can rattle off the names of all the persons who attended the lawn fete of the First M. E. Church in Columbus in 1907." As a result, he filled his work with a mine of incidental information which, while sometimes irrelevant, helped give his writings verisimilitude. Henri Bergson noted that "Humor delights in concrete terms, technical details, definite facts. . . . This is not an accidental trait of humor, it is its very essence."

The Romantic element is only one aspect of Thurber's work and is balanced by a great deal of skillful satire, a genre traditionally associated with Classicism. However, Thomas Wolfe observed that "The best fabulists have often been the greatest satirists. . . . Great satire needs the sustenance of great fable." As examples, Wolfe cited Aristophanes, Voltaire, and Swift; to these we might add Rabelais, Samuel Johnson, Mark Twain, Aldous Huxley, George Orwell, and Thurber himself. Sometimes Thurber combined romanticism and satire, as when he attacked the excesses of scientists and psychologists in their efforts to direct or control the imagination.

Perhaps psychiatrists have helped bring about the decline of fantasy (except in science-fiction) by making it too much a subject for analysis. One psychiatrist told Mrs. Thurber that if he had her husband under treatment for a few weeks, he would cure him of all his drawings. Thurber shrugged this incident aside, but he was highly incensed when the psychiatrist Dr. Paul Schilder analyzed Lewis Carroll and concluded that *Alice in Wonderland* is full of "cruelty, destruction, and annihilation." If carried to their illogical extreme, views such as Dr. Schilder's would destroy imaginative literature almost entirely. "Dr. Schilder's work . . . is cut out for him," wrote Thurber. "He has the evil nature of Charles Perrault to dip into, surely as black and devious and unwholesome as Lewis Carroll's. He has the Grimms and Hans Christian Andersen. He has Mother Goose, or much of it. He can spend at least a year on the Legend of Childe Rowland, which is filled with perfectly swell sexual symbols— from (in some versions) an underground cave more provocative by far than the rabbit hole in Wonderland to the sinister Dark Tower of the more familiar versions. This one piece of research will lead him into the myth of Proserpine and into Browning and Shakespeare and Milton's *Comus* and even into the dark and perilous kingdom of Arthurian legend. . . . When he is through with all this, Dr. Schilder should be pretty well persuaded that behind the imaginative works of all the cruel writing men . . . lies the destructive and unstable, the fearful and unwholesome. . . .'' Dr. Schilder would probably think that Lewis Carroll would have done better to devote himself solely to mathematics or to some other aspect of Reality; but Thurber believed that *Alice* is more valuable; and he wrote that, after all of Tenniel's political cartoons, the illustrations for *Alice in Wonderland* had given him something important to do. In reply to Dr. Schilder, Thurber quoted Dr. Morton Prince, "a truly intelligent psychologist," who says of the creatures of artistic imagination that "Far from being mere freaks, monstrosities of consciousness, they are in fact shown to be manifestations of the very constitution of life."

Certainly Thurber, an extremely careful craftsman and conscious critic of his work, which often underwent two dozen revisions, would not endorse the Freudian theory of the unconscious origins of art as a product of sublimated neurosis. As for Freud's study of humor, Thurber wrote in 1949: "I strongly believe that the analogy between dreams and wit rests on a similarity more superficial than basic, and the psychic explanation of wit fails to take in the selectivity of the artist whose powers of rejection and perfection are greater than his vulnerability to impulse." "Don't you think the subconscious has been done to death and that it's high time some one rediscovered the conscious?" he wrote as caption for a cartoon advertisement of S. N. Berhman's *Rain from Heaven* (1935).

"I have not always, I am sorry to say, been able to go the whole way with the Freudians, or even a very considerable distance," he wrote in 1937. His first book, *Is Sex Necessary?* spoofs the sort of sex books that transform love into nothing more than an inherited behavior pattern with a heavy dose of neuroses. Never caring for the attitude that cherishes neuroses and even considers them a sign of superior sensitivity, Thurber wrote that through the early part of this century "neuroses were staved off

longer, owing to the general ignorance of psychology." Accordingly he found little use for the theories of Dr. Louis E. Bisch, the "Be-Glad-You're-Neurotic" man, whose concepts he dismissed as mere mysticism. Thurber refused to indulge in psychic hypochondria and maintained that the analysts could not have him while he still kept his strength. "We worry so much about being neurotic that we never really delve into our minds," he told W. J. Weatherby in 1961. "Modern psychology and psychiatry have made us all afraid of ourselves," he wrote in the same year. "*Angst* is spreading, and with it mental ailments of whose cause and cure, one authority has recently said, we know little or nothing. But the terminology of psychiatry proliferates to the point that almost everybody now seems to think he is schizophrenic, schizoid, or schizo."

Source: Robert E. Morsberger, "The Romantic Imagination," in *James Thurber,* Twayne Publishers, 1964, pp. 55–59.

Sources

Baker, Russell, Afterword, in *My Life and Hard Times,* by James Thurber, with an introduction by John J. Hutchens, an afterword by Russell Baker, and commentary by Michael J. Rosen, 1st Perennial Classics ed., Perennial Classics, 1999.

Coates, Robert, "James G. Thurber, the Man," in *New Republic,* Vol. LXXVII, No. 993, December 13, 1933, pp. 137–38.

Elias, Robert H., "James Thurber: The Primitive, the Innocent, and the Individual," in *Thurber: A Collection of Critical Essays,* edited by Charles S. Holmes, Prentice-Hall, 1974, pp. 87–100; originally published in the *American Scholar,* Summer 1958.

Long, Robert Emmet, *James Thurber,* Continuum, 1988, p. 107.

Maddocks, Melvin, "James Thurber and the Hazards of Humor," in *Sewanee Review,* Vol. XCIII, No. 4, Fall 1985, pp. 597–601.

Further Reading

Burnett, Michael, "James Thurber's Style," in *Thurber: A Collection of Critical Essays,* edited by Charles S. Holmes, Prentice-Hall, 1974, pp. 75–86.
    Burnett examines the contradictions in Thurber's use of language that lead to the humorous effect of his stories.

Holmes, Charles S., ''James Thurber and the Art of Fantasy,'' in *Yale Review,* Vol. LV, No. 1, October 1965, pp. 17–33.

> Holmes, probably the best known of Thurber's biographers, gives an overview of the author's career.

Kinney, Harrison, *James Thurber: His Life and Times,* Henry Holt, 1995.

> At 1,238 pages, Kinney's biography is one of the most recent and most thorough studies of Thurber's life available.

Morsberger, Robert E., *James Thurber,* Twayne Publishers, 1964.

> This book, part of Twayne's ''United States Authors'' series aimed at the level of high school and college students, presents a concise overview of Thurber's literary career.

The Slump

John Updike

1968

In "The Slump," John Updike uses the national pastime, baseball, as the setting to explore one individual's frustration with the world. The story is told by a professional ballplayer who finds himself, for no identifiable reason, unable to hit as well as he once did. He thinks about why this might be, but not very deeply; for the most part, he accepts this slump as his fate and considers what it says about life in general. The story depicts the superstitious nature of athletes in the way that its narrator hopes for better days without having any hope that anything he can do would make his luck return.

Readers can see in "The Slump" the raw talent that has made Updike one of America's most respected writers for over a half century. The story is meticulously detailed, with sharp observations of even the most seemingly irrelevant actions, raising them to the level of importance. It achieves a philosophical depth that most stories only aspire to. It is, however, very unlike most of Updike's fiction. A typical Updike story plays out in relationships, examining the social expectations that surround most couples. In "The Slump," however, the narrator's relationship with his wife is described, but it is not an integral part of the story. Updike is a master at showing human interaction, and here he shows that he can be just as effective when writing an extended monologue.

"The Slump" was originally published in *Esquire* in 1968. It is currently available in the author's

1972 collection, *Museums & Women*, and is frequently reprinted in anthologies.

Author Biography

John Hoyer Updike was born on March 18, 1932. He was raised in Shillington, Pennsylvania, the only child of Wesley Updike and Linda Grace Hoyer Updike. Updike's father was a mathematics teacher at the local high school and supported his family, which included the author's maternal grandparents, on a meager salary. When John Updike was thirteen, his family could no longer afford to live in Shillington and moved to a broken-down farmhouse ten miles outside of town. In 1950, Updike entered Harvard University on a full scholarship. He was active in the school's literary scene, including being editor of the *Harvard Lampoon*. Before Updike graduated in 1954, he had met and married Mary Pennington, who was to be his wife for twenty-four years, and sold his first story to the *New Yorker*.

Updike was in Oxford, England, in 1955, attending the Ruskin School of Drawing and Fine Art, when he was contacted by the distinguished author E. B. White, who asked him to come to work for the *New Yorker*. He moved his family to Manhattan. Though his writing successfully complemented the magazine's cosmopolitan style, Updike feared that living in the big city would drain his talent, so, after less than two years, when his second child was born, he left his salaried position and moved to Massachusetts, continuing to contribute to the *New Yorker* frequently.

Away from New York City, Updike's writing career prospered. He published a book of poetry in 1958 that failed to attract any critical attention, but his first novel, *The Poorhouse Fair*, was a finalist in for the National Book Award in 1959. That same year, one of Updike's stories was reprinted in *Best American Short Stories of 1959*, and he was awarded a Guggenheim Fellowship. For the next few decades, Updike published at least one book every year and was awarded many major literary awards. He quickly became recognized as one of the preeminent American stylists and a chronicler of the suburban landscape that developed across the country after the end of World War II. Updike is among the nation's most eminent writers in at least four genres: novels, short stories, poetry, and essays. Updike has won many prestigious awards in each of these fields, including the National Book Critics Circle Award, the American Book Award, the PEN/Malamud Memorial Prize, the Caldecott Medal, and several Pulitzer Prizes. His most famous body of work is the ambitious ''Rabbit'' tetralogy, a series of novels that started in 1960 with *Rabbit, Run* and returned to the same central character roughly every ten years, with *Rabbit Redux* in 1971, *Rabbit Is Rich* in 1981, and *Rabbit at Rest* in 1990.

Updike continues to write and publish fiction and poetry. His work continues to appear frequently in the *New Yorker*, with which he has enjoyed an ongoing relationship since he was in his early twenties, and in the *Atlantic*.

Plot Summary

When ''The Slump'' begins, its narrator, a professional baseball player, has already been experiencing trouble with his hitting. The opening line goes right past the subject of a batting slump, leaving readers to understand the subject matter from the story's title, and starts immediately with guesses about what might be causing the problem. The first topic that the narrator suggests is ''reflexes,'' which his coach and the press assume to be causing his problem. He explains that he does not think it is caused by reflexes, though. As evidence for why he discounts this theory, he explains that the night before his wife surprised him in their bedroom with a rubber gorilla mask and he jumped under the bed in less than a second—she had a stopwatch ready and timed his reaction.

He remembers how easy it used to be for him to hit before falling into this slump, how the pitched ball seemed to float in the air before his eyes so that he could see every detail about it clearly. Now, though, the ball is obscured in a cloud, a ''spiral of vagueness.'' He paraphrases the Danish philosopher, Søren Kierkegaard, as saying that ''You can't see a blind spot.'' Aware that his hitting is his strong point as a ballplayer, he reflects on the likelihood, which he has already seen reported in a newspaper, that his team will try to trade him.

One good thing about being unable to hit is that he feels less pressure. He recalls how he used to leave home for the stadium and as he drew closer and closer, he could feel the butterflies in his stomach growing. He thought of himself as a thief, and walking through the corridors to the locker room, he imagined that he was being taken to the electric chair. It seemed like a dream, then, that players he had looked up to all his life recognized him. The whole experience of being on the team had been so amazing to him that he was constantly nervous—"by the time I got into the cage, I couldn't remember if I batted left or right."

Since the slump, however, the pre-game nervousness is gone. He drives to the stadium singing along with the radio, ignores the fans on the street, strides into the stadium, and performs perfectly in the batting cage before the game. When he steps up to the plate to bat, however, he is overcome with self-consciousness and unable to hit at all.

He describes his situation as "panic hunger." It is not the kind of hunger that drives him to achieve what he needs to sustain himself, which is what his detractors say he has lost as he has grown successful. He compares panic hunger to the intensity that a child puts into trying to catch a ball, becoming so consumed with the idea of doing well that he closes his eyes as the ball approaches. He tries to force himself to keep his eyes open, to look at something off in the distance (the example he gives is "some nuns in far left field"), but his eyes keep closing.

The slump that has affected his hitting has affected other parts of his life, as well. He avoids intimate contact with his wife, although he knows that it disappoints and angers her. He rides the lawn mower around the lawn so often that the grass is all dead. Filled with inexplicable dread, he is afraid to see his children trying at baseball. When he goes to Florida with the team, the repetitive sameness of wave after wave hitting the beach reminds him of the endless succession of batting opportunities that he endures in his profession, each one following the others with no meaning or differentiation. He suspects that reading Kierkegaard might lead him to the answer to his dilemma, but when he tries it, he finds himself unable to read: the pages of the book *Concluding Unscientific Postscript* all look blank, an emptiness that he describes as metaphorically resembling "the rows of deep seats in the shade of the second deck on a Thursday afternoon, just a single ice-cream vendor sitting there, nobody around to sell to, a speck of white in all that shade, old Søren Sock himself, keeping his goods cool."

In the end, he reflects on the indignity of his situation. He cannot even get on base by being hit by a pitch because the pitchers do not fear him enough to throw the ball near him; instead, they throw it right up the middle of the plate, where it would be

John Updike

easy to hit if he were not in a slump. For a moment, while thinking about the catchers laughing at him behind his back, he remembers "the old sure hunger" that drove him in his hitting in the old days, but the memory fades quickly, leaving him hopeless again. He is unable to believe in the external things about the game, citing specifically the stadium and the batting averages that are used to measure a batter's success. "[J]ust *you* are there," he muses, "and it's not enough."

Characters

The Ballplayer

The narrator of this story is a professional baseball player. Readers are not given his name or told what league he plays for. They do know, from the very first sentence, that he is famous enough to have his hitting problem discussed in the newspapers. When he was at the top of his game, children waited around the parking lot of the baseball stadium, just trying to get a glimpse of him. He has an attendant to park his car for him at the stadium. Also, the fact that the ballplayers who were famous

Media Adaptations

- John Updike reads several of his own short stories, including "A&P," "Pigeon Feathers," and "Separating," on the audiocassette *American Masters: The Short Stories of Raymond Carver, John Cheever, and John Updike*. It was produced by Bantam Books Audio in 1998.

when he was young now know his name is one more sign that he is famous and that he may have been a star player before his slump began.

Now that he is afflicted with his batting problem, he does not spend his time studying batting technique. Instead, his thoughts about what has happened to him are philosophical. He is a well-read man, with enough education to be familiar with the Van Allen belt and with the writings of Kierkegaard. The connection between his intellectual musings and his slump is made fairly explicit in the story, particularly where his rest on the beach in Florida is associated with losing, which turns immediately to his unsuccessful attempt to read philosophy. It is not clear whether his philosophical nature is actually causing the slump, forcing him to be too conscious of things that he should do naturally, or if he is turning to philosophy as a way of dealing with the fact that his batting is off.

The slump has affected his entire life. He has no physical contact with his wife anymore, causing her to walk right past him "with a hurt expression and a flicker of gray above her temple." He does not play with his children anymore as he did in the past. Opponents no longer fear him, and he himself can no longer enjoy simple pleasures that used to mean much to him. On the other hand, he does have more freedom: In the past, he used to turn down the volume on his radio as he approached the stadium because he was a role model for the children, but now it does not matter who hears him; they would not care anyway. And his slump continues because he cannot care enough about his own performance to make them care.

The Ballplayer's Wife

Trying to help the narrator break out of his slump, his wife tried shocking him, on the night before this story was narrated, by coming into the bedroom wearing a rubber gorilla mask that belonged to one of their children. The fact that she did this as an attempt at therapy is clear from the fact that she brought a stopwatch with her to measure in tenths of a second how long it took him to react. That she thought to time him, and that she thought of this idea to test his reflexes at all, shows that she understands the life of a ballplayer.

She is only mentioned in the narrative in the context of the gorilla mask incident, which comes up a second time when the narrator is talking about dread. He mentions his wife in a mask as an almost erotic image, mentioning that in the old days he would have taken fast, decisive action if she has approached him in such an exotic way; now, she goes away disappointed. And he spends more time outside by himself on the lawnmower than he did before the slump. The third time he mentions the gorilla mask, he thinks that she was probably hinting at his need for a change of pace. Since his interpretation of her action changes throughout the story, with no new input from her, it is difficult for readers to tell her real intentions from those that he assigns to her.

The Coach

The ballplayer's coach is only mentioned in the first sentence, as agreeing with the newspapers and the fans in thinking that the slump is caused by "reflexes." He is conspicuous by his absence: Since coaches are supposed to help athletes play better, the fact that this player in the middle of a slump has so little to say about his coach, and so much to say about Kierkegaard, indicates to readers that his problem stems from philosophical causes.

Themes

Futility

At the end of this story, the narrator notes that he finds it hard to care about his slump. Although he does not care about his own existence, he cannot force himself to believe in the importance of baseball, either. This is given as the final clue to what is bothering him, but it cannot be read as the only or most pervasive cause. He does, in fact, realize the value of some things throughout the story. He longs for the feeling of being important to his wife and children, and he fondly remembers the adulation of fans and other players. He can see things that make life worth living, but he does not know how to attain those things. It is not life but action that he finds futile.

In some way, this speaker seems to feel that futility is a liberating force, freeing him to act only when he knows that nothing important will come of it. He speaks of the tension that followed him from home to the ballpark when he was hitting well, how he had to behave in a certain way for his fans and for the other players. During the slump, though, he drives along, singing, and feels no compulsion to talk to his fans. A telling detail is how well he can hit the ball—just not during a game. "[I]n the batting cage I own the place," he says, noting that hits come as easily to him "as dropping dimes down a sewer." When there is nothing to be gained, his hitting is fine, but when his batting is supposed to count, he realizes that there is no ultimate point, that what he is doing is futile.

Self-Knowledge

At the very start of this story, the ballplayer muses on the fact that everyone who observes his slump says that it is a matter of "reflexes." His inability to hit the ball the way he used to seems to everyone else to be caused by too much thought, as reflexes, like instinct, rely on action that takes place automatically. Though he does not personally accept this theory, he does mention it again in the last paragraph: "for a second of reflex," he says, "I see it like it used to be." In that second, everything seems the way it did back when he was hitting well. He is in control of the situation, paradoxically, only when his body is acting reflexively and his mind does not control it.

Though thought might be holding him back, he knows that reflex alone is not the answer to his problem. He does have reflexes, as evinced by his ability to move quickly when his wife sneaks up on him. When he is forced to move without thinking, he can move as well as ever. His problem is that he cannot not think while playing baseball. He knows the game too well to move reflexively, and he knows himself too well, is aware of how he will react in every situation. This knowledge of himself makes it unlikely that he could ever again act out of pure reflex on the baseball diamond. Pure reflex is only for organisms that do not have the capacity to be self-conscious. As this ballplayer's knowledge of his own situation has grown, he has lost the ability to act as a non-conscious creature would.

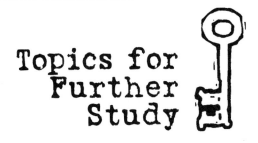

Topics for Further Study

- Research the philosophical theories of Søren Kierkegaard, and then write a letter from Kierkegaard, giving batting advice to this baseball player.

- Study the batting statistics from the most recent season and find a batter who experienced a significant batting slump. Read newspaper reports on the batter, and write your own report on how long it lasted, the theories about what caused it, and what might have finally ended it.

- This ballplayer's wife's trying to startle him with a gorilla mask is reminiscent of the sort of practical jokes that baseball players are famous for. Find out about some famous pranks, and share them with your class.

- Read the 1888 poem "Casey at the Bat," by Ernest L. Thayer. Compare specific lines from that poem with the experience the narrator of this story describes.

Baseball

There is great irony in the fact that this person's philosophical crisis occurs in the game of baseball. Fans of the game consider baseball to be one of the most intellectual sports, requiring strategy and nerve, in addition to physical prowess. Still, its status as America's national pastime means that millions of people enjoy the game without giving much thought to its mental aspect. Like any part of mass culture, baseball is something that does not require much intellectual activity to watch, and so it would at first seem to be an unlikely platform for exploring issues of such depth.

The very fact that there is a common word, "slump," to describe an inability to hit the ball, a condition that is otherwise unexplainable, is a clear sign of baseball's philosophical side. Although many baseball fans would recoil from the idea of studying Kierkegaard, the nature of the sport is such that it addresses the very same issues about the human condition that philosophers have addressed for centuries.

Existentialism

The nineteenth-century philosopher Søren Kierkegaard, who is referred to several times in this story, is credited with having coined the phrase "leap of faith" to describe the philosophical position of having to act even when one knows that action will be futile. He is recognized as being the precursor to the philosophy of existentialism, which is prevalent throughout "The Slump."

At the heart of Kierkegaard's philosophy is the concept of subjectivity. In his book *Concluding Unscientific Postscript,* which is mentioned in this story, Kierkegaard explains the tension between objective reality and subjective reality. According to him, these two concepts will always be at odds with one another and can never be reconciled. In "The Slump," this paradox shows itself in the subjectivity of the individual player and the objectivity of the team that he is a member of, as well as in the subjectivity of the intellect versus the objectivity of physical activity. Another of Kierkegaard's books, *Fear and Trembling,* stresses the dread that is a part of the human condition. This dread comes from realizing that one's fate is always one's choice, even though it might not seem so at times. A ballplayer in a slump, for instance, might look for all sorts of explanations in order to avoid accepting the responsibility for it.

These themes in Kierkegaard's writing carried over into the philosophy of existentialism in the twentieth century. Because of its focus on the balance between the individual's actions and his or her circumstances, existentialism was clearly expressed in literature, and in the 1940s and 1950s a wave of French writers, led by Jean-Paul Sartre and Albert Camus, produced plays and fiction that popularized the existential worldview. In "The Slump," Updike uses his protagonist's awareness of Kierkegaard to draw attention to the existential dilemma at the heart of a ballplayer's inability to hit.

Style

Monologue

This story is constructed as one continuous monologue given by the ballplayer experiencing the slump to an unidentified audience. Unlike most stories, it is not constructed in individual scenes, and it does not contain dialogue between individual characters. Instead, all of the action occurs in the head of the speaker. It is not *shown* to readers but is rather *told* to them.

Narrative

Because the action is set so deeply within this one person's consciousness, the narrative flow of the story shifts freely, more like a person's rambling thoughts than like a structured story. In some cases, this can confuse readers, making them feel that they have stepped into the middle of a situation that has not been adequately explained. For instance, the first paragraph begins, "They say reflexes," without providing any background about who "they" are or why they say this. The second paragraph starts off with "the flutters," as if readers should know what those are. This gives the impression of a narrator who is allowing his mind to wander freely, taking up issues with which he himself is familiar without bothering to explain them to an audience.

Symbol

Though a baseball player's slump is in many ways unique to his particular situation, Updike talks about it in such a general way that readers can draw connections to many different aspects of life. Anyone in any field can know the feeling of being unable to produce, of knowing all the right steps to take but still not achieving the desired results, and of wanting to let instinct, or reflex, guide his or her actions, only to be disappointed with the results. That the narrator of this story is not given a name and is vague about his circumstances leads readers to understand that the narrator is not meant to be thought of as a real human being—that he exists as a symbol for all people facing the sort of existential dilemma that he faces.

In particular, it is easy to see how baseball is used in this story to symbolize Updike's own profession, writing. Not only do the anxieties associated with a batting slump apply to the emotions that a writer with writer's block faces, but the career of the ballplayer in the story parallels Updike's own career. When this story was written, Updike had been famous for almost ten years and was trying to write in new styles. The ballplayer, intimidated by public scrutiny, wishes for "a change of pace" as something that might possibly help him get over his intense self-consciousness, the way that a writer might tackle new subject matter or a new style to get over the sense that he has nothing more to say.

Tone

The rambling, stream-of-consciousness structure of this story leans it in the direction of confusion, as readers are not certain at any time where the narrator is going. He picks up new subjects as they come to him and drops hints about what is on his mind, without feeling any responsibility to explain what he means. The lack of clarity takes some getting used to, forcing readers to adjust their expectations of what a story should do, to accommodate Updike's style.

Readers who are uncomfortable with the confusing aspects of the story are nonetheless compelled by the tone of the work to trust that it does have something to offer. Updike gives this baseball story a very elevated, specific vocabulary. He uses complex sentence structures that indicate intelligence and care. In its tone, this story shows readers that the story is being told by someone who understands what he is talking about, even though the situation that he describes is one of emotional instability. Combined, they render an accurate portrait of a talented individual who finds himself unable to exercise his talent.

Historical Context

According to common belief, baseball was invented by Abner Doubleday, a nineteen-year-old West Point cadet, at Cooperstown, New York, in 1839. Few historians consider that more than a myth, though. Doubleday did in fact set down standardized rules, but the game had been played for decades before his involvement. It is mentioned, for instance, in Jane Austin's novel *Northanger Abbey,* published after her death in 1816, and poet Oliver Wendell Holmes mentioned that he played the game in 1829, before his graduation from Harvard. The game's mysterious origin is just one of the many bits of folklore that have grown up around it. The acceptance of the Doubleday story is a fitting sym-

bol of the relatively young nation's need for a prefabricated tradition. Though it is clearly a derivative of the English game of cricket, baseball has always been thought of as a metaphor for America.

In the 1840s and 1850s, baseball was popular throughout the New York area. It spread throughout both the Union and the Confederacy during the Civil War (1861–1865), which set the stage for the formation of the National League in 1876. Once it was realized that there was a profit to be made by exhibiting professional baseball games, other leagues formed: the American Association in 1881, and the Players' League in 1990. National League managers worked either to bankrupt the other leagues or to absorb their teams by offering other contracts, leaving it briefly the only league by 1891. They remained unchallenged until 1900, when the American League formed, mostly in cities where National League teams had folded and left their fans embittered.

To limit competition between the two leagues and to ensure that they did not violate each other's interests, the American League and the National League joined together through an agreement, creating the Major League Baseball Commission. As a result of this agreement, the team owners were able to control the game's profits throughout most of the twentieth century. Although it was the players with whom the fans identified, whom they cheered in good times and jeered in bad times, the players themselves actually had little control over their lives. They were bought, sold, and traded at the whims of the teams' owners. The two leagues only had eight teams each, and few other countries besides America were interested in the game, so professional ballplayers were very limited regarding where they could ply their trade.

Over the decades, the game's popularity rose and fell, often in step with the world around it. The year 1919 brought the infamous Black Sox Scandal, with gamblers bribing players to lose the World Series, and it also brought the Volstead Act, which outlawed the sale of liquor. Baseball gained a reputation for crime just as bootlegging led to the rise of organized crime throughout the 1920s. During the 1930s, baseball was appreciated as a relatively inexpensive diversion during the Great Depression. In the 1940s, the country turned its attention to the war in Europe, and the game itself became less worthy of attention as its best players left to join the

Compare & Contrast

- **1968:** At the height of the Vietnam War, America is gripped with a crisis of conscience: Millions of citizens, mobilized by a movement started on college campuses, vocally oppose the U.S. actions in Southeast Asia.

  Today: Politicians still fear that popular support for their actions will be split if a military situation is perceived to be "another Vietnam."

- **1968:** Baseball is America's most popular pastime.

  Today: Television viewership for football has eclipsed baseball's audience. Furthermore, millions of Americans now play and watch soccer, which is the world's most popular pastime.

- **1968:** A public figure such as a professional ballplayer can lead a fairly normal life, driving from his house to the stadium, past his fans.

  Today: Since entertainers such as John Lennon (1980) and Selena (1995) were killed, all public figures are aware of the need for added security.

- **1968:** The average major-league baseball player's salary is $19,000. The minimum salary is $10,000.

  Today: Average salaries range as widely as $4,575,000 for members of the New York Yankees to $300,000 for members of the Tampa Bay Devil Rays. The minimum salary in Major League Baseball is $175,000.

service. Baseball regained its popularity during the late 1940s and throughout the 1950s with the advent of televised games.

Its iconic stature in the American culture makes baseball a fitting subject for Updike to approach with the cultural cynicism that pervaded the late 1960s. The baby boom generation, which consisted of those born in America's triumphant years after World War II, was raised to be more inwardly directed than earlier generations: Not only were they free of the economic and military distractions that had engulfed earlier generations, but they were also the first generation of the new consumer culture. Advertisers drew the baby boomers' attention to finding cures for their own problems. At the same time, in the colleges and universities, which were suddenly accessible to record numbers because of government programs to pay tuition for veterans, intellectuals drew their attention to their own enlightenment. This emphasis on the individual led to a skeptical approach to revered institutions. People questioned the government's involvement in Vietnam and, in fact, found that they had been lied to. Writers like Updike questioned the sexual morals that previous generations insisted on and found their repression to be psychologically harmful. The indi-

vidual player, which Major League Baseball always showed as just one piece of a team, a league, and a tradition, was due the sort of psychological scrutiny that Updike gives him in "The Slump."

The first players' union was formed in 1966. It took some time, until the mid-1970s, for the union to win the right for players to successfully control their own contracts. Finally, a player was able to demand as much money as he thought he was worth or go to another team if he thought he was being treated unfairly. This caused a dramatic spike in salaries and ticket prices. As individual players won their freedom, fans' sympathies divided between those who blamed the owners and those who blamed the players for the game's troubles. The perception of major league baseball as an American institution has gradually eroded since the 1970s.

Critical Overview

John Updike has been considered one of America's most important fiction writers since the publication of his first novel, *The Poorhouse Fair*, in 1959. Critics generally categorize him as a witty writer from the *New Yorker* school, acute in his observations and accurate in his diction. His work as a novelist is well respected among his peers. A survey done by the *Sunday Times* of London in 1994, asking a group of distinguished British writers who they thought was the greatest living novelist writing in English, ranked Updike second. (Saul Bellow, another American, ranked first.) James A. Schiff, who reports those survey results in his book *John Updike Revisited*, goes on to list the things that Updike's detractors hold against him: "he writes about the white middle class and epitomizes the comfortably smug white male;" and "he allows his white male protagonists to think or make derogatory statements about anyone and everyone, including women, blacks, gays, and various others." Although these are certainly things that might push Updike out of favor with some critics, others legitimately point to shortcomings such as a vague hollowness to his exquisitely wrought characters. Readers tend to see different things. "The same novel," Bernard A. Schopen wrote in his essay "Faith, Morality and the Novels of John Updike," "might be hailed as a major fictional achievement and dismissed as a self-indulgence or a failure."

"The Slump" is seldom specifically mentioned in criticism of Updike's works. In part, this is because Updike has been such a prolific writer, churning out more than sixty novels, short story collections, poetry collections, and volumes of essays, that there may be space only to mention one or two of the outstanding short pieces. In addition, though, it is written in a style different from most of the author's works. Typical of these is a 1984 survey of Updike's career, for example, in which Robert Detweiler discusses the book *Museums and Women* (mentioned in his book *John Updike*) for six pages and then tacks a paragraph onto the end to cover the "Other Modes" and "Maples" sections of the book, which make up almost half the text.

One of the few critics to specifically mention this particular story is Robert M. Luscher, who mentioned it in *John Updike: A Study of the Short Fiction*. Luscher found:

> The 'Other Modes' . . . fill out the volume, but vary in quality. Updike's considerable stylistic talents receive exercise as he ventures further beyond the traditional narrative, although the weight of his well-chosen words threatens to collapse the slighter subjects.

He goes on to dismiss "The Slump" as a "whimsical sketch," though he does so respectfully, making clear that nothing more should be expected of it than what it turns out to be.

Criticism

David Kelly

Kelly is an instructor of creative writing and literature at several Illinois colleges. In this essay, Kelly considers how readers are to approach an elusive story that seems to intentionally hide its meaning and purpose.

"The Slump" from John Updike's 1972 collection *Museums and Women, and Other Stories* provides readers with a challenge. It is not clear what this piece of writing is supposed to be, only what it is not. It is not an essay or a poem and is probably not really a short story either, though that comes the closest to identifying it. In the book, it is tagged as a "mode." Since a mode is an undefined literary genre, though, identifying it as such does not help much. This is a piece that lacks character development, plot, setting, and any other element that usually builds a short story, indicating that it does not need these things. Still, if there is to be any understanding of "The Slump," then there has to be some understanding of what it is so that readers might at least guess at whether or not it is achieving what it is supposed to do.

Understanding the piece's negative nature starts with seeing its place in the book. *Museums and Women* is divided up into three sections. The first contains the title story, and, presumably, the other ones. It is not clear whether ". . . and Other Stories" means that *all* of the things in the book are stories or just *some* of them are, although, if there are pieces that are not stories, then the title should properly be *Museums and Women, and Other Stories, and Still Other Things*. But they are clearly not all stories. There are the initial fourteen, which, like most of Updike's works in the late 1960s and early 1970s, concern themselves with understated domestic troubles: marriage, sex, destiny, disappointment, and such. There are also five stories at the end of the

A bustling Yankee Stadium, shown here in 1963, represents the popularity of baseball as a national pastime in the ''The Slump''

book, identified as ''The Maples,'' that are concerned with one couple, Joan and Richard Maple, whose stories Updike collected later in his career in *Too Far to Go*. Revisiting characters over and over again, bringing them back for another look at them, is another technique that is common in Updike's work, such as his multiple books about another failing athlete, ''Rabbit'' Angstrom, and the intellectual writer Henry Bech.

Nestled in the middle of all of these stories is the section called ''Other Modes.'' The ambiguity of this phrase is clearly intentional. The pieces

gathered under this heading have an undefined quality that either frees them from conventional expectations or devalues them, rendering them forgettable, like jokes or sketches that were never fully worked out.

The cynical view of the ''Other Modes'' would hold that they are orphan pieces that Updike wrote and had published in magazines around the time that he wrote the stories in this book and that they are included between its covers for no better reason than that he wrote them. Not having enough of these ''mode'' things to fill a book of their own, they

What Do I Read Next?

- Updike's greatest work is considered to be his four-part series of novels about Harry ''Rabbit'' Angstrom, a protagonist that he followed from 1960 through 1990. All of the ''Rabbit'' novels are available in *Rabbit Angstrom: The Four Novels,* published by Knopf in 1995.

- W. P. Kinsella, who wrote the novel that was adapted to the movie *Field of Dreams,* is considered one of the best contemporary fiction writers. Baseball is a constant theme of his stories, as in those in his 1985 collection *The Thrill of the Grass.*

- Mark Harris's novel *Bang the Drum Slowly* is considered a classic of baseball writing. It follows the final season of a baseball pitcher with a dark sensibility similar to the one Updike's narrator displays. Published in 1956, the novel was made available again by University of Nebraska Press in 1984.

- A wide variety of literary perspectives on the game of baseball is represented in *Hummers, Knucklers, and Slow Curves: Contemporary Baseball Poems,* edited by Don Johnson. It was published in 1991 by University of Illinois Press.

---

serve in *Museums and Women* the way empty pages would, to fill up space and make the book sit more imposingly on a shelf. Harsh as this sounds, it seems to be the prevailing critical attitude. These short, experimental pieces are generally avoided by critics. There is enough in Updike's oeuvre that much can be written about his career without ever touching on this brief section of this one book. Even when talking about his work of the sixties and seventies, most writers ignore the ''Other Modes.'' Those who get so specific as to mention this particular book cannot ignore the ''Other Modes,'' but they focus on the pieces that can be identified as short stories and then, perhaps embarrassed, make passing mention of these undefined pieces and get off the subject as quickly as possible. It would be hard to blame them. No matter what the reason for including them in this collection, the pieces in the ''Other Modes'' section are, by definition, undefined, which makes them a blatant challenge to anyone reading them. ''The Slump,'' in particular, balances between obviousness and obscurity in a way that can be maddening.

This much is known, and it is all that is known: There is a baseball player, the narrator, and he once was able to hit well but now cannot. He is intelligent and analyzes his trouble in terms of a broad range of concepts, from physics to philosophy. Specifically,

he seems to think that his hitting dilemma is an existential one, as he mentions the father of existentialism, Søren Kierkegaard, several times. His understanding of his situation is enough to make him dread it but not enough to make his experiences matter to him. He may break out of his problem someday, or he may be trapped in it forever. Updike has clearly, actively, tried to make this a story that defies interpretation, just as readers and critics are inclined, by their nature, to try to interpret it.

If, for instance, this piece were about the ballplayer's marriage, then that would offer a solid enough point of reference, even though it is completely different in tone and style from Updike's other short stories about marriage of the era. It is not, though; at least, it does not seem to be. The main character's wife only shows up once in the story, for a fraction of a second, to give him a shock. And in this one appearance (the first sentence, referred to again in the fifth paragraph), she is hidden in a rubber gorilla mask. She does not qualify as an important character, but she is the closest thing this narrative comes to admitting another character into the ballplayer's world. Her attempt to break through the cloud of angst that surrounds him might not be successful, but it shows that he is not in this thing alone. The people associated with baseball—his coach, the reporters, the

They do not have the daily interaction that the Maples share, but unusual circumstances require unusual actions: His wife, with her gorilla mask and stopwatch, shows a screwy sense of psychological intimacy with the narrator."

other players, and the fans—are pushed even farther away from the center of his consciousness. In a general way, this could be considered a ''marriage'' story by default, because no one else seems to reflect the narrator's mental state back upon him the way his spouse does. They do not have the daily interaction that the Maples share, but unusual circumstances require unusual actions: His wife, with her gorilla mask and stopwatch, shows a screwy sense of psychological intimacy with the narrator.

Of course, the presence of a spouse does not make ''The Slump'' a story about a marriage, any more than it is a story about a car, a radio, or an ice cream vendor, all of which are also mentioned in the course of the story. It only serves to give this piece some recognizable element. This is obviously what Updike was trying to avoid when he wrote it in an unconventional ''mode,'' but it might be necessary. Clearly, the idea is that this piece intends to be considered on its own terms, and not put into a broader context; this is not, however, always practical or useful for helping it achieve its artistic purpose.

There is no forward motion in this piece nor even the sort of hidden growth that many similar experimental pieces of fiction have used to develop a character at the same time that they seem to go nowhere. Even with the talk about ''dread'' and ''reflex'' and ''hunger,'' readers do not find out where this player's slump came from, how long it has lain upon him, or what it will take to ease him. It has to be this way when dealing with an existential dilemma, because the problem is not one that ebbs and flows; it is one of existence. And to that extent, Updike is forced by his subject matter to shun the

basics of storytelling. Without putting it into a context or trying to connect it to other works that they know from the same author, readers come away from ''The Slump'' with nothing but a mood. Facile readers get from this nothing but the general sense that thought equals sadness.

Updike does what he can to subvert the natural inclination that readers and critics might have to label this piece. He puts it in this category called ''Other Modes'' to excuse it from being held to the same expectations that a short story is held to. He avoids plot; he avoids characterization; he avoids conflict. With so much negative about it, the piece can only work if it establishes an identity for itself, on its own terms. The mood is its identity: mournful, pensive, and obsessed with the works of Kierkegaard, who is expected to somehow, someday, provide the cure for this narrator's troubles. ''The Slump'' does not offer a portrait of this man nor even a snapshot of him—just a passing glimpse, which allows readers to absorb his problem and his thoughts on his problem, though even that is clouded because his thoughts are unclear and uncertain and presented in an uneven order. Readers who respect this piece, despite all they do not know, do so out of respect for Updike, trusting that he would not present something that fails to be worthwhile. Skeptics, though, cannot accept the value of an undefined, elusive work without making sure that it has some connection to the world at large.

Source: David Kelly, Critical Essay on ''The Slump,'' in *Short Stories for Students,* Gale, 2004.

John Updike

In the following essay, Updike recalls his beginnings as a writer.

My first books met the criticism that I wrote all too well but had nothing to say: I, who seemed to myself full of things to say, who had all of Shillington to say, Shillington and Pennsylvania and the whole mass of middling, hidden, troubled America to say, and who had seen and heard things in my two childhood homes, as my parents' giant faces revolved and spoke, achieving utterance under some terrible pressure of American disappointment, that would take a lifetime to sort out, particularize, and extol with the proper dark beauty. *In the beauty of the lilies Christ was born across the sea*—this odd and uplifting line from among the many odd lines of ''The Battle Hymn of the Republic'' seemed to me, as I set out, to summarize what I had to say about America, to offer itself as the title of a continental *magnum opus* of which all my books, no matter how many, would be mere installments, mere starts at the hymning of this great roughly rectangular country severed from Christ by the breadth of the sea.

What I doubted was not the grandeur and plenitude of my topic but my ability to find the words to express it; every day, I groped for the exact terms I knew were there but could not find, pawed through the thesaurus in search of them and through the dictionary in search of their correct spelling. My English language had been early bent by the Germanic locutions of my environment, and, as my prose came to be edited by experts, I had to arbitrate between how I in my head heard a sentence go and how, evidently, it should correctly go. My own style seemed to me a groping and elemental attempt to approximate the complexity of envisioned phenomena and it surprised me to have it called luxuriant and self-indulgent; self-indulgent, surely, is exactly what it wasn't—*other*-indulgent, rather. My models were the styles of Proust and Henry Green as I read them (one in translation): styles of tender exploration that tried to wrap themselves around the things, the tints and voices and perfumes, of the apprehended real. In this entwining and gently relentless effort there is no hiding that the effort is being made in language: all professorial or critical talk of inconspicuous or invisible language struck me as vapid and quite mistaken, for surely language, printed language, is what we all know we are reading and writing, just as a person looking at a painting knows he is not looking out of a window. . . .

The writing enterprise that so engaged [my mother] presented it to me first as a matter of graphic symbols; the tangible precise indented forms of those alphabet blocks and the typewriter's smart little leap of imprintation were part of the general marvel of reproduced imagery, of comic strips and comic books and books and magazines and motion pictures. This last looks like the anomalous term in a sequence, the one that must be circled on the aptitude exam, but in fact, in that pretelevision Thirties world, the world of the movies and the world of the popular press were so entwined, and the specific world of Walt Disney so promiscuously generated animated cartoons and cartoon strips and children's books and children's toys, that it all seemed one art. The projector in effect printed with its beam of light the film upon the screen, and the stylized activities one saw there were being simultaneously read in a thousand theatres. A potentially infinite duplication was the essence, an essence wed for me to the smell

> " What I doubted was not the grandeur and plenitude of my topic but my ability to find the words to express it; every day, I groped for the exact terms I knew were there but could not find. . . ."

of inked paper, dead pulped paper quickened into life by the stamped image of Dick Tracy or Captain Easy or Alley Oop; the very crudities and flecked imperfections of the process and the technical vocabulary of pen line and crosshatching and benday fascinated me, drew me deeply in, as perhaps a bacteriologist is drawn into the microscope and a linguist into the teeming niceties of a foreign grammar. . . .

My subsequent career carries coarse traces of its un-ideal origins in popular, mechanically propagated culture. The papery self-magnification and immortality of printed reproduction—a mode of self-assertion that leaves the cowardly perpetrator hidden and out of harm's way—was central to my artistic impulse; I had no interest in painting or sculpting, in creating the unique beautiful object, and have never been able to sustain interest in the rarefied exercise of keeping a journal. I drew, in black and white, exploring the minor technical mysteries of lettering nibs and scratchboard, of washes and benday, and then I drifted, by way of Ogden Nash and Phyllis McGinley and Morris Bishop and Arthur Guiterman, into light verse, and very slowly—not until college age, really—into the attempt to fabricate short stories. The idea of writing a novel came even later and presented itself to me, and still does, as *making a book;* I have trouble distinguishing between the functions of a publisher and those of a printer. The printer, in my naïve sense of literary enterprise, is the solid fellow, my only real partner, and everyone else a potentially troublesome intermediary between him and myself. My early yearnings merged the notions of print, Heaven, and Manhattan (a map of which looks like a type tray). To be in print was to be saved. And to this moment a day when I have produced nothing printable, when I have not gotten any words out, is a day lost and damned as I feel it.

Perhaps I need not be too apologetic about these lowly beginnings. The great temple of fiction has no well-marked front portal; most devotees arrive through a side door, and not dressed for worship. Fiction, which can be anything, is written by those whose interest has not crystallized short of ontology. Coming so relatively late to the novel, as the end-term of a series of reproducible artifacts any of which I would have been happy to make for a living if I could, I find I feel, after completing thirteen of them, still virginal, still excited and slightly frightened by the form's capacity. My assets as a novelist I take to be the taste for American life acquired in Shillington, a certain indignation and independence also acquired there, a Christian willingness to withhold judgment, and a cartoonist's ability to compose within a prescribed space.

Source: John Updike, "Getting the Words Out," in *John Updike: Studies in the Short Fiction,* by Robert M. Luscher, Twayne's Studies in Short Fiction Series, No. 43, Twayne Publishers, 1993, pp. 175–77.

R. B. Larsen

In the following essay, Larsen discusses Updike's mastery of the short story form, focusing on his "lyrical meditation."

The often acerbic critical controversy over the stature of John Updike continues, unabated by the publication of *Rabbit Redux*. It is still too early to tell, of course, how durable will be the total work of a writer so surprisingly fertile and inventive. One thing seems indisputable even now, though: his mastery of the short story form. . . .

Even after the strikingly modish *Rabbit Redux,* the short story seems as significant a part of Updike's achievement as it was for Hemingway and Fitzgerald. Many of Updike's efforts bear the hallmarks of good short fiction in America since Poe: discipline, structural soundness, a unity of theme or effect, a sense of wonder at life—all results of the "care and skill" which, Poe said, the form demands. Yet they do not follow the direction taken early by Poe and almost universally since World War II, the depiction of brooding psychomachia that seems in our time to have transfixed the epigoni of Lawrence and Faulkner. Rather they are content to portray, if not (to borrow Howell's phrase) "the more smiling aspects of life," then at least those nonviolent, sublunary events that form the backbone of contemporary American experience. If Updike's characters

are not happy, their frustrations drive them neither to madness nor to morbidity. The intelligent, rational, yet sensitive minds of the protagonists preclude psychopathic behavior merely as a function of their (albeit sometimes hypertrophic) observation of life's stable minutiae.

It is in the lyrical meditation that Updike allows precise intelligence and linguistic *delicatesse* their greatest play. The *lyrical* (meaning imaginative and image-filled subjective prose-poetry) *meditation* (meaning contemplation of large, problematic areas of human experience) is not a story in the conventional sense: it bears only vestigial "characterization" and makes no concessions to standard devices of "plot." It is more closely related to Hawthornes "pure essays" (our guide Poe's term for such pieces as "Snow-Flakes" and "The Sisters Years") or Washington Irving's sketches (both Updike and Irving had intensive art training and hence exhibit the painterly eye) than it is to something out of *Dubliners* or *Go Down, Moses.* Ranging uninhibitedly but always anchored to a central image or concept, it is often incremental in manner: meaning accrete through small revelations as the story works toward making concrete one or more monadic abstractions. In arriving at illumination it employs what Northrop Frye calls "*dianoia,* the idea or poetic thought (something quite different, of course, from other kinds of thought) that the reader gets from the writer." In arriving there, too, it often requires of the reader a greater mental involvement than he is accustomed to giving the A+B+C plotted story. Yet it is typically neither an exhibition of stylistic dandyism nor the type of solemn lucubration that the word *meditation* sometimes implies: it is, metaphorically, a miniature geography of a region of human experience, elaborated with erudition and wit and a full measure of the author's renowned verbal magic, often partly parodic. Drawing upon story and essay and poem for its form, it succeeds in overcoming the usual limitations of its models: the storyline of the story, the prosaic logic of the essay, the often obscure ellipticality of the poem. It is a sophisticated writer's most sophisticated accomplishment. . . .

Ambiguity itself is one of the many delights of the lyrical meditation. Subsuming whole worlds of experience under the abstractions it engages, it ensures against facile exhaustion of meaning and thus more greatly regards the sedulous reader. Ignoring what are often called the "conventions" of the short story, it is an autonomous form that arrogates to itself what it needs of poetry and the essay and offers, where appropriate, universal problems in place of plot and archetypes in place of character. And in celebrating the concrete and minute in experience as a vital aspect of the human condition, it becomes perhaps the most infrangible accomplishment of an author around whom critical whirlpools will, no doubt, continue to swirl.

Source: R. B. Larsen, ''R. B. Larsen,'' in *John Updike: Studies in the Short Fiction,* by Robert M. Luscher, Twayne's Studies in Short Fiction Series, No. 43, Twayne Publishers, 1993, pp. 197–98.

Robert Detweiler

In the following essay excerpt, Detweiler offers a thematic analysis of the stories in Updike's Museums and Women *collection.*

Museums and Women: *Liminal States*

The title story (originally published in 1969) of this 1972 collection is crafted as a meditative reminiscence by the narrator-protagonist William Young (manifestly an Updike alter ego) on six significant women in his life and their connection to museums he and they have visited. The recounting of his relationships to these six merges with the imagery of four terms he finds evoked by the two key title words—museums and women—conjoined (and which also echo in his name): radiance, antiquity, mystery, and duty. The story proceeds as a developing interplay of this imagery and of the characterizations of the six women in William's life. For example, William's mother, obviously the first woman in his consciousness and the one who takes him to the local provincial museum, ''like the museum'' is for her adolescent son ''an unsearchable mixture of knowledge and ignorance . . . a mystery so deep it never formed into a question,'' while the woman— the sixth one of the story—who becomes his lover shares with him in a New York gallery (probably the Cooper-Hewitt) ''a translucent interval'' and represents to him, along with the museum, ''the limits of unsearchability''—radiance and mystery paired.

Yet the orchestration of images based on the quartet of concepts, and of the depiction of the six women interacting with the narrator in museums, disguises a persistent plot line that surfaces toward the end of the story with clarity and power. The narrator's progression, in his relationship with women, has been from mother love, to adolescent infatuation (with the freckled popular girl in his school), to courtship and marriage, to esthetic reflection (on the eighteenth-century figurine of the sleeping girl), to casual erotic friendship, to an

> *Ambiguity itself is one of the many delights of the lyrical meditation.''*

extramarital attachment. The common denominator in these is the inaccessibility, one way or another, of all of the women, and William's experience with them has centered on his desire both to know them intimately and to preserve their ineffability. His response to them has been like his passion for museums, where ''we seek the untouched, the never-before-discovered, and it is their final unsearchability that leads us to hope, and return.'' One is not surprised, then, to learn that William has had a serious affair with the sixth woman of the story but has chosen what he perceives as duty over mystery and remains with his wife; this situation, described in the final section, constitutes the main conflict of the story's plot.

A seventh female enters the story at midpoint and reappears toward the close to help resolve via imagery what is left unresolved in the literal action: the headless marble Attic sphinx in the Boston museum, the focal point of William's college-days visit there with the girl (at this time marked by ''something mute and remote'') he will marry, is glimpsed again years later when William meets his lover, their affair over, in that same gallery. The sphinx combines the four qualities of radiance, antiquity, mystery, and duty that inform William's striving with women. Headless, she suggests the absence of vision that typifies William's erotic sojourn; interacting with the delicate figurine of the slumbering girl, she spells the blend of fascination, danger and premonition that William feels in his dealings with women; and finally, she contrasts in her classic and ''pagan'' way with the Judeo-Christian imagery that begins and ends the narrative: the imagery of a lost Eden, its portal watched by the archangel rather than a woman with a lion's body. William's mother, the first woman who guides him through the ''paradisiacal grounds'' redolent of Adam's articulating presence, is replaced by William's wife, who seems to him initially to be ''someone guarding the gates''; and in the story's final paragraph, William leaving the museum and his abandoned lover there looks back at the building

> It is portentous that the Maple tales conclude <u>Museums and Women</u>, for virtually all of Updike's fiction written since then stresses the pleasures and agonies of those who love neither wisely nor well."

("the motionless uniformed guard like a wittily disguised archangel") and feels the loss of innocent wonder and the first hints of jadedness from a surfeit of experiencing. Unsearchability can lead to ennui. The narrator expects "to enter more and more museums, and to be a little less enchanted by each new entrance," and that muted anticipation clearly applies to his future with women as well.

The staging of a mood of world weariness at the end of "Museums and Women" is self-conscious design on Updike's part. It recalls the epigram from Ecclesiastes 3:11–13—the biblical text famous for its evocation of "vanity"—that prefaces the collection, and it anticipates other biblical elements that mark stories such as this one. "I Will Not Let Thee Go Except Thou Bless Me," the fifth story of the collection, are also the words spoken by Jacob in Genesis 32:26 to the angel with whom he has struggled throughout the night. That account, erotic in itself, is employed here in quasi-allegorical fashion to deepen a modern tale of desire and departure. The main components of the Genesis account concern Jacob (destined to become an Israelite patriarch) on the way to his brother Esau's land, wrestling an angel of Yahweh. Because of Jacob's formidable strength the angel cannot prevail until he dislocates Jacob's thigh with a divine touch, but even then Jacob holds him in his grip until he is blessed by the angel and christened with the new name of "Israel."

The Jacob figure in Updike's story is Tom Brideson, a computer software expert about to be transferred to Texas with his wife Lou (one of Jacob's wives is Leah) and their children. The Brideson's attend a predeparture party on the eve of

their journey, and there Tom encounters Maggie, his former lover. With her white dress and great white sleeves, she suggests an angel, and her struggles to escape Tom's grasp as they dance are the equivalent of Jacob's contest with the angel. Tom, ironically, does not get the "blessing" from her that he wants—some assurance that she still loves him. Instead, she tells him that he is "nothing," pronouncing his loss of identity instead of a new identity of the sort that Jacob/Israel receives.

But toward its conclusion the story leaves the Genesis model and takes an instructive turn. On the way home Lou reports that Maggie has kissed her "warmly" as she left whereas she was aloof to Tom. The story ends with:

> He must not appear too interested, or seem to gloat. "Well," Tom said, "she may have been drunk."
>
> "Or else very tired," said Lou, "like the rest of us."

What Tom takes as evidence of Maggie's continued affection for him, bestowed on his wife as surrogate, could just as well be a kiss of good riddance or an impulsive gesture of sympathy for his wife. Weariness at the end of this tale is female exasperation at the male's persistent obliviousness to the emotional distress he causes, a masculine failing that attends many of the dissolving relationships inhabiting Updike's fiction.

A more immediately lethal sexual triangle is handled in the brief story "The Orphaned Swimming Pool," barely six pages long. It begins with an elaborate simile that is expanded into an illustrative narration in the paragraphs that follow: "Marriages, like chemical unions, release upon dissolution packets of the energy locked up in their bonding." The imagery also reminds one of atomic fission and could be a punning comment on the breakdown of the "nuclear" family. At any rate, here a swimming pool becomes the literal focus of a divorce in progress, of its aftermath, and of the instability of neighborhood ties in seemingly solid suburbia. The two-year-old pool, at first the locus of the Turners' uxorial pleasures, through Updike's adoption of a scenic point of view mirrors their separation in the neglect it suffers; then as both Ted and Linda Turner vanish during this late-sixties summer, the neighbors take over the pool, and its use extends to strangers exhaustively accounted for in a comic catalogue of over thirty assorted types. This busy traffic represents the energy let free by one couple's separation. The bizarre listing is matched by the spectacle of Tom and a woman trapped inside the house, by the hordes of pool users, during a clandestine visit, so that "the root of the divorce" is spotted as the lovers flee that evening.

When Linda returns home in the fall, divorced, she sees in the pool images of her broken marriage: "The nylon divider had parted, and its two halves floated independently." Above all, "Linda saw that the pool in truth had no bottom, it held bottomless loss, it was one huge blue tear." This could be the tear of weeping or the tear of rending; both ways it signifies the grief over the end of love. Further, the ex-wife's vision of the pool as bottomless likens it to the classical abyss, symbol of humankind's worst fears. This symbolic weight is too much for such an innocuous object as a suburban swimming pool, but it works as a conveyor of the sense of disproportion and unreality that accompanies the breakdown of deep attachments.

In "The Orphaned Swimming Pool" a suburban community attends a long ritual of separation; in "I Am Dying, Egypt, Dying" an international fellowship of travellers imitates a lengthy rite of passage. The thirty-three page tale is one of Updike's longest, comprehensive enough to contain the complexity of interaction between Clem, a wealthy young American from Buffalo, and more than twenty other characters accompanying him on a luxury boat trip down the Nile in 1967 during the Israel-Egypt conflict. One could profitably engage the old "Ship of Fools" motif to interpret this story, for the motley group floating down the river, dressed in often outlandish costumes and indulging in antic behavior, reminds one of the mad passengers of the *stultifera navis* set adrift on European rivers during the Renaissance and constituting a popular theme of iconography. Stock elements of the Ship of Fools symbolism included a wine glass and a naked woman, and Updike reproduces these in scenes of heavy drinking and of the bikini-clad Swedish girl who desires Clem. Yet Clem himself is too sober to fit such a designation, and his neutral demeanor reminds one far more of Robert Musil's "man without qualities"—an apt *typos* for expressing the superficiality and overadaptability supposed to characterize *homo technicus*.

The words comprising the story's title are uttered twice by the dying Antony to Cleopatra toward the close of Act IV of the Shakespearean drama, and it is sharply ironic that the passionate Roman should be made to serve as a forebear of the bland American. Clem is dying in Egypt only in the sense that he seeks to avoid, in his placid but consuming egotism, all experience that could arouse

and unsettle him, and thus the voyage, although it has the trappings of a ritual journey, is for him not a passage that leads to a new stage of being. His *stasis* is stressed, and is carried by two tropes that permeate the narrative. The first (actually two tropes that interact) is the language of mirrors counterposed to that of scratching, and the other is the figuration of parentheses. Clem, of course, is the polished entity who reflects others, without an identity of his own, and the one who resists being scratched—touched in any significant way—by others. And he is the one who exists in parentheses: in a world, and with a provisionary status, that separates him from other people. But the parentheses also mean his "in between state" (a favorite Updike concept), or as the anthropologist Victor W. Turner puts it, his "liminal period" in the rite of passage, the period of transition during which nothing decisive happens. Clem's problem is that he cannot escape this nowhere condition, cannot grow, and condemns himself to an impoverished emotional life.

This story can be read just as profitably as a lightly disguised criticism of United States foreign policy. Viewed from this angle, Clem stands for the rich, blasé, desirable, and enviable America which assumes itself to be at the center of the world's interest, which exerts its great influence globally with an amiable, unwitting destructiveness, and manages always to insulate itself from the worst of human suffering. America's liminal period presents a terrible burden to the rest of humanity, for other nations are spellbound by the wasteful self-absorption of this amorphous giant.

Like "The Orphaned Swimming Pool," "Egypt" concludes with an evocation of the void: "Gazing into the abyss of the trip that was over, [Clem] ... saw that he had been happy." The "abyss" of the voyage must refer to its emptiness; if Clem has found pleasure in this vacuity, he may be even further removed from participation in erotic existence than he was at the start. His ritual passage seems to be a regression.

It would be misleading to imply that all of the other *Museums and Women* tales deal with the disintegration of love relationships. "I am Dying, Egypt, Dying," possibly the most impressive narrative in the collection, is in fact the inability to enter into, rather than sustain, such a relationship. Nevertheless it is not incorrect to view this collection as evidence of Updike's deepening concern, if not to say outright obsession, in the early seventies with deteriorating marital, domestic, and broader social-erotic affections. Four other stories from among the fourteen (including the four just analyzed) comprising the first and major part of *Museums and Women* develop facets of the subject. "The Day of the Dying Rabbit" depicts discord within a family on holiday, with marriage problems threatening in the background; "The Witness" shows a middle-aged man's embarrassing attempt to use an affair as an antidote for a bad marriage; in "Solitare" a husband plays the card game alone while his guilty imagination pits wife against mistress; and "When Everyone Was Pregnant" is a nostalgic trip back to the fifties from the narrator's seventies perspective, evoking young marriages and interlocking domestic lives, and with the predictable theme of infidelity running throughout.

Of the ten stories, some of them experimental, in the middle section called "Other Modes," only one deals with sexuality: the whimsical "During the Jurassic," in which the familiar Updike triangle of desire is acted out at a party attended by lustful dinosaurs. The five stories comprising the final section on "The Maples" are indeed on the subject, describing the continuing decline of Richard and Joan Maple's conjugal fortunes; these stories reappear later in *Too Far to Go* (in which context I will treat them), where in the company of the other Maple tales they make up the chronicle of that couple's marriage and its demise. It is portentous that the Maple tales conclude *Museums and Women,* for virtually all of Updike's fiction written since then stresses the pleasures and agonies of those who love neither wisely nor well. It is, however, short-sighted to conclude, from reading the *Museums and Women* stories, as Donald J. Greiner does, that "marriage is a relic." The marriage bonds are indeed vulnerable to the extreme, but as one learns by the end of *Too Far to Go,* they are also as resilient as anything that exists.

Source: Robert Detweiler, "More Fiction of the Seventies: The Exertions of Eros," in *John Updike,* G. K. Hall, 1984, pp. 140–46.

Sources

Detweiler, Robert, "*Museums and Women:* Liminal States," in *John Updike,* Twayne Publishers, 1984, pp. 140–46.

Luscher, Robert M., *John Updike: A Study of the Short Fiction,* Twayne Publishers, 1993, pp. 103, 105.

Schiff, James A., "Introduction: America's Bourgeois Artist," in *John Updike Revisited,* Twayne Publishers, 1998, pp. 7–8.

Schopen, Bernard A., "Faith, Morality, and the Novels of John Updike," in *Critical Essays on John Updike,* edited by William R. Macnaughton, G. K. Hall, 1982, pp. 195–206.

Further Reading

Greiner, Donald J., *The Other John Updike: Poems/Short Stories/Prose/Plays,* Ohio University Press, 1981.
Greiner puts "The Slump" in the context of Updike's other works of failing athletes, recognizing the author's own background in sports as a solid base for his writing.

Oates, Joyce Carol, "John Updike's American Comedies," in *The Profane Art: Essays & Reviews,* E. P. Dutton, 1983.
This essay, which does not mention "The Slump" by name, still gives a good analysis of Updike's works at the time it was published and his significance to American literature.

Plath, James, ed., *Conversations with John Updike,* University Press of Mississippi, 1994.
This book contains thirty-two interviews with the author, over the course of more than thirty-five years.

Pritchard, William H., *Updike: America's Man of Letters,* Steerforth Press, 2000.
Pritchard traces the roots of Updike's writing back to early American authors, with contemporary references to show the author's influence.

Sweat

Zora Neale Hurston

1926

In 1926, a group of writers from the younger generation of the "New Negro" movement in New York City, including Langston Hughes and Zora Neale Hurston, decided to organize the quarterly magazine *Fire!!* Frustrated by the responsibilities thrust on them by Alain Locke and other leaders of the Harlem Renaissance, these writers wanted to express their own ideas without the artistic constraints of a political agenda. And, although they only managed to publish one issue because of a host of complications, the magazine left behind one of the most lasting legacies of the radical younger generation of black writers, still considered Hurston's best fiction of the period: a short story titled "Sweat."

Now available in the complete collection of Hurston's stories published by HarperCollins (1995), "Sweat" focuses on the turning point in the life of Delia Jones, a washerwoman from Hurston's hometown of Eatonville, Florida. Beginning with an outburst against her abusive husband and finishing with her involvement in his death, the story follows Delia through a transformation, an upheaval of values that Hurston is interested in setting in the context of the Harlem Renaissance in New York City. The author makes use of biblical allusion and African American folk culture to attack issues of gender and oppression that were taboo topics at the time and continue to have a wide significance today.

Author Biography

Born in 1901, Hurston grew up in Eatonville, Florida, a town with an entirely African American population that was a lasting inspiration for her writings. Hurston's mother was perhaps the most important part of this cultural heritage, since she encouraged her daughter's "large spirit" and protected her from the bad influence of her father. Unfortunately, Hurston's mother died when Hurston was a teenager. Soon after her mother's death, Hurston was sent away to school in Jacksonville. She went on to work as a maid for a white family, eventually joined a theatrical troupe, and then attended preparatory school at Morgan Academy in Baltimore.

Hurston continued to work her way through Howard University, the most famous institution for black scholars in the country, from which she graduated in 1924. By this time, Hurston had begun to write short fiction, and the eminent black writers Alain Locke and Charles Johnson had noticed her. Johnson encouraged Hurston to move to New York, where the black artistic and cultural movement later known as the Harlem Renaissance was thriving. Hurston did so and successfully continued to build contacts with key figures of the movement, working as a secretary to the writer Fannie Hurst, until the novelist Annie Meyer offered her a scholarship at Columbia University to study anthropology.

The only black woman at Columbia, Hurston became a leading figure of the New Negro movement, publishing plays and short stories. In 1926, Hurston wrote "Sweat" for *Fire!!,* a magazine that was intended to express the artistic goals of the younger generation of black writers, as opposed to the seasoned and carefully political generation of Alain Locke. Hurston then began to travel to the South and collect folklore that she would use in a book of anthropology titled *Mules and Men* (1935). Hurston's most famous novel, *Their Eyes Were Watching God,* was published in 1937, followed by another anthropological work, her autobiography, two additional novels, and a play.

Hurston failed to support herself by her writings and suffered a decline in popularity during her later years spent in Florida. This was due, in part, to her politics; Hurston's autobiography, *Dust Tracks on a Road* (1942), was severely criticized by leaders of the New York black community because it vocalized the author's opposition to desegregation, as well as other views that were considered outdated.

Hurston continued to publish but became increasingly obscure until her death in 1960 in a Florida welfare home.

Plot Summary

Set in a small all-black Florida town near Orlando, "Sweat" opens with Delia Jones soaking some clothes on a Sunday night. She is wondering where her husband has gone with her horse and buckboard (a simple carriage), when suddenly a bullwhip drops over her shoulder and terrifies her. Her husband, Sykes, then bursts out laughing at this joke he has played, since he is well aware of Delia's fear of snakes, and proceeds to taunt her and kick around the clothes she had put into piles.

Delia tries to ignore him, but Sykes continues to threaten her, saying that she should not be working on Sunday. Although Delia goes to church each week, she cannot manage to deliver clean clothes in time to the white people she works for if, as is considered correct practice, she does no work on Sunday. And so, in contrast to her usual meekness, Delia shouts that she will not lose the house she has worked so hard for and threatens Sykes with a frying pan. Sykes is too surprised to beat her, so he just says he hates skinny women and goes to his portly mistress for the night. Remembering all of the times Sykes wasted her money, slept with other women, and beat her, and realizing that the only thing left to care about is her "lovely" home, Delia goes to sleep. When Sykes finally comes home and kicks her feet out of the way, she resolves to remain indifferent to him.

The next very hot Saturday, Delia passes Joe Clarke's store on her way to deliver the clean clothes and pick up the dirty piles. The porch of the store is the gathering place for the joking, gossiping men of the town, and today they are talking about how Sykes is a scoundrel who beats Delia and runs around on her. But they ask for a melon, instead of following an intention to teach him a lesson, and leave when Sykes shows up with his current mistress, Bertha. Sykes buys her expensive things at the store with Delia watching, indicating how much of Delia's money he regularly spends on his cheating.

A month goes by, with the heat rising and Delia continuing to sweat at her washerwoman work. One day she comes home to find Sykes laughing next to a large wooden box covered with wire and telling her he has brought her something. Delia nearly faints when she sees that it contains a rattlesnake. Despite her pleading, he refuses to kill it and even shows it off to other townspeople. Delia is driven to fury, and at dinner she tells Sykes that she's put up with his beating and stealing, but she isn't going to put up with the snake. He tells her he'll beat her again if she stays around him, and she tells him she hates him like a ''suck-egg dog,'' or a dog that steals eggs and sucks them dry, and threatens to tell the white people about him.

Sykes leaves, and by the time she goes to church the next day, Delia still hasn't seen him. She feels better and comes home singing a spiritual song, but she quiets down when, at the kitchen door, she cannot hear the snake in its box. After using the last match behind the stove and noticing with anger that Sykes had brought his mistress into her house, Delia brings the dirty clothes into the small bedroom to sort them and starts to sing again. But when she goes to take the clothes out of the basket, she suddenly springs back to the door because the viper is lying inside.

Terrified, Delia manages to run out of the house and lie in the barn for an hour before going to sleep. She wakes up to the sound of Sykes demolishing the wooden box, and she crouches beneath the bedroom window. She can hear the rattlesnake whirring inside. Sykes, whose head is clearing from gin, hears nothing until he reaches behind the stove to look for a match. But they are all gone, and Sykes hears the rattling right beneath him, so he leaps up on the bed. Delia can hear a horrible scream as Sykes is being attacked, and she becomes ill. While lying down to recover, she hears Sykes moan her name and gets up to walk towards the door. He crawls towards her and realizes that she had been there the whole time.

Characters

Bertha

Bertha is Sykes's plump mistress, with whom he is openly cheating on Delia. Elijah Moseley calls her a ''big black greasy Mogul'' (this last word referring to the Muslim rulers of India between the sixteenth and nineteenth centuries), a description that connotes some of the white stereotypes and

Zora Neale Hurston

racist caricatures of the time as to what kind of women were attractive to black men. Bertha has picked up a bad reputation in her previous town and carried it to Eatonville; she is bold enough, unlike Sykes's previous mistresses, to call for him at Delia's gate. For three months, she has been living in Della Lewis's disreputable inn, and Delia can tell that Sykes has brought her into their house.

Dave Carter

One of the men on the porch of Joe Clarke's store, Dave mentions that Bertha looks like an alligator when she opens her mouth to laugh. The character of the same name in Hurston's play *Mule Bone* (coauthored with Langston Hughes) is described as a ''Dancer, Baptist, soft, happy-go-lucky character, slightly dumb.''

Joe Clarke

Joe runs the general store on the main street. His character is based on the real man of the same name who ran the general store during Hurston's childhood, and the gathering of people on this porch is an important and omnipresent element in much of her fiction. Eatonville residents gathered there to joke and gossip, but there was also philosophy, politics, and storytelling in their conversations, as

Joe demonstrates in his commentary about men who abuse their wives like "a joint uh sugar-cane," throwing them away when they're finished with them.

Delia Jones

The protagonist of the story, Delia is a washerwoman fighting to keep her house and her sanity. She is a thin woman with sagging, overworked shoulders, and she is deathly afraid of snakes, a fear that her husband cruelly exploits. "Sweat" marks a turning point in her life, when she has finally had enough, and the reader can notice an entirely "new Delia" emerging between the first time she confronts Sykes and his death.

As the men on the porch of Joe Clarke's store remember, Delia used to be a very pretty young woman until her husband began to abuse her. It is clear from lines such as "Delia's habitual meekness seemed to slip from her shoulders like a blown scarf" that she had taken his beatings, unfaithfulness, and squandering of her money without a fight for a very long time. But Delia also says to Sykes, "Ah hates you tuh de same degree dat Ah useter love yuh," and the reader can infer from the vehemence of this outburst that she used to love him quite a lot before they were married fifteen years ago and his cruelty began.

The story does not describe how their marriage came to be so miserable, but Sykes is the main source of Delia's problems. She does not complain about working so hard for white people to pay for her "lovely" home, and Joe Lindsay notes how she delivers the clean clothes every week without fail. Imagery like "Delia's work-worn knees crawled over the earth in Gethsemane and up the rocks of Cavalry many, many times during these months" paints her as a victim, a martyr even, of intersecting oppressions, from the white community and from her husband. She has tried meekness, friendliness, and hard work to get along with Sykes and finally only wants to be left in peace to do her work, to live in the house she has worked for, and to worship on Sundays. It is only when she cannot possibly take the abuse from her husband anymore that she begins to be aggressive towards him and, as a sort of last measure, to refuse to help while he is dying.

Nevertheless, the reader is left contemplating Delia's actions during her husband's death. Hurston seems to emphasize that Delia is driven to this end with no alternative, but she also suggests an element of emancipation and a refusal to bow to conventional ethics in her character. This "new Delia" has changed quite radically, and along with her newfound freedom has come a loss of innocence.

Sykes Jones

The wife beater who is duly punished by the end of "Sweat," Sykes is Delia's husband of fifteen years. Since two months after their marriage, he has physically and verbally abused his wife, as well as frequently cheating on her and wasting her money. He is no longer attracted to skinny women and prefers his mistresses to be portly and, if his current lady is an indication, disreputable. Sykes is a prankster whose fascination with snakes leads to his death by the same creature he caught to exasperate his wife.

The men on Joe Clarke's porch point out that there are plenty of men like Sykes who wring "every drop uh pleasure" out of their wives, cheat on them, and are overbearing and self-important profligates. It is possible that Sykes was not always this way, since Jim Merchant mentions that he used to be very "skeered uh losin'" Delia when they first married. But he has become more brazen and open in his abuse even since the beginning of the story, although Delia's finally standing up for herself seems to halt his beatings.

Some of Sykes's characteristics, particularly his attraction to big women and his money-wasting, were common stereotypes that white people held about black men, reinforced in various racist publications during the time in which Hurston wrote the story. In fact, he embodies a great many bad traits that leaders of the Harlem Renaissance discouraged black authors from portraying, such as heavy drinking, sexual deviance, and irresponsibility. And, at moments such as Delia's threatening to go "tuh de white folks bout *you*," Sykes seems less demonic and more victimized himself as a result of his ignoring white value systems. Indeed, Hurston allows the reader some room to pity him in the closing moment of the story, when his neck is swollen and he has "one open eye shining with hope" despite the fact that his wife has left him to die.

Jim Merchant

Jim comments on Sykes's habit of cheating and relates the time that Sykes tried to seduce his wife. Like the other men gossiping on Joe Clarke's porch, he jokes in heavy Eatonville slang and provides some important insight into the general attitude of the town towards Delia, Sykes, and Bertha.

Elijah Moseley

Elijah is the man from Joe's porch who jeers at Sykes's treatment of women and pesters Joe for a watermelon.

Old Man Anderson

Suggesting that the men whip and kill Sykes, Old Man Anderson does not follow through on his advice to the rest of the men on the porch.

Walter Thomas

Walter remembers that Delia used to be a pretty young woman before she married Sykes.

Themes

Oppression

One of Hurston's central preoccupations in ''Sweat'' is the problem of oppression within the black community. Sykes's ceaseless cruelty towards his wife is by far the most difficult part of Delia's situation, and she must seek emancipation from her tyrannical husband before she tries to address the wider system of racial inequality.

This is not to say that Hurston oversimplifies Delia's problems; her poverty and hard work are inextricably connected with whites, for whom she must work. A major irony in the story is that Delia must work so hard to clean white people's clothes while her own clothes are dirtied with sweat and blood. It is precisely the combination of white racism and spousal abuse that leads Delia to a level of desperation not at all uncommon amongst black women attempting to carry the burden of two forces of oppression at once. Given the reality of her social and economic situation, Delia can no longer remain indifferent to her increasingly abusive husband, as she has attempted to do for fifteen years.

The story does not provide any neat solutions; indeed, Delia's options are quite limited. Hurston is careful to emphasize that a black washerwoman is not able to clean away the abuse of a philandering

and merciless husband while following a strict and meek Christian moral code. As she must work on Sundays (against convention) in order to fulfill the heavy obligations to her white oppressors, Delia eventually finds that she must resort to a conventionally immoral way of dealing with Sykes. Whether she is justified in standing by while he dies, and whether Hurston is advocating a transgression of a widely accepted moral standard, is not entirely clear, but Hurston certainly illustrates the stark desperation of Delia's situation in vivid detail.

The editors of *Fire!!* may have felt that they needed to publish their own magazine in order to bring up these issues at all; the leaders of the Harlem Renaissance did not approve of topics like immorality and oppression within the black community. Wishing to portray blacks as civilized, modern, and virtuous people, Alain Locke and W. E. B. Du Bois were hesitant to highlight conditions that would be detrimental to their agenda. They were interested in trying to decrease the large numbers of black men lynched each year more than they were interested in allowing black writers free rein in their work. But Hurston and her peers professed that they were unwilling to accept any artistic compromise, which is why ''Sweat'' does not compromise in portraying all sides of a black woman's oppressive reality.

Sex and Love

The prominence of phallic snake imagery, as well as the infidelity and the sexual power struggle in the story, makes sex a key theme in ''Sweat.'' When Hurston writes in the opening of the story that ''something long, round, limp and black'' fell on Delia's shoulders, she is playing a prank on the reader in somewhat the same way that Sykes is playing a trick on Delia. This phallic reference is purposefully shocking so it can begin to ask questions about sex and love in the context of the Jones's marriage.

The first thing the reader wonders is why Delia is so terrified of this ''bull whip,'' which falls on her shoulders, emphasizing that it represents the burden of oppression. It soon becomes clear that her fear derives from the beatings to which she has been subjected for fifteen years. Sykes seems to be painted, through the description of his fixation with snakes, as an aggressive rapist figure. Hurston does not, however, treat this theme as a simple complaint about male phallic tyranny. Indeed, the fact that this bull whip is ''limp,'' combined with Delia's insults,

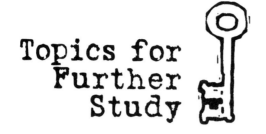

Topics for Further Study

- Read the rest of the material in *Fire!!* How do Hurston's pieces compare with those of her colleagues? Are they operating under the same artistic agenda? Describe the agenda(s) that you observe. Do you find the content radical? If you were a leader of the New Negro movement, how would you evaluate or critique the work of these authors?

- Consider some of the reasons for Hurston's declining popularity and alienation from the literary community. For example, read her autobiography *Dust Tracks on a Road* and review the history of race relations between 1920 and 1960. Discuss why some of her political views might have been unpopular, and explain why you think she came to these conclusions. What led to Hurston's unpopularity besides her stance on certain political issues? Describe the elements of "Sweat" that might have alienated her readership, and explain how the characteristics that later made her unpopular are noticeable, or missing, in the story.

- Listen to some of the music from the Harlem Renaissance, such as Duke Ellington, Count Basie, and especially the lyrics of singers such as Bessie Smith. What do the rhythms of jazz and blues have in common with the writings of Hurston and her colleagues? Compare the character, style, and sexuality of Bessie Smith's songs with Delia Jones and "Sweat," particu-

larly in terms of empowerment and female autonomy. How is Hurston's treatment of black folk culture different from the cultural style preserved in the music? How do they employ similar techniques?

- Hurston underwent a major revival in the 1970s, particularly by the writer Alice Walker. How, and on what grounds, did writers of this period identify with Hurston? Discuss why one might consider Hurston a feminist. Read Walker's *The Color Purple* and compare its themes to those of "Sweat." How have understandings and theories of race and gender changed since Hurston's lifetime? Do you think Hurston's works will continue to be popular in the future? Why or why not?

- Read several historical accounts of the Harlem Renaissance, both from the primary sources and from contemporary analysts. How does "Sweat" fit in with the politics and artistic theories of Hurston's contemporaries? How do her writings reflect the sentiment of the time? Make a case for why she can, or cannot, be fairly called a "New Negro." How does she think of and refer to herself in relation to this term? What impact do you think her writings had on the Renaissance community, and how do you think her career might have differed had she lived during a different moment in black history, such as after the Civil Rights movement?

---

such as calling her husband a "suck-egg dog" whose "black hide" is like "uh passle uh wrinkled up rubber," questions what the author is really saying about Sykes's sexuality.

In his book *Jump at the Sun,* the critic John Lowe highlights these instances of Delia's "verbally emasculating" her husband (a concept related to castration, or taking away "manhood") and argues that Hurston must be thinking about "the emasculation of the black man by a racist, capitalist

society." This suggests a more complex power dynamic between Delia and Sykes than at first seems to be the case; for example, Hurston seems conscious of the impotence Sykes faces as a black man, exhibiting some of the stereotypical traits that leaders of the Harlem Renaissance attempted to shun.

Although she does not seem to be vindicating Sykes, the author is certainly playing with the idea of a reversal of sexual power into the hands of a thin woman who toils ceaselessly for white people. In fact, Sykes's sexuality (associated with black folk values) is his undoing. As Lowe points out, it is when he jumps on the bed, the sexual space in the home, that he is finally poisoned by the representation of his violent sexuality. The manner in which this violent sexuality plays into the conflict of the forces of racial and domestic oppression in the story adds a complex and ambiguous dimension to the couple's sexual power struggle.

Style

Biblical Allusion

Hurston makes a number of allusions to the Bible in "Sweat" that underscore her authorial intentions. Perhaps the most important is the allusion to the Garden of Eden, with the serpent taking on its role of temptation (common to the Western Christian interpretation of the story of Eden) and giving Delia the opportunity to allow for her husband's death. Delia's character may not seem much like Eve's, but Delia does obtain from the serpent the forbidden knowledge of how to disregard convention and subvert Christian morality.

The implications of this allusion are unclear, however. Hurston might be condemning Delia's complicity with the serpent, or she might be praising her ability to bend the rules of Christian morality so that Sykes is punished by his own evil device—an idea Delia expresses as "whatever goes over the Devil's back, is got to come under his belly." This reference to the Devil is one of the phallic references discussed above and highlights the fact that, like the function of sexual imagery in the story, Hurston's biblical allusions are highly ambiguous.

Further complicating the meaning of these allusions are Delia's song about crossing the Jordan, which refers to Joshua leading the nation of Israel across the river, and her crawling "over the earth in Gethsemane and up the rocks of Calvary," which were journeys of Jesus. They place Delia in the role of leading her people to a new destiny, either as a warrior or a martyr, although this becomes much less clear when seen together with her more subversive role as the enabler of the serpent. Perhaps the best way to regard Hurston's biblical allusions is as a method of emphasizing Delia's ability to draw power from all sources available to her and to manifest it in the manner most pertinent to her struggle.

Black Southern Dialect

Hurston is famous for her thorough knowledge of black slang and folk culture, and her use of black southern dialect is an important stylistic device in "Sweat." The dialect itself, aside from portraying the authentic speech patterns of Eatonville, allows Hurston to take ownership of the language. Like Delia, who assumes power through the story by shouting back at Sykes and insulting him, the author gains her own autonomy over the meaning of the text by putting it into the rhythm of her community's speech pattern.

Hurston's ability to switch between Eatonville dialect and technically grammatical English allows her to act as a sort of intermediary and interpreter, bringing southern folk wisdom to New York. The philosophy expounded, for example by Joe Clarke, about using one's wife like sugar cane, is a kind of wisdom very specific to the metaphors, rhythm, and imagery available in Eatonville slang. Relating this, as well as phrases such as "suck-egg dog" (a seemingly contradictory phrase perfect for relating Sykes's violently sexual emasculation) in authentic phonetics gives Hurston authority in her radical politics and themes; she manages to pose as an ambassador of her culture's wisdom. Nonbourgeois black readers might be more willing to accept ideas in this form than in the language of a doctoral student at Columbia, since folk wisdom seems much more tried and true than the whims of an individual, ambitious writer, especially when it is presented in authentic dialect.

Historical Context

Prior to and during World War I, African American demographics underwent a major shift, with over a million black people migrating north. Filled with hope of more jobs and less racial oppression, many black Southerners saw cities such as New York and Chicago as the land of their deliverance, although this was not always true in practice. Instead, blacks largely found it difficult to settle in and, after the war, tended not to benefit economically from the "Roaring Twenties," finding themselves segregated to poor racial ghettos such as Harlem in New York City. The Ku Klux Klan remained active, actually increasing in membership during these years, and segregation was widespread.

What the newly arrived blacks in New York did find, however, between the end of World War I and

Compare & Contrast

- **1920s:** Racism towards African Americans is an extreme problem, in both the southern and northern states. Much of the optimism of blacks moving to the North is turning out to be an illusion. Education is poorly funded, poverty is widespread, and 281 blacks, compared with 34 whites, are lynched during the decade.

  Today: Racial discrimination is illegal, but it has not been completely abolished in practice. The Supreme Court has ruled to continue the process of "affirmative action" in public universities, a sign that the legal system desires to remain committed to equalizing the opportunities afforded to all racial groups.

- **1920s:** The American economy is booming. The stock market is rising at unprecedented rates, and many Americans are becoming rich, although money and jobs are not generally trickling down to the poorer black classes.

  Today: The United States has a powerful economy, but it has failed to completely recover from the downturn coinciding with the September 11 terrorist attacks in New York. Unemployment is particularly high for black workers—over double the jobless percentage for whites.

- **1920s:** Harlem is a burgeoning urban center, full of black artistic achievement and exciting new ideas, but housing is becoming increasingly cramped, and poverty is widespread.

  Today: After a long and severe decline since the 1930s in housing conditions, crime, and poverty, conditions have now drastically improved. Harlem property value is among the fastest rising in New York City, although some people are afraid this has created an unaffordable housing crisis and a negative impact on the local culture.

- **1920s:** Spousal abuse goes largely unpunished, as police and courts rarely have the right to intervene.

  Today: *The Violence Against Women Bill* of 1991 and other measures introduced to protect women within the home are likely to have decreased levels of spousal abuse, but it remains a major problem.

---

the beginning of the Great Depression, was an unprecedented flowering of black art and culture later coined the "Harlem Renaissance." Institutions like the Urban League and the National Association for the Advancement of Colored People (NAACP) were becoming increasingly influential, and black political thinkers such as W. E. B. Du Bois held more power and were much less conciliatory to the white gentry than were their predecessors. Black culture was suffused with the ideology of the "New Negro," which emphasized abandoning traditionalist values and becoming a modern American citizen exercising the right to vote—and cultured leaders like Alain Locke were actively supporting this ideology in their magazines.

But Hurston's reaction to the values of this movement demonstrates that they were not entirely pervasive, especially within the younger generation of writers living in Harlem. When she moved to New York towards the end of the "Great Migration" northwards, Hurston was more idealistic about the unity and agenda of the New Negro movement than she later became. She was invited to New York by Locke himself and proceeded to ingratiate herself with a number of key political and artistic figures in Harlem, writing against Marcus Garvey and in favor of Du Bois and his efforts to lower mortality rates and work for the benefit of his people.

After publishing a short story in Locke's *New Negro* magazine, however, she and some of her peers began to be skeptical about elements of the magazine's artistic agenda, such as its tendency to avoid commonly caricatured folk traits such as black superstition. As Robert Hemenway writes in

Sweat

his literary biography of Hurston, "The established bourgeois position was that black art should avoid reinforcing racist stereotypes by refusing to portray the lowest elements of the race." The magazine *Fire!!* was created to refute these black bourgeois values when they clashed with "pure" artistic goals.

Spearheaded by Hurston, Langston Hughes, and Wallace Thurman, *Fire!!* had major difficulties getting published at all, including a lack of money and a fire in an apartment that destroyed several hundred copies, and the editors managed to publish only one issue before the magazine collapsed. But "Sweat," along with the other pieces published in 1926, was a major achievement for Hurston and her subsection of Harlem Renaissance writers, earning them a little-acknowledged uniqueness within a movement whose leaders wanted to portray a unified front to the country.

Critical Overview

Fire!! received a critical review of mild disinterest. Hurston's biographer Robert Hemenway explains that the editors planned, even hoped, for Du Bois to dislike it because he had previously condemned the notion of apolitical writing and his disfavor would confirm that the magazine was indeed "pure." But Du Bois's NAACP journal simply ignored *Fire!!*, aside from a bland endorsement, leaving the editors actually brainstorming for ways of making the magazine more offensive. Hemenway writes that Benjamin Brawley, "a pillar of the black literary establishment," disliked it intensely. Alain Locke only bothered to censure the magazine's "effete echoes of contemporary decadence" but later praised its "anti-Puritanism." This critical response was the final factor, after all of the difficulties in publication, that led to the magazine's collapse: It was not received as controversial enough to procure any heated condemnation or acclaim.

"Sweat" itself received no major critical attention until Hurston's revival by black feminist writers over fifteen years after her death. All of her writing was very highly regarded during the Harlem Renaissance, and she was thought to be one of the most prodigious writers in her generation, but Hurston rapidly lost her fame and even the ability to publish her works. By the end of her life, she was almost completely ignored by the literary community, in part because of her old-fashioned politics on issues such as segregation. Black feminist writer Alice

Walker was one of the first to champion Hurston's talent, placing a gravestone on the field where Hurston was buried in an unmarked plot and writing about her rediscovery, in essays such as the forward to Hemenway's literary biography of Hurston.

The black feminist criticism that dominated Hurston's revival largely focused on her most famous novel, *Their Eyes Were Watching God*, but critics have also discussed the intersection of race and gender in "Sweat" since the late 1970s. Hemenway discusses "Sweat" as a "remarkable work, her best fiction of the period," portending the "unlimited potential in Hurston's folk material when an organic form grew from the subject matter." John Lowe discusses the sexual and racial politics, as well as the folk roots, of the story in his book *Jump at the Sun,* and other critics tend to discuss it in these terms as well, always setting it in the context of the political climate of the Harlem Renaissance.

Criticism

Scott Trudell

Trudell is a freelance writer with a bachelor's degree in English literature. In the following essay, Trudell examines the place of "Sweat" within the political climate of the Harlem Renaissance.

"Sweat" is an intriguing story in terms of what it is "supposed" to be about, especially in its treatment of racial issues. The key piece of a magazine eager to defy the Harlem Renaissance artistic agenda, the story would have been expected to exercise its artistic freedom and break the taboos of leaders such as W. E. B. Du Bois. Hurston had certainly grown irritated with the pressure from Du Bois and Alain Locke, her former mentor, to write with politics in mind. As she later wrote in *Dust Tracks on a Road*, "from what I had read and heard, Negroes were supposed to write about the Race Problem. I was and am thoroughly sick of the subject." Given this sentiment, one might even expect her to have made a particular effort to spite Du Bois's politicized view of art and write something that would be offensive to the Harlem Renaissance leadership.

And there is evidence that "Sweat" does defy Du Bois's agenda, since it is the story of a conflict between an abusive black man and his wife, one that results in the wife's standing by while her husband

Zora Neale Hurston and musicians Rochelle French and Gabriel Brown in Hurston's hometown Eatonville, Florida, where "Sweat" takes place

dies. As far as the black literary elite in Harlem was concerned, authors were supposed to play down interracial problems and instead help to achieve a unity of purpose and direction for the ideal of the New Negro. In 1925, Locke wrote in the *New Negro* that Hurston and her peers "have no thought of their racy folk types as typical of anything but themselves or of their being taken or mistaken as racially representative." This comment actually comes out of an essay that considers this ignorance a positive sign for the newly developing black consciousness and their unprecedented freedom to write what they wish, but Locke remains condescending towards authors who choose to place the race in this light. One would expect him to find a story like "Sweat" inappropriate and counterproductive to the goals of his movement.

Du Bois, who, unlike Locke, never claimed to be exclusively interested in "art for art's sake," was even more condemnatory of stories with plots he considered unflattering to African Americans. Describing the obligations of black writers to the New Negro movement, Du Bois describes the important political influence of black artists in his article "The Creative Impulse," proclaiming, "Thus all art is propaganda and ever must be, despite the

wailing of the purists." Locke was irritated when literature displayed poor, uneducated blacks, which (he felt) reinforced stereotypes and impeded progress, but Du Bois was irate, especially if they reflected some of the common white stereotypes against blacks. Du Bois was also more specific about the stereotypes to avoid, writing that whites want to see "Uncle Toms, Topsies, good 'darkies' and clowns" and that black writers should refuse to give them anything that could be construed as such.

So it is difficult to see how these black leaders could fail to condemn "Sweat." Sykes in particular has many of the "folk" characteristics of which Locke disapproved, such as a preference for larger women and a problem with wasting money, which many whites placed on blacks as a race. And Du Bois might even have seen Delia as an "Uncle Tom," which refers to the servile title character in Harriet Beecher Stowe's novel and came to be used as a label for blacks who tried to emulate or gain favor with whites. Indeed, Delia says she does not mind dirtying her black skin with sweat and blood in order to clean the clothes of white people, and she actually tells Sykes "Ah'm goin' tuh de white folks bout *you,* mah young man, de very nex' time you lay yo' han's on me." One would expect Du Bois to be

What Do I Read Next?

- Hurston's novel *Their Eyes Were Watching God* (1937) is probably the most important of Hurston's works to read after "Sweat." Also set in Eatonville, it follows the story of Janie Crawford and her clashes with the moral code of the town.

- *The Color Purple* (1982) is Alice Walker's novel about the difficult life of a girl named Celie, whose fortunes finally begin to change with the arrival of her husband's lover in her home. Not only is this highly regarded novel heavily allusive to Hurston's work, it addresses some of the themes of "Sweat" in a more modern and thorough light.

- *The New Negro,* an anthology of some of the most influential writers of the Harlem Renaissance, was published by Alain Locke in 1925. It includes Hurston's short story "Spunk," and it is a superb way to enter the literary world of the time.

- In his controversial history, *Modernism and the Harlem Renaissance* (1987), Houston A. Baker Jr contends that the Harlem Renaissance is unfairly judged by the standards of European modernism and instead should be seen in the light of its own rich discourse.

- *The Collected Poems of Langston Hughes* (1994) provides an excellent range of the accessible and sensitive poet who went on from Hurston's group of friends to become possibly the most celebrated black writer of the century.

- The one published issue of the magazine *Fire!!* was reprinted by the Negro Universities Press in 1970 and again by Fire!! Press in 1982. Its collection of writings by Hurston and her peers reveals the context and medium of "Sweat" as well as a broad sense of their artistic goals.

---

particularly angry that Delia, in a way, carries out this warning, leaving Sykes to his death so she can be left to earn her living as a diligent servant of whites.

In reality, however, Locke and Du Bois ignored the story. Locke made only two short and conflicting references to the entire *Fire!!* magazine, and Du Bois did not even mention it. There was some very negative criticism from Benjamin Brawley, a prominent academic and black leader, but the major players in Harlem Renaissance leadership did not appear to be offended enough to comment.

They could have been purposefully ignoring "Sweat" and the rest of the magazine because they were worried about attracting attention to it, but this does not explain why the *Crisis,* the NAACP journal edited by Du Bois, made a brief and positive announcement of the magazine's publication. It is more likely that Hurston's short story did not offend Du Bois or Locke because it had more in common

with the spirit of the movement than she and her fellow editors of *Fire!!* would have liked to admit. Indeed, a closer look at the thematic implications of "Sweat" reveals, ironically, that it can be read as an allegory for the birth of the New Negro that is distinctly in line with the conception of Locke and Du Bois. To illustrate this point, it is necessary to examine Delia's moral journey, concentrating on the values she denies and gains, and revealing how she comes to be what the black leaders actually meant by a "New Negro."

It is clear that "Sweat" is about some kind of birth. The story is heavily allusive to the Garden of Eden in the Bible, complete with the snake of temptation, and Delia is, in a sense, reborn at the end of the story with a radically different life view. This birth is not a straightforward representation of the Bible, however; it is complicated by other biblical references to the life of Jesus ("over the earth in Gethsemane and up the rocks of Calvary") and to the journey of the nation of Israel under Joshua

---

> "... a closer look at the thematic implications of 'Sweat' reveals, ironically, that it can be read as an allegory for the birth of the New Negro that is distinctly in line with the conception of Locke and Du Bois."

("*Ah wantah cross Jurden in uh calm time*"), by which Hurston begins to develop an allegory of the birth and emancipation of a people that mixes and matches biblical stories suitable for her goals.

In fact, in the role of the prophet or deliverer, Delia undergoes a process of reinterpreting biblical authority, just as she reinterprets the religious custom of not working on the Sabbath, in order to provide herself a realistic and original solution to her difficult life. For example, she reinterprets the "awful calm" she finds after nearly being killed by the snake into the "calm time" for crossing the Jordan, and she reassigns the meaning of her sweaty hard work for white people, in a way, in order to baptize her followers, because a prophet always has followers, in the "salty stream that had been pressed from her heart," the baptismal font of her sweat. But perhaps the clearest example is her reversal of the story of the Garden of Eden by refusing to act in the passive role of Eve and turning the symbol of abusive male power, the snake, against itself.

The allegorical lesson of "Sweat," then, must consist of the value system that Delia gains from this process of reinterpretation and rebirth. And, this is where the story's biblical imagery and allegory connect specifically to the prevailing concept of the New Negro.

The principle value system Delia denies and from which she leads her people away is that of Sykes and his abusive, phallic sexuality associated with the snake. By the end of the story, Delia has not simply retained her "triumphant indifference to all that he was or did"; she has actively and violently allowed what "goes over the Devil's back" to "come under his belly." And her vehement rejec-

tion is not just of Sykes's abuse; it is of all "he was or did"—his laziness, his preference for large women, his money-wasting, and his prankster pleasure-seeking—all of which are symbols of the discriminatory white stereotypes of blacks and the "folk type" that so irritated Locke. Under this allegorical interpretation, the whole point of "Sweat" is to reject the value system of the "old" Negro and start anew. Perhaps this accounts for Locke's indifference to *Fire!!* Its feature piece seems superficially offensive but actually reinforces basic New Negro ideology, such as the importance of entering a new cosmopolitan moral system and denying the folk values that Harlem Renaissance leadership considered detrimental to the image of the race.

It is important to note, however, that "Sweat" also considers the negative consequences of this New Negro rebirth. From the story's treatment of white oppression, for example, it is clear that Hurston is worried about the predominance of Du Bois and Locke's artistic agenda. In rejecting Sykes, Delia is also rejecting a philosophy that, albeit violent and abusive, refuses white oppression as her own does not. When Sykes says, "Ah done tole you time and again to keep them white folks' clothes outa dis house," he is demonstrating independence from white capitalist (and exploitative) values, unlike his wife, and Hurston is sympathetic to this. The critic John Lowe even suggests in his book *Jump at the Sun* that the story laments and condemns Sykes's indirect murder. By this logic, Hurston's allegory of the rise of New Negro philosophy is somewhat ironic or at least ambivalent.

Nevertheless, Hurston's ambivalence about the process she is allegorizing does not prevent her, like Delia, from allowing Sykes's ideology to destroy itself. The reader, and the author, ultimately side with Delia, and the allegory of "Sweat" overturns sympathy with the "old" Negro. Hurston's political statement is subtle about what it affirms, but it does ultimately reinforce the New Negro politics of Locke and Du Bois.

Source: Scott Trudell, Critical Essay on "Sweat," in *Short Stories for Students,* Gale, 2004.

Laurie Champion

In the following essay excerpt, Champion discusses gender oppression in "Sweat," and its symbolically negative outcome.

Even more than "The Gilded Six-Bits," "Sweat" exposes gender oppression by revealing the plight of women in a sexist society. The protagonist, Delia, works long hours washing laundry for white customers, whose economic privilege is contrasted with Delia's economic status: not only can she not afford to hire someone to wash her laundry, but she must also wash wealthy people's laundry to provide for herself. While the story demonstrates the disparity of wealth between the wealthy Winter Park whites and the poor Eatonville blacks, the main plot of the story does not center on this form of economic exploitation, but rather upon how Delia's husband, Sykes, exploits her. Ironically, throughout the course of the story, sweat signifies Delia's exploited labor and Sykes's poisoned mental state that ultimately leads to the physical poisoning that kills him. Additionally, ''Sweat'' exposes gender oppression and economic exploitation by suggesting that ''what goes around comes around.''

The story opens with a technical description of Delia's labor that reveals that she works long hours every day of the week. Early on, the narrative establishes that Sykes both physically and mentally torments Delia. Scolding him for scaring her by sliding across her knee a bullwhip that she thinks is a snake, Delia says she may die from his foolishness. More interestingly, she asks him, ''where you been wid mah rig? Ah feeds dat pony,'' informing him that the pony belongs to her and that she pays for its upkeep. He responds by reminding her that he has told her repeatedly ''to keep them white folks' clothes outa dis house'' and by claiming that she should not ''wash white folks clothes on the Sabbath.'' Although the argument begins with a physical scare, it soon turns to a quarrel about economics. After scolding him for scaring her, Delia reminds him that she owns the pony, the means by which Sykes leaves the house. His rebuke reveals his resentment that Delia owns the material goods he wishes to use to entice Bertha to remain his girlfriend. He promises to give Bertha the house as soon as he ''kin git dat 'oman outa dere.'' Sykes pays Bertha's rent and spends money to take her to Winter Park for dates. He promises her that he will give her whatever she wants: ''Dis is mah town an' you sho' kin have it.'' Significantly, when Delia sees Sykes with Bertha, he is at the store purchasing groceries for her and telling her to ''git, whutsoever yo' heart desires.'' Not only does Sykes spend Delia's money on Bertha, he wants to give Delia's other possessions to her.

Delia develops from a meek woman who acquiesces to Sykes's abuse to one who defends herself both verbally and physically. Although Delia

> '' Similar to the poison that kills Sykes, Delia's sweat represents both literal bodily toxins and symbolic poisons that represent the social system that has caused her to sweat.''

has suffered abuse from Sykes for fifteen years, she has yet to refute him. However, during this particular argument that has turned to economics, her ''habitual meekness slips,'' and she responds to Sykes's verbal abuse with the assertion that she has been washing clothes and sweating for fifteen years to feed him and to pay for her house. Later, when he refuses to remove the snake from the house, she says, ''Ah hates you, Sykes. . . . Ah hates you tuh de same degree dat Ah useter love yuh. Ah done took an' took till mah belly is full up tuh mah neck.'' Significantly, she ends her argument by saying, ''Lay 'roun' wid dat 'oman al yuh wants tuh, but gwan 'way fum me an' mah house'' (emphasis added). Although the story involves a love triangle, the more important conflict is the battle between Sykes and Delia for possession of the house. Delia is much more concerned with protecting her property than she is with redeeming her marriage.

Hoping that Sykes will receive retribution for abusing her, a week before he dies, she says, ''Whatever goes over the Devil's back, is got to come under his belly. Sometime or ruther. Sykes, like everybody else, is gointer reap his sowing.'' Also, announcing that she refuses to leave her house, Delia threatens to report Sykes to the white people. Apparently, this threat scares him, for the next day he puts the snake in Delia's laundry basket. However, Delia does not depend on the ''law'' for justice. She seems to agree with the Eatonville community, which acknowledges both that there ''oughter be a law about'' Sykes and that ''taint no law on earth dat kin make a man be decent if it aint in 'im.'' Depending on forces above the law, Delia allows Sykes's retribution to come to him ''naturally.'' Unlike the conjure that renders poetic justice in many of Hurston's works, Sykes's own action renders justice in "Sweat": the very snake he intends to bite Delia bites him instead.

Sykes's self-inflicted poisoning brings about poetic justice, as he is the victim of his attempt to kill Delia and thus gain possession of the house; but the sweat that comes from Delia's exploited labor is not self-inflicted: it is inflicted upon her by a vile social system that privileges wealthy whites. This vile social system also, to be sure, victimizes Sykes. As Lillie P. Howard points out, Sykes clearly is Delia's antagonist, but part of the reason he resents her is "because her work makes him feel like less than a man. He resents her working for the white folks, washing their dirty laundry, but he does not resent it enough to remove the need for her to do so." Similarly, Lowe argues that although readers empathize with Delia, "the emasculation of the black man by a racist, capitalist society is on Hurston's mind too. . . ."

Critics argue whether or not Delia's refusal to help Sykes after the snake has bitten him exemplifies her spiritual downfall. Lowe says, "Delia's Christian righteousness, evident in the scene when she returns from a 'Love Feast' at church, also seems challenged by her failure to seek help for Sykes after he has been bitten by the snake at the end of the story and by her deliberate showing herself to him so he will know she knows what he attempted and that there is no hope for him." Cheryl A. Wall says, "Delia makes no effort to warn, rescue, or even comfort Sykes. She exacts her revenge but at a terrible spiritual cost. . . . The narrator does not pass judgment. Yet, how will Delia, good Christian though she has tried to be, ever cross Jordan in a calm time?" Contrary to Wall and Lowe, Myles Hurd argues, "Because Hurston exerts quite a bit of creative energy in outlining Sykes's outrageous behavior and in subsequently punishing him for his misdeeds, Delia's virtue is too often easily overshadowed by his villainy." Hurd suggests that because Sykes is a "more dramatically compelling" character than Delia, some "readers overeagerly expect Delia to counter his evil, rather than allow herself to be repeatedly buffeted by it." When readers consider that the sweat, or poison, eventually seeps out of Delia's body, the title of the story suggests that she is not spiritually corrupt. Similar to the poison that kills Sykes, Delia's sweat represents both literal bodily toxins and symbolic poisons that represent the social system that has caused her to sweat. Sykes is possessed by an evil that consumes his soul and eventually kills him; however, Delia remains pure because the sweat, the toxin or poison that represents the social system that exploits her, is released from her body and does not corrupt her physically or spiritually.

In an interesting twist that parallels the snake that bites Sykes instead of Delia, at the end of the story, "the man who has loomed above her through the years now crawls toward her, his fallen state emphasized by the frame of the door and Delia's standing figure; the man who has treated her with continuous contempt and cruelty now hopes for help from her." At the end of the story, Delia notices Sykes looking to her with hope; however, she also realizes that the same eye that looks to her for help cannot "fail to see the tubs" as well. As he lies dying, he is forced to look at the tubs, the tools of Delia's exploited labor. It is significant that while he is in the process of dying from self-inflicted poison, Sykes is forced to observe the tubs, the source of Delia's sweat, symbolizing the poisoned social system. Perhaps the tubs represent for Sykes the very property he had hoped to acquire by killing her because he is reminded of the labor Delia has exchanged for the property. Earlier, in his attempt to kill her and thus gain possession of the house, Sykes places the snake in the laundry basket, another emblem of Delia's exploited labor. Sykes's use of a tool of Delia's labor as a tool for his effort to acquire her property reminds readers that only through intense sweat, exploited labor, has Delia been able to buy a house for herself. However, Delia is determined not to allow Sykes to take possession of the house. In addition to releasing her from his emotional and physical abuse, Sykes's death releases the threat that Delia's house will be taken away from her.

The title "Sweat" refers both to Delia's hard work necessary to survive economically in a society that offers limited employment opportunities to African American women and to the emotional and physical agony Sykes's abuse causes her. As David Headon acknowledges, the story "forcefully establishes an integral part of the political agenda of black literature of this century. . . . Hurston places at the foreground feminist questions concerning the exploitation, intimidation, and oppression inherent in so many relations." Breaking from literature that so often perpetuates stereotypical roles for women, "'Sweat is in fact, protest literature." Hurston simultaneously discourages those who try to reinforce sexist modes of oppression and encourages women to defy sexism by illustrating how those who abuse women are doomed.

Source: Laurie Champion, ''Socioeconomics in Selected Short Stories of Zora Neale Hurston,'' in *Southern Quarterly*, Vol. 40, No. 13, Fall 2001, pp. 79–92.

John Lowe

In the following essay excerpt, Lowe discusses the framework of comic expressions present in ''Sweat.''

Hurston's comic gifts, simmering in ''Muttsy,'' came to a boil with *Fire!!* the magazine issued by the ''New Negro'' group in 1926. ''Sweat,'' the more gripping of her two contributions, details the grim story of hardworking Delia Jones and her no-good, philandering husband, also a devotee of practical jokes. Hurston cleverly turns this aspect of her villain into a structural device, for the entire story turns on the idea of jokes and joking. She begins with one of Sykes's cruel jokes: he throws his ''long, round, limp and black'' bullwhip around Delia's shoulders as she sorts the wash she must do for white folk in order to support herself. Sykes's prank, motivated by Delia's abnormal fear of snakes, begins the sexual imagery that makes the story more complex. Is Delia's fear of the explicitly phallic nature of the snakes a sign of her innate fear of sex or, more likely, a fear that has been beaten into her? What has caused Sykes to seek the beds of other women? The story raises but never really answers these questions, yet suggests Sykes cannot stand his wife's supporting them by washing the soiled sheets, towels, and undergarments of white folks. Lillie Howard thinks that ''whether [Delia] needs Sykes at all is questionable and perhaps he senses this and looks elsewhere for someone who does need him.'' On the other hand, Delia reflects that she ''had brought love to the union and he had brought a longing after the flesh.'' Only two months into the marriage he beats her. Why?

In any case, Sykes's laughter at his wife and her fears fill the story; he continually slaps his leg and doubles over with merriment at the expense of the ''big fool'' he married fifteen years ago. Clearly, his insults deflect attention away from the ''big fool'' he knows he appears to be in the community, as he has never held a steady job himself and depends on Delia for his livelihood. Hurston in this story seems to be developing gender-specific forms of humor, which will be extremely important in *Jonah, Their Eyes,* and *Seraph.*

We may thus notice a difference in the rhetoric employed here. Delia too, although grimly serious in her defiance of Sykes, uses the deadly comic

> When writing this story, she seemed to have learned how intertwined comedy and tragedy were in folk culture and also how the comic was embedded in the cosmic.''

signifying language of female rivalry; referring to her husband's mistress, she states, '''That ole snaggle-toothed black woman you runnin' with aint comin' heah to pile up on *mah* sweat and blood. You aint paid for nothin' on this place, and Ah'm gointer stay right heah till Ah'm toted out foot foremost.''' Later, alone, Delia takes comfort in folk wisdom: '''Oh well, whatever goes over the Devil's back, is got to come under his belly. Sometime or ruther, Sykes, like everybody else, is gointer reap his sowing.'''

The appearance of the communal comic chorus in the personages of the loiterers on Joe Clarke's porch constitutes another significant development in Hurston's craft. When Delia passes by with her pony cart delivering clothes, they render the community's sense of pity for her and contempt toward Sykes, especially regarding his new mistress: '''How Syke kin stommuck dat big black greasy Mogul he's layin' roun' wid, gits me. Ah swear dat eight-rock couldn't kiss a sardine can Ah done throwed out de back do' 'way las' yeah.''' The men's humor rises a notch as they wryly observe that Sykes has always preferred heavy lovers over the thin Delia. Hurston signifies here on jokes in the black community about some men's preference for hefty women. A classic blues expression goes: ''Big fat momma wid de meat shakin' on huh bones / Evah time she wiggles, skinny woman los' huh home.'' The last line should particularly intrigue readers of ''Sweat,'' for Sykes's plot is designed not so much to kill Delia but to secure her property.

Significantly, all of the men on the porch continually chew cane, but they do not throw the knots as usual, which creates a foundation for the extended natural metaphor that Clarke, their leader, uses to summarize the inversion of the story they are actually helping us to read.

"Taint no law on earth dat kin make a man behave decent if it aint in 'im. There's plenty men dat takes a wife lak dey do a joint uh sugar-cane. It's round, juicy an' sweet when dey gits it. Buts dey squeeze an' grind, squeeze an' grind an' wring tell dey wring every drop uh pleasure dat's in 'em out. When dey's satisfied dat dey is wrung dry, dey treats 'em jes lak dey do a cane-chew. Dey throws 'em away. Dey knows whut dey is doin' while dey is at it, an' hates theirselves fuh it but they keeps on hangin' after huh tell she's empty. Den dey hates huh fuh bein' a cane-chew an' in de way.''

This casually brilliant rendering of a tragic truth provides a double irony for readers who know all of Hurston's work, for this same Joe Clarke emerges as a wife-beater himself in "The Eatonville Anthology" and becomes the model for Jody Starks in *Their Eyes,* who treats Janie like a mule he owns. Furthermore, the liquid squeezed out, the receptacle discarded, mirrors the title figuration of a woman's sweat and her weary body.

Normally comic expressions can be used to deadly effect as well. In the heat of August's "Dog Days!," the "maddog" Sykes plays his ultimate and cruelest joke to drive Delia from the house that he has promised to Bertha. He keeps a caged rattle-snake on the porch, knowing Delia fears even earthworms. When she asks him to kill the rattler, he replies with a comically coined word and devastating irony: "'Doan ast me tuh do nothin' fuh yuh. Goin' roun' tryin' tuh be so damn aster-perious. Naw, Ah aint gonna kill it. Ah think uh damn sight mo' uh him dan you! Dat's a nice snake an' anybody doan lak 'im kin jes' hit de grit.'" When Delia's fury overflows into courage, she tells Sykes, "'Ah hates yuh lak uh suck-egg dog,'" and, of course, the imagery seems right, for Sykes's gender is usually associated with dogs, and a "suck-egg" dog would be a predator of women, egg bearers. Hurston would later use the egg and snake symbolism to characterize the couple in *Jonah.*

When Sykes replies with insults about her looks, she replies in kind, joining a verbal duel that finally silences him: "'Yo' ole black hide don't look lak nothin' tuh me, but uh passle uh wrinkled up rubber, wid yo' big ole yeahs flappin' on each side lak uh paih uh buzzard wings. Don't think Ah'm gointuh be run 'way fum mah house neither. Ah'm goin' tuh de white folks bout *you,* mah young man; de very nex' time you lay yo' han's on me. Mah cup is done run ovah.'" Delia here effectively "caps" Joe by verbally emasculating him, in a doubled way. The "wrinkled rubber" seems obvious enough, but the buzzard reference varies her refrain that he is not man enough to support her; he

just preys on her. This speech has much in common with Janie's silencing of Joe in the great scene in *Their Eyes,* but our pleasure in "Sweat" at Sykes's punishment is compromised by the ambiguity of our response throughout the story. Certainly, we feel for Delia, but the emasculation of the black man by a racist, capitalist society is on Hurston's mind here too, and Delia's threat to bring the white folks, whose laundry she washes, down on Joe, partially mitigates our natural inclinations to champion Delia; so does her tendency to taunt Joe about the fact that she brings home the bacon. Delia's Christian right-eousness, evident in the scene when she returns from a "Love Feast" at church, also seems challenged by her failure to seek help for Sykes after he has been bitten by the snake at the end of the story and by her deliberate showing herself to him so he will know she knows what he attempted and that there is no hope for him.

This climax occurs when Joe, trapped in the dark bedroom with the snake he left in Delia's basket, jumps in terror onto the bed, where he thinks he'll be safe; the snake, of course, lies coiled there. In Tennessee Williams's *Cat on a Hot Tin Roof,* Big Mama, advising her daughter-in-law, Maggie, pats the bed she is sitting on and tells her that all the big problems in marriages can ultimately be traced *here;* Hurston, at least in this story, would seem to agree. The final joke on Sykes is that his obsession with male, phallic power, and the way he misuses it in his marriage, finally kills him, in a doubly figurative and dreadfully comic way.

What made this story special? For one thing, it was written after Hurston had been collecting black folklore for several years in the South and returned to live in Eatonville. When writing this story, she seemed to have learned how intertwined comedy and tragedy were in folk culture and also how the comic was embedded in the cosmic. These relationships are always manifest in her best work, like "The Gilded Six-Bits."

Source: John Lowe, "'Cast in Yo' Nets Right Here': Finding a Comic Voice," in *Jump at the Sun: Zora Neale Hurston's Cosmic Comedy,* University of Illinois Press, 1994, pp. 71–79.

Kathryn Lee Seidel

In the following essay, Seidel analyzes Hurston's narrative technique and the metaphor of the working woman as artist in "Sweat."

Zora Neal Hurston's short story "Sweat" (1926) presents a radical transformation of an oppressed black domestic worker who attempts to envision her work as a work of art. The story is remarkable in Hurston's body of work for its harsh, unrelenting indictment of the economic and personal degradation of marriage in a racist and sexist society.

To accomplish this, "Sweat" functions at one level as a documentary of the economic situation of Eatonville in the early decades of the twentieth century. Hurston uses a naturalistic narrator to comment on the roles of Delia and Sykes Jones as workers as well as marriage partners, but ultimately the story veers away from naturalistic fiction and becomes a modernist rumination on Delia as an artist figure. The story's coherence of theme and structure makes it one of Hurston's most powerful pieces of fiction.

Preserved not only as a place but as an idea of a place, Eatonville, Florida, retains the atmosphere of which Hurston wrote. As putatively the oldest town in the United States incorporated by blacks, Eatonville possesses understandable pride in its unique history. When Hurston writes of Eatonville in "How It Feels To Be Colored Me," she implies that her childhood place was idyllic because "it is exclusively a colored town," one in which the young Zora was happily unaware of the restrictions that race conferred elsewhere. However, this gloss of nostalgia can be read simultaneously with "Sweat," published only two years earlier. Although Hurston's biographer, Robert Hemenway, writes perceptively that "Sweat" is a personal story without identifiable local folklore, in the story Hurston reveals the somber and multifaced variations of life in Eatonville in the first part of this century.

Economically Eatonville in "Sweat" exists as a twin, a double with its neighbor, the town of Winter Park. Far from being identical, the twin towns are configured like Siamese twins, joined as they are by economic necessity. Winter Park is an all-white, wealthy town that caters to rich northerners from New England who journey south each fall to "winter" in Florida—"snowbirds," as the natives call them. Winter Park then as now boasts brick streets, huge oaks, landscaped lakes, and large, spacious houses. To clean these houses, tend these gardens, cook the meals, and watch the children of Winter Park, residents of Eatonville made a daily exodus across the railroad tracks on which Amtrak now runs to work as domestics. This pattern has been described in detail by sociologist John Dollard whose study *Caste and Class in a Southern Town* (1937) remains the classic contemporaneous

> " Hurston moves beyond the naturalistic narrator by employing a Henry Louis Gatesian dual focus; she uses the townspeople as a chorus who comment orally on the characters of Delia and Sykes."

account of a small segregated town in the 1920s and 1930s, approximately the time in which the action of "Sweat" occurs. What is unique about Eatonville and Winter Park is that they are not one town divided in two but two towns. Eatonville's self-governance, its pride in its historic traditions, and its social mores were thus able to develop far more autonomously than those in the many towns of which Dollard wrote where the black community had to struggle to develop a sense of independent identity.

In "Sweat" we see the results of this economic situation. On Saturdays the men of the town congregate on the porch of the general store chewing sugarcane and discussing the lamentable marriage of Delia and Sykes Jones. Although these men may be employed during the week, Sykes is not. Some working people mentioned besides Joe Clarke, the store owner, are the woman who runs a rooming house where Bertha, Sykes's mistress, stays, the minister of the church Delia attends, and the people who organize dances that Sykes frequents. Work as farm laborers on land owned by whites is probably available, but it pays very little and is seasonal. Jacqueline Jones points out that in 1900, not long before the time of the story, 50 to 70 percent of adult black women were employed full time as compared to only 20 percent of men. A black man might be unemployed 50 percent of the time. One reason that unemployed men congregated at the local general store was not merely out of idleness, as whites alleged, nor out of a desire to create oral narratives, as we Hurston critics would like to imagine, but there they could be "visible to potential employers," as Jones asserts.

There is not enough work for the men as it is, but the townspeople discuss Sykes's particular aversion to what work is available. Old man Anderson reports that Sykes was always "ovahbearin' but since dat white w'eman from up north done teached 'im how to run a automobile, he done got too biggety to live—an' we oughter kill 'im." The identity of this woman and her exact role in Sykes's life is not referred to again, but if she was a Winter Park woman, then perhaps Sykes worked for a time as a driver for residents there. All the more ironic, then, his comment to Delia in which he berates her for doing white people's laundry: "ah done tole you time and again to keep them white folks' clothes outa this house." The comment suggests that Sykes does not work out of protest against the economic system of Eatonville in which blacks are dependent on whites for their livelihood. Has he chosen to be unemployed to resist the system? Within the story, this reading is fragile at best. The townspeople point out that Sykes has used and abused Delia; he has "squeezed" her dry, like a piece of sugarcane. They report that she was in her youth a pert, lively, and pretty girl, but that marriage to a man like Sykes has worn her out.

In fact, Delia's work is their only source of income. In the early days of their marriage Sykes was employed, but he "took his wages to Orlando," the large city about ten miles from Eatonville, where he spent every penny. At some point Sykes stopped working and began to rely entirely on Delia for income. As she says, "Mah tub full of suds is filled yo belly with vittles more times than yo hands is filled it. Mah sweat is done paid for this house." Delia's sense of ownership is that of the traditional work ethic; if one works hard, one can buy a house and support a family. That Delia is the breadwinner, however, is a role reversal but not ostensibly a liberation; her sweat has brought her some meager material rewards but has enraged her husband. Although she may at one time have considered stopping work so that Sykes might be impelled to "feel like man again" and become a worker once more, at the time of the story that possibility is long past. Sykes wants her to stop working so she can be dainty, not sweaty, fat, not thin. Moreover, he wants to oust her from the house so that he and his girlfriend can live there. Robert Hemenway perceptively notes that Sykes's exaggerated reliance on phallic objects—bullwhips and snakes in particular—is an overcompensation for his "emasculated" condition as a dependent of his wife. Sykes's brutality is a chosen compensation because he does not

participate in the work of the community. He chooses instead to become the town's womanizer and bully who spends his earnings when he has them; he lives for the moment and for himself.

Houston A. Baker's ideological analysis of *Their Eyes Were Watching God* emphasizes what he calls the "economics of slavery" in Hurston's works. This term refers to the historical use of human beings for profit, a potent theme he identifies in African-American authors from Linda Brent and Frederick Douglass to Hurston. In this context, one can point out that Delia's work, difficult as it is, is productive; it allows her to sustain herself (and Sykes) and to become a landowner, a rare situation for blacks, as John Dollard points out. With her house she possesses not only a piece of property, but she also gains the right to declare herself as a person, not a piece of property. Because Sykes has not shared in the labor that results in the purchase of this property, he remains in a dependent state. He is rebellious against Delia whom he feels controls him by denying him the house he feels ought to be his; his only reason for this assertion is that he is a man and Delia is his wife.

Thus, the economics of slavery in "Sweat" becomes a meditation on marriage as an institution that perpetuates possession of women for profit. Indeed, Sykes is the slaveholder here; he does not work, he is sustained by the harsh physical labor of a black woman, he relies on the work of another person to obtain his own pleasure (in this case buying presents for his mistress Bertha). He regards Delia's property and her body as his possessions to be disposed of as he pleases. Sykes's brutal beatings of Delia and his insulting remarks about her appearance are the tools with which he perpetuates her subordination to him for the sixteen years of their marriage.

Sykes has been transformed during his marriage, or perhaps because of it, from contributor to the family economy to the chief recipient of its benefits. Delia is a producer of goods (she grows food) and a provider of services (cooks, cleans); she also works at a service activity that brings in cash. Sykes responds by becoming a consumer. He uses her to buy the goods and services he desires (Bertha's favors, liquor, dances, etc.) rather than using this income to contribute to the family. Because he is a consumer only, he cannot become an owner of real estate, for he has a cash-flow problem. As a result, to use Walter Benn Michaels's terminology, Sykes determines to possess the owner, to regard her body and her property as his possessions. Like the Simon Legrees of abolitionist fiction, Sykes proves his ownership by the brutality he shows toward Delia. His hatred of her rests not on a feeling of inferiority because she owns the house; rather, he hates her because as one of his consumable goods, she ought to be desirable, not sweaty; compliant, not resisting. He prefers Bertha because her fatness suggests an overly fed commodity; like a cow, she has been opulently and extravagantly fed beyond her needs. Sykes desires the large and the luxurious commodity; he does not want what he needs.

Given this hopeless set of economic forces, the story does not sink into a trough of despair, largely because of Hurston's choice of its narrative point of view. While generally Hurston is associated with the lyrical, oral structure of *Their Eyes Were Watching God* (1937), the narrative strategy of "Sweat" is a sophisticated amalgam of the naturalistic narrator and narrative voice that Henry Louis Gates identifies in *Their Eyes Were Watching God* as that of "speakerly text." Gates defines such a text as incorporating oral tradition, indirect discourse, and a transcendent, lyrical voice that is "primarily . . . oriented toward imitating one of the numerous forms of oral narration to be found in classical Afro-American vernacular literature." Gates points out further that in oral tradition the speaker tells the story to a listener who is part of the teller's group; thus, in *Their Eyes Were Watching God,* Janie tells her tale to her friend, Phoeby, with the result that the first-person narrative is subtly shaped by the implied and the explicit dialogue. This type of novel is sharply defined in Alice Walker's *The Color Purple* (1982), in which the epistolary frame embodies the dialogic, oral tradition to which Gates refers. Gates contrasts this narrative mode with that of Richard Wright's *Native Son* (1940). In that work the third-person narrator is a removed authoritative, third commentor who possesses the knowledge of the larger context but does not permit characters to develop self-knowledge. Hurston's speakerly text exists to permit the main character, Janie, to search for self-knowledge, indeed for self, in a way that focuses on central themes but does not rely on the architectural plot scaffolding that characterizes Wright's fiction.

It is important to recognize that the narrative mode of "Sweat" is more similar to that of *Native Son* than *Their Eyes Were Watching God.* In "Sweat" the third-person narrator speaks in past tense about the events in the lives of Delia and Sykes. The narrator's voice is one of an educated observer who has complete knowledge of the sociology of the town of Eatonville, its place as a poor, all-black town in central Florida, and the litany of troubles in Delia's fifteen-year-long marriage. This narrator is, in short, the narrator of naturalism, who sees Delia's life as a short, brutish thing because of the nature of marriage within an economic miasma of poverty and powerlessness. At first glance, the story conforms to Donald Pizer's definition of naturalistic fiction as that which "unites detailed documentation of the more sensationalistic aspects of experience with heavily ideological [often allegorical] themes, the burden of these themes being the demonstration that man is circumscribed." Not only has Delia's life been a stream of "her tears, her sweat, her blood," as the narrator despairingly reports, but her marriage to a womanizer and wife-beater becomes worse when he also adds attempted murder to the list of forces that literally threaten her. This narrative mode allows Hurston a wider context for Delia's misery, the context of the economics of a central Florida community composed of black women who work as domestics in elite, white Winter Park. Hurston's narrator is especially effective when speaking of the setting itself, the long, hot central Florida August that both parallels and contributes to the climax of the story. The narrator gives shape to the natural cycles that influence Delia and Sykes, as in this passage that forms a transition to the story's climax: "The heat streamed down like a million hot arrows . . . grass withered, leaves browned, snakes went blind . . . and man and dogs went mad." But the perils of choosing an omniscient naturalistic narrator sometimes results in heavy-handed didacticism: "Delia's workworn knees crawled over the earth in Gethsemane and up the rocks of Calvary many, many times."

Because Hurston's narrator in "Sweat" has many features of the naturalistic narrator, the question arises as to whether this story itself is naturalistic. Donald Pizer points out that the 1930s was a time when naturalistic fiction such as *The Grapes of Wrath* offered at least partial solutions to the problems besetting the protagonist. One of the remarkable aspects of "Sweat" is Hurston's variation and escape from the naturalistic narrator. In the classic rhetoric of naturalism, characters are often curiously untouched by self-insight, as Pizer points out. In Theodore Dreiser's *Sister Carrie* (1900), for example, Carrie's victimization is unchallenged by anything more than a vague film of discontent that she feels now and then. Delia does fall from a state of relative success only to become brutalized, but she then begins the treacherous journey to self-knowledge and then self-esteem, the very journey that Janie makes in *Their Eyes Were Watching God.* Delia's marriage is far worse than any of Janie's; her economic situation is more impoverished. She does not have a friend like Phoeby or a grandmother to provide support, information, sympathy, and love. Yet Delia does change and grow in spite of her circumstances and her narrator. How does Delia (and Hurston) escape the narrator?

Hurston moves beyond the naturalistic narrator by employing a Henry Louis Gatesian dual focus; she uses the townspeople as a chorus who comment orally on the characters of Delia and Sykes. From them we learn of Delia's former beauty, of Sykes's early infatuation with her, of his difficult and brutal personality. We also learn that the town does not condone this behavior at all, but considers it an anomoly at best that their town should have produced a Sykes. Hurston sets up a dialogue between the narrator and the townspeople, the result of which is a double focus upon central characters. Unlike a Greek chorus, the townspeople are not omniscient; they are, on the contrary, interested in maintaining peace and harmony. They praise Delia's work, regarding her weekly delivery schedule with respect: ''hot or col', rain or shine, jes ez reg'lar ez de weeks roll roun' Delia carries em an' fetches 'em on Sat'day.'' Delia's work has become a predictable ritual for the town. Their reaction clarifies the attitude toward work: Work is admirable; the fact that Delia works on a Saturday and is as predictable as the seasons establishes her as worthy of their respect.

It is her work and her own attitude toward it that ultimately allow Delia to become a person who possesses self-esteem, pride, and the ability to create an ordered and harmonious existence. Delia has created her small world; she has lovingly planted trees and flowers in the garden around her house; her home and garden are ''lovely, lovely'' to her, as the narrator explains. For all her woes, Delia takes joy in her tidy house, her garden, and her work. These images establish the archetypal undertone of the story, that of the Edenic place. Hurston presents Delia's portion of Eden/Eatonville as a female-created place, ordered and beautiful because of the efforts of a woman.

Among Delia's efforts, and the central focus of the story, is her work. Although the stereotype of the mammy is all too pervasive as a symbol of black women's work, Jacqueline Jones points out that the most frequent job for black women in the early twentieth century was not as a full-time domestic in the household of whites. For over 50 percent of working black women, ''washing and ironing clothes provided an opportunity to work without the interference of whites, and with the help of their own children, at home.'' Mothers generally were reluctant to leave their own young children and to tolerate the all too frequent humiliation by their white women employers. Being a ''washerwoman'' was as arduous a task as being a field hand, and thus was of lower status and lower pay than that of a maid or cook within a household—but it did offer a measure of independence.

Jones found that the typical laundry woman collected clothes on Monday, boiled them in a large pot, scrubbed them, ''rinsed, starched, wrung out, hung up, and ironed'' often in the hot days of summer. Starch and soap she paid out of the one or two dollars a week she received. She delivered the clothes on Saturday and collected the next week's if she was lucky; otherwise she had to return on Monday. This pattern matches Delia's, but her work assumes an importance beyond sociological accuracy.

Delia's work acts as a metaphor for the work of the human creator, that is, the artist. Susan Gubar describes metaphors for the female artist in her essay '''The Blank Page' and the Issues of Female Creativity.'' She comments that ''many women experience their own bodies as the only available medium for their art. . . . Within the life of domesticity, the body is the only accessible medium for self expression.'' When we apply these statements to Delia, the sweat of her body, which has laundered, cooked, and scrubbed, is the corporal medium of her art. Her basket of pristine laundry stands as the artistic object created by her body. Her creation exists surrounded by home and garden, a miniature Eden made by a woman.

The laundry is a brilliant and evocative symbol in the story. It is, of course, white, pure white, the narrator reports; its whiteness and purity connote Delia's innate goodness as opposed to the evil darkness of Sykes's snake. The whiteness also indicates that her created object is indeed a blank page waiting for inscription; however, the appropriate inscriber, Delia, must of necessity keep her canvas blank; only Sykes writes upon it with the dirt of his boots and eventually the male object, the snake/penis, that symbolizes his desire to be the controller of the objects Delia's body has created.

The laundry has been created by the sweat and blood of her body; it rests quiet and serene like a tabula rasa, awaiting purposeful fulfillment. Nestled snugly in a basket, the laundry is an object Delia protects and to which she devotes her time, her attention, and her body. The laundry thus functions as a cherished child, the child of their own that Sykes and Delia do not have. One can only speculate that Delia's hard-muscled thinness coupled with the stress of the work itself and the cruelty of her husband have rendered her physically infertile. How much more pregnant, then, the potential fruitfulness of the laundry, the object of Delia's devotion, the object of Sykes's hatred. Had the laundry been literally a child, the story would devolve into a naturalistic tale on child abuse. But Hurston establishes herself as a writer, *the* Afro-American writer of her time and among the greatest in our century, by transcending such a cul-de-sac.

In *Invisible Man,* written twenty-four years after "Sweat," Ralph Ellison's nameless narrator, himself a blank page, ruminates on the qualities of whiteness and blackness in the brilliant section in the paint factory. The whiteness of the paint, considered so desirable, so good, so pure by white customers, results from the minute drops of blackness carefully, artistically added by the black paint makers. Ellison's scene is prefigured in "Sweat." Hurston takes the discourse on whiteness suggested by the laundry far beyond the stereotype that white is right and black is invisible. One could line up the side of the good in the story with Delia, the laundry, and whiteness opposed to Sykes, the snake, and blackness, but this easy dichotomy would overlook Hurston's ultimate accomplishment. The laundry created by Delia does not belong to her. The laundry, her creation, belongs to the white people of Winter Park, her patrons, who will be the ultimate inscribers of it; they will turn the laundry into clothes. Delia has prepared the perfect canvas for her patrons, but she is not able to participate in the use, evaluation, or assignment of worth to the creation. Like Hurston as an artist, Delia depends ultimately on the white patron for recognition. As Hurston was in the late 1920s the companion of Fannie Hurst, a white patron indeed, the story shades into a troubling comment on Hurston's relationship with her employer as a restriction on her art. Delia does not own her art. If the laundry represents a baby, then the baby is not Delia's; it is a white person's baby whom Delia tends so carefully. She is its mammy, creating the child but not owning it. But again, Hurston avoids the simple sociological statement of making the object of Delia's sweat an actual child.

In keeping with the Edenic imagery is the serpent in Delia's house, her husband. Sykes is not an Adam at all; his potential as a mate has been supplanted by the bullwhip he carries, which is the satanic object associated with a snake as it "slithers to the floor" when he threatens to strike Delia with it, as Robert Hemenway has noted. Sykes attempts to destroy everything Delia has created. He begins by complaining that she should "keep them white folks' clothes outa dis house," and purposely kicks the neatly folded stack of white laundry into a dirty, disordered heap. His demand is irrational on a literal level because these clothes are their only source of money. In an ironic way, however, Sykes is reflecting a lingering Adamic need to establish his home as terrain in which he too has power. He owns nothing of his own; the house legally belongs to Delia. His protest against a white-controlled labor system embodies a somber problem for black men, but Sykes's anger and frustration cannot be directed toward the white perpetrators of his situation because he lacks the power to change the status quo. Instead he passes his days with careless pursuits and becomes increasingly violent with Delia. Her response to his violence has been excruciatingly passive, but when Sykes criticizes her work, he is not only protesting against his own economic condition. He has intuitively violated the one object, the laundry, that Delia values about all others.

Sykes's attack on the laundry brings about Delia's first assertion against him in fifteen years of marriage. When she grabs a heavy iron skillet from the stove, she is threatening her husband with a female object used for creation, in this case a cooking pot. Sykes responds by threatening her with the object of male creativity and violence with which he is most familiar, the bullwhip. The choices of these objects reveal that to Hurston, male creativity (the whip) exists only to injure and destroy; female creativity (the pot) *can* be used destructively but is intended primarily to be positive, that is, to cook and create a meal. Thus, women can use their creative power to defend themselves against the destruction that is the only intended use of male power.

The scene acts as a foreshadowing of the couple's climactic confrontation when Sykes brings home in a crate the satanic object of destruction, a snake. He leaves the snake in the kitchen for several days; Delia is terrified and terrorized by the snake, but she repeats her assertive stance by ordering her husband to remove it. Sykes responds by criticizing Delia's appearance. This apparent non sequitur reveals Sykes's attempt to control Delia by reminding her of the role he expects her to play, that of wife/sex object, prettied up and passive for the husband's use. Sykes criticizes her thin, hard-muscled body; he prefers fat women with flaccid bodies. Delia is strong because she works hard, another Sojourner Truth in her ability to work like a man. But as a representative of patriarchal masculinity, Sykes cannot prize Delia for what she is; he expects her to make herself, her body, into the image he prefers.

In the climax of the story Delia picks up the basket of white laundry and sees the snake in it. She drops the basket, runs outside in terror, and huddles in a gully beside a creek; Sykes returns home to the darkened house, picks up the snake's cage, and discards it. In this way the reader realizes that Sykes knew the snake was no longer in the cage; thus, it was Sykes who had placed it in the basket in order to murder Delia. When he goes inside to verify her death, he cannot see the snake in the dark house. Delia must decide whether to call out to warn her husband. If she does, he will live another day to take her life. She can save his life or she can save her own. In placing the snake in the laundry, Sykes has violated Delia's creation; he has disordered her house and finally actually intends to take her life. Delia chooses not to call out; the snake strikes, and Delia is permitted the gruesome revenge of seeing Sykes die before her eyes.

Delia's decision involves not only saving her life but preserving her vision of reality; her alternative choice would be to save her oppressor and thereby perpetuate not only her bondage to him but also to the corrupt, diseased vision of life he represents. As a female artist figure, Delia represents the power of the female artist who must adopt strategies that directly and violently bring change and allow her art to thrive. The debased condition of Sykes and of their marriage, even though it is in part a product of the economic disenfranchisement of black men, is not salvageable in this desperate story. Delia's choice implies that the oppressors of the woman worker/artist must be eliminated because they are evil, that the oppressors will bring about their own destruction. The tension for the black woman of creating art in a milieu controlled absolutely by whites remains unresolved. Hurston's story suggests that women artists must be free to create art and to contribute to a harmonious, ordered world. The issue of the need for a world that suits both men and women remains to be addressed, a task Hurston takes up in her later writing, especially in *Their Eyes Were Watching God* (1937). The issue of the situation of the black female artist remained her lifelong subject.

Source: Kathryn Lee Seidel, ''The Artist in the Kitchen: The Economics of Creativity in Hurston's 'Sweat,''' in *Zora in Florida,* edited by Steve Glassman and Kathryn Lee Seidel, University of Central Florida Press, 1991, pp. 110–20.

Sources

Du Bois, W. E. B., ''The Creative Impulse,'' in *The ''Crisis'' Writings,* Fawcett Publications, 1972, pp. 286–88.

Hemenway, Robert E., *Zora Neale Hurston: A Literary Biography,* Camden Press, 1986, pp. 41–50, 70–73, 148; originally published by the University of Illinois Press, 1977.

Hughes, Langston, and Zora Neale Hurston, *Mule Bone: A Comedy on Negro Life in Three Acts,* Perennial Press, 1991, pp. 1–2.

Hurston, Zora Neale, *The Complete Stories,* edited by Henry Louis Gates Jr., HarperCollins, 1995, pp. 73–85.

———, *Dust Tracks on a Road,* Harper & Row, 1984, p. 206; originally published by J. B. Lippincott, 1942.

Locke, Alain, ''Negro Youth Speaks,'' in *The New Negro,* edited by Alain Locke, Atheneum, 1968, p. 50; originally published by Albert & Charles Boni, 1925.

Lowe, John, *Jump at the Sun: Zora Neale Hurston's Cosmic Comedy,* University of Illinois Press, 1994, p. 74.

Further Reading

Croft, Robert W., *A Zora Neale Hurston Companion,* Greenwood Press, 2002.
   This indexed overview considers Hurston's literary career as a whole and provides a useful reference source for examining the author's short fiction in relation to her other writings.

Gates, Henry L., *Zora Neale Hurston: Critical Perspectives Past and Present,* Amistad Press, 1999.
   This collection of analysis of Hurston's entire body of work provides a series of essays from diverse critical lenses and time periods.

Hurston, Zora Neale, *Zora Neale Hurston: A Life in Letters,* edited by Carla Kaplan, Doubleday, 2002.
   A comprehensive collection of Hurston's letters, this volume is vividly suggestive about her life, writings, and decline in popularity.

Miles, Diana, *Women, Violence, & Testimony in the Works of Zora Neale Hurston,* Peter Lang Publishing, 2003.

Miles's book focuses on some of the most important themes in ''Sweat,'' as evidenced in several of Hurston's other works. It is an excellent resource for readers interested in the most recent theories on the author.

Watson, Steven, *The Harlem Renaissance: Hub of American Culture, 1920–1930,* Pantheon Books, 1995.
Outlining the key elements of the historical movement in Harlem, Watson provides photographs and poetry to illustrate his presentation of the cultural climate at the time.

A Temporary Matter

Jhumpa Lahiri

1998

"A Temporary Matter" was originally published in the *New Yorker* in April 1998 and is the first story in Jhumpa Lahiri's debut collection, *Interpreter of Maladies* (1999). The collection won the 2000 Pulitzer Prize for fiction, a rare achievement for a short-story collection.

The story takes place over five days, beginning March 19, at the suburban Boston home of a married couple, Shoba and Shukumar. During this week, when they must cope with a one-hour power outage each evening, the grief and alienation that the two have suffered since the stillbirth of their child six months earlier builds to a climax.

Author Biography

Jhumpa Lahiri was born in London, England, in 1967. Her parents, natives of Bengal, India, soon moved the family to Rhode Island, where Lahiri grew up. Lahiri's father, Amar, is a librarian at the University of Rhode Island, and her mother, Tia, is a teacher's aide. From childhood, Lahiri made frequent trips to India to visit relatives.

After receiving a bachelor's degree in English literature from Barnard College, Lahiri earned master's degrees in English, creative writing, and comparative studies in literature and the arts, all from Boston University. She went on to earn a doctorate in Renaissance studies at the same university.

"A Temporary Matter" first appeared in the *New Yorker* in 1998 and was among Lahiri's first published stories. It is the first story in the collection *Interpreter of Maladies* (1999), for which Lahiri won the Pulitzer Prize for fiction in 2000. The collection's title story also won an O. Henry award and the PEN/Hemingway award in 1999.

Lahiri lives in Brooklyn, New York, with her husband, Guatemalan American journalist Alberto Vourvoulias, and their young son, Octavio. Her first novel, *The Namesake*, was published in the fall of 2003.

Plot Summary

The story opens with Shoba, a thirty-three-year-old wife, arriving home at the end of a workday. Her husband, Shukumar, is cooking dinner. Shoba reads him a notice from the electric company stating that their electricity will be turned off from 8 p.m. to 9 p.m. for five consecutive days so that a line can be repaired. The date shown on the notice for the first evening of the outage is today's date, March 19. The notice seems to have been mailed.

The narrator mentions that Shukumar has forgotten to brush his teeth that day and often does not leave the house for days at a time, although Shoba stays out more as time goes on. Then the narrator explains that six months earlier, in September, Shoba had experienced fetal death three weeks before their baby was due. Shukumar, a doctoral student, was in Baltimore for an academic conference at the time, having gone only at Shoba's insistence. Shukumar often thinks of the last time he saw Shoba pregnant, the morning he left for the conference. As he rode away in the taxi, he had imagined himself and Shoba driving in a station wagon with their children.

By the time Shukumar had gotten news of Shoba's premature labor and returned to Boston, their baby had been stillborn.

Now, Shoba leaves early each morning for her proofreading job in the city. After work, she goes to the gym. She also takes on extra projects for work that she does at home during the evenings and weekends. Shukumar stays in bed half the day. Because of the tragedy, his academic advisor has arranged for him to be spared any teaching duties for the spring semester. Shukumar is supposed to be working on his dissertation; instead, he spends most of his time reading novels and cooking dinner.

Jhumpa Lahiri

When Shukumar remarks that they will have to eat dinner in the dark because of the power outage, Shoba suggests lighting candles and goes upstairs to shower before dinner. Shukumar notes that she has left her satchel and sneakers in the kitchen and that since the stillbirth Shoba has "treated the house like a hotel." He brushes his teeth, unwrapping a new toothbrush in the downstairs bathroom. This leads him to recall that Shoba used to be prepared for any eventuality. In addition to having extra toothbrushes for last-minute guests, Shoba had stocked their pantry and freezer with homemade foods. After the stillbirth, she had stopped cooking, and Shukumar had used up all the stored food in the past months. Shukumar also notes that Shoba always keeps her bonuses in a bank account in her own name. He thinks that this is for the best, since his mother was unable to handle her financial affairs when his father died.

The narrator explains that Shoba and Shukumar have been eating dinner separately, she in front of the television set, he in front of the computer. Tonight, they will eat together because of the power outage. Shukumar lights candles, tunes the radio to a jazz station, and sets the table with their best china. Shoba comes into the kitchen as the electricity goes off and the lights go out. She says that the kitchen looks lovely and reminisces about power outages in India. She tells Shukumar that at family dinners at her grandmother's house, when the electricity went off, ''we all had to say something''—a joke, a poem, an interesting fact, or some other tidbit. Shoba suggests that she and Shukumar do this, but she further suggests that they each tell the other something they have never revealed before.

Shoba begins the game, telling Shukumar that early in their relationship she peeked into his address book to see if she was in it. Shukumar reveals that on their first date he forgot to tip the waiter, so he returned to the restaurant the next day and left money for him.

The next evening, Shoba comes home earlier than usual. They eat together by candlelight again. Then, instead of each going to a different room, Shoba suggests that they sit outside, since it is warm. Shukumar knows that they will play the game again. He is afraid of what Shoba might tell him. He considers but then discounts several possibilities: that she had an affair, that she does not respect him for still being a student at thirty-five, or that she blames him for being away when she lost the baby.

Shoba tells Shukumar that she once lied to him, saying that she had to work late when actually she went out with a friend. Shukumar tells her that he cheated on an exam many years earlier. He explains that his father had died a few months before and that he was unprepared for the exam. Shoba takes his hand, and they go inside.

The next day, Shukumar thinks all day about what he will tell Shoba next. That evening, he tells her that he returned a sweater she gave him as an anniversary gift and used the money to get drunk in the middle of the day. The sweater was a gift for their third anniversary, and Shukumar was disappointed because he thought it unromantic. Shoba tells Shukumar that at a social gathering with his superiors from the university, she purposely did not tell him that he had a bit of food on his chin as he chatted with the department chairman. They then sit together on the sofa and kiss.

The fourth night, Shoba tells Shukumar that she does not like the only poem he has ever had published. He tells her that he once tore a picture of a woman out of one of her magazines and carried it with him for a week because he desired the woman. They go upstairs and make love.

The next day, Shukumar goes to the mailbox and finds a notice that the electric repairs have been completed early. Shukumar is disappointed, but when Shoba arrives home she says, ''You can still light the candles if you want.'' They eat by candlelight, and then Shoba blows out the candles and turns on the lights. When Shukumar questions this, she tells him that she has something to tell him and wants him to see her face. His heart pounds. He thinks that she is going to tell him that she is pregnant again, and he does not want her to be. She tells him, instead, that she has signed a lease on an apartment for herself.

Shukumar realizes that this revelation has been her planned ending for the game all along. He decides to tell Shoba something he had vowed to himself that he would never tell her. Shoba does not know that Shukumar held their baby at the hospital while she slept. Shoba does not even know the baby's gender and has said that she is glad that she has no knowledge about the lost child. Shukumar tells Shoba that the baby was a boy and goes on to describe his appearance in detail, including that the baby's hands were closed into fists the way Shoba's are when she sleeps. The two sit at the table together, and each of them cries because of what the other has revealed.

Characters

Mr. Bradford

Mr. and Mrs. Bradford are neighbors of Shoba and Shukumar. Shoba and Shukumar see them walking by, arm in arm, on their way to the bookstore on the second night of the power outage. The Bradfords seem to be a happily married couple and as such provide a contrast to Shoba and Shukumar. The narrator mentions that the Bradfords placed a sympathy card in Shoba and Shukumar's mailbox when they lost their baby.

Mrs. Bradford

Mr. and Mrs. Bradford are neighbors of Shoba and Shukumar. Shoba and Shukumar see them on the second night of the power outage, and Shukumar sees them again, through the window, on the last evening of the story. The first time the Bradfords appear, Mrs. Bradford asks Shoba and Shukumar if they would like to join her and her husband on their walk to the bookstore, but they decline.

Shoba

Shoba is a thirty-three-year-old woman who is married to Shukumar. She is described as tall and broad-shouldered. She seems to have been born in the United States of immigrant parents from India, and she has spent considerable time in India visiting relatives. She and her husband now live in a house outside Boston.

Shoba works in the city as a proofreader and also takes on extra projects to do at home. She works out at a gym regularly.

Six months before the time of the story, Shoba's first child was stillborn. This tragedy has changed her habits and her relationship with her husband. While she was formerly a neat and enthusiastic housekeeper and cook, she has become careless about the house and has stopped cooking. The narrator remarks that she previously had the habit of being prepared for anything, from keeping extra toothbrushes on hand for last-minute guests to stocking the freezer and pantry with homemade Indian delicacies.

Shukumar

Shukumar is a thirty-five-year-old doctoral student who is married to Shoba. He is a tall man with a large build. He, too, seems to be an American-born child of Indian immigrants, but he has spent less time in India than Shoba has.

Because of the loss of his child six months earlier, Shukumar has been given a semester away from his teaching duties. He is supposed to use the time to focus on writing his dissertation on agrarian revolts in India. However, Shukumar accomplishes little. He stays in bed until midday, doesn't leave the house for days at a time, and often forgets to brush his teeth. He has spent the past months preparing dinners for himself and Shoba using the foods she has stored in the freezer and pantry.

Themes

Grief

The story takes place six months after the stillbirth of Shoba and Shukumar's first child, and the two are still overwhelmed by grief. Shukumar has withdrawn from the world and seldom leaves the house. He stays in bed half the day, unable to summon the energy and concentration to make progress on his dissertation. Shoba, on the other hand, stays away from the house as much as she can. She used to be an attentive housekeeper and enthusiastic cook, but the house seems to remind her of her loss. According to Shukumar, she treats the house as if it were a hotel and would eat cereal for dinner if he did not cook. The narrator also reveals that Shoba and Shukumar no longer go out socially or entertain at home.

People who suffer the loss of a loved one often go through a period of not wanting to go on living themselves. They may feel unable to make the effort required to go about daily life. Sadness may drown out all positive emotions. This seems to be true for this couple, and especially of Shukumar.

Alienation

Shoba and Shukumar's grief has led them to withdraw from each other. Until the nightly power outages began, they avoided each other. Shoba leaves for work early each morning, returns late, and often brings home extra work to occupy her evenings and weekends. When Shoba is home, Shukumar retreats to his computer and pretends to work on his dissertation. He has put the computer in the room that was to be the nursery because he knows that Shoba avoids that room. She comes in briefly each evening to tell him goodnight. He resents even this brief interaction, which Shoba initiates only out of a sense of obligation.

Shoba and Shukumar do not attempt to comfort or support each other. Each withdraws from the relationship, and they endure their grief as if they were two strangers living in a boardinghouse.

Deception

Through the game that Shoba and Shukumar play of revealing secrets, readers learn that deception has been a theme in their relationship. They have lied to each other, and the lies have been selfish ones—told not to spare the other's feelings but to allow the person telling the lie to escape some discomfort or sacrifice. To avoid having dinner with Shukumar's mother, Shoba lied and said she had to work late. Shukumar told Shoba that he lost a sweater she had given him, when in reality he returned the sweater and used the money to get drunk.

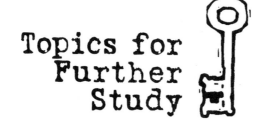

Topics for Further Study

- Shoba recalls visits to her grandmother's house in Calcutta. Do research to learn about living conditions in Calcutta for people at various economic levels. What do you think Shoba's grandmother's house was like? What kinds of memories might Shoba have of her visits there, besides those of power outages?

- A theme that runs throughout Lahiri's body of work is that of the challenges faced by immigrants and children of immigrants who must strive to meld two cultures in their lives. Does this theme appear in "A Temporary Matter"? Explain your answer.

- What is your opinion of Shoba and her actions toward Shukumar? Specifically, what do you think of the way she chose to tell Shukumar that she was leaving him? Was she trying to spare his feelings by breaking the news gently, or was she being manipulative and unfair?

- Do research to learn about the challenges faced by couples who suffer the tragedy of a stillborn child. Shoba and Shukumar's marriage does not survive their loss. How common is this? What are some other difficulties that such couples may face, and what do medical professionals recommend to help prevent or minimize them?

- Lahiri included in the story brief descriptions of both Shoba's and Shukumar's mothers. She accomplished this by having the narrator recall a visit from each woman. Why do you think Lahiri included these recollections? What do they add to the story?

As these examples of deception are revealed throughout the story, it is clear that Shoba and Shukumar's emotional estrangement began before the loss of their baby. They have always dealt with difficult situations and unpleasant emotions by lying and keeping secrets. When Shoba breaks the stalemate that their grief has caused by initiating a deceptive game, she is following an established pattern. Throughout the week of power outages, Shoba appears to be reaching out to Shukumar. In truth, she is engineering her final separation from him.

Style

Realism through Details

Lahiri uses dozens of everyday details to create a realistic context in which the story takes place. When Shukumar recalls the morning he left for Baltimore, he remembers that the taxicab was red with blue lettering. When he wakes up each morning, he sees Shoba's "long black hairs" on her pillow. The crib in the nursery is made of cherry wood; the changing table is white with mint-green knobs. Taken together, such details comprise a world that readers find familiar. The realism of the environment makes the characters who live in it and the events that take place in it seem real as well.

Conflicting Clues

As the story unfolds, Lahiri provides readers with two conflicting sets of clues as to how it might end. Each evening Shoba and Shukumar seem to draw closer to each other both emotionally and physically. As they share long withheld secrets, they hold hands, kiss, and finally make love. It seems as if ghosts that have haunted their marriage are being exorcised.

At the same time, the game that appears to be drawing them together also reveals a past filled with deception. Things have not always been as they seemed between these two people. In addition, readers learn early in the story that Shoba has always been one to plan ahead and that she keeps a separate bank account. Readers are left to wonder whether the pattern of deception will be broken or intensified.

The balance seems to shift decisively in favor of a happy ending when, on the fifth evening, the narrator declares, "They had survived a difficult time." Shoba's silence that evening has been interpreted as the calm after a storm. But that interpretation is as misleading as Shoba's behavior has been. Readers, like Shukumar, have been given mixed signals and only learn at the end which set of clues was reliable.

Historical Context

Indian Americans

According to the 2000 census, there were nearly 1.7 million Indian Americans in the United States at that time. This was more than double the figure for 1990, making Indian Americans the fastest-growing group in the nation. As of 2004, Indian Americans are the third largest group of Asian Americans, after those of Chinese and Filipino origin. California, New York, New Jersey, and Florida are among the states with large numbers of Americans of Indian origin.

Indian Americans are among the best educated and wealthiest of all Americans. In 2000, their median household income was more than $60,000, compared to a median of just over $41,000 for non-Hispanic white Americans. Substantial numbers of Indian Americans work in the high-tech industry and also in various engineering and health care occupations. This is unsurprising given India's strong tradition of education in math and science. In addition, the fact that most Indian immigrants arrive in the United States speaking fluent English is an economic advantage. English is one of the official languages of India, a legacy of its long status as a colony of Britain.

As the number of Indian Americans grows, so does their influence on American culture. Indian foods are increasingly available not only at restaurants—many of them owned by Indian Americans—but also in suburban supermarkets. Many large American cities have at least one Hindu temple. The works of Indian American writers and filmmakers have generally been well received by an American public eager to know more about India and about Indian Americans, who are more and more likely to be among their neighbors and coworkers.

Critical Overview

Interpreter of Maladies, the collection in which "A Temporary Matter" appears, won widespread praise from American critics when it appeared. Besides the nearly universal approval bestowed on the book, the most remarkable feature of the criticism is that nearly every reviewer compared Lahiri to one or more literary predecessors and no two reviewers seem to have linked her with the same writers.

New York Times Book Review critic Caleb Crain declares that "Samuel Richardson's latest heir is Jhumpa Lahiri," a reference to Richardson's eighteenth-century novel *Pamela* in which a household servant is the unwilling object of a wealthy young man's lust. The connection between Lahiri and Richardson is not obvious to all, but Crain also compares Lahiri to Raymond Carver and Ernest Hemingway. "There is nothing accidental about her success," Crain concludes, "her plots are as elegantly constructed as a fine proof in mathematics."

Writing in the *San Francisco Chronicle,* David Kipen sees similarities with Philip Roth and Lan Samantha Chang. Like the former's *Good-Bye, Columbus* and the latter's *Hunger,* Kipen writes, Lahiri's work "transcends mere ethnic exoticism." He praises her use of "simple, familiar tools—subtle characterization, meaningful but never portentous detail."

Ellen Emry Heltzel, writing in *The Oregonian,* calls *Interpreter of Maladies* "an impressive start, signaling the arrival of yet another notable Anglo-Indian writer at a time when, in literary circles at least, India is all the rage." The comment is an implied comparison to Bharati Mukherjee, Chitra Divakaruni, and other writers who deal with themes similar to those found in Lahiri's work.

In general, critics in Asia and other non-Western countries have not been as approving as have Americans. Reviewing *Interpreter of Maladies* in *Time International* magazine, Nisid Hajari writes, "At times the three stories that deal with the souring of love . . . read like journal entries, or schematics to the collapse of a relationship. Their declines are almost too measured, too academic to evoke much sympathy or uncontrived sadness.'' Hajari nevertheless called the collection ''assured and powerful'' and implies that Lahiri's next effort may be an improvement.

Criticism

Candyce Norvell

Norvell is an independent educational writer who specializes in English and literature. In this essay, Norvell discusses the story as ''the interaction between an active woman and a passive man.''

The world that Jhumpa Lahiri creates in ''A Temporary Matter'' is one in which women are in charge. Women act; men react. This state of affairs is a reversal of traditional gender roles in India, the country from which both Shoba's and Shukumar's parents emigrated, and the United States. This role reversal gives the story a strongly modern feel.

Both the author and the critics who analyze her work categorize Lahiri along with other female Indian American writers whose work deals with the cultural conflicts faced by immigrants and their children. But Lahiri's stories in general, and this one in particular, do not seem to grapple with cultural issues as much as with gender issues. The dynamic that drives ''A Temporary Matter'' is the interaction between an active woman and a passive man. It is the kind of situation that today's readers would find credible and compelling whether the characters were children of immigrants or descendants of the Pilgrims.

That Shoba and Shukumar are second-generation Americans of Indian heritage is incidental. They eat Indian food. And when a visit from Shoba's mother is recalled, readers learn that she is a Hindu. But these facts have no impact on how Shoba and Shukumar respond to the loss of their child or behave toward each other. The husband and wife could just as well eat Italian food or fast food, and the visiting mother might just as easily have been a Catholic or a Jew. Shoba and Shukumar are apparently divorced from the religion and traditions of their forebears. Far from struggling to balance two traditions, they have set themselves adrift from all

traditions. They are thoroughly modern and secular, and their story could be the story of any educated thirty-something couple.

Freedom from tradition leaves Shoba and Shukumar to work out the terms of their relationship on their own. Individual personalities, free of cultural restrictions, shape their relationship and their lives. And in this marriage, that fact puts Shoba in the driver's seat.

Although Shoba has been changed by the loss of her child, she has found the strength and determination to restart her life. She goes to her job, and she even works out at a gym. She still has the will to plan ahead and to take the initiative; she simply channels her energy in new directions. Instead of stocking the pantry and planning parties, she carefully plans how to extricate herself from her marriage. She initiates a game designed to gradually open a channel of communication between Shukumar and herself that is wide enough to accommodate the message she has to deliver. At the same time, she finds and leases an apartment for herself. Her response to trying circumstances is to set about changing them.

Shukumar, on the other hand, is a passive victim of those same circumstances. He stays in bed late and does not leave the house or even brush his teeth regularly. He rarely initiates interaction with Shoba; instead, he reacts to her action. When she leaves her gym shoes and satchel in the kitchen, he moves them out of his way without saying anything to her. When Shoba suggests that they eat by candlelight, he searches out candles and lights them. When Shoba starts the game of revealing secrets, it becomes the focus of his days. He spends hours thinking about what she might say to him and what he should say to her that evening. While Shoba is out interacting with the world and creating a foundation for her future, Shukumar languishes. He is engaged with neither the present nor the future. In fact, he is paralyzed.

The roles in this marriage, those of the active woman and the passive man, were established long before the tragedy. Early in the story, readers learn that Shukumar finds Shoba's ability to plan ahead astonishing. In a description of their past trips to a farmer's market, Shoba leads him through the crowds and does all the choosing, haggling, and buying. Shukumar is seen ''trailing behind her with canvas bags.'' Shukumar's trip to the conference in Baltimore, which resulted in his being away at the time of the stillbirth, was made at Shoba's insistence. He had not wanted to go, but he did as she told him to.

What Do I Read Next?

- Lahiri's first novel, *The Namesake* (2003), is a story that began with an incident in the author's childhood. In her parents' Bengali culture, each child has two names, a pet name used by family and friends and a ''good name'' used more formally. Lahiri's first American teacher found her good name too difficult and began using the private, pet name without understanding how inappropriate this was. The incident was such a powerful example of the cultural dissonance experienced by immigrants and children of immigrants that Lahiri made it the starting point of her novel.

- *The Unknown Errors of Our Lives: Stories* (2002) is a collection of nine stories with female protagonists. Its author, Chitra Divakaruni, is an American immigrant from India who explores the same issues as does Lahiri, but from the point of view of the older generation born abroad.

- *The Middleman and Other Stories* (1988), by Bharati Mukherjee, won the National Book Critics Circle Award for fiction in 1988. It is the first story collection published by Mukherjee, who continues to be a prolific writer. The stories deal with the experiences of immigrants to the United States from many nations.

- *Flannery O'Connor: The Complete Stories* (1971) is a collection of all thirty-one short stories by O'Connor, who is widely considered one of the best American short story writers. Lahiri has mentioned O'Connor as a writer whom she admires.

- *Finding the Center: Two Narratives* (1984) contains two personal narratives by Nobel Prize–winning author V. S. Naipaul. Naipaul was born and reared in Trinidad (where his parents had immigrated to from India), and moved to London as a young man. The challenge of straddling cultures is a theme that pervades Naipaul's work and links it to Lahiri's. ''Prologue to an Autobiography,'' the first narrative in *Finding the Center,* explores this theme in some detail.

These incidents and others set the stage for Shoba's manipulation of Shukumar during the week of the power outages. Readers know that Shoba is leading and Shukumar is following long before it is clear where they are going. Shukumar, however, does not even realize that Shoba is leading him until the game has played out.

Shukumar's passive role is not limited to his relationship with his wife. Both Shoba's and Shukumar's mothers make brief appearances in the story through recollections of their visits. Both women share Shoba's active, independent nature, and both dominate and intimidate Shukumar.

Shoba's mother is an immigrant, born and brought up in a Hindu society in which wives were expected to be humble and obedient servants to their husbands. Men led; women followed. Shoba's mother lives in Arizona now. Perhaps not coincidentally,

her husband—Shoba's father—is not mentioned. It is unclear whether he is still living.

Shoba's mother comes to stay for two months after the stillbirth. Although her practice of Hinduism links her to the culture in which she was brought up, she is surprisingly modern and self-sufficient. Not only does she cook dinner every night, as Shoba once did, she also ''drove herself to the supermarket.'' This is more remarkable than it might seem. In another of Lahiri's stories, a Hindu housewife a generation younger than Shoba's mother is not able to drive. Readers learn, too, that Shoba's mother once held a job in a department store.

In traditional Indian society, a woman often goes from being a young wife in a subservient position in her father-in-law's household to being an elderly widow in a subservient position in her son-in-law's household. Therefore, Shoba's mother

> **Although Shukumar hurts Shoba in the end by revealing a devastating secret, he is like a wounded animal whose lashing out is impulsive and, ultimately, ineffectual."**

could be expected to treat Shukumar with deference. But there is nothing subservient or deferential about this woman. Although she is generally polite to Shukumar, when he mentions the death of his child, Shoba's mother says to him accusingly, "But you weren't even there."

Less is revealed about Shukumar's mother. She, too, continues to observe the religious traditions of her homeland. Her visit to Shoba and Shukumar's home is timed to mark the twelve-year anniversary of Shukumar's father's death. What is notable is that Shukumar's mother comes for a two-week stay during which she imposes upon Shukumar, in his own home, certain traditions that mean nothing to him. Further, Shukumar dreads having dinner with his mother without Shoba there "to say more of the right things because he came up with only the wrong ones." Clearly, Shukumar is intimidated by his mother's power to impose her will upon him and by her habit of finding fault with him. Once again, Shukumar is at the mercy of a powerful, take-charge woman.

What lies at the heart of this story is neither a conflict between cultures nor a power struggle between the genders. The two sides are not evenly matched enough to make for a struggle. Although Shukumar hurts Shoba in the end by revealing a devastating secret, he is like a wounded animal whose lashing out is impulsive and, ultimately, ineffectual. Given what has transpired between Shoba and Shukumar, readers have no doubt that she will recover from the blow and make a life for herself. Shukumar's fate is much more uncertain.

Source: Candyce Norvell, Critical Essay on "A Temporary Matter," in *Short Stories for Students,* Gale, 2004.

David Remy

Remy is a freelance writer in Pensacola, Florida. In the following essay, Remy examines Jhumpa Lahiri's use of irony in "A Temporary Matter."

"A Temporary Matter," the first story in Jhumpa Lahiri's debut Pulitzer Prize–winning collection *Interpreter of Maladies,* captures a pivotal moment in a couple's relatively short but eventful marriage. At times absurdly funny, at others heartbreakingly sad, Lahiri's tale examines how a tragic loss can lead to indifference and a breakdown in communication between two people who once loved each other. The author's use of irony in various forms makes the transition even more poignant, for it underscores an element of suspense as it brings about the story's denouement.

Lahiri increases the ironic quality of the story by setting up a situation in which the emotionally distant couple must interact more closely. Because the utility company will turn off the electricity for one hour each night for five consecutive nights to make repairs after a recent snowstorm, Shoba and Shukumar, deprived of their usual distractions, must turn to each other for companionship. To heighten her characters' isolation, Lahiri informs the reader that it is only the houses on the "quiet, tree-lined streets" that experience the nightly power outages and not the shops near the trolley stop.

Although the utility company assures the residents of the neighborhood that the inconvenience is only "a temporary matter," the blackout has a transforming effect on the neighborhood and its residents. Despite the cold, neighbors chat with one another as they stroll up and down the street carrying flashlights. The darkness and cold, fresh air instill a restless feeling while enforcing a sense of community. "Tonight, with no lights, they would have to eat together," says the narrator, describing the situation inside Shoba and Shukumar's house. The power outage forces a change in routine—from voluntary separation to forced interaction.

Ever since the loss of their child in September, Shoba and Shukumar have lived separate lives under the same roof. Within the span of only a few months, they have constructed for themselves a routine structured on the avoidance of each other and the horrible truth that has changed their married life forever. In an effort to delay her homecoming and an inevitable confrontation with her husband, Shoba spends long hours at work and at the gym. Shukumar, on the other hand, remains ensconced on the third floor, ostensibly writing his dissertation. Both husband and wife are depressed, and neither is willing to acknowledge that their marriage has lost something vital, something more than just romance.

Until recently, Shoba had always been neat and tidy, but now she deposits her briefcase in the middle of the hall and leaves her clothes strewn about the room; she is so weary that she does not even bother to untie her shoes before removing them. At thirty-three, she looks ''like the type of woman she'd once claimed she would never resemble.'' Shoba's slightly rumpled appearance reminds Shukumar of a time when she was more carefree and all ''too eager to collapse into his arms.'' Alas, those days are no more, and her rumpled appearance reveals a different attitude toward Shukumar.

The relationship has deteriorated to the point that Shukumar never leaves the house, not even to retrieve the mail, and sleeps until it is almost lunchtime, drinking coffee Shoba had brewed earlier that morning. He cannot find the motivation he needs to finish his dissertation but reads novels instead. Everything in his life seems to have lost color, vibrancy. The love he once felt for Shoba has lost its ardor, for he sees her beauty fading. ''The cosmetics that had seemed superfluous were necessary now, not to improve her but to define her somehow.'' The woman he once loved has disappeared and with her his own passion.

What proves even more ironic is that Shukumar's growing alienation toward his wife is exacerbated by the knowledge that it is reciprocated. The couple has reached a stalemate, an impasse that has quickly led to indifference. The two live separate lives, yet they pretend to participate in a marriage. When Shoba finally stops in to greet him at night, Shukumar tries to look busy. ''Don't work too hard,'' says Shoba ironically, aware, perhaps, that the dissertation is not progressing smoothly. Shukumar seeks to escape his wife's attention by moving his office to the nursery, a place Shoba avoids. ''It was the one time in the day she sought him out, and yet he'd come to dread it. He knew it was something she forced herself to do.'' Shoba and Shukumar occupy separate floors of the house, masquerading as a couple—that is, until the lights go out.

In addition to highlighting the couple's estrangement, the power outage adds an element of suspense as it draws the characters' differences sharply into focus. Eating dinner that first night in the dim glow of birthday candles which Shukumar must light constantly, Shoba is reminded of the

> Thus, Lahiri enhances the story's ironic quality by creating a situation whereby her characters, isolated in darkness yet sustained by the customs of their native land, must confront each other with the truth."

power failures she experienced as a child in India. To pass the time, her grandmother would have Shoba and the other members of her family tell a joke, recite a fact, or tell a story for all to enjoy. Wishing to break the awkward silence between her and her husband, Shoba suddenly has the idea that she and Shukumar should pass the evening in the same manner, the only difference being that they must tell each other something they've never told before. While it is ironic that they never thought to make such personal revelations until the lights go out, the idea of a married couple divulging their deepest secrets to each other adds an air of mystery to the darkness that surrounds them and heightens the suspense of what will actually be revealed.

Upon hearing his wife's idea, Shukumar observes that Shoba ''hadn't appeared so determined in months,'' unaware of the real purpose behind her suggestion. An air of suspense enhances the story further as Shukumar reluctantly agrees to play the game even though he doesn't have a childhood story about India to share. ''What didn't they know about each other?'' he thinks, foreshadowing the story's conclusion. Thus, Lahiri enhances the story's ironic quality by creating a situation whereby her characters, isolated in darkness yet sustained by the customs of their native land, must confront each other with the truth.

At first the revelations are harmless and insignificant. They involve minor intrusions of privacy or lapses in thought, white lies told in brief moments of selfishness, or desperate, unconscious attempts to preserve one's sense of dignity. With each night that passes, the truths that Shoba and Shukumar exchange become bolder and more honest as the couple struggles to relate and communicate. "Somehow, without saying anything, it had turned into this. Into an exchange of confessions—*the little ways* they'd hurt or disappointed each other, and themselves" (emphasis added).

As the nightly game progresses, Shukumar contemplates what he should say to his wife. He seems happy to at last be relieved of the secrets that have burdened him for so long. He is so happy, in fact, that he cannot decide the order in which to make his confessions. Moreover, the thought of what Shoba will say next excites him, creating a sense of anticipation which the reader shares. Each revelation appears to bring them closer together (though, as the story's ironic conclusion demonstrates, any hope of a reunion is beyond reach). "Something happened when the house was dark," says the narrator. "They were able to talk to each other again." This improved communication between Shoba and Shukumar inspires displays of affection long absent from their marriage. She is kind and patient with him, holding his hand in hers to show understanding, whereas he takes even more pride in planning and preparing the meals they now enjoy by candlelight. On the third night, Shoba and Shukumar kiss awkwardly on the sofa like a couple exploring each other's bodies for the first time. On the fourth night, they climb the stairs to bed and make love "with a desperation they had forgotten," apparently having forgiven each other for their acts of neglect and selfishness.

But, on the morning of the fifth night, they receive a notice from the utility company stating that the repairs have been completed early, signaling an end to their apparently rekindled romance. "I suppose this is the end of our game," Shukumar says when he sees Shoba reading the notice. It is ironic that Shukumar should make this statement, because he doesn't know the half of it, for the period of harmony and affection that Shoba and Shukumar have experienced is, like the power outage that brought it about, "a temporary matter," the calm before the storm—the one that heralds the end of their marriage. Together, they have played a game in which they have pretended to want the same things when neither one of them has had the courage to state the obvious: their marriage is over. Moreover, the loss of their child has proved insurmountable, for neither spouse is willing to suffer that kind of pain and sorrow again. "Only he didn't want her to be pregnant again," the narrator says as Shukumar anxiously awaits Shoba's final declaration. "He didn't want to have to pretend to be happy."

As she prepares to make her final revelation, Shoba changes the candlelight ritual, insisting that they leave the lights on, moving them at once to a less intimate but more vulnerable position, since neither is able to hide: "I want you to see my face when I tell you this," she says gently, though she refuses to look him in the eye.

When Shoba tells Shukumar that she has signed a lease for an apartment on Beacon Hill, he understands immediately that the confessions they've made recently have served as a preamble for a far more disingenuous revelation. Shoba has not made her confessions in an attempt to restore their relationship but to prepare herself for a transition to a more independent life. Lahiri uses suspense to heighten the irony of the scene as the reader anticipates Shukumar's reaction.

> It sickened Shukumar, knowing that she had spent these past evenings preparing for a life without him. He was relieved and yet he was sickened. This was what she'd been trying to tell him for the past four evenings. This was the point of her game.

The irony of their situation is painfully clear to see. The "little ways" in which they have disappointed each other have become for Shukumar acts of betrayal, leading to Shoba's final act of betrayal.

But Shoba, in making her latest revelation, has unwittingly brought about a reversal in power—the power to wound—which Shoba thinks is hers exclusively. As though the game were continuing, Shukumar counters Shoba's announcement with one of his own that proves devastating in the end.

Though the death of their child has been difficult for Shoba to accept, there is also an undercurrent of resentment, as expressed by her mother, that the loss would have been somewhat easier to bear had Shukumar been at the hospital for the delivery. Shoba believes that she has experienced her loss alone. Moreover, she seeks consolation in the thought that the baby's gender has remained unknown, therefore preventing her from forming too deep an attachment to her dead child, for, when an ultrasound was taken, Shoba declined the doctor's offer to know the child's sex. "In a way she almost took pride in her decision, for it enabled her to seek refuge in a mystery," says the narrator. But now Lahiri adds a twist, making the revelation that, although Shoba "assumed it was a mystery for him, too," Shukumar knew. Ironically, now it is Shukumar who has the power to wound.

Thus the stage is set for Shukumar's final, heartbreaking revelation. "There was something he'd sworn he would never tell her, and for six months he had done his best to block it from his mind,'' says the narrator, yet the present circumstances weaken Shukumar's resolve to the breaking point. Contrary to what Shoba and her mother believe, Shukumar arrived at the hospital shortly after the baby was born, only to find his wife asleep, and was then taken to see their child with the hope that ''holding the baby might help him with the process of grieving.'' That day Shukumar ''promised himself . . . that he would never tell Shoba, because he still loved her then, and it was the one thing in her life that she had wanted to be a surprise.'' Shoba's decision to move out makes her husband realize that their marriage is, indeed, loveless. There is nothing left to bind him to his promise. Shoba, who is ''the type to prepare for surprises, good and bad,'' finds herself unprepared for the biggest surprise of all.

When Shukumar describes for Shoba how he had held their son, his tiny fingers ''curled shut'' like hers while she sleeps, he sees his wife's face ''contorted with sorrow,'' for, though she has initiated their separation, she fully comprehends the loss that has engulfed them. Without a word, she turns out the lights and sits down at the table, where Shukumar joins her. ''They wept together,'' says the narrator, ''for the things they now knew.''

This poignant scene, at once tender and yet filled with an abandonment marked by despair, could not have been rendered as artfully had the author not led up to the ironic conclusion by delineating the emotional predicament of her characters and creating a sense of suspense in the reader about what would happen to their marriage. In the hands of an author less skilled than Jhumpa Lahiri, the result would have been cool detachment rather than one of profound empathy.

Source: David Remy, Critical Essay on ''A Temporary Matter,'' in *Short Stories for Students*, Gale, 2004.

Sources

Crain, Caleb, ''Subcontinental Drift,'' in *New York Times Book Review*, July 11, 1999.

Hajari, Nisid, ''The Promising Land,'' in *Time International*, Vol. 154, No. 10, September 13, 1999, p. 49.

Heltzel, Ellen Emry, ''A Voice Echoing in the Culture Chasm,'' in the *Oregonian*, July 11, 1999.

Kipen, David, ''Interpreting Indian Culture with Stories,'' in the *San Francisco Chronicle*, June 24, 1999, p. E-1.

Lahiri, Jhumpa, *Interpreter of Maladies*, Houghton Mifflin, 1999, pp. 1–22.

Minzesheimer, Bob, ''For Pulitzer Winner Lahiri, a Novel Approach,'' in *USA Today*, August 19, 2003.

Further Reading

Bala, Suman, *Jhumpa Lahiri, the Master Storyteller: A Critical Response to ''Interpreter of Maladies,''* Khosla Publishing House, 2002.
> Indian literary scholar Suman Bala has collected thirty essays by Indian critics and scholars discussing Lahiri's story collection. The volume is valuable in providing Western readers with Indian perspectives on Lahiri's work.

Jayapal, Pramila, *Pilgrimage: One Woman's Return to a Changing India*, Seal Press, 2000.
> Jayapal was born in Madras in southern India, grew up in Indonesia and Singapore, and came to the United States as a teenager to complete her education. At the age of thirty, Jayapal returned to India for two years with a fellowship that allowed her to travel throughout the country and write about her experiences and observations. Jayapal is an international development specialist, and her narrative is a mixture of scholarly observation and personal narrative—the latter including the hair-raising tale of her son's birth. The book is a useful portrait of India today.

Patel, Vibhuti, ''Maladies of Belonging,'' in *Newsweek International*, September 20, 1999, p. 8.
> In this wide-ranging interview published soon after the publication of *Interpreter of Maladies*, Lahiri answers questions about her relationship to India and her approach to writing.

Zimbardo, Xavier, *India Holy Song*, Rizzoli, 2000.
> Lahiri wrote the foreword to this book of photographs taken throughout India over a fifteen-year period. The forward tells of her childhood visits to Calcutta and her responses to India.

The Ultimate Safari

Nadine Gordimer

1989

Nadine Gordimer's short story "The Ultimate Safari," first published in Great Britain's literary publication *Granta* in 1989, and later included in her 1991 collection, *Jump and Other Stories*, follows the story of an unnamed narrator and her family as they leave their Mozambique village for a refugee camp across the border in South Africa. In an unrecorded talk she gave at the University of the Witwatersrand in Johannesburg in 1991, Gordimer attributed the inspiration for the story to a visit she made to a camp for Mozambique refugees. The so-called "bandits" alluded to by the story's main character and narrator are, presumably, members of Renamo, the Mozambique rebel group that tried for years, with the clandestine support of South Africa, to overthrow Mozambique's Marxist government. By the time the events of this story take place, liberation movements in countries across Africa had long since swept whites from power, with South Africa being the single exception. Throughout the 1970s and 1980s, in an attempt to protect itself and its white power structure, the South African government supported the destabilization efforts of rebels in its black-controlled, neighboring countries by financing armed incursions and raids, such as the ones that the narrator describes in the story.

"The Ultimate Safari," like nearly all of Gordimer's work, addresses the effects South Africa's system of apartheid had on its people and its neighbors. Published in book form the year she was awarded the Nobel Prize for Literature, the story

continues Gordimer's long-standing efforts to gauge the effects of apartheid by delving into the minds of characters of all races and genders; in this case, Gordimer takes on the persona and adopts the voice of a young black Mozambique girl to narrate the family's arduous trek through Kruger Park and to the refugee camp.

Author Biography

Nadine Gordimer was born in Springs, South Africa on November 20, 1923 to Isidore Gordimer, an immigrant Jewish watchmaker, and Nan Myers, who had immigrated to South Africa from Great Britain as a young child. The younger of two girls, Gordimer led a solitary life growing up due to a prognosis, at the age of 10, of heart problems. As a result of her condition, Gordimer's mother put an end to her daughter's strenuous activities, including dancing lessons, pulled her out of the convent school she had been attending, and a hired a tutor for her for three hours a day. From the ages of 11 to 16, Gordimer had very little contact with children of her own age and spent most of her time either with her parents or alone.

Although Gordimer would later describe the severe loneliness she experienced during those years, she used her time to read and write voraciously, and at the age of 13, she published her first short story in the *Johannesburg Sunday Express*. By the time Gordimer was 16, she stopped being tutored entirely, and except for a year of general studies at the University of the Witwatersrand in Johannesburg in 1945, Gordimer never took another class of formal education.

In 1949, the year following the election of South Africa's National Party—the political party that would formalize South Africa's system of racial segregation, or apartheid—Gordimer published her first collection of short stories, *Face to Face*, and a few years later, in 1953, her first novel, *The Lying Days*, was published.

In 1949, Gordimer married Gerald Gavron (also known as Gavronsky), and in 1950 her daughter, Oriane, was born. Gordimer and Gavron divorced in 1952. In 1954, Gordimer married the

Nadine Gordimer

German art dealer, Reinhold Cassirer, with whom she had a son, Hugo. Gordimer and Cassirer remained married until his death in 2001.

In the fifty years since her first book was published, Gordimer has published more than 30 novels, short story collections, and collections of essays that have won numerous awards. Her 1960 collection *Friday's Footprint and Other Stories* won the W. H. Smith Literary Award. Her 1970 novel *A Guest of Honor* was awarded the James Tait Black Memorial Prize; *The Conservationist* received Great Britain's prestigious Booker–McConnell Prize in 1974, as well as South Africa's CNA Literary Prize. In 1991, Gordimer was awarded the Nobel Prize for Literature. Also in 1991, Gordimer published *Jump and Other Stories*, the collection which includes "The Ultimate Safari."

Long regarded as one of South Africa's leading political activists and intellectuals, Gordimer saw many of her books banned in her own country at the time of their publication due to her stance against the apartheid policies of the government. All of her books, including her collection of short stories titled *Loot and Other Stories* (2003)—published nearly a decade after apartheid's official demise—in some way address apartheid or its effects.

Plot Summary

''The Ultimate Safari'' opens with the narrator's cryptic and mysterious statement that tersely sets the tone of the story: ''That night our mother went to the shop and she didn't come back. Ever.'' The narrator of the story, a young black Mozambican girl, never finds out what happened to her mother, or to her father, who had also left one day never to return. The presumption, however, is that both her parents are dead by the time her story unfolds; her people are at war, and her village has been beset by ''bandits'' that have left the villagers destitute and frightened, and all evidence points to those so-called ''bandits'' as the cause of her parents' disappearance.

The story that the girl relates is a deceptively simple one: After losing everything at the hands of the bandits who have repeatedly raided their village, and in fear of their lives, the girl's family—her grandmother, grandfather, and older and younger brothers—set out on a long and arduous trek through Kruger Park, the popular national reserve in northeast South Africa that borders Mozambique and has for years been a tourist destination for rich foreigners wanting the experience of the ultimate African safari.

Along the way, the grandfather, who has been reduced to doing little more than making ''little noises'' while rocking ''from side to side,'' wanders off and is lost in some high grasses and must be left behind. The young girl recounts how little her family had to eat in the park, despite the aromas of campfire grills from the park's tourists. Even the buzzards, she notices, have more to eat than the refugees. Eventually, the remaining family members, all of whom remain nameless throughout the story, are led by the grandmother to a refugee camp where they are given space in a tent in which to live. There the grandmother eventually ekes out a living carrying bricks while the girl attends school. At the story's conclusion, we learn for the first time some of the basic facts about the girl and her family when ''some white people'' come to the camp to film the camp and a reporter interviews the grandmother. For instance, we learn definitively that the girl and her family are black, that they are originally from Mozambique, and that the story has taken place over the course of nearly three years.

''The Ultimate Safari'' is set along the Mozambique–South African border sometime during the 1980s, at a time when Mozambique was ruled by a black Marxist government and South Africa was the lone remaining African country still being run by its minority white population. The ''bandits'' alluded to by the narrator are members of Renamo, the rebel group supported by the white South African government whose goal it was to destabilize Mozambique by pillaging rural villages and causing civil unrest. One of the consequences of these incursions, or ''raids'' as the narrator calls them, was a large-scale exodus by poor villagers from Mozambique into refugee camps that lined the border between the two countries. Many of these refugees languished for years in the camp while South Africa continued its military and economic domination of the region. Some estimates suggest that the civil war that was fueled by Renamo was responsible for a million deaths in Mozambique alone. In 1992, when apartheid was officially abolished and blacks began to exert control over the South African political structure, the destabilizing efforts were halted, though the region continues to suffer the consequences of the years of instability.

Characters

The Bandits

So called by the government, the bandits raided the narrator's village repeatedly, forced her and her family into hiding, and ultimately forced them into the long trek that takes up most of the story. The identity of the bandits is never revealed specifically, although they are presumed to be one of the Mozambique rebel factions supported by the South African government, trying to overtake the government by wreaking havoc in the rural areas.

The Daughter

A young girl of nine or ten when the story opens, the daughter, who is also the story's narrator, reveals very little about herself, but it is through her eyes that the story of her and her family's arduous trek away from their village to the refugee camp is told. She understands very little about the war, or the reasons behind it, except to comment about the fear the bandits have instilled into her people and to describe the effects their raids have had on her life. An astute observer, she conveys much of the tone of the story through her descriptions of the trek: her grandfather rocking to and fro making little noises; flies buzzing on her grandmother's face; her older brother becoming silent like their grandfather. Although we ultimately learn very little about the narrator herself, it is through her descriptions that the story unfolds.

The Father

Although he never appears in the story, the father's absence, and presumed death in the war, is significant as it helps to set the tone of the story, and without him, the narrator's family must survive on their own.

The Grandfather

Once the owner of three sheep, a cow, and a vegetable garden—all of which have been taken away by the bandits by the time the story takes place—the grandfather does little more than rock side to side and make little noises in this story. He is clearly suffering from some form of dementia or the effects of a mental breakdown, and in the course of the trek through Kruger Park, he wanders off through the high grasses, becomes lost, and must be left behind by the family.

The Grandmother

As the matriarch of her extended family that includes her husband and her grandchildren—the narrator, and the narrator's younger and older brothers—the grandmother is the strongest adult character in the story. It is through her vision and leadership that the family is able to escape the danger wrought by the rebels and travel through Kruger Park to a refugee camp across the border. Once her family settles into the refugee camp, she finds work hauling bricks, and she oversees her grandchildren's education.

The Little Brother

Less than a year old when the family is forced to leave their village, the little brother is three when the story ends. In that time he suffers greatly from malnutrition, and as he grows older, his older sister notices that he barely speaks, a result, she believes, of having too little food during their journey.

Media Adaptations

- The Nobel Prize committee maintains a Gordimer web page at http://www.nobel.se/literature/laureates/1991/ with a link to her Nobel Prize speech and other related sites.

- In a separate section of the Nobel Prize web site, at http://www.nobel.se/literature/articles/wastberg/index.html, writer and vice president of International PEN Per Wästberg offers an extensive overview of Gordimer's career.

The Mother

Similar to the father, we know nothing about the mother except that she left one day for the store and never returned, forcing the narrator's grandparents to take over responsibilities for the children during the war.

Themes

Apartheid

Between 1948 and 1992, the Republic of South Africa had an institutionalized system of racial segregation known as "apartheid"—the Afrikaner word meaning "separateness." Effectively stripping all South African blacks, coloreds, and Indians of their citizenship rights, apartheid was instrumental in helping whites to maintain power in the predominantly black country. As countries across Africa regained their independence from Europeans, the South African government, fearing the liberating influence of its recently liberated black neighbors on its own black population, financially and militarily supported the efforts of rebel groups to destabilize neighboring governments. This desperate measure to protect the apartheid system and

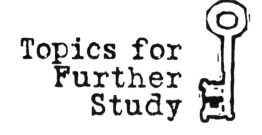

Topics for Further Study

- A major foreign policy concern of the South African government from the 1970s through the end of apartheid in 1992 was the burgeoning liberation and Marxist movements in its neighboring countries. Why was South Africa concerned about these movements? Which countries, in particular, was it most concerned about? What types of policies did the government pursue to contain those movements?

- For years Gordimer was a member of the outlawed African National Congress, or the ANC. Research the history of the ANC under apartheid. What was its political mission? Did its goals change once apartheid was banned? What is the ANC's role in South Africa today?

- Although Gordimer is one of South Africa's best-known writers, because of censorship laws, many of her stories were first published by British and American publications long before they were published widely in her own country. Research the role censorship played in apartheid South Africa. Were there periods of time during South Africa's history when the censorship rules were more strictly enforced than during others? If so, why?

- Look up the term "interregnum," and read Gordimer's essay entitled "Living in the Interregnum" from her collection *The Essential Gesture: Writing, Politics and Places*. To what does Gordimer refer when she talks about the interregnum? Explain how she uses the term in relation to the context of both South Africa and of the world.

- Gordimer is one of the few women writers to have been awarded the Nobel Prize in literature. Research the other women Nobel laureates. Are there any similarities in their writing styles or the subject matters they address? Do politics play a role in their writings?

- In 1968, American writer William Styron was awarded the Pulitzer Prize for his novel *The Confessions of Nat Turner*. Like Gordimer does in "The Ultimate Safari," Styron, who is white, writes from the perspective of a black character. Despite the critical acclaim it received, Styron's book also received widespread criticism for its portrayal of Turner. Research the critical reviews of Styron's book. What were the main reasons for the criticism? Could that criticism also be applied to Gordimer?

---

the white control of the South African economic and political structures resulted in the long-term displacement and deaths of millions of southern Africans over the years. Nearly all of Gordimer's work addresses, in some way, the effects apartheid has had on whites and blacks alike.

Family

Prior to the events of the story, the narrator had lost both her father and her mother to the war. Her grandmother and grandfather took over parenting responsibilities, and when the grandfather lost his only means of livelihood to the bandits, he suffered from a mental breakdown of some sort, and the grandmother took over sole responsibility of raising

the family. It was through the commitment of the grandmother to keeping her family together that the narrator and her siblings were able to trek hundreds of miles across the wilds of Kruger Park to the relative safety of the refugee camp.

Homelessness

One of the major effects of the South African policy of apartheid was the displacement of millions of blacks in the region. In South Africa itself, where apartheid dictated where blacks were legally allowed to live, many poor families were forced to live illegally in shanty towns outside of cities where they hoped to find work, living effectively as homeless people in corrugated iron shacks and temporary structures. In the larger southern African region, many poor villagers were forced by military incursions financed by South Africa to abandon their homes in favor of refugee camps where they lived for years in desperate conditions. At the end of the story, a white reporter asks the grandmother if she ever wants to return home. While the young girl dreams of a day she will be reunited with her mother and grandfather in their home village, the grandmother responds directly by saying, "There is nothing. No home."

Lawlessness

Even though many countries around the world—particularly in Africa—have successfully liberated themselves from their European colonial rulers, most of them are still economically and militarily vulnerable to outside forces. In southern Africa, many of the border areas surrounding South Africa were effectively reduced to anarchy and lawlessness by the repeated incursions by quasi-military groups funded and supported by the South African government. While some of the military groups had legitimate political issues they were addressing, most of them were little more than groups of vigilantes whose sole aim was to destabilize the areas through brutal force that included raids, pillaging, and military attacks. It was this environment of lawlessness that finally forced the narrator and her family to make the arduous trek with other refugee families through Kruger Park and to the refugee camps in South Africa.

Oppression

One of the goals of apartheid was to help whites, who made up less than 20 percent of the South African population, maintain complete economic and military control. The effect of their policies was the widespread oppression of otherwise innocent blacks in both South Africa itself as well as in the neighboring countries.

Racial Conflict

Apartheid effectively contributed to the complete economic and political control by whites of the non-white population in and around South Africa through the institutionalization of race-based classification systems and laws. Apartheid effectively fueled racist tendencies among the populace, and one of the effects was the dehumanization, in the eyes of the white populations, of blacks. Although there is no "racial conflict" per se in "The Ultimate Safari," the widespread racial conflicts that the area had been experiencing for years led to the environment that forced whole families and villages into desperate living situations. Without that racial conflict, it would have been difficult for whites to justify the widespread refugee problem, and there would have been greater pressures for more humane and peaceful solutions to the problems South Africa believed it was facing.

Rites of Passage

The family's trip through the wilds of Kruger Park can be viewed allegorically as a rite of passage for the young narrator. Through the journey, the girl must confront the loss of yet another family member—her grandfather—and she must take over the parenting responsibilities of her younger brother whom she must physically support. The narrator, though she is only 11 years old at the story's completion and although she still clings to the naïve hope that she has a home to return to where her grandfather and mother will be waiting, has begun the process of passing through the rites that will eventually lead her to womanhood.

Role of Women

In a society ruled by war, the women of the villages were forced to take over all parenting responsibilities, becoming both the homemaker and wage earner. In "The Ultimate Safari," the burden of this dual responsibility falls onto the shoulders of the grandmother, who must not only lead her grandchildren to safety, but who must also take over the care of her own husband whose dementia has rendered him useless. To a lesser degree, the narrator must also take over parenting responsibilities by carrying and caring for her infant brother who begins to grow weak from malnutrition during their trek.

Warfare

The warfare that the villages experience in the course of Gordimer's story is "guerilla" warfare; that is, the Renamo rebels trying to overthrow the government do so in ways that create instability in the outlying areas without ever directly confronting the government's military forces themselves. Guerilla warfare is an effective military tool for groups of limited resources, as fewer soldiers are needed to inflict serious damage, and the psychological effects on the population are far greater than they are through conventional warfare.

Style

Diction

Throughout the telling of her story, the narrator of "The Ultimate Safari" employs a simple, colloquial diction with sentences that are sparse and stripped of all ornamentation. In fact, the diction that Gordimer has given the narrator contributes to the surprise readers may experience upon learning that the narrator is a black Mozambique refugee. While the story she tells is consistent with a refugee's experience, her diction hints at her being a young white English-speaking girl. There are no idiomatic expressions, slang phrases, or sentence constructions that hint at the narrator's being black or Mozambican. One effect the girl's diction has is to break down the barrier between the non-African white readers and the narrator: by portraying the girl as being more like her largely white American and European readers, Gordimer has succeed in creating a more sympathetic character than would have otherwise been possible.

Dialogue

Although the narrator summarizes conversations she overhears or is a part of, there is no dialogue to speak of in the story until the final scene when a filmmaker interviews the grandmother. This technique offers perhaps a truer representation of how a girl of the narrator's age would recall conversations, and it also has the effect of giving the story more of a dream-like or mythic atmosphere. By not engaging us directly in the conversations as they happened, the narrator effectively keeps the entire story in her head, presenting it to us entirely from memory. And even with the small amount of dialogue at the story's conclusion, Gordimer chooses not to use quotation marks to set the dialogue off, giving the story the continued dream-like effect.

Imagery

Gordimer uses stark, often-violent imagery to help set the tone of the story and to help us understand the grim circumstances the girl and her family are facing. The narrator, for instance, begins her description of entering Kruger Park by telling of a man in her village who lost his legs to crocodiles, reminding the reader of the dangers lurking before them and adding to the story's menacing tone. Once in the park, she describes the animals surrounding them as being continually on the prowl for food while she and her family have nothing to eat. "We had passed [the vultures] often where they were feeding on the bones of dead animals, nothing was ever left there for us to eat," she tells readers.

Irony

By giving the story the title, "The Ultimate Safari," and by prefacing it with an epigraph from a London travel advertisement luring rich tourists to Africa for the "ultimate safari," Gordimer is employing irony to underscore the vast differences between the wealthy, foreign whites and the poor, black refugees that populate southern Africa. For many people from the narrator's village who were forced out of their homes and into Kruger Park for the arduous journey to the refugee camps, this would certainly be their "ultimate," or last, "safari." Many, such as the narrator's grandfather, would die in the park itself, and many would ultimately die in the refugee camp, never able to see their homes again. Meanwhile, as the group travels through the game reserve that rich European tourists spend thousands of dollars to visit, the roasting meats of the tourists waft by, and the refugee children grow hungrier and hungrier, with less even to eat than the buzzards.

Point of View

By employing the first person point of view, and using a young black refugee girl as the story's narrator, Gordimer is able to imagine for herself and for us what it is to be "the other." Since the story is not told from a third-person omniscient point of view, the experience of being a refugee fleeing war is personalized, and the reader is able to experience not only the facts of the journey, but also, in a limited way, the emotions and personal experiences of the girl herself.

Tone

Gordimer effectively sets the tone of the story with the first two sentences: "That night our mother went to the shop and she didn't come back. Ever." In a quiet, dispassionate, almost distant tone of voice, without a hint of sentiment or pity, the narrator has just reported the presumed death of her mother. The remainder of the story is told in a similar, matter-of-fact way: regardless of how despairing her circumstances are, there is a profound sense of acceptance and fatalism hinted at in the girl's voice. At the same time, the sentences introduce the continual sense of loss that the narrator will experience throughout the course of the story, as well as a menacing aspect. This will be a stark story, one filled with loss and foreboding, and the telling of it will offer very little in the way of analysis or description. One purpose of using this tone to tell the story is to help underscore the girl's overall sense of optimism. At the end of the story she continues to dream of a day she can be reunited, in her home, with her mother, father, and grandfather. The girl, despite her hardships and her bleak surroundings, never gives up hope, however illusory that hope may be.

Historical Context

South African Apartheid

It is impossible to understand Nadine Gordimer's fiction without having an understanding of the system of racial segregation, known as apartheid, under which South Africans lived between 1948 and 1992. Gordimer's work, perhaps more than the work of any other South African writer (including fellow white writers André Brink and J. M. Coetzee), is inextricably linked to her political views and lifelong resistance to apartheid. With the lone exception of an early autobiographical work, all of Gordimer's work addresses the effect of apartheid on South Africans of all classes and races, so much so that the Vice President of International PEN Per Wästberg, writing on the official Nobel Prize web site, calls Gordimer "the Geiger counter of apartheid."

Briefly, apartheid was a system of laws set up by the South African government designed to control the movements of the majority, non-white population. The laws dictated where blacks, Indians, and so-called "coloreds" could live and work and who they could marry. The purpose of apartheid was to allow the minority white population, which comprised less than 20 percent of the population, to consolidate political power and control over the majority population.

As liberation movements during the 1960s and 1970s spread through Africa, many colonial powers lost control of their power bases and were forced to cede power to blacks. South Africa remained the lone exception, and until civil unrest began to spread through the country in the late 1980s and effectively undermine the government's control over the black population, the South African government continued to exert its political hold. However, the liberation movements throughout the continent spread to the South African borders, with Mozambique and Zimbabwe being transformed into black-controlled, leftist governments. As a defensive mechanism designed to keep the ideas of liberation and equality from being spread through its own black population, South Africa financially and militarily supported rebel groups in the border areas of Mozambique and Zimbabwe; throughout the late 1970s and 1980s the rural populations of those countries suffered through the effects of guerilla warfare. Entire villages were uprooted, and refugee camps made up of civilians fleeing the war were established along the South African borders.

This is the political and military background to "The Ultimate Safari." The narrator's family are, by all accounts, nonpolitical rural peasants who are forced into the war. The father is presumably killed in combat, and though the mother's fate is less clear, it is presumed that she was kidnapped or killed by the rebel forces. After a series of rebel raids that have left the villages destitute, the narrator's family, along with other members of their village, are forced to make the long trek through Kruger Park to one of the South African refugee camps.

Censorship and the Works of Nadine Gordimer

As part of the efforts to control its black population, the South African government strictly controlled the news and dissemination of information during much of Gordimer's writing career. The press was either state-run or state-controlled, and severe measures of censorship were taken to control the information coming into and going out of the country. An outspoken critic of censorship, Gordimer saw several of her works banned upon publication, including her novel *Burger's Daughter*, which was banned as a result of the Soweto uprisings. Because of this publishing climate, many of Gordimer's novels and stories, including "The Ultimate Safari" and several other of the stories that make up the collection *Jump and Other Stories*, were published in Great Britain and the United States before being published in her native South Africa.

Ironically, for several years following the demise of apartheid in 1992, Gordimer's 1981 novel *July's People* was banned in a South Africa school district for being "deeply racist, superior and

Compare
&
Contrast

- **1980s:** Apartheid laws are still in effect in South Africa, with the majority population unable to vote or move about freely.

  Today: Apartheid has been abolished, and blacks are allowed to vote in local and national elections.

- **1980s:** Many important works of literature, including works by Nadine Gordimer, are banned in South Africa.

  Today: With the exception of some school districts occasionally calling for the censorship of certain works, South Africans can read and write without fear of official, state-sanctioned censorship.

- **1980s:** Mozambique and Zimbabwe villagers

living along the South African borders are frequently displaced because of the guerilla warfare supported by the South African government.

Today: South Africa has long stopped its incursions into neighboring countries, and villagers are no longer forced away from their homes by guerilla raids.

- **1980s:** The African National Congress, of which Gordimer is a long-standing member, is considered illegal by the government, and its members are considered outlaws.

  Today: The African National Congress, which Gordimer continues to support, is the majority political party in South Africa.

---

patronising. . . .'' The ban, which also affected several other notable works, including Shakespeare's *Hamlet,* was eventually lifted after hundreds of writers from around the world protested, but not before Gordimer publicly compared the school board to the censors of the old apartheid regime.

Critical Overview

Because it was released shortly before Gordimer was awarded the Nobel Prize for Literature, *Jump and Other Stories*, the collection in which ''The Ultimate Safari'' was published, is not considered to be one of Gordimer's major works. Nonetheless, the book received widespread reviews in the major media of the day, and several reviewers remarked specifically on the story itself.

John Banville, writing in the *New York Review of Books,* wrote that the story, one of the ''three fine stories'' in the collection, ''fairly quivers with angry polemic, yet achieves an almost biblical force through the simplicity and specificity of the narrative voice.''

Writing in *America,* Jerome Donnelly writes that the collection as a whole achieves a ''unity'' that is ''remarkable'' considering the multiplicity of voices Gordimer uses, and the ''simple, controlled narrative of wonderment filtered through a mind too unknowing to be terrified generates powerful understatement,'' and that the story moves on ''without indulging the temptation to sentimentalize the moment.''

The Spectator critic Hilary Mantel described Gordimer's new stories as having ''complexity and resonance, sometimes grandeur,'' and that they are all ''worth reading and re-reading.'' She describes the new work ''as trenchant and committed as her novels,'' and the sentences of *''The Ultimate Safari''* as ''stripped down, simplified. . . . ''

Dan Cryer, on the other hand, in a review for *Newsday,* suggested that while much of Gordimer's work had made her ''Nobel Prize–worthy,'' it was important to separate Gordimer's ''superb novels'' such as *A Sport of Nature* and *The Conservationist* from works such as *Jump and Other Stories.* ''The majority of these stories,'' Cryer writes in reference to several of the collections stories, including ''The

Mozambican refugees flee the civil war and resettle at a refugee camp

Ultimate Safari," "achieve the limited objective of bringing the headlines to vivid life."

Critic Jeanne Colleran, in an essay included in the collection *The Later Fiction of Nadine Gordimer,* discusses Gordimer's views that a short story collection, in many ways, is more able to convey the multiple truths of South Africa than a novel due to its ability to represent "the even greater multiplicity of voices, attitudes, and constituencies that comprise South African society. . . ." While much of the collection, with the "obsessive image of recent South African history, the dead . . . children [that] haunt the collection," portrays the dire legacy of apartheid, "The Ultimate Safari," written through the eyes of a young black southern African girl, offers some hope for the future. The girl, despite her refugee status, fully plans to return home where she believes her missing mother and grandfather are waiting.

In a major critical review in the *Journal of Southern African Studies* titled *"Jump and Other Stories:* Gordimer's Leap into the 1990s: Gender and Politics in Her Latest Short Fiction," University of the Witwatersrand professor Karen Lazar contextualizes the collection with respect to South Africa's political climate at the time, as well as Gordimer's previous work. In particular, Lazar is interested in exploring the trajectory of Gordimer's political thought, particularly the evolution of her views of women.

While Lazar believes that the collection shows that Gordimer's political thinking has continued to evolve, Lazar finds her continued representation of women as tending more to the "uni-dimensional" relative to her treatment of men, and that "various aspects of South African womanhood [in *Jump and Other Stories*] are split off, dichotomised and assigned to individual figures, such that the representations of women tend to be truncated, reduced and static, giving women a marginal and decentered status relative to the more lively and layered status of men." While in many respects Gordimer "jumps" into the 1990s with this collection, according to Lazar, Gordimer's sometimes "static" and "truncated" representations of women continue to be a concern.

Criticism

Mark White
White is the publisher of the Seattle-based literary press, Scala House Press. In this essay,

What Do I Read Next?

- Gordimer's essay collection *The Essential Gesture: Writing, Politics and Places* (1988) includes the often-quoted essay "Living in the Interregnum," in which she discusses the role of revolution in the South African political context, and the responsibility she felt as a writer to come to terms with it.

- To fully understand Gordimer's fiction, one must understand her political convictions and how they have affected her growth as a writer. *Conversations with Nadine Gordimer,* published in 1990, gives a good background to Gordimer's evolution as a political thinker and as a writer just prior to her writing of "The Ultimate Safari."

- Of the many novels that Gordimer has written in her career, *The Burger's Daughter* is considered one of her best and was one of her most controversial at the time of its publication. Banned by the South African government, *The Burger's Daughter* follows the story of Rosa Burger, the daughter of a martyred revolutionary leader, as she tries to pursue an apolitical existence of her own.

- Gordimer's story collection *Selected Stories* (1975) offers the full range of Gordimer's style and subject matter. Although some of the stories are thirty years older than "The Ultimate Safari," the collection provides a good overview to the evolution and breadth of Gordimer's writing.

- Like "The Ultimate Safari," J. M. Coetzee's Booker Prize–winning novel, *The Life and Time of Michael K* (1983), tells the story of a black family displaced by war. Coetzee, along with André Brink and Gordimer, has long been considered to be one of South Africa's leading white intellectuals and opponents of apartheid.

White argues that Gordimer's decision not to reveal the race of the narrator in "The Ultimate Safari" resulted in the creation of a more empathetic character with whom her white American and British readers could identify.

The art of "writing in voice," or "writing in character," is a common literary technique that has been used by countless writers over the years. In one of literature's most famous examples, Herman Melville adopts the persona of Ishmael, an itinerant seaman, in *Moby Dick,* and in two of the more popular examples from the late twentieth century, Alice Walker, in *The Color Purple,* adopts the voice of Celie, an uneducated, abused southern girl, and Arthur Golden writes from the perspective of a Japanese geisha in *Memoirs of a Geisha.*

While it is not at all uncommon for a writer to take on the character of someone outside his or her own economic and social status, as Walker did, what is far less common is for a writer to adopt the character of a different ethnic background or race, as was the case with Golden. And least common of all—perhaps because of the highly contentious and politically charged nature of black-white relationships—is when a white writer adopts the voice of a black character, as Nadine Gordimer does in her short story "The Ultimate Safari."

In "The Ultimate Safari," Gordimer, a white South African writer well into her sixties when the story was published, takes on the voice of a young nameless black refugee girl from Mozambique. While Gordimer had written from a black perspective several times throughout her career, what sets this particular story apart is the fact that through most of its telling, the reader is not made fully aware of the narrator's race. While the few details of the story's setting and the narrator's circumstances that are offered from the outset hint strongly that she is black, it is not until the story's final scenes that the girl's nationality and race are confirmed. Gordimer's conscious manipulation of these facts is one of the techniques she uses that ultimately gives this story its poignancy. By keeping the reader uncertain about the girl's background, Gordimer effectively holds out the possibility in the reader's mind, on some level, that the narrator could be "the girl next door" and not simply another distant and nameless African refugee. While this may seem insignificant to the overall meaning of the story itself, in light of the fact that the vast majority of the story's readers at the time of its publication were not only white, but also non-South African, this technique effectively helped Gordimer to maximize the empathy the story's readers felt for the character and effectively contributed to her agenda of enlightening the world to the dehumanizing effects of her country's system of apartheid.

Throughout most of her fifty-year career, Gordimer has used her writing to explore, expose, and oppose South Africa's long-standing system of racial segregation known as apartheid. With the major exception of her early autobiographical work, *The Lying Days*, nearly all of Gordimer's fiction in some way addresses apartheid, so much so that fellow writer and the Vice-President of International PEN Per Wästberg, writing on the official Nobel Prize web site, calls Gordimer "the Geiger counter of apartheid."

Officially struck down in 1992 after nearly 50 years as the government's official policy of racial segregation, apartheid—the Afrikaner word meaning "separateness"—was a system of laws that effectively stripped all South African blacks of their citizenship rights and was instrumental in maintaining white control over the majority black population. However, throughout the 1970s and 1980s, as countries across Africa regained their independence from Europeans, the South African government, fearing that their recently liberated neighbors such as Zimbabwe and Mozambique would encourage liberation movements in its own country, responded by financially and militarily supporting the efforts of rebel groups to destabilize those countries. These desperate measures to protect the apartheid system, which often took the form of military raids into the rural border areas, resulted in the long-term displacement and deaths of millions of southern Africans over the years, with an estimated million deaths accounted for in the Mozambique civil war that was fueled by South Africa. Fleeing from their war-ravaged homes, many villagers who survived the war in Mozambique ended up as refugees in any number of the South African refugee camps.

A related piece of historical information that should also be kept in mind when reading "The

> " By keeping the reader uncertain about the girl's background, Gordimer effectively holds out the possibility in the reader's mind, on some level, that the narrator could be 'the girl next door' and not simply another distant and nameless African refugee."

Ultimate Safari" is that, because of her public opposition to the government, coupled with the overtly political themes of her work, many of Gordimer' stories and novels were banned in her own country at the time of their publication; as a result, the first readers to most of Gordimer's work were usually not South African but rather British and North American. "The Ultimate Safari," in fact, was first published in the British literary journal, *Granta* before being published in book form by American publisher Farrar, Straus, and Giroux in the collection *Jump and Other Stories*. It is with these facts in mind that the techniques Gordimer uses in "The Ultimate Safari" can be best understood.

"The Ultimate Safari" is written in a deceptively simple style. The story's first two sentences— "That night our mother went to the shop and she didn't come back. Ever."—not only set the mysterious and foreboding tone of the story that is about to be told, but they effectively announce Gordimer's style as well. The sentence structure and diction are simple, yet not so simple as to indicate that the narrator is a person of lesser intelligence or capabilities. The narrator speaks in plain, everyday English; there is nothing remarkable in terms of vocabulary, syntax, or dialect that would indicate her to be anything but an English speaker of ordinary intelligence and sensibilities. She does not speak in dialect; she could be from any number of English-speaking locations. And Gordimer leaves few idiosyncratic clues that give her racial, cultural, or ethnic identity away.

Aside from knowing that the story's author is South African, there is little to indicate at the outset of the story that the narrator herself is from the region. She tells us immediately of "the war" and of "the bandits," and she references her "village" and the "bush"—both of which would hint at an African setting of some kind—but because the overall tenor of the narrative voice is anything but African, it is easy to overlook these clues at first reading. As the story progresses, the girl gives us further clues as to the setting with her description of the "dried mealies" her grandmother boils for her and, most importantly, her family's journey through Kruger Park, one of South Africa's popular game parks. Within a few pages, then, we have come to understand that she is in fact from southern Africa, but the overriding sense, as indicated by her narrative voice, is that she is a proper English-speaking girl, and the reader can't help but wonder, on some level, what this girl is doing wandering as a homeless refugee in South Africa.

Of course, since Gordimer writes in English, and her audience mostly comprises English readers, her stories must also be written in English. It would make no sense whatsoever were "The Ultimate Safari" to be written in the girl's native tongue. But when taking on the voice of a character, especially when that voice's "true" voice is non-English, the writer usually provides the reader with early clues as to the narrator's background—whether explicitly through a remark by the narrator or implicitly through his or her choice of diction.

In the case of *Moby Dick,* for instance, the book's very first sentence—"Call me Ishmael."—announces the identity of the narrator, and very shortly thereafter Ishmael describes his background and the reasons for his pending journey. In *The Color Purple,* Celie speaks in a southern black idiom that leaves no question as to her racial or regional identity. In Gordimer's story, until the final scenes in the refugee camp, the narrator provides few clues as to her race or ethnicity. It is in the refugee camp that the narrator finally confirms that she is of African descent, even if the details as to which tribe she belongs are left out. "The people in the village have let us join their school," the narrator says,

> "I was surprised to find they speak our language; our grandmother told me, That's why they allow us to stay on their land. Long ago, in the time of our fathers, there was no fence that kills you, there was no Kruger Park between them and us, we were the same people

under our own king, right from our village we left to this place we've come to."

Yet even here, when she references "our language," the possibility still exists that she is referring to English, and that perhaps this narrative is taking place in a world turned upside down, in a mythical future where the (white) English-speaking families are forced to wander the continent as refugees, and where their land has been carved into artificial political boundaries that separate people of the same tribe and ethnic backgrounds from one another. This possibility is eliminated, however, in the story's final scene when the narrator describes the "white people" who have come to film the refugee camp (implying, of course, that the refugees are not white), and we are told with certainty what her nationality is when a reporter asks of her grandmother, "Do you want to go back to Mozambique—to your own country?"

While Gordimer has always been committed to her writing as a form of art, and not simply as a tool to advance her politics, she has also always been unapologetically committed to using her writing to advance her antiapartheid stance. With her readership being made up of mostly, though not exclusively, British and American whites, and by giving the narrator many of the qualities that a typical young white English or American girl would have—she is observant, articulate, intelligent, selfless, and emotionally even-keeled—Gordimer created a character with whom readers could empathize, but not necessarily pity. Ultimately it is not pity that Gordimer wants to elicit from her readers, but rather she wants her readers to come to a profound understanding of the human toll of apartheid. Holding off until the last possible moment before revealing the girl's race has the effect of giving her white audience every possible reason to feel for the girl as "one of us," rather than reasons to feel sorry for the miserable conditions of yet another poor anonymous black African. In other words, by effectively creating a character who closely resembles her readers, or who at least resembles people with whom her readers were familiar, Gordimer gave her audience the vicarious experience of what it was like to be, or know, a refugee, even if for a brief amount of time.

It should also be noted that, in order for the story to pass as a work of art, and not merely political propaganda or journalism, its narrator must remain true to her character. The fact is that most ten-year-old girls, regardless of their backgrounds, would not necessarily consider their race or ethnicity to be important in the telling of their stories.

Race, nationality, and ethnicity are adult constructs that children become aware of to varying degrees over time, so Gordimer's decision not to have her narrator discuss those issues was as much a decision to create a believable character as it was to create an empathetic one. However, the effect of that decision, regardless of its design, was to create an empathetic narrator.

In one of her more famous essays, "Living in the Interregnum," Gordimer paraphrases Mongane Wally Serote, a black South African poet: "Blacks must learn to talk; whites must learn to listen." By taking on the voice of a young black refugee girl, and by offering her readers the possibility that her voice was not simply "black" but also "universal," Gordimer not only created a black voice that whites could more readily listen to, but she also opened a window for her readers into one of the ugly rooms of apartheid.

Source: Mark White, Critical Essay on "The Ultimate Safari," in *Short Stories for Students,* Gale, 2004.

Nadine Gordimer with Karen Lazar

In the following interview, Gordimer discusses her political affiliations and views as well as her more recent works.

[Karen Lazar:] Nadine, I have some questions to ask you about your involvements as a citizen during the 80s and early 90s, and then a few questions about your more recent work.

In the early 80s, what stirred you to become more deeply involved in political organisations? Which groups were you specifically involved in? I know about ACAG (Anti-Censorship Action Group), but wondered about your other organisational commitments at that time?

[Nadine Gordimer:] What spurred me was a new opportunity to be involved. In the 70s, we had the separatist movement, Black Consciousness, which I understood and sympathised with. There were some whites who were hurt or incensed by it. Even the writers' organisation, PEN, at that time black-led (under the leadership of Mothobi Mutloase but with a non-racial national executive), broke up because of the BC movement. It didn't break up acrimoniously, though it was seized upon by the popular press as having entailed a terrible row. This wasn't so at all. We just decided that we wouldn't carry on as an organisation. The black members had had some pressure brought to bear upon them: we felt that this was not the time for small gatherings of

> In America I'm asked, do you think your Jewish background has influenced you politically? I've thought about it a lot, and I think not. I would hate to think that you have to be Jewish in order to understand racism...."

like-minded people of this nature, that it was rather the time for the consolidation of blacks.

Then, of course, in the 80s, the situation changed. I, like many others, had been in the position where there was no organisation with a public profile that you could belong to, unless you wanted to belong to the Progressive Party, as it was called at the time, or the Progressive Federal Party, as it became. So there were liberal organisations that you could belong to, but nothing to the left of that if you were left-inclined. So I was homeless, so to speak, as a social being. I had, of course, my attachments to the African National Congress (ANC) which I'd had all along, but it was underground. But then, with the formation of the non-racial United Democratic Front (UDF) in 1983, you could openly avow yourself. So I think that was a great encouragement. Here was some sort of organisation to which I could attach myself, which I did, and I met and worked with some wonderful people.

And COSAW (The Congress of South African Writers) formed later in the 80s?

Yes, COSAW formed later. But COSAW too became possible out of the new climate, the feeling that apartheid wasn't made of granite, that it was crumbling, that there was some kind of attrition from within. The UDF surviving without being banned was proof of that. And there was a more confident mood among blacks that it wasn't necessary to maintain this total separatism. The time was right to start a national writers' organisation, so we called together all cultural groups concerned with writing and aspects of writing, including theatre, and had a meeting. Out of that came the Congress of South African Writers.

So that is really how my involvement moved. Running parallel with that I was also becoming more and more involved with the ANC, especially with its cultural side. I was one of the people who went to Botswana to the Culture and Resistance festival, as many of us did. Somehow things were really beginning to move. I also had quite frequent contact with Wally Serote overseas, when he was running the cultural desk of the ANC from London.

During the 80s were there any particular and decisive political events—perhaps trials, funerals, assassinations—which might have shaped your decisions as a writer? I'm thinking, for instance, of your portrayal of Whaila's assassination in A Sport of Nature *and of the graveside scenes in* My Son's Story—*those kinds of scenes in your work.*

Well, the graveside scenes came out of my own several experiences of funerals, one in particular when I experienced teargas for the first time. So that came out of what was going on at the time and my own personal experience of it. What had made me think of Whaila's murder is the assassination of David Sibeko. I had known him virtually as a kid, an adolescent, when he was on the telephone exchange at *Drum* magazine; he first worked there. Then he became active in the Pan Africanist Congress (PAC). He was extremely bright and very charming, and he rose steadily in the hierarchy of PAC. He was one of the people assassinated abroad in the 70s, so that was somehow at the back of my mind. It's interesting how these assassinations first of all took place outside the country—it's a mystery why during that period they were not taking place inside. Now political assassinations in the last few years have taken place inside the country.

I wondered what had been decisive for you, because for me, Eastern Cape leader Matthew Goniwe's assassination in 1985 was a totally decisive event. Perhaps one is ripe at a certain point for a consciousness shift.

It's true, and that event can haunt you. Other events start becoming part of a general category after that.

Moving to the censorship side of things: a Johannesburg advocate mentioned to me that you frequently took part in representations to the Publications Appeal Board on behalf of other writers during the 80s. Which literary texts did you appeal on, and on what grounds?

I can't remember the details, but there were quite a large number of texts we appealed on. I was

there as a member of the Anti-Censorship Action Group, and ACAG would naturally have chosen a writer if it were fiction in question, a journalist for a banned edition of a newspaper, and so on. So it's quite true that I was called upon, and went, a number of times.

What were your impressions of the Appeal Board, especially coming out of your experience of the banning of Burger's Daughter?

Well, that was really very interesting. They were unbelievably polite and positively smarmy. One of the accusations I had made again and again concerned not only the whole principle—I always started with the principle—but also the incredible lack of qualification of these members of the board to make decisions. Members of the Appeal Board would sit facing us, and there was an old retired schoolmaster from Witbank or somewhere, and a retired dentist at one point, I remember, making decisions like this.

I think one of the texts we appealed on was probably Don Mattera's *Azanian Love Song,* a book of poetry, and there were many others.

In the records of the mammoth Delmas Treason Trial of 1986–9, you testify to the peaceful and legitimate nature of the UDF. Your support for the still exiled ANC and your understanding of why the organisation was forced into violence also come through in your testimony.

That was the real purpose of my testimony. It wasn't so much the UDF because most of those on trial were really ANC people. I suppose we can talk about it now. I had been involved in that trial because Terror (Patrick) Lekota was writing a book in the form of letters to his daughter. I was smuggling out bits of it with the help of the lawyers and then going over it with a friend who did a wonderful job of typing it out. I knew the trialists well, particularly Terror and Popo (Molefe).

Did Terror's book ever come to light?

The book did come to light. It was published by some little publisher. It's a pity. It sank like a stone. The interesting thing about it: I would have thought that the idea that came to Terror was inspired by the letters to Indira Gandhi by her father. But he'd never heard of them. It just came to him out of his situation. There were problems because he wasn't near a library and couldn't research or verify the dates or names he couldn't remember. So we did our best with that but it wasn't strong on fact. But it was interesting because it was one of the attempts to write from the people, to see history from the personal point of view rather than from the historian's point of view.

That was my initial access point to the trial. It is customary for the accused to give the names of people they would like to speak for them in mitigation. I was one of the people that they asked for. And I was then very nastily questioned by the prosecutor. I was not used to this. He asked . . . quite bluntly, was Nelson Mandela my leader, and then he said is Umkhonto we Sizwe your Umkhonto we Sizwe? And I said yes. So I suppose in a way that was a watershed in my political development.

Have you, yourself, written anything about the Delmas trial?

No, nothing. Actually it's interesting. I've been to a lot of political trials over my lifetime but I don't think there's a trial in any of my books. Trials are just natural good theatre, aren't they?

If they aren't very tedious.

They can be, yes. But they can make good theatre if you know something about them.

Nadine, when did you actually join the ANC?

Oh, the moment it was legal. You couldn't join before. What you did meant you were with it or not with it. The moment it became possible to do so, a friend and I went down to JISWA which was the Johannesburg Indian Welfare Association (at that time run by a friend of mine, Cas Saloojee and his wife Khadija) because we were told that this was one of the first places where you could get your ANC membership card. So we went down there. He is a good friend, Cas Saloojee, and we were his first two members. That was the end of February 1990.

A few more questions about your perceptions of left politics in the 1980s. In My Son's Story, *Sonny gets marginalised by his comrades in "the movement" for reasons which are not made entirely clear. When did you become aware of splits in the Congress Left, and what splits were you aware of? Is Sonny's "movement" to be associated unequivocally with a UDF/ANC alignment?*

Oh, I think so in response to the latter. It was clear from the kind of things he was doing. The tensions, the splits are there in every political formation and it doesn't require any great feat of imagina-

tion to concoct something with these things. And I'd already done it before on a different scale in *A Guest of Honour.*

At that stage in the late 80s or in the time that My Son's Story *was being written, did you ever believe that any other liberation sectors might come to centrality within South African politics?*

Such as?

Perhaps worker sectors, PAC, alliances of other kinds? The reason that I ask is that I've noticed the pervasive way in which you use the definite article in that novel: "the movement", suggesting that there is no other.

I used the definite article because, to me, the movement did encompass others. I specially didn't want to make it specific. Of course there was certainly the SACP and the ANC and the rising Trade Union movement that were already allied. Although there was no official recognition of this, they were working together. A very significant development for me in the 80s was the recognition of black trade unions. I can't imagine that we would have moved as we did without the worker power. In my youth in that mining town, Springs, the miners were even kept out of the towns. They were so completely cut off from any normal kind of concourse with people in the town (I'm talking about black townspeople too). And then in the 80s I would go down to Braamfontein to the post office or the bank, and out of the National Union of Mineworkers' offices there would come these young men in their T-shirts striding down the pavement. It was to me such a graphic illustration of a huge change. So the Trade Union movement opening up was also important to my thinking. That was clearly encompassed under "the movement".

I think that somehow, the underlying conflict seemed to be between the UDF and the movement: the more direct political forces, ANC, PAC, SACP and so on. I anticipated the kind of thing that happened between the returning ANC exiles and the UDF people in my book *My Son's Story.* Later, when the exiles did come back, one saw people who had done such wonderful work being somehow set aside or getting minor positions.

Did you have any direct contact with FEDSAW (Federation of South African Women), FEDTRAW (Federation of Transvaal Women) or other women's orgnisations during the 80s, or with the documents and speeches emanating from these organisations?

I always received the documents and quite often went to various functions but I was not an active member at all.

Many feminist reviewers and interviewers, including myself, have attempted to draw you out on your opinions of feminism in recent years. Your description of feminism as "piffling" in the early 80s was followed by your recognition that there are some "harder, more thinking" kinds of feminism in the later 80s. What is your opinion, now, of the role that a political feminism may have in our current moment of governmental and constitutional change?

My views have changed, and they've changed because the situation has changed. It's interesting. I can't see any vestiges now of that trivial feminism that I was talking about so disparagingly in the early times because I think it deserved to be disparaged. A tremendous division arose in the mid-70s (about '76) between the concerns of white women and the concerns of black women. I'll never forget the attempts of Women for Peace, which was a good idea although it came out of a "White Lady Bountiful" thing. They did have some meetings and some sort of contact with black women. It was based on the idea that we all have children and what happened in '76 was a threat to children.

But what happened then was that, come November, all these white adolescents were preparing for the matric dance and what was happening in Soweto or Gugulethu and all over the place was that black women were running behind their kids with bowls of water and *lappies* to wash the teargas out of their eyes. There was really no meeting point for these women unless the white women had directly challenged the government, which they were not prepared to do. You can't change a regime on the basis of compassion. There's got to be something harder. I'm not saying that compassion is not necessary in our lives but you can't change a regime that way. I think that's one of the faults of a worthy liberal organisation like Women for Peace. At least you could say that the women had moved along that far but I couldn't see how there could be any common feminism unless white women had truly thrown in their lot with black women, as some of the members of FEDTRAW later did.

And now? What do you make of the gender politics of the current moment?

And now, I think the proof is there. We've got quite a lot of women in Parliament. We have got in place of a white male Afrikaner (which we've had

for generations) a black woman as Speaker. She's also, significantly, a South African Indian which is for me a true demonstration of non-racism. Nobody said she isn't black enough or if they have, I haven't heard it. And I don't think they have said it. I think she is recognised for what she is. And then you have other people like Baleka Kgotsisile and Cheryl Carolus who are in high positions. And there are a number of others. Barbara Masekela is now going to be our ambassador in Paris, and as you talk about it you can think of other names. So they are all evidence of a very important kind of feminism from my point of view.

Another thing I'd like to say is that in the interim Constitution, the strong emphasis on no discrimination on grounds of gender is a very important step of the right kind now. They've brought that up on a level with discrimination on grounds of colour or race.

And you think there's the will to enact that?

I think so, certainly among younger black women and some white women.

Nadine, a few questions on your work. When one looks at some of your portrayals of leftwing or activist women, one can see a kind of physical type coming across. I'm thinking of Joy in "Something Out There" and Hannah in My Son's Story, *both of whom are depicted as sloppy dressers and sexual improbables when compared with your more conventional beauties such as Hillela and Aila. Is your depiction of this "alternative" female aesthetic (the Hannah/Joy kind) based on something you've observed in leftwing circles over the years, or could you suggest where it might come from?*

Oh, of course. These are things that come from observation. I think we all fall into some kind of uniform. I remember years ago arriving in America—I was going to some meeting at Columbia—and I was put up in a sort of residential complex where we were all writers and painters and artists. And it was a year when if you were a writer or painter, you wore black trousers and a black polo-neck sweater and you wore a certain kind of earring and you would not wear another kind. And one day I looked at myself and thought, you're wearing the uniform. So I think this observation comes from simply living among people. Just like the sweater- and-pearls aesthetic: it isn't true of everyone, but it does define a certain kind of woman, doesn't it?

Some critics have commented that your most recent novel, None to Accompany Me *(1994), is surprisingly sombre in mood, given the largely triumphant political period from which it emerges. Could you comment on this?*

Well, I think there's a certain solemnity when, after a long, long time, extraordinary good things happen, when things open up. Sometimes in the last year, I think we've all had what one might call a sense of awe. And I think this probably comes out in that book.

Your portrayal of the consequences of violence, as in Oupa's death in your latest novel, seems to me to be more sustained than in any such portrayals in earlier works.

Yes, because such events became so terrible in view of the fact that we were coming to the end of this struggle against the apartheid regime. You know it's rather like, in war, soldiers being killed while the armistice is being signed somewhere else. It pointed to the tremendous waste that took place over years and years and years, and also to the mindless and criminal violence that has come about in this country as a result of poverty and the conditions of apartheid. So in a way, the prolonged attention to Oupa's death, the whole process of his dying, really encompasses many deaths.

Your protagonist in this latest novel, Vera Stark, moves towards a recognition of the fundamental solitude of the ''self'' as she grows older. At the same time, she withdraws further and further away from sexuality, such that her relationship with her final male companion, Zeph, is a celibate one (even though he is still sexually active—with younger women). Could you perhaps comment on why Vera's eventual life choices are coterminous with a sexual removal from the world? And what might that say about the ageing process for women in our society? Does it exert different stresses on women than it does on men?

There's a different attitude to women's sexuality than there is to men's. It's still not recognised in the way that men's is.

By whom?

By everybody. By other women too, by conventional women. Vera is a strange woman because in some ways she is conventional. She attacks her daily work. Even though it is unconventional work, she goes about it in this rather strict, direct, authoritarian way. She doesn't seem to belong to any women's movement. She's a women's movement in herself, I think. And she bluntly asserts her

sexuality. She even quotes Renoir at one point—''I paint with my prick''. But she has her fill of sexuality, and she works her way through it. She's had a very active kind of sensual life and hasn't cared too much about the morality of it.

So you don't see any loss when she moves away from sexuality?

No, it's a conscious decision. You've said something that many other people miss: they say how lonely she is, but you've said she recognises the ultimate solitude of self. If you're going to make a journey towards that, towards accepting that, then you are shedding some things along the way. She sees the baggage of her life as something which she took on and wanted and wouldn't have been without, but she doesn't want it dragging around with her forever.

And sexuality might have been part of that baggage?

Yes. And of course, who can say? People's sexuality dies down at different ages. Some people seem to be finished with sex in their mid-forties, or fifties. Terrible! Others take on lovers, both male and female, at seventy. It's a matter of the glands, I suppose. Vera genuinely doesn't want another sexual relationship and doesn't resent the fact that Zeph has his little pleasures on the side.

I notice some of your work (stories and sections from novels) have been published over the years in the glossy women's press, such as in Cosmopolitan, Femina *and* Fair Lady. *What is your impression of these magazines?*

Well, I've always had very mixed feelings. Quite frankly I don't read them, though I see them around. But I notice, through the kind of contents they splash on the covers, that they have changed quite a lot. Also you see black faces on the local covers these days. Admittedly, they're usually beauty queens. I haven't seen any of our black women writers or actresses on these covers. But, you know, that is the women's magazine culture: to be a beauty queen is the ultimate ambition. It's rather interesting that women have to be very consciously feminist in order to reject the whole beauty queen thing. I suppose quite a lot of young women do get quite financially independent through modelling.

Incidentally, what do you make of the ANC coming out in support of something like the ''Miss South Africa'' contest?

I suppose this is the kind of thing that political parties do, and the ANC is now a political party. If people say "This is part of the emancipation of blacks", I have no objection to it. It's a little thing. I'm much more worried about us becoming nice big arms dealers.

Nadine, are you a television watcher, and were you watching South African TV and its represention of local politics during the 80s?

No, I never watch it. I'm a newspaper reader.

What newspapers and journals did you subscribe to or read during the 80s, and are you still reading those papers?

During the 80s, the usual local English-language ones (I'm afraid my Afrikaans isn't up to much), and of course the alternative press: *Weekly Mail, New Nation,* etc. And then, literary journals such as *New York Review of Books* and so on. For a long time I used to get *The Observer* and then *The Independent,* and then it just got too much. In recent years, once *The Weekly Mail* started printing pages from *The Guardian,* I thought that will do.

As for local cultural journals, *Contrast* comes to me and *Staffrider* of course (I was involved in that journal in COSAW) and now and then, *The Southern African Review.*

Finally, the mandatory question. Now that we are past South Africa's first democratic election, what are your impressions: of the pace of change, of the receptiveness of South Africans to this change?

I've been pleased, I should say surprised by the receptiveness of South Africans. I think the crisis of expectation which absolutely obsesses people overseas—I can't tell you how many times in America I got questioned about this—is not called for. In my experience, my small experience of talking to grassroots people, and from what I gather from those who do have a big experience of it, what people want is truly basic. I think this has been recognised now in the ANC. It's not recognised by the press, it's not recognised by people who saw April 27, 1994 as the beginning of the millennium. People are not asking for Mercedes Benzes and big houses. You know what they're asking for: a roof over their heads, electricity, education, jobs.

That is nonetheless a tall order for a new government.

It is a very tall order, of course. As for how much has been done, of course it seems too little but

one can't say a start hasn't been made. I think the question of how much can be done how quickly should be explained to the black majority in a different way from the way that it is being explained. When dissatisfaction comes up along the lines that the ANC has bent over backwards to placate whites and done nothing for blacks, I think Mandela answers that very well but he doesn't go into it enough, from my point of view, when he says the placating of whites has cost nothing, that no money has been spent on it. What money there was has been spent on providing electricity, water where it's been possible. . . . This is great. To me it's progress. It's not spectacular but it's progress.

What should be explained much more fully, and is not, to the black majority is the reason why whites have to be soothed and kept in place: because the government, ANC-led, does not want any abandonment of our very complicated economic infrastructure here, such as you saw in other parts of Africa, while there is still insufficient black skill to take over such things. So if there are too many concessions to whites, in terms of tax or keeping them in a certain measure of control of various boards, it could be explained that this is only because you cannot move towards greater prosperity and development without using them. In other words, whites are being used, and they should accept it; we should all accept it. Whites have got things that blacks never had, and they are now being used to help provide these things for others. Of course there's also the question of investment from overseas. And this is not put clearly enough to blacks. If you look at material concessions to whites, what have they been? Nothing, except that white life has been left intact. Also people tend to ignore the quiet, slow (too slow) integration of schools. As far as I know from white and black friends, the kids are now going to school together and there's no problem.

So my feeling is of realistic optimism. Of course, new hitches arise all the time. I turned on the radio at lunchtime, and now the farmers on the borders of Lesotho whose cattle are being rustled have made counterattacks and burned down cattle kraals in Lesotho where they say their stolen cattle have been housed. I heard one of the farmers say that, unless this rustling over the border is stopped, there's going to be bloodshed. Also, a year ago, who would have thought that we would have the problem of illegal immigration which we now have—that we'd have Koreans selling watches in the streets, Zaireans talking French in the streets. Who would have thought this? It's something we couldn't possibly have imagined.

Why do you think this has happened to the extent that it has? Is it that we are seen as a place of bounty or safety relative to these other countries?

Oh absolutely, but we can't afford this. We must think of our own people first, and somehow this has got to be stopped. Of course, this ill becomes somebody like myself who comes from immigrant stock. All of us who are whites here originally do. So who are we to say that the Koreans must be kicked out?

Most whites come from immigrant stock a very long way back.

Precisely, but do you think that really makes such a difference?

I notice that some critics writing for Jewish journals and papers claim that you have denied or suppressed your Jewish origins and your family's immigrant history.

Well I think it's truly based on nothing. I have never denied that I'm Jewish and I've no desire to deny it. For me, being Jewish is like being black: you simply are. To want to deny it is disgusting. It's a denial of humanity. There's no shame in being black and there's no shame in being Jewish. But I'm not religious, I haven't had a religious upbringing, and whether I'm an unbeliever in terms of Jehovah or Jesus Christ to me is the same thing.

Being black in our society surely amounts to a more politically disadvantaged state than being Jewish, for most people anyway?

Yes, of course, much more. I wonder how these Jewish critics feel about Joe Slovo and others, who've put something else first. I've never seen any criticism of them. I'm not sure why it's happened to me! Perhaps writers are always easy targets. In America I'm asked, do you think your Jewish background has influenced you politically? I've thought about it a lot, and I think not. I would hate to think that you have to be Jewish in order to understand racism, just as I would hate to think you have to be black to understand it. It should be something absolutely repugnant and quite impossible for anybody who is a real human being. So, to say I'm not Jewish so I don't care about the Holocaust or I'm not black so I don't care about Sharpeville or all the other Sharpevilles that followed . . . that's appalling.

There are strange little ethnic loyalties, I suppose, that come up. I can't help being pleased, and have been pleased over the years, to think that in South Africa's liberation movements and progressive circles there have been a really disproportionate number of Jews, given the smallness of the Jewish population. I'm rather proud of this. Though of course, you may then get the accusation, as you do in America, that Jews dominate progressive thinking and the press, and so on. So it can be used as a stick to beat you with as well.

Source: Nadine Gordimer with Karen Lazar, "'A Feeling of Realistic Optimism': An Interview with Nadine Gordimer,'' in *Salmagundi,* Winter 1997, pp. 150–65.

Sources

"Anti-Apartheid Author Branded Racist,'' *BBC News Online* at http://news.bbc.co.uk/1/hi/education/1283378.stm

Banville, John, "Winners,'' Review of *Jump and Other Stories,* in the *New York Review of Books,* Vol. 38, No. 19, November 21, 1991, pp. 27–29.

Colleran, Jeanne, "Archive of Apartheid: Nadine Gordimer's Short Fiction at the End of the Interregnum,'' in *The Later Fiction of Nadine Gordimer,* edited by Bruce King, St. Martin's Press, 1993, pp. 237–45.

Cryer, Dan, "Tales of Racial Turmoil and Other Tempests,'' Review of *Jump and Other Stories,* in *Newsday,* September 23, 1991, p. 50.

Donnelly, Jerome, "Summer Fiction—*Jump and Other Stories* by Nadine Gordimer,'' in *America,* Vol. 166, No. 20, June 6, 1992, pp. 518–19.

Gordimer, Nadine, "Living in the Interregnum,'' in *The Essential Gesture: Writing, Politics and Places,* edited by Stephen Clingman, Jonathan Cape, 1988, pp. 261–84.

Jeyifo, Biodun, "An Interview with Nadine Gordimer: Harare, February 14, 1992,'' in *Callaloo,* Vol. 16, No. 4, Fall 1993, pp. 922–30.

Lazar, Karen, "'A Feeling of Realistic Optimism': An Interview with Nadine Gordimer,'' in *Salmagundi,* No. 113, Winter 1997, pp. 150–65.

———, "*Jump and Other Stories:* Gordimer's Leap into the 1990s: Gender and Politics in Her Latest Short Fiction,'' in *Journal of Southern African Studies,* Vol. 18, No. 4, December 1992, pp. 783–802.

Mantel, Hilary, "Irrecoverably Dark, Without All Hope of Day: *Jump and Other Stories* by Nadine Gordimer,'' in the *Spectator,* Vol. 267, No. 8519, October 19, 1991, pp. 43–44.

Wästberg, Per, "Nadine Gordimer and the South African Experience,'' at http://www.nobel.se/literature/articles/wastberg/index.html#2 (on the official Nobel Prize Web Site)

Further Reading

Brink, André, *Reinventing a Continent: Writing and Politics in South Africa, 1982–1995,* Secker & Warburg, 1996.
   One of South Africa's foremost novelists and opponents of apartheid brings together this collection of essays about the role of the writer in South Africa.

Davis, Geoffrey V., *Voices of Justice and Reason: Apartheid and Beyond in South African Literature,* Amsterdam, 2003.
   Davis provides a detailed overview, with an extensive bibliography, of South African writing under apartheid, with a focus on black writers.

Finnegan, William, *A Complicated War: The Harrowing of Mozambique,* University of California Press, 1992.
   A Complicated War is an eyewitness journalistic account of the civil war in Mozambique that was sponsored by South Africa and ultimately killed over a million Mozambicans.

Karodia, Farida, *A Shattering of Silence,* Heinemann, 1993.
   Karodia gives a fictionalized account of the adventures of a young Mozambican girl who loses her family to the civil war in her country.

Vines, Alex, *Renamo: Terrorism in Mozambique,* Indiana University Press, 1991.
   Vines provides an historical overview of Renamo, the rebel movement supported by South Africa that fueled the civil war in Mozambique.

The Underground Gardens

T. Coraghessan Boyle's story, "The Underground Gardens," was first published in the *New Yorker* in the May 25, 1998, issue, and was collected in 2001 in the author's short-story collection *After the Plague*. The story is loosely based on the life of an Italian American immigrant who began digging a huge underground complex on his land in Fresno, California, in the arid San Joaquin Valley, in the early 1900s. Using this historical person and elements of his life as a start, Boyle crafts an optimistic story about an Italian American immigrant whose hopes—including marrying the woman of his dreams—are repeatedly dashed, but who nevertheless perseveres and continues to dream. This story is unlike many of Boyle's works, which poke fun at the human condition or contain large doses of cynicism, sarcasm or other forms of negativity. Instead, Boyle examines positive ideas such as the power of faith and the importance of self-sufficiency. The story is, however, similar to many of Boyle's other works, in that it uses an actual historical event—in this case, Baldasare's digging of his gardens—as a starting point for the narrative. A copy of the story can be found in the Penguin paperback edition of *After the Plague*, which was published in 2003.

T. Coraghessan Boyle

1998

Author Biography

Boyle was born on December 2, 1948, in Peekskill, New York. He has noted that he never read a book

T. Coraghessan Boyle

until he was eighteen. In fact, Boyle never aspired to be a writer. In the 1960s, Boyle enrolled at the State University of New York at Potsdam as a music student. While in school, he took an influential creative writing course, and began reading literature. After graduating in 1968, Boyle taught English in a public high school, which, he has admitted, was mainly to avoid serving in the Vietnam War.

During this same period, Boyle began writing his own short stories and became a habitual user of drugs and alcohol. These two activities culminated in Boyle's short story, ''The OD and Hepatitis Railroad or Bust,'' which was published in the *North American Review*. In 1972, looking to clean up his act—and confident in his abilities as a writer after his story publication—Boyle applied and was accepted to the University of Iowa's prestigious Iowa Writers' Workshop, where he studied under some very influential writers, including John Irving. He earned two degrees from the university, a master of fine arts degree in 1974 and a doctoral degree in 1977.

After graduation, Boyle moved west to teach creative writing at the University of Southern California, a tenured position that he continued to hold as of 2004. In 1979, he published *The Descent of*

Man, a collection of short stories that he had used as his doctoral dissertation. Critics liked the book, which immediately earned Boyle a reputation as a quirky, humorous writer. Boyle cemented this reputation with his first novel, *Water Music* (1981). Over the next two decades, Boyle published seven novels and five more story collections, including 2001's *After the Plague*. This last collection included ''The Underground Gardens,'' which won Boyle an O. Henry Award.

Boyle published the novel *Drop City* in 2003.

Plot Summary

''The Underground Gardens'' begins with a short biography of Baldasare Forestiere, a thirty-two-year-old Italian American immigrant who has survived by his digging skills, which he learned in his father's Italian orchards and which he honed through working as a laborer in American cities. It is the summer of 1905, and Baldasare has purchased seventy acres of central California land through the mail. He is optimistic about this real estate investment. Having heard about the lack of cold weather in California, he assumes that the land will be suited for growing his own vineyards.

Baldasare finds that, while the land never freezes, it is dry and nearly impenetrable, but this does not discourage him. First, he buys the necessary materials and builds himself a small shanty. Then, he uses his agricultural knowledge to find water and dig a well. He plants some seeds, but the hard California land is not fertile enough to produce much. He starts working for another farmer to replenish his savings, and just as he is getting depressed that he will never achieve his dream, he meets Ariadne Siagris, the young niece of a Greek drugstore owner, and falls instantly in love.

Baldasare finds new inspiration, which motivates him to work toward a new dream—marriage to Ariadne. Rain leaks into his flimsy shanty that night, so he digs a cavern the next day, thinking that it will someday be the cellar for the house in which he and Ariadne will live. Yet, as the rain returns, Baldasare moves all of his possessions into the cellar, and begins to fashion an underground house, including a stove and storage shelves. Since there is little laboring work that winter, Baldasare continues adding to his underground residence, digging out hallways and rooms.

His one indulgence is his weekly hamburger at Siagris' Drugstore, where he strikes up an acquaintance with Ariadne. Baldasare observes that Ariadne is not very smart at some tasks, is rapidly putting on weight, and has whiskers on her chin and red blotches on her skin, among other imperfections—but these traits only make Baldasare love her more. For two years, Baldasare continues the pattern of working for other men to make money, digging out his underground house in his free time, and making his weekly visit to see Ariadne. She begins to show interest in Baldasare, especially when he tells her about his spacious twelve-room home. Baldasare finally works up the nerve to ask Ariadne to come see his home, and she accepts.

When he walks to town to pick her up, however, Ariadne is shocked that Baldasare has not come in a carriage, especially since it is particularly hot that day, and she refuses to go with him. The following week, Baldasare rents a cabriolet, and they travel to his underground residence, but Ariadne has been expecting a normal, aboveground house, and refuses to go underground with him. She is furious with Baldasare, and, three days later, Baldasare hears that Ariadne has gotten engaged to another man. Baldasare refuses to give up, however, believing that if he can demonstrate the strength of his love to Ariadne, she will come and see his underground palace and will be interested in him again. In an attempt to get her attention, Baldasare sneaks to the lot behind the drugstore one night and begins digging a heart-shaped hole in the ground underneath Ariadne's window. Although Mr. Siagris and the sheriff try to stop Baldasare, he continues digging until the next evening, when Ariadne's new fiancé and one of his friends beat Baldasare badly.

A week after being released from the hospital, Baldasare gets a new inspiration, which comes to him in a flash. He dreams of *Baldasare Forestiere's Underground Gardens,* a unique set of complex caverns that he envisions spanning the entire area of his seventy-acre plot of land, and which will include fish ponds, a restaurant, a gift shop, and other aspects designed to attract tourists. Although he is still sore from his beating, he begins to dig, intent on achieving this latest dream.

Media Adaptations

- Boyle's novel *Budding Prospects* was produced as an audiobook in 1994 by Books on Tape.

- Boyle's novel *Drop City* was produced as an audiobook in 2003 by Audio Books Unabridged.

- Boyle's novel *A Friend of the Earth* was produced as an audiobook in 2000 by Books on Tape.

- Boyle's novel *The Road to Wellville* was adapted as a feature film in 1994 by Columbia Pictures. The film, written and directed by Alan Parker, featured an all-star cast, including Anthony Hopkins, Bridget Fonda, Matthew Broderick, John Cusack, and Dana Carvey. It is available on DVD and VHS from Columbia Tristar Home Video.

- Boyle's story collection *Without a Hero* was produced as an audiobook in 1994 by Books on Tape.

Characters

Lucca Albanese

Lucca Albanese is another Italian American immigrant, and Baldasare's only friend in California. They meet while working in another man's vineyards.

Hiram Broadbent

Hiram Broadbent gets engaged to Ariadne Siagris after she rebukes Baldasare. When Baldasare tries to get Ariadne's attention by digging a heart-shaped hole under her window, Broadbent and his amateur boxing friend beat Baldasare so badly that he ends up in the hospital.

Baldasare Forestiere

Baldasare Forestiere is an optimistic young Italian American, based on an actual historical figure, who buys a seventy-acre plot of worthless central California land with the intention of growing grapevines. As the youngest of three Italian sons, he will probably not inherit his father's vineyards, and so he has left the comfort of Italy behind to make his own fortune in America. Although his dream of growing vineyards on his new land ultimately fails, Baldasare proves to be very resilient. His second dream is to marry Ariadne Siagris, the niece of old Siagris, a Greek drugstore owner. Baldasare pours his seemingly limitless energy into building a life with Ariadne.

Baldasare digs a cellar, thinking it will become part of the house he will build for himself and Ariadne, but then decides that an underground residence will be more sturdy and impressive. Over the span of a few years, he builds up a relationship with Ariadne, and tells her about his large house. When she finally agrees to see it, however, she does not share his enthusiasm for underground living and, in fact, thinks that Baldasare has duped her. When he hears that Ariadne has gotten engaged to somebody else, Baldasare does not give up, and tries to impress her by digging a heart-shaped hole underneath her window. This act prompts Ariadne's new fiancé, Hiram Broadbent, along with one of his friends, to beat up Baldasare. When Baldasare is released from the hospital, he gets the inspiration for his third and final dream—digging a massive set of underground gardens that will attract tourists and make him rich.

Euphrates Mead

Euphrates Mead, who never appears in the story except in letters, is the man who sells Baldasare his seventy-acre plot of California land.

Ariadne Siagris

Ariadne Siagris is a nineteen-year-old Greek woman, who comes to live with her uncle in California after her parents are killed at a railroad crossing. (In Greek mythology, Ariadne was the daughter of King Minos of Crete, the ruler who sacrificed Athenian youths to a monster known as the minotaur—a creature with the head of a bull and the body of a human. Ariadne helped one of the intended sacrificial victims, the Athenian hero Theseus, to escape from the labyrinth where the minotaur lived by giving the hero a ball of thread.) While living with her uncle, Ariadne works at his drugstore. Despite her education, she is not very good at reading menus or making change, and she begins to put on lots of weight from eating too much at the drugstore. She also develops red splotches on her

skin, along with other imperfections. Through Baldasare's regular weekly visits to the drugstore, Ariadne learns that he has a big house and that he is interested in her. She agrees to see his house, but is mortified when she finds out it is underground. She rebukes Baldasare, refuses to see him, and promptly gets engaged to Hiram Broadbent.

Old Siagris

Old Siagris is Ariadne's Greek uncle, who takes in the young woman when her parents are killed. He is tolerant of Baldasare when he thinks that Baldasare might be able to marry and support Ariadne—and thus remove the financial burden from his own shoulders. But when Siagris learns that Baldasare's big house is underground, he bans Baldasare from his drugstore, and tells him he cannot see Ariadne anymore.

Themes

Faith

While "The Underground Gardens" explores many ideas, the common thread that runs through the story is faith—namely, Baldasare's near-unshakeable faith in his ability to achieve his dreams. "He'd always thought big, even when he was a boy wandering his father's orchards." Recognizing early on that his place in the family assured he would never inherit these orchards, "Baldasare wasn't discouraged—he knew he was destined for greatness." Baldasare initially thinks this greatness will come in a familiar form, as the owner of his own vineyards in America.

The power of his faith is such that Baldasare is not daunted by the tasks necessary to create vineyards in the hard, dry California land. He gets right to work. "He didn't even stop to eat, that first day." Baldasare pursues this first dream with a single-minded passion, fighting the natural toughness of the land with only his pick and shovel. When it becomes clear to him that his land is not suited for vineyards, his dream changes to marrying Ariadne, but the strength of his faith remains the same. "She was the one. She was what he'd come to America for, and he spoke her name aloud . . . and made the solemnest pledge that she would one day be his bride." After Ariadne refuses Baldasare, his aspira-

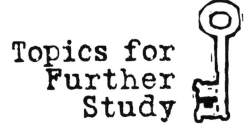

Topics for Further Study

- Research the average life span of an Italian American immigrant in the early 1900s. Discuss some of the sociological factors that determined this average life span.

- Research the caverns, natural or otherwise, that exist today in central California. Write an in-depth report about one set of caverns—other than the Forestiere Underground Gardens—including when it was created, how it was formed, and its estimated value as a modern-day tourist attraction.

- Compare the lives of Italian American immigrants to the lives of other immigrants in America in the early 1900s. Choose the ethnic group that you think had it the worst during this time period. Choose one influential figure from this group and write a biography about this person, including how his or her actions either improved or degraded the ethnic group's reputation.

- Research the average size of a cellar in the early 1900s. Using this research, as well as the size clues given in this story, guess how big Baldasare's cellar is and figure out how many cubic yards of dirt would need to be removed to create this space. Make a chart that compares this volume of dirt to the volumes of several other modern-day structures.

- In the story, Baldasare falls in love with Ariadne while drinking his coffee and eating his hamburger sandwich at Siagris' Drugstore. Research the types of food that would likely be offered in such an establishment in the early 1900s. Create a menu that lists all of these items, including early 1900s-era prices.

tions change again, this time to digging a seventy-acre underground tourist attraction. Yet Baldasare's faith remains strong. In fact, the originality of his latest vision affects him more deeply than either of his previous two dreams. ''It was a complete vision, more eloquent than any set of blueprints or elevations, and it staggered him.''

While Baldasare is able to maintain his faith, even when he is chasing unconventional or lofty dreams, others are not capable of taking this leap of faith. When Ariadne comes to see Baldasare's ''twelve room'' house, she does not see it aboveground and thinks that Baldasare is playing a prank on her and that his house is hidden behind a hill. Baldasare becomes insistent, trying to ''lead her down from the carriage—if only she would come, if only she would see,'' but Ariadne, like the rest of the town, does not have Baldasare's ability to think outside the box and find the beauty in unconventional things. Even Baldasare's friend, Lucca, lacks this vision. Lucca, unlike Ariadne, does come visit Baldasare in his underground residence, but he never thinks of it the way that Baldasare does and, in fact, refers to Baldasare's home in a derogatory fashion. When Baldasare asks Lucca about Ariadne's new fiancé, Lucca says, ''Hell, if you ever came out of your hole, you'd know who I'm talking about.''

Self-Sufficiency

While his faith is strong, Baldasare would not even have a chance to achieve any of his dreams if it wasn't for his self-sufficiency. From an early age, he worked in his father's vineyards, where he learned a variety of digging and agricultural skills, which he hones through his laboring work in American cities. These skills come in handy on Baldasare's California land, where he is able to build a shanty, find an underground water source to supply his well, and ultimately form his underground residence, all without the help of others. Furthermore, he is able to do these things while working long hours in the worst conditions.

This same constancy and discipline also helps Baldasare manage his financial matters. Although the story never discusses this, in order to even come to America, much less buy land, Baldasare would have had to save a fair amount of money. In fact, he is always conscious of his savings, recognizing that the key to survival is to never put himself in a bad financial spot, even if it means putting his dreams on hold, as he has to do three months after arriving on his land. So "when his savings began to dwindle down to nothing, Baldasare became a laboring man all over again." Baldasare has so programmed himself into a self-sufficient mode of financial survival that he is unable to enjoy entertainment as others do. When he and his friend Lucca go to the vaudeville theater, Baldasare is unable to focus on the show, because "all the while he was regretting the two cents the streetcar had cost him and the fifteen-cent admission." Baldasare prides himself on his frugal spending, but proves that he can also go against his nature if it means taking another step toward achieving his dream. For example, when Ariadne refuses to go see Baldasare's house unless he takes her there in a carriage, he obliges. "The following Sunday, though it wounded him to throw his money away like some Park Avenue millionaire, he pulled up to Siagris' Drugstore in a hired cabriolet."

Appearances

To Baldasare, hiring the cabriolet makes it seem like he is trying to appear like a millionaire. Baldasare is a man obsessed with appearances. Baldasare's initial dream is to create vineyards on his American land, not only because he was raised in the business in Italy, but because it fits into his vision of what the American dream should look like. In his mind's eye, he sees "his seventy acres buried in grapes," a large "house of four rooms" for his wife and children, "four sons and three daughters"—in other words, an excessive, unrestricted lifestyle. When he meets Ariadne, she replaces the vineyards as the central focus of his dream, but he is initially discouraged, because of his first, favorable impression of her appearance. "What could he offer her, a girl like that who'd come all the way from Chicago, Illinois, to live with her uncle, the prosperous Greek—a school-educated girl used to fine things and books?" As Baldasare spends more time with Ariadne, he recognizes that, not only is she not as smart as he had thought, but that she also has a number of "imperfections" including a flawed eye and splotches on her skin. He does not mind them. In fact, he thinks they will be an asset to him, and becomes "surer each day that she was his. After all, who else would see in her what he saw? . . . Who but Baldasare Forestiere would come forward to de-

clare himself?" Baldasare assumes that most suitors will only be interested in the physical appearance of their potential brides, and not look beyond imperfections such as mottled skin, as he is doing.

Even Baldasare's final vision—the massive, underground complex of gardens—is based on appearances. In his imagination, he sees, among other things, "a lot for parking the carriages and automobiles of the patrons who would flock there to see what he'd accomplished in his time on earth." For Baldasare, the poor Italian American immigrant, it is not enough to just make money and provide for a family. To be truly successful, he feels that he must build something large and visible that will prove to the world, once and for all, that he "wasn't just another sorrowful Italian laborer with no more means or expectations than the price of the next hamburger sandwich, but a man of substance."

Style

Metaphor

A metaphor is a comparison between dissimilar things that invites readers to see the subject in a new way. In this story, digging is the literal activity of creating a hole by removing dirt. It is also a way of characterizing Baldasare and of revealing his belief system. Ultimately digging is a metaphor for Baldasare's success. "He dug because the earth was there beneath his feet, and men paid him to move it. He dug because it was a sacrament, because it was honorable and holy." Digging is not only his means of making money, it is also the only religion he knows. It is what gives him faith and is the means by which he plans to achieve each of his dreams—the vineyard, impressing Ariadne so that she will marry him, and his underground gardens.

A metaphor becomes more powerful when the metaphorical meaning is the opposite of the standard meaning of the word or concept. Boyle's digging metaphor works in this way.

Normally, people speak of success with upward-focused terms. For example, business owners "build" their organizations and star employees "climb" the corporate ladder. Digging, on the other hand, a downward-focused activity, is associated with lower class laborers and with negative terms in general, as when somebody in a bad situation says they have "dug themselves into a hole." Likewise, criminals are often said to inhabit an "underworld."

The underground world is also, as Baldasare's father tells him as a boy, synonymous with the animal world. *"Men are upright . . . and they have dominion over the beasts. . . . And where do the beasts live, mio figlio? In the ground, no?"* In fact, in the beginning of the story, the city digging work Baldasare has done is described in animal-like terms. "As a young man in Boston and New York he burrowed like a rodent beneath streets and rivers, scouring the walls of subway tubes and aqueducts."

Yet, as Baldasare is faced with the challenge of surviving the harsh California rains, he ignores these stereotypes of underground life, and puts his faith in digging once again. "It took him a while, but the conclusion Baldasare finally reached was that he was no animal—he was just practical, that was all." He starts building his underground residence, thinking that it will impress Ariadne. Unfortunately, while Baldasare sees digging as the way to achieve his dreams, nobody else is able to look past the negative connotations of digging and life underground.

Setting

The setting is also a crucial component of the story. The story is set in the developing American West in the early 1900s, when most of the good land had already been snatched up, and immigrants like Baldasare were left with scraps of infertile real estate. When Baldasare arrives at the train station and asks a farmer for directions to his land, the man's comments indicate that he thinks the land is worthless. "That's where all the Guineas are," he said, "that's where Mead sold 'em. Seventy acres, isn't it? That's what I figured. Same as the rest." The farmer's use of the word "Guinea" underscores the racist attitudes that were aimed toward Italian Americans in this time period. Not many expected Italian American immigrants to succeed in America, even if they had bought land. It was more likely that they would end up working for a more wealthy landowner, as Baldasare has to when his savings start to run out. "He plowed another man's fields, planted another man's trees, dug irrigation channels and set grape canes for one stranger after another." This depresses Baldasare. "He'd dreamed of independence. . . . and what had he gotten but wage slavery all over again?"

Historical Context

Immigration from Italy in the late 1800s and early 1900s

In the story, Baldasare moves to California in 1905, after having emigrated to America from Italy several years before. He was not alone. The last two decades of the nineteenth century and the first two decades of the twentieth witnessed America's biggest period of Italian immigration. The Italians had powerful reasons to leave their homeland. In 1870, following the conquest of Rome and the unification of Italy into one state, many Italians experienced a crushing poverty, brought on by political chaos, overpopulation, and an overabundance of agricultural products that caused a massive deflation in the market. Seeking a better life, many Italians emigrated to other countries. "By the end of the century more than 5.3 million Italians of all ages had emigrated, nearly half a million more than Italy's population growth up to that point," Jerre Mangione and Ben Morreale note in their book *La Storia: Five Centuries of the Italian American Experience.*

Besides poverty, some Italians left home because their opportunities in Italy were limited. In the story, Baldasare realizes that he will never be successful in Italy, because he is not the eldest son. Mangione and Morreale note this trend: "It was the eldest who took charge of the family in the event of the father's death and who became the chief beneficiary of whatever properties the family had." Unfortunately, many Italians left a bad situation to come into a worse one. Many of the immigrants were illiterate, and were too trusting, making them ripe targets for hucksters that only wanted to steal their money by offering to find the immigrants a job or a place to live, and never delivering on either promise. Or, these charlatans worked as agents for employers who sought cheap labor. In some cases, the employer rigged it so that the immigrant owed money for lodgings or work supplies, and made sure that the immigrant's salary was never enough to cover these expenses, thus making the immigrant a

Compare & Contrast

- **1900s:** Although the population shift caused by California's 1849 Gold Rush has slowed, immigrants of all ethnicities continue to come to California, attracted by the promise of land or work.

  Today: More than 30 percent of all foreign-born people in the United States live in California. Since California is a Mexican border state, one of the continuing concerns is the flood of illegal immigration from Mexico. The dangers of unregulated immigration also becomes a hot topic in all of America following terrorist attacks in New York and Washington, D.C., on September 11, 2001, which ignite a war on terrorism and a widespread fear of some foreigners, especially those of Middle Eastern descent.

- **1900s:** Following widespread irrigation of the land in the late nineteenth century, California's agricultural output increases. In addition to vineyards—introduced mainly by European settlers in the mid-nineteenth century—the state also boasts many citrus orchards, such as those for oranges and lemons.

  Today: California grows more than 50 percent of all fruits and vegetables marketed in the United States, and produces more than 90 percent of all domestic wines. The state also produces several specialty crops, including artichokes, avocados, dates, kiwifruit, olives, prunes, and raisins.

- **1900s:** As America's population grows and urban areas expand, cities build subways and other forms of mass transportation, greatly enhancing the modern infrastructure.

  Today: Following the digital revolution of the late twentieth century, fiber optic cables and other forms of modern infrastructure—designed to transport large amounts of data at high speeds—are installed underground and in various buildings in both urban and suburban areas.

---

type of indentured servant. Since many, like Baldasare in the story, did not read or write English, they had little recourse to defend themselves in situations such as these. Mangione and Morreale note: ''In 1885, in an effort to protect foreign workers from unscrupulous hiring agents, Congress enacted the contract labor laws that made it illegal to recruit immigrants before they reached the United States.''

Baldasare Forestiere

Boyle's story features a character named Baldasare Forestiere, who is modeled on an actual Italian American immigrant who came to Fresno, California in the early 1900s. Forestiere's life is shrouded in mystery, and not all of the details are known, or agreed upon. For example, while Boyle's story has Forestiere coming to California in 1905, some sources say it was 1904, some put it as late as 1907, and others simply indicate that it was the early 1900s. Likewise, while the story is correct in saying that Forestiere bought the land in Fresno and gave up on the idea of farming because the ground was too hard and infertile, there is some disagreement on how many acres Forestiere actually bought. Some say seventy acres, as it is in Boyle's story, while others put the number as low as ten—the size of the modern-day Forestiere Underground Gardens, a tourist attraction run by Forestiere's heirs that is registered with the National Register of Historic Places. Most sources agree that Forestiere dug his gardens over a period of about four decades, but not everybody gives the same reason as to why he started in the first place. Some say that Forestiere, like Boyle's character, began the project to escape the weather. But Boyle's story deviates from most accounts, which say that it was extreme heat—not torrential rains—that caused Forestiere to seek underground shelter. According to one legend that has sprung up around the gardens, Forestiere began digging the gardens in an effort to win the love of a woman. This, in fact, may have helped spark Boyle's story and the character of Ariadne. Of course, the only thing that can be certain of is that Forestiere left a unique and massive structure as his legacy, which one can still visit as of 2004.

Critical Overview

Boyle is known for his short fiction. As Denis Hennessy notes in his 1999 entry on Boyle for *Dictionary of Literary Biography,* "Boyle has built his career as a short-story writer on stylistic innovations and inventive subject matter, always displaying his respect for the power of short fiction to entertain." Yet, for all of the critical acclaim he has received for his short stories, not many scholars have commented on "The Underground Gardens" or, for that matter, the collection in which it was included, *After the Plague.*

Those who have reviewed the book, however, have given it high marks. In his 2001 review of the book for *Library Journal,* David W. Henderson calls the stories "wickedly ironic, sometimes poignant, sometimes darkly humorous tales that speak directly to the human condition and to a variety of contemporary social issues." Henderson also notes that the book "is classic Boyle, a work to be embraced by his enthusiasts and one that belongs in most collections of serious fiction." At the same time, he says that "The Underground Gardens" is "Somewhat out of context, but no less touching" than the other stories.

Henderson has good reason to single out "The Underground Gardens," since it is the rare Boyle story that features a protagonist like Baldasare, an optimist who continues to try, even when his dreams fail. As Hennessy notes, Boyle's protagonists are usually deplorable:

> There are no true heroes in Boyle's short fiction. The reader may ask as well if there are any real, memorable characters in his stories or if the cynicism of his stories has obliterated the humanity of the characters.

Still, while "The Underground Gardens" is different in moral tone than many of Boyle's other stories, its historical setting is one that the author has used again and again. As Jon Regardie notes in his 2000 *Los Angeles Magazine* review of Boyle's novel, *A Friend of the Earth,* Boyle practices a "blend of historical fiction and satire that has nabbed

him a fistful of honors." Likewise, in his 1998 review of Boyle's novel *Riven Rock,* for *The Washington Times,* David Patterson noted that the author "loves the era in which this novel is placed. For a satirist the early twentieth century is ripe territory." Patterson also says that "The prejudices of that earlier age were also firmer and perhaps more obvious than our own," a fact that Boyle plays on to great effect in "The Underground Gardens."

Criticism

Ryan D. Poquette

Poquette has a bachelor's degree in English and specializes in writing about literature. In the following essay, Poquette discusses Coraghessan's use of imagery in "The Underground Gardens."

The specific details of the life of Baldasare Forestiere—the Italian American historical figure who spent four decades digging a unique underground complex in Fresno, California, in the early 1900s—are open to debate. As depicted by Boyle's short story, "The Underground Gardens," Baldasare is a hardworking Italian immigrant who comes to America to make his fortune. Imbued with a strong faith in his abilities and a self-sufficient nature, Boyle's Forestiere perseveres even as his initial dreams are crushed and he must find the strength to follow new ones. He is a noble man who has admirable, even heroic qualities. This goes against the assessment of critics such as Denis Hennessy, who notes in his *Dictionary of Literary Biography* entry on Boyle, "The reader may ask as well if there are any real, memorable characters in his stories or if the cynicism of his stories has obliterated the humanity of the characters." When an author chooses to break his or her normal style, it is usually for good reason. By examining the effects of Boyle's use of imagery in "The Underground Gardens" one can begin to understand why the author deviates from his normal practice of writing cynical stories.

"The Underground Gardens" is an extremely visual story. From the very first paragraph, Boyle sets up the two types of imagery that he uses throughout the story which give the tale much of its

A vineyard in San Joaquin Valley, California, in the mid-1900s, similar to the one described in Boyle's ''The Underground Gardens''

power and help define Boyle's interpretation of Baldasare's life:

> As a boy in Sicily he stood beside his brothers under the sun that was like a hammer and day after day stabbed his shovel into the skin of the ancient venerable earth of their father's orchards.

The sun in Sicily is so hot it is ''like a hammer,'' setting up the story's strong environmental imagery. Likewise, Baldasare digs in the ''skin'' of his father's orchards, setting up the story's anatomical imagery. Environmental images are important to the plot of the story. Baldasare's labor background in Italy has prepared and conditioned him to work in Fresno's extreme heat. In fact, he prefers it to the ''sleet and snow'' that he faced working in America's eastern cities. He refers to California's weather as ''good Sicilian heat, heat that baked you right down to the grateful marrow of your happy Sicilian bones.'' His ability to survive in this weather separates this ''sun-seared little man'' from many others, including his intended beloved, Ariadne Siagris, and her family. When Baldasare comes to pick up Ariadne, the ''Siagris children lay about like swatted flies,'' and it is ''too hot to smile, so'' Mrs. Siagris ''grimaced instead.'' And unlike Baldasare,

Ariadne does not see the value in saving money by walking on a hot day. When he comes to pick her up to take her to see his house, she is shocked that he does not have a carriage and that he is expecting them to walk. '''Walk?'' she echoed. ''In this heat? You must be crazy.''

Baldasare is not, however, immune to the effects of the heat. In fact, when he goes against his laboring nature and tries to be something he is not, by dressing up in fancy clothes to impress Ariadne, he is as hot and miserable as the rest of the populace. ''He was wearing his best suit of clothes, washed just the evening before, and the unfamiliar jacket clung to him like dead skin.'' He is also not able to fully escape the cold that he faced in New York and Boston. During a particularly rainy night in his shack, the cold is almost unbearable. ''He was wearing every stitch of clothing he possessed, wrapped in his blankets and huddled over the coal-oil lamp, and still he froze, even here in California.''

These environmental factors, especially the cold, ultimately give Baldasare his initiative to start digging an underground home. During that cold, rainy night, he remembers his work in the tunnels in New York and Boston, ''how clean they were, how warm

What Do I Read Next?

- In "The Underground Gardens," Baldasare lives underground, as his father once told him the animals do. In Boyle's first collection of short stories, *The Descent of Man* (1979), each story examines humanity's reversion to an animal-like state. This quirky collection of stories includes a woman who falls in love with an ape, a man who risks physical harm to win an eating contest, and a group of pillaging Norsemen who burn books—which represent a threat to their barbarian lifestyle.

- Boyle's novel *East Is East* (1991) tells the story of Hiro Tanaka, a Japanese man who comes to the United States to try to find his American father. Like Baldasare, Hiro has visions of finding a new life in America, where he thinks that a mixed-race man such as himself will be accepted. His dreams, however, are thwarted when he lands in Georgia and experiences racism, among other challenges.

- Boyle's novel *The Tortilla Curtain* (1995) focuses mainly on two couples in Southern California—an affluent American family and an illegal immigrant family from Mexico. The book explores the lifestyles, attitudes, and challenges of these two couples, as well as the struggle to keep immigrants out of America, which was itself founded by immigrants.

- Italo Calvino was one of the most quirky Italian writers of the twentieth century. His collection of short stories, *Gli amori difficili* (1970) was translated into English by William Weaver, Archibald Colquhoun, and Peggy Wright as *Difficult Loves* (1984). This collection explores the idea of love in all of its forms.

- *Don't Tell Mama!: The Penguin Book of Italian American Writing* (2002), edited by Regina Barreca, contains selections of Italian American fiction and nonfiction writing from the 1800s to the present. The nearly one hundred contributors include such well-known figures as David Baldacci, Don DeLillo, Jay Leno, Mario Puzo, and Ray Romano.

- Boyle has noted in interviews that one of his professional influences was Latin American writer Gabriel García Márquez. In García Márquez's collection *Doce cuentos peregrinos,* published in Madrid in 1992, the stories feature the trials and tribulations of Latin American characters abroad in Europe. Translated by Edith Grossman as *Strange Pilgrims: Twelve Stories,* the collection was published by Knopf in 1993.

---

in winter and cool in summer, how they smelled, always, of the richness of the earth." Baldasare, a very earthy man and raised to respect the soil, ultimately decides that living in the earth is a more natural choice for him than trying to live the aboveground, conventional life of everybody else.

Anatomical imagery also plays a large role in the story, especially as it relates to Baldasare's passion for Ariadne. Throughout the story, Boyle chooses images that contain undertones of sex or attraction. As a lifelong laborer, Baldasare has developed a toned body, so that when he lifts the handles of his new wheelbarrow, he feels "the familiar flex of the muscles of his lower back." Later, when Baldasare is trying to impress Ariadne and win back her love by digging the heart-shaped hole underneath her window, he wonders if she is watching, but "if she saw the lean muscles of his arms strain and his back flex, she gave no sign of it." Even Baldasare's digging takes on erotic qualities. For example, the day after he meets Ariadne, he begins digging the cellar that he expects will someday be a part of their house, and it is obvious that he is thinking about her in romantic terms while he is working. "The pick rose and fell, the shovel licked at the earth with all the probing intimacy of a tongue."

> To Baldasare, Ariadne's stoutness is a positive sign of her social status. As a poor immigrant, Baldasare has always restricted himself--in eating, spending, and all other aspects of living. To him, success in America means pursuing a robust, unrestricted life, the type of life that Ariadne currently leads."

Images of Ariadne and her anatomy also play prominently in the story, in both subtle and not-so-subtle ways. When Baldasare examines his new Fresno land to try to find a water source, he observes ''the way the hill of his shack and the one beside it abutted each other like the buttocks of a robust and fecund woman.'' This description foreshadows, or predicts, the introduction of Ariadne, who grows in physical size as Baldasare's love grows for her. ''He watched with satisfaction as her hips and buttocks swelled so that even at nineteen she had to walk with a waddle.'' Given the modern American culture, which tends to emphasize thinness, Baldasare's attraction might seem strange to some readers. Yet, to Baldasare, Ariadne's weight is an asset. He remembers one of the women in Italy, Signora Cardino, ''who was said to drink olive oil instead of wine and breakfast on sugared cream and cake.'' To Baldasare, Ariadne's stoutness is a positive sign of her social status. As a poor immigrant, Baldasare has always restricted himself—in eating, spending, and all other aspects of living. To him, success in America means pursuing a robust, unrestricted life, the type of life that Ariadne currently leads. As the word ''fecund'' suggests in the above quote that describes Baldasare's land, Ariadne's girth also represents fertility. Baldasare's dream includes a large family, ''his four sons and three daughters sprinting like colts across the yard,'' and he envisions Ariadne as the mother of these children.

Baldasare has a conviction that no others in the story possess. His passion for Ariadne is so intense that he is unwilling to let it go for any reason, and Boyle underscores this passion through his use of imagery. Unfortunately, Baldasare assumes that Ariadne's feelings for him are equally as strong, failing to recognize that the other characters in the story, including Ariadne, are more superficial than he is. Just as Ariadne expects to be shuttled around in a carriage as opposed to walking, she also is not willing to sacrifice her conventional vision of an aboveground home and accept Baldasare's underground palace.

Yet, even though Baldasare's goals of growing grapevines and marrying Ariadne ultimately prove impossible, and he willingly remains an outsider, he ends the story happier than all of the other characters, who let circumstances dictate their futures. For example, when it is clear to Ariadne that Baldasare is not rich, she promptly marries the wealthy Hiram Broadbent. Though he has money, he is also ''a drunk'' and ''mean as the devil,'' and one suspects that Ariadne's marriage will be less than rosy. Baldasare is the only character who is totally in control of his future. He focuses on digging his underground complex, an activity that is not subject to any environmental or human factors. He is driven by the strength of this final vision, which is almost religious in nature. ''Standing there in the everlasting silence beneath the earth, he reached out a hand to the wall in front of him, his left hand, pronating the palm as if to bless some holy place.'' One expects that Boyle's character will spend decades carving out his underground palace and that he will be happy while he is doing it.

So why did Boyle, who is known for his cynical satires about humans with few redeeming qualities, choose to write a nice little story about a hardworking Italian American immigrant who perseveres and who, given the historical background of the real Baldasare Forestiere, will probably end up succeeding? The answer may come from Boyle's own life. Like Baldasare, Boyle is an outsider, who initially wanted to be accepted by society. In his early career, Boyle yearned to be included among the nation's popular authors, but as Hennessy notes, ''he has never become a household name.'' Like Baldasare, Boyle denied the urge to conform, even if it meant achieving his dream, and has instead stayed true to his own quirky nature. Boyle has been outspoken about his intent to write the way he wants to and has become noted for his unconventional appearance. As Hennessy notes, ''Boyle has created a zany image for himself by accentuating his frizzy hair and wearing punk clothing while affecting a semiserious scowl.'' Given the great lengths to which Boyle goes in the story to label Baldasare an outsider, and the fact that Baldasare is the only truly happy character at the end of the story, it is likely that Boyle gave ''The Underground Gardens'' a positive spin to send the message that outsiders win in the end—regardless of what anybody thinks of their unconventional lifestyles.

Source: Ryan D. Poquette, Critical Essay on ''The Underground Gardens,'' in *Short Stories for Students,* Gale, 2004.

Curt Guyette

Guyette is a longtime journalist. He received a bachelor of arts degree in English writing from the University of Pittsburgh. In this essay, Guyette discusses Boyle's ability to take a story based in fact and transform it into a work of literature.

In his short story ''The Underground Gardens''—part of a collection published in 2001 titled *After the Plague*—author T. Coraghessan Boyle creates what appears to be a fable that is both beautifully written and extremely poignant. A man, inspired by love, begins digging. Using nothing but a pick, shovel, and wheelbarrow, the man—a poor, uneducated laborer—continues his back-breaking toil until he has created a sprawling underground home he hopes will so impress his beloved that she will take his callused hands in marriage. What could be more ''fantastic,'' in the strictest sense of that word? It is like a rapturous dream, the stuff of pure fantasy. That sense of incredibility is carried through to the end as the author seems to opt for a climax that takes a sorrowful chronicle of romantic tragedy and transforms it into something pure and inspirational. Instead of concluding this story on a note of heartbreak when the woman runs from what she perceives as the insanity of the man's enterprise, the protagonist, his body beaten and bones broken but with his spirit still intact, envisions an even more elaborate underground world. Rather than succumb to despair and depression over the loss of his love, the spurned suitor begins clawing his way toward a vision even more impossibly grand than the one with which he began.

Upon reading this story, one is tempted to describe it as ''fabulous,'' meaning that it explores a mythic world where the hero is capable of superhuman feats, much like Hercules performing his twelve labors. There is only one problem with depicting this tale in that way: ''The Underground

> In the process of fulfilling his dream Baldasare Forestiere inspired others, including Boyle himself, who was so moved by the life's work of a poor immigrant that he created a beautiful and moving piece of literature that reads as if it were a fable."

Gardens'' is based in fact. There really was an Italian immigrant by the name of Baldasare Forestiere who, at the beginning of the last century, bought 70 acres of land in California with the intent of creating a vineyard. To his dismay, he learned too late that he had been duped into handing over his life's savings for a piece of property covered with a layer of hardpan rock just beneath the topsoil, making agriculture impossible. But he did not let that setback break his spirit. His body strengthened by years of labor digging subway tunnels in Boston and New York, he did construct an underground home beneath the thick sheet of hardpan with the hopes that his true love would be truly enamored with both his labors and its ingenious results. And, as with Boyle's story, the woman recoils at the thought of living underground and rejects his proposal of marriage. Boyle ends his story with Forestiere experiencing a vision so clear and precise and full-blown that it seems as if it could be divinely inspired. In reality, Forestiere worked for nearly 40 years to bring that vision to fruition, creating a subterranean wonderland of more than 90 rooms spread across seven acres. It is a marvelous, brilliantly conceived structure replete with fruit trees and grapevines, a fishpond, grottoes, and a ballroom.

So, what is it that makes Boyle's story a piece of literature rather than a biographical sketch? As with other of his works, such as the novel *The Road to Wellville*, Boyle takes a real-life character and uses him to explore specific aspects of our society. In this case he touches on a number of issues, including the discrimination and degradation immigrants to this country faced in the past and, often, still face today. Like Forestiere, these people, through their labor and their creativity, rise above the prejudice they face to build a society that is better and stronger than the one that greeted them.

But ''The Underground Gardens'' is more than just a social critique. This story tackles a broader, more universal issue by asking and answering the question: what separates man from other animals. This issue is established in the first paragraph when Boyle writes this of Forestiere: ''As a young man in Boston and New York he burrowed like a rodent beneath streets and rivers, scouring the walls of subway tubes and aqueducts, dropping his pick, lifting his shovel, mining dirt.'' Soon afterward, Boyle depicts the shanty—little more than a ''glorified chicken coop,'' really—that Forestiere had constructed. Boyle writes:

> It was a shelter that was all, a space that separated him from the animals, that reminded him he was a man and not a beast. *Men are upright,* his father told him when he was a boy, *and they have dominion over the beasts. Men live in houses, don't they? And where do the beasts live,* mio figlio? *In the ground, no? In a hole.''*

Given this, it is possible to look upon a man like Forestiere as something less than human, an illiterate beast of burden toiling his entire life beneath the earth, clawing at soil to dig himself an elaborate burrow. He is a man who has no appreciation for the niceties of civilization. Only once does he seek out some form of entertainment, a visit to a burlesque show. But even that he can't enjoy because he so frets over the few cents he feels he has squandered over this lone night out.

In the end, not even love is redemptive. How can it be when it is not returned, even though it is epic and soul stirring? How else would one describe a love that would motivate a man to spend two years digging beneath the ground in an attempt to woo a woman who, at the very best, has more than her share of flaws? And when his beloved Ariadne rejects him because he lives in the ground like some animal and turns instead for marriage to a mean-spirited drunk, how does Forestiere attempt to win her back? With more digging. It borders on insanity, really. Boyle, who writes with beautifully vivid prose, describes with heart-breaking clarity how Forestiere hopes that this girl who is wholly unworthy of such magnificent devotion, this girl with whiskers like a cat and ''hands like doughballs fried in lard,'' will gaze out her window to see his muscles and sinews flex as he sweats and strains to create the mute communication of a heart. It is all he

has to offer, because he is unable to put his words down on paper and spell out his love in a letter.

In the end, what separates man from the animals is his ability to dream. A mole burrows into the ground to create shelter. That, too, is what Forestiere did. The difference is that he did it in the hopes that his efforts would win him the woman of his dreams. And when that failed, instead of caving in to depression, he became inspired simply by an idea itself. He dreamed not just of shelter—that he already had. He dreamed of creating a palace that would stand as a testament to his own particular genius. He dreamed of creating an underground paradise that would let the world know that he had not just survived and toiled during his time on this earth but had created something magnificent that would live on long after he departed. He dreamed of a legacy that would carry his name: Baldasare Forestiere's Underground Gardens. Then he fulfilled that dream, setting him apart not just from the animals but also from many of his fellow men. Few people ever dream with such grandeur, and fewer still ever achieve such greatness.

In the process of fulfilling his dream Baldasare Forestiere inspired others, including Boyle himself, who was so moved by the life's work of a poor immigrant that he created a beautiful and moving piece of literature that reads as if it were a fable.

Source: Curt Guyette, Critical Essay on ''The Underground Gardens,'' in *Short Stories for Students,* Gale, 2004.

Jeff Hill

Hill is a freelance writer and editor who specializes in literature. In the following essay, Hill analyzes the contrasts between the aboveground and subterranean environments in ''The Underground Gardens'' and argues that these elements illustrate Baldasare's achievement of greater self-knowledge and independence.

''The Underground Gardens'' opens with an epigraph that quotes Franz Kafka's story ''The Burrow.'' It's a fitting introduction: ''The Burrow'' features an unnamed narrator (perhaps an animal, but with very human concerns) who, in typically drawn-out Kafka fashion, details his anxieties about his subterranean home. At times, his worries about the security of his burrow and the dangers that lie aboveground grow so extreme that he is unable to approach the opening that leads to the outside world.

Likewise, ''The Underground Gardens'' deals with the division between the world above and the world below. T. Coraghessan Boyle drives this point home with both the larger events of the story's plot and the smaller details of description. When combined, these elements create a rich story that contrasts high and low, up and down. The vertical positioning of people and things is stressed repeatedly. When linked to the larger ideas they stand for, the surface and subterranean worlds become important clues that lead to a deeper understanding of the story and, more specifically, the insight Baldasare gains at its conclusion.

A man buys a plot of inhospitable land. He falls in love. He builds an elaborate underground residence in hopes of winning his beloved, but he loses her. He ends with a vision of making an even more elaborate subterranean palace. These events are interesting in themselves, but what else is at stake? To arrive at an answer, it's necessary to consider larger ideas that might be implied in the concepts of above and below. In other words, if the surface and subterranean worlds are considered as symbols or metaphors, what do they mean?

Those things existing above the ground are generally linked to material success and a conventional domestic lifestyle that includes a comfortable home and a family. Initially, these elements—wealth, home, and marriage—are associated with independence, and they are the very things that Baldasare was denied in Sicily by virtue of his not being the eldest child. It could also be said that these are some of the key ingredients of the so-called American Dream that drew millions of immigrants to the United States.

The subterranean world is treated in two ways: Initially, it's considered a lesser, inhuman place. This is made clear in Baldasare's memories of his father's words:

> *Men are upright,* his father had told him when he was a boy, *and they have dominion over the beasts. Men live in houses, don't they? And where do beasts live, mio figlio? In the ground, no? In a hole.*

But in the course of the story, the underground world takes on a different meaning: it becomes associated with an alternative, creative life that allows Baldasare to utilize and benefit from his true talents.

What makes Baldasare such an interesting character is that he is attracted by both the upper world and the lower one. Early in the story, he envisions his future home as a "house of four rooms and a porch set on a hill." The description is telling: His dream is not only to live atop the ground but to gain

> **"** But the aspect that most attracts him to the underworld is that it allows him to build and create in a way that was impossible on the surface. Art rather than practicality becomes his focus, as he compares his work to the great architecture of the past."

as much elevation as possible. The vineyard he intends to create is likewise a thing of the surface world. Though the vines grow from the soil, the description "seventy acres buried in grapes" emphasizes the plants' aboveground fruit.

There is another part to Baldasare's dream: a family. He pictures it along with his hilltop house— "his wife on the porch, his four sons and three daughters sprinting like colts across the yard." It's a picture-book vision of domestic bliss, and Baldasare clings to this family dream even after his vineyard proves unfeasible. Enter Ariadne. In Baldasare's mind, she's the woman on the porch. Her connection to the aboveground world is made clear by the many "upward" descriptions of her. When the couple walks down the street, Ariadne's height forces Baldasare to "reach up awkwardly" to take her arm. And, despite the weight that goes along with her "stout" size, his perception is that she "floated above her feet like one of the airships the Germans so prized." She also personifies the prosperity and happiness Baldasare expected to find in the United States: "She was the one," he tells himself. "She was the one he'd come to America for." Later he marvels at the "sweet flow of familiar phrases that dropped so easily from her supple American lips."

Then there is the issue of money. It could be argued that one of the reasons that Baldasare fixates on Ariadne is that she is associated with material success, at least compared with his own humble means. But her wealth is also an obstacle. Given Baldasare's poverty, wooing Ariadne does not seem much more likely than creating a vineyard on his hardpan acreage. His thoughts outline the problem specifically:

> What could he offer her, a girl like that who'd come all the way from Chicago, Illinois, to live with her uncle, the prosperous Greek—a school-educated girl used to fine things and books.

To put it in common terms, Ariadne is "above" Baldasare in terms of wealth and social standing. But when he makes his attempt to overcome this obstacle, he does not go up, he goes down—literally. He constructs a large home in the only manner he has available to him—by carving it out of the earth.

In the process, Baldasare discovers that the subterranean world is not as subhuman as his father once declared. Baldasare initially justifies his underground life by saying that "he was just practical," and he notes how the hardpan soil is "impervious to the rain and sun, and more durable than any shingle or tile." But the aspect that most attracts him to the underworld is that it allows him to build and create in a way that was impossible on the surface. Art rather than practicality becomes his focus, as he compares his work to the great architecture of the past. "He could already see a hallway there, a broad grand hallway, straight as a plumb line and as graceful and sensible as the arches the Romans of antiquity put to such good use in their time." His designs steadily grow more elaborate. "When he completed a passage or a room or carved his way to the sky for light, he could already see the next passage and the next room beyond that." There is also a spiritual element to his creativity. He connects his dome-shaped cellar with "the apse of the cathedral in which he'd worshipped as a boy," and at the end of the story he raises his hand to an underground wall "as if to bless some holy place."

Though inspired in the underworld, Baldasare is still faced with the difficulty of integrating his subterranean existence with his romantic quest. At one point he declares that "he was digging for her, for Ariadne," but this is no simple task. To bring together his underground home and an aboveground woman Baldasare must unite two worlds that, throughout the story, are shown to be opposites.

Which is why his plans unravel. Ariadne is bound up with material success and its conventional trappings. She simply cannot conceive of a home in the ground and refuses to consider a marriage that would make her inhabit such a place. (Unlike the mythic Ariadne whose thread gives Theseus a way to escape from the labyrinth, this Ariadne leaves her suitor to his underworld maze.) Boyle masterfully expresses the up and down of this situation in the passage where Baldasare attempts to show Ariadne his home.

> He'd become insistent, and he had his hand on her arm, trying to lead her down from the carriage. . . . He wanted to tell her, but the words wouldn't come, and he tried to articulate it all through the pressure of his hand on her arm, tugging, as if the whole world depended on her getting down from that carriage—and it did, it did!
>
> "Let go!" she cried, snatching her arm away. . . .
>
> He tried to reach for her again—"Please," he begged, "please"—but she jerked back from him so violently the carriage nearly buckled on its springs.

Tug as he might, Baldasare cannot bring the two worlds—above and below—together. This is made doubly clear when he attempts to transfer his subterranean talents up to ground level. In excavating the valentine in the vacant lot, he exposes his greatest gift—his ability to dig—to the surface dwellers. It's to no avail: his work goes unacknowledged by Ariadne, and he receives a beating for his efforts.

These events give an interesting twist on Boyle's vertical metaphors: Ariadne and others in the aboveground world are people of the surface—not only because they desire conventional comforts but because their decisions are ruled by appearances, what's visible on the surface. Ariadne judges Baldasare solely on his wealth as expressed in a large, aboveground house. She gives no consideration to his character or his other accomplishments. Her desire to maintain the appearance of success leads her to choose a man who has "always got money in his pocket" despite the possibility that he's an alcoholic who is "mean as the devil."

These elements are part of a shift in attitude that becomes more pronounced as the story progresses. The tone of the descriptions begins to suggest that perhaps it is those in the upper world that are flawed, rather than the ground dweller. This can be seen when Baldasare ascends "two stories above the ground" to Siagris's walkup residence to pick up Ariadne for their first date. He's greeted by a grim and unpleasant atmosphere rather than "the fine things" he had previously imagined:

> Up here, inside, it was even hotter. The Siagris children lay about like swatted flies, and Mrs. Siagris, her hair like some wild beast clawing at her scalp, poked her head around the corner from the kitchen. It was too hot to smile, so she grimaced instead and pulled her head back out of sight.

The term "beast" plays off the words that Baldasare's father used when dismissing the creatures of the underworld. The scene turns his thoughts on their head and reveals that life can be a beastly affair aboveground, even for "the prosperous Greek." Indeed, the story implies that those farther up the social hierarchy in Fresno are in some sense deficient or diseased. Obesity is common among this group: Siagris's shirt sticks to "the bulge of his belly"; Hiram Broadbent is a "[b]ig, fat man." After her arrival Ariadne grows so large that "she had to walk with a waddle," and she's afflicted with blotchy skin and a perpetual cold.

If the surface world and its inhabitants are flawed, what can be said of Baldasare? The metaphoric implication is that he is "deep," as compared to the superficial people at ground level. Physical appearance is certainly not a high priority for him: Ariadne's "imperfections" seem to accentuate his resolve rather than reducing it. But the depth of his character is better expressed by the insight he achieves at the conclusion of the story.

Rather than being demoralized by his loss of Ariadne and yielding to the "life of disillusionment," he finds new purpose in his vision of the Underground Gardens. He recognizes that love and matrimony were not his real goals after all. Instead, he has decided to cultivate his creative, unconventional existence while abandoning his previous dreams of material wealth and domesticity. Instead of being a monument to his beloved, the Underground Gardens become an end in themselves.

So self-knowledge becomes Baldasare's reward. This fits well with the theme of subterranean digging. It could be said that his excavations serve as a symbol for digging inside himself, finding his true emotions, and discovering what he finds most important. In psychoanalytical terms, it could be said that he mines his subconscious to come to a better understanding of himself and his desires.

Does this mean that he has completely abandoned the American Dream that inspired him originally? Not entirely, because even though he has given up on marriage and seems less concerned with gaining material wealth, another of his goals remains intact. He wants to control his own destiny. "He'd dreamed of independence," the story states at one point, and the vision of the Underground Gardens is certainly a move toward doing things his own way.

The main change that has taken place by the end of the story is that he has rejected the superficial trappings of independence. Baldasare's revised American Dream is not based on getting rich or on being a respectable family man. It's about having the freedom to build a monumental creation so that people could "see what he'd accomplished in his time on earth." Or, more accurately, what he'd accomplished *beneath* the earth, because it's the essential, underlying things that most inspire him.

Source: Jeff Hill, Critical Essay on "The Underground Gardens," in *Short Stories for Students,* Gale, 2004.

Sources

Boyle, T. Coraghessan, "The Underground Gardens," in *After the Plague,* Viking, 2001, pp. 262–80.

Henderson, David W., Review of *After the Plague,* in *Library Journal,* Vol. 126, No. 13, August 2001, p. 168.

Hennessy, Denis, "T. Coraghessan Boyle," in *Dictionary of Literary Biography,* Vol. 218, *American Short-Story Writers Since World War II, Second Series,* edited by Patrick Meanor and Gwen Crane, Gale, 1999, pp. 70–77.

Kafka, Franz, "The Burrow," in *Selected Short Stories of Franz Kafka,* translated by Willa Muir and Edwin Muir, Modern Library, 1952, pp. 256–304.

Mangione, Jerre, and Ben Morreale, *La Storia: Five Centuries of the Italian American Experience,* HarperCollins, 1992, pp. 69, 94, 270.

Patterson, David, "Love and Madness in America," in the *Washington Times,* March 29, 1998, p. 7.

Regardie, Jon, "Boyle's Life," in *Los Angeles Magazine,* Vol. 45, No. 10, October 2000, p. 30.

Further Reading

Cosco, Joseph P., *Imagining Italians: The Clash of Romance and Race in American Perceptions, 1880–1910,* State University of New York Press, 2003.
    Cosco draws on history, literary criticism, and cultural studies to explore the effect of Italian Americans on national identity and vice versa, during the years of 1880–1990, a time when many Italians immigrated to America.

DiStasi, Lawrence, ed., *The Big Book of Italian American Culture,* Sanniti Publications, 1996.
    This book profiles the lives of many famous and ordinary Italian Americans, including a discussion of Baldasare Forestiere and his underground gardens.

Guglielmo, Jennifer, and Salvatore Salerno, eds., *Are Italians White?: How Race Is Made in America,* Routledge, 2003.

> This thought-provoking collection of original essays examines how and why the concept of whiteness became important to Italian Americans, as well as how various immigrants have dealt with racism in American society. The book also explores the contributions that Italian Americans have made to American culture.

Leffingwell, Randy, *California Wine Country: The Most Beautiful Wineries, Vineyards, and Destinations,* Voyageur Press, 2002.

> Although technically a photo travel guide, Leffingwell's book provides an in-depth, illustrated look at California's wine country, including the area of central California where ''The Underground Gardens'' takes place.

McClurg, Sue, and Kevin Starr, *Water and the Shaping of California: A Literary, Political, and Technological Perspective on the Power of Water, and How the Effort to Control It Has Transformed the State,* Heyday Books, 2000.

> In ''The Underground Gardens,'' Baldasare realizes that water is the key to growing his lush grapevines.

> This engaging, multifaceted documentary history of California's water dependence includes more than 200 photos and drawings that illustrate the unique political, economic, and social issues that have surrounded the state's water usage. The book also includes literary selections from some of California's best-known authors.

McWilliams, Carey, *Factories in the Field: The Story of Migratory Farm Labor in California,* University of California Press, 2000.

> First published in 1939, McWilliams's landmark exposé explores the effect of corporate agriculture in California on migrant workers, labor groups and California's economy from the nineteenth century—when much of the available land in California was snatched up—until the 1930s.

Starr, Kevin, *Americans and the California Dream: 1850–1915,* Oxford University Press, 1986.

> In this first book of a multi-part series, Starr explores the early history of California, including the many alluring factors that drew people to the region, such as the Gold Rush. The book is thoroughly researched, and discusses both famous and little-known figures in California history.

You're Ugly, Too

Lorrie Moore

1989

"You're Ugly, Too" by Lorrie Moore was first published in the *New Yorker* in 1989 and was subsequently included in Moore's second collection, *Like Life*, and in several anthologies, including the *The Best American Short Stories, 1989,* the 1997 anthology, *The Penguin Book of International Women's Stories* and *The Best American Short Stories of the Century,* edited by John Updike. "You're Ugly, Too" was Moore's first story to find a home in the *New Yorker,* the magazine considered by many to be the pre-eminent publication for new fiction. According to Don Lee, writing in *Ploughshares,* the story also had the distinction of causing a bit of a stir in the magazine's editorial offices. With the "turgidity" of long-time editor William Shaw still gripping the venerable "institution," *New Yorker* editors pointed out to Moore several "vulgarities" of the writing process she had committed in the story. "All through the editing process, they said, 'Oooh, we're breaking so many rules with this,'" Lee quotes Moore as saying.

Acclaimed for the cutting sarcasm and wit that Moore has come to be known for, "You're Ugly, Too" tells the story of Zoë Hendricks, an unmarried history professor who lives alone in the small Midwestern town of Paris, Illinois, and teaches in the local liberal arts college; the story examines her relationships with men, her students, her sister and, in general, her life. With a sparse plot, Moore's story relies on Hendricks's character and the run-

ning gags and jokes she relentlessly throws at any-one within listening distance to sustain it.

While one of the major themes that "You're Ugly, Too" addresses is obviously sexual relation-ships (throughout much of the story, Hendricks's relationships to men are somehow addressed, either through anecdotes, her biting commentary, or in the story's final scenes at a Halloween party where Hendricks is engaged in a long conversation with a recent divorcé), issues of loneliness, alienation and mortality play a prominent role in the development of Hendricks's character.

Author Biography

Lorrie Moore, born Marie Lorena Moore on February 13, 1957 in Glens Falls, New York, was the second of four children. The daughter of an insurance executive and a former nurse turned house-wife, Moore excelled in her studies and earned a Regents scholarship, which allowed her to enter St. Lawrence University early. While at St. Lawrence, Moore was the recipient of a Paul L. Wolfe Memorial Prize for literature and was also awarded First Prize in a *Seventeen* magazine short story contest for her story, "Raspberries." She graduated summa cum laude from St. Lawrence in 1978.

After a brief stint as a paralegal in Manhattan, Moore entered the master of fine arts program at Cornell University in 1980. Over the next few years, Moore saw several of her stories accepted by such national publications as *Ms, Fiction International,* and *Story Quarterly.* In 1983, Moore sent her collection *Self-Help,* which comprised her master's thesis, to Melanie Jackson, the literary agent of Alison Lurie, one of Moore's teachers at Cornell. Jackson in turn sent the manuscript to Knopf, which immediately bought the collection and published it to rave reviews in 1985.

Moore has been the recipient of several major awards, including a National Endowment for the Arts fellowship in 1989, an O. Henry Award in 1998, and a John Simon Guggenheim Memorial Foundation fellowship. In addition to *Self–Help,* Moore has published two novels, namely *Anagrams* (1986) and *Who Will Run the Frog Hospital* (1994), a juvenile novel titled *The Forgotten Helper* (1987), and two other collections of short stories, which are

Like Life (1990) and *Birds of America* (1998). Moore was also the editor of *I Know Some Things: Stories about Childhood by Contemporary Writers.*

Since 1984, Moore has taught at the University of Wisconsin, Madison, where she holds the Delmore Schwartz Professorship in the Humanities.

Plot Summary

"You're Ugly, Too" is a much more character-driven story than it is a plot-driven one. With a sparse plot, but layered with anecdotes and flash-backs that reveal the main character to be cynical and dismissive in her relationships with nearly everyone in her life, especially men, the story offers a glimpse into the thoughts and daily life of an unmarried Midwestern history professor who flies to Manhattan to spend Halloween weekend with her younger sister.

Although narrated in the third person, "You're Ugly, Too" is told from the point of view of Zoë Hendricks who, when the story opens, has been teaching at Midwest colleges for four years. Her first teaching stint was in New Geneva, Minnesota, or "Land of the Dying Shopping Mall" where "[e]veryone was so blond . . . that brunettes were often presumed to be from foreign countries." Her liberal arts students in Paris, Illinois, where she currently teaches—"by and large good Midwest-erners, spacey with estrogen from large quantities of meat and cheese . . . [who share] their parents' suburban values . . . [and who seem] to know very little about anything. . . . "—do not fare much bet-ter in her eyes. Known for her eccentric behavior—students complain about her singing in class, for instance, and when asked by one student what perfume she is wearing, Hendricks replies, "*Room freshener*"—she is tolerated by her "department of nine men. . . ." After all, the department had recently faced a sex-discrimination suit and the men are in need of a "feminine touch to the corridors."

Hendricks lives alone in Paris and has had poor luck in meeting men. Of the three men she has dated since moving to the Midwest, the first was a Paris bureaucrat who surveyed his own pectorals while driving and who became incensed when she brushed an ant onto his car floor. "Now it's going to lay eggs in my car!" he complained. Her second date concluded his emotion-filled critique of a piece of museum art by saying, "A painting like that. . . . It just makes you sh——t." And her third and final date was with a political science professor who liked to go on double dates with friends so he could flirt and play footsie with their wives in restaurants.

One of Hendricks's characteristic features is that she loves to tell jokes, often at the expense of her immediate audience. In fact, she is writing a book on humor, and her entire life, and this story, seems to be held together with one joke after another. Her jokes usually have a sarcastic and cynical edge to them, and she usually tells them with utter disregard for the situation. Even when severe abdominal pains force her to undergo ultrasound tests that we are all but told reveal a perilous growth inside of her, she is relentless in her sarcasm. Her favorite joke, which is the source of the story's title, is about a man who is told by his doctor that he has six weeks to live. The man says he wants another opinion. "You want a second opinion? OK," says the doctor. "You're ugly, too."

"You're Ugly, Too" comprises anecdotes and flashbacks that effectively paint Hendricks as a cynical, dismissive, lonely and possibly depressed character. The only "action" in the story takes place when her younger sister, Evan, invites her to Manhattan where Evan and her boyfriend are hosting a Halloween party. At the party, Evan introduces her to Earl, a recent divorcé, who is dressed as a naked woman with "large rubber breasts protruding like hams." Wearing a bonehead costume ("It's this thing that looks like a giant bone going through your head," she had told her sister), Hendricks engages in conversation with Earl, who wants to talk about love and relationships. Hendricks, however, dismisses him by replying with lies, vague allusions, and a long story that ends with the protagonist shooting herself in the head. Earl seems defeated, barely able to keep up with her wit and seeming irreverence, and at one point shakes his head in disbelief and says, "You know, I just shouldn't try to go out with career women. You're all stricken. A guy can really tell what life has done to you. I do better with women who have part-time jobs." Earl then turns to lean on the railing of the twentieth floor balcony, and after a snide exchange of comments, Hendricks performs her final joke of the story by shoving him from behind, forcing his arms to slip off the railing and his beer onto the streets below. "Just kidding," Hendricks tells the horrified man dressed as a naked woman, "I was just kidding."

Lorrie Moore

Characters

Charlie

Charlie is Evan's boyfriend. Described as "independently wealthy [with] an amusing little job in book publishing," Charlie spends his time at home watching football games on a television that gets fuzzy reception and has a ritual of undressing at night in which "he kicks up his leg and flips the underwear in the air and catches it." It is in Charlie's Manhattan apartment that the Halloween party takes places where Zoë meets Earl.

Earl

Earl is the date Evan arranges for Zoë at the Halloween party. He arrives to the party dressed as a naked woman with "large rubber breasts protruding like hams." Earl has recently gone through a divorce, and throughout the evening he attempts to engage Zoë in conversation about love, only to be continually interrupted by her sarcastic quips and vague allusions. Earl is a photographer who worries aloud about the effect the photographic chemicals are having on him. At one point in the evening, after repeated attempts at having a comprehensible discussion with Zoë, Earl gives up and says, "You're not at all like your sister." And in final defeat he

Media Adaptations

- A recording of Lorrie Moore reading "You're Ugly, Too" can be found in the audio version of *The Best American Short Stories of the Century,* edited by John Updike. Published in 1999 by Houghton Mifflin, an abridged version of the collection is available on cassette and an unabridged version is available on CD.

announces aloud that he shouldn't go out with "career women" anymore. "You're all stricken," he says and adds that he'll be better off "with women who have part-time jobs."

Evan Hendricks

Evan Hendricks is Zoë's younger sister, five years out of college, who lives in Manhattan with her boyfriend, Charlie. Evan has a part-time job arranging photo shoots of food and lives in Manhattan in "a luxury midtown high-rise with a balcony and access to a pool. . . ." Evan sets her sister up with Earl at the party and just prior to the party announces to Zoë that she and Charlie are getting married.

Zoë Hendricks

The main character in the story, Zoë Hendricks teaches American history in a small liberal arts college outside Paris, Illinois. Considered eccentric or simply misunderstood by both her students and her administrators, she often interjects seemingly irreverent statements to conversations and has been known by her students to sing aloud as she enters class. Cynical and sarcastic, Hendricks loves jokes, but the punch lines are often lost on her audiences. Her response to every situation—whether it is a date with a colleague or the ultrasound tests she undergoes due to the severe abdominal pains she has been experiencing—is to make joke or sarcastic comments. Her favorite joke, and the source of the

story's title, is about the doctor who tells his patient that he has six weeks to live, and when the patient asks for a second opinion, the doctor says, "You're ugly, too."

As a single woman, she has unsuccessfully tried dating local men, but the only two men she seems to care for are her postman, who delivers her "real letter[s], with real full-priced stamp[s], from someplace else," and a cab driver, whom she has gotten to know from the repeated trips she took to the airport in order to leave town. When her sister Evan invites her to Manhattan for a Halloween party, Hendricks accepts, and it is there that she meets Earl, a friend of her sister. In her long talk with Earl on the balcony, Hendricks lies to him repeatedly about herself and offers him her cynical views of love and relationships.

Jerry

Called "Jare" by Zoë, Jerry is the town's only cabbie and one of Zoë's two favorite men. He gives her cut rates on her rides, and while dropping her off for her flight to New York to see her sister, he admits that he's never been on a plane or an escalator before. Jerry represents one of Zoë's few links to the world outside Paris, Illinois.

The Mailman

Like Jerry the cabdriver, the mailman is also one of Zoë's few links to the world outside her small town of Paris. Zoë lives for the daily arrival of the postman, "that handsome blue jay" who will deliver her letters which she'll read over and over again in her bed.

The Students

Zoë considers her students to be "by and large good Midwesterners, spacey with estrogen from large quantities of meat and cheese" who share the "suburban values" of their parents and who have been given "things, things, things" by their parents. Zoë shows very little respect for her students, often chiding them with what she believes to be ironic remarks but which one student points out are sarcastic. "Illinois. It makes me sarcastic to be here," Zoë admits to her sister. Her students are one of the many excuses Zoë uses to escape Paris as often as she is able.

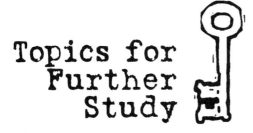

Topics for Further Study

- In his 1992 book *Talents and Technicians: Literary Chic and the New Assembly-Line Fiction,* John E. Aldridge criticizes writers such as Lorrie Moore for tending ''to treat the personal life [of their characters] as if it were a phenomenon existing totally apart from society and without connotations that would give it meaningful relevance to a general human condition or dilemma.'' Do you think this criticism applies to ''You're Ugly, Too''? Are there social forces behind the problems Hendricks is facing, or do you agree with Aldridge that Moore treats Hendricks's life as something apart from her social context?

- In her snide remarks to her undergraduate students in Paris, Illinois, Hendricks believes she is being ironic, but her students accuse her of being sarcastic—an accusation Hendricks eventually accepts. Research the definitions of ''sarcasm'' and ''irony.'' What is the difference between the two terms, and do you agree with the students that Hendricks is being sarcastic? Where, if anywhere, can you find irony in ''You're Ugly, Too''?

- The history department Hendricks teaches for recently faced a sex-discrimination suit, and Hendricks is the only woman currently teaching there. Research the male-female ratios in academia in general, and in history departments in particular. Is Hendricks's experience unique, or are women widely represented as professors in academia? What are the male-female ratios among teachers in liberal arts colleges in the Midwest? Are they significantly different from those in Northeast schools?

- While Hendricks may be simply considered to have an eccentric personality, there is some indication that she may suffer from any number of mental or emotional disorders. *The Diagnostic and Statistical Manual of Mental Disorders–Fourth Edition,* published by the American Psychiatric Association, is the main reference used by mental health professionals and physicians to diagnose mental disorders. Also referred to as the *DSM–IV,* the reference helps professionals determine if patients are suffering from any number of depressive conditions, such as major depression, dysthymia, or bipolar disorder. Using the *DSM–IV* as your source, research the symptoms of major depression, dysthymia, and bipolar disorder to determine whether or not Hendricks suffers from any of those conditions.

Themes

American Midwest

The American Midwest, known for its lack of ethnic diversity and socially conservative values, bears the brunt of many of Hendricks's remarks and observations. Her town of Paris, Illinois, is one of ''those Illinois towns with the funny names'' people have to escape from every so often; her students in Paris are ''by and large good Midwesterners'' who seem ''to know very little about anything.'' The students at her first college in New Geneva, Minnesota, or the ''Land of the Dying Shopping Mall'' where everyone was ''so blond . . . that brunettes were often presumed to be from foreign countries,'' fare no better in Hendricks's eyes. There everyone was expected to be a ''Heidi'' who would ''lug goat milk up the hills and not think twice'' and who would never complain. These Midwestern characteristics are the antithesis of Hendricks's personality; they lead her to tell her sister, ''Illinois. It makes me sarcastic to be here,'' and they contribute to her alienation.

Academia

Academia has long been accused of being a bastion of male values. Hendricks teaches American history for a small liberal arts college in Illinois. Her department, which recently faced a sex-discrimination suit, is made up of nine men who put up with her eccentricities because of the ''feminine touch'' she contributes to the atmosphere. This male environment, coupled with students she feels have little intellectual abilities, also contribute to Hendricks's overall sense of alienation.

Alienation

Hendricks lives alone, does not feel connected to the culture of the Midwest, has had no luck meeting men, and is not respected or understood by her students or her colleagues. Her constant cynicism and snide comments underscores the lack of connection she feels with her surroundings, and the only people she seems to connect with are her postman, who delivers mail ''from someplace else,'' and her cab driver who takes her to the airport on her regular escapes from her small Midwest town.

Loneliness and Isolation

At Christmas, Hendricks gives large tips both to the cab driver who takes her to the airport for her frequent weekend escapes and to the postman who delivers her letters which she reads again and again in her bed. Every Tuesday she phones her sister in New York and often flies to visit her on weekends. She also has her television in her bedroom, a self-admitted ''bad sign,'' and she has not had a successful date since moving to the Midwest. The loneliness and isolation Hendricks experiences are partly the result of the disconnection she feels from her surroundings and possibly due to issues of emotional and mental instability that the story hints at.

Mental and Emotional Instability

Although there is no explicit discussion of Hendricks being unstable, nevertheless she makes several inappropriate comments and performs several questionable acts that can possibly be attributed to mental or emotional instability. Many of the sarcastic comments she makes to her students are professionally inappropriate and border on being hurtful, and her sharing of stories that end in a violent suicide or death seems to hint at larger issues of depression she may be experiencing. At her home she tacks a sign to a tree in her backyard that says, ''*Zoë's Tree*''; she returns a mirror to the store because it had been frightening her ''with an image of a woman she never recognized''; and she also returns an Oriental rug because she convinces herself that the Chinese symbols on it say ''*Bruce Springsteen.*'' While some of these acts may merely indicate an ''eccentric'' personality, others, such as

her final act of shoving Earl against the balcony rail 20 stories above the street, push the boundaries of eccentricity and reveal a woman who is out of control with her emotions and who does not have the ability to know when a joke goes too far.

Absurdity and Meaninglessness

One of the reasons for Hendricks's constant barrage of jokes could be her inherent nihilism, her view that life is essentially absurd and meaningless. If others don't understand her or her jokes, or if the jokes backfire, it doesn't matter because, in her opinion, life is essentially meaningless anyway. A telling moment in the story to indicate that Hendricks suffers existentially occurs when she describes to herself the trick to flying safe. Never buy discount tickets, she suggests, and ''tell yourself you [have] nothing to live for anyway, so that when the plane crashed it was no big deal.'' And if the plane doesn't crash, by the time the cab arrives to take you and your baggage away, you will have had time to ''come up with a persuasive reason to go on living.''

Illness

Hendricks is clearly suffering from what could be a serious illness. Severe abdominal pains force her to undergo ultrasound tests. While the results of the test are not revealed, at one point the technician becomes ''suddenly alert'' with his machine ''clicking away,'' and Hendricks is convinced that she has a ''growth.'' She decides not to mention the test to her sister, but during the Halloween party, she is forced to leave her conversation with Earl because of her pain, and her stories and jokes are full of allusions to death.

Mortality

The title of the story is taken from Hendricks's favorite joke, which is about a patient who is told by the doctor that he has six weeks to live. Throughout the story, Hendricks alludes to death—either her own or that of someone she knows. At one point, just prior to her ultrasound tests, she tells her sister that she feels like she's dying—a statement Hendricks intends more literally than her sister can understand.

Irony

Throughout the story, Hendricks makes her students and her dates the brunt of her jokes. Somewhat smugly, she believes she is being ironic, using "gently layered and sophisticated" wit in their telling, but ironically, her students, whom she believes "know very little about anything," understand the difference between irony and sarcasm and accuse Hendricks of the latter, which Hendricks ultimately admits to. Another ironic aspect of the story relates to Hendricks's existential crisis. Many of her stories and quips point to her belief in the ultimate meaninglessness of life; if she does in fact have an abdominal growth and if she is in fact dying, as she believes, Hendricks may have a chance to discover first-hand whether life does in fact have meaning.

Sexual Relationships

One one level, "You're Ugly, Too" is about a woman trying to find love, but through her actions and the stories and jokes she tells, it is clear that Zoé has little faith that men and women can live or love together harmoniously. At the hospital, she wonders aloud with the technician performing her ultrasound test whether the rise of infertility in the country is the result of "completely different species trying to reproduce." Indeed, from her descriptions of her dates, and from her final interaction at the Halloween party with Earl, it seems that Hendricks believes that men and women are not ultimately made for one another and that healthy sexual relationships, particularly if the woman is to retain her own sense of individuality and identity apart from the man, are impossible.

Role of Women

One of the underlying issues in Hendricks's life is connected to the fact that she is unmarried, that she has yet to take on the role of "wife," and she refuses or has the inability to be a "good date" for the men she meets. "Oh, my God. . . . I forgot to get married," she sarcastically tells her sister, who will soon reveal her own marriage plans to Hendricks. However, she is able, as expected of her, to add a "feminine touch" to her mostly male history department. Hendricks is obviously cynical about traditional female roles; she prefers to live her life as she pleases with utter disregard for the opinions of others. When her cutting remarks and sarcasm become too much for Earl at the Halloween party, he blurts out, "You know, I shouldn't try to go out with career women. You're all stricken. . . . I do better with women who have part-time jobs." He later turns away from Hendricks and mumbles, "Live and learn," to which Hendricks responds by saying, "Live and get dumb." While her final act of shov-

ing Earl against the balcony railing can be seen as the act of an unstable personality, it can also be interpreted as Hendricks's response to Earl's complaint that "hormones" metaphorically being sprayed around is preventing men from wanting to have intercourse with women, as if the man's desire is the all-important part of the equation while the woman has no say in the matter.

Style

Style

Throughout "You're Ugly, Too," Moore uses flashbacks, jokes, and anecdotes to complete Hendricks's character. Although the story's plot is sparse, the reader is given ample details of the protagonist's dates, her relationships with her students and colleagues, and her feelings for her geographic surroundings that effectively fill in her psychology and personality.

Tone

"You're Ugly, Too," seen through the point of view of the main character, is told in a witty, often sarcastic and glib tone. Hendricks's views of her surroundings—her students, the Midwest, and the men she's dated—are revealed through cutting and sarcastic anecdotes and jokes. Even her trip to the hospital for ultrasound tests that may reveal a fatal growth is described with wit and sarcasm. This tone acts to underscore her generally morbid and cynical view of her life.

Point of View

Although the story is narrated in a third person omniscient point of view, "You're Ugly, Too" is told through the eyes of Zoë Hendricks, the story's main character. Through the telling of stories and jokes, the reader is given a deep understanding of Hendricks's daily life and personality.

Setting

"You're Ugly, Too" takes place in Paris, Illinois, where Hendricks lives and works, and in New York City, where her sister and her sister's boyfriend live. The Midwest, known for its conservative values, is the target of many of Hendricks's sarcastic comments and the source of much of her isolation and loneliness. Although no date is given, references to the singer Bruce Springsteen reveal that the story is set in contemporary times.

Historical Context

Women and Academia

In the 1980s, women were greatly outnumbered by men as faculty members, accounting for only 27 percent of all academic faculty, according to *Academic Women Working towards Equality* (Bergin and Garvey Publishers, 1987). This number was an increase of about 5 percent over the period 1942–1962, according to the same study. By contrast, women reached their peak in terms of representation among faculty members in 1879–1880 when they made up 36 percent of all faculty in U.S. colleges and universities. According to the National Resource Council's *Humanities Doctorates in the United States, 1991 Profile* (National Academy Press, 1994), about one-third of all PhD candidates in History between 1981 and 1988 were women.

Detection of Tumors

Ultrasound imaging, also known as ultrasonography, is a non-invasive medical imaging technique that uses high frequency sound waves and their echoes to help physicians get an inside view of soft tissues and body cavities. By the 1980s, ultrasound had been widely available to clinics and hospitals for years and was the method of choice for diagnosing abdominal-related pains. Magnetic Resonance Imaging, or MRI, had just been approved by the Food and Drug Administration in 1984, but because of its costs would not be widely used for diagnosis for at least another decade.

Critical Overview

"You're Ugly, Too," first published in 1989 in the *New Yorker,* was included in Moore's second collection of short stories, *Like Life.* The consensus of critics at the time of its publication was that it helped to cement Moore's growing reputation as a masterful short story writer known for her engaging wit.

However, several reviewers also noted that, while Moore's strengths were obvious and many, the wit expressed in her writing often came at the expense of an emotional depth to her characters, and her stories revealed a lack of thematic diversity: most of her stories in the new collection, like her previous work, were about middle-class, educated, single women looking for love.

Writing in the *Chicago Tribune,* the National Book Award winning author John Casey called the collection "a dazzler" with "witty (and sometimes wisecracking) narration [that is] wonderfully theatrical. . . ." While Casey notes that all of Moore's characters in *Like Life* "want both solitude and love," a quandary that is not a new one, "Moore brings her own variations to [the quandary], her own comic talent and her own eloquence." Writing in the *Houston Chronicle,* reviewer Sally Poivoir also points to Moore's comic tendencies, stating that in her "search for the authentic, Moore's lantern is humor. Humor in every form and of every degree, from the most abject pun to the subtle insinuation of a vast cosmic joke, from tender irony to mocking contempt to total devastation."

Although critic Dan Cryer, writing in *Newsday,* concludes that Moore's voice is "badly needed" in fiction, *Like Life* is "both a cause for celebration and concern." While the stories themselves are "full of sharp observation and stylistic grace," they reveal that Moore may be in a "thematic rut" with the "single women's anxiety over finding lasting love" being her predominant concern. Cryer writes that there is a "danger . . . that [Moore's] smart, articulate career women quipping their way out of pain may come to seem interchangeable."

Boston Globe reviewer Matthew Gilbert called *Like Life* a "deceptively complex" collection that "contains a moving emotionality that was previously banned" in Moore's work. "In [*Like Life*], the laughter turns to tears. The stories are not merely witty, they are relentlessly tragic."

However, *Los Angeles Times* reviewer Merle Rubin disagreed, stating that though Moore's writing provided "enough verbal glibness to provide material for all the stand-up comics in Los Angeles," she has "very little ability to create convincing characters or tell stories that invite us to suspend our disbelief as we read them or to brood upon them after they've been read." Rubin concludes his review by praising "her flair at doing what she does," but warning that "when style becomes this stylized, it is likely to prove a fad.'' And in a generally positive review, the *Christian Science Monitor* criticizes Moore's one-liners, ''[h]owever entertaining they may be,'' for being ''distracting.''

As for the story itself, if reviewers mention it at all, it is to discuss the similarities between Hendricks and the characters Moore had created in her other work. The reviewer for the *Christian Science Monitor,* for instance, writes that Hendricks, like most of Moore's characters, ''teeters on the edge of rationality,'' while Matthew Gilbert, in the *Boston Globe,* writes that Hendricks, like many of Moore's other characters, ''is married to pure isolation.''

Although ''You're Ugly, Too'' itself has not been critiqued extensively, it has been widely anthologized since it was first published in such collections as *The Scribner Anthology of Contemporary Short Fiction* and the highly regarded anthology, *The Best American Short Stories of the Century* edited by John Updike.

Criticism

Mark White

White is the publisher of the Seattle-based literary press, Scala House Press. In this essay, White argues that, while Moore displays an extraordinary gift of language in "You're Ugly, Too," she does not reveal the sources of her character's anguish and therefore leaves little for the reader to empathize with.

Lorrie Moore's ''You're Ugly, Too'' is a witty and sometimes hilarious account of an unmarried woman who, like so many of Moore's fictional creations, is unable to connect with men—or with anybody else, for that matter. With Moore's signature barrage of one-liners, jokes, and what critic John W. Aldridge, in his critique of Moore in *Talents and Technicians: Literary Chic and the New Assembly-Line Fiction,* calls ''other ludicrous dislocations of language,'' it is easy to understand the acclaim that Moore and this story have received.

However entertaining her style may be, reading Moore can ultimately be a frustrating experience. While she has an obvious knack for creating memorably eccentric and disassociated characters (especially women characters), and while she displays a pyrotechnic touch of language that makes those women smolder with a clarity and intensity rarely seen in contemporary fiction, Moore generally keeps her readers in the dark as to the causes of their predicaments. It is never quite clear if Moore's women are genetically predisposed to live a life of isolation and loneliness or whether there are larger cultural or social forces at play. Do her women merely have bad luck with men, or are they rebelling, subconsciously or not, against society's expectations of how they should behave in sexual relationships? More often than not, it is as if Moore keeps her characters hermetically sealed from their surroundings, allowing them to be influenced only by their own internal clocks and thoughts. And even at that, her readers can never be certain if there are more serious bio-chemical or psychological issues beyond mere ''eccentricity'' that are driving these women to the precipice of spinsterhood.

Zoë Hendricks, the leading woman in ''You're Ugly, Too,'' is a typical Moore creation: a remarkably eccentric but possibly clinically depressed woman who, for whatever reasons the reader can never know, lives a life utterly alone, with only her wit and her jokes to accompany her.

That Zoë Hendricks is an extraordinary, though not necessarily likeable, character is inarguable. An east coast transplant teaching American history in a Midwest college, Hendricks seldom lets an opportunity for a snide remark or joke elude her. When a student asks her about her perfume, she retorts that it's ''*Room freshener*''; when another student tells Hendricks that she wants her history major to be meaningful, Hendricks snaps, ''Well, there's your problem.'' She relates seemingly irreverent stories at the most inappropriate occasions that conclude in suicide or violent death, and she tells drawn-out lies to her dates for no apparent reason. With impeccable timing, she often reduces her audience to various states of incredulity, disgust, and disdain. Her final act of pushing Earl against the balcony railing, her final ''joke'' in ''You're Ugly, Too,'' is little more than a physical manifestation of what she had been doing to him the entire evening through dialogue: pushing him, pushing him, and pushing him some more until he metaphorically and literally has no place left to go.

When Hendricks first began teaching in Paris, she thought she was using ''irony, something gently layered and sophisticated'' in her joking. But ironically, her students, whom she believes ''know very

What Do I Read Next?

- *Self-Help* (1985), Lorrie Moore's first collection of short stories, largely consists of her master's thesis at Cornell, where she studied under the writer Allison Lurie. Many of the stories in *Self-Help* are written in the second person and display the wit and humor that Moore has come to be known for.

- *Who Will Run the Frog Hospital?* (1994) is Moore's second and most accomplished novel. In it, a disillusioned, middle-aged woman vacationing in Paris looks back to her girlhood in a small Adirondack tourist town near the Canadian border.

- Allison Lurie, who mentored Moore at Cornell, won the Pulitzer Prize in 1985 for *Foreign Affairs,* a novel about two academics living and working in France. Fred Turner is an attractive, twenty-nine-year-old English professor and Vinnie Miner is an English professor in her 50s, divorced and not that pretty, but they share many needs and passions.

- Raymond Carver, considered by many to be the master of minimalist fiction, is often mentioned as a precursor to Lorrie Moore. *Where I'm Calling From: New and Selected Stories by Raymond Carver* includes a wide selection from Carver's career.

- In an interview with freelance writer Lauren Picker in *Newsday,* Lorrie Moore calls Alice Munro's collection of stories *Open Secrets* "one of the greatest books of the century."

- In *Talents and Technicians: Literary Chic and the New Assembly-Line Fiction,* John W. Aldridge takes a critical look at writers in the 1980s, such as Moore, whom he believes were committed to a style of fiction that was largely nihilistic with little connection to the world surrounding them.

---

little about anything," understand the difference between irony and sarcasm and accuse her of the latter, and Hendricks is eventually forced to concede their point and admit to her sister, "Illinois. It makes me sarcastic to be here."

Hendricks does not derive pleasure from her behavior; her incessant joking is what Aldridge calls "a kind of sublimated scream ... anxiety displaced into jokes that Moore and her characters incessantly make but at which no one is laughing." And what is Hendricks anxious about? For starters, she is extremely lonely. She lives by herself in a "rather empty" house that she bought; her television, which she watches at all hours, is in her bedroom, a self-admitted "bad sign." She lives for the mailman, "that handsome blue jay," who brings her letters "from someplace else" which she then takes to her bedroom to read "over and over." And her dates, of which there have only been three since she moved to Paris, are miserable failures. The men she meets may as well speak ancient Greek for all

the success she has in communicating with them. And although she talks with her younger sister Evan every Tuesday and visits her regularly, Hendricks does not communicate much better with her. "I'm going out of my mind," Hendricks tells Evan at one point, very possibly intending the statement to be taken more literally than her sister has the capacity or willingness to do, and shortly before the ultrasound test that would reveal what may be a tumor growing inside of her, Hendricks resorts to another cliché, thus glossing over the stark truth she may be trying to convey, when she tells her, "I feel like I'm dying."

If Hendricks is like others, she has probably used phrases such as "I'm going out of my mind" and "I feel like I'm dying" countless times in her life as the innocuous figures of speech they are normally intended to be. In the context of this story, however, it is conceivable that in both cases she literally means what she says. But for reasons that Moore never makes clear, Zoë Hendricks, a liberal arts history professor whose first chapters on her book on presidential humor have been generally "well received," seems to have the ability to speak only in clichés to describe her feelings, or through jokes to communicate to the world, and the reader is never certain what she is actually trying to convey.

In effect, Hendricks is a character who suffers from loneliness but does not have the communication or social skills to escape that state, a predicament that is, of course, self-generating: the more she fails to communicate, the lonelier she gets.

But why exactly is Hendricks so lonely? Why is she unable to build any lasting relationships, with either men or women? This is one of the frustrating aspects of reading "You're Ugly, Too": the reasons behind Zoë Hendricks's situation are unclear, and as a result, her abject loneliness and alienation are mere window dressing to her character, evoking little sympathy from the reader.

It is not entirely true that Moore does not offer some reasons behind Hendricks's situation, but what she gives is inadequate. Moore suggests that the Midwest, known for its conservative customs and lifestyles, is one factor to consider. "You had to get out of them occasionally, those Illinois towns with the funny names: Paris, Oblong, Normal," the story opens. And if living in Paris as an expatriate east coast academic and an eccentric one at that is not difficult enough, to make matters worse, Hendricks is a woman in an otherwise all-male department. Her reaction to this situation is reflected succinctly by one of her students in a faculty evaluation: "*Professor Hendricks has said critical things about Fawn Hall, the Catholic religion, and the whole state of Illinois. It is unbelievable.* "

However, neither regional dislocation nor her all-male department can be blamed entirely for Hendricks's predicament. She has not been served a prison sentence, after all; she was not forced to move to Paris to begin with, and her purchase of a house can easily be interpreted as a commitment to establishing roots. And regardless of whether or not Paris is making her miserable, is it truly possible that there is not a single human being in the college, in the town itself, or in the surrounding area with whom she can relate on some level? Another dislocated easterner, for instance? And if geographic and cultural isolation are the problems, how does one explain Hendricks's dismal failure at connecting with Earl, an east coast photographer and divorcé, at Evan's party in New York?

> " Zoë Hendricks, the leading woman in 'You're Ugly, Too,' is a typical Moore creation: a remarkably eccentric but possibly clinically depressed woman who, for whatever reasons the reader can never know, lives a life utterly alone, with only her wit and her jokes to accompany her."

With regard to her professional situation, despite her being the only woman in her department, there is no indication that she is either being unfairly treated or has expressed any complaints. In fact, the obvious lack of respect she shows toward her students should raise eyebrows in her department and cause Hendricks at least some worry about job security, but her colleagues seem indifferent.

No, there is something besides her geographic and professional environment that is causing Hendricks these feelings of isolation. One clue may be found in Evan's response to Hendricks when Hendricks tells her she is losing her mind. "You always say that," Evan replies, "But then you go on your trips and vacations and then you settle back into things and then you're quiet for a while and then you say you're fine, you're busy, and then after a while you say you're going crazy again, and you start all over."

In other words, according to Evan, Hendricks is on an emotional or psychological roller coaster. Although the story does not offer anything more than suggestions of biochemical or psychological instability, the suggestions are numerous. While tacking a "*Zoë's Tree*" sign to a backyard tree may be a sign of innocent eccentricity, her returning of the Oriental rug to the store because she convinced herself that the symbols on it said "*Bruce Springsteen*," and the return of the pine chests because they reminded her of baby caskets, and the return of the mirror because it kept "startling her with an image of a woman she never recognized,'' are acts that push the envelope of eccentricity into the mail boxes of the unstable. In this light, her seeming obsession with stories and images of death begin to make sense: Hendricks may very well be clinically depressed, or worse. But again, Moore only provides hints, with nothing for readers to grasp; there is no conscious discussion or thought about these possibilities. In fact, the possibility exists that Hendricks is, ultimately, nothing more than a mean-spirited, eccentric, and lonely academic who deserves all the isolation she gets.

Ultimately, what ails Hendricks is that she is, for all intents and purposes, a nihilist; she believes in nothing and sees little meaning in life. Her trick, for instance, to flying safely ''is to tell yourself you had nothing to live for anyway, so that when the plane crashed it was no big deal.'' And by the time the time the cab arrives to take you and your luggage away, make sure you've ''come up with a persuasive reason to go on living.'' It is easy, then, to understand her scornful attitudes to her students and her biting response to the young woman who wants her history major to mean something. Believing in *anything* is a problem for Hendricks.

Still, none of this is enough to evoke the sympathy necessary for the reader to feel anything but curious disdain for Hendricks. Nihilism is the result of other forces—social, psychological, spiritual, metaphysical. Explaining Hendricks's nihilism on any of these grounds could provide ample information for the reader to empathize with her, but Moore only offers her readers the products of Hendricks's nihilism—her jokes, her sarcasm, and her dismissive treatment of humanity.

While this ultimately leads to a frustrating experience in reading ''You're Ugly, Too,'' it is the exact reading Moore seems to want for her stories. In an interview with the *Paris Review,* Moore calls her stories ''a kind of biopsy of human life.'' As far as ''You're Ugly, Too'' is concerned, ''biopsy'' is the perfect metaphor. The purpose of a biopsy is, after all, to test for a malignancy in tissue. The source of the cancer, if it exists, and its possible treatments, are revealed through a series of other tests. The biopsy simply answers the question, ''Is the tissue cancerous?''

''You're Ugly, Too'' is Moore's biopsy of Zoë Hendricks—a lonely, unmarried, woman who has only her wit to keep her company. The results of this biopsy reveal that Hendricks is being eaten alive by profound psychological, emotional, spiritual, and,

very likely, physical cancers. But whether these cancers are treatable or not, or whether any reader actually cares, are questions Moore's biopsy is not designed to answer.

Source: Mark White, Critical Essay on ''You're Ugly, Too,'' in *Short Stories for Students,* Gale, 2004.

Catherine Dybiec Holm

Dybiec Holm is a freelance writer and editor. In this essay, Dybiec Holm looks at the theme of sadness in ''You're Ugly, Too,'' a theme which Moore accentuates through use of cynical humor, nuanced observation of the human condition, and description.

Lorrie Moore, in talking about her short stories and novels, has admitted that her work has an underlying theme of sadness. Her narrative is often overlaid with tones of cynicism, one-liners, and wisecracks, which suggest sadness below the surface. Certainly, this appears to be the case in ''You're Ugly, Too,'' an acclaimed short story from Moore's collection *Like Life.* How, then, does Moore keep a reader engaged? Sadness alone will not hold all readers. Part of the effectiveness of Moore's writing lies with her detailed, nuanced observation about the human condition, via her characters and her descriptions. Moore's observations about the human psyche are fascinating. But it's the edgy interplay between acerbic humor and the darker aspects of the human experience (despair, anger, grief, realization) that make this story unique. This interplay accelerates throughout the story, showing the reader the sadness of the character's life and of life in general.

As reviewer Ralph Novak of *People Weekly* says of Moore's writing, Moore is ''effective with indirect approaches'' and ''her stories are usually thick with insight and laugh-first, think-later humor.'' In ''You're Ugly, Too,'' this is immediately evident in protagonist Zoë's observations and feelings about living in the Midwestern United States. Moore finds original ways to make observations here that manage to convey cynicism, disdain, and wry humor all at once. These observations are motivated by sadness, ever a part of the world in this story. Moore takes the reader below the surface. Instead of Zoë simply saying, ''Illinois. It makes me sarcastic to be here,'' Zoë goes to great lengths in the beginning of her stay in the Midwest to insist to herself that she is being ironic rather than sarcastic, even when talking about sarcasm. Irony, to Zoë, is subtle and seems more appropriate to a sophisticated New Yorker in exile rather than more blatant sarcasm. Both sarcasm and irony, however, reflect a deeper despair on the part of the character. This kind of observation on the part of Moore makes Zoë a fascinating character. It's exactly the kind of thought anyone might have in the protagonist's situation. But such nuances do not always get captured so well in writing.

Humor and sadness are interwoven throughout the story so skillfully that the reader is not aware of the transition from one to the other. Moore leads the reader from wisecracking observations to the sharp edge between sadness and madness, and it's what keeps story tension high. Zoë's Midwestern students are ''spacey with estrogen from large quantities of meat and cheese,'' complacent, unnerved by Zoë's brunette hair, and ignorant about the geography of the east coast. Zoë compares the Midwestern tendency to repeatedly insist that ''everything is fine'' to the worldview of a sort of archetypal or stereotypical Heidi. But Heidi doesn't stand in front of broken copiers and threaten to slit her wrists. Zoë has discovered her ''crusty edge,'' and in the scene that quickly follows, with teacher and student (who has a ''big leather bow in her hair, like a cowgirl in a TV ranch show''), Zoë slams it to the girl, telling the student that it's her problem if she wants ''her history major to mean something.'' Zoë's had it; she's realized that she'll never fit into the Midwest and will never completely understand it.

So that the reader isn't completely estranged from Zoë, Moore soon gives a sense of Zoë's vulnerability (still motivated by sadness, however). Vulnerability is actually suggested earlier in the story, when Zoë skips into class singing all two verses of ''Getting to Know You.'' It is difficult to tell at this point in the story whether Zoë's behavior is spurred by cynicism, frustration, vulnerability, or all of these. As the story progresses, however, Moore gives the reader a clearer picture. This happens not so much in the description of the three men Zoë tries to date in the Midwest. Instead, it is presented in smaller, everyday ways. Narrative such as the following shows her actions as intensely human, whether motivated by loneliness, sadness, or a sense of personal insignificance in the world: ''Zoë lived for the mail, for the postman, that handsome bluejay, and when she got a real letter . . . she took it to bed with her and read it over and over.''

Zoë stares with longing over the interior decorating magazines that her mother sends; remnants from a family that could not afford what the maga-

> "Moore leads the reader from wisecracking observations to the sharp edge between sadness and madness. . . ."

zines suggested. But when Zoë attempts to decorate her own house, the ideas don't quite take hold. Most unnerving is Zoë's reaction to her reflection in a newly purchased mirror: ''Most times she just looked vague . . . 'You look like someone I know,' she had been told . . . sometimes she seemed not to have a look of her own.'' Zoë returns the mirror, scared by thoughts of insignificance or the nullification of personal identity. In a *Ploughshares* article about Moore, Don Lee notes that the author, as a child, ''fretted, quite literally, about her insubstantiality.'' Reviewer Sybil Steinberg of *Publishers Weekly* refers to Moore's characters' ''quiet desperation and valiant searches for significance.'' In ''You're Ugly, Too,'' the character's desperation has subtly been building since the beginning of the story and is nicely alluded to in Zoë's reaction to the mirror.

The skill with which Moore plays with story time (perhaps purposefully) imitates Zoë's tendency to deflect crisis with jokes or sarcasm. Always, however, the character's sadness drives her cynical humor. Zoë does not quite get to the center of certain issues; she cannot face the certain despair of looking at these issues straight on. For example, during her ultrasound procedure she jokes about the word ''ultrasound'' and babbles about infertility, although it is obvious that she is completely worried about her health and the consequences of the tests.

Zoë approaches difficult issues tangentially. While Zoë is well aware of the sadness in her own life, she somehow can't bring herself to burden those she is closest to (her sister Evan, for example) with in-depth discussions of some of the strange or frightening things Zoë is facing. She evades her sister's questions about her dating life and can't quite come out and tell Evan that she will be having an ultrasound. When the ultrasound is mentioned, the reader knows that the stakes have suddenly shot through the roof for Zoë and for the story. The sentence is presented and constructed in an emphatic way ("The ultrasound Zoë was keeping a secret, even from Evan"). The construction of the sentence (object ahead of subject) gives the wording added impact, which it deserves. The irony is that this character can hardly bear to face these huge aspects of sadness in her life herself, even though she's ready and willing to deflect everything or express herself with a cynical joke. Reviewer Ralph Novak calls Moore "so effective with indirect approaches," and this point in the story is a stellar example of such a tactic. Much like a cynical joke-teller, Zoë and Moore come at sadness indirectly, but the reader is always aware of its pervasive presence.

Zoë and Moore continue to juxtapose humor and sadness, but it feels as if now, at this point in the story where the stakes are out in the open, both protagonist and author become more forthcoming and direct about the sadness. Even the humor has more bite, reflecting more at stake for Zoë. Zoë finds a particular joke (from which the story takes its title) "terribly, terribly funny," even though the first part of the joke deals with someone who has only six weeks to live. Perhaps it is no accident that Moore uses a word like "terribly" rather than a bland "very." There is something terrible about the joke and its consequences. Zoë's life, for the reader, has taken on a hard, new edge. This seems reflected by the sad wave of the cabdriver who reveals the smallness of his world. When Zoë ends the scene with her philosophy of flying, her humor has turned completely acerbic ("you had nothing to live for anyway" and "keeping [the plane] aloft with your own worthlessness"), and one is no longer sure of this character's fuzzy boundary between humor and intense sadness.

More and more, the reader gets a taste of the author's and Zoë's reflections on relationship. Much of this is accomplished through Moore's attention to telling details. Evan's boyfriend comes home and watches "fuzzy football." He kicks his underwear in the air and gets into bed. These details are funny yet sad and tell the reader more in a few words than Evan could if she had she gone on to describe the monotony of her relationship in more explicit ways. Zoë also reveals her obsession with relationship with a few telling details that Moore slips in: "the toad-faced cicadas . . . like little caped men" and the "size fourteen shoes" on the doorstep, indications of her lack of a relationship. These details are placed next to another starkly sad realization—"as soon as you think you've got the best of both worlds

. . . it can suddenly twist and become the worst of both worlds."

Again, Moore deflects the reader from lingering too long in sadness, just as Zoë tries to use humor to avoid facing her despair. Evan doesn't seem to hear what Zoë has just said about "the worst of both worlds" and abruptly changes the subject. Zoë cuts short a story of mismatched lovers. Moore saves this for later, when Zoë gives the man at the party the full force of her edgy humor/anger, and tells the man the sad story in its entirety.

The party scene is the rawest part of the story, and both the bite of the humor and the depth of Zoë's desperation are accelerated during this scene. True to Zoë's and Evan's fears about marriage, Evan dresses for the Halloween party as a hausfrau and later regrets it. Earl represents the epitome of what frustrates Zoë about the dating life; appropriately, his costume seems to make a mockery of women. Zoë, in a subconscious way, contrasts Earl's female representation with her own costume choice, but the reader does not pick up on this until Earl compliments her "bone" and she compliments (in a sarcastic manner) Earl's "tits." Typically, Earl interrupts Zoë's recitation of her favorite joke, and gives it an ending which has overtones of sex and victory ("I finally f——ked her") rather than overtones of self-perception and defeat ("You're ugly, too"). Earl talks of wanting physical contact, and Zoë is reminded of gorillas smacking each other when they've been in a cage together for too long. All during the conversation between Earl and Zoë, Moore lets us see Zoë's thoughts. These are detailed, honest, and despairing; the kind of tangential mind-jumps any human might make in Zoë's place. Zoë is complex, and Moore's descriptions help us see Zoë as a subtle, layered woman.

To Zoë, Earl represents the most frustrating aspects of men. The reader feels Zoë's irritation when Earl laments dating career women ("A guy can really tell what life has done to you. I do better with women who have part-time jobs."); the reader feels her scorn when Earl talks about female hormones and "men screwing rocks." Moore convinces the reader that Zoë really meant to push Earl off the balcony, even though, in typical Zoë and Moore fashion, Zoë insists that she was only kidding. The entire story represents an edgy interplay between cynicism and sadness, and this instance in the climax of this story is the strongest illustration of Moore's strange, jarring, story dynamic.

Source: Catherine Dybiec Holm, Critical Essay on ''You're Ugly, Too,'' in *Short Stories for Students,* Gale, 2004.

Ericka Marie Sudo

Sudo is currently pursuing a master's degree. In this essay, Sudo explores stereotypes found in Lorrie Moore's ''You're Ugly, Too.''

In ''You're Ugly, Too,'' Lorrie Moore presents the story of a female character who is a mixture of tradition and modernity. She presents a new style of writing about women that is colorful and charismatic, portraying women with true emotional baggage and reaching readers on a more personal level. Her characters are drawn in a streamlined and uncluttered way. In fact, critics are split between finding fault with the characters because they lack traditional development and finding Moore's representation of women with real faults incredibly refreshing. Moore reaches readers by constantly changing the roles through which her male and female characters interact and by writing about women and their perceptions of men. In ''You're Ugly Too,'' she accomplishes this with various devices, stereotypes, and symbols.

In ''You're Ugly Too,'' Moore creates a character, in Zoë Hendricks, who reveals her humanity through her flaws. Moore uses italics to identify pieces of information that are crucial in defining her characters and enhancing character development. Early in the story, Moore's narrator reveals, ''*Professor Hendricks is often late for class and usually arrives with a cup of hot chocolate which she offers the class sips of.*'' This makes explicit the metaphor that, as a professor, Zoë comes to class equipped with ''a cup of knowledge'' to share with her students. Some time later, we hear one of her students say to her, ''You act . . . like your opinion is worth more than everybody else's in the class.'' Consequently, the reader can see that, as a teacher, Zoë has fallen into the ''I come to teach you, you don't come to teach me'' trap, which shows that Zoë is an average woman with real human flaws. This is just one of many ways that shows that Zoë is the average woman.

Zoë's personality is revealed by her humor and Moore's projection of skepticism onto female characters. Zoë considers her humor to be ironic, but her students consider it sarcastic—an opinion that Zoë eventually comes to accept. In fact, Zoë's humor is sarcastic and cynical, which reveals her pessimistic view of life and dark humor. The joke that Zoë uses to cope with the abdominal growth is revealed as

> Moore's story depicts a female driven satire that is a result of mismatched roles or stereotypes that some women, like Zoë, combine, as they search for who they are.''

Zoë drives home from the ultrasound procedure. The punch line, ''You're ugly, too'' when the patient asks for a second opinion from the doctor is referenced in the title of the story. Zoë finds this joke hilarious because the punch line of the doctor's second opinion, a matter-of-fact statement, is not an answer to her original serious question. Instead, it serves to illuminate the fact that the doctor is offended because the patient feels that he needs another opinion. One can see that the doctor's response to Zoë is similar to Zoë's response to her students in her class and that the doctor's and Zoë's opinions are no longer matter-of-fact. Moore's use of italics to reproduce the thoughts of Zoë's student— ''You act like your opinion is worth more than everyone else's in the class''—puts Zoë in the place of the patient and the student, and Zoë realizes that the shoe is on the other foot now. The joke shows Zoë getting tangled in a web of her own thoughts, just as we do in the real world. Michelle Brockway, a writer for *Poets and Writers,* describes Moore's characters in the following way: ''Intelligent and well-meaning as the next guy, wisecracking, willfully illogical, these men and women invariably trip over life's accepted wisdom and assurances—only to come up . . . slack-jawed, gawking at an endgame replete with unanticipated incongruities.'' This description could be used to describe the multiple female roles that Zoë embodies.

Moore's story depicts a female driven satire that is a result of mismatched roles or stereotypes that some women, like Zoë, combine, as they search for who they are. The use of stereotypes in a satirical manner brings an ironic tone to her representation of Zoë as a hopelessly lonely woman. According to the stereotype of the traditional woman represented by Heidi, Zoë is a disappointment in society's eyes because she has not fulfilled the traditional expectation of a happy marriage with several children.

However, Zoë does not try to remedy her situation through marriage. A prime example is the interaction between Zoë and Earl, the man dressed as a naked woman. Zoë's attitude is not typical of the woman longing for a male companion, especially as she switches between playing the aloof already-divorced-though-never-married woman and the almost homicidal bonehead at the party. Jumping between non-traditional female roles may occur because Zoë does not know how she is expected to act or what society will classify as an acceptable and desirable flirtation. She experiments with her roles, playing off the reactions Earl gives her. Moore exaggerates a simple conversation to prove how non-traditional responses from Zoë are awkwardly received by others. Moore effectively uses the contrast of modern independent woman and the stereotypical Heidi by using satire in the character of Zoë toward the archaic image of woman.

Particularly intriguing is the explanation of Heidi. Moore illuminates the notion of conflict between the expectations of modern woman and the traditional passive woman. "You were never to say you weren't fine thank you and yourself. You were supposed to be Heidi. You were supposed to lug goat milk up the hills and not think twice. Heidi did not complain. Heidi did not do things like stand in front of the new IBM photocopier, saying, 'If this f——king Xerox machine breaks on me one more time, I'm going to slit my wrists.'" Zoë represents the struggle between the woman that was and the woman that is, including her struggle with society's reaction to the transition between the two types. Moore infers that people typically expect Heidi—the woman who was—and few see or accept the woman who is, or so Zoë believes. Zoë is a representation of the struggle of woman to transcend the Heidi of yesterday to be the woman of today, who does not live for chores to support others, but rather stands before modern technology and cusses until she is emotionally satisfied. As technology advances, so do women. The Heidi stereotype humorously contrasts archaic expectations of woman with current demands on her and her current reality.

In addition, Moore uses Zoë symbolically in another way, to show a darker side of the typical woman that is no laughing matter. A harsh reality presents itself privately to Zoë in the form of an unidentified growth in her abdomen. Robin Werner of Tulane University categorizes the quest to identify Zoë's growth as Zoë's struggle to find herself. As a woman who has not yet "solidified" her life by becoming a wife and bearing children and staying home and doing the dishes, Zoë is confused by how people react to her reality and how she reacts to the reality of others. The abdominal growth may be a symbol of Zoë's unspoken self-doubts. Though Zoë's reality of being utterly alone is obvious, she harbors a secret that represents all the fears of any woman who shares Zoë's longing for company. She refuses to tell even her sister, Evan, though at times she seems to want to. Fear and self-consciousness may vary in degree from woman to woman, but, in the end, every woman experiences them. Zoë does not want to attract attention to the elephant in the room—her isolation—but she cannot help but fixate on it. Admitting that she is utterly alone may just touch the surface of the accumulation of insecurities that she has because she does not fit the mold of Heidi—one stereotype of the traditional woman.

Moore represents Zoë as an ordinary woman with very real human flaws, as a type or symbol of the modern woman. Zoë stands in contrast to the stereotype of Heidi, the traditional woman, the woman who used to be, who had no flaws, who lived for others, made no demands to have her own needs satisfied, and never complained. Zoë is seeking the acceptance that Heidi received when her behavior was socially accepted, but she cannot or will not do what Heidi did to achieve that acceptance. Zoë tries several non-traditional female roles to try to gain acceptance, but these do not give her a sense of satisfaction. Her repeated attempts elicit mixed reactions from society, which she does not know how to process into a new attitude or behavior that fits the mold. A conflict is set up within Zoë over who she should be, and this conflict grows like a tangible growth inside her. The growth symbolizes not only the conflict between the traditional and the modern woman but Zoë's doubts, the modern woman's doubts about herself, about her ability to measure up to Heidi. Nevertheless, Zoë as the modern woman does not want to do what Heidi did: she does not want to lose her identity in the process of pleasing others, and by not achieving the acceptance she desires, she becomes a symbol of frustration and sadness.

Moore upsets ideal romanticism by using Zoë to explore what might happen to a woman who does not get married and have 2.7 children and a white picket fence. One would traditionally expect a love story, as she states it is, to end with something wistful and romantic. Instead, Zoë gives the story an ugly spin by having the heroine commit suicide. As the reader is stunned by this unexpected outcome, Moore illustrates that not every story and not every life has a happy ending. Don Lee, editor of the literary journal *Ploughshares,* in his article "About Lorrie Moore: A Profile," encapsulates Moore's own assessment of her work: "While Moore's fiction is renowned for its wit and humor full with repartee, pithy one-liners, and wisecracks, she considers the essence of her stories sad." Zoë's character in the end is ultimately sad, as exemplified by her confusion in how to act in response to Earl's reactions. What is not clear is what she wants from Earl; perhaps she does not know. In her attempt to deal with society's response to her lifestyle, Zoë represents the antithesis of the woman who has it together, the woman all women are expected to be. Zoë becomes the symbol of the modern woman who is caught between fulfilling the stereotype of the traditional woman, Heidi, and being who she really is, someone who cannot give what others expect or get what she wants.

Source: Ericka Marie Sudo, Critical Essay on "You're Ugly, Too," in *Short Stories for Students,* Gale, 2004.

Erin McGraw, Lorrie Moore, and Richard Burgin

In the following panel discussion excerpt, Moore discusses her views about and experiences with writing short stories.

Erin McGraw: As soon as we start talking about the short story, the long shadow of the novel shades our conversation. After all, the short story is only short in comparison with longer works, and through the twentieth century the novel has been generally considered fiction's most ambitious and important form. Nobody talks about wanting to write the great American short story (though maybe people should). Instead, we get opinions such as this, from E. L. Doctorow's introduction to *Best American Short Stories 2000:*

> While there are exceptions—Isaac Babel or Grace Paley, for example, writers-for-life of brilliant, tightly sprung prose designedly inhospitable to the long forms—we may say that short stories are what young writers produce on their way to first novels, or what older writers produce in between novels. The critic will hold title to all its estates, and the novel is a major act of the culture.

Well. How are we to respond to this assured assertion placed in the introduction to a collection of short stories that novels, not stories, are a major act of the culture?

Richard Burgin: I take exception to Doctorow's remark. I'm thinking of something Isaac Bashevis

> "A lot of short story writers are interested in the idea of a collection. I'm not, so much--at least not for myself. For me, each story comes separately and I don't even know if there ever will be another story after I write one. I don't know. I'm starting from scratch every time."

Singer, who wrote masterful novels *and* stories, said. He felt that a novel really was a story, just a longer, more complicated story. And he felt as a simple matter of logic that a novel would, as a rule, have more mistakes in it than a story. I think he said that Tolstoy's *War and Peace* had many more aesthetic mistakes than his "The Death of Ivan Ilych," and I would agree. So, in that sense, I think he was arguing that a story is a more perfect form, or perfection can be more readily approached, and perhaps even have the illusion of being achieved there than in the novel.

And I am thinking of another important writer in my life, with whom I also had the good fortune to do a book of conversations, Jorge Luis Borges. He, of course, felt the same way. He's famous for not writing a novel. So that would be my initial response to Doctorow's statement. Also, it occurs to me that if time is infinite, and literature keep proliferating with it, it's going to be increasingly attractive for writers to write and readers to read short stories to get any sense of this monster of literary history that just won't stop. And that in the future writers even very good writers, will be lucky to be remembered for even a single short story or perhaps for a single line. I suggest this just from the point of view of literary ecology, one might say.

Moore: I've never been on a panel before, so I don't know when I'm supposed to speak. Now?

I do think there's this idea afloat in the culture, which is an erroneous one, that the short story is suited to our diminishing attention spans. But there's a kind of organic wholeness that a short story requires which contradicts that idea. One can, if necessary, read a novel in five-minute increments. One cannot read a short story that way. So as time fragments and gets scarcer, and our attention spans supposedly diminish, the short story is not something that can rush in and fill the gap. The short story will be a casualty.

The short story is written in a manner similar to the way it's read, which is all at once. At some point in a short story the writer sits down and writes it all the way through from beginning to end. Whether it's on the eleventh draft or on the first draft, there's a wholeness to it, a momentum to it, a seeing of it all the way through from beginning to end. And when you sit and read a short story you read from beginning to end. You don't read five minutes here and there. But novels are checked in and out of, and they're checked in and out of by the novelist. A novelist can even sit down and work on it for ten minutes, and then go away, and work on it ten minutes the next day, too. That's how you can read novels as well, even if it's not ideal.

I don't really know what my point is except to argue against the particular idea that short stories are convenient for our shortened attention spans. They really are the opposite of that, I think. You need thirty-five, forty minutes to read a good short story, whereas you don't necessarily need that to continue reading a novel. And forty uninterrupted minutes are sometimes, perhaps increasingly, difficult to come by.

McGraw: You know, earlier this week the critics Charles May and Susan Lohafer gave their own panel. And Charles, who's read everything, was talking about what he says was his preference for reading a collection of stories over a novel—just assuming books of equal merit. Which I found astonishing. I think it's hard to read a book of stories. It's much, much easier to sit down and read a novel. After fifty pages you know what the terrain is. . . .

Audience Member: I have a question that changes the subject, is that okay? If the novel is something that began in eighteenth-century England and developed from there, you could call the short story a newer form. Unless you see an alliance between the short story and the folktale, the colloquial oral tradition that goes back infinitely. How do you see it? Do you see the short story as a newer kind of twentieth-century form, or do you see it as connected with that old, old tradition?

Moore: Me? I see it as a more oral form. It's confined to a physical idea, to sitting down, telling in a single sitting, receiving in a single sitting. It's very much attached to that idea of your body, your half-hour sitting, your hearing in a single shot. I always thought the first collection of stories was *The Decameron,* which goes way back. And those stories are incredible. And they don't seem all that different from what writers, short story writers, are trying to do now. And *The Decameron,* that first collection, makes explicit in the frame the idea of sitting down, and hearing stories, and telling stories. And then it also makes explicit the sense of disaster that's surrounding this storytelling, that storytelling is one way we keep ourselves alive, to celebrate our living, if not our lives.

Burgin: I suppose one could argue there are stories in the Bible, aren't there? Isn't the Bible full of little short stories really?

McGraw: Yeah, but I like the big stories in there, too.

Moore: Outside the parables of the New Testament, however, it doesn't make explicit the idea of storytelling which *The Decameron* does.

McGraw: Like *A Thousand and One Nights,* too, which is sort of pleasant because it's weird.

Audience Member: And how about *The Canterbury Tales*?

McGraw: *The Canterbury Tales.* Yes, absolutely.

Audience Member: I think, related to this, I was at a conference where a woman was talking about short story collections. And she mentioned yours, Ms. Moore, as well as *The Canterbury Tales,* countering people who say a short story can't tell about life. And what she was saying is that you should look at these collections as a whole, like *The Canterbury Tales,* that it really is a short story cycle. And I thought in some ways it's an interesting concept, but it also undercuts the short story itself, as it pushes toward this idea that it has to be large, that it has to be something from which you can take away an understanding of human life. That you can't took at an individual story and learn something from it. And I wonder what you thought of that way of approaching a collection, especially since you write stories separately, and only later put them in a collection.

Moore: A lot of short story writers are interested in the idea of a collection. I'm not, so much—

at least not for myself. For me, each story comes separately and I don't even know if there ever will be another story after I write one. I don't know. I'm starting from scratch every time. Eventually, when you have enough short stories you can sort of see what they have in common, and see how they form a collection. They form a temporal document. Over a ten-year period these were your obsessions and your concerns; here are your little summaries of life. And you put them together and give them a title. Now, then, afterward someone else can come along and just read them as or see them as a collection, or see the collection as a genre, or as a form. I'm not that interested in that, except maybe with respect to other people's collections.

I think the danger, also, as a writer, of seeing stories as a collection, is that it starts to corrupt the genesis of the story. If you're trying to find a story that fits the other stories, there's some kind of corruption that's already gone on. It's a worrisome idea. I was just talking to a writer who was actually doing that in his collection. He said he had a story that he was going to fit in and—

Burgin: Mix and match.

Moore:—link, link the theme of this story and that story. But he was getting stuck. Well, of course, he would get stuck because he's making something else. He's removed from the original impulse of writing a story.

Burgin: That's what the editors try to do later, with a story. I really like what Lorrie is saying about the individual stories and the potential corruption of a collection. I also think that a single good story can tell us just as much about ''life'' as a single good novel.

First of all, novels don't tell us what ''life'' is. They talk about a section of it, a little bit of the writer's personal emotional real estate, as it were, but hardly the entire earth. So, thinking of one example off the top of my head, Faulkner's great story ''That Evening Sun'' tells me personally a lot more about racism, among other things, than Harper Lee's novel *To Kill a Mockingbird,* which was not a bad novel. But, you know, as far as learning something about life, I think this single short story teaches a lot more and is a far more powerful aesthetic document than Lee's novel or many other novels about racism. You don't need a collection of stories to illuminate reality. One really good one will do it.

Jim Schiff: I have a question. Since you all not only read a good deal of short fiction but write it, I wanted to get a sense of some of the differences you see in the two forms, between the short story and the novel. And just going over some of the things that have been said over the last week, I know that Charles May, when he was here, was talking about the short story not really having much to do with realism. I think he felt like the novel had a lot more to do with realism. And, I think, even going back to when Updike was here, I mean if you look at the Rabbit novels they're full of sociological data and details. They're very contemporary, maybe even more so than his stories. And I remember somebody else talking about the passage of time and how a Tolstoy novel obviously conveys that passage of time in a way that short stories don't, I think, or at least does it differently. So I wonder what kind of differences you see in how the two forms operate?

Burgin: Erin, why don't you take it? You haven't spoken in a while.

McGraw: Well, you've got me thinking about Alice Munro. Because nobody writes stories that cover more time than Alice Munro does. And she tends to do it, I think, in lurches. You'll spend a great deal of time in a long scene in an Alice Munro story, and then vault ahead, with no transition at all, ahead or backwards fifty years, or you'll get a space alien or something. And I don't think that she is all that unique in using the story form as a way to hopscotch through time, though few do it so audaciously as Munro. She is such a case by herself.

Moore: She is unique.

McGraw: Yeah, and she's wonderful.

Moore: Someone once said that Munro does start out every time to write a novel, and I don't believe this, so maybe I shouldn't repeat it, but someone believes it: that Munro's stories start off with the ambition to be a novel, then they somehow get distilled down. Which, if true, is perhaps why they don't resemble anyone else's stories: they have an unusual handling of time. I mean, time is usually more the subject and the medium of novels than of short stories. But Munro has a kind of story that has always had the satisfactions and elements of a novel. And it's because she's started off with novelistic ideas and just ended up, I think, with a kind of sculpture in the end. I think that's how she creates her narrative time, sort of sculpturally. And she ends up with something that's a long short story that's not like anybody else's. . . .

Audience Member: Yes. What about the collections of linked stories? I mean, *Winesburg, Ohio, The Joy Luck Club,* there's a bunch more. *Go Down, Moses.* Is it a fad? Is it another genre? What is it?

Burgin: I think it can work commercially just by some of those examples. It's not something I've ever done. But I know some writers want to do that because they figure, "Well, I can sell each story individually, and sell the book as a whole." So, you know, it has that commercial dimension to it or whatever else you want to call it.

Audience Member: Are you interested in that?

Burgin: I don't have a particular interest. They haven't been among the best story collections that I've read, the so-called theme stories. They get tiresome because they're repetitive. You know, every story collection you pick up, there's going to be two or three stories of personal victimization and adultery in the suburbs. But eleven of them? I mean, it gets a little old.

Moore: I think those kinds of linked stories are novels, and they're just taking a story collection as their structure—I mean a novel can take any structure it pleases, and a novel-in-stories is taking the structure of stories and just linking them together. *Lives of Girls and Women,* which is Alice Munro's second book, is that. And it's just astounding. And there are other ones, too, obviously. But I think they're novels essentially. But the experience of reading them is much more like reading short stories. And they're written so carefully. Each of the "chapters" is a story complete unto itself. Sort of beautiful. In a way it's more accomplished than either a novel or a collection of short stories because it's done both things.

Audience Member: But then it does seem like a training ground for a would-be novelist. I know Pam Houston tried, well, she did write a collection of short stories, but they were linked stories. But what was interesting was that all the same characters were in each story. So you could read it as a short story. But I think, in her mind she felt that, well, I can't speak for her, but I think the idea was, "Yes I need to write a novel, and maybe if I do it this way it will be a novel." I don't know if that is why her memoir or short stories are linked. But it seemed to me something that was actually edging toward a novel, but didn't quite make it.

Audience Member: A Peruvian writer, Laura Risco, originally wrote a collection of short stories, and all the short stories had a little girl. And then

after she presented them to the editor in Peru, the editor suggested to link the short stories, and then it ended up like a novel. And it was a successful novel.

Moore: I think that happened with Amy Tan's book, *The Joy Luck Club.* She offered it up as stories initially, right? And the editors said, "We need this to be a novel."

Audience Member: There's that book of Alice Munro's, *The Beggar Maid.*

Moore: The Beggar Maid is like *Lives of Girls and Women.*

Audience Member: I read somewhere that she wrote a lot of those stories where the characters did all, in fact, have different names. And she said something about—

Moore: "Who am I kidding?"

Audience Member: Yeah. Like she was standing in the grocery store, literally, or something, and said, "They're all the same person." And they had to do something to the galleys. It was ready to go, and they had to get it out for the Christmas trade in Canada. And she said that if you look at it carefully there are some mistakes, a pronoun here or there, something's wrong in one or two of the stories where they rushed to get it out and to make those changes. Yeah, yeah, I've never looked closely enough to see if I could find the mistakes.

Moore: Her publisher must have fixed the mistakes in subsequent printings. . . .

Audience Member: I think there's one point that needs to be made about the short story, and that's how we can experience it. How the story can exist for us. And the reading last night was a case in point. That is, my reading of the story and the author's reading of the story are two different things. I've long known, of course, that everybody reads a story differently from the next person. So that with a short story, you can hear the whole thing, the whole definition of something you can read in one sitting is likely true. And that's okay, that's not a bad definition, actually, for a short story.

And so we can listen to the whole thing and hear the whole thing. But not only can we hear the whole thing, we can hear the writer herself, in this case, reading the whole thing. And last night, when Lorrie was reading "Dance in America," it became a different story and I watched and followed it in the book. You made some changes, in case you didn't notice.

Moore: Oh I noticed.

Audience Member: And you put in some "he saids" and "she saids" that weren't there. Were you reading from the text?

Moore: You're every writer's nightmare!

Audience Member: Well, I'm interested in how writers represent their stories aloud. Because we get back to the old notions that all of our fiction is basically oral. And when you read a story I think you have to hear a voice telling it to you. And if you can hear the author, in this case, it makes it a different kind of story. For instance, last night your story was funnier than I'd thought it was. I'd thought it was kind of sentimental when I read it. And you can hear the details repeating in it. And you can hear the whole story's implicit in the first line. And it comes home in the end and you can hear that. You can't do that with a novel.

Burgin: No, that's a really good point you're making.

Audience Member: And so, so it's like Walter Benjamin's notion of aura. What's the authentic reading of this story? What should we hear, and what should we be perceiving when we read this? How does it exist? And when you hear the author read it, it's something else. And certain other things came out where you could hear the parts are being juxtaposed as you went along, and you could hear the connections. And so, I think, the great defense of the short story is that it takes us back, close to the oral tradition. And secondly, it's something we can experience as a whole. And it's something that the artist herself, or himself, can present to us, something that you can't do with the novel. You've got to have breaks in reading the novel. You've got to stop some place. You can't just read seven hundred pages of a Pynchon at the same time.

McGraw: Desirable though that might be.

Audience Member: But at any rate, the short story is something that, it seems to me, is one of our most extraordinary forms of literature because of the fact that we can hear the whole thing at one time. That we can hear the writer present it to us, too, which I think is invaluable. That's why all this stuff is worthwhile. To bring people, writers, here to read them, to see how the writers represent what's on the page. And it's surprising what will happen. I'm sorry, I'm lecturing. But it's surprising the way some writers sometimes can't read their own stuff. And it's sometimes surprising how good things are

by the way the writers read them. So I think that it's not just the voice in the story, it's also how the writer himself, or herself, hears this thing, and then represents it to us. And we can perceive that in one sitting, at one time. And that's why I think the short story is so very important, and why it stays around.

Moore: I think it's a musical form, which perhaps ties it to performance. That is a very important point. And it does connect, again I think, more with theater, more with poetry, more with music. Whereas novels are not connected with those things, are not performed successfully that way. I will add that when a writer reads his or her own work the writer is seldom offering up his or her own reading as definitive or exemplary, the way the story should be read, or must be read, or the way it should exist. When I write a story I'm hearing a voice that I can't actually reproduce in a room for anyone. When I read it out loud I'm doing my best, but it's just not even very close to how I want the thing to sound, but it's my attempt. But I'm so pleased that you felt the story was improved by the reading, and that means I have somehow at least gone in the right direction. But the writer hearing his or her own voice reading the work is always disappointed. It's not really the perfect voice you want to hear for the perfect reading.

Burgin: I agree with Lorrie. I also feel that when I read from my story collections I'm not offering a definitive reading. And, like Lorrie, I also will make little changes that aren't in the printed text. So maybe what I'm offering is my definitive reading at that moment, because it's always evolving. And that's something tying in with some of what you said, and some of what Lorrie said, about the short story being somehow related to performing arts. Just like an orchestra will play Stravinksy's "Rites of Spring," or Mahler's Second, or whatever, a little differently each time, that's what's going to happen in the short story. Because even though there's a version between covers, that doesn't mean that it ends. It still exists in the writer's mind and you'll get these subtle changes. If not in actual language or words being omitted or added, in the inflection in the way one reads it. In that sense it is a kind of evolving performing art in a way that, just because of the logistics you alluded to, a novel isn't.

McGraw: And sometimes you're just off. Sometimes you read it and you know you've muffed it. You've screwed up words, or you didn't, you couldn't get yourself present enough to do a good job. The actor Richard Shiff read a story of mine a year ago, and I was flabbergasted. He read that story much better than I ever have. He was getting laughs, oh! And I've really studied that. And I have been trying to imitate his reading of my story because he did it better. So, I very much think that a public reading of a story is a performance and that we are not trained as performers. We are trained to be solitary people who sit in a room.

Audience Member: Well, you have to become a performer, then, if you're going to read them in public. Because you have to respect your reader and your audience.

McGraw: Well, sure. And how many of us have sat through deadly readings where you're like this [looks at her watch] that whole time?

Moore: I have to say I've felt the opposite experience with actors and actresses reading my work. I have found it unbearable because it was too actressy, too performed. There is another sort of place that you're trying to get to when you read your work aloud. And I can't exactly get to it, but neither can a number of actresses. So it's not just about being an actress. It's some other level that the story has to live on, which actors sometimes bypass and writers can't quite get to.

Audience Member: Getting back to the question of political correctness. Erin mentioned that often it is the narrative point of view which controls the narrative of the story. But there is this strange, irony-impaired point of view in our culture, that the writer, whether a short story writer or whatever, is always announcing his own point of view in everything that he says. And that the voice of the story is always the voice of the person behind the story.

Burgin: Yes, it's unfortunate that that exists because that's one of the pressures, I think, that, subliminally at any rate, make writers write politically correct stories where the "right people" are always noble and wise. It's because of this fear that, "Oh, well, no one would even think that I'm just writing a story, so I can't have my characters use this word or think those thoughts."

Audience Member: Nobody could imagine that this is just a character I'm writing about. They're always saying, "Keith!"

Jim Schiff: You know, I agree with the point about political correctness and see how that operates. But I also wonder if there's something counter to that. I mean in terms of *The New Yorker,* how that's changed from the pre-Gottlieb years, in terms

of what you can say, and so on, and the outrageousness of humor with a number of Lorrie's stories and George Saunders and others. So I wonder if there's something working against that also.

McGraw: Thank you for saying that. I understand what you're getting at Keith, but I'm startled to hear you talk about American literature as being an irony-free zone. Because my experience is that most American literature is drenched in irony. I would like to see rather less of it.

Burgin: Yes, ironists have their own political correctness.

McGraw: Yes, yes!

Burgin: The compulsive ironists are totally unaware of their own cliches. They're only aware of writing they deem to be too earnest.

Audience Member: Well I'm thinking of the fear of the reader. There's often a fear of the reader's reaction.

McGraw: Have you ever feared the reader's reaction, Lorrie?

Moore: Maybe I should, but no. I have a fear of my own reaction. I'm sort of out of this conversation, I guess. I don't really know what any of you are talking about. I don't feel an invisible fence of political correctness that I'm confined by. I feel like when you write a story you're just going out there, and you're on this journey, not this frightened little tour around your yard. So I don't know. I don't feel those things as a writer.

Burgin: Well, the writer shouldn't feel them. I'm saying these are cultural forces.

Moore: Political correctness should be, and mostly is, I think, a movement toward sensitivity and openness, not away. I have to say that I did just write a tiny piece of nonfiction that I dashed off in an hour and after it appeared several people said to me, "Oh, did the anti-defamation people call you yet?" So I went, "Really?" One can offend when one isn't aware of it, and then be made aware. That's OK. I think that afterwards it's good to, you know, have the conversation if, in fact, you have stepped on some toes and you didn't realize it. But no, one shouldn't censor oneself. But one should be as intelligent as possible and not get defensive about carelessness.

Burgin: But I'm saying these forces are out there among editors, among publishers, among people who are on awards committees and professors who determine the courses that are taught at universities, and finally, not hearing anything else but that, readers themselves. And eventually some of that trickles back, and affects some of our less courageous writers, as opposed to you, Lorrie.

Audience Member: This is going fully on something that Rebecca asked, and that Lorrie partly touched on, too, when you were talking about reading sort of experimental short stories back in the seventies. Do you see, as far as trends go, and big established names in short story writing, do you see length becoming a trend with them. For instance, Alice Munro, her earliest stories in *Dance of the Happy Shades* were much shorter than what she's doing now, in the last book for instance. She keeps getting longer, and longer, and longer. And that's not a complaint. Even somebody like Ann Beattie, who was one of the so-called minimalists when that term was especially derogatory, she's even working longer. And in her just-published collection, *Perfect Recall,* the stories are the longest I've ever seen her write. And even Amy Hempel who works really, really tiny, tried a novella in her last book. Do you see that? Does that have something to do, possibly, with being established and with feeling free to work longer? Or is that a trend among younger, more inexperienced writers as well?

Moore: I have no idea. I don't think an artist makes these decisions in response to trends, careers, editors, magazines. I think they have something they want to write, and they find a form that can best contain it. The long short story is a wonderful form. Ethan Canin works really well within that form. He's written some of the best, as have Stanley Elkin and Andre Dubus. And Alice Munro was always working in that length. In *Lives of Girls and Women,* there's a very long story called ''Baptizing,'' which is one of her best stories. I think the long story is hardly new.

Audience Member: Yeah. I'm just wondering because of Carver and Beattie, that sort of trend from the seventies into the eighties that was very small, compact, pared down stories. Very few adjectives, very short, compact sentences. So I'm just wondering because that seems to be gone from stories you see nowadays. I mean, you don't see those in *The New Yorker* anymore.

Moore: You don't?

Audience Member: I don't see them as much anymore. Or maybe I'm just not reading them.

Moore: I know *The New Yorker* has space constraints like it's never had. So I think the long story is not going to work happily with any commercial magazine if it's not working well in *The New Yorker.* So maybe among literary magazines you'll find the long short story more often.

Audience Member: So a twenty to twenty-five page manuscript that was okay before is now way too long. I think to tell that you have to keep your story shorter to fit in the constraints of today's lack of available space is really a shame.

Burgin: That's something you have to resist, again, like political correctness. You just have to write what you want and let the chips fall as they may.

McGraw: Well, that's what I was about to ask you, Richard. You're seeing all these things cross your desk. Are you seeing a lot of long stories that can't find a place in the slicks, or are you seeing very tight stories á la Carver that are also not, by and large, showing up in the slicks?

Burgin: I think I see all kinds of them. We get about six thousand a year and pretty much see a lot of different kinds. I couldn't generalize really.

McGraw: Fink. You're exactly the one who should be generalizing. Carol?

Audience Member: I have a dim-witted question and an impertinent question. The dim-witted question is, since all three of you have written in both forms, I'm wondering what you feel you can do in a short story that you can't do in a novel and vice versa?

Moore: This metaphor has been used by so many people but it seems the most accurate to the experience of writing short stories versus writing novels. A short story is like a love affair. It's got this quick excitement to it and closure; one throws oneself into it, and then is done with it. I'm not going to continue to describe a love affair. But the novel is much more like marriage. It's a daily, daily struggle, taking place over years. It's work, as everyone tells you about marriage, but forgets to tell you about novel writing. And there are all kinds of other metaphors you can come up with. I once thought that the short story was like a biopsy. You know, you go in, and you get a kind of layered sample of the body. And that a novel was more like cloning. You started with some cells, and you had to grow, over time, the whole body.

For short story writers I do think that writing short stories is just much more satisfying. You know, all the rewards are faster. The sense of accomplishment is there. And you can feel, you can internalize the form, you've written more short stories, always, than novels and so you feel familiar with the form. And there's a kind of happiness and, I don't know, a sense of familiarity with the whole thing. And novel writing is just painful. It's mysterious and it's just never ending. Short story writers working on a novel are always in great pain. But sometimes, as Erin was saying, you have something you need to explore that won't fit into a short story. It has different parts. It may have different points of view. It may have two different themes, two different worlds. It may have time as its subject. And so you just need to work in the novel form. It's a miserable business. . . .

Source: Erin McGraw, Lorrie Moore, and Richard Burgin, "The State of the Short Story," in *Boulevard,* Vol. 17, No. 1–2, Fall 2001, pp. 1–27.

Sources

Aldridge, John W., "Anguish as a Second Language," in *Talents and Technicians: Literary Chic and the New Assembly-Line Fiction,* Charles Scribner's Sons, 1992, p. 110.

Blades, John, "Lorrie Moore: Flipping Death the Bird," in *Publishers Weekly,* Vol. 245, No. 34, August 24, 1998, pp. 31–32.

Brockway, Michelle, "The Art of Reading Lorrie Moore," in *Poets and Writers,* Vol. 28, No. 5, September/October 2000, pp. 16–19.

Casey, John, "Eloquent Solitudes: The Short Stories of Lorrie Moore Address Life's Essential Loneliness," Review of *Like Life,* in *Chicago Tribune,* May 20, 1990, p. 3.

Cryer, Dan, "Bittersweet Quest for a Lasting Romance," Review of *Like Life,* in *Newsday,* May 21, 1990.

Gaffney, Elizabeth, "Lorrie Moore: The Art of Fiction CLXVII: An Interview with Lorrie Moore," in the *Paris Review,* Vol. 43, No. 158, Spring–Summer 2001, pp. 57–84.

Gilbert, Matthew, "*Like Life:* Moore's Clever and Complex Set of Stories," Review of *Like Life,* in *Boston Globe,* May 23, 1990, p. 51.

Lee, Don, "About Lorrie Moore," in *Ploughshares,* Vol. 24, Nos. 2–3, Fall 1998, pp. 224–29.

"Lives on a Short-Story Roller Coaster," in *Christian Science Monitor,* August 2, 1990, p. 12.

Novak, Ralph, Review of *Like Life,* in *People Weekly,* Vol. 33, No. 20, May 21, 1990, pp. 43–44.

Picker, Lauren, "Talking with Lorrie Moore: Humor and Heartbreak," in *Newsday,* October 30, 1994, p. 40.

Poivoir, Sally, "In Lithe, Insolent Prose, a Challenge from Lorrie Moore," Review of *Like Life,* in *Houston Chronicle,* May 20, 1990, p. 24.

Rubin, Merle, "Lean Cuisine for Picky Palates: *Like Life* Stories by Lorrie Moore," in *Los Angeles Times,* June 3, 1990, p. 11.

Steinberg, Sybil, Review of *Like Life,* in *Publishers Weekly,* Vol. 237, No. 8, February 23, 1990, pp. 205–06.

Werner, Robin A, "Lorrie Moore," in *Dictionary of Literary Biography,* Vol. 234, *American Short-Story Writers Since World War II, Third Series,* edited by Patrick Meanor, Gale, 2001, pp. 205–13.

Further Reading

Gelfant, Blanche H., ed., *The Columbia Companion to the Twentieth-Century American Short Story,* Columbia University Press, 2000.

   This comprehensive reference guide to twentieth century short stories includes over 100 pages of thematic essays that focus on the form of the short story as well as stories from over 100 writers.

Updike, John, and Katrina Kenison, eds., *The Best American Short Stories of the Century,* Houghton Mifflin, 1999.

   Updike, one of America's leading short story writers, co-edited this critically-acclaimed anthology that includes writers from the entire twentieth century.

Williford, Lex, and Michael Martone, eds., *The Scribner Anthology of Contemporary Short Fiction: Fifty North American Stories since 1970,* Simon and Schuster, 1999.

   This is an eclectic anthology of contemporary short stories written by American writers, including Lorrie Moore.

Glossary of Literary Terms

A

Aestheticism: A literary and artistic movement of the nineteenth century. Followers of the movement believed that art should not be mixed with social, political, or moral teaching. The statement ''art for art's sake'' is a good summary of aestheticism. The movement had its roots in France, but it gained widespread importance in England in the last half of the nineteenth century, where it helped change the Victorian practice of including moral lessons in literature. Edgar Allan Poe is one of the best-known American ''aesthetes.''

Allegory: A narrative technique in which characters representing things or abstract ideas are used to convey a message or teach a lesson. Allegory is typically used to teach moral, ethical, or religious lessons but is sometimes used for satiric or political purposes. Many fairy tales are allegories.

Allusion: A reference to a familiar literary or historical person or event, used to make an idea more easily understood. Joyce Carol Oates's story ''Where Are You Going, Where Have You Been?'' exhibits several allusions to popular music.

Analogy: A comparison of two things made to explain something unfamiliar through its similarities to something familiar, or to prove one point based on the acceptance of another. Similes and metaphors are types of analogies.

Antagonist: The major character in a narrative or drama who works against the hero or protagonist. The Misfit in Flannery O'Connor's story ''A Good Man Is Hard to Find'' serves as the antagonist for the Grandmother.

Anthology: A collection of similar works of literature, art, or music. Zora Neale Hurston's ''The Eatonville Anthology'' is a collection of stories that take place in the same town.

Anthropomorphism: The presentation of animals or objects in human shape or with human characteristics. The term is derived from the Greek word for ''human form.'' The fur necklet in Katherine Mansfield's story ''Miss Brill'' has anthropomorphic characteristics.

Anti-hero: A central character in a work of literature who lacks traditional heroic qualities such as courage, physical prowess, and fortitude. Anti-heroes typically distrust conventional values and are unable to commit themselves to any ideals. They generally feel helpless in a world over which they have no control. Anti-heroes usually accept, and often celebrate, their positions as social outcasts. A well-known anti-hero is Walter Mitty in James Thurber's story ''The Secret Life of Walter Mitty.''

Archetype: The word archetype is commonly used to describe an original pattern or model from which all other things of the same kind are made. Archetypes are the literary images that grow out of the ''collective unconscious,'' a theory proposed by psychologist Carl Jung. They appear in literature as incidents and plots that repeat basic patterns of life. They may also appear as stereotyped characters. The ''schlemiel'' of Yiddish literature is an archetype.

Autobiography: A narrative in which an individual tells his or her life story. Examples include Benjamin Franklin's *Autobiography* and Amy Hempel's story ''In the Cemetery Where Al Jolson Is Buried,'' which has autobiographical characteristics even though it is a work of fiction.

Avant-garde: A literary term that describes new writing that rejects traditional approaches to literature in favor of innovations in style or content. Twentieth-century examples of the literary *avant-garde* include the modernists and the minimalists.

B

Belles-lettres: A French term meaning ''fine letters'' or ''beautiful writing.'' It is often used as a synonym for literature, typically referring to imaginative and artistic rather than scientific or expository writing. Current usage sometimes restricts the meaning to light or humorous writing and appreciative essays about literature. Lewis Carroll's *Alice in Wonderland* epitomizes the realm of belles-lettres.

Bildungsroman: A German word meaning ''novel of development.'' The *bildungsroman* is a study of the maturation of a youthful character, typically brought about through a series of social or sexual encounters that lead to self-awareness. J. D. Salinger's *Catcher in the Rye* is a *bildungsroman*, and Doris Lessing's story ''Through the Tunnel'' exhibits characteristics of a *bildungsroman* as well.

Black Aesthetic Movement: A period of artistic and literary development among African Americans in the 1960s and early 1970s. This was the first major African-American artistic movement since the Harlem Renaissance and was closely paralleled by the civil rights and black power movements. The black aesthetic writers attempted to produce works of art that would be meaningful to the black masses. Key figures in black aesthetics included one of its founders, poet and playwright Amiri Baraka, formerly known as LeRoi Jones; poet and essayist Haki R. Madhubuti, formerly Don L. Lee; poet and playwright Sonia Sanchez; and dramatist Ed Bullins. Works representative of the Black Aesthetic Movement include Amiri Baraka's play *Dutchman,* a 1964 Obie award-winner.

Black Humor: Writing that places grotesque elements side by side with humorous ones in an attempt to shock the reader, forcing him or her to laugh at the horrifying reality of a disordered world. ''Lamb to the Slaughter,'' by Roald Dahl, in which a placid housewife murders her husband and serves the murder weapon to the investigating policemen, is an example of black humor.

C

Catharsis: The release or purging of unwanted emotions—specifically fear and pity—brought about by exposure to art. The term was first used by the Greek philosopher Aristotle in his *Poetics* to refer to the desired effect of tragedy on spectators.

Character: Broadly speaking, a person in a literary work. The actions of characters are what constitute the plot of a story, novel, or poem. There are numerous types of characters, ranging from simple, stereotypical figures to intricate, multifaceted ones. ''Characterization'' is the process by which an author creates vivid, believable characters in a work of art. This may be done in a variety of ways, including (1) direct description of the character by the narrator; (2) the direct presentation of the speech, thoughts, or actions of the character; and (3) the responses of other characters to the character. The term ''character'' also refers to a form originated by the ancient Greek writer Theophrastus that later became popular in the seventeenth and eighteenth centuries. It is a short essay or sketch of a person who prominently displays a specific attribute or quality, such as miserliness or ambition. ''Miss Brill,'' a story by Katherine Mansfield, is an example of a character sketch.

Classical: In its strictest definition in literary criticism, classicism refers to works of ancient Greek or Roman literature. The term may also be used to describe a literary work of recognized importance (a ''classic'') from any time period or literature that exhibits the traits of classicism. Examples of later works and authors now described as classical include French literature of the seventeenth century, Western novels of the nineteenth century, and American fiction of the mid-nineteenth century such as that written by James Fenimore Cooper and Mark Twain.

Climax: The turning point in a narrative, the moment when the conflict is at its most intense. Typically, the structure of stories, novels, and plays is one of rising action, in which tension builds to the climax, followed by falling action, in which tension lessens as the story moves to its conclusion.

Comedy: One of two major types of drama, the other being tragedy. Its aim is to amuse, and it typically ends happily. Comedy assumes many forms, such as farce and burlesque, and uses a variety of techniques, from parody to satire. In a restricted sense the term comedy refers only to dramatic presentations, but in general usage it is commonly applied to nondramatic works as well.

Comic Relief: The use of humor to lighten the mood of a serious or tragic story, especially in plays. The technique is very common in Elizabethan works, and can be an integral part of the plot or simply a brief event designed to break the tension of the scene.

Conflict: The conflict in a work of fiction is the issue to be resolved in the story. It usually occurs between two characters, the protagonist and the antagonist, or between the protagonist and society or the protagonist and himself or herself. The conflict in Washington Irving's story "The Devil and Tom Walker" is that the Devil wants Tom Walker's soul but Tom does not want to go to hell.

Criticism: The systematic study and evaluation of literary works, usually based on a specific method or set of principles. An important part of literary studies since ancient times, the practice of criticism has given rise to numerous theories, methods, and "schools," sometimes producing conflicting, even contradictory, interpretations of literature in general as well as of individual works. Even such basic issues as what constitutes a poem or a novel have been the subject of much criticism over the centuries. Seminal texts of literary criticism include Plato's *Republic,* Aristotle's *Poetics,* Sir Philip Sidney's *The Defence of Poesie,* and John Dryden's *Of Dramatic Poesie.* Contemporary schools of criticism include deconstruction, feminist, psychoanalytic, poststructuralist, new historicist, postcolonialist, and reader-response.

D

Deconstruction: A method of literary criticism characterized by multiple conflicting interpretations of a given work. Deconstructionists consider the impact of the language of a work and suggest that the true meaning of the work is not necessarily the meaning that the author intended.

Deduction: The process of reaching a conclusion through reasoning from general premises to a specific premise. Arthur Conan Doyle's character Sherlock Holmes often used deductive reasoning to solve mysteries.

Denotation: The definition of a word, apart from the impressions or feelings it creates in the reader. The word "apartheid" denotes a political and economic policy of segregation by race, but its connotations—oppression, slavery, inequality—are numerous.

Denouement: A French word meaning "the unknotting." In literature, it denotes the resolution of conflict in fiction or drama. The *denouement* follows the climax and provides an outcome to the primary plot situation as well as an explanation of secondary plot complications. A well-known example of *denouement* is the last scene of the play *As You Like It* by William Shakespeare, in which couples are married, an evildoer repents, the identities of two disguised characters are revealed, and a ruler is restored to power. Also known as "falling action."

Detective Story: A narrative about the solution of a mystery or the identification of a criminal. The conventions of the detective story include the detective's scrupulous use of logic in solving the mystery; incompetent or ineffectual police; a suspect who appears guilty at first but is later proved innocent; and the detective's friend or confidant—often the narrator—whose slowness in interpreting clues emphasizes by contrast the detective's brilliance. Edgar Allan Poe's "Murders in the Rue Morgue" is commonly regarded as the earliest example of this type of story. Other practitioners are Arthur Conan Doyle, Dashiell Hammett, and Agatha Christie.

Dialogue: Dialogue is conversation between people in a literary work. In its most restricted sense, it refers specifically to the speech of characters in a drama. As a specific literary genre, a "dialogue" is a composition in which characters debate an issue or idea.

Didactic: A term used to describe works of literature that aim to teach a moral, religious, political, or practical lesson. Although didactic elements are often found in artistically pleasing works, the term "didactic" usually refers to literature in which the message is more important than the form. The term may also be used to criticize a work that the critic finds "overly didactic," that is, heavy-handed in its delivery of a lesson. An example of didactic literature is John Bunyan's *Pilgrim's Progress.*

Dramatic Irony: Occurs when the reader of a work of literature knows something that a character in the work itself does not know. The irony is in the contrast between the intended meaning of the statements or actions of a character and the additional information understood by the audience.

Dystopia: An imaginary place in a work of fiction where the characters lead dehumanized, fearful lives. George Orwell's *Nineteen Eighty-four,* and Margaret Atwood's *Handmaid's Tale* portray versions of dystopia.

E

Edwardian: Describes cultural conventions identified with the period of the reign of Edward VII of England (1901–1910). Writers of the Edwardian Age typically displayed a strong reaction against the propriety and conservatism of the Victorian Age. Their work often exhibits distrust of authority in religion, politics, and art and expresses strong doubts about the soundness of conventional values. Writers of this era include E. M. Forster, H. G. Wells, and Joseph Conrad.

Empathy: A sense of shared experience, including emotional and physical feelings, with someone or something other than oneself. Empathy is often used to describe the response of a reader to a literary character.

Epilogue: A concluding statement or section of a literary work. In dramas, particularly those of the seventeenth and eighteenth centuries, the epilogue is a closing speech, often in verse, delivered by an actor at the end of a play and spoken directly to the audience.

Epiphany: A sudden revelation of truth inspired by a seemingly trivial incident. The term was widely used by James Joyce in his critical writings, and the stories in Joyce's *Dubliners* are commonly called ''epiphanies.''

Epistolary Novel: A novel in the form of letters. The form was particularly popular in the eighteenth century. The form can also be applied to short stories, as in Edwidge Danticat's ''Children of the Sea.''

Epithet: A word or phrase, often disparaging or abusive, that expresses a character trait of someone or something. ''The Napoleon of crime'' is an epithet applied to Professor Moriarty, arch-rival of Sherlock Holmes in Arthur Conan Doyle's series of detective stories.

Existentialism: A predominantly twentieth-century philosophy concerned with the nature and perception of human existence. There are two major strains of existentialist thought: atheistic and Christian. Followers of atheistic existentialism believe that the individual is alone in a godless universe and that the basic human condition is one of suffering and loneliness. Nevertheless, because there are no fixed values, individuals can create their own characters— indeed, they can shape themselves—through the exercise of free will. The atheistic strain culminates in and is popularly associated with the works of Jean-Paul Sartre. The Christian existentialists, on the other hand, believe that only in God may people find freedom from life's anguish. The two strains hold certain beliefs in common: that existence cannot be fully understood or described through empirical effort; that anguish is a universal element of life; that individuals must bear responsibility for their actions; and that there is no common standard of behavior or perception for religious and ethical matters. Existentialist thought figures prominently in the works of such authors as Franz Kafka, Fyodor Dostoyevsky, and Albert Camus.

Expatriatism: The practice of leaving one's country to live for an extended period in another country. Literary expatriates include Irish author James Joyce who moved to Italy and France, American writers James Baldwin, Ernest Hemingway, Gertrude Stein, and F. Scott Fitzgerald who lived and wrote in Paris, and Polish novelist Joseph Conrad in England.

Exposition: Writing intended to explain the nature of an idea, thing, or theme. Expository writing is often combined with description, narration, or argument.

Expressionism: An indistinct literary term, originally used to describe an early twentieth-century school of German painting. The term applies to almost any mode of unconventional, highly subjective writing that distorts reality in some way. Advocates of Expressionism include Federico Garcia Lorca, Eugene O'Neill, Franz Kafka, and James Joyce.

F

Fable: A prose or verse narrative intended to convey a moral. Animals or inanimate objects with human characteristics often serve as characters in fables. A famous fable is Aesop's "The Tortoise and the Hare."

Fantasy: A literary form related to mythology and folklore. Fantasy literature is typically set in non-existent realms and features supernatural beings. Notable examples of literature with elements of fantasy are Gabriel Garcia Marquez's story "The Handsomest Drowned Man in the World" and Ursula K. LeGuin's "The Ones Who Walk Away from Omelas."

Farce: A type of comedy characterized by broad humor, outlandish incidents, and often vulgar subject matter. Much of the comedy in film and television could more accurately be described as farce.

Fiction: Any story that is the product of imagination rather than a documentation of fact. Characters and events in such narratives may be based in real life but their ultimate form and configuration is a creation of the author.

Figurative Language: A technique in which an author uses figures of speech such as hyperbole, irony, metaphor, or simile for a particular effect. Figurative language is the opposite of literal language, in which every word is truthful, accurate, and free of exaggeration or embellishment.

Flashback: A device used in literature to present action that occurred before the beginning of the story. Flashbacks are often introduced as the dreams or recollections of one or more characters.

Foil: A character in a work of literature whose physical or psychological qualities contrast strongly with, and therefore highlight, the corresponding qualities of another character. In his Sherlock Holmes stories, Arthur Conan Doyle portrayed Dr. Watson as a man of normal habits and intelligence, making him a foil for the eccentric and unusually perceptive Sherlock Holmes.

Folklore: Traditions and myths preserved in a culture or group of people. Typically, these are passed on by word of mouth in various forms—such as legends, songs, and proverbs—or preserved in customs and ceremonies. Washington Irving, in "The Devil and Tom Walker" and many of his other stories, incorporates many elements of the folklore of New England and Germany.

Folktale: A story originating in oral tradition. Folktales fall into a variety of categories, including legends, ghost stories, fairy tales, fables, and anecdotes based on historical figures and events.

Foreshadowing: A device used in literature to create expectation or to set up an explanation of later developments. Edgar Allan Poe uses foreshadowing to create suspense in "The Fall of the House of Usher" when the narrator comments on the crumbling state of disrepair in which he finds the house.

G

Genre: A category of literary work. Genre may refer to both the content of a given work—tragedy, comedy, horror, science fiction—and to its form, such as poetry, novel, or drama.

Gilded Age: A period in American history during the 1870s and after characterized by political corruption and materialism. A number of important novels of social and political criticism were written during this time. Henry James and Kate Chopin are two writers who were prominent during the Gilded Age.

Gothicism: In literature, works characterized by a taste for medieval or morbid characters and situations. A gothic novel prominently features elements of horror, the supernatural, gloom, and violence: clanking chains, terror, ghosts, medieval castles, and unexplained phenomena. The term "gothic novel" is also applied to novels that lack elements of the traditional Gothic setting but that create a similar atmosphere of terror or dread. The term can also be applied to stories, plays, and poems. Mary Shelley's *Frankenstein* and Joyce Carol Oates's *Bellefleur* are both gothic novels.

Grotesque: In literature, a work that is characterized by exaggeration, deformity, freakishness, and disorder. The grotesque often includes an element of comic absurdity. Examples of the grotesque can be found in the works of Edgar Allan Poe, Flannery O'Connor, Joseph Heller, and Shirley Jackson.

H

Harlem Renaissance: The Harlem Renaissance of the 1920s is generally considered the first significant movement of black writers and artists in the United States. During this period, new and established black writers, many of whom lived in the region of New York City known as Harlem, published more fiction and poetry than ever before, the first influential black literary journals were established, and black authors and artists received their first widespread recognition and serious critical appraisal. Among the major writers associated with this period are Countee Cullen, Langston Hughes, Arna Bontemps, and Zora Neale Hurston.

Hero/Heroine: The principal sympathetic character in a literary work. Heroes and heroines typically exhibit admirable traits: idealism, courage, and integrity, for example. Famous heroes and heroines of literature include Charles Dickens's Oliver Twist, Margaret Mitchell's Scarlett O'Hara, and the anonymous narrator in Ralph Ellison's *Invisible Man*.

Hyperbole: Deliberate exaggeration used to achieve an effect. In William Shakespeare's *Macbeth,* Lady Macbeth hyperbolizes when she says, ''All the perfumes of Arabia could not sweeten this little hand.''

I

Image: A concrete representation of an object or sensory experience. Typically, such a representation helps evoke the feelings associated with the object or experience itself. Images are either ''literal'' or ''figurative.'' Literal images are especially concrete and involve little or no extension of the obvious meaning of the words used to express them. Figurative images do not follow the literal meaning of the words exactly. Images in literature are usually visual, but the term ''image'' can also refer to the representation of any sensory experience.

Imagery: The array of images in a literary work. Also used to convey the author's overall use of figurative language in a work.

In medias res: A Latin term meaning ''in the middle of things.'' It refers to the technique of beginning a story at its midpoint and then using various flashback devices to reveal previous action. This technique originated in such epics as Virgil's *Aeneid.*

Interior Monologue: A narrative technique in which characters' thoughts are revealed in a way that appears to be uncontrolled by the author. The interior monologue typically aims to reveal the inner self of a character. It portrays emotional experiences as they occur at both a conscious and unconscious level. One of the best-known interior monologues in English is the Molly Bloom section at the close of James Joyce's *Ulysses.* Katherine Anne Porter's ''The Jilting of Granny Weatherall'' is also told in the form of an interior monologue.

Irony: In literary criticism, the effect of language in which the intended meaning is the opposite of what is stated. The title of Jonathan Swift's ''A Modest Proposal'' is ironic because what Swift proposes in this essay is cannibalism—hardly ''modest.''

J

Jargon: Language that is used or understood only by a select group of people. Jargon may refer to terminology used in a certain profession, such as computer jargon, or it may refer to any nonsensical language that is not understood by most people. Anthony Burgess's *A Clockwork Orange* and James Thurber's ''The Secret Life of Walter Mitty'' both use jargon.

K

Knickerbocker Group: An indistinct group of New York writers of the first half of the nineteenth century. Members of the group were linked only by location and a common theme: New York life. Two famous members of the Knickerbocker Group were Washington Irving and William Cullen Bryant. The group's name derives from Irving's *Knickerbocker's History of New York.*

L

Literal Language: An author uses literal language when he or she writes without exaggerating or embellishing the subject matter and without any tools of figurative language. To say ''He ran very quickly down the street'' is to use literal language, whereas to say ''He ran like a hare down the street'' would be using figurative language.

Literature: Literature is broadly defined as any written or spoken material, but the term most often refers to creative works. Literature includes poetry, drama, fiction, and many kinds of nonfiction writing, as well as oral, dramatic, and broadcast compositions not necessarily preserved in a written format, such as films and television programs.

Lost Generation: A term first used by Gertrude Stein to describe the post-World War I generation of American writers: men and women haunted by a sense of betrayal and emptiness brought about by the destructiveness of the war. The term is commonly applied to Hart Crane, Ernest Hemingway, F. Scott Fitzgerald, and others.

M

Magic Realism: A form of literature that incorporates fantasy elements or supernatural occurrences into the narrative and accepts them as truth. Gabriel Garcia Marquez and Laura Esquivel are two writers known for their works of magic realism.

Metaphor: A figure of speech that expresses an idea through the image of another object. Metaphors suggest the essence of the first object by identifying it with certain qualities of the second object. An example is "But soft, what light through yonder window breaks?/ It is the east, and Juliet is the sun" in William Shakespeare's *Romeo and Juliet*. Here, Juliet, the first object, is identified with qualities of the second object, the sun.

Minimalism: A literary style characterized by spare, simple prose with few elaborations. In minimalism, the main theme of the work is often never discussed directly. Amy Hempel and Ernest Hemingway are two writers known for their works of minimalism.

Modernism: Modern literary practices. Also, the principles of a literary school that lasted from roughly the beginning of the twentieth century until the end of World War II. Modernism is defined by its rejection of the literary conventions of the nineteenth century and by its opposition to conventional morality, taste, traditions, and economic values. Many writers are associated with the concepts of modernism, including Albert Camus, D. H. Lawrence, Ernest Hemingway, William Faulkner, Eugene O'Neill, and James Joyce.

Monologue: A composition, written or oral, by a single individual. More specifically, a speech given by a single individual in a drama or other public entertainment. It has no set length, although it is usually several or more lines long. "I Stand Here Ironing" by Tillie Olsen is an example of a story written in the form of a monologue.

Mood: The prevailing emotions of a work or of the author in his or her creation of the work. The mood of a work is not always what might be expected based on its subject matter.

Motif: A theme, character type, image, metaphor, or other verbal element that recurs throughout a single work of literature or occurs in a number of different works over a period of time. For example, the color white in Herman Melville's *Moby Dick* is a "specific" *motif,* while the trials of star-crossed lovers is a "conventional" *motif* from the literature of all periods.

N

Narration: The telling of a series of events, real or invented. A narration may be either a simple narrative, in which the events are recounted chronologically, or a narrative with a plot, in which the account is given in a style reflecting the author's artistic concept of the story. Narration is sometimes used as a synonym for "storyline."

Narrative: A verse or prose accounting of an event or sequence of events, real or invented. The term is also used as an adjective in the sense "method of narration." For example, in literary criticism, the expression "narrative technique" usually refers to the way the author structures and presents his or her story. Different narrative forms include diaries, travelogues, novels, ballads, epics, short stories, and other fictional forms.

Narrator: The teller of a story. The narrator may be the author or a character in the story through whom the author speaks. Huckleberry Finn is the narrator of Mark Twain's *The Adventures of Huckleberry Finn.*

Novella: An Italian term meaning "story." This term has been especially used to describe fourteenth-century Italian tales, but it also refers to modern short novels. Modern novellas include Leo Tolstoy's *The Death of Ivan Ilich,* Fyodor Dostoyevsky's *Notes from the Underground,* and Joseph Conrad's *Heart of Darkness.*

O

Oedipus Complex: A son's romantic obsession with his mother. The phrase is derived from the story of the ancient Theban hero Oedipus, who unknowingly killed his father and married his mother, and was popularized by Sigmund Freud's theory of psychoanalysis. Literary occurrences of the Oedipus complex include Sophocles' *Oedipus Rex* and D. H. Lawrence's "The Rocking-Horse Winner."

Onomatopoeia: The use of words whose sounds express or suggest their meaning. In its simplest sense, onomatopoeia may be represented by words that mimic the sounds they denote such as "hiss" or "meow." At a more subtle level, the pattern and rhythm of sounds and rhymes of a line or poem may be onomatopoeic.

Oral Tradition: A process by which songs, ballads, folklore, and other material are transmitted by word of mouth. The tradition of oral transmission predates the written record systems of literate society.

Oral transmission preserves material sometimes over generations, although often with variations. Memory plays a large part in the recitation and preservation of orally transmitted material. Native American myths and legends, and African folktales told by plantation slaves are examples of orally transmitted literature.

P

Parable: A story intended to teach a moral lesson or answer an ethical question. Examples of parables are the stories told by Jesus Christ in the New Testament, notably ''The Prodigal Son,'' but parables also are used in Sufism, rabbinic literature, Hasidism, and Zen Buddhism. Isaac Bashevis Singer's story ''Gimpel the Fool'' exhibits characteristics of a parable.

Paradox: A statement that appears illogical or contradictory at first, but may actually point to an underlying truth. A literary example of a paradox is George Orwell's statement ''All animals are equal, but some animals are more equal than others'' in *Animal Farm*.

Parody: In literature, this term refers to an imitation of a serious literary work or the signature style of a particular author in a ridiculous manner. A typical parody adopts the style of the original and applies it to an inappropriate subject for humorous effect. Parody is a form of satire and could be considered the literary equivalent of a caricature or cartoon. Henry Fielding's *Shamela* is a parody of Samuel Richardson's *Pamela*.

Persona: A Latin term meaning ''mask.'' Personae are the characters in a fictional work of literature. The persona generally functions as a mask through which the author tells a story in a voice other than his or her own. A persona is usually either a character in a story who acts as a narrator or an ''implied author,'' a voice created by the author to act as the narrator for himself or herself. The persona in Charlotte Perkins Gilman's story ''The Yellow Wallpaper'' is the unnamed young mother experiencing a mental breakdown.

Personification: A figure of speech that gives human qualities to abstract ideas, animals, and inanimate objects. To say that ''the sun is smiling'' is to personify the sun.

Plot: The pattern of events in a narrative or drama. In its simplest sense, the plot guides the author in composing the work and helps the reader follow the work. Typically, plots exhibit causality and unity and have a beginning, a middle, and an end. Sometimes, however, a plot may consist of a series of disconnected events, in which case it is known as an ''episodic plot.''

Poetic Justice: An outcome in a literary work, not necessarily a poem, in which the good are rewarded and the evil are punished, especially in ways that particularly fit their virtues or crimes. For example, a murderer may himself be murdered, or a thief will find himself penniless.

Poetic License: Distortions of fact and literary convention made by a writer—not always a poet—for the sake of the effect gained. Poetic license is closely related to the concept of ''artistic freedom.'' An author exercises poetic license by saying that a pile of money ''reaches as high as a mountain'' when the pile is actually only a foot or two high.

Point of View: The narrative perspective from which a literary work is presented to the reader. There are four traditional points of view. The ''third person omniscient'' gives the reader a ''godlike'' perspective, unrestricted by time or place, from which to see actions and look into the minds of characters. This allows the author to comment openly on characters and events in the work. The ''third person'' point of view presents the events of the story from outside of any single character's perception, much like the omniscient point of view, but the reader must understand the action as it takes place and without any special insight into characters' minds or motivations. The ''first person'' or ''personal'' point of view relates events as they are perceived by a single character. The main character ''tells'' the story and may offer opinions about the action and characters which differ from those of the author. Much less common than omniscient, third person, and first person is the ''second person'' point of view, wherein the author tells the story as if it is happening to the reader. James Thurber employs the omniscient point of view in his short story ''The Secret Life of Walter Mitty.'' Ernest Hemingway's ''A Clean, Well-Lighted Place'' is a short story told from the third person point of view. Mark Twain's novel *Huckleberry Finn* is presented from the first person viewpoint. Jay McInerney's *Bright Lights, Big City* is an example of a novel which uses the second person point of view.

Pornography: Writing intended to provoke feelings of lust in the reader. Such works are often condemned by critics and teachers, but those which can be shown to have literary value are viewed less harshly. Literary works that have been described as pornographic include D. H. Lawrence's *Lady Chatterley's Lover* and James Joyce's *Ulysses.*

Post-Aesthetic Movement: An artistic response made by African Americans to the black aesthetic movement of the 1960s and early 1970s. Writers since that time have adopted a somewhat different tone in their work, with less emphasis placed on the disparity between black and white in the United States. In the words of post-aesthetic authors such as Toni Morrison, John Edgar Wideman, and Kristin Hunter, African Americans are portrayed as looking inward for answers to their own questions, rather than always looking to the outside world. Two well-known examples of works produced as part of the post-aesthetic movement are the Pulitzer Prize-winning novels *The Color Purple* by Alice Walker and *Beloved* by Toni Morrison.

Postmodernism: Writing from the 1960s forward characterized by experimentation and application of modernist elements, which include existentialism and alienation. Postmodernists have gone a step further in the rejection of tradition begun with the modernists by also rejecting traditional forms, preferring the anti-novel over the novel and the anti-hero over the hero. Postmodern writers include Thomas Pynchon, Margaret Drabble, and Gabriel Garcia Marquez.

Prologue: An introductory section of a literary work. It often contains information establishing the situation of the characters or presents information about the setting, time period, or action. In drama, the prologue is spoken by a chorus or by one of the principal characters.

Prose: A literary medium that attempts to mirror the language of everyday speech. It is distinguished from poetry by its use of unmetered, unrhymed language consisting of logically related sentences. Prose is usually grouped into paragraphs that form a cohesive whole such as an essay or a novel. The term is sometimes used to mean an author's general writing.

Protagonist: The central character of a story who serves as a focus for its themes and incidents and as the principal rationale for its development. The protagonist is sometimes referred to in discussions of modern literature as the hero or anti-hero. Well-known protagonists are Hamlet in William Shakespeare's *Hamlet* and Jay Gatsby in F. Scott Fitzgerald's *The Great Gatsby.*

R

Realism: A nineteenth-century European literary movement that sought to portray familiar characters, situations, and settings in a realistic manner. This was done primarily by using an objective narrative point of view and through the buildup of accurate detail. The standard for success of any realistic work depends on how faithfully it transfers common experience into fictional forms. The realistic method may be altered or extended, as in stream of consciousness writing, to record highly subjective experience. Contemporary authors who often write in a realistic way include Nadine Gordimer and Grace Paley.

Resolution: The portion of a story following the climax, in which the conflict is resolved. The resolution of Jane Austen's *Northanger Abbey* is neatly summed up in the following sentence: "Henry and Catherine were married, the bells rang and every body smiled."

Rising Action: The part of a drama where the plot becomes increasingly complicated. Rising action leads up to the climax, or turning point, of a drama. The final "chase scene" of an action film is generally the rising action which culminates in the film's climax.

Roman a clef: A French phrase meaning "novel with a key." It refers to a narrative in which real persons are portrayed under fictitious names. Jack Kerouac, for example, portrayed various his friends under fictitious names in the novel *On the Road.* D. H. Lawrence based "The Rocking-Horse Winner" on a family he knew.

Romanticism: This term has two widely accepted meanings. In historical criticism, it refers to a European intellectual and artistic movement of the late eighteenth and early nineteenth centuries that sought greater freedom of personal expression than that allowed by the strict rules of literary form and logic of the eighteenth-century neoclassicists. The Romantics preferred emotional and imaginative expression to rational analysis. They considered the individual to be at the center of all experience and so placed him or her at the center of their art. The Romantics believed that the creative imagination reveals nobler truths—unique feelings and attitudes—than those that could be discovered by logic or by scientific examination. "Romanticism" is also used as a general term to refer to a type of sensibility found in all periods of literary history and usually considered to be in opposition to the principles of classicism. In this sense, Romanticism signifies any work or philosophy in which the exotic or dreamlike figure strongly, or that is devoted to individualistic expression, self-analysis, or a pursuit of a higher realm of knowledge than can be discovered by human reason. Prominent Romantics include Jean-Jacques Rousseau, William Wordsworth, John Keats, Lord Byron, and Johann Wolfgang von Goethe.

S

Satire: A work that uses ridicule, humor, and wit to criticize and provoke change in human nature and institutions. Voltaire's novella *Candide* and Jonathan Swift's essay ''A Modest Proposal'' are both satires. Flannery O'Connor's portrayal of the family in ''A Good Man Is Hard to Find'' is a satire of a modern, Southern, American family.

Science Fiction: A type of narrative based upon real or imagined scientific theories and technology. Science fiction is often peopled with alien creatures and set on other planets or in different dimensions. Popular writers of science fiction are Isaac Asimov, Karel Capek, Ray Bradbury, and Ursula K. Le Guin.

Setting: The time, place, and culture in which the action of a narrative takes place. The elements of setting may include geographic location, characters's physical and mental environments, prevailing cultural attitudes, or the historical time in which the action takes place.

Short Story: A fictional prose narrative shorter and more focused than a novella. The short story usually deals with a single episode and often a single character. The ''tone,'' the author's attitude toward his or her subject and audience, is uniform throughout. The short story frequently also lacks *denouement*, ending instead at its climax.

Signifying Monkey: A popular trickster figure in black folklore, with hundreds of tales about this character documented since the 19th century. Henry Louis Gates Jr. examines the history of the signifying monkey in *The Signifying Monkey: Towards a Theory of Afro-American Literary Criticism,* published in 1988.

Simile: A comparison, usually using ''like'' or ''as,''of two essentially dissimilar things, as in ''coffee as cold as ice'' or ''He sounded like a broken record.'' The title of Ernest Hemingway's ''Hills Like White Elephants'' contains a simile.

Social Realism: The Socialist Realism school of literary theory was proposed by Maxim Gorky and established as a dogma by the first Soviet Congress of Writers. It demanded adherence to a communist worldview in works of literature. Its doctrines required an objective viewpoint comprehensible to the working classes and themes of social struggle featuring strong proletarian heroes. Gabriel Garcia Marquez's stories exhibit some characteristics of Socialist Realism.

Stereotype: A stereotype was originally the name for a duplication made during the printing process; this led to its modern definition as a person or thing that is (or is assumed to be) the same as all others of its type. Common stereotypical characters include the absent-minded professor, the nagging wife, the troublemaking teenager, and the kind-hearted grandmother.

Stream of Consciousness: A narrative technique for rendering the inward experience of a character. This technique is designed to give the impression of an ever-changing series of thoughts, emotions, images, and memories in the spontaneous and seemingly illogical order that they occur in life. The textbook example of stream of consciousness is the last section of James Joyce's *Ulysses*.

Structure: The form taken by a piece of literature. The structure may be made obvious for ease of understanding, as in nonfiction works, or may obscured for artistic purposes, as in some poetry or seemingly ''unstructured'' prose.

Style: A writer's distinctive manner of arranging words to suit his or her ideas and purpose in writing. The unique imprint of the author's personality upon his or her writing, style is the product of an author's way of arranging ideas and his or her use of diction, different sentence structures, rhythm, figures of speech, rhetorical principles, and other elements of composition.

Suspense: A literary device in which the author maintains the audience's attention through the buildup of events, the outcome of which will soon be revealed. Suspense in William Shakespeare's *Hamlet* is sustained throughout by the question of whether or not the Prince will achieve what he has been instructed to do and of what he intends to do.

Symbol: Something that suggests or stands for something else without losing its original identity. In literature, symbols combine their literal meaning with the suggestion of an abstract concept. Literary symbols are of two types: those that carry complex associations of meaning no matter what their contexts, and those that derive their suggestive meaning from their functions in specific literary works. Examples of symbols are sunshine suggesting happiness, rain suggesting sorrow, and storm clouds suggesting despair.

T

Tale: A story told by a narrator with a simple plot and little character development. Tales are usually relatively short and often carry a simple message. Examples of tales can be found in the works of Saki, Anton Chekhov, Guy de Maupassant, and O. Henry.

Tall Tale: A humorous tale told in a straightforward, credible tone but relating absolutely impossible events or feats of the characters. Such tales were commonly told of frontier adventures during the settlement of the west in the United States. Literary use of tall tales can be found in Washington Irving's *History of New York,* Mark Twain's *Life on the Mississippi,* and in the German R. F. Raspe's *Baron Munchausen's Narratives of His Marvellous Travels and Campaigns in Russia.*

Theme: The main point of a work of literature. The term is used interchangeably with thesis. Many works have multiple themes. One of the themes of Nathaniel Hawthorne's ''Young Goodman Brown'' is loss of faith.

Tone: The author's attitude toward his or her audience may be deduced from the tone of the work. A formal tone may create distance or convey politeness, while an informal tone may encourage a friendly, intimate, or intrusive feeling in the reader. The author's attitude toward his or her subject matter may also be deduced from the tone of the words he or she uses in discussing it. The tone of John F. Kennedy's speech which included the appeal to ''ask not what your country can do for you'' was intended to instill feelings of camaraderie and national pride in listeners.

Tragedy: A drama in prose or poetry about a noble, courageous hero of excellent character who, be-

cause of some tragic character flaw, brings ruin upon him- or herself. Tragedy treats its subjects in a dignified and serious manner, using poetic language to help evoke pity and fear and bring about catharsis, a purging of these emotions. The tragic form was practiced extensively by the ancient Greeks. The classical form of tragedy was revived in the sixteenth century; it flourished especially on the Elizabethan stage. In modern times, dramatists have attempted to adapt the form to the needs of modern society by drawing their heroes from the ranks of ordinary men and women and defining the nobility of these heroes in terms of spirit rather than exalted social standing. Some contemporary works that are thought of as tragedies include *The Great Gatsby* by F. Scott Fitzgerald, and *The Sound and the Fury* by William Faulkner.

Tragic Flaw: In a tragedy, the quality within the hero or heroine which leads to his or her downfall. Examples of the tragic flaw include Othello's jealousy and Hamlet's indecisiveness, although most great tragedies defy such simple interpretation.

U

Utopia: A fictional perfect place, such as ''paradise'' or ''heaven.'' An early literary utopia was described in Plato's *Republic,* and in modern literature, Ursula K. Le Guin depicts a utopia in ''The Ones Who Walk Away from Omelas.''

V

Victorian: Refers broadly to the reign of Queen Victoria of England (1837–1901) and to anything with qualities typical of that era. For example, the qualities of smug narrow-mindedness, bourgeois materialism, faith in social progress, and priggish morality are often considered Victorian. In literature, the Victorian Period was the great age of the English novel, and the latter part of the era saw the rise of movements such as decadence and symbolism.

Cumulative Author/Title Index

Nationality/Ethnicity Index

African American

Baldwin, James
  The Rockpile: V18
  Sonny's Blues: V2
Bambara, Toni Cade
  Blues Ain't No Mockin Bird: V4
  The Lesson: V12
  Raymond's Run: V7
Butler, Octavia
  Bloodchild: V6
Chesnutt, Charles Waddell
  The Sheriff's Children: V11
Ellison, Ralph
  King of the Bingo Game: V1
Hughes, Langston
  The Blues I'm Playing: V7
  Slave on the Block: V4
Hurston, Zora Neale
  The Eatonville Anthology: V1
  The Gilded Six-Bits: V11
  Spunk: V6
  Sweat: V19
Marshall, Paule
  To Da-duh, in Memoriam: V15
Toomer, Jean
  Blood-Burning Moon: V5
Walker, Alice
  Everyday Use: V2
  Roselily: V11
Wideman, John Edgar
  *The Beginning of
      Homewood:* V12
  Fever: V6
Wright, Richard
  Bright and Morning Star: V15
  *The Man Who Lived Under-
      ground:* V3

  *The Man Who Was
      Almost a Man:* V9

American

Adams, Alice
  The Last Lovely City: V14
Agüeros, Jack
  Dominoes: V13
Aiken, Conrad
  Silent Snow, Secret Snow: V8
Alexie, Sherman
  *Because My Father Always Said
      He Was the Only Indian Who
      Saw Jimi Hendrix Play ''The
      Star-Spangled Banner'' at
      Woodstock:* V18
Anderson, Sherwood
  Death in the Woods: V10
  Hands: V11
  Sophistication: V4
Asimov, Isaac
  Nightfall: V17
Baldwin, James
  The Rockpile: V18
  Sonny's Blues: V2
Bambara, Toni Cade
  Blues Ain't No Mockin Bird: V4
  The Lesson: V12
  Raymond's Run: V7
Barth, John
  Lost in the Funhouse: V6
Barthelme, Donald
  The Indian Uprising: V17
  *Robert Kennedy Saved from
      Drowning:* V3

Beattie, Ann
  Janus: V9
Bellow, Saul
  Leaving the Yellow House: V12
Berriault, Gina
  The Stone Boy: V7
  Women in Their Beds: V11
Bierce, Ambrose
  The Boarded Window: V9
  *An Occurrence at Owl Creek
      Bridge:* V2
Bisson, Terry
  The Toxic Donut: V18
Bloom, Amy
  Silver Water: V11
Bowles, Paul
  The Eye: V17
Boyle, Kay
  Astronomer's Wife: V13
  Black Boy: V14
  The White Horses of Vienna: V10
Boyle, T. Coraghessan
  *Stones in My Passway, Hellhound
      on My Trail:* V13
  The Underground Gardens: V19
Bradbury, Ray
  There Will Come Soft Rains: V1
Brown, Jason
  Animal Stories: V14
Butler, Octavia
  Bloodchild: V6
Butler, Robert Olen
  *A Good Scent from a Strange
      Mountain:* V11
Capote, Truman
  A Christmas Memory: V2

Subject/Theme Index